The Blackwell Cultural
Economy Reader

The Blackwell Cultural Economy Reader

Edited by

Ash Amin and Nigel Thrift

Blackwell
Publishing

Editorial material and organization © 2004 by Blackwell Publishing Ltd

350 Main Street, Malden, MA 02148-5020, USA
108 Cowley Road, Oxford OX4 1JF, UK
550 Swanston Street, Carlton, Victoria 3053, Australia

First published 2004 by Blackwell Publishing Ltd

Library of Congress Cataloging-in-Publication Data

The Blackwell cultural economy reader / edited by Ash Amin and Nigel Thrift.
p. cm. – (Blackwell readers in geography)
ISBN 0-631-23428-4 (alk. paper) – ISBN 0-631-23429-2 (pbk.: alk. paper)
1. Economics–Sociological aspects. I. Amin, Ash. II. Thrift, N. J. III. Series.

HM548.B58 2003
306.3–dc21

2003051820

A catalogue record for this title is available from the British Library.

Set in 10/12pt Sabon
by Kolam Information Services Pvt. Ltd, Pondicherry, India
Printed and bound in the United Kingdom
by TJ International Ltd, Padstow, Cornwall

For further information on
Blackwell Publishing, visit our website:
http://www.blackwellpublishing.com

Contents

Acknowledgments

The editor and publishers wish to thank the following for permission to use copyright material (some of which has been excerpted for editorial reasons):

1   McRobbie, Angela (1998) "A Mixed Economy of Fashion Design." In *British Fashion Design*. Routledge, London, pp. 89–101, 191, 193, 196–7. Reprinted by permission of Taylor and Francis Books Ltd.

2   O'Riain, Sean (1999) "Net-Working for a Living: Irish Software Developers in the Global Workplace." In Michael Burawoy, Joseph A. Blum, Sheba George, Zsuzsa Gille, Teresa Gowan, Lynne Haney, Maren Klawiter, Steven H. Lopez, Sean Thayer, and Millie O'Riain, (eds.) *Global Ethnography: Forces, Connections and Imaginations in a Postmodern World*. University of California Press, Berkeley, pp. 175–202, 352–5, 358–9, 361–3, 366–72. Reprinted by permission of the University of California Press. Copyright © 2000 by the Regents of the University of California.

3   Vann Katie and Bowker, Geoffrey C. (2001) "Instrumentalizing the Truth of Practice." *Social Epistemology*, 15 (3), pp. 247–62. Reprinted by permission of Taylor & Francis Ltd (http://www.tandf.co.uk/journals).

4   Callon, Michel, Meadel, Cecile and Rabeharisoa, Vololona (2002) "The Economy of Qualities." *Economy and Society* 31 (2), pp. 194–217. Reprinted by permission of Taylor & Francis Ltd (http://www.tandf.co.uk/journals).

5   Tsing, Anna (2000) "Inside the Economy of Appearances." *Public Culture*, 12 (1), pp. 115–29, 134–44. Copyright © 2000 by Duke University Press. All rights reserved. Used by permission of the publisher.

6   MacKenzie, Donald (2001) "Physics and Finance: S-Terms and Modern Finance as a Topic for Science Studies." *Science, Technology and Human Values*, 26 (2), pp. 115–34, 138–44. Copyright © 2001 by Sage Publications Inc. Reprinted by permission of the Sage Publications Inc.

7   Knorr Cetina, Karin and Bruegger, Urs (2002). "Traders' Engagement with Markets: A Postsocial Relationship." *Theory, Culture, and Society*, 19 (5/6), pp. 161–85. Copyright © 2002 by Sage Publications Inc. Reprinted by permission of Sage Publications Inc.

8   Varese, Frederico (2001) "Varieties of Protectors." In Frederico Varese, *The Russian Mafia*. Oxford University Press, Oxford, pp. 55–72, 223–8, 260–2, 264–70, 272–3. Reprinted by permission of Oxford University Press.

9   Lapham, Lewis H. (1998) "The Agony of Mammon." In Lewis H. Lapham, *The Agony of Mammon: The Imperial World Economy Explains Itself to the Membership in Davos, Switzerland*. Verso, London, pp. 1–2, 7–19, 23–30, 33–9, 41–6, 48–51. Reprinted by permission of Verso Books.

10 Miller, Peter (2001) "Governing by Numbers: Why Calculative Practices Matter." *Social Research* 68 (2), pp. 379–96. Reprinted by permission of *Social Research*.

11 Stoller, P. (2002) "African/Asian/Uptown/Downtown." In P. Stoller, *Money Has No Smell: The Africanization of New York City*. Chicago University Press, Chicago, pp. 45–63, 189–91, 207–17.

12 Hughes, A. (2000) "Retailers, Knowledges and Changing Commodity Networks: The Case of the Cut Flower Trade." *Geoforum* 31, pp. 175–90. Copyright © 2000 by Elsevier. Reprinted by permission of the publisher.

13 Murdoch, Jonathan and Miele, Mara (2003) "Culinary Networks and Cultural Connections: A Conventions Perspective." In Hughes, A. and S. Reimer (eds.) *Geographies of Commodity Chains*. Pearson Education, London. Reprinted by permission of the publisher.

14 Miller, Daniel (1998) "Making Love in Supermarkets." In Daniel Miller, *A Theory of Stopping Polity*, Cambridge University Press, Cambridge, pp. 15–36, 158, 171–5. Reprinted by permission of the publisher.

15 Clarke, Alison J. (1998) "Window Shopping at Home: Classifieds, Catalogues and New Consumer Skills. In Daniel Miller (ed.) *Material Cultures: Why Some Things Matter*, University College London Press, London, pp. 73–99. Reprinted by permission of Taylor and Francis Books Ltd. (UCL Press) and the University of Chicago Press.

16 Geismar, Haidy (2001) "What's in a Price? An Ethnography of Tribal Art at Auction." *Journal of Material Culture*, 6 (1), pp. 25–47. Copyright © 2001 Sage Publications Ltd. Reprinted by permission of Sage Publications Ltd.

17 Crang, Philip (1994) "It's Showtime: On the Workplace Geographies of Display in a Restaurant in Southeast England." *Environment and Planning D, Society and Space* 12, pp. 675, 678–94, 696–704.

18 Hochschild, Arlie (1983) "Feeling Management: From Private to Commercial Uses." In Arlie Hochschild, *The Managed Heart*. University of California Press,

Berkeley, pp. 89–126, 255–6, 270, 274, 291. Copyright © 1983 Arlie Hochschild. Reprinted by permission of the University of California Press.

19 Law, Lisa (2000) "Negotiating the Bar: Sex, Money and the Uneasy Politics of Third Space." In Lisa Law, *Sex Work in Southeast Asia*. Routledge, London, pp. 44–61, 129, 132–8. Copyright © 2000 Lisa Law. Reprinted by permission of Taylor & Francis Books Ltd.

20 Denton, S. and R. Morris (2001) "A Joint's a Joint." In S. Denton and R. Morris, *The Money and The Power: The Making of Las Vegas and its Hold on America*. Vintage, New York, pp. 358–67, 370–3, 375–8, 380–8.

21 Lury, Celia (1999) "Marketing Time with Nike: The Illusion of the Durable," *Public Culture*, 11, 3: pp. 499–526. Copyright © 1999 by Duke University Press. All rights reserved. Used by permission of the publisher.

Every effort has been made to trace copyright holders and to obtain their permission for the use of copyright material. The authors and publishers will gladly receive any information enabling them to rectify any error or omission in subsequent editions.

Introduction

We live in an unusual historical period in that the business of economic analysis has become associated not just with one discipline, but with one part of one discipline. Economics, and in particular, neoclassical economics, rules the roost. However, there are at least some signs that this hegemony is beginning to break down or at the very least is beginning to fray at the edges. The reasons for this are clear. New accounts of the economy have been produced, accounts that not only challenge the dominance of neoclassical economics, but also question what counts as economy.

This book can be seen as both a contribution to this growing body of heterodox economic knowledge, and also as an extension of it. Until quite recently, heterodox approaches still took on the terms of trade of economics, concentrating their attention around the conceptualization of a separate sphere of social life called "the economy," a sphere which was lorded over by distinctive and systemic rules and driven by the imperatives of resource production, allocation, and distribution. For example, in institutional and evolutionary economics, the main task has remained that of honing or improving accounts of an unproblematically presented economic realm (e.g., value, profit, distribution, surplus), rather than challenging the ontological status of the economy and the dominance of an economic worldview.

Similarly, in socioeconomics, the ambition has been to reveal the variety of ways in which the economy is socially embedded (e.g., by considering how qualities such as trust and reciprocity operating in networks of interpersonal relations affect economic efficiency), rather than to argue that the social and the economic are woven together as a single and inseparable fabric (thereby questioning what economic efficiency might mean in isolation). In turn, while certain political economy critiques of the neoclassical orthodoxy demonstrate that capital is a social relation (e.g., profit is based on class exploitation or the social division of labor), they usually continue to accept such strong assumptions of systemic rationality and order that they too often oust non-rational, performative impulses (from desire to radical uncertainty) from being given their due consideration (Joseph 2002).

More far-reaching accounts of the economy and the economic have, of course, always existed, from those of Gabriel Tarde, Max Weber, or Theodor Adorno who,

each in their very different ways, noted the ethical-cum-psychic orders that characterize different economic systems, to those of Georg Simmel, Walter Benjamin, and
Georges Bataille who, equally differently, showed how enchantment and obsession
propelled accumulation. But it is only recently that a genuine ambition for change
has come about in so many different disciplines at once.

There are many reasons for this new ambition. We will identify just six. The first is
a profound mistrust across the world of what the business of economy and the
accompanying discourse of economics have wrought. The current world economic
horizon includes the wreckage of so many hopes and dreams that it was almost
inevitable that people would begin to search for alternative understandings of what
counts as prosperity and economic well-being.[1] The second reason relates to the
first. There is increasing frustration in parts of the policy community that orthodox
economics has provided at best partial accounts of the current state of affairs,
leading to a search for policy alternatives drawn from outside orthodox economics
that is being conducted with some urgency (Leyshon, Lee, and Williams 2003).[2]

In turn, this ambition has led to a much greater recognition of plural ways of
organizing the economy and plural ways of meeting economic need. Thus, third, the
sheer diversity of economic organization has become clear in a way that has never
been the case before. While it is true that Weber and others were acutely aware of the
cultural specificity of Western economic modes of thinking, it has taken much longer
to accept that such differences are not anomalies, even though the principles of, for
example, Islamic and Buddhist economics now inform the economic practices of
large parts of the world.[3] And, back in the West, it has become almost normal to
refer to varieties of capitalism rooted in different histories of institutional and
cultural practice.

A fourth reason for this ambition is the rise of interdisciplinary work, which has
led to a heightened exchange of different knowledges of the economic, including the
various theorizations of economic knowledge itself. For example, work within
economics, which has traditionally explained learning in terms of perfections of
rational behavior, has been leavened over the years by work in cognitive psychology
that distinguishes between different types of rationality and learning (e.g., substantive rationality and rule-based learning, versus procedural rationality and adaptive
learning). More recently, these understandings have been jolted by work in social
studies of science, economic anthropology, and business studies, which show that a
significant amount of learning is the product of embodied knowledge, the cognitive
unconscious, and practical action. A noticeable development has been the attempt to
combine these insights into a general interdisciplinary perspective on economic
knowledge (Callon 1999; Amin and Cohendet 2004).

Fifth, there has been a growing frustration with the narrow range of methods that
are considered legitimate by orthodox economics, and especially the current emphasis on the countable, the modellable, and the predictable. For example, in business studies, such an approach makes it difficult to understand a number of crucial
dimensions of the workings of firms, from their uses of knowledge and rhetoric,
through the role of "soft skills" like leadership to the bite of various monopoly
practices. Similarly, businesses know that there are profits to be made from the
insights of market research based on participant observation of consumers, discussions in focus groups, the practical semiotics of advertising and consumer magazines,

and video diaries. Of course, the hold of formalism and calculus remains strong – and no doubt it has its place – but this hold is weakening in the face of regular misdiagnosis and the availability of knowledge from, as it were, the ground up.

Sixth, and most importantly for the concerns of this book, there has been an explosion of interest across academe in matters cultural. It was perhaps inevitable that some of this interest would flow over into the economic sphere, given the sheer numbers of academics involved in the cultural turn, which expressed itself as either a more limited ambition to take up cultural aspects of the "economy" (e.g., consumption as a cultural practice), or a more far-reaching ambition to rework the economy as a cultural artifact. The result is an efflorescence of work that this book is designed to reflect and give a coherent voice to. Though, to begin with, this work might have been described as simply gap finding, adding cultural inflections to various economic topics, that phase has now passed and new and interesting hybrids are appearing (Du Gay and Pryke 1999).

The New Settlement

The production, distribution, and accumulation of resources – loosely the pursuit of prosperity – have always been a cultural performance. However, since the late nineteenth century in particular, with the rise of a separate profession of economics and a set of specifically economic knowledges, such performance has either been neglected or actively denigrated (Hodgson 2001). This Reader seeks to put back that which should never have been taken out.[4] This is no easy task because prevalent social description has come to take for granted the idea that there are separate spheres of activity called culture and economy. The book challenges this settlement by showing how the pursuit of prosperity is a hybrid process of aggregation and ordering that cannot be reduced to either of these terms and, as such, requires the use of a unitary term such as cultural economy.

We had originally thought to begin this introduction with a series of examples that showed the ways in which economies are becoming more culturally driven or more culturally embedded. Thus, we might have shown how the continuing rise of cultural industries based on the mass commodification of culture had breathed new life into the economy (e.g., through new markets in tourism, leisure, media, arts, music, books), created all manner of new forms of enterprise (from Internet giants such as Amazon, to a market for impresarios), and played a major role in economic regeneration in many parts of the world (e.g., in the urban renewal of some old industrial cities, the impact on the profile of exports from small countries like Sweden of preeminence in global popular music, national programs around the developing world based on cultural tourism). Again, we might have shown how the consumption preferences and status demands of a new global middle class have propelled the rise of a lucrative fashion and design industry that is supported by an extensive and elaborate infrastructure (made up of magazines, advertising, international travel, lucrative offshoots like spectacles, designer architecture, and consumer servicing of one sort or another). One more example might have linked economy to ethics. Thus, the slow food movement that first arose in Italy is now rapidly spreading to other European countries. This movement rejects the culture of fast food, and taps deep into sensibilities of tradition, community, holism, work–life balance, and taste, as the ground for a new economics of staple needs. Equally, we could have considered the rise of the Fair Trade movement that has attempted to ethically reconfigure modern Western consumer preferences with some interesting results.

Out of this host of examples, and no doubt many others, we have decided to fix on just one to show the way in which economy and culture are inextricably intertwined: the case of the quite extraordinary rise and rise of the Sport Utility Vehicle (SUV). In general, the system of automobility, which has become a threat to the very atmosphere of the planet, is a paramount example of the cultural and the economic moving in lockstep (Sheller and Urry 2000). But the case of the SUV makes the point in a way which is somewhere between tragedy and farce – and parody. Beginning with vehicles like the Jeep Cherokee and the Ford Explorer in the 1980s, these vehicles have gradually become a major segment of the US car market, earning record profits for their makers.[5] They have grown larger and larger (hence the Jeep Grand Cherokee), culminating in the General Motors Hummer H2, modeled on the military Humvee, and have been taken up by more and more car manufacturers (including foreign car companies like BMW, Mercedes, and Lexus). Yet these cars have been generally condemned by environmentalists for their appalling record on fuel economy (which for some models can be as little as 10 mpg) and for the fact that by being classified as light trucks they avoid federal automobile fuel efficiency regulations. Thanks in large part to the growth of this segment of the market, the average fuel economy of American cars is currently at its lowest for two decades, at about 21 mpg. Given that the United States represents 5 percent of the population but uses 25 percent of its oil, this propensity to consume light trucks and lots of gasoline is a major problem for the world, both in terms of resource depletion and greenhouse effects. Again, these cars have also been castigated by road safety experts for being no safer than other smaller cars and for being particularly susceptible to problems like rollover (Bradsher 2002).

Why such "economic" success? The reason can be found in the way in which the "cultural" buttons of the large number of affluent families[6] that now constitute the main market for SUVs have been able to be pushed by the car manufacturers. Four of these buttons have proved particularly important. One, paradoxically, is safety. Drivers, and perhaps especially women, feel safe in SUVs. They are up high and surrounded by a cage of steel and, especially for those families with children, they seem to offer a kind of domestic fortress – but on the road. A second related button is fear of crime. In part, SUVs also seem to function psychologically as armored cars: Bradsher (2002) claims that they are often designed to look as menacing as possible so as to allay their occupants' fear of crime and violence. Then, third, cars in general have become platforms for large amounts of equipment, which it is much easier to fit into bulky SUVs. Fourth, through concerted advertising campaigns, SUVs have become associated with glamor and power. Added to these factors, high income families care little about gasoline prices and so are inured to price rises in what is anyway a low gasoline price environment.

The economic-cum-cultural spell of SUVs is now being fought against by various ethically attuned alliances. For example, the National Religious Partnership for the Environment (NRPE), an alliance of Christian and Jewish groups, has written to 100,000 congregations in the US calling from the pulpit for people to cut fuel consumption, is training clergy to speak out on green issues, and has started an advertising campaign to ram the message home.[7] NRPE asks "What would Jesus drive?" and the answer is clearly not an SUV. Whatever the case, the Bush administration is currently considering a proposal to require SUVs and other light trucks to achieve higher rates of fuel efficiency in a response that again is both economic and cultural.

It is clear from an example like this that stripping out the so-called cultural so as to leave the so-called economic pure and ready to be analyzed makes no sense, since it inevitably leaves out of the explanation some of the most important motive forces. But, more than this, trying to break the two apart produces epistemic monsters which try to repress their own mixed origins in a way which is already all too familiar in other fields.

It should already be clear, then, that this book is not in the business of simply adding a cultural filigree to what in the end is still held to be an economic core. Neither is it in the business of arguing that there are immanent economic laws that play themselves out in a medium called culture (i.e., that the economy is culturally embedded). Nor is it interested in showing that matters cultural are mobilized for economic gain (e.g., the mobilization of culture for profit). Rather, the argument of this book is that the pursuit of prosperity must be seen as the pursuit of many goals at once, from meeting material needs and accumulating riches to seeking symbolic satisfaction and satisfying fleeting pleasures. For most of the time these goals are pursued through hybrid and temporary coalitions, but set against the background of various kinds of ordering frame, from the swathe of regulations that order the conduct of competition to the mundane ordering of everyday economic life through various crucial infrastructures such as roads, pipes, and cables.

This book is intended to concentrate on a new phase in the history of cultural economy approaches. In the beginning, writers in the field tended to employ what we might call an additive model, in which all that was attempted was to add a cultural element to an economic explanation. Indeed, this position is still held by those who believe that without a strict demarcation of the cultural and the economic, often parsed as the interpretive and the instrumental, analytical power is lost (cf. Ray and Sayer 1997). Some possible shortcomings of this approach led to the deployment, instead, of what we might call a synthetic model, in which culture and economy became partners. This is the dominant position currently, with much work paying attention to illustrating, as we have already seen above, the way in which "culture" impinges on the "economic." However, more recently a certain amount of dissatisfaction with this approach (and not least its tendency to transfer inappropriate models from one domain to another) has also surfaced, leading to what might be called a hybrid model in which the two terms, culture and economy, are dispensed with, and instead, following actor–network theory and similar approaches, attention focuses on different kinds of orderings (cf. Callon 1999, Latour 1999, Hassard and Law 1999).

This new position is still struggling to find an exact vocabulary for its analysis of the steps through which economic quantities and qualities are formed. What is certain is that this is more than simply analyzing each moment in a production or consumption process, and then seeing how it is culturally inflected and how the cultural inflection affects economic "outcomes." Rather, it is an attempt to identify the varied impulses and articulations through which value is formed, added, and circulated; summing to what can only be described as a cultural economic ensemble with no clear hierarchy of significance. These impulses and articulations are not only plural and mixed, but also performative, since they involve not only following the rules of the game but also constantly establishing new rules.

Such an approach emphasizes the sheer variety of actors – human and non-human – involved in modern economic transactions and organizational arrangements, and the ways in which expertise is constantly being redistributed among them. Seller prices in a given commodity market, for example, might be seen as the combined product, and shifting power of influence, of long-term supply and demand trends, the decisions of major sellers (Tool 1991), the parameters of trading standards and regulations, the work of forecasts and forecasting tools, imaginaries of desire and desirability, the symbolic power of the product, and the machinations of trading arrangements and trader strategies. This approach has been particularly fruitful in analyzing the formation and maintenance of markets of all kinds, and especially the way in which the economic knowledge that transpires becomes a horizon of expect-ation that is itself constitutive. Most obviously, we see these insights worked out in a series of close-hatched ethnographies of the global financial markets, where fluctu-ations in the markets and the standards of worth that are applied to the highly profitable gleanings from those fluctuations are the result of complex compromises arising out of the circulation of information and knowledge among many actors, from speculators and traders to databases and small proto-artificial intelligences (e.g., Knorr-Cetina 2000, Miyazaki 2003, Riles 2003). However, the approach works just as well in analyzing smaller scale markets, and especially those that have been built up using formal economic knowledge (e.g., famously, market ex-pectations in the French strawberry market are based on a particular model of markets, such that the economic and cultural horizons fuse) (Callon 1999).

A Brief History of Cultural Economy

In this section we want to trace out some of the possible approaches to cultural economy that are currently circulating. In undertaking that task, we need to be aware that these approaches all have a history, which could be recounted as the lineage of cultural economy. But we want to make it clear that this is a fragmented history, full of stops and starts, rather than a definite and definitive narrative.

The first approach stresses the centrality of *passions*. Pre-nineteenth century European economic thought was often concerned with economic principles as a means of overcoming what was seen as a surfeit of passions in the conduct of daily life. Economic rationality would damp down passion and produce a more "civil-ized" mode of conduct; so, for example, engagement in productive work would head off the kinds of violent encounters – from war to duels – which were an all too prevalent feature of eighteenth-century life. Later on, in the course of the nineteenth century, a romantic reaction to this civilizing conception of the economy sets in. The economy itself comes to be seen as a negative passion for accumulation of the kinds revealed in the practices of hoarding by misers and in the theoretical writings of Marx. Many analyses argued that hedonistic behavior and other forms of passion needed reintroduction in a world whose only passion had become accumulation.

What we see then is a shift in register, but in both cases, the economy is seen to be intimately associated with the expression of passion.

The second approach is loosely related to the first, in that it focuses on so-called *moral sentiments*. It is often forgotten that Adam Smith not only wrote *Wealth of Nations*, but also *Theory of Moral Sentiments*. For Smith, as for so many writers of his time, the practice of œconomy was also the practice of moral judgment and worth. Economic value could never be divorced from moral value. Smith saw that the entanglement in modern society of a moral order of sympathy – participation in the feelings of others – with economic individualism as the driving force of wealth creation, cushioning the worst effects of pure self-interest.[8] Such injunctions have a very long history, casting in some cases a long shadow into the present. For examples, the principles of hard work, honest commercial relations, and trust that guide the trading practices of faith-sensitive Muslim entrepreneurs draw deep into Qur'anic injunctions on giving false oaths, correct weight, and goodwill in transactions (Stoller 2002). Moral judgment also abounds in the choice over different types of economic system or subject. For example, in a long line of socialist economic thought running from Marx and Ruskin to Lenin and Chayanov, a clear distinction is drawn between the moral worthiness of labor for social utility and social need and the degenerative effects of labor based solely on production for profit. Similarly, in nineteenth-century French writing on poverty, the economic condition of the poor is judged as a condition of moral descent, with remedial actions such as alms and charitable support justified less in terms of labor market or other economic imperatives than as a weapon against moral turpitude and social degeneracy (Procacci 1978).

The third approach identifies *knowledge* as a key motive force in the practice of economy. Going back even to the work of Smith and Marx on the division of labor, we can see a meditation on how different forms of knowledge – mental and manual – can be deployed in order to produce optimal accumulation. While Marx and Smith were chiefly concerned with the link between knowledge and capitalist efficiency (Sohn-Rethel 1978), another equally long parallel tradition has been concerned with showing how knowledge inculcated in the habits of work, tacit practices, machinery and tools, institutionalized norms, and cultural understandings acts as the motor of economic prosperity. The assertion here is that the economics of prosperity hinge around the qualities of knowledge distributed across a variety of mediums, which, taken together, count as a cultural resource with profound economic weight. This is most evident in the work of Veblen at the turn of the last century, who argued that because of the strong interdependence between "habits of thought" and "habits of life," there can be "no neatly isolable range of cultural phenomena that can be rigorously set apart under the head of economic institutions." Interestingly for our purposes, he thus concludes that "an evolutionary economics must be the theory of a process of cultural growth as determined by the economic interest" (Veblen 1990: 77).

The fourth approach, also in no small measure traceable to Veblen, stresses that learning and economic change in general can be likened to *evolution*. The evolutionary metaphor, drawing on the work of Darwin, Lamarck, and Spencer, has a long history of use and abuse in economic thinking since the mid-nineteenth century. Learning (and learning how to learn) is seen as a means of transmission of culture in non-linear, path-dependent, and institutionally specific ways. This process of evolutionary transmission is conceptualized in terms of "habits of thought" and "habits of life" that act as a culturally inscribed "genetic" template guiding economic behavior across societies and through time. Evolutionary thinking was one of the key ways in which a historicist current was injected back into a predominantly equilibrium-based economics, thereby reasserting the centrality of the kind of dynamics that allowed a space for cultural explanations.

The fifth approach considers the kinds of *disciplines* necessary to produce competent economic actors. It is an approach that has very practical antecedents in the work of writers such as F. W. Taylor, who were mainly concerned with minute analyses of bodily movement as ciphers for increased productivity. Later in the twentieth century this kind of approach was supplemented by other forms of bodily accountancy that paid more attention to non-quantifiable factors such as worker satisfaction, which, it was argued, were themselves important aspects of productivity. Literature in this tradition itself depended heavily on the presence of a framework of countability that, with the rise of accountancy and similar technologies, acted as a fundamental frame within which economies could be thought. These very acts of measurement made it possible to establish a culture of governance that acted as a precondition for the establishment of notions of economic rationality now so beloved of neoclassical economics. They also formed a powerful narrative of corporate control, by providing a discourse of "objective" number through which economic decisions could be made disinterestedly and through which aberrant behavior could be identified and judged.

The sixth and final approach focuses on *symptoms*. Interpretations of Euro-American economies as symptoms of general economic modes or models have been a constant of cultural life since at least the time of Adam Smith. These economic readings have had powerful cultural effects. One only has to think of the work of Marx and Engels to see the way in which such readings are able to reinscribe how cultures see themselves as a single functioning economic system, which, in turn, is returned to these cultures as an established economic and cultural fact. This is exactly how Marx and Engels were able to project nineteenth-century English capitalism – despite all its peculiarities – as a world economic standard and its class culture as the only culture. Exactly the same can be said of the pioneer experiments by F. W. Taylor and Henry Ford in the US early in the twentieth century with principles of mass production and mass consumption, which not only served as a model of accumulation for the rest of the world to copy or measure up to, but also as a way of life pivoted around the individual (as specialized worker and as fulfilled consumer).

All these lineages have continued to exist, but as a disorganized field; one that has been marginalized by the weight of marginal economics and computational knowledge, by political economy and the rationality of structure, and by the general neglect of economic processes within cultural studies. Though certain organized subdisciplines have emerged as a partial counterweight – and most notably economic sociology, economic anthropology, economic geography, and economic psychology – they have exerted very little influence on mainstream economic thought. However, there is an opening here that might be widened, since mainstream marginalist economic thought has itself continued to evolve, even as it has become hegemonic. So, for example, mainstream economics has developed an interest in so-called behavioral finance, which takes note of, and works with, findings from psychology, which are often far removed from the rational assumptions of marginalism. Similarly, recent methodological work on complex systems, simulation modeling (including agent-based modeling), certain forms of game theory, and intersubjective economics has produced a gradual drift from rational and calculative assumptions.

The Current Map of Cultural Economy

Contemporary work in cultural economy may be understood as being concerned with the processes of social and cultural relations that go to make up what we conventionally term the economic. No particular subdiscipline can claim dominance in this emerging field. Rather, it is a hybrid field consisting of impulses arising from a number of different disciplines, including economic sociology, cultural studies, social studies of finance, business and management studies, economic anthropology, and cultural geography, and a whole series of different methodological strategies as diverse as semiotics, ethnography, social studies of science, and theories of practice.

The early days of the approach – some ten years or so ago – were marked by an emphasis on distinctively economic topics with a strong social but weak cultural tinge, such as trust, the sociology of networks, and transaction-rich environments, including markets. This approach continues to flourish, as is evident from the surfeit of books published on the "soft" inputs that drive knowledge capitalism and the cultural industries (Burton-Jones 1999), on the powers of social capital and reflexivity in all areas of economic life (Cohen and Prusak 2001, Storper 1997), and on how trust and associational ties help to lubricate efficiency and economic creativity (Nooteboom 2002).

However, another strand of work in cultural economy has grown in profile, broadening substantially beyond these topics and representing a very different style and approach. This work is more process oriented, more culturally inflected, and more directed towards actual practices. In turn, the intellectual bounty from this work has been a much better appreciation of the economy as cultural practice and of culture as economic practice, for example through understandings of the narrative elements of many modern economies, which are inherent to notions of learning and knowledge acquisition in firms, and the emotional investments made by consumers in mundane but crucial practices such as shopping or investing. This shift has itself has been enabled by the growth of a heterodox series of interdisciplinary networks that have striven to bring together things formerly held apart (e.g., more interaction between socioeconomists and cultural anthropologists). There is, in itself, an interesting geography of interdisciplinarity, which deserves further study (for example, in social studies of finance, US economic sociologists have joined with French engineers and German and British practitioners of the social study of science).

What is interesting is how many of the themes we identified in the preceding section are resurfacing in the most recent work (see table 1).

Let us begin by considering the question of passions. Here we see, on a theoretical level, increasing appeal to the work of writers such as Deleuze and Guattari on immanence and potentiality that, in turn, is based on notions of affect and time,

Table 1 A map of contemporary cultural economy approaches

Themes	Contemporary emphases		
Passions	Subliminal energies, e.g., libido of capitalism (Deleuze and Guattari, Hardt and Negri)	Obsessional consumption (Bataille)	Passion to represent, e.g., brands (Lury)
Moral sentiments	Moral orders of conventions (Thevenot and Boltanski)	Constructedness of markets (Callon)	Ethical economies
Knowledge	Tacit knowledge (M. Polanyi)	Embodied knowledge and things that speak (Law, Latour)	Knowing in communities of practice (Wenger, Knorr-Cetina)
Evolution	Metaphors of economy (Mirowski and McCloskey)	Emergence and complexity (Delorme, Metcalfe)	Variety and redundancy (Grabher and Stark)
Power	Discipline (Mitchell, Rose)	Measurement (Miller)	Corporate narratives (Pine and Gilmour)
Symptoms	Information economy (Castells)	Consumer society (Bell)	Simulation (Baudrillard)

taken from the work of Spinoza in the seventeenth century. Such work stresses movement and process, and is often assumed to fit a mobile, libidinal and quick acting capitalism (Hardt and Negri 2001). Such an emphasis also overlaps with work of an older root that stresses the obsessional and excessive nature of accumulation, as found in the work of writers such as Bataille (1985), who noted the achievements of obsessive consumption. Not all of this entire strand of thought stays at the abstract level. For example, Lury's work on brands draws on notions of quick time within which brands have a transitory existence within the arc of perception; an existence that gives brands a grip on consumers that hardly registers but is still very powerful.

The moral sentiments approach continues to have a grip on current economic discourses, but as a practical ethical dimension of the everyday economy. Reframed in this way, the new work points to the way in which particular ethical justifications are bound up with particular economic practices. So, for example, contemporary work on economic conventions by writers such as Boltanski (Boltanski and Thevenot 1991, Boltanski and Chiapello 1999) is concerned with the identification of multiple orders of moral justification, which provide both motivation and explanation for participants (e.g., the contemporary emphasis on connectivity can be understood as the birth of a new order of justification in, and of, the economy). In turn, such an approach produces a much more variegated account of what constitutes economic practice and the construction of values. It pays particular attention to the utter constructedness of apparently pure economic entities like markets, and also relates to parallel work by writers such as Callon (1999), which stresses how market mechanisms are, in fact, long chains that can, and do, vary massively in terms of both their rules and their infrastructures. There are, then, multiple orders of ethics that drive the economy, many of which are not conventionally regarded as ethical. For example, it is easy to think of organic food production, fair trade, or workplace democracy as having ethical dimensions, but it is just as possible to think of the market and all other orderings of the economy as having these dimensions too.[9]

Moving on to the question of knowledge, it is increasingly stressed that not only knowledge capitalism but also capitalism in general is powered by tacit knowledges that are to be found in both cognitive and non-cognitive realms. This work finds a common ancestor in the central insight of Michael Polanyi that we know more than we can tell, through what he calls both mental and bodily knowledges. In turn, this insight has been used to build up a whole industry based on the auditing of knowledge as an asset class and the means by which knowledge assets can be enhanced and added to by learning and innovation (e.g., Nelson 1993, OECD 2000). One of the most fruitful means of grasping these insights has been provided by work on communities of practice, which tries to understand the full richness of such processes by attending to the ethnographic minutiae of knowledge transmission/translation in concrete workplaces – from insurance offices to laboratories (Wenger 1999, Brown and Duguid 2000, Knorr-Cetina 1999). Still more recent work has looked at the so-called para-ethnographic minutiae of knowledge transmission/translation in concrete workplaces, by concentrating on those "mute mobiles" in which so much economic knowledge is carried and through which so much economic life is now conducted – paper, chairs, texts, numbers, computers, software, and so on (Latour 1999, Law 2002, Thrift 2003a, Harper and Sellen 2001).

One of the central insights of work on knowledge, learning, and innovation has been the extreme importance of initial conditions in dictating subsequent outcomes. There is a direct link here with the long tradition of thinking of economics in evolutionary terms. However, in new evolutionary thinking, the cultural aspects of evolution are given more weight in three ways. First, there is an acute consciousness of the historical progress of evolutionary metaphors; commentators such as Mirowski (2002) and McKloskey (1998) have shown the power of these metaphors in economic thinking and organization (e.g., rhetorics of selection and adaptation, or assumptions of rational progress) and the way in which they are adapted to historical and geographical circumstances.[10] Second, the current sense of evolution stresses to a much greater degree – in line with developments in evolutionary theory itself and a much greater understanding of the history of evolutionary metaphors – notions of emergence, complexity, and autopoesis, showing how they work to order and sustain what have become highly variegated and complex economic systems (Loasby 1999, Foster and Metcalfe 2001, Delorme 2001). Third, particular population aspects of evolutionary theory tend to be emphasized. For example, notions of variety and redundancy in the selection environment have become of prime importance in explaining phenomena as diverse as the growth of project modes of working, differences in national and regional economic systems, and the mobilization of latent potential (Grabher 2002, Louca 1997). Here, what may often seem to be initially random cultural perturbations can turn out to be crucial competitive advantages as, for example, in the putative role that extended family and kinship ties have played in the dynamism of overseas Chinese economic networks.

Power is one of the key aspects of the cultural economy approach. However, in contemporary literature, the understanding of power is increasingly associated with discursive approaches and especially the work of Michel Foucault and followers such as Rose (1999). Such work tends to stress two particular aspects of economic formations. One aspect is the narration of the economy as found in features as diverse as stories of corporate power and advertising scripts, where the narration works as a cultural template of what it takes to become powerful, and, in turn, is an act of enrolment of allies and warning to competitors (Pine and Gilmore 1999). The other is the formation of "economic subjects" who have been configured to perform in, and understand, particular modes of discipline, subjects that are both subject to particular discourses and creators of them. More recently, notions of discourse have been broadened out to include not only words and deeds but also the object world which channels, and very often gives form to, utterances, and in doing so, produces powerful ordering impulses, which have heretofore been neglected, such as measurement standards and algorithms (Miller 1995)

The final mode of contemporary cultural thinking on the economy consists of symptomatic readings of the overall economic trajectories of Western societies. As we have already indicated, these kinds of readings have been popular since the days of Adam Smith. However, a recognizably cultural economic approach probably dates from Daniel Bell's work on the consumer society and the related growth and influence of the service sector in the 1960s. More recent variants have tended to stress culturally diffracted technological developments. For example, Castells' (2000) work on the information economy produces an account of a world in thrall to various cultural appropriations of information technologies. Castells takes the media into his account in a number of ways as a result. Other narratives go further. For example, Baudrillard (1994) argues that digital media technologies presage a society based on the absolute power of simulation. Work on the image therefore becomes a prime activity of capitalism.

Mapping an Emergent Field

Cultural economy is in the process of re-figuring every aspect of the value chain, from production through to consumption. In this book, we look at the various cultural transubstantiations of the economic by following this value chain, in six steps. We begin with cultural economy readings on the world of production, followed by readings on finance and money, economic regulation, commodity chains and consumption – all very much the heartland of conventional economic analysis. Then, in order to show that the cultural economy approach extends and enlivens the field of what is conventionally understood as the economic, we have also added a section on the economy of passions.

We have chosen essays that are not only exemplifications, but also stand in their own right as seminal and in some cases path-breaking contributions. Two caveats need to be registered immediately. One is that we have only included contributions that address the Euro-American sphere or its influence. We believe that including just a few contributions from elsewhere, which is all that space would allow, would have produced a misplaced tokenism. Another book is necessary to deal with the South, which would include important contributions such as those by anthropologists and postcolonial scholars on the cultural economy of indigenous knowledges, non-Western moral orders, non-market rituals and exchange networks, and alternative modernities (e.g., Thomas 1999). A second caveat, again for reasons of shortage of space, is that we have had to exclude certain important topics, since including them would have left us with only one or two illustrative readings under each heading, producing a thinness of content that would have damaged our very attempt to give body and weight to the field. These topics might have included waste generation and disposal, tourism and mobility, the rise of specialized market segments like children's toys (cf. Thrift 2003b), nature and the environment, new forms of property (and especially the new rules of possession being built into entities like software, the radio spectrum, and the genome), the body in all its myriad forms, queer economics (e.g., the pink pound and the difference it makes), the cultural circuit of capital (made up of institutions like business schools, management consultants, management gurus, and the media), trust and social capital, and risk.

Production

Part one includes four readings that illustrate different aspects of the cultural economy approach to production. The first two readings are caught up in the day-to-day existence of workers. In chapter 1 Angela McRobbie shows the way in which the principles of craft design can still exist if workers are willing to make economic compromises in pursuit of cultural goals. McRobbie's fashion workers frame themselves as members of a cultural elite, even though to do so, they have to be willing to self-exploit in ways which she shows are unlikely to benefit them in material terms over the long run. Seán Ó'Riain, in contrast (chapter 2), burrows into the lives of a set of Irish software developers working for American firms. Ó'Riain shows the complex temporal and spatial strategies that these workers have to follow in order to produce kudos for themselves in firms that are strung out between many locations. At the same time, he also shows what a complex cultural object software is, made up of many compromises, which often defy the logical templates it is meant to follow, and comprise many different skills that are both social and technical (Thrift and French 2002). These compromises also arise from extraordinarily heterogeneous associations of things, people, ideas, and other actors that need to be brought into alignment in order to produce an object (see Law (2002) for a detailed account of the vast material–semiotic assemblages involved in the production of the doomed TSR 2 aircraft).

Chapter 3 focuses on the cultural economy of corporate learning and innovation. Over the last 40 years, management practices have taken their own cultural turn, as a result of the growth of new intermediaries like business schools, management consultancies, management gurus, and the business media. Integral to this growth has been the circulation of management ideas. One of the most important of these recent ideas is the notion of the "community of practice" as the key site of innovation and learning in firms (as opposed to the kind of approaches that locate innovation and learning as the product of knowledge possessed by gifted people or technologies). Originating from work in the 1980s by such writers as Jean Lave, "community of practice" was meant to encapsulate a whole series of ideas from practice theory. It has subsequently become a key management tool, through its canonization in influential journals such as the *Harvard Business Review* (Wenger and Snyder 2000). However, in the course of canonization and application, certain elements of practice theory were dropped for the sake of portability and convenience. The result has been the instrumentalization of the idea, as documented in chapter 3 by Vann and Bowker; an instrumentalization which, it could be argued, was both necessary for the idea to travel and, at the same time, came loaded with compromises that violated a number of the fundamental tenets of the practice theory approach.

Chapter 4, by Callon et al., makes clear that in the service economy, the kinds of issues set out in the previous chapters are not epiphenomenal, but part of the production process itself. More and more products depend upon notions and perceptions of quality, which are inscribed into them by a whole set of intermediaries. In considerable detail, Callon et al. set out the steps by which this process takes place, and the crucial role that reflexivity plays at all points.

Finance and Money

One of the most expansive aspects of cultural economy has turned out to be the study of money in all its forms through detailed ethnographic research. Part of the reason for this is the cultural hold that money has on Euro-American societies, which is clearly of the strongest order and yet its impact and workings are still often very difficult to define. One reason for this is that money is regarded as an economic entity *par excellence*, whose workings are smooth, fast, and rule-driven. Yet the fund of ethnographic research that has now been built up tells a very different story – of the importance of improvisation, manipulation, and the ability to grasp the moment (Buenza and Stark 1999). Chapter 5 by Anna Tsing works mainly at the macro-scale to make these points. She shows how opportunistic individuals and corporations, working in concert with political interests, can manipulate investor expectations and investment behavior in the world gold markets. This behavior amounts to a kind of financial depredation that, however, is rarely counted as such, cloaked as it is in talk of legitimate versus illegitimate manipulations that provides a sense of regulated and orderly practice.

A particularly important element of the formation of cultural economy has been the injection of ideas from science studies and the sociology of science more generally. Drawing particularly on ideas developed in these fields, money and finance have been likened in recent work to a series of networks within which the hard graft of material semiotics takes temporary place. A particular challenge has been presented to those studying money and finance by the fact that so much of the conduct of money and finance depends upon non-human actors – from formulae to screens and from keyboards to electronic contacts. Taking these non-human actors seriously has led to some major advances. Chapter 6 by Donald MacKenzie looks at the dramatic performativity of one particular economic formula and its ability to move markets, accumulate wealth, and then lose it. However, a good part of the business of financial markets is much less visible than this, a stricture that applies in particular to many kinds of vital day-to-day systems of operation and regulation (for example, clearing systems and other forms of netting). Similarly, in Chapter 7, Karin Knorr Cetina and Urs Bruegger illustrate how central the computer screen has become in the conduct of foreign exchange markets, now traded largely via electronic broking and dealer-to-dealer contact systems. This assemblage of a highly distributed and rapidly changing space of global transactions onto the screen is no simple process of objectification. It produces a constant demand to fill the gaps thrown up by the screen, which is more than a technical operation, since it involves the technical mobilization of various persons. It may well be that, as a result, we are entering a world of "post-social" forms which are beginning to step into the place of conventional social relations, which emphasize thickness and meaningfulness. The result is that markets can no longer be understood as human collectivities, but instead, are based on a kind of specialized mimetic reflexivity.

Economic Regulation

Another key area has proved to be the different forms of economic regulation that populate the world. Despite all the alleged toughness of economic rule making and following, there is substantial cultural variation in both practice and value. Nothing illustrates this contention better than the informal modes of regulation that have grown up in emerging economies, where the state is a comparatively weak actor whose activities have to be supplemented (or displaced) by various private forms of regulation, or where the state has been actively drawn into illegal or shady economic activities. Such lacunae provide fertile ground for cultural traditions that may have been previously submerged under the aegis of the centrally planned state. As Frederico Varese shows in chapter 8, inadequate state regulation in Russia has produced numerous opportunities for the Mafia to thrive, guide state action, and provide a livelihood for large numbers of people.

Regulation as a cultural practice is not simply a "disease" suffered by those who lack formal structures, but can everyday feature of all forms of regulation, including the workings of the world's mot prestigious institutions. From the commanding heights of capitalism, regulation obviously appears to be a different matter. In chapter 9 the journalist Lewis Lapham, well known for his work on the American upper class, extends his gaze to the coteries of capitalist and government functionaries that run the world economy. He shows the way in which marginalization is not just an economic, but also a cultural phenomenon, made up of quasi-imperial judgments about the value and worth of different nations, arranged according to entrepreneurial and other kinds of norms, which are continually reproduced in discursive spaces like Davos in Switzerland, where some of the benevolent rich and powerful come together to extol their own virtues and to instruct others fortunate enough to be allowed in to the event on proper economic conduct.

The contours of power are highly visible in Lapham's chapter, but a lot of regulatory power also resides in presuppositions about how the world is which are so widely held that they are never challenged. Foremost among these must surely be the importance of number and the associated values of calculability and precision. Another important element of cultural economy has been the attempt to make the values of countability transparent. Peter Miller's chapter on accountancy is a particularly revealing example of why number matters, how arbitrary many of its practices actually are, and the power that can be deployed by those who lay claim to understanding it. As recent accountancy scandals show, number is often a movable feast masquerading as an immovable standard.

Commodity Chains

Spanning the globe are a whole series of transactional networks which allow commodities to be transferred from one market to another, in the process very often being transformed both materially and semiotically. Much exciting work has been carried out recently on the nature of these commodity chains and the transformations they are able to effect. Stoller's ethnographic study of West African market traders in New York (chapter 11) shows that these global networks do not have to be the preserve of large transnational corporations. Even those with relatively little economic where-withal are able to participate, by weaving together consumer demand in the West with trading opportunities in Africa and Asia. These skilled arbitrageurs have to have cultural skills in order to produce economic opportunities: skills of being attuned to Western markets, skills of intercultural negotiation, skills of tuning in to global trading opportunities, and skills of improvisation.

However, it is of course the case that the vast bulk of trade along commodity chains is carried out in larger and more organized structures than those that Stoller's traders normally tap. In chapter 12 Hughes uses the example of the cut flower trade between Kenya and the supermarkets of the West to show the concentrated work of connection that needs to be continually reproduced in order to not only produce profits, but also to preserve perishable goods in a form that consumers located thousands of miles away from producers will find appealing. A vital element in these chains of connection is the ability to read a continually changing market and to make this reading count across the chain of links. Hughes shows how this ability is as much a process of cultural interpretation and depends on a rich variety of intermediaries to do the cultural work.

Clearly, these commodity chains are spatially inflected and built up from below, through located values, symbols, products and practices. In chapter 13 Murdoch and Miele document one particular contrast, that between fast food trade networks and the so-called slow food movement. This movement is trying to rework the predominant cultural registers of food in the West by changing judgments on the worth of food and consumption. It therefore values the sensual pleasures of taste and smell, and the temporal pleasures of gradual gratification by attempting to create local spaces of production and consumption that are fitted to these pleasures. Interestingly, the chapter thus shows that economic value and worth in both fast and slow food markets is built around a cultural valuation rather than vice versa; an "order of worth" encoded into material arrangements in commodity chains.

Consumption

One of the areas where the cultural economy approach has made most impact has been in the study of consumption. For a considerable time, an alliance of anthropologists, geographers, and sociologists has been concerned with trying to show that the economics of consumption are culturally constructed by considering the broad canvas of "commercial cultures," in recognition of the degree to which Western culture and commerce have gone hand in hand for many centuries (cf. Jackson et al. 2000). Daniel Miller has been a key worker in this area, trying to marry material culture approaches with ethnography in order to understand modern Western consumption. In particular, he has been concerned to outline the key emotional origins of shopping practices. In chapter 14 he develops an argument that shopping is beset by obligations to others, many of which might well be described as bonds of love. The variegated set of shoppers that he follows nearly all display an acute awareness of the needs and wants of others as they shop: economic relations are necessarily social relations.

In chapter 15 Alison Clarke shows some of the same impulses taking shape in the context of home shopping. Focusing on mail order catalogues, she shows the different economies of regard that are associated with even the humble catalogue: senses of authenticity, foppery, and affluence circulate even in these outlets, and drive some consumers to display what almost might be conceived of as compulsive behavior. The economy of regard clearly lies at the heart of the responses of firms in the mail order business, as elsewhere, but the particular dimension has often escaped conventional economic accounts. Even in the humblest outlets for consumption, the same kinds of behavior can be found, with the result that different kinds of consumer conventions often apply (see, for example, Crewe and Gregson's (1998) study of the cultural economy of car boot sales, where forms of sourcing, circulation, transaction and pricing are quite different from those found in more conventional outlets, but where values like thrift continue to have a hold).

In chapter 16 Haidy Geismar studies a market in which that history is formalized and becomes a part of the price mechanism. She is particularly acute on the importance of auction mechanisms in so many markets, a set of mechanisms that is again expanding as a result of the Internet. By taking as her main topic the sale of tribal art, Geismar also shows the degree to which value is made from the colonial entanglement of objects, which in turn has produced senses of cultural authenticity that have become the basis of a new form of "soft" cultural imperialism that defines cultural worth by price.

Finally, it is important to remember the actual practices of retailing, including the myriad workforces that are employed in acts of sale. In chapter 17 Philip Crang points to the different performances that are required of retail employees according to the context in which they find themselves. By drawing on his own ethnography of restaurant work, Crang is able to show the multiple personas that waiters need to adopt in order to be attuned to the practice of sale. In particular, he shows the degree to which reflexivity has become a vital part of the act of serving, especially as Euro-American societies, driven by the media, have ratcheted up expectations of what constitutes good practices of eating and serving.

Economy of Passions

Part six aims to show the extraordinary affective investments that are made in commercial cultures that are often depicted as hyper-rational or even sterile. Crang shows the emotional work that is involved in working in certain kinds of restaurants. Arlie Hochschild's classic work (chapter 18) makes the same point, but then extends it by showing the degree to which this emotional work is now a matter of explicit training, so that employees are able to participate more fully and more effectively in the act of sale. Using the example of flight attendants, she shows the growing expectation that employees will be emotionally literate, and the stresses and strains that this expectation produces. She also shows the way in which both employee and customer participate in a fantasy of service to which they both subscribe – though often to wildly varying degrees.

This fantasy is fully realized with the case of sex workers, outlined in chapter 19 by Lisa Law. Here, the act of exchange and the act of sex are clearly one and the same thing, but that instrumentalism has to be concealed in a play of calculated subservience. In Law's analysis, which focuses on bar workers in the Philippines, this act is complicated still further by the intercultural nature of these kinds of transactions. Here, what we see is the charge of sexual desire converted into the raw currency of exchange.

The case of sex workers in Southeast Asia can be seen as only one part of a massive illicit global economy trading on passions like sex, drugs, and gambling. This economy comes together in certain strategic sites around the world, of which one of the most notable is Las Vegas. What is striking about the Las Vegas outlined in chapter 20 by Denton and Morris is the degree to which its prosperity has become central to the prosperity of the American economy, driven by systematic alliances between casino owners, politicians, criminals (from US syndicates to the Japanese Yakuza), the urban elite, and property magnates, which have, if anything, become more deep seated. After reading chapter 20 it is difficult to be quite so judgmental about how anomalous the situation outlined by Frederico Varese really is.

It would of course be impossible to produce a book on cultural economy that does not address the rise and rise of the cultural industries as an integral part of Western economic formations. Chapter 21 concentrates on the archetypal cultural industry of advertising, the industry that is often considered to be at the center of modern consumer capitalism. Celia Lury's interest is in the brand, that here and not-here icon, which stands for so much and for so little. Focusing on the Nike swoosh, Lury argues that the brand has effectivity because it triggers a response in that very small space of time before cognition takes hold. Using video evidence she shows the way in which the brand acts as a kind of halo around numerous activities in modern life, framing them rather than giving them meaning. We are all continually being lightly touched by brands and this brush with cultural economy has now become an integral part of not only what we consume, but also who we are.

Conclusion

This is a book that acts as both a summary of what has so far been achieved in the expanding field of cultural economy and as a ground for further work. The field continues to rapidly evolve, so that it is not just filling out every dimension of what is conventionally regarded as the economic with cultural filigree, but is also producing new senses of the economic, which heretofore have not existed. There is much still to do, but we hope that this book will create more adherents who will have the wherewithal to do it.

NOTES

1   Of course, many economists would argue that it is the improper application of economic knowledge that has brought us to this pass.
2   For example, considerable policy interest has grown in psychometric tools of assessing risk and hedging against uncertainty, in measuring and building social capital as the mainspring of economic regeneration strategies, in processes of tacit knowledge formation and creative improvisation in order to unlock business innovation and adaptation.
3   However, there are obvious interesting intertwinings with orthodox Western economics. For example, Maurer's work on the spatial distribution of Islamic economic theory includes key sites in Leicester and San Francisco, powered by experts who have been trained in both Islamic and Western orthodox principles of economics. Similarly, Islamic principles have a tendency to appear as a weapon of moral sanction in President Mahathir's Malaysia rather than as the foundation of the country's industrialization program.
4   Even Alfred Marshall, often invoked as a founding figure by many practitioners of economics narrowly defined, was clear that the discipline should be broadly defined. His *Principles of Economics*, first published in 1890, opens with this statement: "Political economy of economics is a study of mankind in the ordinary business of life; it examines that part of individual and social action which is most closely connected with the attainment and with the use of material requisites of well-being. Thus, it is on the one side a study of wealth; and on the other, and more important side, a part of the study of man" (Marshall 1961: 1).
5   The pre-tax profit margins on an SUV are currently about $8,000 compared with a figure close to break-even on smaller cars.
6   Brought forth in part by rising income inequality
7   The car manufacturers have taken the NRPE campaign seriously. Bill Ford has met the NRPE leaders, while Chevrolet has sponsored a series of rock concerts, called "Chevrolet Presents: Come Together and Worship," a move which failed to impress the NRPE director who was quoted as saying that "It encourages Christians to buy cars, many of which despoil God's creation" (Rushe 2002: 18).
8   "In the race for wealth, and honor, and preferments [man] may run as hard as he can, and strain every nerve and every muscle, in order to outstrip all his competitors. But if he should jostle, or throw down any of them, the indulgence of the spectators is entirely at an end. It is a violation of fair play which they cannot admit of. This man is to them, in every respect, as good as he: they do not enter into that self-love by which he prefers himself so much to this other, and cannot go along with the motive from which he hurt him" (Smith 1759, pt. ii, sec. ii, ch. 2; cited in Morrow 1969: 48).
9   Similarly, these orders come with hopes and dreams that might be considered to have a religious dimension (see Maurer 2002).
10 Mirowski (2002) shows how these evolutionary metaphors bear a complex relation to other families of metaphors, and especially machinic and linguistic metaphors.

REFERENCES

Amin, A. and Cohendet, P. (2004) *Architectures of Knowledge: Firms, Capabilities and Communities*. Oxford: Oxford University Press.
Bataille, G. (1985) *Visions of Excess: Selected Writings 1927–39*. Manchester: Manchester University Press.
Baudrillard, J. (1994) *Simulacra and Simulation*. Ann Arbor: University of Michigan Press.

Boltanski, L. and Chiapello, E. (1999) *Le Nouvel esprit du capitalisme*. Paris: Gallimard.

Boltanski, L. and Thevenot, L. (1991) *De la justification. Economies de la grandeur*. Paris: Gallimard.

Bradsher, K. (2002) *High and Mighty. SUVs: The World's Most Dangerous Vehicles and How They Got That Way*. New York: Public Affairs.

Brooks, D. (2000) *Bobos in Paradise: The New Upper Class and How They Got There*. New York: Simon and Schuster.

Brown, J. S. and Duguid, P. (2000) *The Social Life of Information*. Boston, MA: Harvard Business School Press.

Buenza, D. and Stark, D. (1999) "Tools of the trade: The socio-technology of arbitrage in a Wall Street trading room." Mimeo, Center on Organizational Innovation, Columbia University.

Burton-Jones, A. (1999) *Knowledge Capitalism*. Oxford: Oxford University Press.

Callon, M. (ed.) (1999) *The Laws of the Markets*. Oxford: Blackwell.

Carrier, J. and Miller, D. (eds.) *Virtualism: A New Political Economy*. Oxford: Berg.

Castells, M. (2000) *The Rise of the Network Society*, 2nd edn. Oxford: Blackwell.

Cohen, D. and Prusak, L. (2001) *In Good Company: How Social Capital Makes Organizations Work*. Boston, MA: Harvard Business School Press.

Crewe, L. and Gregson, N. (1998) "Tales of the unexpected: Exploring car boot sales as marginal spaces of contemporary consumption." *Transactions of the Institute of British Geographers*, 23, 39–53.

Delorme, R. (2001) "Theorizing complexity." In J. Foster and J. S. Metcalfe (eds.) *Frontiers of Evolutionary Economics: Competition, Self-Organization and Innovation Policy*. Cheltenham: Edward Elgar.

Du Gay, P. and Pryke, M. (eds.) (1999) *Cultural Economy: Cultural Analysis and Commercial Life*. London: Sage.

Foster, J. and Metcalfe, J. S. (eds.) (2001) *Frontiers of Evolutionary Economics: Competition, Self-Organization and Innovation Policy*. Cheltenham: Edward Elgar.

Frank, T. (1997) *The Conquest of Cool: Business Culture, Counterculture and the Rise of Hip Consumerism*. Chicago, IL: University of Chicago Press.

Frank, T. (2001) *One Market Under God: Extreme Capitalism, Market Populism and the End of Economic Democracy*. London: Secker and Warburg.

Grabher, G. (ed.) (2002) *Special Issue: Productions in Projects: Economic Geographies of Temporary Collaborations, Regional Studies*, 36, 3, May.

Hardt, M. and Negri, A. (2001) *Empire*. Cambridge, MA: Harvard University Press.

Harper, R. and Sellen, A. (2001) *The Myth of the Paperless Office*. Cambridge, MA: MIT Press.

Hassard, J. and Law, J. (eds.) (1999) *After Networks*. Oxford: Blackwell.

Hodgson, G. M. (2001) *How Economics Forgot History*. Routledge: London.

Jackson, P., Lowe, M., Miller, D., and Mort, F. (eds.) (2000) *Commercial Cultures*. Oxford: Berg.

Joseph, M. (2002) *Against the Romance of Community*. Minneapolis: University of Minnesota Press.

Knorr-Cetina, K. (1999) *Epistemic Cultures: How the Sciences Make Sense*. Chicago, IL: University of Chicago Press.

Knorr-Cetina, K. (2000) "The market as an object of attachment: Exploring postsocial relations in financial markets." *Canadian Journal of Sociology*, 25, 141–68.

Latour, B. (1999) *Pandora's Hope: Essays on the Reality of Science Studies*. Cambridge, MA: Harvard University Press.

Law, J. (2002) *Aircraft Stories*. Durham, NC: Duke University Press.

Leyshon, A. and Thrift, N. J. (eds.) (1997) *Money/Space*. London: Routledge.

Leyshon, A., Lee, R., and Williams, C. (eds.) (2003) *Alternative Economic Spaces*. London: Sage.

Loasby, B. (1999) *Knowledge, Institutions and Evolution in Economics*. London: Routledge.

Louca, F. (1997) *Turbulence in Economics*. Cheltenham: Edwar Elgar.

McKloskey, D. (1998) *The Rhetoric of Economics*, 2nd edn. Madison: University of Wisconsin Press.

Marcus, G. (ed.) (1998) *Corporate Futures: The Diffusion of the Culturally Sensitive Corporate Form*. Chicago, IL: University of Chicago Press.

Marshall, A. (1961) [1890] *Principles of Economics*. Lomdon: Macmillan.

Maurer, B. (2002) "Repressed futures: Financial derivatives' theological unconscious." *Economy and Society*, 31, 1, 15–36.

Mirowski, P. (2002) *Machine Dreams: Economics Becomes a Cyborg Science*. Cambridge: Cambridge University Press.

Miyazaki, H. (2003) "The temporalities of the market." *American Anthropologist*, 105.

Morrow, G. R. (1969) *The Ethical and Economic Theories of Adam Smith*. New York: Augustus Kelley Publishers.

Nelson, R. (1993) *National Systems of Innovation*. Oxford: Oxford University Press.

Nooteboom, B. (2002) *Trust: Forms, Foundations, Functions, Failures, and Figures*. Cheltenham: Edward Elgar.

OECD (2000) *Knowledge Management in the Learning Economy: Education and Skills*. Paris: Organization for Economic Cooperation and Development.

Pine, J. B. and Gilmore, J. (1999) *The Experience Economy*. Boston, MA: Harvard Business School Press.

Procacci, G. (1978) "Social economy and the government of poverty." *Ideology and Consciousness*. 4 (autumn), 55–72.

Ray, L. and Sayer, A. (eds.) (1997) *Culture and Economy after the Cultural Turn*. London: Sage.

Riles, A (2003) *Real Time: Governing the Market after the Failure of Knowledge*. Chicago: American Bar Foundation.

Rose, N. (1999) *Governing the Soul: The Shaping of the Private Self*. London: Routledge.

Rushe, D. (2002) "On Wall Street: Jesus wouldn't drive a gas-guzzling truck." *Sunday Times Business*, November 24, p. 18.

Scott, A. J. (2000) *The Cultural Economy of Cities*. London: Sage.

Sheller, M. and Urry, J. (2000) "The city and the car." *International Journal of Urban and Regional Research*, 24, 737–57.

Sohn-Rethel, A. (1978) *Intellectual and Manual Labour*. London: CSE Books.

Stoller, P. (2002) *Money has no Smell: The Africanization of New York City*. Chicago, IL: Chicago University Press.

Storper, M. (1997) *The Regional World*. New York: Guilford Press.

Thomas, N. (1999) *Possessions: Indigenous Art/Colonial Culture*. London: Thames and Hudson.

Thrift, N. J. (1997) "The rise of soft capitalism." *Cultural Values*, 1, 29–57.

Thrift, N. J. (2003a) "Remembering the technological unconscious." *Environment and Planning: Society and Space*, 21. Forthcoming.

Thrift, N. J. (2003b) "Closer to the machine? Intelligent environments, new forms of possession, and the rise of the supertoy." *Cultural Geographies*, 16 forthcoming.

Thrift, N. J. and French, S. (2002) "The automatic production of space." *Transactions of the Institute of British Geographers*, NS, 27, 3, 309–35.

Tool, M. (1991) "Contributions to an institutionalist theory of price determination." In G. M. Hodgson and E. Screpanti (eds.) *Rethinking Economics: Markets, Technology and Economic Evolution*. Aldershot: Edward Elgar.

Veblen, T. (1990) [1919] *The Place of Science in Modern Civilization*. New Brunswick, NJ: Transaction Publishers.

Wenger, E. (1999) *Communities of Practice*. Cambridge: Cambridge University Press.

Wenger, E. and Snyder, W. M. (2000) "Communities of practice: The organizational frontier." *Harvard Business Review*, Jan.–Feb., 139–45.

Part I Production

Chapter 1

A Mixed Economy of Fashion Design

Angela McRobbie

On the Dole

For most of the interviewees, being on the dole was a taken-for-granted part of the experience of being a fashion designer, not unlike the periods actors spend 'resting' between jobs. For the designers these periods were, in the first instance, tied up with going on the business enterprise scheme which required that applicants be unemployed for a minimum period of thirteen weeks before becoming eligible. This scheme became the official route for young designers setting up in business. Its existence ameliorated the reality of 'signing on' and, once they were on the scheme, they suddenly moved in status from being unemployed to being 'fashion designers'. The scheme got young graduates off the dole since, as we have already seen, few received job offers of any type in the months following graduation. Over the eight year period since they had left college many found themselves reapplying to the scheme until it was withdrawn by the government in 1994.

Originally the scheme was designed to support small businesses in their first year of operation, after which the young entrepreneur was expected to be able to manage without the supplement of £40 and later £50 a week. When it became evident that this was not long enough to create a healthy cash-flow the scheme was extended a further year. Of the young designers only one had not been on the EAS (and this was because she couldn't raise the £1,000). Five had reapplied after an interval in employment, and one designer had also been on an equivalent scheme during her time working in France. The young designers who later ended up on the brink of bankruptcy with substantial debts, or had actually declared themselves bankrupt, had no alternative but to go back on the dole. Despite this heavy reliance upon the dole as a kind of fallback mechanism, the graduates were signing on for relatively short periods of time. For most, being unemployed was a temporary gap in their careers. None had been fully unemployed for a stretch of more than nine months, and they tended to use these periods to renew contacts in the business, and to rethink their futures in fashion. In addition, while signing on they took on some freelance work which was paid 'cash in hand' to supplement their dole. This activity in the hidden economy was not so much a matter of criminal intent, more a means of surviving and getting back into work. Like many young people living in London they knew that dole payments were not sufficient to live on, never mind provide the kind of resources needed to look for a new job. Making dresses for a stall in Camden Market or helping out as a stall assistant, or making clothes for friends in the club scene, allowed the young designers the opportunity of keeping in touch with the industry until they found a proper job. This was also a way of negating or overcoming the reality of being unemployed.

Even the established, well-known designers, of whom three out of eight acknowledged their experience of signing on at Job Centres, treated the dole in a matter-of-fact way. The stress of keeping their businesses going, knowing that they were making losses, and the exhaustion and anxiety of dealing with the banks as they headed towards bankruptcy, meant that retreating from business by going on the dole felt like a temporary unburdening of responsibility. Helen Storey describes her experience of being on the dole as follows:

> What does it feel like when the need to run has gone? ... I now deal in the small, in the detail of pennies rather than the rounding-up of thousands. I am down to collecting premier points from that supermarket and Income Support of £25 a week. It's during the day that I miss the part of me I thought I knew ... there is me, and the rest of the long-term unemployed. (Storey 1996: 2)

Signing on the dole has become an expected and routine aspect of life in the creative sector. The fashion designers, like so many other workers in the culture industries, know that they will experience periods out of work. But because they have such an investment in the kind of work they do, they adjust to this rather than confront the possible reality of failure. They neutralize being on the dole so that it comes to signify the spaces between work, almost like days off. It is assumed that everybody has been on the dole at some point and going from the dole into the spotlight of success is as much a part of fashion mythology as it is in the music industry. The moment that a band who have eventually had a hit can celebrate being able to 'sign off' is paralleled in fashion with the point at which the designer can also 'sign off'. Fashion history, like pop history, is full of stories like that of the internationally recognized Bodymap team preparing for their 1984 catwalk collection while still having to sign on and working from the kitchen table. This kind of folklore destigmatizes unemployment while also confirming the artistic integrity of the designer.

Despite this reliance on the dole as, at least, a fallback mechanism, these young people can hardly be described as dependent upon welfare or benefits. Their periods of unemployment were intermittent and they sought to find ways of getting off the dole. Nor were they in any sense intentionally fraudulent in their claims. Rather, they recognized that occasional freelance payments or the odd few days' work here and there could hardly allow them to sign off and eat. This poses urgent questions about the sustainability of employment and 'regular' work in these increasingly casual creative fields and the consequences of shifts in unemployment benefits as dole in 1996 is transformed into a 'jobseeker's allowance' with a workfare component.[1]

Dole is understood, then, not simply as being without work and therefore having to find any job, but rather as a stretch of time which is to be filled with activities aimed at getting back into fashion and creative work. This is a particular way of managing the uncertainty and risks of working in the creative field. Dole becomes another temporary contract. However, if being on the dole is bearable for short periods, this is only possible because the graduates are young and without major financial responsibilities such as children or mortgages. Theirs is a high-risk strategy. The day-to-day existence which their occupational choice forces upon them means that they have to suspend or put on hold major decisions in their personal lives, and it also leaves them underinsured and ill-equipped to cope with unexpected illnesses or accidents.

Stall-holding

Just as everybody in fashion design seems to have spent some time on the dole, so almost everyone has been a stall-holder at some time. Indeed, getting a stall was and is the standard route into setting up as a fashion designer in the United Kingdom. It is almost a *rite de passage*. It also offers relative ease of access. With a sewing machine and a few other pieces of equipment, and enough capital to buy fabric, the young designer can enter this market. And the availability of such units in most of the large cities provides access to a market of (mostly young) consumers and, also, tourists. Fifteen of the young designers, and six out of eight of the established designers had, at some point in their careers, a lease or a share in a unit or stall in one of the fashion retail markets. For many this proved a more expensive and labour intensive option than they had imagined. At the same time, with £40 a week from the EAS it was the best way of trying to get recognized as a 'name' designer. Having a stall allowed the designer to produce a range of 'own label' stock without having to rely on other retailers placing orders and then adding a substantial mark-up onto the price. It also allowed the designers to set their own working pace and they could adjust their output according to what was selling well at any one point in time. In addition to this, without being tied to an order they could vary fabric and quality according to their cash-flow.

This kind of stall-holding arrangement frequently relied on two or three young designers working together. They would share the rent of a unit at one of the London street markets and spend one half of the week designing and making up the clothes and the rest of the week selling them. Alternatively, they would supply a unit with an agreed number of items each week and be paid by the stall-holder on the basis of how well the clothes sold, with only a small mark-up going to the stall-holder. While initially exciting, in that it meant the graduates could immediately call themselves designers with their 'own label', this actually proved to be very exhausting work, especially when the designer was also either doing the production work at home with the help of friends or family, or else relying on the services of a single machinist to make up the clothes on this rapid production line. Once again contrary to their own public images many of the designers were also doing the sewing.

For a small number of the designers interviewed, this cottage-industry style of working was the best option for staying in business but, for others, the rising rent of the unit or stall or the slow volume of sales from these kinds of outlets put them out of business (in 1994 Hyper Hyper rents were running at £900 a month). If the stock did not sell quickly the designer was left with it, still having to fund a further range in the hope that it would sell more easily. In effect, the designer was carrying all the costs and all the risks. It was at this stage in their careers that two of the designers, Ruth A. and Anna T., abandoned independent design work each with debts of over £20,000. But for those who did well with a unit, it was a transitional stage to acquiring a proper shop, and a more fully-fledged business. Three of the better-known designers who participated in this study had retained a stall even when they had other outlets, on the basis that the stall provided them with a more immediate response to new ideas, and also allowed them to produce slightly cheaper ranges for a younger market. Having a stall was a way of keeping in touch with the club scene and with youth culture.

The merchandising manager of the Hyper Hyper store in London, which provided rented stall space for up to seventy young designers (until 1997 when it relocated a few doors down the street and renamed itself Hype DF), described how she helped the young stall-holders to develop a more stable and reliable turnover. She was surprised by how little they knew about marketing, promotion and production. To be offered a unit in the shop the designer must have already produced three collections and must be able to present the merchandising manager with a whole range, including a minimum of twenty-five items. Under her advice they would then 'edit' this down to a range which fitted both the pricing levels in the store and the outlook of the market it served. While a shared unit provided a valuable outlet for young designers, one of the main difficulties in sustaining or developing this further as a way of working in fashion lay in the high cost of renting a stall. A stall at Camden Market at a cost of £250 for the weekend was a good deal cheaper, as was Kensington Market and also Portobello Road, but this also meant that the clothes were cheaper and so the returns smaller.[2] In addition, the kind of support and advice given to stall holders at Hyper Hyper was not available elsewhere.

Having a space at Hyper Hyper was a more professional and less informal arrangement, the costs were higher but so were the prices of the clothes and therefore the possible returns to the designer through sales. And as we have seen, to be offered a unit at Hyper Hyper the designers already had to have established some kind of reputation, so entrance to this market was not as direct as it was elsewhere. In all cases, however, producing for this kind of outlet soon led to a make or break moment, since to move out of a unit and into a proper shop, or to be able to work independently as a designer for stockists or for wholesalers, required a good deal more capital upfront than the returns from having a stall provided. So at this point the young designers were forced to think and plan more strategically about what it would take to build on this as a business foundation. Of my sample of young designers only three, at the time of the interview, had retained a unit-style of outlet. Gaby T. had a shared unit at Portobello Market which was producing a small but relatively steady income; Rachel F. had made a conscious decision to stay small and focus on selling from Hyper Hyper while also producing individual items to order; and Celia M. was one of the longest remaining and best-known designers based in Hyper Hyper. All three of these designers knew who they were producing for in these outlets. Celia had a cheaper line of clothes made specially for the club market; Rachel specialized in party dresses for stylish young professionals; and Gaby was producing slightly cheaper versions of her freelance work for 'young, working mums in the Notting Hill area'. All three also benefited from the tourist trade which these market outlets attracted.

Shop Assistants

At the time of the interviews, only two out of the eighteen respondents were sales assistants, and a third was a shop manageress. Ruth A. was pleased to get the job in an upmarket designer outlet in Knightsbridge after she was forced out of business with spiralling debts. Although she was not employed in a design capacity, her experience and knowledge of design were useful in her work. During the three years she had been working in this boutique she had paid off most of her outstanding debts and was beginning to be able to make more of a contribution to the flat she shared with her partner. It was, as she put it, a relief not to have the responsibility of running her own business. She also felt she was able to learn much more about the fashion business in her capacity as manageress than in the more stressful and isolated role as young designer. Philippa D. had applied unsuccessfully for several jobs as design assistants after her attempts on the EAS failed. Eventually she was employed by Coates and Storey but was made redundant a year later when the company was forced to lose staff. After another period on the dole she was employed as a sales assistant at Laura Ashley. This was a step back since obviously it provided her with no opportunities to develop her design skills, but it did pay her a regular salary and she was considering applying to their management training scheme, which would mean abandoning hopes of returning to her design work in the meantime. Finally, Nana F. also worked as a shop assistant even though her official title was design assistant. She was one of the few students who had no savings or parental support to fall back on following graduation and for this reason she was not able to consider looking for work abroad. Nor was she able to go on the EAS, although she did spend a few months unemployed after graduating. This experience forced her to look for a job in the industry and she spent three years with a wholesale company before finding work with a company who produced under its own label for a number of outlets across London. The promise was that Nana would work her way through the various parts of the group to the point where she could take on responsibility for the design work. However, after four years this still had not happened and when interviewed she was looking after the unit the company had at Hyper Hyper. All three graduates who worked as sales assistants or shop manageresses felt that the work they were doing was less taxing and certainly less creative than they would have originally wished. At the same time, they were less concerned to project the strong and emphatic sense of self which the other designers did as a matter of course. They did not share that sense of themselves as 'stars'.

However, the shift into retail and retail management for design graduates is not an insignificant transition, even if it means giving up the dream of design celebrity. Paul Smith, the most successful of United Kingdom independent fashion retailers, indicated (in informal discussion) that this was a wise step for graduates, and that he himself had several design graduates working on his own shopfloor. As a progressive employer, he was committed to training people to be able to work at various levels within his company. This was not a route into design but a good means of using the skills and knowledge of design graduates in more flexible ways, given the difficulty so many of them had in making a living independently.

Teaching

All of the established designers had been guest lecturers at a number of different art colleges and, at the time of interview, one designer had actually moved onto a part-time teaching contract whereby she taught two days a week in the fashion design department at one of the London colleges. Of the more recent graduates, those who had either gained the most publicity as designers or had graduated with a first-class degree all found themselves doing some part-time teaching. Only Jasmine S. had seriously considered moving towards a more full-time career in teaching. She had come to this decision once again through the stress and exhaustion of trying to run her own business and then reconciling herself to the idea of combining a number of design-related activities, one of which would be teaching.

Jasmine S. occupies a kind of emblematic status in this study. Her career pattern best exemplifies the experience of the British fashion designer working through the 1980s and into the 1990s. Having gained great success and attracted a good deal of publicity as a talented young designer she had, at the peak of her career, two outlets in London, one in Hong Kong and a substantial order book from all the main department stores in the United Kingdom and New York. Three years later she had lost everything and had to begin all over again. Her working week at the time of interview comprised teaching for two days, working freelance for another two days for Jones, one day for Pied à Terre and, at the weekends, returning to her own work. In this respect, Jasmine was actually following a time-honoured tradition. Many of Britain's best-known designers move from running their own business to going back to the academy. (Wendy Dagworthy, who in the late 1970s and early 1980s was one of the leading figures in British fashion design, is currently head of fashion at Central St Martin's.) Teaching provides a degree of income security for designers as it has also done historically for fine artists, filmmakers and others in the creative fields. But to be offered posts like these it is, of course, necessary to have an established reputation and, for designers, this means success in running their own companies with their own labels.

Own Label

What designers aspire to is being able to concentrate entirely on their own creative work. This usually means designing a range which, carrying their own name or label, they will then oversee into production and from there to the retailers and stockists who have placed the order. Having your own label also means being able to put on a show at the London collections, thus attracting the attention and publicity of the fashion press and media. All eight of the well-known designers interviewed had achieved this prominent position, although not all of them were able to sustain this level of success. In fact, of the eight only five were still trading in the same capacity by the following year. Celia M. gave up the business in 1995, in order to spend time developing a career in music; Coates and Storey also went out of business in 1995 and, when I interviewed her, Jasmine S. was in the process of re-establishing herself as a freelance designer having achieved great success as an 'own label' but still having reached the brink of bankruptcy the previous year. Another three of the companies were reputed to have been rescued by lucrative contracts from bigger textile companies such as Coates Viyella and Courtaulds, or by freelance contracts with Marks & Spencer. Of course, it is a small sample but this pattern does correspond to the forecast provided by the Kurt Salmon study carried out for the British Fashion Council in 1991. Despite the fact that it was looking at the fashion design industry at its late 1980s peak, it predicted that of the 150 companies surveyed many would not exist in the same shape in the next couple of years. The economic analysis conducted by Salmon estimated that many of these were unsustainable, something we will return to in the final section of this chapter.

'Own label' work appears to be viable only when it is supported by other more profitable activities. The most successful of the companies considered here, Paul Smith and Whistles, remain, and have always been, retailers first and designers second. Paul Smith's turnover is an enormous £142 million (1997 figures). Smith is also remarkable for having the biggest selling menswear range in France as well as seventy-eight shops or outlets in Japan alone. Whistles is way behind this but nontheless has twenty stores nationwide and has recently opened three outlets in Japan. In contrast to this, for their own label work to continue, designers such as Betty Jackson, Ally Capellino and what was Coates and Storey have all been reliant on freelance work, consultancies or other forms of support or sponsorship, while English Eccentrics have undergone various slimming down operations over the last two to three years. The issue then is the significance and role of 'own label' work.

If it is 'own label' work which creates a fashion design industry, is this industry one which literally sparkles for its major participants for a few short years before they 'burn out' or retreat with financial losses while other new talent rushes in to enjoy the limelight? Or is 'own label' work the only way in which the designers, working flexibly for a number of companies and also perhaps doing some teaching, can hold onto the notion of their personal creativity, even if they can only get back to it irregularly and produce for a tiny market? Is 'own label' the necessary fiction which fashion needs in order to exist? All but one of the young designers produced an own label collection, or at the very least a range bearing their own name or label, for a stall or unit like those available in Kensington Market, Camden Market or Hyper Hyper. But for most respondents this proved difficult to sustain on the longer term. At the time of the interviews only Rachel F. was able to continue with this kind of work without resorting to freelance work for another company. She only managed this by keeping her overheads and her costs low, and this in turn meant that she often worked to order in a dressmaking capacity. Her own label was relatively unknown to those outside her small group of clients and her range was more or less restricted to evening-or party-wear. She virtually made her name on the basis of one dress which was featured in an advertisement and subsequently ordered by a number of celebrities. She made more money out of this dress alone than from all her other pieces put together, another indication of just how unpredictable fashion livelihoods are.

Freelance and Consultancy Work

Freelance and consultancy work proved the most common way of earning a modest, but relatively reliable, income as a fashion designer. Of course it left the designer responsible for his/her own equipment and other overheads, and as a self-employed person he/she was also responsible for paying into insurance plans. Being freelance meant being hired by a larger design company or retailer to work on a fee basis. If the relationship became regular the designer might find him/herself paid on a retainer basis. The freelance had to forgo the right to use his/her own name or label and had to produce work to go into production under the label of the company. (In some cases the clothes carry a double credit, for example, Jasper Conran for Debenhams.) This kind of arrangement has become increasingly common since the early 1990s when so many designers went out of business. It was recognized within the industry that there was a consumer demand for clothes with a higher design content. A handful of big companies, including the retailer Marks & Spencer and the textile conglomerate Coates Viyella, initiated schemes which funded designers on a freelance basis to produce work which would then go out under the main company label. With Coates Viyella these schemes also included playing a role as sponsor or backer to the smaller design unit. One of the more established but still small design companies, Ally Capellino, was able to avoid going under (so it was rumoured) through the collaboration and partnership provided by this much larger company. As another designer commented: 'They gave her the money to exploit her brand name so it must be worth something to a big company like that.' Ally Capellino's personal assistant explained the relationship with Coates Viyella in rather different terms:

> It gave us an advertising budget and each season it supports a catwalk show and a promotional brochure. They also give us access to their own in-house public relations which means we don't have to employ an agent or a press secretary. As a two-way project it is good for them and good for us. We have a minimum five-year contract and we can use their tremendous knowledge of fabrics and production. They don't say what we have to do design-wise, it's very much a matter of what we want to do. For our diffusion range we have full use of their small factory and all the technical facilities are available. It's taken us out of the recession, touch wood, and it also allows us hopefully to plug into much bigger international licensing deals, that's the idea. It allows us to work more on design and not have to do everything else. (Personal Assistant to Ally Capellino, interviewed June 1995)

More often, the designer would be invited to produce a range or a collection for a bigger chain store or for a smaller high-fashion outlet such as Jones in Covent Garden. What this meant in effect was a more profitable design company buying in the talent of an individual designer. Jasmine S. has worked under such an arrangement producing clothes for Jones' own label for the last couple of years. This allowed her to continue to work in a creative capacity without having to shoulder the burden of running her own business.

But while this kind of practice seems like a good solution to the insurmountable problems many of the designers experienced having set up by themselves, and while it also allows a higher design input to filter into mass market clothes, the obvious question is how many designers can win contracts like these? Is it necessary to have already established a brand name in order to be offered a contract of this type? The answer to this seems to be yes. Many of the respondents referred to other designers who had been successful and become well known but a few years later had gone out of business and were now working on this kind of basis for a range of companies. So freelance work of this type was an available option, but only to those who had already earned their place in the fashion scene. This suggests something of a predatory relationship on the part of the big companies. They tend not to take a risk with young design graduates to whom they would have to pay a salary and then allow to experiment. Instead, the companies leave it to the graduates to make a name for themselves, perhaps run into financial difficulties and even go out of business altogether. Once that kind of groundwork has been established, they might consider sweeping in and rescuing them on the understanding that they both use and relinquish their 'brand name'. Companies will only consider taking this up as an option if they can be sure it will pay off: 'Named designers are simply an added bonus. Competition is extremely fierce and the differentiating factor any supplier can offer when they are competing for business at Marks & Spencer is design' (Sally Smith of Coates Viyella, quoted by Brampton 1994: 40–1). This constitutes what can best be understood in sociological terms as a kind of competitive post-Fordist practice (or flexible specialization) within the over-arching terms of a more conventionally Fordist enterprise. Marks & Spencer now provide for both a mass market with their standard ranges made in runs of hundreds of thousands, and also for a smaller design-oriented, or segmented (or niche), market. They do this by bringing in design talent on a freelance basis direct and also through their suppliers. These designers produce high-quality short runs of a handful of key items which then enhance Marks & Spencer's reputation as a store which can deliver simultaneously to the widest variety of fashion consumers. Helpful though this may be to designers who are finding it hard to stay in business, the commitment of the big companies or the key suppliers is highly selective, short term and involves relatively few risks or substantial investment. What this also shows, and this is an important feature in the overall analysis, is that the designers are themselves placed uncertainly as very small, often one-person businesses within a competitive capitalist industry where the stronger, bigger companies are able to determine the conditions of work for their freelance labour force as well as their own employees.

A Company Job

Relatively few of the interviewees had worked in a design capacity as a full-time employee for a major fashion company. Given that it was quite clear that the big companies prioritized their own profits first and considered creativity much lower down the agenda, and that they frequently 'ripped off' the designers by copying their clothes and then manufacturing them on a mass basis which meant that their economies of scale could allow them to sell them cheap, most of the young designers had strong views about how the larger companies operated. There was a high degree of distrust, they saw larger companies as interested only in profits and willing to forgo quality and design input in order to keep costs down. They also agreed that one of the major problems working for fashion companies was having to compromise with fabrics and work with inferior materials which inevitably spoilt the overall look of the item, no matter how well-designed it was. Some of the respondents were put off working as a paid employee after spending a relatively short time in this kind of job:

> My nightmare came true and I had to take an agency job with W. I was an in-house designer for over two months, they paid quite well but I did not enjoy the work. There was no scope for putting in your own ideas. It was all grey-suited men. W. is a dinosaur, you have to fit in because you cannot change it. (Gillian P.)

What this indicates is the scale of the investment young designers have in developing their creativity and their own ideas in their work. As it happens, this same graduate, having left W. to teach part time and do freelance work, in fact ended up, at the time of the interview, with a salaried job for a German fashion company. Its strong reputation for quality in design meant that she did not feel that she had entirely compromised her design integrity. She was also able to pay off all the debts she had accumulated when working on her own label collection. Opting for a salaried job was also by this stage a realistic choice, given that she had experienced almost every one of the categories of work in fashion outlined in this chapter. Other company jobs were viewed in fairly negative terms:

> I was approached by a guy setting up a new company. He had a shop and a shop designer and he wanted me to provide the clothes. But he also wanted me to contribute £10,000 on an equity share scheme and then he also wanted me to work for him on a tiny wage. In the end it seemed he just wanted a young girl with some cash upfront to sit and sketch and do the design work. I really wasn't interested. (Terry G.)

More attractive to the graduates was a job with a well-known British designer. Even if this paid minimal wages, this kind of work counted as good experience and brought young designers closer to the heart of the fashion industry. One of the graduates was working for Coates and Storey at the time of the interview. She was a lot more enthusiastic about being an employee and described in detail the variety of jobs she was doing:

> Working with Helen and Caroline is terrific, it's completely non-hierarchical and although I've only been here a year I have been involved in almost every stage of the whole process. I'm seeing garments through from the very beginning and I've been learning a lot about the business side of things. Much more than I ever learnt at college. I've also been doing castings for the shows and I've written some press releases, and I've also had some experience in the shops. (Adele B.)

However, in 1995 when Helen Storey and Caroline Coates were forced to call in the receivers, this young woman's job disappeared too. Overall, the graduate designers felt disappointed by the experience of working for bigger fashion companies for the simple reason that they felt that their design skills were not being developed or even used in any way. They were not opposed to salaried work as such but the investment they had in their own talent and in their creativity as 'young designers' encouraged them to find work in areas where this could be further developed rather than put on hold indefinitely.

In conclusion, this chapter has shown the young graduates of fashion design to be trained to work all hours in a flexible, freelance or self-employed capacity, but unprepared for the economic reality of this kind of work. Their willingness and motivation in this respect are apparent, but their ability to create successful small businesses on the basis of the support provided through a number of government-funded schemes (for example, the EAS) or other schemes (such as the Princes Trust) is strictly limited. Moreover, the time scale within which they can reach relatively high levels of success (with their names becoming well known through press and television coverage) only to head rapidly towards bankruptcy or the closure of the business, is remarkably short, on average between three and five years. On the other hand, this stage of setting up as a small business enterprise is important, even necessary, in establishing a name and a reputation and can be seen as a transitional stage. The graduate is caught in a no-win situation. Developing personal talent and creativity soon after graduation is a way of maintaining some kind of public visibility and it can only be done by producing 'own label' work. However, this runs the risk of accumulating huge debts and being forced to work at such a pace that illness and exhaustion are almost inevitable. And the take-home pay is often minimal. Their turnovers are low and frequently they only stay in business by paying themselves on a pocket-money basis.

Working abroad for a well-known fashion house certainly counts as useful experience because generally there is some opportunity to do design work, but these opportunities tend to be short term and, as Lucille Lewin (founder of Whistles) pointed out (in informal discussion), the fashion capitals (Milan, Tokyo, Paris and New York) are expensive to live in 'and not terribly friendly cities for young British graduates'. This current study shows how the graduates doing this kind of work found the fashion culture in *haute couture* ('haute culture' as Bourdieu (1993: 132) aptly put it) to be elitist, hierarchical and exploitative. Such a reaction demonstrates British fashion to be something different from this *haute couture* tradition, a cultural phenomenon suffused instead with elements of the popular: music; multiculturalism; youth culture. What we are left with at this stage is a micro-economy of fashion design. What we see is a sprawling network of uncoordinated, even chaotic, activities. It is therefore all the more surprising that these actually add up to something significant. This is creative work whose distinctive, not to say peculiar characteristics, mean that it connects with and depends upon the *postmodern* image industries which translate the design work into visual images and then circulate them for consumption in this form, regardless of their existence as real objects for sale in the shops, and the (almost) *premodern* sewing machine (and hand-finishing) which remain the tools of the trade. At the same time, it is the truly *modern* ethos of being a struggling, if not starving artist which provides the graduates with an idea of who they are and what they are doing. This combination shows fashion to be an unstable phenomenon, which contains not just traces of the past but is actually founded on elements which span almost two centuries. This is what I mean by a 'new kind of rag trade'.

NOTES

1   The Jobseeker's Allowance replaced 'dole' in 1996. Claimants are expected to attend for
    interviews arranged for them at the Job Centres and allowance can be withdrawn if they
    fail to take up job offers. This makes it difficult, if not impossible, for designers to use the
    dole as a means of trying to re-establish a place for themselves in fashion while 'officially'
    unemployed.
2   According to two successful stall-holders the average volume of sales from a weekend stall
    (Friday, Saturday and Sunday) at Camden Market is approximately £1,000.

REFERENCES

Bourdieu, P. (1993) *Sociology in Question*. London: Sage.
Brampton, S. (1994) 'The Adoration of St Michael'. *Guardian Weekend*, 8 October: 40–2.
Storey, H. (1996) *Fighting Fashion*. London: Faber and Faber.

Chapter 2

Net-Working for a Living: Irish Software Developers in the Global Workplace

Seán Ó'Riain

In 1992 I took the path followed by many young Irish people at that time and emigrated to the United States. In my case I left Dublin for Berkeley, California, to get a PhD in sociology. Within a year or two I found myself beginning to study the Irish software industry from 6,000 miles away in Silicon Valley. Through interviews with managers in Silicon Valley companies with operations in Ireland, I investigated the dynamics of foreign investment in the Irish software industry. E-mail correspondence with managers of Irish companies in Dublin directed me to their Silicon Valley offices, where I learned the basic history of the emergence of an Irish-owned software industry which was now itself becoming increasingly globalized. These contacts and other Irish people I knew in California put me in touch with Irish software developers working in the Silicon Valley area.

In the mid-1990s many of the young emigrants of the late 1980s and early 1990s were returning home, encouraged by the booming "Celtic Tiger" economy. In early 1997 I followed these global connections and returned to Ireland to carry out more detailed research. It was time to live for a while inside one of the global workplaces that constituted the industry I was studying. I spent twelve weeks as a technical writer and sometime tester on a software development team in USTech, a United States transnational corporation well established in Ireland. During this time I participated fully in the work of the team and wrote a user guide for our product, which was installed on the system as on-line help for users of the system. I sat in the same cubicle as the rest of the team, attended team meetings, and interacted closely with them on a regular basis on decisions regarding the user guide. After an initial period of suspicion of my motives, which may return once they read this chapter, the team members were very welcoming and helpful to me. Indeed, the regular flow of contract personnel in and out of the team meant that I became a relatively well-established team member.

By the time I came to work at USTech in Ireland I had made many of the connections and followed many of the transnational career paths which were such a big part of my coworkers' experience. The five long-term members of the team were employees of USTech but were working on a contract designing a product for Womble Software, a spin-off from USTech headquarters in the United States. My own life in the social sciences had mirrored the experiences of my friends on the Womble team – educated on different sides of the same college campuses, working at home and abroad on emerging meanings and logics, one foot in local culture, the other in the global economy. Software had seemed like a distant world until my ethnography revealed the many aspects already familiar to me from life in the Irish knowledge-worker diaspora.

During the time I spent with the Womble team, I uncovered a characteristic set of structures and dynamics of this global workplace. Although we sat at the center of a wide array of local and global connections and of multiple career trajectories, the cubicle space we shared came to dominate our lives. The experience of local space was intensified for us, even as we sat in a global workplace. Time, too, was intensified as the project deadline became the defining element of our work and, to some extent, social lives. Out of this intensification of time and space emerged cooperation, innovation, and career success, but also burnout, individualism, inequality, and pressures on family. It is these dilemmas and tradeoffs that constitute the "contested terrain" of the global informational workplace.

It is 4:15 in the afternoon. On the wall of the software test group in the Irish offices of USTech, a prominent Silicon Valley computer company, there are four clocks. At the moment they show that it is 8:15 a.m. in Silicon Valley, California, 10:15 in Austin and Fort Worth, Texas, and 11:15 in Montreal, Canada. Silicon Valley has just "opened for business," and the software developers and managers in Ireland begin a hectic few hours of discussion with their American counterparts. The row of clocks evokes a smoothly working global economy, held back only by time zones, and a software operation which seamlessly manages a variety of transnational connections.

I hurry downstairs, as I have a conference call to the United States at 4:30 p.m. Irish time (8:30 a.m. their time in Silicon Valley). Thirty minutes later I am sitting in an open-plan cubicle, along with five members of a software development team. Employed by USTech, they are developing a software product for a Silicon Valley start-up company called Womble Software. I have been writing a user guide for the product and am deep in discussion with Jane, the technical-writing editor in Silicon Valley, and Ramesh, an immigrant to the United States from India and the "chief architect" of the program, who is in St. Louis in the heart of middle-America. As my manager comes into the team area, I put the conference call on the speaker phone. Now the whole "Womble team" can hear the conversation.

As the conversation unfolds, so does the mime drama around me, as the team reacts to the flow of global communication into this cubicled "local" space. When Ramesh suggests adding new features (creating more work for the developers around me), there is an explosion of displeased sign language, including a variety of abusive gestures directed at the speaker phone. Since Ramesh can hear everything on our end, this pantomime is conducted in complete silence. I have a hard time not bursting out laughing. When Jane points out to Ramesh that it is difficult to write a user guide when the final screen designs for the software program have not been decided upon (a common complaint within the development team two weeks before the product is released), there is an explosion of mimed cheering and barely controlled laughter around me.

This is just another day in the global informational workplace, a workplace which is home to increasing numbers of employees around the world. The dominant image of these workplaces is that of places lifted out of time and space, places where communication and innovation are free from the drag of local cultures and practices and untainted by power relations. Robert Reich argues that new information and communication technologies make it possible and even necessary to reorganize firms into "global webs" and employees into global telecommuters.[1] For Reich, these webs operate smoothly, destroying constraints of space and social structure, moving in conjunction with the ever-circling hands of the clocks on the USTech wall. The global workplace is "lifted out" of its temporal and spatial contexts and becomes a "pure" space for communication based on shared rules of interaction and understanding.[2]

Others argue that this perspective is too benign. The speeding up of the global economy destroys local space – the fact that Ramesh and the Womble team can participate in the same conversation at the same time means that they essentially share the same social and economic space, despite the physical distance between them. Time annihilates space, melting away "solid" local places into the "air" of the global economy.[3] This is not a neutral process, however, as the once autonomous local space of the worker is increasingly dominated by global corporations and the ever more rapid pace of economic life under capitalism.[4] Ramesh's presence – a phone call, e-mail message, or plane trip away – undermines the autonomy provided these workers by their local space.

The Womble team is certainly connected to other global workplaces – including Silicon Valley and St. Louis on this particular afternoon. They also experience the pressure of the global economy through the demands of Ramesh for new features. However, local space is not destroyed by these global connections. The Womble cubicle takes on a culture of its own, manifested in the mimed hostility to Ramesh's suggestions, but also in the information-sharing, problem-solving, and solidarity-building within the team on an everyday basis. In fact, the demands of the global economy for increased flexibility and specialized learning actually make the local context and interactions of the global workplace even more critical. Efficient production and constant innovation require the construction of shared physical spaces where workers can interact and communicate on a face-to-face basis and where shared goals and meanings can be created and maintained.[5]

Global connections bring the pressures of the world economy into the heart of workplaces such as the Womble team cubicle. However, these pressures actually make local space and social context all the more important. The speed-up of time and the extension of social space across physical distance in the global economy do not destroy space but in fact intensify the impact of space in constituting successful global workplaces.

However, this does not herald a return to an era of workplaces dominated by localized social relations. This is because the importance of local social relations to innovation creates a dilemma for the global corporations that rely on this innovation. The local character of their work teams is essential to their efficiency but also poses a problem of regulating such localized relations from a distance. Ramesh may be aware that his proposals are not meeting with happy grins on the other end of the phone, but he is also unable to directly regulate the team's behavior because of his distance from the team and his only partial incorporation into the social space of the team. The typical managerial answer to this dilemma of control in the global workplace is to attempt to control the instrument of speed-up and pressure within the global economy – time itself. The politics of the contemporary workplace is increasingly the politics of time.[6]

The most important instrument used to control time in the global workplace is the project deadline. Although Ramesh cannot control the everyday behavior of the Womble team, the parameters within which the team can operate are set by the demands of the deadline: the team members have a great deal of autonomy in how they work, but the supervisor looking over their shoulder is time itself, with every decision measured against its impact on meeting the deadline. Ramesh's requests for new features are not considered on their technical merits but on the basis of their impact on the team's ability to meet the deadline. Even as the importance of space is intensified in the global workplace, so too is time, in its manifestation as the dominant mode of control in these workplaces. Global workplaces are subject to a process of what I call time-space intensification.

This chapter explores in detail the characteristic structures and dynamics of the global workplace under conditions of time-space intensification. The first part of the analysis shows the dilemmas posed for innovation in the global workplace due to the pressures placed on it by the intersection of the high-mobility careers of software developers and highly mobile software firms. It documents how intense cooperation in localized workplaces makes it possible for such highly mobile workers and firms to forge an alliance in the pursuit of innovation and profit. A tension persists within this structure, however – a tension between place-bound cooperation based on group solidarity and individual careers based on high rates of mobility between firms and places. This tension is reconciled through the dynamics of the workplace, which are analyzed in the second part of the chapter. The period prior to the project deadline is one of team solidarity and cohesion, while the post-deadline phase is characterized by the fragmentation of the team as they use their social networks to position themselves for the next moves in their careers. The globalization of the information technology (IT) industry is seen to result not in a virtual economy but in a global industry organized around and through certain key places and regions. Within these global workplaces, relations among workers constantly cycle through phases of cohesion and fragmentation, as worker solidarity is mobilized for purposes of innovation but disarmed by the structure of careers in the labor market. The globalization of knowledge workplaces becomes an object of tension and conflict in those workplaces; globalization is neither simply an ever-expanding process of increasingly pure communication and innovation nor an inexorable advance of the dominance of capital. Power relations in these workplaces are forged out of the interplay of mobility and place and time and space, forms of interplay that are examined through the rest of this chapter.

This chapter argues, therefore, that as the workplace stretches out across national borders, local spaces such as the Womble team cubicle become all the more crucial to the operation of the global economy. Overcoming the constraints of international time differences allows organization across time and space, but poses new problems of control from a distance – problems which are solved by the intensification of time through work-team deadlines. Global informational workplaces are characterized not by the disappearance of time and space as realities of work life, but by their increasing importance and intensification.

Dilemmas of the Global Workplace

Neither do these workplaces emerge tabula rasa onto the global stage, as a response to the prompting of the global market. In fact, the Womble team is the outcome of state development strategies, changing corporate structures and strategies, and the emergence of new industries organized around knowledge creation. Indeed, the routine phone and e-mail arguments between Ramesh and the Womble team would bring a glow to the heart of many industrial development agency officials in Ireland. The formation of connections to the global economy by attracting foreign high-technology investment has been the cornerstone of Ireland's industrial policy since the late 1950s. The connection to the United States has been particularly crucial – over 400 United States companies have located in Ireland, and some three-quarters of jobs in electronics and software in Ireland are in foreign-owned companies. Through the 1970s and 1980s, transnational electronics and computer hardware firms located primarily low-level functions in Ireland and developed few links to the local economy.[7] Many of the transnational corporations used Ireland as an "export processing zone" within the European market, taking advantage of low tax and wage rates and Ireland's position within European Union tariff barriers. Irish plants were at best weakly integrated into the core activities of the corporate parents, as the typical Irish operation's activities were routine and relations with the parent hierarchical.

However, the past five to ten years have seen a shift in the nature of the activities and the character of some of the foreign investment in Ireland.[8] Encouraged by the state industrial development agencies, many hardware operations began to grow software development centers as the information technology industry moved toward a focus on software and software became the strategic technology for these corporations. Local managers, usually Irish-born, were able to carve out strategic positions for their operations within the parent companies, although their position always remained precarious. In cases such as USTech, local managers often developed relationships with customers well before discussing these new lines of business with their colleagues at headquarters. In recent years, subcontracting and business partnership relationships between United States and Irish firms have expanded and the two economies have become increasingly closely integrated. Indeed, the apparent shortage of computer skills in Silicon Valley was one of the reasons why the Womble software contract went to the USTech Ireland office. Companies such as USTech Ireland were still limited by their place in the international corporate structure and often still concentrated on testing, support, and consulting software work rather than on the strategic software development tasks. However, many were able to develop small- to medium-sized software development teams, closely integrated with the parent's operations.

USTech is well established in Ireland, having located there over fifteen years ago and becoming one of the early success stories of Irish industrial policy. For many years it was one of Ireland's primary computer hardware production operations, with a reputation for high quality. The hardware manufacturing operations of USTech Ireland were dismantled, with massive layoffs, in the early 1990s, leaving local management scrambling for the operation's survival and turning to a complete reliance on the local pool of software skills. Their links to the global economy have subsequently diversified, with a proliferation of customers, partners, and internal corporate sponsors replacing their previous model of reporting directly to a single office in the United States. The software development contract for Womble reflects this change, as there was little opportunity within the previous corporate structure for such arrangements.

Womble Software itself is a perfect example of the "global web" corporate structure, which Reich argues is becoming the norm. Formed as a spin-off from a large hierarchical corporation, the company is partly owned by the four founders, partly by USTech itself, partly by a major customer, and the rest by a venture capital fund in Silicon Valley. It has no more than fifteen employees of its own. The development team is based in Ireland and is officially contracted to provide software development services to Womble. The screens for the program are conceptualized by Ramesh, but all the development work necessary to turn them into computer graphics is done in a small graphic-design house just outside San Francisco. The helpdesk staff, which users reach if they call with a problem, is staffed by the trained employees of a helpdesk contracting company. The technical writers who write the on-screen help for users are all hired on a contract basis. In place of more rigid, hierarchical organizational structures, we have a shifting web of connections forged into a relatively fleeting alliance.

Mobility and connections in the global labor market

Womble is not only, however, the prototype of the "global web" organization but also conforms to a new model of computer-industry careers. In this model the dominant metaphor of IBM's promise of lifetime employment has been replaced by the image of the freewheeling Silicon Valley engineers who expect little from their employers and will jump ship for more money or more challenging work at the drop of a hat.[9] Both of course are stereotypes, but there is more than a grain of truth in the emergence of cross-firm careers as the dominant pattern in software companies in Silicon Valley and in Ireland.[10] These trends are intensified by a shortage of experienced personnel in most countries' software industries.[11] Certain skills are in particularly high demand – including the Unix, C++, database, and Java skills of the employees in the Womble team. The variety of local and global connections of the team reinforces the tendency toward mobility by providing the channels of information about new opportunities and the social contacts for facilitating moves to those emerging areas. Negotiating the commitment of highly mobile employees becomes the critical dilemma facing software firms, a dilemma which is addressed in the following sections of this chapter.

In industries such as software the typical career pattern now involves a number of moves between organizations, and there has been a clear shift from internal labor markets to job-hopping between firms. When employees stay with the same firm, their tasks and level of responsibility change on a regular basis. Furthermore, professional migration into both the United States and Ireland has been increasing, with transnational intrafirm and interfirm careers expanding. As can be seen from the career histories described above, the high mobility career pattern, with employees feeling little attachment to the employer (or, conversely, the firm to the employee) has become a reality for these particular software developers. Even in a still "semiperipheral" region like Ireland, the careers of such software developers have converged quite significantly with those of their counterparts in the leading high-technology regions such as Silicon Valley or global cities such as New York and London. A survey of 250 software firms in Ireland in 1997 revealed that a quarter of the firms had had employee turnover of 25 percent or more in the previous year.[12]

These trends were evident in the experience of the Womble software team members. Including myself, the team consisted of six people during the time I was there. Séamus, the team leader, had been at USTech for seven years. In that time he had held four completely different positions – working as a computer test engineer, software systems test engineer, information systems support, and software development team leader. The rest of the team had been assembled over the prior six to eighteen months. Conor, six months out of college, still received job postings from his college career-counseling service every two weeks. If he follows the industry pattern he will most likely leave USTech after eighteen months or so, when another software company will be glad to pay him well for his skills and experience.

Jim and Paul were employed on a contract basis. Dan had also been a contractor and took a pay cut of almost 50 percent when he accepted a permanent post in order to get a mortgage from the bank. Paul's history is one of a "software cowboy," using a series of lucrative short-term contracts to see the world without being tied down by business, social, or personal obligation. Jim and Dan have pursued a different path, having at times been employees, contractors, entrepreneurs, or several of these at the same time. The lines between employer, self-employed, and employee begin to blur in such careers.

Transnational experience is a major part of the developers' careers. Dan is originally from Hong Kong and came to Ireland to study, subsequently pursuing a career in software. Almost all the contractors who worked with the team while I was there had emigrated at one point or spent a significant amount of time working on contracts abroad. Indeed, it is the contractors who are most openly dependent on mobility for their career advancement. They are usually brought in for their quite specialized skills and are often given tasks working on relatively self-contained parts of the system being designed. Their need to communicate with other team members may be minimal, although their ability to do so remains a critical part of their effectiveness. Sometimes, contractors stay with a team for a relatively long time. Jim, a contractor, had been with the team for longer than the two permanent staff and had successfully resisted efforts to make him take a permanent position. Indeed, he was the de facto deputy team leader. Mobility across organizational, employer/employee, and national boundaries has therefore been central to these workers' careers and is understood by all to be the background to workplace interactions and relationships.

Mobility is also the team members' key bargaining chip with their employers. One lunchtime, Conor, Michael, the group manager, and I ended up sitting together. We had somehow got onto the topic of the difficulty of getting people for the jobs that were available within USTech. Conor went into great detail on the job offers he had received on leaving college and on the ever-improving job market for graduates, until Michael quietly finished his lunch and left. Conor turned to me and asked: "What did you make of that? I wanted him to know there are plenty of other jobs out there. What I didn't say is that I've been getting job offers every two weeks through the college."

Mobility is the dominant career strategy within the software industry as a whole and within the Womble software team. There are also, however, constraints on the mobility system for both the firm and the employee. The firm will sometimes try to get contractors with crucial product knowledge to become permanent employees so that their knowledge is kept within the organization. In the Womble team, Dan had gone permanent because he had to get a mortgage, whereas Jim, already having a mortgage, was able to resist the efforts of the project managers to have him become a permanent employee. Nor are employees completely free to exercise their mobility. Companies are reluctant to pay employees if they threaten to leave, as they are likely to set a series of threats in train which may spiral out of control. However, companies will make exceptions on occasion as long as they can avoid having other employees learn about them. In general, the threat of mobility serves as a latent possibility, which keeps the company's attention focused on getting training for key employees, increasing their pay, and so on, in order to forestall ideas of leaving.

Employees must also be careful not to get a reputation for being unlikely to stay at a company. "If you look at a CV and see that someone has moved every nine months or so, you have to wonder if they'll stay here any longer than that. But if they stay two or three years, then you know they will contribute something" (Séamus). The degree of demand for a developer's particular skills is the critical factor that affects his or her bargaining power through mobility. "When I was in Belfast, you would be on contract if you couldn't get a permanent job. Here, you would be permanent if you couldn't go on contract. It's just a question of how many jobs there are" (Paul). This can even override the threat of lost reputation if the demand is high enough: "They mightn't think you'll stay, but if they need you badly enough they'll hire you anyway!" (Paul). Industry norms have developed around the "proper" forms of mobility – mobility between jobs is not unlimited but requires a strategy that must be carefully managed.

Mobility is therefore taken for granted as an element of the composition of software teams such as the Womble team. Relations with coworkers develop in the context of a constant awareness that the members of the team might be dispersed at short notice. This can happen either by corporate decision (the team beside us was disbanded overnight when USTech in Silicon Valley halted development of the product on which they were working) or through the decision of individuals to leave the team. Mobility, then, is a double-edged sword – the advantage to employees of being able to leave with few repercussions is balanced against the lack of constraints on companies' changing employees' responsibilities and even getting rid of them (within the bounds of the law). Indeed, the Womble team was itself largely disbanded when development work was moved back to the United States and fully disbanded when Womble itself went out of business. These advantages and dangers are all the more significant for contract employees, given their complete lack of formal job security. These highly fluid conditions threaten the ability of software developers to work together in a cohesive way on a common project. The intensification of space in the global workplace provides some of the critical elements of the answer to this organizational dilemma.

Putting work in its place

While software developers may move quite regularly from job to job, they have an intense relationship with each other once in a particular job. In informational and design work, the labor process is usually organized in the form of teams working closely together on specific projects. Some see these as "virtual" teams interacting purely through cybertechnologies – the process of generating cooperation among employees is assumed to be unproblematic.[13] Indeed, Ramesh himself subscribed to the theory of the virtual economy in a "Thank You" e-mail message he sent to the contract graphic-design firm in California:

> Our project team was truly an international virtual-team, with up to 8 hours of time-zone difference among the different team members. We expected you to work at such a hectic pace, yet, we also demanded extreme flexibility from you in all respects. It is very rare that anybody of your caliber would be able to excel on both these fronts.

However, Ramesh had misread his own organization. Members of such teams are usually located in close proximity to one another, as this allows the team to handle the complex interdependencies among them through easy and constant communication and allows them to build a coherent collective identity, which becomes the basis of cooperation within the team.

The sheer volumes of information and the dependence of each member of the team on the design decisions of the others makes the easy interaction of the team members critical. As Jim at USTech worked on the user interface screens he would intermittently call over to Paul two desks away: "What did you call the course number variable, Paul? I can't find it," "Are you working on the database at the moment? It's a bit slow," "Who's doing the security screens?" The questions and answers are discussed on the way to and from breakfast and lunch, although by common consent rarely during the meal itself.

By contrast, information flows to the United States can be patchy and tend to be limited to broad strategic decisions. A developer in Silicon Valley would have great difficulty in developing this product with the team around me in Ireland. Indeed, my own easy ability to ask the developers around me for information fifteen times a day contrasts with the difficulties I have sharing information with Jane in Silicon Valley, a process that sometimes left me idle for mornings or afternoons as I waited to be able to call her in the United States to clear up some minor misunderstandings. Where such transnational "virtual" relationships work, they are constantly supplemented by travel to meet the team or teams in the other country. Ramesh was a regular visitor to the USTech Ireland office. Distance also clearly limits how much employees can learn from their colleagues. The experience of working in close physical proximity with the more experienced and skilled developers teaches others the skills and tricks that turn a computer science graduate into an effective and innovative programmer.[14]

The accountability of team members to one another is also much more easily sustained in face-to-face interactions than in "virtual" communications. Problems can arise even in the most apparently "flat" and non-hierarchical of organizations. I was caught in a bind during the conference call when Ramesh asked me, an untrained technical writer with a long and largely irrelevant training in sociology, "Seán, are you happy with the proposal to put the toolbar in the help box?" While I was being formally asked to participate in a design decision, the social structure of this global organization made me think first not of the implications of my decision for the system itself but of my loyalties to the fuming developers around me. Even the periodical visits of Ramesh to Ireland did not solve the problems of miscommunication and alienation felt by the Irish team. As Michael, the business manager of the group, said, "Having a remote manager has made getting a process of communication in place a lot more difficult." Problems which would require solution in a face-to-face context can be swept under the carpet or become a figure of fun in a context where communication is by phone and the Internet.

The issues that can be resolved in a daily phone call to the United States are those relating to the strategic technical decisions, which were hotly debated with Ramesh every day by Séamus, the team leader, and even by the other members of the team. E-mail was generally used within the team to pass on relatively routine information to one another – whether that was between the team members or between Séamus, the team leader, and Ramesh. On one occasion, although we sat fewer than 10 feet apart, Conor and I exchanged a series of e-mails about problems I had found with the program and the fixes he had made – without ever turning around to speak to one another. Only when it became clear that one of the problems was more complex than it appeared did we discuss the issue face to face. E-mail also appeared to be a valuable tool for allowing the team members to stay in touch with their friends throughout the industry. I was able to combine my membership in the "global ethnography group" with participation in the Womble team, largely unbeknownst to anyone else on the team. Other team members seemed to use e-mail similarly – every now and then someone would read out a joke they had been sent by a friend or tell us about the bonuses being offered at other companies for recruiting a new employee. Overall, while face-to-face interactions were critical to conveying complex information or to building and sustaining trust, computer-supported communication seemed "especially suited to maintaining intermediate-strength ties between people who cannot see each other frequently."[15]

USTech is situated in one of the areas best known for information technology in Ireland. In a city that is attractive to the young people who dominate the software industry, USTech also benefits from access to a large pool of local skilled labor and from the connections of the Womble team members to the broader "culture of innovation" within the region. The Womble team members, especially those who have had more mobile career patterns, have many connections to people throughout the local industry and often recount stories of people they know in common, people who could be hired by the team, other developers they met around the city and discussed their work with, and so on. Their high-mobility careers are also sustained through social ties to others in the industry who can provide the team members with information on job opportunities and can provide formal or informal recommendations to employers regarding the team members' competence. It turns out that both the high-mobility careers and the face-to-face interactions which mitigate the corrosive effect of that mobility on workplace cohesion are supported by the emergence of this regional "innovative milieu."[16]

Face-to-face interaction, localized social relations, and electronic networks each structure the global workplace in important but different ways. Clearly, face-to-face interaction does not guarantee good communication or cooperative working relationships. However, it makes it a lot easier than trying to achieve these across eight time zones and numerous digital interactions. Ease of communication and mutual accountability at "work" ensure that spaces defined by face-to-face interaction remain a critical component of the global workplace, even as virtual spaces proliferate.

A globalized local culture

These globalized workplaces also take on a distinct culture, which reinforces the cooperation and cohesion produced by the organization of work itself. In many ways even these human paradigms of the global economy are "global locals," bringing distinct "local" cultures to the global stage and remaking both global and local social relations in the process. This small open-plan team area may be a globalized space but it is one that has a clearly defined local identity and that interacts with the global economy with caution and at times with difficulty. Some have argued that such tensions between the local and the global are born out of a traditionalist resistance by the local to the cosmopolitanism of the global.[17] However, the Womble team does not resist the global in and of itself but contests how the global should operate, showing disdain for the mismanagement of the global by the remote managers.

This can be seen most clearly in their perceptions of American software developers and managers. As an Irish manager at USTech told me:

> The test group here was the best in the corporation and they were really saving USTech with their customers in the field. So we had all these American managers coming over telling them they were the greatest and how they were the best thing since sliced pan. That's OK the first time, but after a while the people here started saying among themselves "Quit the bullshit – if you think we're so great, give us a raise or at least buy us a few pints."

This disjunction was shown up dramatically after one particular bout of complaining about the United States managers of the team. Séamus, the team leader, summed up the relationship to the United States parent ironically:

> *Séamus:* It's not as if there's "us and them" or anything... It's not even that, it's just "them" really!
> *Jim (wearily):* Yep, they're the enemy!

Nonetheless, the Irish managers and developers tended to work very successfully with their American counterparts, accepting some aspects of United States corporate culture while maintaining a clear rejection of many aspects of the Americanized environment in which they find themselves.

The developers themselves regard their team culture as homogenous, despite the fact that Dan is from Hong Kong:

> *Jim:* What would we do if a black guy joined the group? Who would we pick on?
> *Conor:* Or a woman?
> *Jim:* Séamus, you can't ever hire a black woman!
> *Seán:* There's always Americans to pick on...
> *Séamus:* Yeah, but they're too easy. There's no challenge in that. [Laughter.]

The mention of a "black guy" was largely rhetorical, as I never heard any comment within the team directed against "black-guys." The team culture was clearly masculine, and there is no doubt that this culture could be self-perpetuating.[18] "American" is also somewhat ambiguous in this context, as Ramesh, the "American" with whom the Womble team members have the most interaction, is originally from India. On a different occasion, three members of a different team discussed their Indian boss in the United States with Conor and me:

> *Pat:* We have one too – Ranjit.
> *Conor:* Ranjit – that sounds like something out of Aladdin.
> *Peter:* [Says something imitating Ramesh's accent.] That's racist, that is. [Criticizing himself, very serious about it.]
> *Bob:* Yeah, that's an "ism," that is. That's racism.
> *Pat:* They're [Indian software developers] probably over there saying "those bloody Micks."
> *Aidan:* Yeah, saying "drinking pints of Guinness over their computers."

"Difference" on a global scale is an everyday part of these software developers' milieu, although it is negotiated within a strong, homogenous local culture. This was evident in the team's relationship to Dan (from Hong Kong). In fact, while the culture of the team was strongly male and Irish, members of the team were highly aware of this global culture, and most would criticize racism and sexism that they saw elsewhere. On one occasion, two other team members and I were both shocked and amused on hearing Dan racially slander a visiting technical trainer who was Pakistani. "The other" was accepted as an everyday part of life for Irish software developers and helped to define the team identity. When Dan revealed his own criticisms of another Asian ethnic group, this disrupted our assumption of a single "other" and was both surprising and funny to Dan's team members. It revealed that Dan's behavior and attitudes regarding race were subject to different rules than those of the Irish-born team members.

While the team members worked relatively easily with people of a variety of national, ethnic, and racial backgrounds, they consciously maintained a strong local team culture. Operating in the global workplace required them to work with and around "difference" but, by the same token, the less hierarchical forms of economic domination in the global workplace allowed them to maintain their local culture within these global connections. There is also a strong pragmatic element in this ability of people from different backgrounds to work together in the global workplace. One of the Womble Software managers took us out for a meal when she was visiting from the United States. Halfway through the evening I commented to Pat, a contractor, "She seems OK, decent enough," to which Pat replied, "Well, when you come to discover the jungle you have to play with the natives."

Not only are the Womble developers "global locals," but they also think of themselves as such. Their highly mobile careers and relatively fleeting association with one another in the workplace demand an intense experience of a shared space and culture in order for them to create a cohesive work team. The team members use elements of a shared culture from outside the team to create this solidarity, but are also able to accommodate aspects such as Dan's non-Irish racial and ethnic background into the team through the overriding emphasis on work and technical competence. While these local team cultures can be exclusionary of women and other ethnic groups, as indicated in the quotes above, they are also flexible enough to accommodate the presence of such others within the domin-ant team culture when necessary. Place, mobility, and the global workplace are not necessarily in tension with one another, as they might appear to be on first glance, but are in fact symbiotic, underpinning one another's importance and sustainability.

In short, globalization does not mean the end of place. Instead, it creates places which are increasingly "between" other places and have ever-deepening connections to other places. The high-mobility career pattern that is typical of the software industry poses a threat to the work team cooperation, commitment, and cohesion necessary for innovation. What I have called the intensification of space through the dense social networks of the team and the region provides a solution of sorts to this dilemma. However, local networks also serve to reproduce mobility, as developers use their connections to engineer their next career moves. Mobility and place sustain one another but also remain in tension within the structure of the global workplace. In order to understand how this tension is resolved, we need to go beyond the intensification of space in the structure of the global workplace to an analysis of the dynamics of that workplace, dynamics that are set in motion by the control, regulation, and intensification of time.

The Dynamics of the Global Workplace

The mechanism for controlling the software development team is the project dead-line. As it is impossible for the final design specifications to provide solutions to every issue faced by the team, and as the actual work done by the team is difficult for management to supervise directly, the deadline becomes the focus of both manage-ment and team efforts. "Do what needs to be done to get this specification working by the deadline" is the broad task of the team. The deadline represents the first point in the development process when both team and management will be able to examine the entire working product. The deadline is the mechanism by which management brings the intensification of time into the heart of the team. It is also an attractive mechanism of control, since direct management authority over the work process is undermined by the employees' superior expertise and by their need for rapid communication and cooperation. In contrast, time can be regulated through the use of the deadline, with only a limited local managerial presence, and with relatively little ongoing exercise of managerial authority. This deadline becomes the stimulus that sets the dynamics of time-space intensification in motion in the global workplace – leading to a pre-deadline phase of team introversion and a post-deadline phase of extroversion.

The Womble team schedule had three main phases: a beginning period of "normal work," a hectic middle period before releasing the product at the deadline, and a final period of rest and negotiation after the deadline and the release had passed. The character of the team and the issues it faced changed as the team members went through these stages of the cycle together. I joined the team in the hectic pre-release phase and left them as the post-release phase wound down.

Introversion before the deadline: A team against the world

In the weeks before March 1, the release date for our product, life in the Womble cubicle becomes busier and busier. The team works longer hours and becomes more and more isolated from the life of the company around it. Internally, the team becomes more cohesive, communication becomes more urgent, technical arguments take on a new edge, and any delay or new instruction from outside the team is met with a barrage of criticism. The graphics for the screens of the system (what the user sees when using the system) are delayed in coming in from the graphic-design house outside San Francisco. The Womble developers grow more and more impatient, furiously criticizing management and the graphic designers for their incompetence. The time allotted for particular development tasks is counted first in weeks and then in days. From time to time, a particular problem is put aside, to be dealt with in the period set aside for fixing the initial bugs in the system, a period between March 1 and March 10. Such postponements create some dissatisfaction among the developers:

> Conor: We're all tired. We've been at it for two months really. It's a lot of pressure. Something every day. There's no time to take a day and research something. We need a week to go over some of the bigger issues, have some meetings, go over things, you know. There's some dodgy code in there too.

While not as long as the hours worked by some other software development firms in Ireland, the work hours do start to creep up toward sixty a week. Séamus, the team leader, works constantly, often late into the evening and the night.

Weeks earlier, Conor had told me:

> I've a feeling this is the calm before the storm. My attitude when it's calm is get out of here at 4 or 5, 'cause when it gets busy... You have to draw the line yourself as far as hours go, you have to say once in a while "Sorry I have something on tonight, I can't stay." You have to keep your standard hours around thirty-nine/forty. If you let your standard hours go up to forty-five, then they'll still come to you and ask you to do a few extra hours that evening. They won't think about that extra six hours you're doing as part of your standard. It's up to yourself to draw the line.

As the deadline nears, however, he ends up staying late and coming in two weekends in a row. While not pleased by having to work these long hours, they are largely accepted as the industry norm. In the Irish economy as a whole, managerial and professional workers, especially in small firms, tend to work the longest hours and work a great deal of unremunerated overtime, according to a recent study: "Ireland may be a long way from the Japanese or North American patterns of executive working time, which involve managers working particularly long hours…as a normal feature of managerial careers, but the trajectory of change is in this direction." The authors of this study argue that the same findings apply to professional workers, although the trend is somewhat weaker.[19] Among the team members, proposed legislation limiting working hours is discussed ironically:

> *Séamus:* I wonder does Ramesh know about the European Social Charter limiting the working week? Forty-three hours per week or something.
> *Conor:* Great!
> *Jim:* It's forty-eight.
> *Conor:* Fuck, that long?
> *Jim:* Yeah, forty-eight for each company, forty-eight for Womble, and forty-eight for USTech!

Such hours and constant pressure take their toll – the week after the release I bumped into Paul on our way in to work:

> *Paul:* I was feeling crap lately 'cause I've been under a lot of pressure and everything. But now I feel great after having that day off.

The impact on the developers' personal lives is also clear from a conversation weeks later before Ramesh arrived in Ireland to take us to a promised celebration dinner:

> *Jim:* Maybe we'll all meet up. I hope he doesn't meet my wife. She has it in for him.
> *Séamus:* Herself and Linda should get together so. They have a lot in common actually – they're both vegetarians too.
> *Seán:* Except when it comes to Ramesh! [Laughter.]
> *Jim:* I see you've met my wife!

However, what appeared to be deep antagonism to Ramesh during the pre-release stage faded away in the post-release phase. While the developers' complaints about management's making their life more difficult persisted, their intensity waned so that when Ramesh came on a visit to Ireland after the release he was quite warmly welcomed (he was also quite well liked by the team members on a personal basis). Apparently, however, the complaints did not fade as quickly for the developers' families, who experienced only the long hours and intense demands on their personal lives without sharing in the collective team "buzz" of getting the product out in time and of working well together.

While attempting (with little success) to limit their hours, the developers also tried to protect themselves against the follies of management in other ways. The team responded to the pressures from Ramesh and the outside world by turning in on themselves, by becoming increasingly introverted. Having a manager on the other side of the world allowed the team, including the team leader, to screen information from management in order to let the team balance the technical and time demands to their own satisfaction. Having encountered a particularly thorny problem, the team finally found a solution:

> *Jim:* So we're going to do that then. Ramesh never needs to know about it. So we can have it set up the way we want it, and he'll have it the way he wants too.
> *Paul:* So we're going to do it the sneaky bastard way.
> *Séamus:* I like the sneaky bastard way!
> *Paul:* And Ramesh never needs to know.
> *Séamus:* No, no. Well done, gentlemen!
> *Jim:* Just don't say anything about this on Monday when Ramesh is here!

In many cases the reason for this screening of information was to avoid Ramesh's interference with a solution which the team considered to be the most technically effective. At other times, the goal was to avoid any extra tasks being given to the team before the deadline. On one occasion. Ramesh sent an e-mail about a problem in the database they were using. Not realizing that Dan had been working on this issue for a while now, Ramesh set aside a day the week before the release for Dan to work on it.

> *Jim:* Dan will have that done today.
> *Seán:* So what about the day Ramesh is setting aside for it next week?
> *Jim:* Oh God, I'm not going to tell him we already have a solution. He's already expecting it to slip a bit, so if we get it in on time he'll be really happy. I think we're a little bit ahead of schedule, but he thinks we're a bit behind, so that suits us.

In general, team members were careful to protect themselves from undue interference from headquarters in the United States and left the negotiation of deadlines and larger technical issues to Séamus, the team leader. As Conor advised me when I had sent an e-mail to Ramesh about a problem in the "help" screens:

> Be careful what you send to Ramesh. Cc it to Séamus, or, better yet, send it to Séamus first; let him decide. That's what I do. You have to look after your own behind first, you know. I try to get involved as little as possible with Silicon Valley; I give it to Séamus. That way I have a buffer between me and the United States.

The team could also use the Product Technical Specification (PTS) as a rhetorical device with which they could, if necessary, justify not doing certain tasks. The technical specification for the product was a detailed document outlining the technical basis and logic of the system and supposedly defining the key aspects of the actual development process. However, in contrast to the expectations of formal models of software engineering, the specification document was necessarily vague in places and could not capture all the technical dilemmas that arose during the development process.

Dan, sitting beside me, constantly justified his resistance to certain new tasks that arrived before the deadline with the refrain "If it's not in the specs, I'm not doing it."

On one occasion, Jim and Paul discussed a new requirement for the system that had come from Ramesh in an e-mail that morning:

> *Jim:* Is it in the specs?
> *Paul:* No.
> *Jim:* Well, screw it then; we don't need to do it.

However, they later came up with a solution to the problem, which they knew was not strictly compatible with the technical requirements of the PTS but which would solve the problem satisfactorily. In this case they were willing to drop their apparent dedication to following the specs in order to try to slip a different solution past Ramesh:

> *Paul:* I have a feeling we're going to get screwed on this. I think the thing to do is to keep our mouths shut, do this what I'm doing now, present it to them without saying anything, and then if they come back saying "We're not supporting that," then OK. 'Cause if I just say it to him, he'll just say "Noooo..."
> *Jim:* Yeah, he does that.

At times the dissatisfaction extended into banter about collective action among the employees. When new changes to the computer graphics for the screens arrived one week before the deadline, the team was furious:

> *Conor:* I'm going on strike.
> *Seán:* That'll make history, the first strike in the software industry.
> [Dan laughs ironically.]
> *Conor:* You know what last-minute changes means: it means you work your arse off.
> *Dan:* If it's something we've agreed already, I'll work my ass off. But if it's last-minute changes I won't. It has to be reasonable, or else it's "See you later."

Later, at breakfast, Conor brought up the issue again:

> *Conor:* I'm going on strike. I say, "In with the union!"
> *Jim:* Well if it's minor changes to what we still have to do, then we'll do it. But if it's changing stuff we've done already, then we're not doing it.

The others on the team agreed. Conor's view was that the developers themselves were not an elite, as it was the companies that were making the real money. Of course, software developers are generally relatively well paid:

> *Jim:* Maybe we should join SIPTU [the largest national union] and get union rates. But who wants that kind of pay cut?

Conor was, however, the only team member who put the complaints of the team in the language of collective action. Despite the close ties between the team members and the generous cooperation and help they gave to one another, the solidarity of the team was cast almost entirely in negative terms, terms that grew out of their need to protect themselves from the interference of management and less competent designers and developers, in order to get a technically good job done under reasonable conditions. This was achieved largely by controlling the flow of information out of the team as best they could. Collective efforts to negotiate what such reasonable conditions might be were not on the agenda, as industry norms around hours, unreasonable deadlines, and so on were rarely challenged. However, as the team comes together to resist the pressures of time intensification, they created the team cohesion and work intensity that allowed them to meet the challenges of innovation in the global economy. Ironically, it was the team's resistance to corporate interference that created the conditions under which the team managed to meet corporate innovation goals.

Extroversion after the deadline: A team in the world

After the release the team goes into temporary collapse, with the work pace slowing dramatically. As work starts to pick up again, I notice that the solidarity of the team in the pre-deadline, introverted phase has fractured somewhat. During the period after the release individual team members begin to negotiate their roles in the next phase of product development. The team begins to fragment as the focus of the team members shifts from getting the work done to building their careers: the team members become extroverted, looking outward to their future opportunities within and beyond the team.

The next deadline is three to four months away and requires the implementation of the system in the Java programming language. This move to Java is critical for the product, although difficult because it is a new language. People with Java development skills are in short supply and many products with which the Irish teams work do not have Java "drivers," which are needed in order to work with a system designed in Java. From the team members' point of view, this is a great opportunity: training in Java and experience in developing a complex product in the language will greatly enhance their appeal in the labor market.

However, the distribution of such opportunities for training and for valuable experience is not determined by the technical requirements of the product. It is an object of negotiation within the team, negotiation that takes place through the social networks among team members and between team members and the team leader and managers. The issue is rarely mentioned publicly, let alone discussed collectively. Furthermore, the move to Java is a gradual one and each stage produces different sets of conflicts.

The move to Java represents an opportunity for the Irish team, but also a threat. As the team moves to a new technical phase in the development, an opportunity opens for Womble Software to relocate the development work. Despite the Irish team's advantages of knowledge and experience of the system, there is still a danger that development work could move back to the United States. One team meeting discussing the move to Java produced the following exchange:

> *Michael (Business Manager):* We have to get a Java person in Ireland. Ramesh has someone in the United States, but we can't let that happen. We can't let it go there.
> *Paul:* Yeah, you don't want to let the development stuff leak back to the United States. If it starts it'll all end up back there eventually.

The Irish team scrambles to gather together Java skills and to give Ramesh the impression that we have more skills than we do. Later it is my clear impression that Ramesh is aware of the limited level of skills in the Irish team but that he has developed a trust in the Irish team's ability to get up to speed on Java in time.

Of course, merely keeping the Java work in Ireland does not solve the issue of how exactly the need for Java knowledge will be solved for the team. This issue arises first in relation to a totally different problem. The system with which we work needs to be able to run on computers with Apple's Macintosh operating system. At present, our system cannot do that. One quick way to achieve this is to buy a particular software product. However, this will add £2,000 to the cost of each copy of our product for Mac. Instead, it is decided to adjust some parts of our system using Java, which will achieve two goals: make the system work on Mac and begin the process of implementing the system in Java. The team must look for a contract developer who can do this work before the release date.

> *Michael:* I think we'll have to get a contractor. Pat is up there with the porting team at the moment. He should be able to do it.
> *Jim:* yeah, Pat is very good.
> *Michael:* Under normal circumstances we'd put that 2,000 into training somebody on the team so that they could do it, but we don't have the time at the moment because of the release date coming up. So I think we should get Pat.

There are usually multiple ways to incorporate new skills and sources of knowledge into the team. The strategy of buying a product made by another company, a product that embodies that knowledge, is rejected in this case due to its cost. Training current employees is always an option but is often overlooked in the hectic development schedule. No one can be spared for a week-long course with the deadline hanging over the team. The team also missed out on other training opportunities while I was there due to this pressure of time. Finally, bringing in someone with the necessary knowledge is chosen as the strategy, less than satisfactory in the long term but necessary given the time constraints.

The issue of hiring contractors versus training employees is of course a sensitive one:

> *Conor:* Be careful we don't keep getting contractors to do Java stuff and none of us get to go to the training on it.
> *Jim:* Sure, I know. I'm thinking if we get someone on Java he'll have lots of ideas about things to do in Java, and that'll create lots of work for us to do in Java.

This strategy poses a particular danger to the team: while contractors may come only for a short while, they often stay longer as they develop knowledge of a particular piece of the product or become valuable to the team in a particular area. Even I, as a novice technical writer, become valuable: having developed a knowledge of the system, I will be able to write the help materials for future editions more quickly than some professional "tech writers" with no knowledge of the product.

This tension between contract and permanent employees becomes clear in the negotiation of team members' roles around opportunities for working with Java. It is in this internal competition for Java work that the fragmentation of team solidarity and the shift from an introverted to an extroverted orientation within the team is clearest. When Paul, a contractor, declares that he is starting to teach himself Java and wants to do a Java implementation of his part of the system, this meets with some (private) concern from some other members of the team: "I thought he was just here to do that section of the system and not to do this Java stuff." Dan is particularly worried about the involvement of contractors in Java work to the exclusion of permanent employees:

> *Dan:* The three contract people are doing Java and the two permanent people are doing everything else. It is not right. Conor and myself were told in our one-on-one reviews with Michael that the permanent people would get Java training. They would get priority over the contractors. Michael said that they didn't want to give it to the contractors first 'cause they could just leave and take it somewhere else. But that's not how it's going to be – over the next few months they will be doing Java, and we will be doing everything else. I was talking to Conor about it yesterday. He is aware of it.
>
> *Seán:* Will you say anything about it?
>
> *Dan:* What can I say? My attitude is if something is wrong and I can't change it, then I just leave and go somewhere else. It's as simple as that. It doesn't make sense from USTech's point of view. They are paying all this money for contractors, and they are not paying for training for permanent staff. In the end they just pile up the costs for themselves. It's crazy from USTech's point of view. And from my point of view. [Laughs ironically.]

Dan did eventually talk to Séamus, the team leader, about this and received assurances that he would be doing Java work. Paul's growing interest in other advanced technical areas also helped defuse the situation to some extent. However, the negotiations continued as I left. Indeed, on Ramesh's second visit he treated the whole team to a dinner and a night out on the town. Each one of us, as we sat over dinner and wound our way through the city streets, discussed our future roles with Ramesh. I talked over the possibility of doing some further technical writing on a contract basis once my fieldwork was over. Paul discussed his hopes to do some field consulting on the product, Jim and Paul their plans to work on a new technical area of the product, and Conor his desire to do work with Java in a particular application of our system. Indeed, we also put in a good word with Ramesh for each other where the different roles seemed complementary. Even while competing over certain areas of the work, the team members helped each other out in others.

The team solidarity of the pre-release phase becomes more fractured as opportunities for training and learning become a focus of conflict within the team. However, the conflict is submerged and operates through a complex set of social networks and shifting alliances among team members. These ties interact with the formal categories of permanent and contract employees to produce a politics of learning and skills within the team. These local dynamics are intimately connected to the nature of the opportunities in the global market for knowledge embodied (in this case) in the skills of United States developers and the products (software tools) available to carry out certain tasks.

The pre-release phase reveals the nature of the local and global solidarities of the team, with local solidarities increasingly pitted against global interference, as the local team fights for the space to achieve the "global" goal of releasing a good product in the way that they see fit. The post-release phase reveals more schisms within the team and shows how the local team is forged out of a range of alliances among local and global employees and managers. The mobility of team members through various learning paths, both within the team and outside it, is negotiated in this phase, laying the foundation for the next pre-release phase, which is three to four months away.

Time-Space Intensification

The emergence of a global information economy has transformed the character of the workplace for many employees, including those within informational industries such as software. Many authors argue that the globalization of work destroys place and locality, creating placeless "virtual" work. Against this view, this chapter has argued for a concept of globalization that emphasizes the organization of the global economy through particular places and regions and the critical importance of patterns of mobility of people, information, and resources within and between these regions. These changes in the territorial organization of capitalism interact with an organizational restructuring characterized by the decentralization of work and firms. While some authors argue that these organizational changes will bring relative equality and a rough and ready economic democracy, this chapter has shown that new forms of power operate within these new organizational forms. Ethnography reveals that we cannot simply deduce concrete social practices and power relations from a particular organizational and territorial work structure. Instead, we find that a new ground is emerging upon which the struggles of the global informational economy will be waged – a new set of social identities, resources, interests, and issues is created, which will be the basis of the politics of the global workplace in the years to come.

This new "contested terrain" of the global workplace is a system of time-space intensification where workers experience not the "end of time and space" but their ascent to a new level of intensity. Space is intensified by the necessity of local cooperation and the increased use of project teams in the face of the challenges posed by the global economy. Time becomes an ever more pressing reality in the deadline-driven workplace. This time-space intensification shapes the structure of both work and careers in the global workplace. Careers are built using mobility between firms to bargain for improved wages and access to technical learning, and these mobile careers only increase the importance of close interactions and strong local cooperation while working on any particular project. Out of these underlying structures emerges a set of dynamics, organized around the project deadline, which give the global workplace its dynamism but also generate certain costs and dilemmas for the participants. Conflicts over these dilemmas of time-space intensification constitute the new politics of the globalization of knowledge work.

What will be the central controversies on this new contested terrain? The two phases of time-space intensification create characteristic advantages and dilemmas for knowledge workers such as the software developers in this chapter, for firms such as USTech and Womble Software, and for workers' families, software users, and the other (largely invisible) social actors beyond the industry with an interest in its social organization. While these dynamics and dilemmas have been recognized for some time in the information industries, globalization intensifies them.[20]

Certain characteristic organizational problems are likely to emerge: these are the internal organizational dilemmas of time-space intensification. In the pre-release phase, the introversion of the team, the intensification of time, and the pressures imposed by the deadline create the conditions that lead to employee burnout – manifested in the case I have described in the exhaustion of the team members up to and after the deadline and also in the decision made by Ramesh (some five months after I left the team) to resign due to overwork. This creates problems for the organization, as the team's introversion cuts it off from the rest of the organization and raises the danger of organizational involution and the distancing of teams from one another, even teams working on related technical or business issues. For the Womble team, this can be seen in the antagonistic attitude to the graphics team in California, a set of relationships which, if more cooperative, could have been very valuable in improving the product under development.

In the post-deadline phase, the solidarity fragments and team members begin to look elsewhere for future opportunities. The extroverted phase is when employees can turn to the labor market to gain the rewards of their new-found expertise and the organization can assemble a new group of employees with new sets of skills and resources into a project team for the next phase of the development effort. However, there is also a significant cost associated with the high levels of employee turnover within the industry. The accumulated knowledge derived from the development of the Womble software product, which has built up within the team, is now dissipated throughout the industry. This constitutes a significant loss of firm-specific knowledge from Womble's point of view and also a loss of the effort put into developing effective working relationships within the team. There are therefore clear organizational costs attached to failure to address these internal dilemmas.[21]

Time-space intensification also causes certain external social dilemmas. The pressure and introverted character of the pre-deadline phase, and the resulting insulation of workers and the organization of their work from any kind of broader social accountability, make it difficult to reconcile the team structure and team culture with broader social concerns. This is manifested in at least two areas. The most directly obvious is the work–family nexus, where work demands come to dominate family life, leaving very little space for workers to negotiate alternative work and family time arrangements. Secondly, as technology increasingly penetrates our everyday social practices, the involvement of users in decisions regarding these technologies becomes more and more crucial. But the isolation and insulation of the developers during their most creative and innovative phase militates strongly against any meaningful interaction with prospective users of the product from outside the team. To the extent that we might fear the arrival of the Weberian "iron cage" in the form of a society dominated by large, centralized organizations, there is some promise in the decentralized organizational forms compatible with this high-mobility system. However, although organizations no longer have the same rigid bureaucratic structures insulating them from social accountability, the intensification of time ultimately results in a similar outcome.

The post-deadline phase of high mobility creates a very high degree of volatility and insecurity in the labor market so that employees lack strong employment guarantees. This is not currently a major issue in the Irish industry, given the generally very high demand for software skills. Even in the current tight labor market, "employment security" gives way to "employability security."[22] However, when career gains are based on the threat of mobility, this seems inevitably to lead to increased labor market inequality, as the threat to leave is only effective when replacing the employee is difficult. As it is inherently based on scarcity, the limits of mobility as a universal career strategy are clear. This seems likely to be a contributing factor to the spiraling wage inequality in Ireland over the past ten years.[23]

These internal and external dilemmas of time-space intensification are all the more crucial given that the economic success of the Republic of Ireland over the past ten years has been built upon the success of industries such as software.[24] The politics of the conference call became the new politics of the global workplace – distant yet closely integrated into operations in the core, less hierarchical but nonetheless subject to new forms of power relations. As these global workplaces spread through economies such as Ireland's, the dilemmas of time-space intensification will become central economic and social issues for societies incorporated into new, deeper processes of globalization. The value of global ethnography is its ability to reveal these dilemmas as aspects of a "contested terrain" of globalization, rather than as inevitable outcomes of an apolitical process.

NOTES

1   Robert Reich, *The Work of Nations*.
2   Anthony Giddens, *The Consequences of Modernity*. Giddens argues that globalization occurs in a process of *time-space distanciation*, as space and time are "distanciated" from (lifted out of) their local contexts. There are two main mechanisms through which this happens: the use of *symbolic tokens* (universal media of exchange/interaction such as money) and of *expert systems* (shared bodies of technical knowledge that can be applied in a wide variety of contexts).
3   See Marshall Berman, *All That Is Solid Melts Into Air*; David Harvey, *The Condition of Postmodernity*; and Manuel Castells, *The Rise of the Network Society*. Harvey argues that globalization is characterized by a process of *time-space compression*, in which the speed-up of time in the global economy also serves to compress the autonomy of local space and social context, as different places are integrated into an increasingly universal capitalist economy.
4   See Barry Bluestone and Bennett Harrison, *The Deindustrialization of America*; Michael Burawoy, *The Politics of Production*; and Harley Shaiken, *Mexico in the Global Economy*.
5   We might refer to this perspective as *time-space embedding*, as embeddedness of workplaces in their local social contexts appears to provide a solution to the speed-up of the global economy, giving the successful workplaces some insulation from these pressures and perhaps even re-embedding time itself in local contexts. See Michael Piore and Charles Sabel, *The Second Industrial Divide*; AnnaLee Saxenian, *Regional Advantage*; and Michael Storper, *The Regional World*.
6   See Leslie Perlow, *Finding Time*, and "Boundary Control," for detailed empirical analyses of these issues in a software workplace.
7   Eoin O'Malley, *Industry and Economic Development*.

8   For a more detailed analysis of this process, see Seán Ó Riain. "The Birth of a Celtic Tiger?," "An Offshore Silicon Valley?," and "Remaking the Developmental State."

9   IBM's employment guarantee collapsed with a reduction of 140,000 in a workforce of 400,000 between 1986 and 1993. For an analysis of "corporate culture" in such workplaces, see Gideon Kunda, *Engineering Culture*.

10 See Saxenian, *Regional Advantage*, and Baron, Burton, and Hannon, "The Road Taken."

11 Office of Technology Policy, *America's New Deficit*.

12 Seán Ó Riain, "Remaking the Developmental State." See also Saskia Sassen, *The Global City*, and Saxenian, *Regional Advantage*, for discussion of labor markets in agglomerated industries in core regions.

13 Reich, *The Work of Nations*.

14 Much of this learning, especially in a team context, derives from what Jean Lave and Etienne Wenger call "situated learning." See Lave and Wenger, *Situated Learning*.

15 Barry Wellman et al., "Computer Networks as Social Networks," p. 231.

16 For a discussion of this concept and a review of a variety of examples, see Manuel Castells and Peter Hall, *Technopoles of the World*.

17 See, for example, Rosabeth Moss Kanter, *World Class*, and Manuel Castells. *The Rise of the Network Society*.

18 For a more detailed analysis of these processes, based on a case study of a software company in Ireland in the mid-1980s, see Margaret Tierney, "Negotiating a Software Career."

19 Brian Fynes et al., *Flexible Working Lives*, p. 138.

20 For a classic account of these dynamics in a computer design workplace in the 1970s, see Tracy Kidder, *The Soul of a New Machine*.

21 For an organizational and management theory perspective, see Brown and Eisenhardt, "The Art of Continuous Change."

22 See Kanter, *World Class*, for a discussion of this concept as developed in a study of a software company in Massachusetts.

23 For a detailed analysis of trends from 1987 to 1994, see Alan Barrett, Tim Callan, and Brian Nolan, "Rising Wage Inequality, Returns to Education and Labour Market Institutions."

24 For a more detailed analysis of the growth of the Irish software industry, with particular reference to its potential and to the limits of state–society alliances in shaping the industry's development and impact, see Ó Riain, "Remaking the Developmental State."

REFERENCES

Baron, James, M. Diane Burton, and Michael Hannan. "The Road Taken: Origins and Early Evolution of Employment Systems in Emerging Companies." *Industrial and Corporate Change* 5 (1996): 239–75.

Barrett, Alan, Tim Callan, and Brian Nolan. "Rising Wage Inequality, Returns to Education and Labour Market Institutions: Evidence from Ireland." *British Journal of Industrial Relations* 37 (1999): 77–100.

Berman, Marshall. *All That Is Solid Melts Into Air: The Experience of Modernity*. London: Penguin Books, 1982.

Bluestone, Barry, and Bennett Harrison. *The Deindustrialization of America*. New York: Basic Books, 1982.

Brown, S., and K. Eisenhardt. "The Art of Continuous Change." *Administrative Science Quarterly* 42 (1997): 1–34.

Castells, Manuel. *The Rise of the Network Society, Vol. 1: The Information Age*. Oxford: Blackwell, 1996.

Castells, Manuel, and Peter Hall. *Technopoles of the World*. New York: Routledge, 1994.

Fynes, Brian, Thomas Morrissey, William K. Roche, Brendan J. Whelan, and James Williams. *Flexible Working Lives: The Changing Nature of Working Time Arrangements in Ireland*. Dublin: Oak Tree Press, 1996.

Giddens, Anthony. *The Consequences of Modernity*. Stanford, CA: Stanford University Press, 1990.

Harvey, David. *The Condition of Postmodernity: An Enquiry into the Origins of Cultural Change*. Oxford: Blackwell, 1989.

Kanter, Rosabeth Moss. *World Class: Thriving Locally in the Global Economy*. New York Simon and Schuster, 1995.

Kidder, Tracey. *The Soul of a New Machine*. New York: Avon Books, 1981.

Kunda, Gideon. *Engineering Culture*. Philadelphia, PA: Temple University Press, 1998.

Lave, Jean, and Etienne Wenger. *Situated Learning: Legitimate Peripheral Participation*. Cambridge: Cambridge University Press, 1993.

O'Malley, Eoin. *Industry and Economic Development*. Dublin: Gill and Macmillan, 1989.

Ó Riain, Seán. "The Birth of a Celtic Tiger?" *Communications of the ACM* 40 (1997) 11–16.

—— "An Offshore Silicon Valley?" *Competition and Change* 2 (1997): 175–212.

—— "Remaking the Developmental State: The Irish Software Industry in the Global Economy." PhD dissertation, University of California, Berkeley, 1999.

Perlow, Leslie. "Boundary Control: The Social Ordering of Work and Family Time in a High-Tech Corporation." *Administrative Science Quarterly* 43 (1998): 328–57.

—— *Finding Time*. Ithaca, NY: ILR Press, 1997.

Piore, Michael J., and Charles F. Sabel. *The Second Industrial Divide: Possibilities for Prosperity*. New York: Basic Books, 1984.

Reich, Robert B. *The Work of Nations*. New York: Vintage, 1991.

Sassen, Saskia. *The Global City*. Princeton, NJ: Princeton University Press, 1991.

Saxenian, AnnaLee. *Regional Advantage*. Cambridge, MA: Harvard University Press, 1994.

Shaiken, Harley. *Mexico in the Global Economy*. San Diego, CA: Center for United States–Mexican Studies, 1990.

Storper, Michael. *The Regional World: Territorial Development in a Global Economy*. London: Guilford Press, 1997.

Tierney, Margaret. "Negotiating a Software Career: Informal Work Practices and 'The Lads' in a Software Installation." In *The Gender–Technology Relation: Contemporary Theory and Research*, edited by K. Grint and R. Gill, pp. 192–209. London: Taylor and Francis, 1995.

Wellman, Barry, Janet Salaff, Dimitrina Dimitrova, Laura Garton, Milena Gulia, and Caroline Haythornthwaite. "Computer Networks as Social Networks." *Annual Review of Sociology* 22 (1996): 213–38.

Chapter 3

Instrumentalizing the Truth of Practice

Katie Vann and Geoffrey C. Bowker

Knowledge of the Knowledge of Labour For Sale

To speak of the commercialization of epistemology is to speak of the commodification of knowledge about knowledge. To speak of the construction of knowledge
about knowledge is to invoke the convergence of interests around the object that this
'knowledge about' constructs.[1] The configuration of interests makes this object, and
the object so made holds the interests together. In this way, to speak of the commercialization of epistemology is to invoke a configuration of instrumentalizations of
the object posited through epistemological endeavours.

Not that the meaning of the object has to be the same for the interests that it
holds together. Its meaning must be malleable enough to be incorporated into the
different shapes of different lives, but be robust enough to provide fodder for its
incorporation.

This practical ambivalence of objects created as knowledge gives life to the political
economy of academic research: it is difficult to survive in the ivory castle making
knowledge that few recognize or are interested in, though it is possible to survive even
if others use the object differently. Thus, to speak of the commercialization of any
knowledge is to speak of the mapping of a commercial logic onto an already complicated political economic process at work among interest formations. Commercialization of knowledge follows the footpath of its many instrumentalizations.

We want to consider the commercialization of a particular knowledge about
knowledge. Specifically, we want to trace a particular configuration of interests
that appear to have been built around a concept of 'practice'.[2] 'Practice', often
associated with Marx's term 'praxis', has become an increasingly regular invocation
within the social and historical sciences since the 1960s, marking an analytical turn
away from structural functionalist approaches.[3] A concept of practice was developed in particular ways through the efforts of social scientists working in educational research and research on work, to develop a theory of learning and knowledge
production. Jean Lave's seminal *Cognition in Practice* (1988) accomplished important work along these lines.

We want to mark a movement of this orientation into a management-consulting domain, where it has been commercialized. Today, the locution 'communities of practice' is often invoked as a term for the kinds of social learning formations to which Lave called attention. A key moment of the trajectory we mark is a book by Etienne Wenger, a colleague and previous co-author of Lave (Lave and Wenger 1991). Wenger's *Communities of Practice* (1998) popularized a concept of practice in the managerial domain, a process whose contours are suggested in a blurb for his book.

> The idea that an organization is a constellation of 'communities of practice' is a genuine breakthrough, and that overused word 'breakthrough' is merited. It is an idea that has profound implications for what it takes to run a successful organization in our frenetic, chaotic times. In this book, Etienne Wenger lays the groundwork for the kind of thinking that will be necessary for any surviving organization in the twenty-first century. Wenger and the IRL are redefining the cutting edge. And they are right! Pay attention! Please! (Blurb by Tom Peters, author of *Circle of Innovation*)

In the trajectory we mark, a particular knowledge about knowledge has become robust enough to be instrumentalized differently. In Lave's work it is instrumentalized as part of a critique of normative psychological testing at use in formal educational assessment. More recently, the locution 'practice' has travelled into organizational management consulting communities, and has been transformed into an acronym – 'CoPs' – to refer to social formations that are either recognized as such by managers or intentionally created in organizations in hope that benefits may be garnered from the learning and knowledge production processes that communities of practice are said to instantiate.[4] One service that commercializes an interest in communities of practice frames the matter thus:

> New economic growth continues to be centered on the ability to leverage corporate knowledge. Although nearly every company practices some form of knowledge management, very few are able to fully leverage knowledge to drive bottom line results. Much of this failure stems from the inability to identify preexisting knowledge communities ... Best Practices, LCC's knowledge exchange 'Knowledge Alliances: Driving Sales, Service, and Innovation Through Communities of Practice' will identify the practices used at leading companies ... Through the insights shared in this study, our firm can help your company successfully realize the full value of its knowledge communities. (Best Practices, LLC)

In pointing to this trajectory, we mean to explore how a concept of practice is re-instrumentalized and reconfigured as a commercial object with specific uses. We trace one strand in a much larger configuration of interests and enquire how practice is instrumentalized in a particular academic formation, how it is there constructed as an object of knowledge, and how it is re-instrumentalized as a commercial object. Each mode of instrumentalization reflects imperatives of the two communities in their respective, particular historical moments. It appears that as we move between the two social formations, 'practice' is configured first as an instrument of a dereifying critical theory, and then as an instrument of economic value creation. We consider this configuration of interested relations and how knowledge about knowledge is transformed as it moves between the two. The commercialized object with which we are concerned is a concept of the knowledge of labour. To know about the knowledge of labour is to know something about the creation of value creating labour. This knowledge comes to have value for those who control labour, and it is this value to which the commercial process is mapped.

Practice as the Object of a Scientific Epistemology

To enter the case more deeply, we juxtapose two descriptions of organizational design, articulated roughly thirty years apart, in which we see two very different pictures of knowledge to be utilized by managerial communities. Compare:

> An organization can be pictured as a three-layered cake. In the bottom layer, we have the basic work processes – in the case of a manufacturing organization, the processes that produce raw materials, manufacture the physical product, warehouse it, and ship it. In the middle layer, we have the programmed decision-making processes, the processes that govern the day-to-day operation of the manufacturing and distribution system. In the top layer, we have the non-programmed decision-making processes, the processes that are required to design and redesign the entire system, to provide it with its basic goals and objectives, and to monitor its performance. (Simon 1960: 40)

with:

> We know that the most valuable knowledge often resides where we are least able to see or control it: on the front lines, at the periphery, with the renegades. Companies that embrace the emergent can tap the logic of knowledge work and the spirit of community. Those that don't will be left behind. (Brown and Gray 1995)

These two pictures – one of work organization as fixed hierarchy, the other of work organization as fluid emergence – rest on very different epistemological commitments. Knowledge *happens* differently and is forged by different kinds of people in each scenario. The crucial difference seems to turn on their respective ideas about the relation between knowledge as a kind of action on one hand, and pre-given structure on the other. The first proposes a structure – like a cake – composed of levels. The levels are differentiated by how structure in the form of a programme can determine decision making at each. The text notes that programmed knowledge occurs in routine, repetitive decisions and organizations develop specific processes for handling them. Non-programmed knowledge occurs in one-shot, ill-structured novel policy decisions. These are handled by general problem-solving processes (Simon 1960). The difference is to be reflected in the hierarchical structures of the organization.

The image here is that the form that knowledge takes can be pre-specified. The content of some decision making is traceable to knowledge in the form of a pre-given programme, whereas other decision making is ill-structured and must occur in the shot of the moment. The structure of the cake relies on the ability to distinguish between where and by whom structured and ill-structured problem solving will be carried out. And distinguishing this relies on an epistemological commitment: structure in the form of a decision-making programme (rules) can, in pre-specifiable

cases, determine the content of decision making. These pre-specifiable cases constitute the bottom layers of the cake. Like a stage of puppets following the movements
of their strings, the lower levels of the cake are where structure does its work: rules
are made and followed. Something above, a programme, is in control.

The second picture, of work as fluid emergence, by contrast invokes the image of
organization as a cauldron of knowledges bubbling up all over the place. There is no
pre-given programme determining where it might turn up next. Thus, Brown and
Gray suggest that 'the real genius of organizations is the informal, impromptu, often
inspired ways that real people solve real problems in ways that formal processes
can't anticipate. When you're competing on knowledge, the name of the game is
improvisation, not standardization' (Brown and Gray 1995). The creation of knowledge – *real* knowledge – does not follow formal, pre-given standards of action. It is
inspired in spite of them and the hierarchies they imply. A renegade real is out there
busting at the seams: it is out of control.

The scenarios contrasted here espouse two very different commitments about the
relationship between pre-given structure and knowledge-bearing action. The picture
of work organization as fluid emergence has proliferated in management theory
discourse over the past five years, and provides a resource for the sales pitch of
consulting firms considered to be innovative in their outlook.

It seems to us that the intelligibility of the transition relies upon important changes
on the epistemological scene that have emerged in American academia since the
1960s.[5] Jean Lave's *Cognition in Practice* carried out important work along these
lines. An anthropologist concerned with questions of learning and education, Lave
was working in response to then extant functionalist paradigms in psychology and
educational assessment. In her account, functionalism regards society

> as a set of macrostructures in place, a fait accompli to be internalized by individuals
> born into it. Consensus – shared norms, values, and culture more generally – is the
> foundation of social order. (Lave 1988: 7)

Lave's efforts to counter functionalism were informed by her readings of Giddens
and Bourdieu, of whom she provided the following quotes:

> we have to avoid any account of socialization which presumes either that the subject is
> determined by the social object (the individual simply as 'moulded' by society); or, by
> contrast, which takes subjectivity for granted as an inherent characteristic of human
> beings, not in need of explication. (Giddens 1979; quoted in Lave 1988)

> We shall escape from the ritual either/or choice between objectivism and subjectivism . . .
> only if we are prepared to inquire into the mode of production and functioning of
> the practical mastery which makes possible both an objectively intelligible practice
> and also an objectively enchanted experience of that practice. (Bourdieu 1977; quoted
> in Lave 1988)

These texts were important points of departure for Lave. They pointed toward a
theory of 'practice' somewhere between structuralist and phenomenological accounts.[6] They are 'critical of functional (and also phenomenological) problematics'
and are

> concerned with dialectical synthesis, and assume the partially determined, partially
> determining character of human agency... Their work recommends the study of social
> practice in spatial and temporal context. For the synthetic character of these theories
> makes it difficult to argue for the separation of cognition and the social world. (Lave
> 1988: 16)

The task for Lave then was to articulate a synthetic theory of learning as practice.

Practice seems to have interested Lave as a window through which to view a deeply political issue. She articulated a relationship between functionalism as a particular social theoretic position, on one hand, and, on another, a 'web of relations' between internalism as a theory of learning and institutionalized systems of formal education.

> Functional theory permeates rationales, explanations, and the organization of schooling
> in American society, and imbues much of anthropological, educational, and psycho-
> logical theory with its particular logic... In particular, it is enacted in schools by their
> claim to treat all children alike... and its view that unequal ranking is an epiphenom-
> enon of differential merit... the functionalist position contains a theory of learning: in
> particular, that children can be taught general cognitive skills (e.g. reading, writing,
> mathematics, logic, critical thinking) if these 'skills' are disembedded from the routine
> contexts of their use... Schooling reflects these ideas at a broad organizational level, as
> it separates children from the contexts of their own and their families' daily lives. At a
> more specific level, classroom tests put the principle to work: they serve as a measure of
> individual, 'out of context' success. (Ibid.: 8–9)

By contrast, Lave was after a practice theory of learning that would accord legitim-acy to different knowledges in addition to those that would be prescribed by such normative functionalist models. Such an approach would have political implica-tions. It would reveal the extent to which meritocratic social relations are predicated on particular normative commitments that are embedded in the apparatus of scien-tific psychological testing being utilized as a formalized means of assessing students' performances. Experimental tasks were derived from normative models that foster a 'static, objectified conceptualization of processes of reasoning, a transformation that occurs between their initial formulation and their incorporation into experimental procedures' (ibid.: 37). Such an approach to formal education is guided by the normative orientation of the experiments: 'so long as evaluation of subjects' per-formance is the goal, and it is to be achieved by comparison to an ideal view of correct understanding, then the experimenter must determine what will constitute correct problem solutions... The task then becomes to get the subject to match the experimenter's expectations' (ibid.).

Here Lave was calling attention to reificatory tendencies of the normative experi-mental models. The internalist tradition is associated with the reification process owing to its reliance on pre-given, normative models of cognitive skills, the decon-textualization of action from its everyday forms for the purposes of testing, and the reduction of social processes to internal mental states thought to precede the testing situations. Practice thus emerges as an approach that attempts to show that the ascription of internal mental states to experimental subjects relies on the construc-tions of the scientist, and that human life has a social texture which the functionalist/

internalist methodologies are incapable of seeing. 'Practice' emerges as an instrument of a de-reifying, critical social theory crafted to problematize the prominence of normative functional models as formal educational assessment techniques. It is de-reifying precisely in how it distances itself from the normative impositions of 'structure' as found in the functionalist framework through an appeal to a living process that such impositions would have obscured.

But there is more at stake here than an appeal to a politics of knowledge about learning. Creating a concept of practice to do this critical political work would require a characteristically scientific move. For it is not just that the functionalist paradigm undergirds meritocratic educational relations with ethically repugnant social consequences; that it fosters competitive relationships among children which they will come to expect in their future as wage earners; that it supports stratified social relations of relative human value and access to social wealth; or even that it configures very particular aspirations and elevates them to the status of universal necessities. Meritocracy fostered by the use of a functionalist apparatus is problematized, instead, in virtue of the fact that it rests upon an epistemologically flawed science. In its place is erected a non-reifying science of practice, a contextual science with an alternative object of investigation and an alternative technique.

Tough work, given a division of intellectual labour – specifically that between psychology and anthropology – as institutionalized in the production relations of the academy. Lave saw such a division of labour as one which effectively

> legislates away major questions about social diversity, inequality, conflict, complementarity, cooperation and differences of power and knowledge, and the means by which they are socially produced, reproduced and transformed in laboratory, school, and other everyday settings. (Ibid.: 10)

To debunk both the academic division of labour and the normative testing apparatus that it supports, a theory of learning as practice had to establish that culture and social organization matter to psychological life in ways different from those suggested by internalist models. That is, functionalism/internalism has an account of the 'social'. But as a component of learning, this social is a *content* – a *fait accompli* to be internalized. Here, psychological assessment is concerned with whether this internalizeable content is seen to be coming back out of the subject through performance on tasks. Assessment wants to know what a masterful puppet the subject is. Such a science needs no anthropological comprehension of puppets, because they are all the same except in the degree to which they reproduce the movement of the strings, the programme, the *fait accompli* to be internalized.

But if learning is seen as a *creative process* that is different from internalization, and if culture and social organization are seen as fundamental to this process, then the study of learning cannot proceed on the basis of the academic division of labour between psychology and anthropology.

> If everyday experience is the major means by which culture impinges on individuals and vice versa, then functionalist and social practice theories imply different answers to questions about *what* cognitive activity is the appropriate object of analysis. In traditional cognitive experiments subjects' performance on laboratory tasks are compared to a normative model, to an ideally meritocratic performance. In practice, theory

> attention shifts to everyday activity, which becomes both the measure of the experi-
> menter's ability to design generalizable experiments, and the source of explanations for
> varieties of performance in those experiments...This motivates...a different set of
> problems and questions than the study of virtuoso performance and people's failures to
> produce such performances. (Lave 1988)

It seems here that the inadequacy of the internalism/formal education web is framed
as an effect of the incorrectness – the 'ecological invalidity' – of a science of
assessment that is predicated on functionalist logic. Indeed, at stake here is a
question of what it is that a good science of knowledge making *studies* and *how*
its investigation will be carried out. Working against the politics of functionalism
works hand in hand with building an alternative scientific object and an alternative
scientific technique. For example, Lave does a lot of work along these lines in her
critique of a study of mathematical reasoning among grocery shoppers, from which
a practice approach would be distanced.

> Capon and Kuhn began with a Piagetian model of formal operational approaches to
> ratio comparison. There is no evidence that the lived-in world directly influenced their
> choice of research topic, in fact it appears the other way around: given a determination
> to study proportional reasoning, they asked themselves, 'where would you find ratio
> comparisons in a mundane situation?' Unit price comparisons in the supermarket had
> this form, and met the ideals of formal operational arithmetic and good consumer
> behavior at the same time. It did not lead Capon and Kuhn to observational research
> inside a supermarket, nor did the location of their experiment outside a supermarket
> lead them to investigate how grocery shopping activity might have shaped arithmetic.
> (Ibid.: 114)

Lave differentiated her study: 'It began with an ethnographic question, "what sort of
math occurs in grocery shopping?" It led to observation in the supermarket and the
singling out of best-buy problems because they looked rather like "real math" (a
point at which normative conceptions of mathematical knowledge shaped the
construction of this experiment)' (ibid.). Here, to understand learning is not just
to understand a process different from the internalization of structure: it is also to
understand learning by using a particular knowledge-creating method.

To call into question the credibility of the web of relations supported by functionalist logic, Lave appeals to a particular truth that the functionalist methodology is
unequipped to see. The internalist theory hinges on a reifying methodology that
conceals the reality of human learning as a social phenomenon. The inadequacy of
the internalist methodology is constructed here through an appeal to a *lived mode*
of human experience to which the internalist methodology is ill-equipped to gain
access. In its place, an anthropological/ethnographic science is proposed. Appealing
to an ethnographic reality becomes a means to debunk the internalist science, and
this reality is accordingly a means of political critique. To study practice is to study a
lived-in world. It is to see a reality that the normative model will have missed. It is an
ethnographic seeing that does not impose normative reifications, and that, as such,
sees a kind of pre-reified, knowledge-bearing subject. This is to engage a particular
politics. Educational assessment predicated on a contextual science with a new
object would constitute a web with an alternative politics. But it is also to build a

scientific object. The 'object' of this science is 'practice' and works as an instrument of political critique.

In this way, an epistemology of practice entails a set of claims about how people learn and how knowledge is shared among social actors. According legitimacy for this description, however, the articulation of the theory contrasts its own epistemic foundations as scientific methodology with that of another. In this sense, practice epistemology depends crucially on the legitimation of a repudiation of internalist methodological commitments. This means that the development of the practice theory of knowledge entails two epistemic moments, or an epistemological othering at two levels. At the first level, a distinction is articulated between an internalist theory of knowledge and a practice theory of knowledge. At the second level, an internalist scientific methodology is distinguished from one deemed appropriate for a science of practice. Here, it is an epistemological commitment about what is real and a concomitant theory about what a science of the real consists of.

This double epistemological movement is later taken up by Lave and Wenger, where the critique of functionalism continues:

> Conventional explanations view learning as a process by which a learner internalizes knowledge, whether 'discovered,' 'transmitted' from others, or 'experienced in inter-action' with others. This focus on internalization does not just leave the nature of the learner, of the world, and of their relations unexplored; it can only reflect far-reaching assumptions concerning these issues...Learning as internalization is too easily con-strued as an unproblematic process of absorbing the given, as a matter of transmission and assimilation. (Lave and Wenger 1991: 47)

What interests us here is how it is not necessarily Lave's, or Lave and Wenger's, political position on meritocratic social relations that attends the spread of the science they build. Rather, what spreads is the science as such. This invites us to think about the ways in which 'practice' as a scientific object is maintained across different communities where it is instrumentalized differently. Even though the instrumentalizations of the object differ, each acquires power precisely through its appeal to the credibility of the science that posits the object (practice) that it instrumentalizes. Publication strategies employed for this book emphasize its uniqueness and relative credibility as a mode of science.

> In this volume, Lave and Wenger undertake a radical and important rethinking and reformulation of our conception of learning. By placing emphasis on the whole person, and by viewing agent, activity, and world as mutually constitutive, they give us the opportunity to escape from the tyranny of the assumption that learning is the reception of factual knowledge or information. The authors argue that most accounts of learning have ignored its quintessentially social character. (Ibid.: back blurb)

The pitch focuses on differentiating the science of practice from a tyrannical conventional assumption. We are not told exactly what the assumption is. Nor are we told of the politics of the social relations that the assumption upholds. We are told that this obscure and incredible assumption is 'ours' and that the theory developed in the book we hold is an important correction of it. And the corrective science we find inside the book is supported by appeal to an ethnographic seeing.

Ethnographic studies of apprenticeship emphasize the indivisible character of learning and work practices. This, in turn, *helps to make obvious* the social nature of learning and knowing. (Ibid.: 61; our emphasis)

Re-instrumentalizing the Truth of Practice

A repudiation of conventional understandings of learning is carried into the Wenger text. It moves with a concept of practice across communities, where an expanded configuration of interests is identified:

if we believe that productive people in organizations are the diligent implementers of organizational processes and that the key to organizational performance is therefore the definition of increasingly more efficient and detailed processes by which people's actions are prescribed, then it makes sense to engineer and re-engineer these processes in abstract ways and then roll them out for implementation. But if we believe that people in organizations contribute to organizational goals by participating inventively in practices that can never be fully captured by institutional processes, then we will minimize prescription, suspecting that too much of it discourages the very inventiveness that makes practices effective. We will have to make sure that our organizations are contexts within which the communities that develop these practices may prosper. We will have to value the work of community building and make sure that participants have access to the resources necessary to learn what they need to learn in order to take actions and make decisions that fully engage their own knowledgeability... A social theory of learning is therefore not exclusively an academic enterprise. While its perspective can indeed inform our academic investigations, it is also relevant to our daily actions, our policies, and the technical, organizational, and educational systems we design. A new conceptual framework for thinking about learning is thus of value not only to theorists but to all of us. (Wenger 1998: 10–11)

This provokes the extension of an interest formation. It simultaneously retains a sense of the kind of de-reifying celebration of ingenuity that we saw in Lave, but it begins to re-frame practice as a kind of asset. The subject of practice is not a puppet and, as such, it is worth promoting. The epistemic orientation proposed here is relevant to academic investigation and it is relevant to the design of organizations. The value of knowledge about practice can spread.

The practical ambivalence of practice as the object of a scientific epistemology can be illustrated if we consider two narrativizations of Julian Orr's *Talking About Machines* (1996). Orr pursued the notion of practice in his ethnographic study of technical workers, and contended that conventional studies of work rely too heavily on definitions of work that are supplied by managers and business administrators. In such definitions, 'work' is defined as work for which workers are paid, as is determined by managerial conceptions of those activities deemed necessary for production. Orr argued that the epistemic credibility of such definitions is arguable at best. More likely, they give a skewed perception of work and do not include all the activities that are 'really essential to production'. By contrast, Orr identified the activities that are really essential to production with a kind of really real that he had witnessed in the ethnographic present:

The work done by the technicians I studied is often very different from the methods specified by their management in the machine documentation. There is clearly a disparity between the tasks that they are told to accomplish and the means that are said to be adequate to the task. The technicians choose to give accomplishing the task priority over use of the prescribed means, and so they resolve problems in the field any way they can, apparently believing that management really wants accomplishment more than strict observation of the prescriptions for work. (Ibid.: 149).

Stephen Barley[7] wrote the foreword to Orr's book and emphasized its rich ethnographic description of 'what people do and how they do it'. Here, a politics dereification reminiscent of Lave's work is engaged:

Orr documents and develops the important and counterintuitive notion that technical knowledge is best viewed as a socially distributed resource that is diffused and stored primarily through an oral culture...[he] puts the flesh of everyday life on Lave and Wenger's idea of a community of practice, an idea that promises to contribute significantly to both occupational and organization studies because it enables us to talk about occupational dynamics in situations that lack the institutional supports that sociologists normally attribute to recognizable occupations...We learn from this book that technicians' work is not what their managers believe it to be...This is because Orr shows us the dignity, the intelligence, the skill, and the dedication that photocopier technicians bring to their work. He rescues what they do and who they are from an invisibility by showing us a piece of their world. (Ibid.: xiii–xiv)

Orr's study became a key player in the narrativization of the communities of practice trope for the managerial community. It was discussed in the article by Brown and Gray for *Fast Company* magazine – written to boost work at Xerox PARC for the business community. There, different aspects of Orr's study of the photocopy technicians are emphasized:

The story begins in the 1980s. We were looking for ways to boost the productivity of the Xerox field service staff. Before deciding how to proceed, we launched a study. An anthropologist from the Xerox Palo Alto Research Center (PARC), a member of the work-practices team, traveled with a group of tech reps to observe how they actually did their jobs – not how they described what they did, or what their managers assumed they did. That research challenged the way Xerox thought about the nature of work, the role of the individual, and the relationship between the individual and the company. It was the first shot in a revolution. (Brown and Gray 1995)

Brown and Gray emphasize the existence and importance of 'real work', drawing on such phrases as: 'observe how they actually did their jobs – not how they described what they did, or what their managers assumed they did'. Looking closely affords a glimpse at how *real* people solve *real* problems. A special, revolutionary science is at work here; it sees a real beneath assumptions and descriptions. Practice, this real, is some real that is different from workers' own self-understandings *and* from managers' understandings of them.

It seems to us that there is an important transposition of the epistemological 'other' of the theory of practice that we saw in Lave. The normative expectations of the functionalist assessment techniques are transposed into the organizational formalizations of work that are predicated on managerial conceptions. There is a real known by a science of practice and there is a non-real posited in the formalizations informing organizational structure. A management consultant working in this vein quotes Brown in a moment in which the science of the real – versus some unreal kind of knowledge – is celebrated:

> corporations must provide support that corresponds to the real needs of the communities of practice...This approach draws attention away from abstract knowledge and cranial processes and situates it in the practices and communities in which knowledge takes on significance. (Brown, quoted in Community Intelligence Labs (COIL) consulting services)

The reference to abstract knowledge and cranial processes seems to be situated here as a repudiation of internalist epistemology whose dubiousness is thrown into relief by an appeal to a 'real'. Far more than just two different theories about how knowledge happens in the world, the pictures of organizational knowledge as fixed hierarchy and fluid emergence hinge on two very different kinds of science. Unlike de-contextualizing laboratory experiments, or process flows drawn in top-floor managerial boardrooms, there is a science of the real that busts at the seams. This science is available to inform organizational design, and it is for sale.

This aspect of the development of the practice theory of knowledge has important consequences for the particular way in which the new epistemology is instrumentalized within the managerial community. The theory of knowledge currently becoming the primary axis of the commercial offerings of these firms implicitly relies on the repudiation of the kind of science on which internalist accounts of knowledge were based. And the angling of the ethnographic science toward work is an important moment of the commercialization of the concept of practice, because in this context the object of ethnographic seeing begins to take on an identity as a workplace organizational reality that exists apart from the process by which it is queried, and it becomes a kind of ready-made object in the world that has no genetic relation to the sorts of organizational structures that the normative science that Lave debunked would have framed as the *fait accompli* to be internalized. In other words, 'practice' becomes an already-there thing in the world that is created by the subjects of practice and not by the organizational structures that posit the subjects of practice as objects of organizational knowledge. In this sense, in the re-narrativization of 'practice' by managers selling their knowledge of it, the science of the real is taken up but the politics of de-reification is not. It seems to us that this is to forget a crucial aspect of the work that the concept of 'practice' did for Lave: to bring into view the power of an apparatus of seeing to constitute the object that it comes to comprehend. But it is also the case that in building a science Lave posits an 'object' ('practice') which is amenable to becoming a ready-made thing in the world that exists as such *apart* from the process by which it is known. This amenability is part of what it takes to be the object of a 'science'.

Practice as Hybrid: A Dilemmatic Object of Management

As 'practice' is re-instrumentalized, the organizational structures built through abstractive management techniques become the analogue to the normative preconceptions of the experimental scientists in Lave's story. Knowledge-bearing practices in organizations are thus framed as a kind of autonomous force whose genetic relation to organizational structure is obscured. In its form as practice, knowledge does not follow the programmes of conventional organizational abstractions; rather, it becomes a kind of natural force. As one consultant states:

> CoP is a phrase coined by researchers who studied the ways in which people naturally work and play together. In essence, communities of practice are groups of people who share similar goals and interests. In pursuit of these goals and interests, they employ common practices, work with the same tools and express themselves in a common language. Through such common activity, they come to hold similar beliefs and value systems. (From Collaborative Visualization Project, quoted in COIL)

Here, practice seems to have been naturalized, not predicated upon the artefacts of abstractive managerial techniques.[8] It seems to take on a kind of power and autonomy in spite of management. An article in *Datamation* highlights the naturalness and autonomy of practice. The article is called 'Harvesting your workers' knowledge', and states that 'communities of practice form and share on the basis of pull by individual members, not a centralized push of information' (Manville and Foot 1996). A *Fortune Magazine* article suggests that communities of practice 'emerge of their own accord' and described them as being 'responsible to themselves. No one owns them. There's no boss ... People join because they have something to learn and to contribute. The work they do is the joint and several property of the group – *cosa nostra*, "our thing"' (Stewart 1996). In Brown and Gray's narrativization of Orr's study, they described a technology that was introduced to the technical reps to facilitate their interactions as a 'free flowing knowledge democracy, much like the natural, informal collaborations among tech reps' (Brown and Gray 1995).[9]

What concerns us about the movement of 'practice' into the workplace is how the object of an ethnographic science becomes a 'real' that is then counterposed against the abstractions of a conventional management science. In this movement the subject of practice becomes not just a particular, legitimate knowledge-bearing being, but also, *as such*, the new target for a non-conventional management science. It is the knowledge of a kind of pre-reified ethnographic object.

Here, the services sold invoke the power of a realist, de-reifying science; but then the de-reification aspect is held in reserve and at the same time superseded by a focus on the value implications of the reality that a *flawed* science of knowledge would have obscured. An instrumentally ambiguous object, practice has value for many communities, and in the hands of a management consultant, the value is decidedly commercial.

> A Community of Practice is formed with an intention to add value by directly collaborating, using one another and outside resources, to learn and teach each other... The purpose of a CoP is to develop a body of actionable knowledge; to learn and contribute

through sharing information on challenges and best practices in four broad management areas that lead to customer delight... Competitive advantage comes to the companies best able to act on the knowledge forged in Communities of Practice. These
companies recognize that they live in a rich and dynamic environment of opportunities.
For them, competitive advantage stems principally from collaborative, coevolving
relationships with a network of other contributors and stakeholders. (Global Gateways
consulting services)

A putative science of the real crafted to debunk the functionalist framework is
transformed into a means through which to act on practice as the locus of economic
value creation. This knowledge then is invoked as a sales pitch by managers who
deal in CoPs. We see this kind of work exemplified in narrativizations of Wenger's
book for the management community. For example, a book blurb crafted to sell
Wenger's (1998) release states:

The terms of debate about 'knowledge management' and 'learning organization' are
slowly, and finally, turning from issues of information and technology to those of
human capabilities – and the sources of motivation, creativity, and problem-solving
skills that create real value in the new economy. Wenger is light years ahead in
understanding these sources, and the critical importance of informal communities and
'social learning' in fostering them. This book is an elegant, subtle treatise that will
redefine all managerial conversations in this arena, and reward anyone wrestling with
the design and leadership of future organizations. (Wenger 1998; blurb by Phillip Brook
Manville, Partner, McKinsey and Co.)

The impetus is to locate locally constructed knowledges as loci of economic value.
A concept of practice is re-inscribed with a market rhetoric in which the leveraging
of social actors' knowledge-bearing practices for the purposes of industrial competitiveness emerges as the key imperative.

New economic growth continues to be centered on the ability to leverage corporate
knowledge. Although nearly every company practices some form of knowledge management, very few are able to fully leverage knowledge to drive bottom line results.
Much of this failure stems from the inability to identify and leverage preexisting
knowledge communities. (Best Practices LLC Knowledge Exchange)

Grasping practice, grasping a real that is already there, thus emerges as a means
toward an innovative managerial strategy. As practice travels from Lave through
Wenger into the managerial community, the 'value' of locally constructed knowledges is tweaked. In Lave, the impetus is to accord equal social legitimacy to forms
of knowledge other than those that would be prescribed by the meritocratic normative experimental model. The real in Lave's practice, used to debunk functionalist
meritocratic testing paradigms, now becomes a real that is the locus of economic
value creation. The dignity, intelligence, skill and dedication marked by Barley
are precisely the objects that the successful company must learn to exploit. In the
process of re-inscribing practice and hooking it up with different imperatives, the real
of a science of practice is reconfigured as labour in its form as nature.
    However, there is clearly a movement in two directions of the practice to be
instrumentalized for purposes of industrial competitiveness. On one hand, the

take up of the practice epistemology in the new community effectively brackets out the extent to which in the initial 'discovery' of 'communities of practice' the latter were found to be flourishing precisely in response to organizational structures that already existed. At this level, practice is framed as a natural, autonomously emergent source. Managerial communities are then set the challenge of 'nurturing' and 'harvesting' this natural source: it becomes a resource. At this level, it is possible to *provoke* the autonomously emergent source that is referred to. In his article for *Systems Thinker*, Wenger captured this dual movement poignantly:

> Just because communities of practice arise naturally does not mean that organizations can't do anything to influence their development. (Wenger 1997)

The vacillation of practice, now natural, now created, presents a dilemma for the management of practice. It happens both in spite of and because of the 'abstracted' and imposed-from-above structuring of work. There is both an out-of-control abundance in nature and a need for this nature to be structured. The re-instrumentalization of the practice epistemology thus entails not only the construction of nature, but also enacts paternalistic relation to nature through which its artificiality and dependence is simultaneously maintained.

> Shadowy groups called communities of practice are where learning and growth happen. You can't control them – but they're easy to kill . . . If you can't manage communities of practice, managers can still help them . . . Fertilize the soil, but stay out of the garden. (Stewart 1996)

In other words, practice is a real and natural force (and not an artificial human idealization), but it must grow as *nature cropped*.

The practice trajectory urges us to go beneath the formal representations of work that are often created by managers, accountants and functionaries of the educational assessment regimes, to study that which busts at their seams. The latter often goes unnoticed in rationalistic descriptions that are constructed for purposes of long-term planning and accounting. These rationalizations are precisely those reifications that practice theory aims to expose *as such*, and from which the real of action is hoped to be rescued.[10] But interestingly, conventional bureaucratic divisions of labour were precisely the conditions under which 'practices' have always emerged, whether identified or not. For organizational structure – from the managerial abstraction to the stratification of expertise – is not just a pre-given, normative apparatus that sets expectations and misrepresents the contours of knowledge as practice (like in Lave's critique of functionalist psychological assessment). It is also an aspect of the very lived social context that the knowledge-creating subjects of practice inhabit. CoPs must already have been there in order for a practice theory to have any salience – notwithstanding the flawed – corrected science. But this also means that formalized managerial abstractions were there as well. In this way, the solutions that the CoP consultants aim to offer are in important respects a configuration of social conditions that already existed.

Bruno Latour (1993) has written about the general process whereby we project a social fact onto nature, and then 'discover' that it is out there in the world, which justifies its adoption. In order for this shell game to work, the right hand cannot know what the left hand is doing – the act of projection needs to be kept separate from the act of discovery. For example, the theory of evolution as adumbrated by Darwin codes a set of social relations described, *inter alia*, by Malthus, but the principle of survival of the fittest is then read back into political discourse as an independently discovered fact about nature. Work in social studies of science is concerned to call attention to this generative, powerful shell game.

The commercialized science of the real sees a hybrid that is predicated upon historically specific industrial social relations. It is marked in Wenger's 1998 text, although it is in some respects obscured. Indeed, there are two subtly different notions of practice at work in this text. For example, consider this description:

> The contrast detailed here is one between organizational design and lived practice. From this perspective, there are two views of an organization. (1) the designed organiza-tion, which I will often call the 'institution' to distinguish it from the organization as lived in practice. (2) the practice (or, more accurately, the constellation of practices), which gives life to the organization and is often a response to the designed organization. (Wenger 1998: 241)

Then consider this one:

> practice is always social practice. Such a concept of practice includes both the explicit and the tacit. It includes what is said and what is left unsaid; what is represented and what is assumed. It includes the language, the tools, the documents, the images, the symbols, well-defined roles, specified criteria, codified procedures, regulations, and contracts that various practices make explicit for a variety of purposes. But it also includes all the implicit relations, tacit conventions, subtle cues, untold rules of thumb, recognizable intuitions, specific perceptions, well-tuned sensitivities, embodied under-standings, underlying assumptions, shared worldviews. Most of these may never be articulated, yet they are unmistakable signs of membership in communities of practice and are crucial to the success of their enterprises. (Ibid.: 47)

'Real work' and 'the designed organization' are distinguished, but then there is also a clear sense here that practice is an emergent relationship between the two: they are both quite 'real'.

Consultants working in the name of communities of practice mark this in their recommendations that managers should 'enable people to do what they are already doing'. This reflects a contradictory movement at work in the re-instrumentalization of the theory of practice that is underwritten by the realist epistemology: that the recommendations depend upon the logic of a set of social conditions that already exist. In other words, although new management regimes attempt to create commu-nities of practice, they will always have already been there under conditions predi-cated upon traditional managerial practices. Managerial instrumentalization of the concept of practice is a tricky business because its practical implications look very much like business as usual, but also because the balance between nature and culture in the real named by 'practice' keeps tipping to the other side from which you look at it. The trick of good management has been precisely to deny publicly the CoP and to erect a formal model of tasks, which *sub rosa* permits the CoP to flourish. The science of practice enables something familiar.

> Look closely at the inner workings of any company and you'll discover gaps between official work process – the 'ideal' flows of tasks and procedures – and the real-world practices behind how things actually get done. These gaps are not problems that need fixing; they're opportunities that deserve leveraging. (Brown and Gray 1995)

And formal, hierarchical relations of authority are not, moreover, framed simply as part of this leveraging act; they are framed as being *supportive* of informal knowledge production practices as well.

> Most communities of practice exist whether or not the organization recognizes them... Certainly, in order to legitimize the community as a place for sharing and creating knowledge, recognized experts need to be involved in some way, even if they don't do much of the work. (Wenger 1997)

When Wenger and others put practice on the market, the critical intent may be to undermine familiar social relations of power. But it appears the reverse: the CoP concept appears instead to be engaged in an intensification of the previously existent logic of organization. Because in spite of the recognition of the multiplicity of knowledges and their values, formal organizational structures of authority, skill and valuation (meritocracy?) are not debunked. They seem to persist in the work of making and banking on hybrids. To sell knowledge of this practice is to offer something like the cake and eat it too.

NOTES

1 Isabelle Stengers suggests that the 'truth' of scientific findings is predicated upon a relationship of forces that are organized around it: 'An interested scientist will ask the question: can I incorporate this "thing" into my research? Can I refer to the results of this type of measurement... In other words, can I be situated by this proposition, can it place itself between my work and that of the one who proposes it?' (Stengers 1997). Latour (1988) deals with this issue when he discusses Pasteur's mobilization of forces around microbes. Microbes become 'real' scientific objects through the various interests (commercial and otherwise) that converge on them.

2 Although 'epistemology' is typically construed as a speculative, philosophical enterprise, in this chapter we will be treating it as a science. This move is principled for reasons discussed in the next section.

3 See Ortner (1994) for a history of this movement; see Bonnell and Hunt (1999) for more recent developments in this field.

4 Interntionally created social formations, CoPs have emerged in companies such as Intel, Dow Chemical, National Semiconductor, Xerox, British Petroleum, IBM and Monsanto. Consulting firms specializing in this approach often facilitate their development. E-commerce platforms have been constructed with a view to enabling CoPs, and web discussion groups from which one can acquire research results pertaining to communities of practice formations can be joined for fees ranging from $8 K to $12 K.

5 We will not give an adequate treatment of these changes here. We note only that they involve a broad renunciation of functional models of society. The renunciation finds leverage variously through notions alternative to 'structure', such as 'subjectivity', 'culture' and 'practice'.

6 She wrote: 'practice theory, which treats macrostructural systems as fundamental, and focuses on relations between structure and action, is thus not to be confused with a phenomenological view, which treats social systems as (only) epiphenomena of inter-subjectively constituted experience. That both focus analysis on the details of everyday practice should not obscure the essential differences between them' (Lave 1988: 193, footnote 7).

7 An organizational scientist and the editor of the ILR Press series on Technology and Work at the time Orr's book was published.

8 This positioning of practice as nature is interesting if considered from the standpoint of Marx's discussion of the social category of abstract labour. He suggests that abstract labour power is a social category whose form of appearance is the generalization of historically particular concrete labours as transhistorical substance (Postone 1993). The recoding of particular knowledge-bearing practices as natural resonates as a mode of such hypostatization. It seems to us that an analysis of commercialization process needs to elucidate the social process through which apparently transhistorically valid categories are historically specific, and to elucidate how such historically specific categories come to be seen as ontologically grounded, or historically non-specific. Recording particular concrete labours of communities of practice as nature might be seen as a crucial moment in its generalization as abstract labour power.

9 This was the 'Eureka' system: 'an electronic "knowledge refinery" that organizes and categorizes a database of tips generated by the field staff. Technically, Eureka is a relational database of hypertext documents. In practice, it's an electronic version of war stories told around the coffee pot – with the added benefits of an institutional memory, expert validation, and a search engine' (Brown and Gray 1995).

10 Such unveiling is not new to labour sociology. Kusterer (1978) made similar claims by recourse to a 'neophenomenological' study of work, and complicated notions of 'skill' that rested on such categorizing practices as those found in the department of labour. 'The problem with these labels,' wrote Kusterer, 'is that the use of the "unskilled" label has led to a gross underestimation of the amount of working knowledge actually necessary in these jobs. There is no such thing as unskilled work. This term demeans the workers involved, and it misleads all who seek to understand the nature of their work' (see also Roy 1959; Burawoy 1979).

REFERENCES

Best Practices, *Best Practices, LCC* website, available online: http://www.best-in-class.com/research/communities/Accessed January 2001.

Bonnell, V. and Hunt, L. (eds) (1999) *Beyond the Cultural Turn*. Berkeley, CA: University of California Press.

Bourdieu, P. 1977, *Outline of a Theory of Practice*. Cambridge: Cambridge University Press.

Brown, J. S. and Gray, E. S. (1995) 'The people are the company.' *Fast Company*, available online: http://www.fastcompany.com/online/01/people.html

Burawoy, M. (1979) *Manufacturing Consent: Changes in the Labor Process under Monopoly Capitalism*. Chicago, IL University of Chicago Press.

Community Intelligence Labs (COIL), available online: http://www.co-i-l.com/coil/index.shtml/Accessed January 2001.

Giddens, A. (1979) *Central Problems in Social Theory: Action, Structure and Contradiction in Social Analysis*. Berkeley, CA: University of California Press.

Global Gateways, available online: http://global-gateways.com/communit.htm/Accessed January 2001.

Kusterer, K. (1978) *Know How on the Job: The Important Working Knowledge of 'Unskilled' Workers*. Boulder, CO: Westview Press.

Latour, B. (1988) *The Pasteurization of France*, trans. Alan Sheridan and John Law. Cambridge, MA: Harvard University Press.

Latour, B. (1993) *We Have Never Been Modern*. Cambridge, MA: Harvard University Press.

Lave, J. (1988) *Cognition in Practice: Mind, Mathematics and Culture in Everyday Life*. Cambridge: Cambridge University Press.

Lave, J. and Wenger, E. (1991) *Situated Learning: Legitimate Peripheral Participation*. Cambridge: Cambridge University Press.

Manville, B. and Foote, N. (1996) 'Harvesting your workers' knowledge'. *Datamation*, July, 42 (13).

Orr, J. (1996) *Talking About Machines: An Ethnography of a Modern Job*. Ithaca, NY: Cornell University Press.

Ortner, S. (1994) 'Theory in anthropology since the 60s'. In N. Dirks, G. Eley, and S. Ortner (eds) *Culture, Power, History: A Reader in Contemporary Social Theory*. Princeton, NJ: Princeton University Press, pp. 372–411.

Postone, M. (1993) *Time, Labor, and Social Domination: A Reinterpretation of Marx's Critical Theory*. Cambridge: Cambridge University Press.

Roy, D. (1959) '"Banana Time" job satisfaction and informal interaction.' *Human Organization*, 18, 158–68.

Simon, H. (1960) *The New Science of Management Decision*. London: Harper and Row.

Stengers, I. (1997) *Power and Invention: Situating Science*, trans. P. Bains. Minneapolis: University of Minnesota Press.

Stewart, T. (1996) 'The invisible key to success.' *Fortune Magazine*, August, 5, 134 (3).

Strategic Initiatives Inc., website: http://www.strategicinitiatives.com/index.html. Accessed January 2001.

Wenger, E. (1997) 'Communities of practice: Learning as a social system.' *Systems Thinker*, available online: http://www.co-i-/.com/coil/knowledge-garden/cop/lss.html

Wenger, E. (1998) *Communities of Practice: Learning, Meaning, and Identity*. Cambridge: Cambridge University Press.

Chapter 4

The Economy of Qualities

Michel Callon, Cécile Méadel, and Vololona Rabeharisoa

As Charles Smith, one of the pioneers of 'new' economic sociology, so rightly pointed out, forms of organization of economic markets and their modes of functioning are becoming an explicit issue for multiple actors and especially for economic agents themselves (Smith 2000). Markets evolve and, like species, become differentiated and diversified. But this evolution is grounded in no pre-established logic. Nor is it simply the consequence of a natural tendency to adapt. Economic markets are caught in a reflexive activity: the actors concerned explicitly question their organization and, based on an analysis of their functioning, try to conceive and establish new rules for the game.

This reflexivity is evident mainly in the proliferation of hybrid forums in which the functioning and organization of particular markets (e.g. transgenic colza or breast cancer predisposition gene tests) are discussed and debated (Callon, Lascoumes and Barthe 2001).[1]

'Forums' because they are public spaces, the specific structuring of which is yet to be defined. 'Hybrid' for two reasons. The first is the variety and heterogeneity of the actors involved. In debate on the organization of markets we find: professional economists from different schools of thought, anthropologists and sociologists; economic actors (industrialists, consumer associations and social movements protesting against the increasing control of certain centres of power, etc.); international or national organizations such as the IMF, IRDB and ERDB which have their say in the structuring of markets; specialists of intellectual property, experts in management techniques and, more and more often, researchers in the life or natural sciences. The second reason they are hybrid is because the questions raised concern the economy,[2] politics,[3] ethics,[4] law[5] and, finally, even science.[6]

In these hybrid forums it is impossible to separate or dissociate the different components of the issues, even for the sake of simplifying the analysis. The forms of organization of markets defended by the actors engaged in the controversy vary, depending on those actors' political or ethical points of view or the way in which they evaluate the reliability of scientific facts or the efficacy of available technology.

Isolating problems and solutions that could be considered purely economic would lead to socially illegitimate solutions.[7]

There is nothing new about markets being the subject of debate and their modes of organization depending on (non-commercial!) transactions between groups with differing and sometimes even opposing views and interests. Studies attesting to this are starting to become available, although they are still too few (Dumez and Jeunemaître 1998, Gao 1998, Miller 1998, Cochoy 1998). What seems to be new is the fact that the locus of these debates and resulting decisions is more and more frequently (relatively) open public arenas.

One of the most visible consequences of public debates on questions that tend usually to be monopolized by specialists (or by professional decision makers who rely on expert opinions) is the resulting redistribution of competencies and the increasing role granted to economic agents themselves. Professional economists no longer have the direct or indirect monopoly (assuming they did ever have it) on authorized and legitimate discourse. This does not mean that they are excluded from the debate. On the contrary, they are cordially invited to participate, but they are no longer alone. Next to them we find not only specialists from other scientific disciplines (anthropologists, sociologists, political scientists and, depending on the nature of the markets under consideration, biologists, chemists or climatologists) but also, and above all, the actors concerned with the markets under discussion. Economists, sociologists and biologists can no longer confine themselves to an outdated form of epistemology. The actors are now colleagues whom they have to take into consideration and who contribute in their own right to the production of knowledge and its transcription in reality, which sometimes ends up corresponding to theories about it.[8] The forum creates an arena in which the great divide between specialists and laypersons is redistributed. It creates material conditions for co-operation between laboratory research performed by experts and specialists, on the one hand, and research 'in the wild' that makes it possible for laypersons to be vigilant and sometimes prompts them to propose guidelines for new research (Callon, Lascoumes and Barthe 2001).

As far as it concerns markets and their organization, this reflexive – because collaborative – research should progressively be focused on a small number of questions, including what I suggest calling the qualification of products. Real markets and the agents inhabiting them have in common with the stylized markets of economics textbooks the same core question: the classification of goods offered to consumers. Economic agents devote a large share of their resources to positioning the products they design, produce, distribute or consume, in relation to others. Any theoretical and formal description of a market starts with the inevitable statement: take goods p1, p2, p3, etc., without which no stylized model would be possible. How could we talk about supply and demand, in practical or theoretical terms, if there were no agreement, at least tacit or even imaginable, on the list of products and their characteristics?[9] How could we describe, in practice and theory, the structures of competition within the same market, or between related markets, if relations of similitude or dissimilitude between the goods that circulate could not be established?[10]

One of the most visible manifestations of this shared concern (how to classify and position goods) is reflected in the upsurge in debate on the concept of a service. The distinction between manufactured goods and services, which has generated recurrent and endlessly open debates, is becoming central again, probably because it is at the heart of a set of questions on the transformation of the economic system and/or on the appearance of new models of growth and regulation (Gadrey 2000). Whether one talks about the new economy, the information economy, the knowledge economy or even, more directly, of the service economy, one is expressing the possibility of a profound transformation of the rules by which markets function, a transformation that is thought to be related essentially to radical changes in the characteristics of the goods traded.

Our view in this chapter is that the emerging convergence between the interests of researchers and the preoccupations of economic agents, around the question of services, warrants encouragement and clarification. It is likely, eventually, to promote the constitution of hybrid forums in which new forms of organization of economic activity could be discussed. To show the advantages of such convergence, I shall take a detour via the general question of the definition of goods and products. Then, based on both the economic tradition and on sociological and anthropological work, we shall put forward a product definition that will lead us, in the second part, to show the active and reflexive role of economic agents in the qualification of products. This will enable us to demonstrate the emergence of new forms of competition and to emphasize the advantages of the concept of a service for describing and explaining them. We suggest calling this new form of organization of markets the economy of qualities.

The key argument in this chapter is the suggestion that, in the economy of qualities, which can also be called the service economy, because the questions posed by researchers and economic agents are to a large degree identical, cooperation between them is inevitable. The organization of markets becomes a collective issue and the economy becomes (again) political. One of social science's objectives might be to contribute, as far as possible, to that development.[11]

The Product as a Variable: Conflict and Negotiation Around the Qualification of Goods

What is a product? When one consults political economics textbooks one is struck by the diversity of terms used to denote the objects of commercial transactions.[12]

Faced with this semantic proliferation and resulting imprecision, it is out of the question to try to control the use of concepts, especially since each of them sheds particular light on the reality in question. To better understand the emergence of new forms of organization of markets and new modes of competition, it nevertheless seems useful to make a distinction – necessarily arbitrary but nevertheless rooted in etymology – between a good and a product (two concepts which are often used interchangeably in the vocabulary of economic theory).

Talking of a good means emphasizing the fact that the aim of any economic activity is to satisfy needs (what is good, sought after, wanted). Qualifying these goods as economic means adding that their production and circulation involve the mobilization of necessarily rare resources, or that these goods can be attached to property rights which are transferable from one agent to another. The concept of an economic good implies a degree of stabilization of the characteristics that are associated with it, which explain why it is in demand and why, being wanted as such, it is traded.

A product, on the other hand, is an economic good seen from the point of view of its production, circulation and consumption. The concept (*producere*: to bring forward) shows that it consists of a sequence of actions, a series of operations that transform it, move it and cause it to change hands, to cross a series of metamorphoses that end up putting it into a form judged useful by an economic agent who pays for it. During these transformations its characteristics change.

The product is thus a process, whereas the good corresponds to a state, to a result or, more precisely, to a moment in that never-ending process. As an economic good a car is an object, a thing with a well-defined shape, which is used to meet specific needs and which has an established value in a market context. But it is more than that. It is also an object that has a life, a career. Seen from the angle of its conception and then production, it starts off by existing in the form of a set of specifications, then a model, then a prototype, then a series of assembled elements and, finally, a car in a catalogue that is ordered from a dealer and has characteristics which can be described relatively objectively and with a certain degree of consensus. Once it is in the hands of its driver the car continues moving, not only on roads but also, later, for maintenance purposes to workshops, then to second-hand dealers. At times it becomes again an object on paper, which takes its place alongside other cars in the guide to second-hand car prices in specialized magazines.

The product (considered as a sequence of transformations) describes, in both senses of the term, the different networks co-ordinating the actors involved in its design, production, distribution and consumption. The product singles out the agents and binds them together and, reciprocally, it is the agents that, by adjustment, iteration and transformation, define its characteristics.

Once the distinction between goods and products has been established, the question of their relations remains. These can be considered from a dual point of view: that of the process of qualification of goods and that of the product considered as a strategic variable.

To deepen and enrich the proposed distinction between product and good, we shall start with the definition of a good, as given in most economics manuals. 'A good can be described as a bundle of characteristics: quality, location, time, availability, consumer's information about its existence and . . . so on. Each consumer has a ranking over the mix of variables' (Tirole 1989: 96). In other words, a good can be defined by a combination of characteristics that establish its singularity. This singularity, because it stems from a combination, is relational. In fact, the selected characteristics can be used to describe other goods, with which relations of similitude or proximity are likely to be established. Defining a good means positioning it in a space of goods, in a system of differences and similarities, of distinct yet connected categories.[13]

How are these characteristics established, which make it possible to say that two goods are relatively similar but different or else totally dissimilar and radically incomparable?

First, these properties are not observed; they are 'revealed' through tests or trials which involve interactions between agents (teams) and the goods to be qualified. The fact that a wine is syrupy, that it matures with age, that it has a high or low alcohol content, that it comes from the Médoc region or Touraine are all properties that will be used to characterize it but which, to be identified and objectified, require the implementation of certified tests and the realization of codified measurements.[14] The same applies to a car. Its road-holding, engine capacity, consumption and comfort, the resistance of its paint to corrosion and its delivery time are all parameters that, to be appreciated, evaluated and objectified, need a battery of tests, test benches, approved measurement instruments, documents guaranteeing traceability, etc. The characteristics of a good are not properties which already exist and on which information simply has to be produced so that everyone can be aware of them. Their definition or, in other words, their objectification, implies specific metrological work and heavy investments in measuring equipment. The consequence is that agreement on the characteristics is sometimes, in fact often, difficult to achieve. Not only may the list of characteristics be controversial (which characteristics ought to be taken into consideration?) but so also, above all, is the value to be given to each of them. Once agreement has been reached it will be characterized by a degree of robustness if the procedures used were objective.

Second, the definition of these characteristics is modified as the product develops and changes. The characterization of a vehicle in the research laboratory is obviously not the same as that on the sales brochure distributed by the dealer, even if the two lists of characteristics are related. It is also different from the one proposed to a sub-contractor who designs and manufactures parts.

The notion of a characteristic in its standard sense (and particularly in the definition proposed by Tirole) tends to mask both the existence of progressive metamorphoses of the product and the necessity for successive investment to organize the trials required for characterization. That is why we prefer talking of qualities and of a (continuous) process of qualification–requalification, for they are simply two sides to the same coin. All quality is obtained at the end of a process of qualification, and all qualification aims to establish a constellation of characteristics, stabilized at least for a while, which are attached to the product and transform it temporarily into a tradable good in the market.[15]

A good is defined by the qualities attributed to it during qualification trials. These qualities are therefore twofold. They are intrinsic: the good is engaged in the qualification trial and the result obviously depends on the good in question. But they are also extrinsic: not only are the qualities shaped by the device used to test and measure the good (and therefore depend on the choice and characteristics of that device) but their formulation and explanation also generate evaluations and judgements which vary from one agent to the next. The notion of quality has the advantage of closely binding these two meanings and of including the classical question in both economics and economic sociology of the hierarchy of comparable goods (as when one talks of the quality of a service or second-hand car). Talking of quality means raising the question of the controversial processes of qualification, processes through which qualities are attributed, stabilized, objectified and arranged. It therefore consists of giving oneself the means to go, with no solution of continuity, from the good to the product, from the result to the process and its organization.

Being by definition variable, the *product* is a strategic variable for the different economic agents engaged in the process of its successive qualifications

–requalifications. Seen from the point of view of its conception, a good, as noted above, moves through different stages: the Twingo presented by Renault's design department has qualities which will progressively be transformed and adjusted, until the version available on the market is obtained. That final version will, moreover, have qualities that differ depending on the place in which it is sold, the year in which it is licensed, the fact of being first- or second-hand, and so on. Products, to borrow Appadurai's apt expression, are goods with a career (Appadurai 1986). Conversely, goods are (temporarily) stabilized products. In the former case, the list of qualities is open; in the latter, it is (temporarily) closed.

The process of qualification–requalification, as described by the good/product twosome, is at the heart of the dynamics of economic markets. It was on the existence of this very process that Chamberlin (1946) based his theory of monopolistic competition. He started with the idea, proposed above, that the qualities that allow goods to be differentiated from one another constitute a very open list. They may be characteristics that common sense would automatically describe as intrinsic, but may also be brands, packaging or special recipients, particular sales conditions such as location, seller's reputation or personal relations between the salesperson and customers. Chamberlin underscored the fact that all these qualities constitute the good in the following striking sentence: the customer buys not only the 'material' good but also the reputation and honour of the seller. Even if Chamberlin does not explicitly say so, this means that all these qualities have the same ontological status, and that it would be wrong to distinguish between primary and secondary qualities, for example, or between the 'real' good and its successive presentations. Yet, Chamberlin adds, these qualities which define a good and make it possible to position it in relation to other goods are not established once and for all. They have the strange characteristic of being constituent of the good but nonetheless reconfigurable.

Chamberlin's conclusion is essential in our argument. The good, as a moment in the life of a product, as a configuration likely to vary in a continuous process of qualification–requalification, must be considered as an economic variable in the same way that prices are:

> By variation (of the product) we may be referring to a modification of the quality of the product itself – technological changes, new model, better raw materials; we may mean the packaging or a new recipient; or, finally, we may mean better and more friendly service, a different way of doing business.

In his introduction to the French translation, Perroux stresses the point. He notes that, for the firm, the ability to modify the list of qualities is a strategic resource since it is a matter of positioning the good in the space of goods (a space comprising all possible dimensions and qualities).

Expressed in our categories, the good, a point in time in the career of a product which starts before it and continues after it, is an economic variable in its own right, which the different economic agents can manipulate to suit their strategic goals.[16]

Of what do these manipulations consist? Or, put differently, what are the economic implications of the qualification–requalification of products? Once again, we turn to Chamberlin, for his answer here is also central to our approach. The qualification of goods is at the heart of economic competition and the organization of markets. According to him, the establishment of the list of qualities of a good involves the linking up or, rather, the co-construction of supply and demand. With hindsight this mutual adaptation between what a firm proposes and what consumers want always seems somewhat miraculous. Chamberlin points out that it is based on a double movement. On the one hand, it leads to a singularization of the good (so that it is distinguished from other goods and satisfies a demand that other goods cannot meet). On the other hand, it makes the good comparable to other existing goods, so that new markets are constructed through the extension and renewal of existing ones. Different and similar, singular and comparable, such is the paradoxical nature of the economic goods constituting the dynamics of markets.

It is of course economic agents, from either the supply or demand side, or involved in either distribution or marketing, that construct these singularities and substitutabilities. The challenge which they share and which divides them is to establish this difficult adjustment between a supply and a demand that is formed around a list of qualities – an adjustment that is temporary and constantly threatened because it operates against a background of substitutability and comparability. The good relates to a certain structuration of competition which acts both as a constraint and a resource for the collective qualification–requalification of products.

This strategic game of positioning or, as we proposed, of qualification–requalification of goods, has two important consequences for forms of organization and modalities of competition.

First, the contrast between a situation of monopoly and one of pure competition no longer has meaning. Through construction, a product is always both singular and similar to other products, because it is immersed in a space of qualities that makes comparisons possible. Chamberlin proposed the concept of monopolistic competition to describe this dynamic. Chamberlin synthesizes this point in the following assertive statement, often cited: 'It is to be recognized that the whole is not a single market, but a network of related markets, one for each seller.'[17] From this point of view, consumers are just as active as the other parties involved. They participate in the process of qualifying available products. It is their ability to judge and evaluate that is mobilized to establish and classify relevant differences. There is no reason to believe that agents on the supply side are capable of imposing on consumers both their perception of qualities and the way they grade those qualities. Interactions involving complex and reciprocal influences, to which we shall return, are the rule rather than the exception.

Second, and Chamberlin makes this point in passing, the requalification process can be carried out either 'gradually and unconsciously', taking into account the reactions of the different agents involved, or in an organized manner. In the latter case, economic agents, that is the firm, but also the spokespersons of intermediaries and consumers, are explicitly defined as being involved in the strategic management of product qualification. They attempt to answer the following questions: how are products positioned in the sphere of goods? How are they distinguished from other goods and to what extent can they be substituted, at least partially, for some of them? This strategic management starts from the design stage and is seen as a governable process in which all agents participate, from the research and design departments right down to the end users, through the production, purchasing and marketing divisions.

The Economy of Qualities

To consider the qualification of goods as one of the central issues in the dynamic organization of markets, makes the situations in which this qualification –requalification constitutes an explicit challenge for all the agents involved particularly interesting. For reasons that will emerge clearly further on in this chapter, we suggest using the term 'economy of qualities' for this (dynamic) economy of the product (as opposed to a more static economy of the good) in which the modalities of the establishment of supply and demand, and forms of competition, are all shaped by the organized strategies deployed by the different actors to qualify goods. These highly reflexive markets are organized around two structuring mechanisms: the singularization of goods and the attachment of goods to (and detachment from) those who consume them.

The singularization of goods

The economy of qualities is based above all on the singularity of the goods offered to consumers. In other words, what is sought after is a very close relationship between what the consumer wants and expects, on the one hand, and what is offered, on the other. Many authors have emphasized these interactions between supply and demand, as well as the personalization of products they allow and the progressive adjustments to which they give rise.[18] But the perspective adopted here, that of the qualification of goods, allows us to enrich and complete existing analyses.

Let us consider the question from the demand side first: how do consumers perceive differences between products and how do they evaluate them? In other words, how do they qualify products and classify them by giving them an order of preference?

The answer to this question should avoid the explanation that immediately comes to mind, which accepts the idea of a radical separation between supply and demand, with the product serving simply as an intermediary between the two. In this widespread view, the qualities of products are intrinsic characteristics, inseparably attached to the products. Consumers are supposed to perceive these qualities (hence, the importance of information) and it is assumed that the way in which they appreciate, evaluate and classify them depends on their own preferences. The latter can be considered as strictly individual (as in the standard neo-classical model) or (as in the extreme sociologizing version) related to membership of a group or social class that tries to distinguish itself or form an identity by adopting a position in relation to the preferences of other groups.[19] From our point of view, this is impossible. The qualities of a product depend on the joint work of a host of actors and there is no reason to believe that consumers do not participate, like the other actors concerned, in the objectification of those qualities.[20]

How, in these conditions, can we explain consumers' participation in the qualification of the goods for which they (finally) express a demand? The best way of avoiding difficulties associated with the traditional concept of preference is to introduce the more realistic and now well-documented concept of distributed cognition (Hutchins 1995, Mallard 1996). The perception of differences and their evaluation, a dual operation that constitutes the exercise of judgement, implies a consumer immersed in a socio-technical system of which the different elements will each, in its own way, participate in the implementation of that dual operation. Cochoy's ethnography of supermarket customers is very instructive from this point of view (Cochoy forthcoming).

Cochoy is interested in the particularly disturbing case in which the consumer has to choose between two almost identical products.[21] As he shows, this situation is very common. Moreover, advertisements often influence the paradox by adding a strange injunction: between these two identical products choose ours! Chamberlin was right. The singularization of a product, which allows its attachment to a particular consumer, is obtained against a background of similitude. The difference that enables a product to capture the consumer always involves the prior assertion of a resemblance which suggests an association between the consumer's former attachments and the new ones proposed.

How do consumers manage to grasp differences when products are so similar? How can I explain why I choose a Philips VCR rather than a Sony or, even more ordinarily, fruit yoghurts made by Danone rather than Nestlé? To explain why and how consumers end up opting for one or the other, Cochoy points to the part played by two decisive mechanisms:

- The establishment of a socio-cognitive arrangement that situates the different products in relation to one another: a particular point on a shelf; packaging, the semiotic analysis of which shows that it helps simultaneously to characterize the product and to compare it with other seemingly similar products; and references added by the distributor. Advertising, studied so well by Chamberlin, is another element in this apparatus. Consumers are not alone, facing a product, left to determine its qualities. They are guided, assisted by material devices which act as points of reference, supports, affordances in which information is distributed.

- But consumers also have a life outside the supermarket. For example, they have a family. The products they buy are tested in their home; collective evaluations are made; learning takes place, which gives rise to evaluations. More broadly, our consumers are caught in social networks in which tastes are formed, discussed and imitated. Moreover, these networks are not purely social. Tests and evaluations are always based on material devices in which bodies are involved (Teil 1998, Thévenot 1993). The lessons learned from them are sometimes synthesized in lists that consumers draw up with the people they live with before going shopping. When faced with a shelf offering a profusion of similar products, the list will enable them to rely on elements external to the situation. For some products and markets our consumers can also consult magazines or guides produced by specialists or consumer associations (Mallard 2000). In the case of high tech goods or, more generally, products that are difficult to qualify (because objective tests are more difficult to set up), these intermediaries play a crucial part, in some cases going so far as to organize what Hatchuel (1995) calls a prescriber's market. We thus see the complexity of the process of judgement through which properties are attributed to products and evaluations are made. It is always, as Chamberlin so clearly saw, through the comparison and explanation of differences that these judgements are made. Such comparisons and explanations suppose the existence of a complex socio-technical device that supports the consumer in her evaluation work.

Let us now turn to the supply side. It has in common with demand the obsession with positioning products. How is it possible to ensure that consumers identify properties that they then evaluate positively? This question is crucial, as the consumers' attachment and consequent profits depend on the answer. This clearly explains why all the firm's activities and those of everyone involved in it turn around the positioning and qualification of the product. And the only way to go about it is by trial and error and the progressive learning it allows: trying some positions, observing consumers' evaluations, trying to clarify their judgements, taking them into account when repositioning the product, etc.[22] As we have seen, and Chamberlin stressed this point, this work of requalification can concern either what common sense would tend to consider to be the materiality of the product (orange juice, its acidity, the origin of the pulp) or its presentation (its wrapping, its position on the shelf or advertisements for it). Yet, in the approach adopted here, there is no reason to distinguish between the two. In both cases what counts is the qualification of the product: one involves work on the orange; the other involves work on the bottle, its label or its place on the shelf. But, from the point of view of interest to us here, there is no need to distinguish between these two types of qualification that contribute equally to the singularization of the product.[23]

The distinction between supply and demand is useful for emphasizing the symmetry and similitude of behaviours of the different economic agents engaged in qualification. Yet it does have a major drawback: it makes the anonymous and collective work of market professionals invisible, despite the key role they play in the qualification–requalification of products. In the mass market these professionals working behind the scenes are legion and far more numerous than omnipresent designers, packagers or merchandisers. Cécile Méadel and Vololona Rabeharisoa (1999) followed the career of orange juice from the orange groves of southern Spain to the display of the juice in a bottle in a range on a shelf. Different actors come onto the scene at different stages in the orange juice's career: the taster who, in close collaboration with the buyer, stabilizes the properties of the juice when production first begins; the sales manager who displays the plastic from which the bottles are made; the advertising agency and its brief; the marketing services and the market surveys that prompt it to segment supply and demand so as to take into account profound changes; the tasting sessions organized with different panels of uninformed consumers or informed professionals who are put into a position to reveal their tastes and judgements (Méadel and Rabeharisoa 2001). All these people working on qualification share a product which they shape and transform: the orange and its juice constitute their world. But they are simultaneously in a distant relationship. They pass the product around and on to the next in line so that, on the basis of work already done, they can propose and prepare other qualifications. The final adjustment is always in the hands of the newcomer (Barrey, Cochoy and Dubuisson 2000). That is why the co-ordination of these professionals is difficult:

the maintenance of their difference is essential but too much distance could cause errors as the product moves between them. All in all, what is being produced is a progressive 'profiling' of products that, through successive adjustment and iteration, ends up profiling both the demand and the consumer.

This profiling which, when successful, results in the qualities of products corresponding exactly to those that consumers want, is concluded with consumers' attachment to the goods they buy and consume: it is that particular bottle, that orange juice, that the customer in the supermarket prefers. This attachment – to a singularized product cannot be disassociated from the configuration – through supply and demand – of an apparatus of distributed cognition in which information and references are spread out between many elements. The consumer's preferences are tied into this apparatus. This is why they can be both stable and reconfigurable.

Detachment and different attachment

All attachment is constantly threatened. This mechanism is central in the question under consideration here. Competition between firms occurs precisely around this dialectic of attachment and detachment. Capturing, 'attaching' consumers by 'detaching' them from the networks built by rivals is the mainspring of competition.

How does this form of detachment occur? Answer: by getting consumers to requalify the different products offered to them, that is, by repositioning a product in such a way that it becomes visible to consumers, so that they are prompted to embark on a new effort at evaluation.[24] One can speak of a calculative supply. But calculations do not simply concern prices and profits. They are mainly about products and their qualities.

A fairly simply way of understanding how this requalification operates is by turning once again to the demand side and adapting March's (1994) distinction between decision making based on consequences (logics of consequences) and routine decision making (logics of appropriateness). It would be a mistake to have to choose between two opposite conceptions of the economic agent in general and the consumer in particular. Agents who follow routines and those who calculate and decide on the basis of the consequences of their choices, both exist. Moreover, those same agents, for example supermarket customers, generally swing from one position to the next, rapidly and sequentially.

Attached consumers are ones who are caught up in routines. They are driven by the distributed apparatus of qualification. The differences they perceive and the evaluations they make are stabilized, objectified. They buy goods, the qualities of which they are familiar. They grade them and then use those scales. In the case of the supermarket, consumers functioning according to routines push their trolleys around, always use the same list, when they use one at all, and go from shelf to shelf, never hesitating on the choice of the products they buy. It is always the same information that is mobilized and treated by the collective to which they belong.

Consumers engaged in the requalification process hesitate. They wonder what they should buy, are puzzled when faced with an impressive range of orange juices or when they notice a new product standing out among the others.

How does this switch operate? How is the same consumer, caught until then in routines, turned into a decision maker? This is where one needs to turn to the supply side and towards professionals of qualification. They constantly try to destabilize consumers, to extract them from routines and prompt them to reevaluate the qualities of products, hoping that that requalification might be favourable to them.

Cécile Méadel and Vololona Rabeharisoa take the example of an orange-juice producer whose sales declined. To remedy the situation it decided to launch a product requalification project with the aim of changing the position of its products in the market. The origin of the oranges, the taste of the juice and its packaging (among other things) were changed. But customers still had to be informed of these changes. The strategy chosen, both simple and common, clearly illustrates the nature of the mechanisms at play in this switch. To the questions: 'How to break the consumers' attachment to their favourite brands? How to extract them from the routines they follow with a certain delight, and get them to grasp the bottle without thinking?' the solution devised by (re)qualification professionals offered an exemplary answer. The strategy consisted of reactivating the network in which customers were immersed by focusing, for example, initially on those consumers who were accompanied by their children. The idea was to attract the children's attention by means of a prominent feature, for example a bottle offering a free Pokemon. The child would predictably detach herself from her father, pull him by the arm, force him to leave the routine he automatically followed, and put him in front of a product which, strictly speaking, he had not seen. A discussion between father and child would follow, which was likely to end in a purchase and, eventually, in attachment to a new brand. If the children's network were effective, the new attachment would spread well beyond that single family unit.

This scene, so ordinary and obvious, is instructive. By acting on the collective in which consumers are immersed, that is, by giving weight to children's evaluation, the supplier is in a position to attach consumers after detaching them from another network in which they are caught. The orange juice proposed, one quality of which is perhaps the slightly sweeter taste but which has, above all, a connection with the Pokemon network, has been differentiated and has attached a new consumer. This clearly illustrates the general mechanism we wish to describe. It is through a reconfiguration of the socio-cognitive apparatus (the new orange juice stands out on the shelf and modifies the circle of those with whom customers are to interact and deliberate in revising their preferences and finally ending up with new judgements and evaluations) that detachment and reattachment are effected.

In the economy of qualities, this struggle for attachment and detachment is at the heart of competition. It entails the collective (re)qualification of the products that become strategic variables. The positioning of products and the shaping of preferences are endogenous variables that agents manipulate and calculate.[25] What we propose to show now is that the modalities of the organization it implies resemble those of the service economy as described by Jean Gadrey.

Service Activities as the Basis of the Economy of Qualities

Until now the validity of the subject of this chapter has been general. At no point have we raised the question of the distinction between material goods and service provision. The process of (re)qualification, whether it concerns an insurance contract, home care for the aged, a transport service, a fruit juice, a motorcar or an apartment, follows the same logic. Forms of competition that are set up and centre around the struggle for attachment and detachment of customers to the goods offered to them likewise follow the same logic. Is it useful and of any interest, in these conditions, to revive problematic distinctions? Why not stick to the good/product twosome, rather than adding confusion by introducing criteria that flirt with metaphysics, like those of materiality or non-materiality of products?

That could be a possible strategy. But it would have the drawback of overlooking the concerns of actors who talk increasingly about services or service relations, stressing the importance of users and the quality of the services offered. The service economy exists in reality, in official classifications and in the categories used by agents. Ignoring that would run counter to our aim, which enjoins us to consider those agents as competent colleagues who know what they are saying and doing. It would also amount to not seeing that the economy of qualities, as defined above, easily encompasses what actors call service provision. What we should like to suggest hereafter is precisely that what we mean by the term 'service' or 'service activity' increasingly corresponds to forms of organization of markets in which the qualification of products is a central and constant concern. Perhaps the service economy is just another name given to the economy of qualities by the agents concerned and certain economists.

To demonstrate this in rough terms, let us start with Jean Gadrey's (2000) definition. According to him, any purchase of services by an economic agent B (individual or organization) is a purchase from an organization A of the right to use, for a specified period, a technical or human capacity possessed by A to produce (on agent B or on the goods that agent possesses) useful effects that do not have the form of new economic entities. On the basis of this definition, Jean Gadrey suggests distinguishing three service logics: *request for intervention*, *making available* and *show*, the definitions of which can be summarized as follows:

- In the case of the logic of a request for intervention, B (for example, the owner of a car) addresses a request for intervention to A who is the owner of a set of human and technical capacities (the garage or mechanics workshop) the mobilization of which will allow B's demand to be satisfied.
- In the case of the logic of making available, B, based on a simple decision, uses a technico-human capacity which functions and which A makes available to B in mutually agreed conditions.[26] Examples of such logics are transport, telephone and electricity.
- In the case of a show (or spectacle), B decides to attend, in conditions proposed by organization A or negotiated with it, a human performance (a play, an amusement park, a show on a river cruise, etc.) generally supported by technical devices.

The advantage of this definition, and of the resulting classification into three logics, is that it clearly demonstrates the link between service activities and the economy of qualities. The particular frame of the service relationship in which the service provision takes place has two consequences. First, it facilitates the setting up of the (reflexive) work through which the different agents engaged in the process pose and solve the problem of the singularization of products. Second, it facilitates the formulation and implementation of strategies aimed at managing consumers' attachment to and detachment from the products offered to them.

In his definition, Jean Gadrey introduces the key concept of socio-technical capacity. This socio-technical capacity consists of human competencies and material devices that have been designed and arranged in a way in which they can be mobilized in order to achieve desired results. In the request for intervention logic, it consists of a set of means for the purpose of investigation, control, maintenance and reparation, which combine instruments and machines but also specialized technicians who are mobilized in an organized way to produce the expected effects on B. In the making available logic, this technical capacity, often invisible to the user, may be considerable, as in the case of connection to electricity, telecommunications or the domestic water supply network. B, by lifting her telephone receiver, opening a tap or switching on her washing machine, sets in motion a complex arrangement of humans and non-humans whose actions have been adjusted in relation to one another and prepared for mobilization at any time and at any point of access to the network. The property of that socio-technical capacity is sometimes shared between different owners. A car rental network makes available its vehicles, its rental sales agents, its agencies and its maintenance and insurance services, but also takes advantage of the road infrastructure (a public good) that will enable its customers to travel about. In the logic of show, the manager of a theatre or amusement park and the organizer of a pleasure cruise on the Seine group together a series of participants, each of whom plays a part in a script or scenario prepared in advance and the realization of which would be impossible without the engagement of material mediums participating actively in the show (the Seine and the boat are needed, as are the theatre, its stage and comfortable seats, the projector: each of these non-human entities contributes, in its own unique way, to the show) (Akrich 1992).

In all these situations the beneficiary B acquires – and this is what the commerical transaction is about – a right to (specified) use of that socio-technical capacity. It is to repair B's car that the garage is mobilized. It is to enable her to light her apartment that the turbines generate electricity year after year, that agencies carefully monitor her consumption and that high-tension lines criss-cross the countryside. It is for the audience's pleasure that the actress repeats her monologue for the hundredth time, that the usherette leads people to the seats they have reserved on the Internet, etc. Service provision consists in the effects produced by the mobilization and reasoned use of this socio-technical capacity.

Thus defined, service provision is not radically different from other forms of goods placed on the market.[27] But, owing to the key importance it gives to the relationship between the socio-technical capacity (in the seller's hands) and the customer (who uses it), it allows greater reflexivity on activities of qualification and singularization. What we have suggested calling a socio-technical device, a device that enables us to think of qualification in terms of distributed cognition, is in fact very similar to what Gadrey calls socio-technical capacity. In the case of service provision, this socio-technical device occupies a central place, for the success of the service depends on it directly and quasi-perceptibly. This can be expressed differently by emphasizing the fact that service provision, by allowing consumers to use this socio-technical capacity, organizes a system of action in which consumers participate personally in order to benefit from that use. In the course of the interaction thus constructed, they become elements in this system of action. They act, react and, most importantly, interact, thus gradually constructing and clarifying their preferences. Service provision is a machine (sometimes a machination) designed to reveal what customers want and progressively to construct the irreducible singularization of their demands along with their satisfaction.

It is with the use of new information and communication technologies that this logic of singularization reaches its peak. Take the pragmatic case of the Internet user. When she goes onto the Web through a portal, the Internet user is faced with a distributed cognition device that, in every sense, is comparable to the one described when we presented a supermarket customer hesitating in the choice between several orange juices. She first chooses between different providers and then between the different services proposed by the chosen provider. Most of her activity will consist of qualifying (i.e. classifying, evaluating and judging) the products offered to her, by comparing and relating them to others. This qualification, the generality of which we discussed above, is even more present, in a purer form, in the case of the Internet. With information renewed on the screen, with links and cross-references and with scroll menus that multiply options from which users can and must choose, the Internet is a machinery that is entirely oriented towards the singularization of products. Whether the user is visiting the site of a supermarket or Club Internet, this qualification takes place within a distributed cognition device. But, in the latter case, it takes place through programs whose only function is to provide and link information so that consumers are in a position to make choices.

Not only do providers create and provide this system in which Internet users are immersed, they are also in a favourable position to monitor users, observe their preferences and, based on these observations, singularize the products offered to them. E-commerce companies hope to base their competitive lead on their ability constantly to observe customers making choices, linking products and showing their preferences. Since they are able to record customers' previous purchases and their reactions to new offers, suppliers end up knowing as much as customers themselves do about what they want and expect. This shared knowledge, which evolves as new experiences accumulate, is based on consumers' engagement in a socio-technical device with which they interact and evolve.

In service provision, as defined by Gadrey, business is structured around this qualification process made possible by the establishment of the device and by the right granted to the customer to use it. From this point of view, new ICTs make an irreplaceable contribution. Between the supermarket X and E-bay there is a difference not of nature but of degree. By mobilizing new ICTs, e-commerce makes the qualification and requalification of products the central concern in service provision.[28] The work of attachment is an obsession explicitly shared by all the actors, including the end user. Paraphrasing La Boëtie, we could talk of consumers' voluntary attachment to the products they qualify in close interaction with supply intermediaries, whether they are human or non-human. It is not by coincidence that, to describe these opportunities provided by e-commerce to qualify the user-consumer's position, the two contradictory words 'independence' and 'dependence' are used: independence, because the Web multiplies openings, facilitates comparisons, etc.; dependence because it conversely promotes singularization and the attachments it allows.[29]

We could multiply examples and consider the logics of show and intervention in order to demonstrate that service provisions are always part of the economy of qualities, because they focus on socio-technical capacities or devices, and promote their mobilization by customers prompted to participate in the process of qualifying the products intended for them. This is just one way of saying, in a more precise form, that what is important in the service business is the relationship or, rather, system of relationships which, on a material and collective basis, organizes the qualification of products. The emblematic nature of services is increasing even further with the development of information networks and computer technology.

The second characteristic of service provision, as defined by Jean Gadrey, is the character, both lasting and limited in time, of the consumer's right to use the socio-technical device. This temporal framing facilitates the reasoned control and management of operations of attachment, detachment and reattachment. It constitutes a sound base for the establishment of lasting relations, constantly re-evaluated, between service provider and customer.

Take the case of the car market. As Jean Gadrey points out, buying a car is fundamentally different from renting one.[30] Of what does this difference consist? Obviously, of the consumer's lesser attachment to the product he consumes. As the owner of his car he will have to make greater investments to detach himself than if he were simply renting the car. A weaker attachment enables him, moreover, to participate more actively (because more frequently and on the basis of more recent experiences) in the singularization of the product he buys. Seen from the service provider's point of view, rental enables him to concentrate on qualification of the product and on its renegotiation to answer questions such as: what are observable uses? How do they evolve? In what kind of business is such or such a type of customer?

This example, which has a general value, shows that the joint advantage for consumer and supplier in establishing a lasting use of the socio-technical capacity, while setting a limit in time to the relationship, is that it allows the increasingly intense and profound qualification of products and the singularization they afford. This relationship simultaneously encourages agents to focus on the returns from ongoing experience and to take them into consideration when renewing the contract and the service.

This collective work on the qualification of products and, consequently, on users' attachment, implies consumers who are calculating rather than set in routines. This in itself implies a risk, for consumers with routines are unquestionably an advantage in the short term for the service provider: they remain attached, loyal, reliable. On the other hand, any attempt to experiment with what they want and hence to model their preferences is more difficult, if not impossible. In an economy where competition concerns the qualification of products (for the purpose of their singularization and the consumers' attachment), a 'routinized' consumer[31] is a constant threat since interaction that has been interrupted can be taken up and re-established by a rival, who will thus adopt a position to detach the consumer by giving him back his ability to calculate, in order to swing him, with his active and calculated participation, towards new attachments.

The paradox is clear. In the economy of qualities it is preferable for the service provider to co-operate with the consumer and therefore to deal with a calculating consumer, at least on a regular basis without long intervals in between. This is possible only by limiting the periods of routine attachment and by constantly calling into question the singularization of products proposed in order to launch new negotiations and adjustments of their (re)qualification. Service provision, as defined by Jean Gadrey, facilitates the detailed and regular management of this delicate balance between attachment and detachment. The right to use socio-technical capacities belonging to the service provider, for a limited period of time: this definition describes a frame that allows compatibility and complementarity between the entanglement of personal relations (and the collective deliberations they allow), on the one hand, and the possibility for agents to get out of these relations, to detach themselves in order to evaluate the advantages of new attachments, on the other.

Conclusion

The organization of economic markets and the formulation of their rules of functioning are an increasingly explicit issue not only for social scientists and political decision makers but also for economic agents themselves. The upsurge of this reflexive activity is reflected in particular in the emergence of what we have suggested calling the economy of qualities. In this economy, inhabited by actors who are real professionals in product qualification and the profiling of goods, consumers are constantly prompted to question their preferences and tastes and, finally, through the explicit debates that that implies, their own social identity. As the anthropology of consumption has so clearly shown, classifying products, positioning them and evaluating them inevitably leads to the classification of the people attached to those goods. Consumption becomes both more rational (not that the consumer is more rational but because (distributed) cognition devices become infinitely richer, more sophisticated and reflexive) and more emotional (consumers are constantly referred to the construction of their social identity since their choices and preferences become objects of deliberation: the distinction of products and social distinction are part of the same movement). As for suppliers, one of their main concerns is to facilitate and organize to their own advantage this process of (re)qualification.

The functioning of the economy of qualities involves the establishment of forms of organization that facilitate the intensification of collaboration between supply and demand, in a way that enables consumers to participate actively in the qualification of products. The establishment of distributed cognition devices, intended to organize real-life experiments on preferences, tends to blur habitual distinctions between production, distribution and consumption. Design, as an activity that crosses through the entire organization, becomes central: the firm organizes itself to make the dynamic process of qualification and requalification of products possible and manageable.

In the economy of qualities, competition turns around the attachment of consumers to products whose qualities have progressively been defined with their active participation. The dynamic of reflexive attachment implies consumers who are calculating, that is, capable of perceiving differences and grading them, and who are accompanied and supported in this evaluation and judgement by suppliers and their intermediaries. Competition between firms plays on the formatting of socio-technical devices which, distributing and redistributing the material bases of cogni-tion, format the bases of calculation and preferences.

We have suggested that the economy of services, especially where new ICTs are involved, is emblematic of this economy of qualities. It is reflected in forms of organization and competition that encourage reflexive behaviours in actors, espe-cially those relating to the qualification of goods. The beneficiary and service provider co-operate closely in the singularization of the services proposed. To be sure, the modalities of this co-operation differ, depending on the logic. In the logic of intervention, the consumer adjusts to the socio-technical device whereas in the logic of making available it is the device that goes to the user. In the logic of representation the two meet each other halfway, so that forms of life and emotions are shared. Having the user at one's place, being at his place or building a place to be with him: in all three cases, the economy of goods gives way to an economy of relations.

It has been possible to demonstrate the emergence and diffusion of the economy of qualities, and to suggest the existence of a link between this economy of qualities and what is commonly called the service economy, owing to a frame of analysis that can be traced back to Chamberlin and sociological and anthropological work on markets. This dual detour has led to the observation that it is possible to bring together the preoccupations of actors who, in the economy of qualities, devote a large part of their resources and cognitive capacities to the qualification of goods, on the one hand, and questions that certain economists and sociologists ask, on the other. This link attests to the reflexive dimension of the economy of qualities. Once established, it should promote the constitution of hybrid forums capable of holding debates on the organization of markets, which have become all the more open both to debate and governance as they deliberately inscribe themselves in a service economy that uses new ICTs on a massive scale.

NOTES

1 Smith gives the example of e-commerce where the organization of auctions is constantly the object of debates, experiments and evaluations. These markets are highly reflexive (see also Giddens 1998).
2 The issues debated are, for example, the granting of property rights, the setting of prices, the organization of competition, the regulation of international trade and the modalities of intervention by public authorities.
3 As, for example, questions of national independence and sovereignty or of social equity.
4 The organization of markets and ethical considerations cannot be dissociated in the case of biotechnologies. Can human organs be transformed into merchandise and, if so, under what conditions? Should the cloning and commercialization of secondary products be allowed? Should genetic tests be allowed as a condition for insurance contracts?
5 Here again, biotechnology multiplies subjects of controversy, such as, for example, those on the conditions of gene patentability.
6 Socio-technical controversies analysed by science studies more and more frequently include the subject of markets, for non-human entities constantly flow over established frames, producing externalities that have to be taken into account. By crossing the barriers of species, do prions connect two markets, that of beef and that of aquaculture salmon, previously considered to be separate? What protocol should be chosen to establish

incontestable figures for the impact of greenhouse gases on global warming or to calculate possible penalties?

7   When talking of the social acceptability of technologies, one has to include social technologies and talk of the social acceptability not of markets in general but of a particular form of market.

8   The social sciences, like the other sciences and perhaps even more than them, are performative. They contribute to the existence of the realities they describe. Being aware of this performative dimension implies a reflexivity that should lead specialists to agree to collaborate with the actors themselves.

9   The aggregation of demand is not a theoretical problem; it is above all a practical problem that has to be solved by economic agents. The solutions devised are multiple. For a suggestive analysis, see Salais and Storper (1993).

10 Apart from Chamberlin, and White (1981), very few authors have considered the products of their qualification as strategic variables for economic agents. We note, however, the significant and original contributions of the French school and especially of Salais (Salais and Storper 1993), Eymard-Duvernay (1994) and Thévenot (1989).

11 In his introduction to *The Laws of the Markets*, Michel Callon (1998) emphasized the performative role of the economic sciences, going so far as to say that economic activities are embedded in economics'. This expression should not be misunderstood. Two observations warrant attention. First, economics as a discipline is not alone in accomplishing this performing and framing. It is helped by other disciplines in the social sciences but also, and above all, by the actors themselves and especially by professionals of the market (marketing specialists, accountants, managers, etc.) who readily mobilize lasting material devices to make these frames irreversible. (As Weber remarked, there could be no possible encounter between supply and demand without technical and material arrangements such as the supermarket with its shelves and tills, etc.). Second, the role played by economics as a discipline increases along with hybrid forums within which the organization of markets is debated, and which supply a vast audience for specialists who were previously more or less in the background.

12 Economic agents have reappropriated this concept which had disappeared from the vocabulary of political economics. In the service sector today engineers and sales people frequently talk of use values as opposed to utility.

13 The incommensurability of goods (as in the classical example of butter and cannons or in that of wine and canvas between which the agents in economics textbooks establish necessarily random preferences) is an outcome of the classifications themselves. In reality, it is by a series of small gaps, tiny shifts, that, starting with a given category of goods, we end up with one or more radically different categories. In its great wisdom, economic theory leaves agents to answer the question by introducing concepts such as that of crossed elasticity.

14 As we shall see below, not all the properties of products are necessarily obtained in metrological networks. For a subtle analysis of the different mechanisms, see Bessy and Chateauraynaud (1995).

15 One of the advantages of this definition is that it enables us to apply the same analysis to the production of 'bads' – the name traditionally given to 'goods' that produce negative externalities.

16 Economic theory distinguishes between markets where agents are 'price takers' and those where they are 'price makers'. This distinction could, and should, be extended to products by contrasting markets where agents are 'product takers' and markets where they are 'product makers'.

17 White is one of the only authors to have followed the programme thus outlined by Chamberlin. This programme jettisons the two concepts of monopoly and competition,

which, as ideal types, are simply useless and even result in a profound lack of comprehension of the functioning of real markets. Chamberlin synthesizes his demonstration as follows:

Price adjustments are, in fact, but one phase, and often a relatively unimportant phase, of the whole competitive process... The fact of such competition should at least be brought into the open by including the 'product' as a variable in the problem... For a complete picture, indeed, each element of the 'product' should be regarded as a separate variable. (Chamberlin 1946: 73)

It is interesting to note that, in Appendix C to his book, Chamberlin discusses at length the seminal article by Hotelling (1929) in which that author lays the foundations of an economy of quality (products differ according to a variable which is the seller's location).

18   We borrow the concept of singularization from Karpik (1989). It is preferable to the more common one of personalization or customization, for it maintains the unity of a process which concerns goods and agents in such a way that they cannot be dissociated. Yet the economy of quality studied by Karpik tends to prefer configurations in which the main issue is the quality of products (e.g. a lawyer's or teacher's service). By choosing to talk of an economy of qualities, we consider the most general case in which it is the (necessarily multidimensional) qualification of products and especially the processes of their (re)qualification that are the key issue. This enables us to include all productive operations in the analysis without neglecting forms of competition.

19   For an exhaustive review of the literature on preferences, see Cochoy (forthcoming). He shows the limits of the classical approaches of Samuelson, of Sen, of Ackerloff and of Lancaster, and highlights the importance of situations in which the qualities of products are variables and their characterization is dynamic.

20   A cogent demonstration of this was made by Smith (1989) in his work on public auctions.

21   As he shows, this situation is only a particular case of a more general paradox, studied for a long time: that of Buridan's donkey.

22   One of the emblematic forms of this life-size experimental work is that of supermarkets, from every point of view identical to ordinary supermarkets but transformed into real laboratories in which a number of parameters can be varied and in which customers' behaviours are observed in detail.

23   The definition of a good as a 'bundle of characteristics' is very valuable, for it establishes no ranking of characteristics.

24   The consumer in question is not necessarily the final user. The process of (re)qualification involves many stages. At some of those stages markets may be organized, binding a supply and a demand around the good thus defined.

25   The concept of calculation must be understood here very generally, as proposed by Michel Callon in The Laws of the Markets. Calculating implies (a) that different options are open, (b) that conceivable decisions are known, and (c) that it is possible to associate each decision with the realization of a particular option. As shown, these situations simply framing. It is easy to check whether distributed cognition devices, considered above, produce such frames. Saying that markets are reflexive is obviously not asserting that agents are calculating (they are always calculating to some degree, but in different ways); it is emphasizing the fact that the design and implementation of framing devices become key concerns for the different agents involved.

26   Again according to Gadrey, 'the conventions and contracts corresponding to them consider in general (a) that A is responsible for the smooth functioning of the capacity in question, according to prevailing standards, and (b) that B must use these capacities

well. In terms of property law he does not have the right to use and abuse them as he feels fit.'

27   Gadrey shows, however, that there are economic differences between the purchase of socio-technical capacities and the purchase of their use (modalities of appropriation, storage, evaluation of production and of performance, etc.).

28   Qualification is at the heart of the customer's strolling around in a supermarket, along the rows of shelves. With the Internet and e-commerce, it becomes the very matter of market relations. E-consumers scroll menus and supermarket clients stroll around in alleys.

29   In the case of the Web, these attachments are inscribed in navigation software which proposes bookmarks but also favourites to go to.

30   Between these two eventualities there exists a whole series of intermediate situations. For example, contracts can be drawn up in which the user is not the owner but may become the owner after a predetermined number of years. Clauses can also be added which provide for replacement cars in case of breakdowns or maintenance. The product becomes more complex; it becomes a 'bundle of qualities' that allow singularizations and differentiations *ad libitum*.

31   Thomas (1991) says 'entangled'. On the relationship between entanglement and disentanglement (calculation), see Callon (1998).

REFERENCES

Akrich, M. (1992) 'The de-scription of technical objects: shaping technology/building society', in W. Bijker and J. Law (eds) *Studies in Sociotechnical Change*, Cambridge, MA: MIT Press, pp. 205–24.

Appadurai, A. (1986) *The Social Life of Things: Commodities in Cultural Perspective*, Cambridge: Cambridge University Press.

Barrey, S., Cochoy, F. and Dubuisson, S. (2000) 'Designer, packager et merchandiser: trois professionnels pour une même scène marchande', *Sociologie du Travail* 42 (3 Numéro spécial: les professionnels du marché): 457–82.

Bessy, C. and Chateauraynaud, F. (1995) *Experts et faussaires: Pour une sociologie de la perception*, Paris: Métailié.

Callon, M. (ed.) (1998) *The Laws of the Markets*, Oxford: Blackwell.

Callon, M., Lascoumes, P. and Barthe, Y. (2001) *Agir dans un monde incertain, Essai sur la démocratie technique*, Paris: Le Seuil.

Chamberlin, E. H. (1946) *The Theory of Monopolistic Competition: A Reorientation of the Theory of Value*, 5th edn, Cambridge, MA: Harvard University Press.

Cochoy, F. (1998) 'Another discipline for the market economy: marketing as a performative knowledge and know-how for capitalism', In Callon (1998) pp. 194–221.

——(forthcoming) *L'âne du Buridan et l'économie du marché: Essai d'anthropologie du marché*.

Dubuisson, S. (1998) 'Regard d'un sociologue sur la notion de routine dans la théorie évolutionniste', *Sociologie du Travail* 40 (4): 491–502.

Dumez, H. and Jeunemaître, A. (1998) 'The unlikely encounter between economics and a market: the case of cement industry', in Callon (1998), pp. 222–43.

Eymard-Duvernay, F. (1994) 'Coordination des échanges par l'entreprise et qualité des biens', in A. Orléan (ed.) *Analyse économique des conventions*, Paris: PUF.

Gadrey, J. (2000) 'The characterization of goods and services: an alternative approach', *Review of Income and Wealth* 46 (3).

Gao, B. (1998) 'Efficiency, culture, and politics: the transformation of Japanese management in 1946–1966', in Callon (1998), pp. 86–115.

Giddens, A. (1998) *The Third Way,* Oxford: Blackwell.

Hatchuel, A. (1995) 'Les marchés à prescripteurs', in A. Jacob and H. Warin (eds) *L'Inscription sociale du marché,* Paris: L'Harmattan, pp. 223–4.

Hotelling, H. (1929) 'Stability in competition', *Economic Journal* 39 (41).

Hutchins, E. (1995) *Cognition in the Wild,* Cambridge, MA: MIT Press.

Karpik, L. (1989) 'L'economie de la qualité', *Revue Française de Sociologie* 30: 187–210.

Mallard, A. (1996) 'Les instruments dans la coordination de l'action', thèse, Ecole des mines de Paris.

—— (2000) 'La presse de consommation et le marché: Enquête sur le tiers-consumériste', *Sociologie du Travail* 42 (3 Numéro spécial: les professionnels du marché): 391–411.

March, J. G. (1994) *A Primer on Decision Making: How Decisions Happen,* New York: Free Press.

Méadel, C. and Rabeharisoa, V. (1999) *Consommateurs et produits alimentaires: la construction des ajustements. Partie II: Le consommateur mis en bouteille. L'équipée de Pampryl et Bangua.* Paris: CSI.

——(2001) 'Taste as a form of adjustment between food and consumers', in R. Coombs, K. Green, A. Richards and V. Walsh (eds) *Demand, Markets, Users and Innovation,* Cheltenham: Edward Elgar.

Miller, P. (1998) 'The margins of accounting', in Callon (1998), pp. 174–93.

Salais, R. and Storper, M. (1993) *Les Mondes de production,* Paris: Editions de l'EHESS.

Smith, C. W. (1989) *Auctions: The Social Construction of Value,* New York: Free Press.

——(2000). 'Understanding real markets: confronting old fallacies, emerging possibilities and imminent challenges', unpublished manuscript.

Teil, G. (1998) 'Devenir expert aromaticien: y a-t-il une place pour le goût dans les goûts alimentaires', *Sociologie du Travail* 40 (4): 503–22.

Thévenot, L. (1989) 'Equilibre et rationalité dans un univers complexe', *Revue Economique* 2: 147–97.

——(1993) *Essais sur les objets usuels: Propriétés, fonctions, usages. Les objets dans l'action. De la maison au laboratoire.* Raisons Pratiques 4, Paris: Editions de l'EHESS, pp. 85–111.

Thomas, N. (1991) *Entangled Objects: Exchange, Material Culture and Colonialism in the Pacific,* Cambridge, MA: Harvard University Press.

Tirole, J. (1989) *The Theory of Industrial Organization,* Cambridge, MA: MIT Press.

White, H. (1981) 'Where do markets come from?' *American Journal of Sociology,* 87: 517–47.

Part II   Finance and Money

Chapter 5

Inside the Economy of Appearances

Anna Tsing

Indonesia's profile in the international imagination has completely changed. From the top of what was called a "miracle," Indonesia fell to the bottom of a "crisis." In the middle of what was portrayed as a timeless political regime, students demonstrated, and, suddenly, the regime was gone. So recently an exemplar of the promise of globalization, overnight Indonesia became the case study of globalization's failures.

This essay brings us back to the months just before Indonesia so drastically changed, to canoe at the running edge of what turned out to be a waterfall, and thus to think about a set of incidents that can be imagined as a rehearsal for the Asian financial crisis as well as a minor participant in the international disillusion that led to the Suharto regime's downfall. In 1994 a small Canadian gold prospecting company announced a major find in the forests of Kalimantan, Indonesian Borneo. Over the months, the find got bigger and bigger, until it was the biggest gold strike in the world, conjuring memories of the Alaskan Klondike and South Africa's Witwatersrand. Thousands of North American investors put their savings in the company, called Bre-X. First-time investors and retired people joined financial wizards. Whole towns in Western Canada invested The new world of Internet investment blossomed with Bre-X. Meanwhile, Bre-X received continuous coverage in North American newspapers, especially after huge Canadian mining companies and Indonesian officials entered the fray, fighting over the rights to mine Busang, Bre-X's find. The scandal of Indonesian business-as-usual, opened to public scrutiny as corruption, heightened international attention and garnered support for Bre-X. But, in 1997, just when expectation had reached a fevered pitch, Busang was exposed as barren: there was nothing there. Gasps, cries, and law suits rose from every corner.

The Bre-X story exemplifies popular thinking about the pleasures and dangers of international finance and associated dreams of globalization. The story dramatizes North–South inequalities in the new capitalisms; it celebrates the North's excitement about international investment, and the blight of the South's so-called crony capitalisms: business imagined not quite/not white. Painting Southern leaders as rats fighting for garbage, the story also promises new genres of justice for the Northern investor who dares to sue. Finance looks like democracy: the Internet, they say, opens foreign investment to the North American everyman. But the Bre-X story also narrates the perils of the downsized, overcompetitive economy: the sad entrepreneurship of selling worthless stock certificates on-line.

Most salient to my concerns about the specificity of global economic promises is the genre convention with which Bre-X started its own story, and by which it was finished off. Bre-X was always a performance, a drama, a conjuring trick, an illusion, regardless of whether real gold or only dreams of gold ever existed at Busang. Journalists compared Busang, with its lines of false drilling samples, to a Hollywood set. But it was not just Busang; it was the whole investment process. No one would ever have invested in Bre-X if it had not created a performance, a dramatic exposition of the possibilities of gold.

Performance here is simultaneously economic performance and dramatic performance. The "economy of appearances" I describe depends on the relevance of this pun; the self-conscious making of a spectacle is a necessary aid to gathering investment funds. The dependence on spectacle is not peculiar to Bre-X and other mining scams: it is a regular feature of the search for financial capital. Start-up companies must dramatize their dreams in order to attract the capital they need to operate and expand. Junior prospecting companies must exaggerate the possibilities of their mineral finds in order to attract investors so that they might, at some point, find something. This is a requirement of investment-oriented entrepreneurship, and it takes the limelight in those historical moments when capital seeks creativity rather than stable reproduction. In speculative enterprises, profit must be imagined before it can be extracted; the possibility of economic performance must be conjured like a spirit to draw an audience of potential investors. The more spectacular the conjuring, the more possible an investment frenzy. Drama itself can be worth summoning forth. Nor are companies alone in the conjuring business in these times. In order to attract companies, countries, regions, and towns must dramatize their potential as places for investment. Dramatic performance is the prerequisite of their economic performance.

Yet conjuring is always culturally specific, creating a magic show of peculiar meanings, symbols, and practices. The conjuring aspect of finance interrupts our expectations that finance can and has spread everywhere, for it can only spread as far as its own magic. In its dramatic performances, circulating finance reveals itself as both empowered and limited by its cultural specificity.

Contemporary masters of finance claim not only universal appeal but also a global scale of deployment. What are we to make of these globalist claims, with their millennial whispers of a more total and hegemonic world-making than we have ever known? Neither false ideology nor obvious truth, it seems to me that the globalist claims of finance are also a kind of conjuring of a dramatic performance. In these times of heightened attention to the space and scale of human undertakings, economic projects cannot limit themselves to conjuring at different scales – they must conjure the scales themselves. In this sense, a project that makes us imagine globality in order to see how it might succeed is one kind of "scale-making project"; similarly, projects that make us imagine locality, or the space of regions or nations, in order to see their success are also scale-making projects. The scales they conjure come into being in part through the contingent articulations into which they are pushed or stumble. In a world of multiple divergent claims about scales, including multiple divergent globalisms, those global worlds that most affect us are those that manage tentatively productive linkages with other scale-making projects.

One of the chief puzzles of globalist financial conjuring is why it works. We've all seen advertisements for hamburgers, express mail, or computers bridging cultures across the globe. But it's one thing to offer a stylish picture of diversity, and another thing to figure out how entrepreneurial projects actually manage to affect people who may not pay them any mind. Conjuring is supposed to call up a world more dreamlike and sweeter than anything that exists; magic, rather than strict description, calls capital. The puzzle seems deeper the more the material and social worlds to be reshaped and exploited are geographically, culturally, and politically remote from financial conjuring centers. How do the self-consciously glossy and exaggerated virtual worlds conjured by eager collectors of finance become shapers of radically different peoples and places? My frame highlights contingent articulations in which globalist financial conjuring links itself with regional and national scale-making projects, making each succeed wildly – if also partially and tentatively. It seems likely that successfully conjuring the globe is possible, at least now, only in thick collaboration with regional and national conjurings; certainly, financial conjuring has been deeply implicated in promises of making regional and national dreams come true.

Often, globalist financial conjuring supports the most bizarre and terrible of national and regional dreams. Certainly this was the case in the Bre-X story. Finance capital became linked with greedy elite dreams of an authoritarian nation-state supported by foreign funds and enterprises; this is a nation-making project I call franchise cronyism to mark the interdependence of corruption and foreign investment. These in turn became linked with migrant dreams of a regional frontier culture in which the rights of previous rural residents could be wiped out entirely to create a Wild West scene of rapid and lawless resource extraction: quick profits, quick exits. To present this rather complicated set of links, I offer a diagram (Figure 5.1). Diagrams by their nature are over-simplifications, and this one is certainly no exception. Indeed, I have named each of the three scale-making projects I discuss in a self-consciously joking manner. Yet the playfulness is also a serious attempt to focus attention on the specificity and process of articulation. Finance capital is a program for *global* hegemony; franchise cronyism is one particular *nation*-making project;

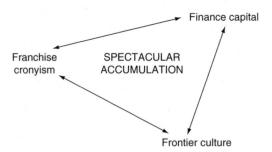

Figure 5.1 F-C articulations in the economy of appearances. This diagram is both serious and a joke.

frontier culture is an articulation of a *region*. Each is a scale-making project with its sights set on a different scale: global, national, and regional. The links among them cross scales and strengthen each project's ability to remake the world. At the same time, not one of these three projects is predictable or ubiquitous in the world. Coming together as they did for a moment in Suharto's Indonesia, they created a great fire. Looking back, we see that they didn't create an evolutionary ladder to the stars. Isn't this sense of specificity and contingency in globalist claims what scholars and social commentators need most to bring into view?

"Yes, We Are Still in Business"

Bre-X was the brainchild of a Canadian stock promoter named David Walsh. Walsh dropped out of high school at the end of tenth grade and soon joined a Montreal trust company, rising quickly to become the head of the investment department. After thirteen years, he left to try to form his own trust company. Three unsuccessful years later, he agreed to start an office in Calgary for another firm, only to quit the next year. From then on, Walsh worked to set up his own companies: first, the oil-oriented Bresea Resources Ltd. (named after his sons Brett and Sean) and then, in 1985, Bre-X Minerals Ltd., which from the first aimed to find gold.[1]

Gold mining had become a profitable industry in the 1970s when the United States ended the gold standard, and the price of gold, which had been held constant at $35 per ounce for many years, skyrocketed, hitting $850 per ounce in 1980. Canadian companies rushed to take advantage of the new gold prices by exploring not only in the Canadian West but around the world. Junior mining exploration companies, whose goal is to find the minerals that can be exploited by major companies, sprouted by the dozens. Toronto became the world's mining finance capital. In 1997 there were 1,225 publicly traded mining companies in Canada, and mining stocks represented 21.5 percent of all trades on the Toronto Stock Exchange.[2] In this industry, the line between various kinds of expertise is thin: geologists (with salaries supplemented by stock options) must be promoters to raise the money to finance their mineral finds, market analysts must be geologists to evaluate those finds, and stock promoters must explain their offerings in geologically convincing terms. Canadian preeminence in mining depended on both its mining history and its position as a center of mining finance.

For a stock promoter like David Walsh to become president of a gold exploration company was not unusual in this climate. Consider the trajectory of the president of Barrick Gold, Canada's biggest gold-mining company. Peter Munk is a high-flying but not always successful entrepreneur. In the 1950s he founded a television and hi-fi company that crashed, leaving the government of Nova Scotia in deep debt; he went on to build hotels on South Sea islands funded by Saudi Arabian princes. Nothing in his background gave him expertise in minerals. In 1986, however, he bought a worked-over mine in Nevada. It turned out to be the most profitable gold mine in the world, pushing Munk's company into a leading position.[3] Peter Munk was "a dreamer who became a king."[4] In this context, David Walsh's little enterprise made sense.

In 1988 Walsh listed Bre-X on the Alberta Stock Exchange at 30 Canadian cents per share. His wife Jeanette supported the household by working as a secretary. The family bought on credit, and, over C$200,000 in debt, both David and Jeanette Walsh declared personal bankruptcy in 1992. Bre-X shares sometimes fell as low as 2 cents; in his 1991 annual report, David Walsh wrote, "Yes, we are still in business." In 1993, however, Walsh pulled together some money for a trip to Indonesia. There he met with Dutch-born geologist John Felderhof, who had achieved some fame in identifying the Ok Tedi copper and gold mine in Papua New Guinea in 1967, but had suffered hard times in the 1980s. Felderhof agreed to help Walsh find gold in Kalimantan and contacted Filipino geologist Michael de Guzman for the project. Filipino geologists had been in much demand in Indonesia because of their experience, education, and regional savvy. De Guzman brought several Filipino associates to the team.

Mining properties were cheap and available in Indonesia in the early 1990s because the Australians, who had come in some ten years before in their own wave of national mining speculation, were trying to get out. Felderhof had worked for some Australian companies and had witnessed the financial boom and bust in which mineral exploration was begun and then abandoned, promising or not. He convinced Walsh to form a partnership with an Indonesian entrepreneur to buy an old Australian claim around the creek called Busang in East Kalimantan, and Walsh raised the money to drill some holes. The results were disappointing, and by December 1993 they were about to close the property. Then, early in 1994, de Guzman struck gold. Walsh was quick and effective in informing investor newsletters and brokerage firms. Felderhof's estimates grew bigger and bigger. In 1993, Bre-X was trading at 51 Canadian cents a share; by May 1996, stocks were trading at C$286.50, accounting for a ten-to-one split. In April, Bre-X had been listed on the Toronto Stock Exchange; in August, the stock was listed in the United States on NASDAQ; in September, it was also listed on the Montreal Stock Exchange. By then the company's market capitalization was over 6 billion Canadian dollars. Awards started to roll in: Mining Man of the Year for Bre-X president David Walsh; Explorer of the Year for chief geologist John Felderhof. On March 9 and 10, 1997, Bre-X officers and geologists were feted in awards dinners and ceremonies at the Prospectors and Developers Association of Canada meetings. They were at the height of their success.

Conjuring

On March 19, 1997, Michael de Guzman fell 800 feet from a helicopter into the rainforests of Kalimantan. Although up to that point he had been considered little more than the Filipino sidekick, at the moment of his death de Guzman became the company, his face displayed everywhere in the news media over charts of the company's finds and stock prices. If Bre-X had been a big story before, it was truly dramatic now.

Mysteries abounded. A suicide note was found in which de Guzman wrote that he couldn't stand the pain of hepatitis. But he was an optimistic man and in quite good health. What happened to the third man the other Filipino geologists had seen enter the helicopter? Rumors circulated like wildfire. One Philippines scholar confided to me, "When I heard about the watch found in the helicopter, I had to find out what kind it was. When they said 'Rolex,' I knew he was murdered. No Filipino gangster would dispose of his victim without first removing his Rolex." A sign, a trophy. The trouble was, the scene was cluttered with signs, clues, false leads. Wives of de Guzman who knew nothing of each other's existence cropped up everywhere: in Manila, Jakarta, Manado, Samarinda.[5] Rumors circulated that de Guzman had parachuted into Zurich.[6] When a corpse was finally found, the face and much of the body had been devoured by wild pigs. Multiple autopsies failed to establish the identity of the body beyond controversy: could Bre-X have changed the fingerprint on his employee identity card? Did the dental records match? And where were his geologist friends when it was time for the funeral?[7]

It was at this point, too, that the gold deposit at Busang came to seem just as mysterious. Bre-X had been drilling core samples at Busang since 1993; by 1997 some sites looked like "Swiss cheese."[8] As Busang became famous, industry professionals came to visit. Bre-X president Walsh later complained, "Virtually every mining geologist, analyst went to the site, but I never received one letter or phone call during that whole period that something was amiss over in Indonesia."[9] The "analysts" Walsh refers to were mining stock analysts, and, indeed, dozens visited the site, each fueling investors' attraction with more glowing reports. But in March 1997 the American company Freeport-McMoRan sent their assayers as the "due diligence" element of their agreement to become partners with Bre-X at Busang. Freeport found nothing. Furthermore, they claimed that the kind of gold in Bre-X's samples was inappropriate for the site: it was stream-rounded alluvial gold instead of igneous gold. Bre-X's assay methods were now open to question. Rumors flew of plots and cover-ups, and the price of Bre-X stocks roller-coastered. Perhaps Freeport was making false claims to take over the property. Perhaps Bob Hasan, an Indonesian partner, was buying up cheap stocks at a bargain-basement price. Why else had he taken out a bank loan to log just in this area, just at this time?[10] Perhaps New York investors were trying to beat out Canadians.[11] The gamble drew stock speculators into the fray, and on April 2 trading was so intense that it closed down the computer system at the Toronto Stock Exchange.[12] On May 3, however, the independent test report arrived. Its finding: *no* economic gold deposit. The ballooning stock swap immediately deflated; Bre-X stocks were officially worthless.[13] Yet what are we to make of the mysteries?

I am not a journalist, and my concern does not involve just which gold miners and which Indonesian government officials and which stock market participants knew about or participated in various conjuring acts. I'm more interested in the art of conjuring itself, as practiced not only by Bre-X officers and employees but also by the analysts, reporters, investors, and regulators who formed their retinue. I am struck by two counterintuitive observations. First, mystery, rumor, and drama did not come to Bre-X just at the tail end of its ride; these qualities marked the Bre-X story from its beginnings. Rather than closing Bre-X down, mystery and drama kept Bre-X alive and growing; it was only when an official report stopped the show that the company died. Second, Bre-X is not the only company that has required spectacle to grow. Bre-X seems typical of the "junior" Canadian mineral exploration companies that it has helped usher into the international spotlight – except, of course, it was more successful at first and later more despised. Junior companies don't have the equipment or capital to take their mining ventures very far. They must make a big splash, first, to attract enough investors to keep prospecting and, second, to bring in big mining companies to buy out their finds.

One can draw the net wider. The mystery and spectacle Bre-X cultivated is representative of many kinds of companies in which finance capital is the ruling edge of accumulation. Such companies draw investments through drama. And the importance of drama guarantees that it is very difficult to discern companies that have long-term production potential from those that are merely good at being on stage. The charismatic and dramatic attraction of international finance capital was a key feature of Southeast Asian development strategies during the so-called economic miracle. After the 1997 financial crisis we were told to distinguish between the real and the fake, but does not the whole design of these accumulation strategies work against our ability to draw this line? As in a beauty contest, artistry and drama are necessary to compete; spectacle and mystery, playing equally across the line of the real and the fake, establish the winning reality of performance.[14]

Bre-X initially attracted investors because of the excitement of the reports coming out about Busang. From the very first, Bre-X was in the news, and journalists constantly wrote about Busang. The success with which Bre-X attracted investors depended on these reports and particularly on the ways they used and elaborated tropes that brought the Bre-X find into other circulating stories of wealth, power, and fulfillment. Some of these stories were colonial adventure tales: the search for hidden, uncounted riches in remote places. *Maclean's*, a Canadian magazine, wrote: "Two, four, and then maybe six million ounces will be pulled from Busang annually. There has never been an El Dorado like this."[15] Other stories told of frontier independence and the promise of wealth "at the end of a miner's rainbow," as the *New York Times* put it, where "independent-mindedness" led miners to "forbidding jungles" in search of the "century's greatest gold strike."[16] There were stories of science in the service of human innovation. There were stories of war and conquest – "the battle for Busang" – recalling the French and the United States in Vietnam, and Bre-X became, repeatedly, a "rumble in the jungle," and then, eventually, a "bungle" or a "jumble" in the jungle.[17]

There were also pervasive stories of underdog charisma. After announcing the Busang find, Bre-X had to fight for the rights to mine it. The story of little Bre-X up against the big North American mining companies and the big Indonesian establishment gathered an overwhelming response, ushering in Bre-X's greatest period of popular investment. When US ex-president George Bush and Canadian ex-prime minister Brian Mulroney put pressure on Jakarta at the request of a big company, Bre-X's David Walsh, with his high school education, his beer belly, and his ineptness, looked like David up against Goliath. He made such a convincing "little guy" that after the scam was exposed many refused to believe him responsible. As *Fortune* magazine's reporter wrote, "Even now I have trouble believing that Walsh participated... Walsh looked more like some poor schlemiel who had just won the lottery and couldn't locate his ticket."[18]

Stockholders, too, contributed to the stories swirling around Bre-X.[19] Bre-X established an Internet presence early on, with stories posted on their website; meanwhile, investors' chat lines buzzed with Bre-X news.[20] The more controversy swirled around Bre-X, the more investors talked and exchanged rumors, extending, too, dreams of wealth, conspiracy theories, reinterpretations of the mining geology and engineering, and romances of unexpected underdog advantage. On the Internet, dramatic presentation was often clearly the point. As one *Silicon Investor* contributor wrote about the Bre-X Internet thread, "The theater is open. The stage is set 24 hrs. a day. There is always an audience."[21]

One Internet contributor signed herself "Ole49er," reminding readers that the Wild West is never far from discussion of Bre-X. A Canadian shareholder with whom I spoke explained that Canadians were excited about the chance to invest in minerals in Indonesia because of the symbolic importance of mining in Canada as well as a national anxiety about the closing of the frontier. Environmental regulations in Canada, he explained, made it difficult to mine profitably in the last wide open spaces of the Canadian West. Yet those open spaces might be pursued abroad in foreign lands. As a substitute frontier, Bre-X's Kalimantan continued the excitement of the frontier story of Canada's development.

CoWs

CoWs are Contracts of Work. No mining company can extract minerals in Indonesia without one. Like animals, CoWs come in generations. The first CoW was a much revered and singular ancestor, granted to Louisiana's Freeport-McMoRan to mine in Irian Jaya.[22] Succeeding generations of CoWs have become more differentiated, more limited, more finely detailed.[23] Yet as they develop, they continue to be icons, even fetishes, held up to show the relationship between the Indonesian nation and the world. Ideally, they guarantee that resource extraction activities work in the interests of the Indonesian nation as well as the mining company. They specify the conditions that create mutual benefits shared between the nation and its foreign investors.

CoWs are magical tools of the national elite. Although merely paper and ink, they conjure a regular income for the Indonesian nation-state. Their terms must be secure and attractive by international standards, or they will not draw capital. But if they meet these standards, they can also conjure the funds that allow the nation-state to produce itself as what one might call a "miracle nation": a nation in which foreign funds support the authoritarian rule that keeps the funds safe. I earlier called this "franchise cronyism." In exchange for supplying the money to support the national leaders who can make the state secure, investors are offered the certainties of the contract, which ensures title to mineral deposits, fixes taxation rates, and permits export of profit.

The CoW guarantees that investors are not working with "dictators." As one Canadian Bre-X investor explained to me, in investing his modest funds he always avoided the countries of dictators. This was the reason the Bre-X investment seemed reasonable. I was confused: what is a dictator? As we talked, I realized that a dictator is a foreign ruler who interferes with Canadian investment. Indonesia's President Suharto was not a dictator, at least before Bre-X. As Bre-X president David Walsh put it, his company – like other Australian and Canadian mining companies in the 1980s and 1990s – targeted Indonesia "by virtue of its geological setting, favorable investment climate and political stability."[24]

Other nations could be and were imagined in Indonesia. Suharto's New Order regime emerged violently in 1966 from an earlier scene of diverse and competitive programs for making the nation, and from the start the regime depended on the repression of other Indonesian national visions through censorship and militarization. Political quietude was nurtured, too, through internationally sponsored "development," which came to refer to programs of state expansion dedicated to convincing diverse local people of the unified national standards of state power. Through "development" the state conceived a legal framework to claim the nation's resources and make them available for foreign expropriation, thus amassing the materials through which its version of the nation could prosper.

When investment capital began to circulate wildly across national boundaries in the 1980s, the Indonesian elite was ready for it. They beckoned to the mining sector, saying: "There are still vast tracts of unexplored land in Indonesia. For those who dare to venture, Indonesia offers immense possibilities."[25] The Australians came. One Indonesian ex-mining official candidly admitted that these were "irresponsible investments" with "rubbish technology." When the Canadian companies followed in the 1990s, it was more of the same: "It's a repetition of history. It's not really a gold rush. It's rather a stock market rush."[26] Yet the government transformed the stock market rush into a gold rush by offering it regional frontiers in the making. The regime gave the companies Contracts of Work, despite their irresponsibility. The CoWs wrote away local rights. Military men deployed to enforce CoWs felt encouraged to start their own entrepreneurial schemes, creating a model of government in which administrators by definition doubled as entrepreneurs who, supported by kickbacks, freed up resources for investors, including themselves. Civil servants became franchise entrepreneurs, too, learning to conjure the miracle nation locally. It was they who sanctioned the mass migration of illegal small loggers and miners that kept the regional economy afloat while bigger investors took out bigger resources and profits. In this escalating mobility and lawlessness, the mysteries of the search for buried treasure became possible. Whether gold was there or not, the economy could grow, spurred on by fabulous dreams.

By the 1990s the Suharto regime began to take for granted its domestic stability and international support. The work of disguising official kickbacks as sound investment policy seemed already complete. Perhaps this is how to understand how the set performance of the miracle nation could have been allowed to deteriorate into dramatic excess. Drama ultimately embarrassed the Suharto regime, allowing investors to label it corrupt. At the same time, it provided a moment of opportunity for investors, who could maneuver within the new embarrassments of national performance to gain a better position for themselves. No investors did better than Bre-X and its rivals in opening up those dramatic cracks and making them visible on international news screens. However unselfconscious the manipulation, it seems clear that the over-the-top drama of franchise cronyism set off around Bre-X allowed the Bre-X investment bubble to last far longer than it could have otherwise, drawing out the drama from the 1994 announcement of gold to the 1997 death of de Guzman. This drama popularized the Bre-X story, vastly enlarging investment.

In January 1994 Barrick Gold offered to buy a stake in Bre-X. Barrick was conducting an aggressive campaign of acquisitions in an attempt to become the world's biggest gold-mining company.[27] As mentioned above, Barrick's CEO, Peter Munk, was a risk taker who made his fortune by a chance buy of a Nevada mine, which turned out to be a fabulous mother lode. Barrick had targeted Indonesia as a possible site for high-profit, low-cost mining, and Bre-X's Busang was just Barrick's kind of buy.

When Bre-X turned him down, Barrick moved into the cracks of the Indonesian regime, working the connection between greed and vulnerability that their nation-making performances had produced. The high-powered politicians on Barrick's advisory board pressured the minister of mines and energy, and even President Suharto.[28] Barrick then approached the president's daughter, Tutut, a tycoon in road construction contracts. He offered her Busang's construction contracts, and she pushed the minister of mines to negotiate a Barrick–Bre-X split in which the government would control 10 percent of the mine, Barrick 70 percent, and Bre-X 20 percent. Bre-X was vulnerable because they had begun drilling without a CoW; now the ministry pulled out even their temporary exploration permit to clinch the deal.[29]

Bre-X stockholders went wild with anger. In the glare of their dissatisfaction, the drama escalated. Placer Dome, another Canadian company, made a better bid.[30] Meanwhile, Bre-X made a spectacular play by approaching the president's son, Sigit, and offering him 10 percent of the mine plus an eye-catching 1 million dollars per month to push their case. Whether naive, as read at the time, or unimaginably clever, this move took the performance of franchise cronyism to its extreme limits, offering the investment drama a new life. Now Suharto's children were pitted against each other publicly.

Barrick continued to have government support until it gained a new opponent: Indonesian entrepreneur Bob Hasan, the longtime friend and golfing buddy of the president, and the man who best knew how to mimic foreign investors' ploys to enlarge his own empire. Hasan played the patriot of the miracle nation, arguing passionately that the enrichment and empowerment of national elites is the first principle of national interest. Barrick irritated him by sending in North American politicians, and he railed against their "cowboyisms," which made Indonesia look helpless under the American thumb.[31] Meanwhile, he managed to acquire a 50 percent share in Bre-X's Indonesian partner.[32]

The game was almost over when President Suharto asked Bob Hasan to work out what to do with Bre-X, and yet this, too, was a moment of momentous drama. Bre-X stockholders were at the edge of their seats. Activist stockholder George Chorny wrote a public letter to Hasan, reminding him that it was Bre-X that had discovered the gold. "It's not any of the guys at Barrick or Placer. It's not the Indonesian government. All the Indonesian government did was to welcome the people of Bre-X to come into their country with open arms to explore this jungle, this desolate jungle in the middle of nowhere."[33] For Chorny, the frontier is always already empty. But Hasan had a different perspective; making the frontier was a national responsibility. Hasan dismissed both Barrick and Placer Dome and brought in the regime's favorite company, Freeport-McMoRan. In Hasan's solution, Freeport-McMoRan would take 15 percent of the mine and become sole operator; the Indonesian government would take 10 percent; Hasan's companies would take 30 percent; and the remaining 45 percent would remain with Bre-X. Backed to the wall, Bre-X signed gracefully.[34]

Freeport, unlike Bre-X and even Barrick, was not in the business of spectacular accumulation, the economy of appearances. Freeport worked with its own cultural logic of investment and development, which, at least at this period, differed from that of Bre-X. Freeport was no mining "junior," amassing capital to finance further exploration. Instead, it had established itself as a big, solid outpost of "American civilization" in Indonesia. As CEO Jim Bob Moffett put it, "We are thrusting a spear of economic development into the heartland of Irian Jaya."[35] Freeport built residential neighborhoods in Irian Jaya reminiscent of US suburbs; Moffett performed Elvis Presley imitations during Christmas visits. Freeport's culture of business, then, offered Americanization rather than "frontier discovery" as a model of profitability.

Freeport had long since gained its miracle deal from the Suharto regime. Its personal Contract of Work far exceeded the benefits of all other investors. In turn, Freeport was the largest source of investor tax revenue for the Indonesian government. It had spent an enormous amount of money developing its Grasberg mine in Irian Jaya, where it depended on the support of the army to keep local residents properly behaved. In 1995, however, riots closed the mine; in 1996, Irian tribal leaders sued the company for environmental destruction and human rights abuses, and the Overseas Private Investment Corporation (an agency of the US government) cancelled the company's risk insurance because of its environmental policies. In 1997, then, Freeport was busy living down international accusations of environmental and social irresponsibility in Irian Jaya. It needed a green profile and solid production results, not an economic miracle.[36] In this spirit, Freeport sent in a sober team to assess the gold at Busang. There was nothing there. "It makes me sick every time I think about it," said Jim Bob Moffett, Freeport's CEO.[37] Following a few impressive last gasps, the spectacle wound down and collapsed. Said Bre-X president David Walsh, "Four and a half years of hard work and the pot at the end of the rainbow is a bucket of slop."[38]

On Spectacular Accumulation

What does this story tell us about transnational finance and its globalist aspirations? In the midst of their dramatic roles, the major players usefully remind us of the stage they have laid. Like Bob Hasan, I am struck by the North American character of the dreams and schemes of investment that swirled around Bre-X. With Bre-X stockholders, I marvel at the ability of Indonesian nation makers to usurp an economic process that has been imagined as fiercely independent from national controls. And as for the Kalimantan landscape, it is hard not to mourn: the pot at the end of the rainbow is a bucket of eroding mud, damaged forests, and mercury-poisoned rivers. Slop indeed.

It was the Canadian imagination of the combined frontier of investment and mining that made this drama possible. The mining industry has been historically important to Canada's economy and identity. By the 1980s its locus had shifted from mining *in* Canada to mining *for* Canada. It represented opportunity, potential prosperity, and the sense of initiative in national character. Bre-X's run from the bottom of the Alberta Stock Exchange to the top of the Toronto exchange and into the world was a source of pride for many Canadians. As much as for profit, Canadians invested for reasons of national pride.[39]

Yet the national specificity of attraction to investments disappears in the excitement of commitments to globalism in the financial world. When one thinks about finance in the Bre-X case, there was nothing worldwide about it at all; it was Canadian and US investment in Indonesia. Yet it is easy to assimilate this specific trajectory of investment to an imagined globalism to the extent that the global is defined as the opening-up process in which remote places submit to foreign finance. Every time finance finds a new site of engagement, we think the world is getting more global. In this act of conjuring, *global* becomes the process of finding new sites. In the force field of this particular globalism, Canadian national dreams are reimagined as transcendent, circulating, beyond culture.

Despite the enormous coercions and seductions of financiers, which aim to make the whole world ready for investment, there is great particularity not only in the reasons a Canadian might want to invest but also in the places where he or she can invest. In the 1990s, when the dreams of the Indonesian elite linked with those of Canadians to jointly conjure the promise of gold, Indonesia became one of those places. Images of remote wild places that could make independent-minded Canadians rich and free touched Indonesian visions of a miracle nation, a nation that could come into being in the arms of foreign finance. Flying in the face of financiers' fantasies of making the nation disappear before the greater mobility of capital, the magic of the miracle nation, waving its CoWs, asserted itself as the only door to North American investment. CoWs, as I have argued, are not merely mechanical adjustments of economic affairs. They are fetish objects, charged with conjuring the miracle nation in the face of competing, threatening alternative visions that unless warded off might come to control the apparatus of the state. From investors' perspectives, they are charged, too, with the security of profit and property. As a gift, they remake the identities of both giver and receiver, vitalizing the miracle nation and its globalist speculators.

For the aspirations of international investors and national elites to emerge as more than a moment's daydream, however, they must be made tangible on a regional landscape. They must engage people, places, and environments. The antilocal culture of Kalimantan frontier regionalism nurtured and raised up both the miracle nation and Canadian speculation. Here is a truly cosmopolitan scene, where varied dreams are jumbled together, naming and renaming creeks, valleys, routes, and towns. The dreamers jostle, fight bitterly, and patronize each other. As they make their own new places, these, too, are knocked away. Even old residents become aliens, as the familiar landscape is transfigured by trauma, danger, and the anxiety of the unknown. Here mystery can flourish, and unexpected discoveries can be made. Unimagined riches can be found because the layout of wealth and poverty is unsettled, unimagined. Impossible promises cannot be ignored. On this landscape, the economy of appearances seems so real that it must be true.

When the spectacle passes on, what is left is rubble and mud, the residues of success and failure. People with other stakes and stories will have to pick up the pieces.

At the intersection of projects for making globes, nations, and regions, new kinds of economies can emerge. In the Bre-X drama, globalist commitments to opening up fresh sites for Canadian mining investments enabled Indonesian visions of a miracle nation at the same time as they stimulated the search for mining frontiers. The program of the miracle nation offered speculators security as it forced potential frontier regions into lawless violence and abolished customary tenure. When Kalimantan responded by developing a wild frontier, its regional reformation confirmed the proprietary rights of the miracle nation. The Kalimantan frontier could then appeal to globalist speculation, offering a landscape where both discovery and loss were possible. Three scale-making projects came together here: the globe-making aspirations of finance capital, the nation-making coercions of franchise cronyism, and the region-making claims of frontier culture (figure 5.1). Globalist, nationalist, and regionalist dreams linked to enunciate a distinctive economic program, the program of spectacular accumulation.

Spectacular accumulation occurs when investors speculate on a product that may or may not exist. Investors are looking for the appearance of success. They cannot afford to find out if the product is solid; by then their chances for profit will be gone. To invest in software development requires this kind of leap: software developers sell their potential, not their product. Biotechnology requires a related if distinctive leap of faith to trust the processes of innovation and patenting to yield as-yet-unknown property rights and royalties. Real estate development requires an assessment of desirability and growth, not demonstrated occupancy; it sells investors attractiveness. In each of these cases, economic performance is conjured dramatically.[40]

I use the term *spectacular accumulation* mainly to argue with evolutionary assumptions in popular theories of the ever changing world economy. According to regulation theorists, "flexible accumulation" is the latest stage of capitalism. Flexible accumulation follows Fordist production as barbarism follows savagery, that is, up a singular political–economic ladder. David Harvey's writing has made this conceptualization influential among anthropologists, who suggest correlated changes in culture, spatiality, and scale to go along with this evolutionary progression.[41] Thus, too, we imagine evolutionary changes in the making of space and time. With Harvey, anthropologists have begun to imagine a worldwide condensation of space and time in which spaces grow smaller and times more instantaneous and effortless. Consider, however, the space-time requirements of Bre-X's spectacular accumulation: space is hugely enlarged: far from miniature and easy, it becomes expansive, labored, and wild, spreading muddy, malarial frontiers. Time is quickened, but into the rush of acceleration, not the efficiency of quick transfers. It is not effortless; if you can't feel the rush and the intensity, you are missing the point, and you'll keep your money at home. Moreover, this spectacular accumulation does not call out to be imagined as new. It is self-consciously old, drawing us back to the South Sea bubble and every gold rush in history. In contrast with flexible accumulation, its power is not its rejection of the past but its ability to keep this old legacy untarnished.

I have no desire to add yet another classificatory device to the annals of capitalism. Instead, my point is to show the heterogeneity of capitalism at every moment in time. Capitalist forms and processes are continually made and unmade; if we offer singular predictions we allow ourselves to be caught by them as ideologies. This seems especially pressing when considering the analysis of scale. At the end of this century, every ambitious world-making project wants to show itself able to forge new scales. NGOs, ethnic groups and coalitions, initiatives for human rights and social justice: we all want to be creative and self-conscious about our scale-making.

We want to claim the globe as ours. In this context, rather than ally myself with globalist financiers to tell of *their* globe. I want to trace how that globe comes into being both as a culturally specific set of commitments and as a set of practices. The investment drama of the Bre-X story shows how articulations among globalist, nationalist, and regionalist projects bring each project to life. In the spirit of serious but joking diagrams, I offer an acronym to refocus your attention (figure 5.2). The particularity of globalist projects. I am arguing, is best seen in the contingent articulations that make them possible and bring them to life: these are APHIDS. Articulations among Partially Hegemonic Imagined Different Scales.

Often we turn to capitalism to understand how what seem to be surface developments form part of an underlying pattern of exploitation and class formation. Yet before we succumb to the capitalist monolith called up in these analyses, it is useful to look at the continual emergence of new capitalist niches, cultures, and forms of agency. For this task. Stuart Hall's idea about the role of articulation in the formation of new political subjects is helpful. New political subjects form, he argues, as preexisting groups link and, through linking, enunciate new identities and interests.[42] Social processes and categories also can develop in this way. I have used this insight to trace the spectacular accumulation brought into being by the articulation of finance capital, franchise cronyism, and frontier culture. While each of these linked projects achieved only a moment of partial hegemony, this was also a moment of dramatic success. Soon after the events I have narrated, Indonesia's economy precipitously collapsed; the miracle nation was discredited as a site for investment, and the articulation fell apart.

Afterward, analysts scrambled to describe the difference between good and bad investments. They recognized that the Busang saga had contributed in a small way to the Indonesian crash. But they ignored or refused its allegorical quality: Bre-X offered a dramatic rendition of the promises and perils of the economic miracle attributed, in Indonesia and beyond, to globalization.[43]

As the century turns, the field of anthropology has taken on the challenge of freeing critical imaginations from the specter of neoliberal conquest – singular, universal, global. Attention to contingency and articulation can help us describe both the cultural specificity and the fragility of capitalist – and globalist – success stories. In this shifting heterogeneity there are new sources of hope, and, of course, new nightmares.

**Globalist projects
come into being
as
APHIDS**

APHIDS=
Articulations among
Partially **H**egemonic
Imagined **D**ifferent **S**cales

Figure 5.2 APHIDS. This acronym is both serious and a joke.

NOTES

1   This version of the much told story is taken from Douglas Goold and Andrew Willis, *The Bre-X Fraud* (Toronto: McClelland and Stewart, 1997).

2   Diane Francis. *Bre-X: The Inside Story* (Toronto: key Porter Books, 1997), p. 24. The $850/ounce price is from the *Privateer Gold Pages*, which reviews the recent history of government, interstate, and private uses and prices of gold.

3   Jennifer Wells, "King of Gold," *Maclean's*, December 9, 1996, 32–40.

4   Peter Newman, "Peter Munk: A Dreamer Who Became a King." *Maclean's* December 9, 1996, 42.

5   Peter Waldman and Jay Solomon, "Geologist's Death May Lie at Heart of Busang Mystery." *Wall Street Journal*. April 9, 1997, A10.

6   "Rumors Swirl around Bre-X," *Ottawa Citizen*, March 25, 1997, on-line version.

7   The autopsy results are discussed in the following news items: "Buried Body Not Geologist: Report," *Ottawa Citizen*. April 10, 1997, on-line version; Michael Platt, "Dead or Alive?" *Calgary Sun*. April 11, 1997. CANOE on-line version: "Foul Play Fears Haunt Geologist." *Calgary Sun*. April 19, 1997. CANOE on-line version: "Family Accepts Autopsy." *Calgary Sun*. April 21, 1997. CANOE on-line version; "ID Challenged." *Calgary Sun*, August 5, 1997, CANOE on-line version; "Print Identified as De Guzman's." *Calgary Sun*. April 24, 1997, CANOE on-line version. Bondan Winarno *Bre-X: Sebungkah emas di kaki pelangi* (Jakarta: Inspirasi Indonesia, 1997), pp. 134–5 discusses the theory that although de Guzman, wore false teeth, the corpse had natural teeth.

8   Nisid Hajari, "Is the Pot at the End of the Rainbow Empty?" *Time*. April 7, 1997. 149 (14). on-line version.

9   "Ultimate Betrayal: Bre-X Boss Says Pair Ruined Dream." *Calgary Sun*. October 12 1997. CANOE on-line version.

10 Joe Warmington, "Bre-X Takeover Claim." April 6, 1997, and "Bank on More Intrigue." April 8, 1997, *Calgary Sun*. CANOE on-line version.

11 Joe Warmington, "Yanks Waiting: Americans Ready to Gobble up Bre-X Shares." *Calgary Sun*. April 13, 1997. CANOE on-line version.

12 David Jala. "Frenzy Stuns Market." *Calgary Sun*. April 2, 1997, CANOE on-line version.

13 Strathcona Mineral Services conducted the independent technical audit. In the words of the report:

> We very much regret having to express the firm opinion that an economic gold deposit has not been identified in the Southeast zone of the Busang property, and is unlikely to be. We realize that the conclusions reached in this interim report will be a great disappointment to the many investors, employees, suppliers, and the joint-venture partners associated with Bre-X, to the Government of Indonesia, and to the mining industry elsewhere. However, the magnitude of the tampering with core samples that we believe has occurred and the resulting falsification of assay values at Busang, is of a scale and over a period of time and with a precision that, to our knowledge, is without precedent in the history of mining anywhere in the world. (Graham Farquarson [Strathcona Mineral Services]. "Busang Technical Audit: Interim Report." reproduced in *Gatra*, May 17, 1997: 27)

14 Ross McLeod gives considerable weight to the Bre-X affair in bringing on the Indonesian financial crisis by undermining investor confidence. He writes, "Perhaps the most significant recent event to crystallize attitudes on the part of the general public, the intellectual

and business elite, and the foreign investment community regarding the direction in which government had been heading was the so-called Busang saga." See "Indonesia's Crisis and Future Prospects," in Karl Jackson (ed.) *Asian Contagion: The causes and Consequences of a Financial crisis* (Boulder, Co: Westview Press), p. 215. In my view, although the Bre-X saga did not in itself shake the Indonesian economy very much, it *dramatized* issues of what came to be called, following Philippine precedent from the 1980s. "crony capitalism."

15   Jennifer Wells, "Greed, Graft, Gold." *Maclean's*, March 3, 1997, 40.

16   Anthony DePalma, "At End of a Miner's Rainbow, A Cloud of Confusion Lingers," *New York Times*, March 31, 1997, A1.

17   Jennifer Wells, "Rumble in the Jungle," *Maclean's*, February 3, 1997, 38–9: Bre-Xscam. com website, "The Bungle in the Jungle"; Michael Platt, "Rush Hour in the Jungle," *Calgary Sun*, May 23, 1997.

18   John Behar, "Jungle Fever," *Fortune*, June 9, 1997, 123.

19   Goold and Willis (*The Bre-X Fraud*, p. 207) write about the Canadian scene: "Because so many small investors held Bre-X stock, virtually everyone knew someone who had won or lost money. Their stories, often exaggerated, played out across the country. In this environment, any rumour had legs."

20   "On Silicon's popular net forum Techstox, Bre-X dominated for months. More than 4,000 new people a day were searching for Bre-X information, and more than 700 items were being posted about the company for all to read" (Francis, *Bre-X: The Inside Story*, p. 153).

21   David Zgodzinski, "Bre-X: The Battle between Bulls and Bears on SI," *Silicon Investor*, May 4, 1997.

22   In April 1967 Freeport Indonesia was granted a tax holiday, concessions on normal levies, exemption from royalties, freedom in the use of foreign personnel and goods, and exemption from the requirement for Indonesian equity. The terms were changed slightly in 1976, canceling the remaining eighteen months of the tax holiday and allowing the Indonesian government to purchase an 8.5 percent share (Hadi Soesastro and Budi Sudarsono, "Mineral and Energy Development in Indonesia," in *The Minerals Industries of ASEAN and Australia: Problems and Prospects*, ed. Bruce McKern and Praipol Koomsup [Sydney: Allen and Unwin, 1988], pp. 161–208).

23   More restrictive second-generation and less restrictive third-generation CoWs were introduced in 1968 and 1976, respectively, 1986–7 marked the Australian "gold rush" in Indonesia and introduced fourth-generation CoWs, with "one year of general survey ending with 25% relinquishment of concession area; three years of exploration with 75% relinquishment by the end of the fourth year; an Indonesian partner in the CoW; and equity divestment after five years of operation so that ideally after 10 years of production the local partner holds 51%" (Carolyn Marr, *Digging Deep: The Hidden Costs of Mining in Indonesia* [London: Down to Earth, 1988], p. 16). Fifth-generation contracts began in 1990, with tax incentives and low tariff property taxes. A 1992 law required foreign investors in frontier areas to reduce their equity shares to a maximum of 95 percent within five years and to 80 percent within twenty years (Marr, *Digging Deep*, p. 17). Sixth-generation CoWs, requiring environmental impact assessments, were offered in 1997 (Bondan Winarno, *Bre-X: Sebungkah emas di kaki pelangi*, p. 28).

24   Wells, "Greed, Graft, Gold." 42.

25   Dr. Soetaryo Sigit, ex-Director General of Mines, "Current Mining Developments in Indonesia," quoted in Marr, *Digging Deep*, p. 26.

26   Rachman Wiriosudarmo, quoted by Wells, "Greed, Graft, Gold," 41.

27   Goold and Willis, *The Bre-X Fraud*, pp. 99–100.

28   US ex-president Bush wrote Suharto to express his "highly favorable" impression of Barrick (Wells, "Rumble in the Jungle").

29   Wells, "Greed, Graft, and Gold."

30   By this time, it was clear to all the players that the Indonesian government was calling the shots. Placer Dome sent their bid directly to the president (John McBeth and Jay Solomon, "First Friend," *Far Eastern Economic Review*, no. 8, February 20, 1997: 52–4).

31   Hasan's perspective was developed in a context in which other Indonesians were calling for greater national control of Busang. Islamic leader Amien Rais, for example, argued that the gold "should be kept for our grandchildren in the 21st century" (cited in Francis, *Bre-X: The Inside Story*, p. 130). Bondan Winarno (*Bre-X: Sebungkah emas di kaki pelangi*, pp. 84–94) details nationalist claims.

32   Hasan's investments during this period are detailed in McBeth and Solomon, "First Friend."

33   Quoted in Jennifer Wells. "Gunning for Gold," *Maclean's*, February 17, 1997, 52.

34   Bre-X president David Walsh said he was settling with an arrangement that reflected "Indonesia's political, economic, and social environment" (Richard Borsuk, "Bre-X Minerals Defends Pact with Indonesia," *Wall Street Journal*. February 2, 1997, B3a).

35   Cited in Marr. *Digging Deep*. p. 71.

36   The history of Freeport-McMoRan is the subject of a forthcoming book tentatively titled *Corporate Power and Civil Society: The Story of Freeport-McMoRan at Home and Abroad* by journalist Robert Bryce and anthropologist Steven Feld. For Freeport's arrangements with the Indonesian government, see n. 22; Francis, *Bre-X: The Inside Story*, p. 129; and Goold and Willis. *The Bre-X Fraud*. pp. 113–14. Marr. *Digging Deep*, details Freeport's Irian operations, with special attention to the mine's history of environmental problems and human rights abuses.

37   Quoted in Behar. "Jungle Fever," 128.

38   "Ultimate Betrayal: Bre-X Boss Says Pair Ruined Dream," *Calgary Sun*. October 12, 1997, CANOE on-line version. David Walsh died of a stroke on June 4, 1998. He spent the last months of his life fighting class action suits and trying to clear his name (Sandra Rubin, "Obituary: David Walsh." *Financial Post*, June 5, 1998, CANOE on-line version).

39   The importance of small, popular investment in Bre-X highlights the importance of this national agenda. "At its peak in May 1996, 70 percent of Bre-X's 240 million shares were in the hands of individual investors" (Goold and Willis, *The Bre-X Fraud*, p. 239). This contrasts with a more ordinary Canadian company, which might have 30 percent of its shares owned by individuals. According to Goold and Willis (p. 105), in 1996 Bre-X had 13,000 shareholders, including pension funds and insurance companies. According to Francis (*Bre-X; The Inside Story*, p. 199), about 5 percent of Bre-X trading was from outside Canada and 90 percent of all Bre-X trading was conducted on the Toronto Stock Exchange (p. 197).

40   It is important to remember that it is possible to make a great deal of money out of speculation even if the product comes to nothing. Bre-X shareholders made money merely by selling their shares while the price was still high. The outspoken investors Greg and Kathy Chorny, for example, sold two thirds of their stock for C$40 million and lost a comparatively minor sum on remaining shares (Francis, *Bre-X; The Inside Story*, p. 196). At the end, smart investors made money by "short selling," that is, borrowing Bre-X shares from brokers, selling them, and returning them by buying them back at a lower price. Goold and Willis (*The Bre-X Fraud*, p. 221) report that 5.5 million Bre-X shares were sold short. Francis (*Bre-X: The Inside Story*, p. 203) reports that the investment bank Oppenheimer and Co. made C$100 million shorting Bre-X stock. Meanwhile,

other firms and individuals, including Quebec's public pension fund and the Ontario Teachers Pension Plan Board, lost major amounts of money (Goold and Willis, *The Bre-X Fraud*, p. 248).

41   David Harvey, *The Condition of Postmodernity* (Oxford: Blackwell, 1989).

42   Stuart Hall, "On Postmodernism and Articulation: An Interview with Stuart Hall," edited by Lawrence Grossberg, in *Stuart Hall: Critical Dialogues in Cultural Studies*. ed. David Morley and Kuan-Hsing Chen (London: Routledge, 1996), pp. 131–50.

43   Other Bre-X allegories have been suggested – for example, that greed blinds everyone's eyes (Goold and Willis. *The Bre-X Fraud*, p. 267), or that the international flow of money means business must deal with "exotic and troublesome regimes" (Francis, *Bre-X: The Inside Story*, p. 232). Outside of Canada, the allegorical reading arose that this was just the way of Canadian business, where stock exchanges are a "regulatory Wild West" (quotation attributed to the US mass media in Bondan Winarno, *Bre-X: Sebungkah emas di kaki pelangi*, p. 208). My reading refuses the distinction between the seeing and the blind to point to the money being made even in a scam. I also emphasize the exotic and troublesome nature of capitalism itself – both in and beyond Canada and Indonesia.

Chapter 6

Physics and Finance: S-Terms and Modern Finance as a Topic for Science Studies

Donald MacKenzie

Some time in the summer of 1994 (the exact date is not known), the Intel Corporation made a disturbing discovery. Its new Pentium Processor contained a flaw in the design of its divide unit. The flaw was a small one: in the worst case, it affected the fourth significant decimal digit in the result of a division, and the pattern of binary digits that triggered it was extremely rare, occurring only once in 9 billion random divides. Nevertheless, the Pentium chip was rapidly becoming the dominant processor in personal computing, and Intel had to take the divide bug seriously. Two of its scientists, H. P. Sharangpani and M. L. Barton (1994), took on the task of discovering where divisions matter. Given the pervasiveness of the personal computer, their task amounted to an inquiry into the arithmetical foundations of high modernity. In what areas of modern life, they had in effect to ask, is the use of arithmetic and specifically division intensive enough that a small, rare error could have serious effects? They quickly ruled out applications of personal computers such as electronic mail or word processing, in which the divide bug would never be encountered, and also found that spreadsheet users would be affected by it at a rate much lower than those of physical failures of the processor or of memory chips. In only two areas did divisions really matter. One, of course, was engineering and scientific applications, but even there, in most cases, "meaningful inaccuracies in the end-result will only be seen once in about 1,000 years" (ibid: 16). The other, according to Sharangpani and Barton, was "financial engineering" (p. 28). Traditional, standard financial calculations "such as present values, annuities, depreciations" (p. 24) would be little affected. But divisions did matter, Sharangpani and Barton found, in the valuation of options and "complex securities." These financial applications were so divide intensive that circumstances could be envisaged in which the flaw might be encountered as often as once a week. In the single most pessimistic sentence in a generally reassuring report, Sharangpani and Barton wrote, "The problem may manifest itself significantly in those programs for valuing the most complicated financial instruments" (p. 27).

The techniques of financial engineering that were vulnerable to the divide bug were all new: the oldest of them, the Black-Scholes option pricing equation, was published only in 1973. But within little more than two decades these techniques had blossomed to become among the most important calculations performed in the high-modern world.[1] Quite independently of the Intel inquiry, the finance theorist Mark Rubinstein wrote, also in 1994, that the Black-Scholes equation, along with its extensions, was "perhaps...the most widely used formula, with embedded probabilities, in human history" (p. 772).

Yet the mathematicized world of finance theory and financial engineering is almost terra incognita to science studies. There is one significant study of the emergence of modern finance theory by a sociologist of science: Whitley (1986). His article is in part a criticism of the theory: "The oft-repeated claims to be doing 'positive' scientific research in this area reproduce elementary philosophical errors promulgated by many economists" (p. 160). Nevertheless, his study offers a useful historical review and an interesting contrast between the success of finance theory and the relative failure of "operations research" (the other most highly mathematicized specialism within business schools) in providing relevant training and a professional identity for practitioners while sustaining a coherent program of theoretical and empirical work. Aside from Whitley's article and a historical discussion of the concept of "efficient markets" by Walter (1996), the only historical treatments of modern finance theory are by practitioners (especially Bernstein 1992, 1996; Bouleau 1998) rather than by historians of science. Although historians of economics have raised relevant matters – in the light of my title, Mirowski (1989) is particularly pertinent – they too are only just beginning work on finance theory (see Mehrling 1999). There has been sporadic interest by general sociologists (especially Baker 1984 and Abolafia 1996) in financial markets, but sociologists of science are only just awakening to the interest of finance theory. A. Javier Izquierdo Martín, Vincent-Antonin Lépinay, Yuval Millo, and Fabian Muniesa have begun research in the area, but little of their work has so far been published, although see Izquierdo (1998, forthcoming) and Muniesa (2000).[2] Perhaps the most impressive work to emerge (at least in part) from the sociology of science is the detailed ethnographic study of trading and traders used by Knon-Cetina and Brügger to introduce a phenomenological perspective into economic sociology (Knorr-Cetina and Brügger forthcoming; Brügger and Knorr-Cetina forthcoming; Brügger 2000); this work, however, has so far said little about markets as a place not just of social interaction but also of the application of mathematical theory.[3]

My purpose in this chapter is to argue for an end to the neglect of finance theory and financial engineering by science studies and to encourage the intensification of the current awakening of interest. If science studies is to fulfil its promise, it must grapple with the myriad ways in which high modernity is a scientific and a technological society: finance theory and its practical applications to the financial markets are among the most important such ways. Financial markets must play a central role in any sensible account of high modernity and of globalization; if high modernity is a "risk society" (Beck 1992), then financial risk – the management of which is a key high-modern industry – is a crucial aspect. Yet the wider sociological profession has a tendency not to open scientific and technological "black boxes": for the limited extent to which even the best general sociologists do this when writing about the financial markets, see Boden (2000) and Castells (2000). The central claim of science studies is that modernity cannot be understood properly unless its black boxes are opened; the study of finance theory and of financial engineering offers a potentially crucial test for this claim.

An improved understanding of high modernity via the application of science studies to finance theory and financial engineering is an immodest aspiration. It is, therefore, necessary immediately to emphasize the limited contribution offered by this chapter. My aim here is threefold. First, I draw attention briefly (and largely in the hope that others will take up these topics) to three demarcations. One is the boundary of economics and the gradual move of financial markets from being a peripheral and even suspect topic to becoming a central one. Another is the distinction between private and public knowledge, the subject of crucial boundary work (see Gieryn 1999). A final demarcation is that between legitimate trading and gambling.

Second, I shall explore Barry Barnes' (1983) contrast between N-type (natural kind) and S-type (social kind) terms. My argument, which parallels, albeit in different terminology, what Michel Callon (1998) has argued for economics more generally, is that finance is a domain of S-type terms. Finance theory is a science and financial engineering is a technology, but there are differences between finance and a natural science such as physics, at least as the latter is ordinarily conceived, and between financial engineering and engineering's more "physical" disciplines. These differences, I argue, are usefully captured by the notion of S-type terms.

The characteristic of S-type terms is the existence of feedback loops between the terms and their referents. My third aim, therefore, is a preliminary examination of some of those loops via a general discussion (which suggests that these loops are typically performative; i.e., they increase the validity of finance theory's assumptions).

Finance Theory and the Financial Markets

Before I turn to those three main tasks, however, the reader may find some background information helpful. Given the long-established nature and importance of stock markets, particularly in the United States and Great Britain, it is not surprising that much of early finance theory (in the 1950s and 1960s) focused on understanding the behavior of stock prices and the principles of rational selection of portfolios of stock. Key was the development of the "random walk" model of stock prices, which, in the words of Fama (1965:34)

> says that the future path of the price level of a security is no more predictable than the path of a series of cumulated random numbers. In statistical terms the theory says that successive price changes are independent, identically distributed random variables. Most simply this implies that the series of price changes has no memory, that is, the past cannot be used to predict the future in any meaningful way.

Tightly linked to the random walk model and to its generalization, the martingale,[4] or "fair game" model, was the "efficient market hypothesis," which asserted that mature capital markets, such as those of the United States, were "efficient" in the sense that prices within them "always 'fully reflect' available information" (Fama 1970:383). (The link between the two ideas is that if the current price of a stock reflects all currently available information, then its future price movements will be shaped only by new information, which by virtue of its being new, is by definition unpredictable.) Alongside these developments was the theory of "portfolio selection," originally developed by Harry Markowitz (1952). Markowitz's student, William Sharpe, along with John Lintner and Jack Treynor, developed what became known as the Capital Asset Pricing Model, in which the key determinant of the expected rate of return on a stock is the stock's β, the covariance of its price with the overall level of the market (see, for example, Sharpe 1964). The key issue was diversification: the idiosyncratic risk of a particular stock could be diversified away but not the generic risk of overall market fluctuations. Rational investors would therefore require higher expected returns to hold stocks with a high β, a high correlation with the overall market, than low-β stocks.[5]

The emergence of modern finance theory was part of a revolution that had a major impact on an older, largely pre-theoretical, and often explicitly relationship-based world of finance. Recalls investment manager and participant historian Peter L. Bernstein (1992),

> Before the revolution, [the individual clients of] our family-oriented business would come to us and say, "Here is my capital. Take care of me." As long as their losses were limited when the market fell, and as long as their portfolios rose as the market was rising, they had few complaints. They came to us and stayed with us because we understood their problems and the myriad kinds of contingent liabilities that all individuals must face. They recognized that we shared the delicate texture of their views about risk. We joked that we were nothing more than social workers to the rich.

To Bernstein and others, the academic theory of financial markets that had begun to develop in the 1950s and 1960s seemed "alien and unappealing...abstract and difficult to understand...It seemed...to demean my profession as I was practicing it" (ibid: 10, 13). Initially, for example, advocates of the random walk model were "greeted in some Wall Street quarters with as much enthusiasm as Saddam Hussein addressing a meeting of the B'nai Brith" (Malkiel 1996: 159). Gradually, however, the random walk model, portfolio selection, and the Capital Asset Pricing Model were adopted by a wide variety of practitioners (see Bernstein 1992: 233–306). The most telling indicator of practitioners' acceptance of finance theory was the emergence in the 1970s of "tracker funds," in which the effort to beat the market by picking promising stocks was abandoned in favor of holding all the stocks making up a market index such as the Standard and Poor's (S&P) 500.

Much more rapid in its adoption by practitioners was the theory of option pricing developed by Fischer Black and Myron Scholes (1973) and Robert C. Merton (1973). An option is a contract that gives the right but not the obligation to buy ("call") or sell ("put") an asset such as a block of shares at a given price on, or up to, a given future date. Black, Scholes, and Merton showed that if returns on the underlying asset followed a continuous-time random walk, then the pattern of returns on an option could be replicated exactly by a continuously adjusted portfolio of the asset and government bonds and/or cash. In an efficient market, therefore, the price of an option had to be the cost of the replicating portfolio. If their prices diverged, an arbitrage opportunity existed: in other words, there was risk-free profit to be made by buying the cheaper and selling the dearer of the two. As arbitrageurs did this, their purchases would raise the lower price and their sales would lower the higher price: arbitrage would eliminate any difference between the price of an option and the cost of the replicating portfolio.[6] At the start of the 1970s, options were "specialized and relatively unimportant financial securities" (Merton 1973: 141): the market in them was limited in volume and ad hoc. It amounted to less than one-thousandth of the volume of the New York Stock Exchange, and

> when an investor wishes to buy a contract he contacts his broker who contacts a member of the Put and Call Dealers Association who acts as a clearing agent, seldom buying or selling options for his own account. These dealers will contact or be contacted by other brokers who sell options for clients. (Ibid: 141)

Because of the time-consuming and complicated nature of these arrangements, "large orders are difficult if not impossible to fill and even small orders may take time to fill" (Black and Scholes 1973: 409, 416).

What gave the work of Black, Scholes, and R. C. Merton its practical significance were two factors. The Chicago Board of Trade, originally an agricultural commodities exchange, spun off the Chicago Board Options Exchange, which opened in April 1973 in what had been the smoking lounge of the Board of Trade, "a limited space that had been converted for the purpose. Soon traders were standing on counters because there was no room on the floor" (Bernstein 1992: 225–6). Such was the success of the new exchange that the Board of Trade soon had to build the Options Exchange its own trading floor, in delightful metaphor suspended above the floor in which trading in futures on physical commodities took place:

> The old trading floor of the Board of Trade occupied an enormous space, about five stories high, with architecture and decoration appropriate to the importance of the commodities traded there. A new floor was suspended between the old floor and the ceiling, and in 1976 that floor of 30,000 square feet became the home of the Chicago Board Options Exchange. (Ibid)[7]

The work of Black, Scholes, and R. C. Merton quickly became an essential resource for traders on the floor of the Options Exchange. All three were involved in supplying market participants with theoretical prices; "soon traders were valuing options on the floor of the [Chicago Board Options] exchange, punching half a dozen numbers into electronic calculators hard-wired with the formula" (Passell 1997: D4). Use of a theoretically based valuation formula rather than simple intuition had intangible as well as practical benefits: "option dealers had newfound respect" (Falloon 1998: 227). The second factor lending significance to Black, Scholes, and R. C. Merton's work was that their underlying methodology, along with the sophisticated mathematics of continuous-time stochastic analysis (e.g., see Itô 1987) introduced into finance theory by R. C. Merton, could be applied not just to the call options originally traded on the Chicago Board Options Exchange, but also to a wide range of financial derivative products (a "derivative" is a product the value of which depends on the price of another asset). To value a derivative and to hedge its risks, suggested Black, Scholes, and R. C. Merton, find the replicating portfolio of more basic assets. By the 1990s the resultant techniques were wide ranging and formidably sophisticated (e.g., see Wilmott 1998 or Hull 2000).

The elaboration of the techniques of Black, Scholes, and R. C. Merton interrelated closely with the development of financial derivatives markets. The Chicago Board Options Exchange was the second modern derivatives market: in the previous year, 1972, the Chicago Mercantile Exchange, like the Board of Trade originally an agricultural commodities exchange, set up the International Monetary Market, trading in currency futures. Soon the Board of Trade itself was trading financial derivatives, and the great success of the Chicago markets attracted international replicants. The London International Financial Futures Exchange (LIFFE), closely modeled on the Chicago markets, began trading in September 1982. As late as 1986, US exchanges still hosted 90 percent of organized derivatives trading, but since then LIFFE, the Frankfurt-based Deutsche Terminbörse (DTB, now EUREX), the French Marché à Terme des Instruments Financiers (MATIF), the remarkably successful Brazilian BM & F exchange, and a variety of other exchanges saw the "American system" of finance develop momentum overseas.[8] By 1996, greater than 60 percent of world derivative-exchange trading was taking place outside the United States (Steinherr 1998: 170–3). Alongside these organized exchanges, a huge market also developed in "over-the-counter" derivatives, traded directly between institutions. Perhaps the most important of these, because they had no exchange-traded equivalent, were swaps, contracts to exchange two income streams, such as fixed-rate interest and floating-rate interest on the same notional principal sum. By the end of the 1990s, trading volumes on the world's organized derivatives exchanges and over-the-counter market were huge. The total notional amount of derivative contracts outstanding worldwide at the end of June 1999 was $98.7 trillion.[9] Those who have difficulty imagining the magnitude of this figure might note that it is equivalent to some $16,000 for every person on earth. Although "notional amounts" overstate the economic significance of derivative contracts,[10] the derivatives markets are nevertheless of great economic importance.

Demarcations

Three demarcations are key to the development of modern finance theory and financial markets. The first is the boundary of economics as a discipline. For most of the twentieth century the stock market was a research topic of dubious legitimacy within economics. Famously, John Maynard Keynes ([1936] 1964) scathingly compared stock-market investment to a newspaper competition in which contestants win prizes if their judgment of the attractiveness of faces matches the average judgment of all contestants: "we devote our intelligences to anticipating what average opinion expects the average opinion to be" (p. 156).[11] Nor was the great ideological opponent of Keynesianism, Milton Friedman, initially disposed to accept as "economics" Markowitz's development of a theory of the optimum allocation of investments, telling Markowitz at the beginning of his PhD defense, "Harry, I don't see anything wrong with the math here, but I have a problem. This isn't a dissertation in economics, and we can't give you a PhD in economics for a dissertation that's not economics."[12] The eventually Nobel prize–winning paper on option pricing by

Fischer Black and Myron Scholes (1973) was initially rejected, without refereeing, by the *Journal of Political Economy* on the grounds that it was "too specialized" (Black 1989: 7). Finance was and is a specialism predominantly within business schools, not economics departments, and "at most universities, the business school and economics faculties barely greeted each other on the street," comments Peter Bernstein (1992: 46). Chicago and MIT were among the few exceptions and became the key sites for the development of modern finance theory. Even as finance has gained legitimacy within economics, with the leading finance theorists winning Nobel Prizes, some traces of division remain. Merton H. Miller (1998: 1), one of those Nobel laureates, wrote that "the huge body of scholarly research in finance over the last forty years falls naturally into two main streams . . . the Business School approach to finance and the Economics Department approach."[13]

With the stock market a marginal topic in economics, it is not surprising that the origins of the random walk model lie outside the subject. It was first put forward by the French mathematician Louis Bachelier (1900), one of Henri Poincaré's students (Cootner 1964: 17–78), and then independently by the statisticians Holbrook Working (1934) and Maurice Kendall (1953). Later developments came from statistician Harry Roberts (1959) and astrophysicist M. F. M. Osborne (1959). The first economist to contribute centrally to the topic was Paul Samuelson, who began work on it in the mid-1950s, although Sidney Alexander (1961) (see Bernstein 1992: 107) also had long-standing interests in the topic. What Roberts (1959: 3) called "the traditional academic suspicion about the stock market as an object of scholarly research" may well have been caused in part by the dubious legitimacy of stock markets themselves. They were implicated in the Great Depression and, after the latter, had for decades been seen as risky investments. "After twenty-three years, stock prices were still one-third below their 1929 peak," but it "was not just the disaster that turned people off; it was also the association of the market with wrong-doing by people in high places" (Bernstein 1992: 42). From the 1950s onward, however, the legitimacy of the stock market grew, and large quantities of data on stock price movements became available, as did the necessary computer power for their analysis. Although the institutional separation of much of finance theory from economics departments remained, finance gradually moved to become a central topic, indeed arguably one of the "crown jewels" of neoclassical economics.

A second demarcation, this time concerning the markets themselves rather than the theoretical analysis of them, has been important to their recovery of legitimacy: the distinction between public and private knowledge. That insider trading ought, from an economic point of view, to be illegal is far from clear and has been the subject of much debate. It is perfectly reasonable to argue, for example, that with insider trading, "stock prices better reflect information" (Leland 1992: 859) and markets are in that sense more efficient: insider knowledge, after all, is likely to be fresh knowledge and more reliable than market rumor. Nevertheless, the sense that a "fair" market in stocks requires a ban on insider trading gained hold in the United States and has gradually spread to other jurisdictions, with, in consequence, delicate "boundary work" (Gieryn 1999) being necessary to maintain and police the distinction between private and public knowledge (see Boyle 1996: ch. 8).

A third crucial demarcation is between legitimate trading and gambling. In 1936 Keynes could write, "It is usually agreed that casinos should, in the public interest,

be inaccessible and expensive. And perhaps the same is true of Stock Exchanges"
(Keynes [1936] 1964: 159). That a financial market is not a casino is key to the
former's claim to legitimacy, but more is at stake in the maintenance of the boundary
than cultural acceptability alone. Legal prohibitions on gambling have been strong
in most parts of the United States, and in Britain, although gambling is permitted,
gambling debts are not legally enforceable. It is thus critical to the practical feasibil-
ity of financial markets that their activities be distinguishable legally from gambling.
Significant initial obstacles to the emergence of financial derivatives markets were
caused by the way in which the distinction between gambling and trading in
futures[14] on physical commodities had traditionally been drawn. The Chicago
Board of Trade, for example, had for many years used Illinois law prohibiting
gambling in its battles against the incursion of "bucket shops" into the futures
market. The key distinction the board sought to have enforced legally was between
the contracts it traded, which could be settled by delivery of a commodity such as
grain, and those, typical of the bucket shops, that could be settled only in cash. The
former were legitimate; the latter, the board argued, were simply wagers on price
movements and so constituted gambling and were illegal. The distinction was a
contested one: the futures-trading activities of the board itself were on occasion
ruled to be gambling despite the possibility of settlement by physical delivery, and
decisions of lower courts had to be appealed – successfully – to the US Supreme
Court (Ferris 1988: ch. 8).[15] To take the possibility of physical delivery rather than
mere cash settlement as a defining characteristic of a legitimate futures trade became
problematic as the Chicago markets moved from agricultural commodities to financial ones. The issue has gradually been resolved in both the United States and United
Kingdom by carefully framed legislation – legal boundary work, one might call it –
legitimizing contracts that have to be settled in cash, but initially, it was a significant
constraint on and shaper of the development of financial markets. In the late 1960s
leading figures in the Chicago Board of Trade, then still a physical commodities
exchange, sought to expand its activities into the financial sphere by developing a
market in futures on the Dow Jones Industrial Average. However, because an index
is an abstraction, such a contract could be settled only in cash, and the leading
securities lawyer they consulted, Milton Cohen, advised them that the idea was
"likely to run afoul of . . . Illinois State gambling laws" (Falloon 1998: 210). The idea
of an options exchange was settled on as likely to be less problematic legally: a
contract for an option on a particular stock could, at least in principle, be settled by
delivery of stock certificates, not just in cash.

As the legal demarcation between trading and gambling was redrawn, barriers to
cash settlement disappeared, and futures and options contracts on abstract quantities such as indexes became unproblematic: indeed, a general characteristic of the
development of the financial markets has been a growth in the degree of abstraction
of the assets being traded. In wider cultural terms, however, the issue of the
boundary between gambling and trading has not entirely vanished. It has been
reopened in recent years above all by the development in the United States of day
trading, in which amateur traders seek to make quick profits (usually on the stock
market, especially NASDAQ, rather than in derivative markets) by buying and
selling assets within short periods of time. Day trading has been made possible by
declining transaction costs and the possibility of executing transactions electronic-

ally: a key development was NASDAQ's Electronic Small Order Execution System, introduced in 1985. There is anecdotal evidence to suggest that many day traders are "momentum traders" who hope to spot market "trends," buying as prices start to rise and selling as they start to fall. In the words of the General Accounting Office (2000: 9), "As a result of their trading strategies, day traders are not considered to be investors. They do not pay close attention to such factors, as price/earnings ratio or investing and earnings models, which investors are taught to follow." The issue of the status of day trading was dramatically highlighted in July 1999, when a mentally disturbed day trader in Atlanta, Georgia, who had run up large losses, killed his family and people at two day-trading firms.

N-Type and S-Type Terms

The various demarcations and boundary work surrounding finance theory and the financial markets indicate a variety of ways in which science-studies approaches could be applied in this area. Another, arguably deeper, reason why finance theory and financial engineering are of interest can best be elucidated by Barry Barnes' (1983) distinction between N-type terms and S-type terms. An N-type, or "natural kind," term is one in which the application of the term to a particular entity can be thought of as a process in which the empirical properties of the entity are judged against a pattern, and the term is applied or not applied according to the perceived closeness of fit. Consider, for example, the term *leaf*. An individual's socialization, what he or she "has been shown of leaves, and told of them, is presumably crucial to an understanding" of what he or she "takes to be leaves." But the "empirical characteristics of a putative leaf are then sufficient to decide whether or not it matches the pattern" (ibid: 525). In contrast, with an S-type, or "social kind," the process of concept application is "performative" (Austin 1962). The simplest, most obviously performative case of an S-term is the situation in which a particular individual is "entitled to *pronounce* any entity an S, or any entity of kind A an S, and thereby *make* it an S" (Barnes 1983: 526). A minister of religion, for example, has the right in appropriate circumstances to *make* a man a "husband," and a woman a "wife," simply by pronouncing them to be "husband" and "wife." To say, to hand signal, or to type "sold" or its equivalent in a financial market is to make a sale (see Brügger and Knorr-Cetina: forthcoming). That something is referred to as an "S" is what makes it an S (Barnes 1983: 525–6).

Of course, there will in many cases not be a single accepted authority nor a clearcut procedure by which S-type references are made to "stick," and then the elementary form of "performative utterance" (Austin 1962: 6) turns into the full complexity of sociology. Consider, for example, even a simple case of whether a social actor is powerful: "John is the leader of the gang. He is the leader because the members know him to be the leader, and act routinely on the basis of what they know" (Barnes 1988: 49). He can be powerful without there being an authority to designate him as such; his power and members' beliefs about his power are mutually constitutive. His power may be doubted, questioned, wax, and wane. The key point, however, is that in both the simplest and the most complicated and contested situations, S-terms have self-referential and self-validating (or occasionally self-invalidating) aspects. As Austin (1962: 6) puts it, "To name the ship *is* to say (in the appropriate circumstances) the words 'I name, &c.'. When I say, before the registrar or altar, &c., 'I do,' I am not reporting on a marriage: I am indulging in it." If "I name this ship," or "I do," or "sold" describe anything, they describe themselves, and by uttering them, one makes them true: they are self-referring, self-validating speech acts. Again, naming, marriage, and selling are simple cases. In more complex cases, the loops of self-reference and self-validation are more complicated: "One must typically expect a tangle of diverse and conflicting usages... [a] spaghetti junction" (Barnes 1988: 526). But if we are dealing with an S-term, the loops are there, creating, and perhaps undermining, its validity.

The notions of N-terms and S-terms are ideal types, and the distinction does not correspond to the demarcation between the natural sciences and other forms of knowledge. The past three decades of the social studies of science can be summarized as the discovery of the S-aspects of apparent N-terms, but those who doubt that the natural sciences contain S-terms need consider only measurement. The property of being the standard meter, for example, is an S-term: a bar, or collection of other physical phenomena, is the standard meter because the relevant authorities have designated it the standard meter. Arguably, our field's enthusiasm for discovering the S-aspects of terms led to underemphasis on their N-aspects, perhaps because it is often thought, quite wrongly, that if a concept were an N-term it would somehow escape sociological analysis (see Barnes, Bloor, and Henry (1996) and Latour (1999) for – radically different – approaches to the sociological analysis of scientific terms that encompass their N-aspects). This, however, is not a debate that need detain us here, because the issue I wish to raise is most easily conceptualized by setting aside complications and focusing on the key point: that S-terms are constituted by loops of self-reference and self-validation. As Hacking (1992: 190) puts it, some "human kinds" (a notion roughly equivalent to S-terms) "differ from those routinely thought of as natural kinds. The classification of people and their acts can influence people and what they do directly. And I believe this is true only of people... Human kinds have feedback, a looping effect."

For many practical purposes, an individual can often ignore S-terms' loops of self-reference and self-validation and, thus, in effect, treat S-terms as if they were N-terms. If the gang is big enough and the loops stable enough, that a particular individual is the leader can seem a fact of the same type as the fact that the individual has brown eyes. In current Euro-American societies, we have for some time been able to be confident that a piece of paper treated as money today will also be treated as money tomorrow. The self-validating inference loop that constitutes money has become so taken for granted as to be invisible. The patterns of belief that constitute money become evident only when those beliefs become precarious in times of social collapse or hyperinflation. Because of the frequent invisibility of S-loops and because of the dominance of what one might call the epistemology of N-terms, influential positions within sociological theory have frequently ignored the loops of self-reference and self-validation; the Durkheimian treatment of "social facts" is an example. One of the few exceptions (at least within mainstream sociology and prior to the 1960s) is a classic paper by Robert K. Merton (1949) on "the self-fulfilling prophecy." Merton's paper begins with "a sociological parable": the failure of a bank. A rumor that a bank is unsound causes depositors to withdraw their money; others observe these withdrawals and seek to withdraw in their turn, and eventually the rumor of the bank's insolvency makes itself true. Merton goes on to diagnose the role of self-fulfilling prophecy in a variety of aspects of social life, in particular "ethnic and racial prejudices." Whites often excluded blacks from trade unions on the grounds that they were strike-breakers and prepared "to take jobs at less than prevailing wages." By excluding them from unions, they "invited a series of consequences which indeed made it difficult if not impossible" for many blacks to avoid being strike-breakers and taking jobs at low wages (ibid: 182).

R. K. Merton's analysis of self-fulfilling prophecies is insightful and, in its diagnosis of the foundations of ethnic prejudice, impassioned and ahead of its time. Nevertheless, as Barnes (1988: 537–8) points out, it does not go quite far enough. Implicit, and sometimes explicit, in Merton's analysis is an emphasis on the pathological aspect of self-fulfilling prophecy: a solvent bank is made insolvent by a false rumor. Self-fulfilling prophecy can indeed be a "vicious circle in society" (Merton 1949: 193), but as Barnes points out, the creation of a sound bank is as much a self-fulfilling prophecy as the creation of an insolvent one. "The presence of deposits makes the 'bank' a safer one, one better able to attract deposits. Further deposits flow in. Growing convictions of security are the basis for yet more convictions of security" (Barnes 1983: 538). What Merton (1949: 180) calls "belief in the validity of the interlocking system of economic promises men live by" is as much a self-fulfilling prophecy as belief in its invalidity. The virtuous circles of social life are as much self-fulfilling prophecies as the vicious ones. Indeed, as Barnes points out (1983: 538; see also Barnes 1988: 1995), "the tendency for reinforcing systems [of S-type inferences] to persist" makes intelligible "the development and stabilization of custom" and provides a potential solution to the problem of social order quite different from, say, the classical Parsonian solution that has been undermined by ethnomethodological critique (see Heritage 1984).

Finance, S-Terms, and Efficient Markets

That finance is a domain of S-terms is in one sense self-evident: it is a domain of money, and money is quintessentially an S-term. Going beyond that banal observation, however, requires investigation of the potential feedback loops between finance theory and its object of study, and that is a task that has seldom been attempted (the major exception is in the work of Merton 1992, discussed below). Most discussion of finance theory is framed, implicitly, by N-epistemology. Consider, for example, the efficient market hypothesis. Even the most sophisticated contributions to the debate about its validity (such as Shleifer 2000) typically frame the question as one of the degree of fit between markets as empirical entities and the hypothesis as pattern. That markets are historically changing entities and that their characteristics may be influenced by the pervasiveness of belief in the hypothesis are not usually considered. All sorts of interesting lines of empirical enquiry are thereby blocked. For example, how are the feedback loops between the hypothesis and the markets to be characterized? Day traders' momentum trading, for instance, is predicated implicitly on disbelief in the random walk and martingale hypotheses (I know of no study of what proportion of traders have actually heard of the hypotheses), because the belief that one can spot trends implies that how a stock has reached its current price helps predict the future movements of that price. If enough day traders believe in trend spotting and momentum trading and if they form a large enough part of the market (by 1999, day trading was estimated to form 10 to 15 percent of the overall volume of trading on NASDAQ),[16] then their trading activities may actually create trends: the purchases of those who think they have spotted a rising trend may cause prices to continue to rise. If that were the case,[17] it would constitute positive feedback (disbelief in the efficient market hypothesis creating phenomena at variance with it). Nevertheless, it seems plausible that the predominant pattern is negative feedback – that the search for pricing anomalies from which to profit causes those anomalies to disappear; in other words, that the activities of those who believe the market not to be efficient help make it efficient.[18] It is interesting to speculate about the opposite situation – would markets that almost all participants believed to be efficient (and in which, for example, they simply invested in index funds) actually become inefficient?[19] – but belief in the efficient market hypothesis is not yet sufficiently widespread to make this other than a speculation.

The Performativity of Finance Theory

One of the few commentators on the financial markets to emphasize their "S-ness," which he calls "reflexivity," is the financier George Soros (1998). "In the social sciences," writes Soros, "thinking forms part of the subject matter whereas the natural sciences deal with phenomena that occur independently of what anybody thinks" (p. x). Soros suggests an incompatibility between an emphasis on reflexivity and "prevailing theories about efficient markets and rational expectations" (p. 41). That, however, need not be the case. As we have seen, the feedback loops between belief or disbelief in the efficient market hypothesis, and actions in the financial markets probably tend to eliminate phenomena at variance with the hypothesis. More generally, it seems perfectly plausible that S-ness of finance theory is predominantly performative.

Consider, for example, Black-Scholes-Merton option pricing theory.[20] The centerpiece of this is the famous Black-Scholes equation for pricing an option. Let V be the value of an option, S the price of the underlying asset, σ the volatility (standard deviation) of the asset price, r the risk-free rate of interest, and t time. Black, Scholes, and Merton showed that

$$\frac{\partial V}{\partial t} + \frac{1}{2}\sigma^2 S^2 \frac{\partial^2 V}{\partial S^2} + rS\frac{\partial V}{\partial S} - rV = 0$$

The boundary conditions and, hence, solution are given by the nature of the option. This "looks" like physics. The Black-Scholes equation is a form of the heat equation

$$\frac{\partial u}{\partial t} = \frac{\partial^2 u}{\partial x^2}$$

where u is temperature, t is time, and x is a spatial variable (distance along a bar, say): the transformation needed to make the Black-Scholes equation take this form is given in Black and Scholes (1973: 643). The underlying model of asset price movements is

$$dS = \mu S dt + \sigma S dZ$$

where μ is the "drift" of the asset price and Z is a variable whose increments over successive time periods are independent and whose increment between times t_{i-1} and t_i follows a normal distribution with mean zero and variance $t_i - t_{i-1}$. Again, that is familiar to physicists: it is the standard stochastic model of Brownian motion, of the movements of a tiny particle subject to minute, random collisions. Indeed, the mathematical similarity of physics and finance has led to a significant migration in recent years of physicists into the latter field.

Finance, however, is not physics: the balance of N-type and S-type terms in the two fields is different. The dominance of N-type epistemology makes this remark sound like a criticism of finance theory, but it is not. Consider the assumptions underpinning the standard derivation of the Black-Scholes option pricing equation, which are typical of much of modern mathematical finance theory. These include not just the Brownian-motion assumption about asset price movements but also, for example, (1) the assumption that the composition of the replicating portfolio can be revised continuously without incurring transaction costs in doing so (in other words, that in any given time interval, however small, an asset sale or purchase can be made at the prevailing market price); (2) the assumption of the possibility of borrowing or lending indefinitely large amounts of money at the risk-free rate of interest; and (3) the presence of arbitrageurs able to exploit, and thus eliminate, any discrepancy between the prices of an option and of its replicating portfolio.

At the start of the 1970s, when Black, Scholes, and Merton were producing their analyses of option pricing, the empirical validity of these assumptions was at best dubious. Stock market transactions, for example, were expensive; they could be relatively slow to implement. Most market participants could borrow only limited amounts and at significantly higher rates of interest than they could earn by lending; the extent to which arbitrageurs were present is uncertain, and high transaction costs and the sporadic, ad hoc nature of the option market meant arbitrageurs would have encountered significant difficulties implementing arbitrage strategies. When Black and Scholes (1972) analyzed the options market as it then existed, they found that the writers of options "obtain favorable prices" and their purchasers unfavorable ones, as judged by the model, while "there tends to be a systematic mispricing of options [as against the model] as a function of the variance of returns on the stock." Options on "high variance securities tend to be underpriced, and . . . contracts on low variance securities tend to be overpriced" (pp. 413–15). These discrepancies persisted, Black and Scholes pointed out, even though in principle they offered opportunities for profitable arbitrage. High transaction costs meant that apparent arbitrage opportunities did not really exist, and trading at prices other than those suggested by the model was therefore stable (pp. 409, 416).

The opening in April 1973 of the Chicago Board Options Exchange began to change this situation. Initially, prices on the exchange still differed sharply from Black-Scholes-Merton values. The key difference, however, was that arbitrage opportunities were identified – the model served as "a benchmark for arbitrage" (Steinherr 1998: 28) – and in a continuous, liquid market, in which participants had access to substantial amounts of capital, arbitrage opportunities were actually exploited.[21] Although the detailed history of the use of the Black-Scholes-Merton model on the Chicago Board Options Exchange remains to be investigated, it appears that the key arbitrage was "spreading": if, according to the model, one option was overpriced and another on the same stock was underpriced, arbitrageurs would sell the overpriced and buy the underpriced option. In the early months of the exchange, arbitrage profits were available from spreading (Galai 1977), and pursuit of them would have drawn prices toward their Black-Scholes values. The model was also incorporated into the risk-management procedures of the firms providing traders' capital.[22] Indeed, the model seems soon to have been used directly to set prices. Fischer Black (1975) produced and sold to market participants sheets showing the Black-Scholes values of options for different stock prices, volatilities, times to expiry, and exercise prices. One option theorist, Mark Rubinstein, recalls starting to trade options on the Pacific Stock Exchange in 1976 and being struck by the exact correspondence of the posted price of the options he was trading with Black's sheets.[23] "Traders now use the formula and its variants extensively," wrote Black (1989). "They use it so much that market prices are usually close to formula values even in situations where there should be a large difference: situations, for example, where a cash takeover is likely to end the life of the option or warrant" (p. 8).

Over the past three decades, then, the typical assumptions of finance theory have become empirically more realistic. Some of the processes involved have nothing directly to do with finance theory. The development of information and communication technologies has increased the speed with which trades can be executed and greatly reduced their cost. The free-market political climate of the 1980s' United States and United Kingdom played its part, particularly the "Big Bang" deregulation of the City of London by Mrs. Thatcher's government, which opened up the city's cartels to competition and thus greatly lowered transaction costs. The origins of other processes increasing the veridicality of finance theory's assumptions are simply unclear. The key innovations of "repo" and "reverse repo" were found in the US bond market in the 1980s but are now found in the UK market as well. A repo, or repurchase agreement, involves organization A borrowing money from organization B to buy bonds that are held by B as collateral for the loan. When A sells the bonds, it repurchases them from B. Reverse repo involves A borrowing bonds from B, selling them, delivering the proceeds to B, and eventually A repurchasing the bonds and returning them. The institutions of repo and reverse repo make it possible to borrow or to lend huge amounts at very close to the risk-free rate of interest, so making a key assumption of finance theory far more realistic, but they have yet to attract their historian, so their origins remain unclear.[24]

Crucially, however, finance theory itself has played an important role in its assumptions becoming more realistic. The growth of arbitrage, for example, was greatly encouraged by the huge success of the bond arbitrage desk headed by John Meriwether at the investment bank Salomon Brothers. Developing close links with academic finance theory (and hiring, for instance, Robert C. Merton's student Eric Rosenfeld), Meriwether and his team contributed enormously to Salomon's profits by identifying and exploiting arbitrage opportunities.[25] Their success was quickly noted by others, and both the number of arbitrageurs and the capital available to them grew rapidly. Because arbitrage is the key finance-theory mechanism by which price discrepancies are eliminated, this is a clear instance of the theory's performative aspect. More generally, Black-Scholes-Merton option pricing theory and its many developments facilitate the introduction of new derivative products by showing how they can be priced and how their risks can be hedged. The new products increase the completeness of the markets (in the sense that insurance against a greater range of risks can be purchased), and the construction and adjustment of replicating portfolios to hedge the risks of the new derivative products increase the liquidity of the markets in the underlying assets.

As noted above, nearly all those writing about finance theory discuss it in N-terms and fail to notice these performative, S-aspects. That the main exception, Robert C. Merton, should be the son of Robert K. Merton, theorist of the self-fulfilling prophecy, is surely not coincidental. As noted above, Robert C. Merton's key technical innovation was the introduction to finance theory of the rigorous mathematics of stochastic processes in continuous time: Itô calculus permitted Merton to replace Black and Scholes' original derivation of the option pricing equation, based on the Capital Asset Pricing Model, with a different derivation, not dependent on this model but based on the demonstration that the hedge offered by the replicating portfolio is exact, if the latter is adjusted continuously. Merton is sharply aware that the mathematics of continuous time is only an approximation to the reality of the markets: even in 2000, there is still a finite time interval between the decision to revise a portfolio and the implementation of the revision. But this and other assumptions of finance theory are becoming more realistic, argues Merton: the "financial-innovation spiral" of new products, new markets, greater completeness, increased volume, and lower transaction costs pushes toward "the theoretically limiting case of zero marginal transaction costs and dynamically complete markets" (Mason et al. 1995: 19). As the spiral evolves, argues Merton (1992: 470), "reality will eventually imitate theory."

Conclusion

Much of what is said here is speculative. Nevertheless, I hope that I have convinced the reader that modern finance offers intriguing material for science studies research. It is among the most thoroughly scientized parts of high modernity and, although I have not emphasized the point here, also among the most technologized. A modern financial market, such as the Chicago markets, is a sociotechnical system: the pit remains a place of the body, in which voices and hand signals still make deals, but surrounding the pit and increasingly encroaching into its domain are information and communication technologies. In other markets the pit has already vanished, leaving a system that is technological throughout. The finance theory deployed in these sociotechnical systems is among high modernity's most sophisticated mathematical products and, if Intel's analysis of the implications of the divide bug is correct, arithmetically the most intensive among them.

What adds to finance theory's interest to science studies, I have argued, is that the balance of N-terms and S-terms within it is different from, say, physics. S-terms and S-loops, present in all sciences, play a particularly constitutive role in finance theory. In a culture saturated with the prejudice that S-terms are epistemologically inferior to N-terms, that sounds like a criticism, but it is not. Physics too has its world-making and not merely world-describing aspects, as Hacking (1983) and Galison (1997) have shown us, but this is even more the case for finance theory. That finance theory makes a world rather than just describes a world adds a wider significance to its study. It is performative (as Callon 1998 would predict) but not uniformly and straightforwardly performative. The S-loops of the financial markets are complex, and as yet incompletely understood; theory's interaction with them can have unexpected effects, just as any form of social action can have unanticipated consequences (Merton 1936). Finance theory's world making exists in tension with forces undermining and resisting that world. The consequent dialectic is at the core of the economic history of high modernity; that, above all, makes finance a compelling object for science studies.

NOTES

1   The Pentium divide bug is, of course, also of interest from quite a different point of view: that of design faults in computer systems. It is treated from that perspective in MacKenzie (forthcoming, chapter 7). "High modernity" is Anthony Giddens' (1990) term.

2   The collection in which the latter appears (Kalthoff, Rottenburg, and Wagener 2000) contains a variety of interesting material.

3   The main empirical focus of this work is the foreign exchange spot market, which is much less mathematicized than, for example, the options market.

4   A martingale is a stochastic process in which the expected value of a variable, conditional upon its current value, is its current value. In a game of chance that is a martingale, the expected value of a player's net gain is thus zero, and hence, the game is "fair." Financial markets are not held to be martingales in an absolute sense but to be martingales with respect to some other processes, which may, for example, include an expected general upward drift of prices. For an accessible account of "equivalent martingale measures," see Hull (2000: 498–522).

5   This exceedingly brief survey is, of course, nothing like comprehensive: it omits, for example, the important contributions of Franco Modigliani and Merton H. Miller (see Modigliani and Miller 1958; Miller and Modigliani 1961).

6   This is a brief summary of the outcome of what was actually a complex historical development involving several converging lines of work, to which I hope to return in a future paper.

7   The origins of the Chicago Board Options Exchange are described in Falloon (1998: 207–27). Again, I hope to return to the history of the Chicago Board Options Exchange in a future paper, co-authored with Yuval Millo.

8   Steinherr (1998: ch. 2) refers to "the American model of finance"; I prefer "system" because of the historical echo of the nineteenth-century "American system of manufactures" (see Hounshell 1984).

9   Data from the Bank for International Settlements: www.bis.org.

10   Swaps, for example, are valued by the notional principal sum, although this is not in fact ever exchanged and serves only to determine the magnitude of the income streams that are exchanged.

11   To the modern game theorist, this is perhaps a suggestive formulation. Nevertheless, I do not think that Keynes, writing in 1936, had this in mind.

12   Harry Markowitz, personal communication to Peter L. Bernstein, quoted in Bernstein (1992: 60).

13 I am grateful to Professor Miller (1998) for a copy of this unpublished typescript, which continues, "The characteristic Business School approach tends to be what we would call in our jargon 'micro normative.' That is, a decision maker, be it an individual investor or a corporate manager, is seen as maximizing some objective function, be it utility, expected return or shareholder value, taking the prices of securities in the market as given. In a Business School, after all, that's what you're supposed to be doing: teaching your charges how to make better decisions. To someone trained in the classical traditions of economics, however, the famous dictum of the great Alfred Marshall stands out: 'it is not the business of the economist to tell the brewer how to make beer.' The characteristic Economics Department approach thus is not micro but macro normative. Their models assume a world of micro optimizers and deduce from that how the market prices, which the micro optimizers take as given, actually evolve" (pp. 1–2).

14 A "future" is an exchange-traded contract for the purchase and sale of an asset at a given price on a given future date.

15 I owe this reference to Yuval Millo.

16 General Accounting Office (2000: 2).

17 I know of no academic studies of the effectiveness of momentum trading in current markets, but in early 2000, market participants told me that funds following momentum strategies had recently been achieving significant excess returns.

18 For example, empirical studies of the efficient market hypothesis found what were claimed to be excess returns to small stocks, an effect that was concentrated in the month of January. Since 1985, however, "both the small firm effect and the January effect seem to have disappeared" (Shleifer 2000: 19). That might quite conceivably be because of efforts to exploit them.

19 Bernstein (1992: 134–5) believes they would.

20 There is an accessible account of this in Wilmott (1998), from which the exposition and notation used here are largely borrowed.

21 Mathew Gladstein, personal communication to author, New York, November 15, 1999.

22 Myron Scholes, personal communication to author, San Francisco, June 15, 2000.

23 Mark Rubinstein, personal communication to author, Berkeley, California, June 12, 2000. I am grateful to Professor Rubinstein for sample copies of Black's sheets and other unpublished material.

24 There is a brief discussion in Dunbar (2000: 104–5).

25 Dunbar (2000); Perold (1999: A2).

REFERENCES

Abolafia, M. Y. 1996. *Making markets: Opportunism and Restraint on Wall Street.* Cambridge, MA: Harvard University Press.

Alexander, S. S. 1961. "Price movements in speculative markets: Trends or random walks." *Industrial Management Review* 2 (2): 7–26.

Austin, J. L. 1962. *How To Do Things With Words.* Oxford: Clarendon Press.

Bachelier, L. 1900. "Théorie de la spéculation." *Annales de l'Ecole Normale Supérieure*, third series 17: 22–86.

Baker, W. E. 1984. "The social structure of a national securities market." *American Journal of Sociology* 89: 775–811.

Barnes, B. 1983. "Social life as bootstrapped induction." *Sociology* 17: 524–45.

—— 1988. *The Nature of Power.* Cambridge: Polity Press.

—— 1995. *The Elements of Social Theory.* London: UCL Press.

Barnes, B., D. Bloor, and J. Henry. 1996. *Scientific Knowledge: A Sociological Analysis*. London: Athlone Press.

Beck, U. 1992. *Risk Society: Towards a New Modernity*. London: Sage.

Bernstein, P. L. 1992. *Capital Ideas: The Improbable Origins of Modern Wall Street*. New York: Free Press.

—— 1996. *Against the Gods: The Remarkable Story of Risk*. New York: Wiley.

Black, F. 1975. "The option service: An introduction." Unpublished typescript.

—— 1989. "How we came up with the option formula." *Journal of Portfolio Management* Winter 4–8.

Black, F. and M. Scholes. 1972. "The valuation of option contracts and a test of market efficiency." *Journal of Finance* 27: 399–417.

—— 1973. "The pricing of options and corporate liabilities." *Journal of Political Economy* 81: 637–54.

Boden, D. 2000. "Worlds in action: Information, instantaneity and global futures trading." In *The Risk Society and Beyond: Critical Issues for Social Theory*, edited by U. Beck, B. Adam, and J. van Loon. London: Sage.

Booth, T. 1998. "Why Costas Kaplanis had to sell." *Institutional Investor*, October: 12–16.

Bouleau, N. 1998. *Martingales et marchés financiers*. Paris: Jacob.

Boyle, J. 1996. *Shamans, Software, and Spleens: Law and the Construction of the Information Society*. Cambridge, MA: Harvard University Press.

Brügger, U. 2000. "Speculating: Work in financial markets." In *Ökonomie und Gesellschaft Jahrbuch 16. Facts and Figures: Economic Representations and Practices*, edited by H. Kalthoff, R. Rottenburg, and H. Wagener, 229–55. Marburg, Germany: Metropolis.

Brügger, U. and K. Knorr-Cetina. Forthcoming. "Global microstructures: The interaction practices of financial markets." *American Journal of Sociology*.

Callon, M., ed. 1998. *The Laws of the Markets*. Oxford: Blackwell.

Castells, M. 2000. "Information technology and global capitalism." In *On the Edge*, edited by W. Hutton and A. Giddens. London: Cape.

Cootner, P., ed. 1964. *The Random Character of Stock Market Prices*. Cambridge, MA: MIT Press.

Dunbar, N. 2000. *Inventing Money: The Story of Long-Term Capital Management and the Legends Behind It*. Chichester: Wiley.

Falloon, W. D. 1998. *Market Maker: A Sesquicentennial Look at the Chicago Board of Trade*. Chicago, IL: Board of Trade.

Fama, E. F. 1965. "The behavior of stock-market prices." *Journal of Business* 38: 34–105.

—— 1970. "Efficient capital markets: A review of theory and empirical work." *Journal of Finance* 25: 383–417.

Ferris, W. G. 1988. *The Grain Traders: The Story of the Chicago Board of Trade*. East Lansing: Michigan State University Press.

Galai, D. 1977. "Tests of market efficiency of the Chicago Board Options Exchange." *Journal of Business* 50: 167–97.

Galison, P. 1997. *Image and Logic: A Material Culture of Microphysics*. Chicago, IL: University of Chicago Press.

General Accounting Office. 2000. *Securities Operations: Day Trading Requires Continued Oversight*. Washington, DC: General Accounting Office, GAO/GGD-00-61.

Giddens, A. 1990. *The Consequences of Modernity*. Cambridge: Polity Press.

Gieryn, T. F. 1999. *Cultural Boundaries of Science: Credibility on the Line*. Chicago, IL: University of Chicago Press.

Hacking, I. 1983. *Representing and Intervening: Introductory Topics in the Philosophy of Natural Science*. Cambridge: Cambridge University Press.

—— 1992. "World-making by kind-making: Child abuse for example." In *How Classification Works*, edited by M. Douglas and D. Hull. Edinburgh: Edinburgh University Press.

Heritage, J. 1984. *Garfinkel and Ethnomethodology*. Cambridge: Polity Press.

Hounshell, D. A. 1984. *From the American System to Mass Production, 1800–1932: The Development of Manufacturing Technology in the United States*. Baltimore, MD: Johns Hopkins University Press.

Hull, J. C. 2000. *Options, Futures, & Other Derivatives*, 4th edn. Upper Saddle River, NJ: Prentice-Hall.

Itô, K. 1987. *Kiyosi Itô: Selected Papers*. Edited by D. W. Stroock and S. R. S. Varadhan. New York: Springer.

Izquierdo, M. A. and A. Javier. 1998. "El declive de los grandes números: Benoit Mandelbrot y la estadística social." *Empiria: Revista de Metodología de Ciencias Sociales* 1: 51–84.

—— Forthcoming. "Reliability at risk: The supervision of financial models as a case study for reflexive economic sociology." *European Societies*, special issue on the new economic sociology in Europe.

Kalthoff, H., R. Rottenburg, and H. Wagener, eds. 2000. *Ökonomie und Gesellschaft, Jahrbuch 16. Facts and Figures: Economic Representations and Practices*. Marburg, Germany: Metropolis.

Kendall, M. G. 1953. "The analysis of time series, Part 1: Prices." *Journal of the Royal Statistical Society* 96: 11–25.

Keynes, J. M. [1936] 1964. *The General Theory of Employment, Interest and Money*. New York: Harcourt Brace.

Knorr-Cetina, K. and U. Brügger. Forthcoming. "The market as an object of attachment: Exploring postsocial relations in financial markets." *Canadian Journal of Sociology* 25.

Latour, B. 1999. *Pandora's Hope: Essays on the Reality of Science Studies*. Cambridge, MA: Harvard University Press.

Leland, H. E. 1992. "Insider trading: Should it be prohibited?" *Journal of Political Economy* 100: 859–87.

Lowenstein, R. 2000. *When Genius failed: The Rise and Fall of Long-Term Capital Management*. New York: Random House.

MacKenzie, D. 2000. "Fear in the markets." *London Review of Books*, April 13: 31–2.

—— Forthcoming. *Mechanizing Proof: Computing, Risk and Trust*. Cambridge, MA: MIT Press.

Malkiel, B. G. 1996. *A Random Walk Down Wall Street*. New York: Norton.

Markowitz, H. 1952. "Portfolio selection." *Journal of Finance* 7: 77–91.

Mason, S. P., R. C. Merton, A. F. Perold, and P. Tufano. 1995. *Cases in Financial Engineering: Applied Studies of Financial Innovation*. Englewood Cliffs, NJ: Prentice-Hall.

Mehrling, P. 1999. "The vision of Hyman P. Minsky." *Journal of Economic Behavior & Organization* 39: 129–58. Meriwether's sequel adopts similar style. 1999. *Wall Street Journal* December 17: C1, C19.

Merton, R. C. 1973. "Theory of rational option pricing." *Bell Journal of Economics and Management Science* 4: 141–83.

—— 1992. *Continuous-Time Finance*. Cambridge, MA: Blackwell.

Merton, R. K. 1936. "The unanticipated consequences of purposive social action." *American Sociological Review* 1: 894–904.

—— 1949. "The self-fulfilling prophecy." In *Social Theory and Social Structure*, 179–95. New York: Free Press.

Miller, M. H. 1998. "The history of finance: An eye-witness account." Unpublished typescript.

Miller, M. H. and F. Modigliani. 1961. "Dividend policy, growth and the valuation of shares." *Journal of Business* 34: 411–33.

Mirowski, P. 1989. *More Heat than Light. Economics as Social Physics: Physics as Nature's Economics*. Cambridge: Cambridge University Press.

Modigliani, F. and M. H. Miller. 1958. "The cost of capital, corporation finance and the theory of investment." *American Economic Review* 48: 261–97.

Muniesa, F. 2000. "Performing prices: The case of price discovery automation in the financial markets." In *Ökonomie und Gesellschaft, Jahrbuch 16. Facts and Figures: Economic Representations and Practices*, edited by H. Kalthoff, R. Rottenburg, and H. Wagener, 289–312. Marburg, Germany: Metropolis.

Osborne, M. F. M. 1959. "Brownian motion in the stock market." *Operations Research* 7: 145–73.

Passell, P. 1997. "2 get Nobel for a formula at the heart of options trading." *New York Times*, October 15: D1, D4.

Perold, A. 1999. "Long-Term Capital Management, L. P." Boston, MA: Harvard Business School Publishing, N9-200-007 to N9-200-009.

Roberts, H. V. 1959. "Stock market 'patterns' and financial analysis: Methodological suggestions." *Journal of Finance* 14: 1–10.

Rubinstein, M. 1994. "Implied binomial trees." *Journal of Finance* 49: 71–818.

Scholes, M. S. 2000. "Crisis and risk management." *American Economic Review* 90: 17–21.

Sharangpani, H. P. and M. L. Barton. 1994. *Statistical Analysis of Floating Point Flaw in the Pentium™ Processor (1994)*. N.p.: Intel Corporation, 30 November.

Sharpe, W. F. 1964. "Capital asset prices: A theory of market equilibrium under conditions of risk." *Journal of Finance* 19: 425–42.

Shleifer, A. 2000. *Inefficient Markets: An Introduction to Behavioral Finance*. Oxford: Oxford University Press.

Soros, G. 1998. *The Crisis of Global Capitalism: Open Society Endangered*. London: Little, Brown.

Steinherr, A. 1998. *Derivatives: The Wild Beast of Finance*. Chichester: Wiley.

Walter, C. 1996. "Une histoire du concept d'efficience sur les marchés financiers." *Annales HSS* 4 (July–Aug.): 873–905.

Whitley, R. 1986. "The rise of modern finance theory: Its characteristics as a scientific field and connections to the changing structure of capital markets." *Research in the History of Economic Thought and Methodology* 4: 147–78.

Wilmott, P. 1998. *Derivatives: The Theory and Practice of Financial Engineering*. Chichester: Wiley.

Working, H. 1934. "A random difference series for use in the analysis of time series." *Journal of the American Statistical Association* 29: 11–24.

Chapter 7

Traders' Engagement with Markets: A Postsocial Relationship

Karin Knorr Cetina and Urs Bruegger

The Market as an Object of Attachment

Current market theories conceptualize the market essentially in three ways: (1) as a price-setting mechanism consistent with equilibrium conditions, where individual decision makers already in possession of the relevant information adjust their behavior and output to a price at which supplies are exhausted and demands are satisfied (Marshall 1936: 270; Frances et al. 1991: 6; Becker 1976: 8); (2) as a mode of coordination that contrasts with hierarchies and networks: while rules and authority constitute the central coordinating mechanism of hierarchies, and trust and cooperation that of networks, the mechanism operating in markets is price competition (Coase 1937; Williamson 1975; Thompson et al. 1991; Frances et al. 1991: 15); (3) as a form of action (exchange) embedded in social relations (Granovetter 1985; Swedberg 1997: 162). The first concept corresponds to the neoclassical approach in economics, the second exemplifies the transaction cost approach, and the third corresponds to the new economic sociology, whose premise is that social networks based on kinship, friendship, and trust influence economic transactions and sustain economic relations (Lie 1997: 349; Carruthers and Uzzi 2000: 489). The field as a whole adopts a disaggregate stance which emphasizes market units, their decision-making processes and relationships, and the market technique of achieving coordination. This micro-economic and "deconstructive" epistemology has the virtue of permitting the deployment of well-developed action models and of network analyses that converge with the embeddedness assumption. It also has drawbacks, however. Economists' rational action models and sociologists' network analyses tend to tell us more about their particular focus (networks and utility maximization) than about actually existing markets and the specific relationships they breed.[1] They also ignore the aggregate dimension of some markets; the ways, that is, in which information flows and trading transactions aggregate within technological environments to form complex wholes that are perceived as lifeforms in their own right by participants.

In this chapter we draw attention to a particular market variant, the foreign exchange market, and one of its specific characteristics, namely that it is a global market entirely exteriorized and embodied on computer screens. With an average daily turnover of $1.5 trillion, it has also been the world's largest and fastest-growing financial market over the last decade (Bank for International Settlements 1998: 1–3). Unlike other financial markets, the foreign exchange market is not organized mainly in centralized exchanges but derives predominantly from inter-dealer transactions among dealers situated on the trading floors of global investment banks. Traders are the major operators in international currency markets, and they are interlinked by high technology communication in real time, handing on their "books", when accounts are not closed in the evening, from time zone to time zone. Traders in interbank currency dealing do not broker deals but trade for their bank's account via electronic broking systems and direct dealer-to-dealer contact disengaged from local settings. As collective disembodied systems generated entirely in a symbolic space, these markets epitomize contemporary high technology professional culture.

They also exemplify, we maintain, what have been called "postsocial relationships" elsewhere (Knorr Cetina 1997, 2001). The goal of this chapter is to illustrate and theorize such relationships which, we think, obtain between traders and the market on screen. Since these markets are exteriorized and concentrated on screen, traders not only participate in these markets, they relate to them as a complex "other" with which they are strongly, even obsessively, engaged. The term "post-social relationships" refers to new kinds of bonds such as those constructed between humans and objects. Nonhuman objects have an increased presence and relevance in contemporary life. This presence can be glossed from the recent bodies of literature devoted to them: examples are the literature on information and communication technologies (e.g., Turkle 1995; Heim 1993), on the return of "nature" and the demands of the natural environment (e.g., Sheldrake 1991; Serres 1990), on consumer objects (e.g., Baudrillard 1996; Ritzer 1999; Miller 1994), markets (e.g., Smith 1981, 1999; White 1981; Baker 1984; Abolafia 1996), and scientific and technological things (Callon 1986; Latour 1988, 1993; Pickering 1995; Rheinberger 1997; Haraway 1991). Many authors are aware of the fact that the influx of some of these objects and object-worlds into the social world has brought profound change to the way we work and spend our spare time. But it may also bring profound change to the structure of relationships, and call for the rethinking of sociality along lines that include objects in the concept of social relations. Such forms of binding self and other are what we call "postsocial"; they are postsocial in that they refer to circumstances where interaction, space, and even communication appear to mean something different from the accustomed understanding of these terms, though we are only beginning to analyze these meanings (an example is computer-mediated interactions in virtual space – e.g., Stone 1996: 36ff.; Hornsby 1998; Jones 1998). But they are also postsocial in that they step into the place of more traditional human bonds, which become a sort of legacy environment for postsocial relations. One distinctive characteristic of contemporary life might be that perhaps for the first time in recent history it appears unclear whether, for individuals, other persons are indeed the most fascinating part of their environment – the part they are most responsive to and devote most attention to (see also Turkle 1995). In regard to relations with objects the idea of a postsocial form rests on the intuition that individuals in some areas relate to (some) objects not only as "doers" and "accomplishers," of things within an agency framework but also as experiencing, feeling, reflexive, and remembering beings – as bearers of the sort of experiences we tend to reserve for the sphere of intersubjective relationships.

For traders, the most fascinating part of their environment is the market – with which they appear to be excessively engaged not only during working hours but also during evenings and weekends. Traders sometimes describe this intense engagement in interviews and conversations (Schwager 1992), but this literature fails to account for it. In this chapter we offer a framework for conceptualizing traders' engagement with the market as an instance of the wider phenomenon of postsocial relationships. A crucial component of this conception which we want to discuss up front is the computer "screen", by which we also mean the dealing and information systems it embodies. We take the screen to be an appresentational device that enhances and routinizes such relationships. We have borrowed the term "appresentation" from Husserl (1960: §49–54) to suggest that the screen brings a geographically dispersed and invisible market close to participants, rendering it interactionally or response-present. Before the introduction of the screen, interbank currency markets were network markets: transactions were conducted in the bilateral mold via the phone or telex, and most of the traders' time was spent finding out "where the market was" (see below). Any coordination that did come about was limited to those moments and parties involved in particular connections. The market nested in territorial space; it lay hidden in a transnational banking network of institutions that did not share the same information. The screen exteriorized, assembled, and aggregated these dispersed exchange relations. After the introduction of screens the market became fully available and identified as a separate entity in its own right for the first time – with prices, interests, and the relevant information all visually indicated on screen. The market on screen is a "whole" market and a global presence; it subdivides into different information feeds and dealing systems, but these are configured to form a global picture framed by the boundaries of the screen, which also serves as a medium for transactions.

The argument we make is that the exteriorization, assemblage, and contextualization of "the market" on screen construe the market, which at one time was dispersed among isolated and specific human connections, as an external "life form" to which traders relate in sometimes adversarial forms of bonding while at the same time remaining able to "enter" the life form and to become part of it. In other words, the transfer of the market onto the screen has meant that traders are now able to simultaneously position themselves inside the market in the sense of becoming players in its overlapping networks, and to relate to the market on screen as an exteriorized other, a sort of master-being that observes all transactions and includes their contextual conditions and motivations. Thus the screen is a crucial element in our discussion, a means of "objectification" and a precondition for a relational regime. More needs to be said, however, about this relational regime. The question which lies at the core of the notion of a postsocial relationship as one that encompasses engagements with non-human others is, how can we dissociate the notion of a relationship, and indeed of sociality, somewhat from its fixation on human groups? In answering this question we will start with the notion of the mirror image self, which accommodates such relations with non-human others; we will distinguish this notion from the I-you-me system derived from Mead, Freud, and others, which places the self more strongly in the context of society than the first notion does. We claim that several developments in contemporary social transitions make it plausible to consider the mirror image conception of the self as better suited to characterizing self-feelings and self-problems in contemporary Western societies than the I-you-me system. Linking this argument to a notion of postsocial relationships, we maintain that traders' engagement with markets is based on a match between the self as a sequence of wantings and an unfolding object that provides for these wants through the lacks it displays. In this account, the "hooking" power of the market derives not only from the embodiment on screen that we have emphasized so far, but also from the dynamic and incompleteness markets display. When considering the market as a life form, traders make explicit the temporal and unfolding character of real markets.

An important element of our account of postsocial selves and relationships is the notion of lack or wanting. We maintain that in contemporary society the lack-wanting system as an interpersonal dynamic is becoming institutionally elaborated and implemented in several contexts, among them that of trading. Studies which focus on the psychological or interactional dimensions of a phenomenon often exclude from the work discussions of macro-level factors, and vice versa, thereby maintaining a strict separation between the micro- and the macro-context. In this research we draw upon psychological models capable, we believe, of enriching sociological concepts of relationships, while at the same time examining the institutional translation of the dynamic of the self on trading floors and locating the discussion in the framework of transformation theories concerned with changes in the social order.

Putting the Market on Screen

The domain in which we want to test the ideas about postsocial object relations in this chapter is that of foreign exchange markets as exemplified by interbank currency trading in large, global investment banks. The data presented in this study derive from participant observation and interviews on the trading floor of a Swiss bank that has continuously been ranked as one of the top five or seven most profitable banks worldwide by reported foreign exchange trading revenues over recent years (*FX Week*, 1998).[2] The bank's global presence involved, in 1999, a staff of 14,500 working in 60 offices in 30 countries on 6 continents. The foreign exchange markets studied have a specific global form, which is not based on the penetration of countries or individual behavior but instead rests on the establishment of bridgehead centers of institutional trading in the financial hubs of the three major time zones: in New York, London, Tokyo, and, since the group to which the investment bank belongs is Swiss, in Zurich. Institutional investors in these regions are linked up with the global bank through "open" or immediate access phone lines. The bank's relevant centers and facilities are also connected through elaborate "intranets" – internal computer linkages that extend across the globe. The intranets include electronic information and brokerage services provided exclusively for institutional customers by firms such as Reuters, Bloomberg, and Telerate. Foreign exchange deals through these channels start in the order of several hundred thousand dollars per transaction, and reach up to a hundred million dollars and more. The deals are made by traders, financial managers, fund managers, central bankers, and others who want to avert or hedge against adverse currency moves, who want to profit from expected currency moves, or who need currency to help them enter or exit transnational investments.

About 200 traders engaged in stock, bond, and currency trading worked on the floor in the global investment bank observed. Currency traders sit at "desks" consisting of a row of several (6–12) single desks. They have a range of technology at their disposal, including a "voice broker" (the voice of a broker coming out of an intercom system continuously shouting prices and demanding deals) and a screen-like phone. Most conspicuous, however, are the up to five computer screens confronting each trader, displaying the market and serving to conduct trading. When traders arrive in the morning they strap themselves to their seats, figuratively speaking, they bring up their screens, and from then on their eyes will be glued to that screen, their visual regard captured by it even when they talk or shout to each other, their bodies and the screen world melting together in what appears to be a total immersion in the action in which they are taking part. The market composes itself in these produced-and-analyzed displays to which traders are attached. "It" exists only on screen, where it has a distinctive written surface or what one might call a gestural "face-in-action."

What does the "it" consist of? The central feature of the displays and the center-piece of the market for traders are the dealing prices displayed on the "electronic broker" (EBS), a special screen and automated dealing service that sorts orders according to best bids and offers. It displays prices for currency pairs (mainly dollars against other currencies such as the Swiss franc or the euro), deals being possible at these prices. Traders frequently deal through the electronic broker, which has largely replaced the "voice broker" (real life broker); the price action there is also central to the prices they make, as "market makers", for callers approaching them on the "Reuters dealing", another special screen (and computer network) through which they trade. On the Reuters dealing, deals are concluded in and through "conversa-tions" conducted on screen. These resemble e-mail message exchanges for which the Reuters dealing is also used in and between dealing conversations. On a further screen traders watch prices contributed by different banks worldwide; these prices are merely indicative, they express interest rather than being dealing prices as such. Traders may also watch their own current position in the market (e.g., their being long or short on particular currencies), the history of deals made over recent periods, and their overall account balances (profits and losses over relevant periods) on this or another workstation at their disposal. Finally, the screens provide headline news, economic commentary and interpretations which traders watch. An important source of information which also appears on these screens, but is closer to traders' actual dealing in terms of the specificity, speed, and currentness of the information, are internal bulletin boards on which participants input information (for a more detailed discussion of "screen work", see Knorr Cetina and Bruegger 2000).

The thickly layered screens provide the core of the market and most of the context. They come as close as one can get to delivering a stand-alone world that includes "everything" (see below) for its existence and continuation: at the center the actual dealing prices and incoming trading conversations, in a second circle the indicative prices, account information, and some news (depending on the current market story), and further headlines and commentaries providing a third layer of information. As suggested before, the market was not always on screen. Screens began to "appresent" (Husserl 1960: §49–54) a dispersed and dissociated matrix of interactions and interests only in 1973, when the British news provider firm Reuters first launched the computerized foreign exchange system "Monitor", which became the basis for this electronic market. By using the term "appresentation", which we have explained above, we also mean to emphasize that the screens do not, in their core elements, *r*epresent a reality "out there", but are constitutive of it. The screens appresented the market only gradually, however, first providing only indicative prices and news. Actual dealing remained extraneous to screen activities and was conducted over the phone and telex until 1981, when dealing services also developed by Reuters went live (Read 1992: 283 ff.). Yet from the beginning, Monitor radically changed one aspect of dealing: it answered the question as to *where the market was*, i.e., what the prices of currencies were and who might be wanting to deal. Prices originally differed from place to place and had to be ascertained afresh for every deal through long and painful processes of phoning up banks and waiting for lines when going through operators for overseas calls. After the introduction of Monitor, prices suddenly became available globally to everyone connected, in a market that functioned between countries and between continents. To reiterate: before the market-on-screen, there existed dispersed networks of trading parties entertaining business relationships. After the introduction of the computerized screen quotes, "the market" acquired a presence and profile of its own, and its own temporal and other properties.

It needs to be emphasized that we are not speaking metaphorically when we point out that the market-on-screen has a presence and profile in its own right. The screen encapsulates the market in the sense that traders must conduct the vast majority of their deals on screen, if they are to remain in the market (they may revert to the telephone as a way of finding out prices and linking up with customers in cases of prolonged computer failure). The market on screen also has its own self-assembling and -integrating features (for example, best prices worldwide are selected and displayed), its own calculating routines (for example, accounts are maintained and prices may be calculated), and self-historicizing properties (for example, price histories are displayed, and a multiplicity of other histories can be called up) – all of which turn it into a being with its own identity and profile. The electronic programs and circuits which underlie this screen world assemble and implement on one platform the previously dispersed activities of different agents; of brokers and bookkeepers, of market-makers (traders) and analysts, of researchers and news agents. In a sense, *the screen is a building site on which a whole economic and epistemological world is erected*. It is not simply a "medium" for the transmission of other interactions.

The Market as a Deep and Liquid Object

Consider, for a moment, this epistemological world. The screens present, we said, information and knowledge: bulletin boards display traders' and analysts' world-wide confidential observations of market players' activities and any other events pertinent to dealing, while news and commentary provided by firms such as Reuters,

Bloomberg, Telerate, and CNN represent information. Knowledge is also implicated in the deals traders make – for example, market moves by "smart money" (important traders and institutions capable of moving large amounts of money) tell participants where the market might be going and what is "on its mind" (see also Smith 1981). What is perhaps less obvious is that the prices, the centerpiece of what a market is for traders, are also "carriers of knowledge". Already in the 1940s, the economist Hayek argued that the economy consists of "dispersed bits of incomplete and frequently contradictory knowledge which all the separate individuals possess", and that "only the price mechanism can collect and aggregate such knowledge" (Hayek 1945: 524). What Hayek pointed out, and what today's "efficient market theory" spells out, is that information is contained in prices; for example, an interest rate change in the US may be reflected in the price of the dollar immediately, and in fact before it is officially announced, as market participants anticipate the rate change. Traders embody their own knowledge in the prices they make and they also "read" prices, trying to derive knowledge from them.

Markets-on-screen, then, prices, news items, and deals included, are knowledge constructs or epistemic objects. Why is this important? Because it points to the essential elusiveness of markets, to their incompleteness of being, which is transposed into a continuous knowledge project for participants. From a theoretical point of view, the defining characteristic of the market as an object is its *lack of "objectivity" and completeness of being*, its *non-identity with itself*. Markets are always in the process of being materially defined, they continually acquire new properties and change the ones they have. The speed with which this happens may be called, borrowing a notion from participants, the ontological *liquidity* of markets. This liquidity corresponds to participants' economic behavior: a dispersed mass of participants continues to act, events continue to occur, policies take hold and have effects. Markets are objects of observation and analysis because they change continually; and while they are clearly defined in terms of prices, news, relevant economic indicators, and so on at any given moment, they are ill-defined with respect to the direction they will take at the very next moment and in the less immediate future, which is what counts in speculation. They also cannot be reduced to known groups of players. Traders differentiate between "their networks" of contacts, which they may consider as a subset of the market, and the market, which has a large anonymous component. As one trader put it, "(the market) is probably like 99.99999 percent anonymous." A market's *depth* is what one might see as the extension of this independent collective behavior and the reach of its implications and consequences. The following quote gives an inclusive definition of the market which brings out this depth. The territorial disputes between economics, sociology, and psychology over market definitions all *melt* into a sort of *markets are everything* in which the focus can shift from aspect to aspect:

> KK: What is the market for you, is it the price action, or is it individual participants, or –?
> RG: Everything. Everything.
> KK: Everything? The information?
> RG: Everything. Everything. How loudly he's screaming, how excited he gets, who's selling, who's buying, where, which center, what central banks are doing, what the large funds are doing, what the press is saying, what's happening to the CDU, what the Malaysian prime minister is saying, it's everything – everything all the time.

The quote comes from an experienced trader who had worked in several countries, including ones in the Far East, before coming to Zurich. Note that his "the market is everything" refers precisely to the manifold things that one finds on screens, the news and news commentary, the confidential information about what some major players are doing, and the prices. In the following quote, the bank's proprietary trader (a trader who is not trading for his own account but speculating for the bank) sums up this depth of the market by referring to it as a *life form* and *greater being*, a being that is sometimes coherent but at other times dispersed and fragmented. The market as a "greater being," as an empirical object of ongoing activities and effects, continually transforms itself like a bird changing direction in mid-flight, creating the unfolding identity of the market and the anticipation problem traders confront:

> *LG:* You know it's an invisible hand, the market is always right, it's a life form that has being in its own right. You know, in a sort of Gestalt sort of way () it has form and meaning.
> *KK:* It has form and meaning which is independent of you? You can't control it, is that the point?
> *LG:* Right. Exactly, exactly!
> *KK:* Most of the time it's quite dispersed, or does it gel for you?
> *LG:* A-h, that's why I say it has life, it has life in and of itself, you know, sometimes it all comes together, and sometimes it's all just sort of, dispersed, and arbitrary, and random, and directionless and lacking cohesiveness.
> *KK:* But you see it as a third thing? Or do you mean the other person?
> *LG:* As a greater being.
> *KK:* ()
> *LG:* No, I don't mean the other person; I mean the being as a whole. And the being is *the* foreign exchange market – and we are a sum of our parts, or it is a sum of its parts. ()
> *KK:* I want to come back to the market, what the market is for you. Does it have a particular shape?
> *LG:* No, it changes "shape" all the time.
> *KK:* And what is shape referring to () for you?
> *LG:* Well, the shape is the price action. Like this (pointing at screen) tells me – short-term trading. You know, try and buy here, sell here, buy here, sell here, buy here, sell here.

Theorizing the Self as Structure of Wantings

Having said something about the objectuality of markets and their character as incomplete things and knowledge projects, we now want to consider notions of binding that are applicable to the domain investigated. Generally speaking, sociality is about forms of grouping, binding and mutuality or reflexivity among humans. The challenge we face, with the present argument, is to dissociate the notion of a relationship, and of sociality, somewhat from its fixation on human groups. This "loosening up" of the concept of sociality need not start from scratch. Mead, among others, discussed communication with non-human objects, and before Mead, James and Cooley (McCarthy 1984; Wiley 1994: 32 ff.). Yet Mead modeled all communication on interpersonal communication, which he also saw at the root of what makes the self a self: a reflexive process of interpersonal role taking, involving first significant, and then generalized human others. Markets, of course, are not non-human others; but what brings them nonetheless close to objects and organisms is that they are ungoverned aggregates of anonymous human behavior and behavioral effects. What one needs to accomplish, then, is to test formulations that focus on the binding mechanism or the iterability and continuation of the tie rather than on the specific significance of human others. The guiding metaphor we have chosen draws on Lacan rather than Mead. It is that *binding (being-in-relation, mutuality) results from a match between a subject that manifests a sequence of wantings and an unfolding object that provides for these wants through the lacks it displays.* The wants are never fulfilled but are led on by a continually renewed lack of object.

We have already provided some substantiation for this formula on the object's side. An identifying characteristic of a financial market in the present context, we said, is its changing, unfolding character; its lack of completeness of being, and its non-identity with itself. The lack of completeness of being is crucial: markets have their moments of fixedness when prices "lock," but behind such fixed facades they always prepare to mutate, and at times explode, into something else. Markets are as much defined by what they are not (but might become) as by current states; what traders encounter on screens are stand-ins for a more basic lack of object. The idea we now need to make plausible is that subjects – traders – can be characterized by a structure of wantings oriented to the lack of object of the market. Let us first consider how subjects tend to be conceived of as social selves in the sociological literature and then turn to Lacan to discuss the alternative model we propose.

In Mead's model, which is also roughly similar to thoughts of Peirce and Freud, the self is composed of an ego and an inner censor. Mead called the inner censor the "generalized other," by which he means the internalized norms of the community or society. The generalized other is closely coupled in Mead's terminology with the "me"; the self as object and as the intrasubjective conformist past of the self. At the opposite end of the generalized other and the me lies what Mead calls the "I," the spontaneous, unpredictable, disobeying side of the self. The I has the power to construct reality cognitively, and by redefining situations, can break away from the me and the norms of society. The me and the generalized other can be likened to Peirce's "you"; Peirce held the you to be a critical self that represented society and to which all thought was addressed. These notions are also roughly similar to Freud's super-ego, the rule-carrier which functions as a regulative principle in an internal dynamic of morality and deviance. In Mead's theory the self first originates from such a dynamic. The internal conversations we engage in when we think are transformed versions of interpersonal communication. The self arises from role taking, from taking the perspective of the other first interpersonally, when engaged with a close caretaker, and then also intrapersonally. Wiley (1994: 34, 44), combining Mead and Peirce, elaborates this structure into what he calls the I-you-me system of the self.

Now the second model. It understands the self not as a relation between the individual and society but as a structure of wantings in relation to continually renewed lacks. The notion of the self as a structure of wantings can be derived from Lacan (e.g., 1975), but it can also be linked to Baldwin and Hegel.[3] Like Freud, the psychoanalyst Lacan is concerned with what "drives" the subject, but he derives this wanting not as Freud did from an instinctual impulse whose ultimate goal is a reduction in bodily tension, but rather from the mirror stage of a young child's development. At this stage the child becomes impressed with the wholeness of his or her image in the mirror and with the appearance of definite boundaries and control – while realizing that she/he is none of these things in actual experience. Wanting or desire is born in envy of the perfection of the image in the mirror (or of the mirroring response of the parents); the lack is permanent, since there will always be a distance between the subjective experience of a lack in our existence and the image in the mirror, or the apparent wholeness of others (e.g., Lacan and Wilden 1968; Alford 1991: 36).

The two conceptions may seem similar in that both emphasize the discrepancy between the I and a model-image of the self, but they are in fact quite different. From the idea of the self as composed of an inner censor results an ego subjected to feelings of guilt, experiencing rebellion and attempting to "live up" to social expectations. In contrast, the self as a permanently reiterated lack gives rise to the desire, also permanent, to eliminate the lack. The former model would seem to result in actions that are perpetually curtailed as an ego attempts to adapt them to internalized norms; it will also result in deviant actions that transgress boundaries of which the actor is well aware. The second model yields actions spurred on by the unfulfill-ability of lacks, or by new wants opening up simultaneously with the (partial) fulfilment of old ones. In the first model, the actor's free fall from society is continually broken as he catches himself (or is caught by others) in compliance with social rules and traditions, and returns to their ontological security. In the second case, no society of this sort is in place any longer to provide ontological security. The "you" is the idealized self in the mirror or the perfect other. The actor would seem to be freed of any guilt complexes; but he or she is like a wanderer perpetually in search of something, stringing together objects of satisfaction and dismantling the structure again as he or she moves on to other goals.

With the first model we can associate primordial social relations of a kind that foster normative models, compliance, and security. With the second model we can perhaps associate postsocial relations. To be sure, the two conceptions of the self make most sense in conjunction; in Western societies, both the I-you-me system of the socialized self and the lack-wanting system of the reflexive (mirror image) self would seem to identify important features of identity. However, one may also claim that the lack-wanting system is better suited to characterizing self-feelings and self-problems in a general way in contemporary societies than the I-you-me system. To historicize the argument, one might venture the hypothesis that the lack-wanting system of self-formation is in the process of displacing and reshaping the I-you-me system. Why would this be the case? Possible reasons for such a scenario are not difficult to come by. If the lack-wanting system describes contemporary selves better than the I-you-me system, then this might result at least in part from the problems of primordial social relations, which no longer offer the kind of normative models and tight structures of social control that are needed to give rise to an inner censor and a dynamic of guilt and rebellion, compliance and transgression. The liberalization of partnership and family life which Lasch (1978), Coleman (1993), Beck and Beck-Gernsheim (1994, 1996) among others describe, the detraditionalization of education and the individualization of choice (Gross 1994), all conspire to prevent a strong I-you-me dynamic founded on the internalization of a censor from develop-ing. Mead, Freud, and others contributing to the I-you-me model were not only proposing abstract theories of the self. Their conceptions were also rooted in existence, in particular patterns of attachment and socialization practices which are no longer dominant in contemporary society.

To conclude this section, we want to make one point about the model we have foregrounded. While the mirror idea appears plausible as a characterization of fictive external elements around which we build an ego as a life project, it may be less plausible when it is applied in the way Lacan intended it, as a description of what happens to the infant when it first recognizes itself in a real mirror. As Anderson (1983), Wiley (1994: 172), and others have stressed, no one knows what the child experiences at this stage, and what the consequences of this experi-ence are. We need not find Lacan's account of the lack of subjectivity as rooted in the child's narcissistic relationship to him/herself persuasive in order to find the idea of a structure of wanting plausible. The latter is simply a convenient way to capture the way wants have of continually searching out new objects and of moving on to them – a convenient way, if you wish, to capture the volatility and unstoppability of desire. The idea of a structure or chain of wantings has the advantage of bringing into view a whole series of moves and their underlying dynamic rather than isolated reasons, as the traditional vocabulary of motives and intentions does. Plainly, one can make the argument that these moves, or the unstoppability of wants, is continu-ally re-incited by the lures and images that society generates, and this is what we will do next. Accordingly, the self need not be seen as frozen into a lacking subjectivity for life at the mirror stage. It is at least as plausible to conceive of lacks in a more sociological idiom as permanently recreated by relevant institutional processes in a post-industrial society.

The Institutional Translation of the Lack-Wanting Structure

We can tie together the self as a structure of wanting and structural characteristics of contemporary Western societies by thinking of how the mirror has become exterior-ized and reflected in a broad range of social and economic roles. For the analysts concerned with self-formation, the mirror is either a physical mirror or the care-takers' activity of "back-projecting"; their activity of "reflecting," like a mirror, the child's being by responding to it as a person and by articulating and defining the child's behavior in relation to parental idealizations and expectations. The source of the power of the mirror lies not in the cognitive superiority or objectivity of the judgments made but in its projection of an (idealized) image that differs from the subject's self-feeling and self-experience. The mirror reveals the subject to him/herself as a piece of unfinished business composed of ever new lacks. In today's societies this sort of projection is no longer only supplied by primary reference persons who do their work in the initial stages of life. The mirror is instituted in the media and other displays which project images and stage "wholeness," and it is permanent: the media provide a continual flow of images of the sort Lacan attributes to the early childhood. These images are present in the shopping malls or "cathedrals of consumption" Ritzer analyses (1999: 8 ff.), and in simulations, the life-like reality processes in a purely symbolic space in which many of the insufficiencies of real life can easily be forgotten and erased (Turkle 1995; Baudrillard 1983). To a considerable extent, the lack-wanting dynamic has changed hands altogether and appears now to be articulated by complicated and dispersed machineries of professional image production – of industries that produce movie stars and fashion models, TV programs and films, shopping catalogs and advertisements.

The dynamic is also articulated, we maintain, in work contexts, notably those in which the Marxist sense of "alienation" as the worker's estrangement from skilled activity and control over the productive process (e.g., Berger et al. 1974: 24) is not or no longer archetypically represented. It is not only the media and the consumption imperative to a capitalist economy which sustain the search for self (e.g., Miller 1994), but also certain avenues of work, for example expert contexts such as those provided by science and technology (a specific recent example is that of software and Internet development companies). The assumption we make is that the self as a structure of wanting becomes articulated in work contexts when the subject has agency in relation to objects – when object relations are possible – and when objects are of the kind described, that is when they are unfolding structures of absences. In these contexts the mirror effect results not from a physical mirror or from another person's or model's back-projections (though this may also be the case, see below), but from the (work) object that reflects back on the subject. What interests us here is the trading context, to which we now turn. These contexts use, or perhaps we should say take advantage of, the lack-wanting dynamic: they provide an organized context for giving "lack" a precise institutional and personal meaning that directs unspecific wants towards clear goals. To make this plausible we will first say something about the traders' agency, which we think is a precondition for their engagement with the market, and then illustrate the institutional articulation of lacks in this context.

Though traders work for global investment banks they are not robbed of individual choice and the possibility for self-realizing action. If anything, their work provides for a gain rather than a loss of ego. Traders, we said, are the key operators in foreign exchange markets. Traders do not broker or mediate deals but are "market makers," meaning they take their own positions (they buy and sell currencies), trying to gain from price developments while also offering trades to other participants, thereby providing liquidity to the market and sustaining it, if necessary against their own position (see also Baker 1984: 779; Abolafia 1996: 2). Though traders are set limits by their bank on losses and the volume of currencies they can trade, they are not constrained by any view the bank may adopt on the development of currencies, but back their own views on the currencies they trade. Indeed, as participants confirm, it is quite common for the trading book and the bank's proprietary position to be at odds with one another (see also Goodhart 1988: 456). The shift in agency from the firm to the trader this implies manifests itself in the readiness of banks to move their trading operations to global cities like London (Sassen 1991; Thrift 1996) in search of pools of competent actors who can provide this agency. A more general indication of the agency traders retain is the legal and commercial deregulation of these markets, the lack of a social censor, one might say, who restrains activities and prescribes their direction.

One articulation of this agency can be associated with the need, for these traders, to win and not just to do their job in a routine fashion. As Abolafia has emphasized, "the trading floor is not understood as a place to satisfice, footdrag, or merely survive, as in other organizational settings. It is a place to win" on the basis of making money (1998: 10). He calls "the sheer raw enjoyment of winning" a secondary goal of excitement and mastery, a goal of "deep play" (Geertz 1973: 433) beyond the obvious goal of money. Traders often comment on this enjoyment and indeed on their engagement with the market when they say they "work, relax, eat, and literally sleep with the markets," or when they respond as follows to questions about their reason for trading (Schwager 1992: 60, 65 ff.)

> S: With trading consuming most of your day, not to mention night, is it still fun?
> L: It's tremendous fun! It's fascinating as hell because it's different every day.
> S: Would you still trade if there were no monetary remuneration?
> L: Absolutely. Without question, I would do this for free. I'm 36 years old, and I almost feel like I have never worked. I sometimes can't believe I am making all this money to essentially play an elaborate game. On the other hand, when you look at all the money I have produced over the years, I've been vastly underpaid.

Such claims are substantiated by ethnographic observations which show traders to take lunch at their desk and to spend long hours on the floor (from approximately 7 a.m. to 6 p.m.), after which they keep track of the markets through hand-held Reuters screens or by watching the markets on CNN and other specialized channels at home. What these observations suggest is that trading affords agency not only in the sense of the practice of skills or power but also in the sense of providing for the *continuation* of wantings, directed towards a market that displays itself as an *unending* series of new challenges. Let us consider these challenges, of which some flow directly from the market, while others emanate from star traders' exemplary activities, and yet others are articulated by the bank on the basis of an assessment and interpretation of a market's track record in the past.

To begin with the last kind, consider that traders are not only confronted with the general requirement that they make money for the bank but are also in fact given precise target values indicating how much they should earn, or in the lack-wanting idiom, how much they lack. These values are determined once a year on the basis of their previous earnings and the condition of the market. Note that these values provide traders with a benchmark in relation to which they can measure the degree to which they have succeeded with the market. Traders attempt to surpass these goals with a view to a second, more personal goal: that of obtaining an ever-higher bonus (whose size depends on their own and the bank's performance) and of accumulating personal wealth. The personal and institutional specification of "lack" as a lack of wealth and market earnings is joined by a third specification, a lack related to "character." Trading room culture involves a star system according to which some traders rank far above others in terms of the money they make and the trading skills attributed to them. The star trader in Zurich trades the most important currency pair on the trading floor (dollars against Swiss francs); his daily turnover may be as high as several billion dollars, his daily "P&L" lies between half a million profit or loss for the bank, and his budget exceeds that of others. His desk is centrally located on the floor, he is in constant communication with the chief trader who sits at a desk next to him, and he displays a number of (personalized) characteristics pertinent to his reputation. Some of these are described in the following quote from a colleague:

X makes prices all day, he makes the market. He wants to make dollar–Swiss and not dollar–mark, since dollar–Swiss is smaller; dollar–mark is too big, no single trader could make the market. X's strength is that he can "bull" his position through. He can tuck his heels in and sit on his balls longest. When others have long quit, he still pushes on. That is his strength.

Other traders measure themselves against the performance and behavior of the "stars" in their business. Star traders provide the self with a mirror and model image, even when the image is, from an observer's viewpoint, negative. As one chief trader said:

If you have a dollar–Swiss dealer who behaves like a pig you can be sure that within two months everyone behaves like a pig, because he functions like…a model…and his behavior affects the whole dealing room.

Traders, then, are made aware of their lacks by their star colleagues on the same trading floor and by the management which calculates what they lack in real money. This last calculation can be broken down into daily and even moment-to-moment assessments, a point that warrants separate attention. Spot traders (those exchanging currencies directly rather than dealing in longer-term instruments such as options or futures) close their accounts in the evening, at which point what they have earned or lost during this day is credited to their record. They can also inspect how they stand with every trade, and indeed tend to be fully aware of "how they add up" at all times during trading. Direct lacks in this respect are the losses they make and their "shortness" on a currency in speculative trading (going short means selling more of a currency than one has available in one's account in the hope of buying the currency back at a lower price later). Losses in particular are associated with fear and terror, as suggested by traders' vocabulary in the context of such losses:

I got shafted, I got bent over, I got blown up, I got raped, I got stuffed/the guy stuffed me, I got fucked, I got hammered, I got killed.

Beyond indicating the dangerousness of some lacks, the vocabulary displays traders' emotional engagement with the market by portraying it in terms of physical assaults. Participants appear to be viscerally plugged into the screen reality, and to experience the dangers of intersubjectivity in terms of the penetration of their bodily preserves.

One interesting effect of conceiving this variety in terms of lacks is that it becomes plausible that the lacks need to be managed if the subject is to address them constructively rather than to be overwhelmed by them. This is where the chief trader comes into the picture as a kind of monitor who sees one of his main tasks as building up traders' confidence when the lacks (losses, failures to gain money, being beaten) seem overwhelming. Chief traders also attempt to manage wantings, for example by bringing traders down to earth when they feel like "masters of the universe" after a series of lucky strokes. In that situation, chief traders attempt to puncture dealers euphoria by putting lids on their risk-taking behavior and trying to steer them away from high risks (Bruegger 1999: 282). In the language of lacks, risk-taking means the calculated acceptance of possible future lacks in return for the chance to overcome a lack. Trading, of course, nearly always implies risks. But this means that in this area, future lacks are reflexively built into the very strategies of action adopted to overcome lacks – a theme that fits well with the idea of *continued* lacks that can never be fulfilled. To put this differently, traders not only confront lacks, they turn "lacking" into a sophisticated game or pratice, a domain of shifting, increasing, decreasing, predicting, hiding, and delaying lack.

We now want to return to the object towards which the wants are directed, the market. Recall that the market is independent of the subject and that it displays its own lacks. Participants, we said, see the market as a life form that they cannot control, even though they are part of it, and may influence prices at times. But they are a very small part of an anonymous mass of exchange behavior and effects. The market was said to be 99.99999 per cent anonymous, "because the part that I see, that I can claim I have first-hand knowledge of, is extremely small." If a message on the bulletin board said "Bought 50 mark–Swiss for Scandi prop. desk" the trader knew the amount and the commodity, but not the price and the Scandinavian buyer. He appreciated the information he got, but this information was nearly always incomplete: "I get some information (from the bulletin board and the screens) but not 100 per cent of the information." Historically, as indicated before, putting markets on screen eliminated a major lack, that of knowing "where the market is" (what the prices are). But the screen created new lacks of information in a faster, more liquid and global market. The literal "wants" of the market are expressed on screen; they are the conversation-initiating price questions emanating from world-wide financial institutions. As we shall emphasize in the next section, these literal "wants" are not simple dealing orders but messages in need of decoding in a context of market knowledge; they display their own lack of information before they become deal requests. Traders attempt to "read" these questions with respect to the dealing intentions (buying or selling) of the calling party and with respect to their implied market-(price-)transforming significance; and in their responses to these wants they are trying to fulfill their own lacks. A second layer of lacks indicated on screens concerns the vast area of market knowledge to which traders orient in forming a "view" of the market; the lack refers to the incompleteness of this infor-mation just illustrated.

A point to note here is that the lacks displayed on screen are specific; through the insufficiencies they display, they suggest what is lacking (in the case illustrated above, the price and the buyer of a commodity), who might have the answer and which way to look further if necessary. One aspect of the notion of a lack as used here *is* the direct and indirect signifying capacity of the visual and textual signals that indicate a lack. As a signifying object, the market structures desire, or provides for the continuation of the structure of wanting on the trader's side. On the subject's side, most lacks experienced were equally specific: examples are the annual profit goal, the possible losses in every trade and in the daily account balance, currency shortness, and bonus-related lacks as measured against last year's bonus, other traders' bonuses, possible offers by other banks, and personal calculations of worth in terms of the money earned for the bank. The specificity of lacks in the present context may account for the traders' sense that control is possible and their engagement is worthwhile in the face of the equally present sense of being further challenged. This points again to the continuity of the engagement implied by the notion of relationship.

We can now conclude this section by spelling out once more what we mean when we say traders' engagement with markets corresponds to a postsocial object relationship. Binding, we said, results from the accomplishment of a match between a sequence of wantings and an unfolding object that provides for these wants through the lacks it displays. A postsocial relationship occurs when the self as a structure of wanting loops its desire through the object and back, on a continuing basis. In this movement, the self is endorsed and extended by the object (recall that traders need to prove themselves against the market, to "show character" in it, and so on), which also provides for the continuation of the structure of wanting through its lacks. Binding here consists in the phenomenon that the subject takes over the object's wants – as a structure of wanting, the subject becomes defined by the object. Conversely, the articulation of the object, the market, is looped through the subject: as a structure of lacks, of the questions it poses and the things that "it" needs, the market receives the kind of extension that the subject determines. In the present case, market continuation literally depends, we said, on market makers' readiness to deal, even if they stand to lose money. But the market also becomes substantively defined by the way market makers decide to engage in market continuation.

The Market as an Object That Can Be Entered by Traders

The notion of a postsocial relationship we have outlined rests on the structural affinity between a subject's wants and an unfolding object. This structural affinity fulfills one condition of a relationship, which is that it should continue over time and not be reducible to an action or a short experience. The significance of the formal correspondence we have claimed to exist lies in what this correspondence facilitates – a potential binding of a subject to an object in which the two sides feed and sustain one another. But when a binding relationship comes about, it always involves more than a formal correspondence. We have already indicated this by pointing to the semiotic dimension of trading: for the relationship to continue, the object must not only have lacks but must be *signaling* what it still lacks and the subject must be *interpreting* these signals. In this section we want to enrich our account of traders' engagement with the market by taking a deeper look into the process of interpretation – and at traders' experiencing, feeling, remembering, and responding to the market by means of "identifying" with it, a feature we tend to reserve for the sphere of intersubjective relationships. The phenomenon we need to pay attention to, if only briefly, is that traders not only relate to markets as an external life form in its own right, they are also able to "enter" this life form cognitively and emotionally, and to become part of it. The basis for entering the market is economic position-taking; becoming part of the market economically entails and in fact demands an attempt at cognitive understanding and the development of a feeling for the market. We have not drawn on Mead's concept of the self in this chapter, maintaining that a less socially conceived self may better capture self-feelings and relationships in a postsocial environment. But we can turn to Mead's famous role-taking formula in search of a concept by means of which to account for traders' quest for understanding. Traders, we maintain, interpret market signals by putting themselves in the position of the market. They thereby deepend their relationship with a being they do not automatically understand and whose behavior they try to apprehend by cognizing and visualizing its needs and dispositions.

How do traders "enter" the market? When spot traders open their account in the morning and start buying and selling currencies, they refer to this as position-taking. "If you're taking a position," they say, "you are part of the market." Only then do they develop "an interest in it" and "leap" into it; they switch from being outside to "being in the market". As one participant said, "Until you have taken your first position home and tried to go to sleep at night and woken up with a loss staring you in the face, you'll never know if you can make it" (Abolafia 1998). But when traders are "in the market" they not only have a stake in its (further) development, they also start experiencing the world from the viewpoint of a market element. On this level, position-taking in trading is a rather literal enactment of the sort of role-taking Mead envisaged when he talked about taking the position of a generalized or specific other. The market, of course, is a generalized, collective other. Being in the midst of it with a particular currency to sell or buy without loss while trying to make profit is what makes traders indicate to themselves the potential strategies of others:

> When I trade I try to find out where the market hurts, what is hurting it . . . how is the market positioned.

> () If I have a long position, () and everyone else is long dollars, and the dollar doesn't want to go any higher, then the dollar will go down. Because if one guy then sells dollars, the other one who buys them doesn't want to keep them, so he also sells. But he already has a lot of dollars that he also wants to sell now. Then there is an erratic, accelerating movement which can only happen when people collectively are on the wrong side. Then I try to imagine what hurts the market, and I try to feel my way into these worst-case scenarios, and to hedge my portfolio accordingly.

Thus traders take the position of the market from the vantage point of their own position in it, observing and imagining what others might be doing that creates a "hurting market" (a falling and perhaps failing market). In the following quote, the chief option trader talks about position-taking in terms of his developing a "feeling for the market":

> You are part of the market, you notice every small shift, you notice when the market becomes insecure, you notice when it becomes nervous, you notice the strong demand . . . You notice also that the demand is much greater than the supply. All this [amounts to a] feeling [for the market]. When you develop this feeling, and not many people have it, the capacity to feel and sense the market, [etc.].

> When someone feels the market, then they can anticipate [it] and can act accordingly. When you are away from the market, and you lack this feeling [for it], then it's incredibly difficult to find it again.

Position-taking, then, encompasses the full spectrum of economic, cognitive, and emotional meanings. When position-taking is added to the structural affinity between subject's (traders') wants and an unfolding market, the idea of conceiving of traders' engagement with the market as a postsocial relationship becomes more salient. A full-blown relationship also includes elements of reciprocity. The Meadean formula which we have used to construct a more complex model of traders' engagement with the market contains a reflexive loop. In person-to-person interactions, the self takes the perspective of the other but the other also takes the position of the self, looking at the self's expectations toward him/her and responding to the self accordingly. Mead thought that this sort of reflexivity also obtains in some measure when we communicate with physical things which are capable of responding to our propositions:

> An engineer who is constructing a bridge is talking to nature in the same sense that we talk to an engineer. There are stresses and strains there which he meets, and nature comes back with other responses that have to be met in another way. In his thinking he is taking the attitude of physical things. He is talking to nature and nature is replying to him. Nature is intelligent in the sense that there are certain responses of nature toward our action which we can present and which we can reply to, and which become different when we have replied. It is a change we can then answer to, and we finally reach a point at which we can cooperate with nature. (Cited in Beckert 2000: 21)

This sort of reciprocity can also be found in the market, where it includes several tangled components. Other market participants may consider a trader's position in the market when they have any indication of it, as they at times do, from electronic messages, observations, or direct involvement in the deals being made – and they will respond accordingly. Other traders may also simply imagine market moves by particular participants on the basis of prior histories of involvement, special information, etc., and, third, they may imagine what the market is doing as a collective entity, acting upon the hypothesis of a market consensus or of mass behavior that includes our original trader. The response of these "others" will not necessarily be communicated directly to our trader but will more likely show on screen, where it becomes part of the market-on-screen as an entity in its own right. Thus, though personal reactions to market events in the sense of other traders' taking the position of the market do play a role in bringing about reciprocity, market interaction does not revert to interpersonal interaction but retains the quality of a trader-to-screen/ market interaction. To some degree, programs implementing the market-on-screen also watch a trader's moves, and may react to it in ways that affect the screen reality (for example, they can implement stop losses, that is sales of a currency when the price drops below a pre-specified limit). As these scenarios indicate, the reciprocity between trader and market-on-screen is there but it is somewhat skewed, since traders and the market as an object on screen do not do the same thing – for example, traders engage in position-taking, whereas a technologically created market aggregates reactions and implements programs. Nonetheless, it is plain that the sort of mutuality we have spelled out is constitutive of the market process. In fact, accomplished economists and market participants (e.g., Soros 1994) have pointed out forms of market reflexivity that rely on this mutuality.

To conclude this section and the chapter, we should note that we can see participants' envisaging the attitude of the "other" as a second way to help us conceptualize traders' engagement with the market as not only work, or instrumental action, but also as a postsocial relationship and form of sociality with objects. The Meadean formula of position-taking specifies *how* a chain of (subjective) wantings becomes related to an object's (the market's) lacks and thus supplements our initial conceptualization of binding. It also details the epistemic and emotional takeover that one can watch on a trading floor: of traders orienting their mind and a significant fraction of their sensory equipment to the life-form of the market – to its glaring and eye-catching presence on screens, its continual vocal demands and its rousing, sometimes galvanizing, effects on other traders. "The movements of the trading floor respond to the movements of the market as if roped together," as a former trader put it (Lewis 1989: 59). Relational thinking of the Lacanian kind may help understand the primordial dimensions of this connectedness. The institutional translation we have given of lacks and wantings is sociologically important: it sustains a view of contemporary society as one in which particular models of the self become institutionally articulated and in which major transitions in relational engagements are taking place. The shift from social to postsocial relations we have posited in this chapter is not the only way of envisaging these transitions, but it is one that is especially apposite to our understanding of sociality. This view of things does not stand in contrast or contradiction to accounts of current transitions as shifts from industrial to post-industrial life, from nation-states to global societies or from modernity to postmodernity. What it stands in contrast to, perhaps, are concepts of the social that have been worked out in the past but may be losing some of the salience they once had. Social relationships and environments as we knew them may become legacy environments – last in a line of succession of cultural forms before contemporary changes, bequeathing to us notions of a human world and solidarity which we need to refashion, or at least to readjust, to new environments.

NOTES

1   Several analysts have pointed out the phenomenological diversity of markets and called for a "multiple market" approach (Zelizer 1988; see also Lie 1997: 354; Smith 2000; Mirowski 2001: ch. 8).
2   By September 1999, 81 interviews of approximately one and a half hours with traders, salespeople, and analysts on trading floors had been conducted and transcribed. The study is also based on one year of continuous participant observation and, in addition, ten shorter periods ranging from several days to a week since 1997 and still ongoing. The study is embedded in a larger effort also involving the investigation of the history of financial markets (Preda 2000), analysts in large banks' research departments (see Mars 1998; Knorr Cetina and Preda 2001), the analysis of financial documents (see Knorr Cetina 2001), and the investigation of what we call "global microstructures" (see Knorr Cetina and Bruegger 2000).
3   Baldwin and Hegel's notions of desire are summarized by Wiley 1994: 33. See also Hegel 1979 (1807) and Baldwin 1973 (1899).

REFERENCES

Abolafia, M. Y. (1996) *Making Markets: Opportunism and Restraint on Wall Street.* Cambridge, MA: Harvard University Press.
Abolafia, M. Y. (1998) "Opportunism and Hyper-Rationality: The Social Construction of Economic Man on Wall Street," unpublished manuscript.

Alford, C. F. (1991) *The Self in Social Theory*. New Haven, CT: Yale University Press.

Anderson, B. (1983) *Imagined Communities*. London: Verso.

Baker, W. E. (1984) "The Social Structure of a National Securities Market," *American Journal of Sociology* 89 (4): 775–811.

Baldwin, J. M. (1973 [1899]) *Social and Ethical Interpretations of Mental Development*. New York: Arno Press.

Bank for International Settlements (1998) "Central Bank Survey of Foreign Exchange and Derivatives Market Activity in April 1998: Preliminary Global Data."

Basle, Switzerland.

Baudrillard, J. (1983) *Simulations*. New York: Semiotext(e).

Baudrillard, J. (1996) *The System of Objects*. London: Verso.

Beck, U. and E. Beck-Gernsheim (1994) *The Normal Chaos of Love*. Cambridge: Polity Press.

Beck, U. and E. Beck-Gernsheim (1996) "Individualization and 'Precarious Freedoms': Perspectives and Controversies of a Subject-Oriented Sociology," pp. 23–48 in P. Heelas, S. Lash, and P. Morris (eds.) *Detraditionalization: Critical Reflections on Authority and Identity*. Oxford: Blackwell.

Becker, G. S. (1976) *The Economic Approach to Human Behavior*. Chicago, IL: University of Chicago Press.

Beckert, J. (2000) "Economic Action and Embeddedness: The Problem of the Structure of Action," paper presented at the Stockholm Conference on Economic Sociology, June 2–3.

Berger, P., B. Berger, and H. Kellner (1974) *The Homeless Mind: Modernization and Consciousness*. New York: Vintage Books.

Bruegger, U. (1999) "Wie handeln Händler? Akteure der Globalisierung," unpublished PhD dissertation. University of St Gallen, Switzerland.

Callon, M. (1986) "Some Elements of a Sociology of Translation: Domestication of the Scallops and the Fishermen of St. Brieuc Bay," pp. 196–233 in J. Law (ed.) *Power, Action and Belief: A New Sociology of Knowledge?* London: Routledge and Kegan Paul.

Carruthers, B. and B. Uzzi (2000) "Economic Sociology in the New Millennium," *Contemporary Sociology* 29 (3): 486–94.

Coase, R. (1937) "The Nature of the Firm," *Economica* 4: 386–405.

Coleman, J. (1993) "The Rational Reconstruction of Society: 1992 Presidential Address," *American Sociological Review* 58: 1–15.

Frances, J., R. Levacic, J. Mitchell, and G. Thompson (1991) "Introduction," pp. 1–23 in G. Thompson, J. Frances, R. Levacic, and J. Mitchell, *Markets, Hierarchies & Networks, The Coordination of Social Life*. London: Sage.

FX Week (1998) June 1, 9 (22).

Geertz, C. (1973) *The Interpretation of Cultures*. New York: Basic Books.

Goodhart, C. (1988) "The Foreign Exchange Market: A Random Walk with a Dragging Anchor," *Economica* 55: 437–60.

Granovetter, M. (1985) "Economic Action and Social Structure: The Problem of Embeddedness," *American Journal of Sociology* 91 (3): 481–510.

Gross, P. (1994) *Die Multioptionsgesellschaft*. Frankfurt: Suhrkamp.

Haraway, D. (1991) *Simians, Cyborgs, and Women*. New York: Routledge.

Hayek, F. A. (1945) *Individualism and Economic Order*. London: Routledge and Kegan Paul.

Hegel, G. W. F (1979 [1807]) *Phenomenology of Spirit*. Oxford: Oxford University Press.

Heim, M. (1993) *The Metaphysics of Virtual Reality*. Oxford: Oxford University Press.

Hornsby, A. (1998) "Surfing in the Net for Community," pp. 63–106 in P. Kivisto (ed.) *Illuminating Social Life*. Thousand Oaks, CA: Pine Forge Press.

Husserl E. (1960) *Cartesian Mediations*. The Hague: Nijhoff.

Jones, St. G. (ed.) (1998) *Cybersociety 2.0. Revisiting Computer-Mediated Communication and Community*. Thousand Oaks, CA: Sage.

Knorr Cetina, K. (1997) "Sociology with Objects. Social Relations in Postsocial Knowledge Societies," *Theory, Culture & Society* 14 (4): 1–30.

Knorr Cetina, K. (2001) "Postsocial Relations: Theorizing Sociality in a Postsocial Environment," pp. 520–37 in G. Ritzer and B. Smart (eds.) *Handbook of Social Theory*. London: Sage.

Knorr Cetina, K. and A. Preda (2001) "The Creation and Incorporation of Knowledge in Economic Activities," *Current Sociology* 49(4): 27–44.

Knorr Cetina K. and U. Bruegger (2000) "Global Microstructures: The Interaction Practices of Financial Markets," *American Journal of Sociology* 107 (4): 905–50.

Knorr Cetina K. and U. Bruegger (2001) "Transparancy Regimes and Management by Content in Global Organizations: The Case of Institutional Currency Trading," *Journal of Knowledge Management* 5 (2): 180–94.

Lacan, J. (1975) *The Language of the Self*. New York: Dell.

Lacan, J. and A. Wilden (1968) *Speech and Language in Psychoanalysis*. Baltimore, MD: Johns Hopkins University Press.

Lasch, C. (1978) *The Culture of Narcissism*. New York: W. W. Norton.

Latour, B. (1988) *The Pasteurization of France*. Cambridge, MA: Harvard University Press.

Latour, B. (1993) *We Have Never Been Modern*. Cambridge, MA: Harvard University Press.

Lehmann-Waffenschmidt and K. H. Müller (eds.) *The Socio-Economics of Long-Term Evolution: Advances in Theory, Complex Modeling, and Methodology*. Berlin: Fakultas Verlag.

Lewis, M. (1989) *Liar's Poker*. New York: Norton.

Lie, J. (1997) "Sociology of the Markets," *Annual Review of Sociology* 23: 341–60.

McCarthy, E. D. (1984) "Toward a Sociology of the Physical World: George Herbert Mead on Physical Objects," *Studies in Symbolic Interaction* 5: 105–21.

Mars, F. (1998) "Wir sind alle Seher. Die Praxis der Aktienanalyse," unpublished dissertation. Faculty of Sociology, University of Bielefeld.

Marshall, A. (1936) *Principles of Economics*. London: Macmillan.

Miller, D. (1994) *Modernity – An Ethnographic Approach*. Oxford: Berg.

Mirowski, P. (2001) *Machine Dreams: Economics Becomes a Cyborg Science*. New York: Cambridge University Press.

Pickering, A. (1995) *The Mangle of Practice*. Chicago, IL: University of Chicago Press.

Preda, A. (2000) "Financial Knowledge and the Science of the Market in England and France in the 19th Century," pp. 205–29 in H.-J. Wagener and R. Rottenburg (eds.) *Facts and Figures: Economic Practices and their Rhetorical Form*. Marburg: Metropolis.

Read, D. (1992) *The Power of News: The History of Reuters*. Oxford: Oxford University Press.

Rheinberger, H.-J. (1997) *Toward a History of Epistemic Things*. Stanford, CA: Stanford University Press.

Ritzer, G. (1999) *Enchanting a Disenchanted World*. Thousand Oaks, CA: Pine Forge Press.

Sassen, S. (1991) *The Global City*. Princeton, NJ: Princeton University Press.

Schwager, J. D. (1992) *The New Market Wizards: Conversations with America's Top Traders*. New York: HarperCollins Publishers.

Serres, M. (1990) *Le Contrat naturel*. Paris: Editions François.

Sheldrake, R. (1991) *The Rebirth of Nature*. London: Rider.

Smith, C. W. (1981) *The Mind of the Market*. London: Croom Helm.

Smith, C. W. (1999) *Success and Survival on Wall Street: Understanding the Mind of the Market*. New York: Rowman & Littlefield.

Smith, C. W. (2000) "Understanding Real Markets: Confronting Old Fallacies, Emerging Possibilities and Imminent Challenges," paper presented at the International Workshop "The Culture(s) of Financial Markets," Department of Sociology and Bielefeld Institute for Global Society Studies, University of Bielefeld, November 10–11.

Soros, G. (1994) *The Alchemy of Finance*. New York: Wiley & Sons.

Stone, A. R. (1996) *The War of Desire and Technology at the Close of the Mechanical Age*. Boston, MA: MIT Press.

Swedberg, R. (1997) "New Economic Sociology: What Has Been Accomplished, What Is Ahead?" *Acta Sociologica* 40: 161–82.

Thompson, G., J. Frances, R. Levacic, and J. Mitchell (1991) *Markets, Hierarchies & Networks, The Coordination of Social Life*. London, Thousand Oaks, CA and New Delhi: Sage.

Thrift, N. (1996) *Spatial Formations*. London: Sage.

Turkle, S. (1995) *Life on the Screen*. New York: Simon and Schuster.

White, H. (1981) "Where do Markets Come From?" *American Journal of Sociology* 87: 517–57.

Wiley, N. (1994) *The Semiotic Self*. Chicago, IL: University of Chicago Press.

Williamson, O. E. (1975) *Markets and Hierarchies: Analysis and Antitrust Implications*. New York: Free Press.

Zelizer, V. (1988) "Beyond the Polemics on the Markets: Establishing a Theoretical and Empirical Agenda," *Sociological Forum* 3: 614–34.

Part III   Regulation

Chapter 8

Varieties of Protectors

Frederico Varese

If the demand for protection that accompanies the spread of market transactions is not met by the state, a demand for *alternative* sources of protection is then expected to arise. It cannot, however, be argued that demand will inevitably be met, otherwise we will yield to functionalist reasoning.[1] Lack of protection implies that there will be more opportunities to meet that demand, and hence that meeting it will be more profitable than elsewhere. However, *demand* for alternative sources of protection alone is not sufficient to explain the emergence of protection agencies. A *supply* of people trained in the use of violence must also be present on the market.[2] If the laws of a country do not pose enough constraints on the activities of such a supply, individuals trained in the use of violence not only meet the demand for protection, they can also force it on reluctant customers through the use of violence.

Was such a supply present in Russia at the time of the transition to the market? In order to answer this question, we first need to focus on two resources needed in this trade, violence and weapons.

The ability to make credible threats is crucial to the role of a protector. He must be able to inflict punishment. The violent resources available to him to inflict punishment must be greater than the combined violent resources of those parties he protects. Both parties must know that in case of 'misbehaviour', punishment is feasible and, for the protector, not too costly.[3] People trained in the use of violence are therefore in great demand in this market. They usually come from a few specific quarters. Vigilantes, ex-soldiers, private guards, prison inmates, bandits, and individuals who enjoy violent activities provide a pool of potential suppliers.[4] To organize an efficient firm providing protection, it is also necessary to have a minimal level of equipment, most importantly weapons. Below, I review the evidence for Russia that points to the presence of both people trained in the use of violence who became suddenly unemployed at the time of the transition, and a vast amount of weapons easily available.

The greater the amount of unemployed, the higher the chance of finding among the newly unemployed people trained in or accustomed to using violence. It has been estimated that over the three-year period 1987–9 economic reform was responsible for 3 million people losing their jobs in industry, only 20 per cent of whom were offered suitable alternative employment.[5] Prime Minister V. Chernomyrdin stated that unemployment in Russia stood at 4.5 million at the end of 1991.[6]

A number of servicemen were made 'redundant' in the early 1990s. At the end of January 1992, Viktor Barannikov, chief of Russia's security service, announced a cut in staff from 36,000 to 2,800, a reduction unprecedented in KGB history. Those retired include chauffeurs, medical personnel, highly skilled specialists (in particular 'code crackers' and experts in computer security).[7] Twenty-five thousand officers of the former Soviet Army were dismissed on political grounds in 1991. The Russian Defence Ministry's press officer announced on 2 February 1993 that between 40,000 and 50,000 officers would be discharged every year.[8] The Army newspaper *Krasnaya Zvezda* published data on cadre officers' discharges for 1992–4, as shown in table 8.1. In November 1996, President Yeltsin ordered 15 per cent of Russian army personnel to be cut during 1997.[9] A series of dismissals affected the police as well. For example, in the period 1987–8, 25,000 policemen were discharged on various grounds, and a further 32,000 were dismissed in 1989.[10] This led the force to be understaffed. Moscow's Main Department for Internal Affairs was short of about 4,000 agents in 1989. Officers were also underpaid and left of their own will. The best-trained and equipped forces of the MVD were offered a three-year contract and a miserable 200 roubles a month in 1989.[11] In the first six months of 1990, over 100 skilled law enforcement experts in the Khabarovsk Territory left their jobs because of low salaries.[12] An Interior Ministry spokesman voiced the concern that the Ministry lacked 60 per cent of skilled experts considered necessary to effectively fight organized crime, and that the equipment available to officers was 'just nothing to talk about'.[13] According to figures revealed at a closed conference on organized crime by Russian Interior Minister Viktor Erin, 63,000 professionals left the militia in 1992 and one in every five of them 'went over to the enemy'.[14]

The collapse of the Soviet Union also led to the collapse of the network of sports clubs supported by the regime. Some sportsmen – such as wrestlers, weightlifters, bodybuilders, and boxers – were in a position to sell their services on the market for protection.

Sport was greatly valued by the Soviet Union. It was regarded as 'the active relaxation of the workers' and 'the way to develop the individual harmoniously'.[15] In 1978, 52 million (one-third of the total population in the 10–60 age group) were

Table 8.1   Reasons for discharge of officers from Russian Military, 1992–4

Reason for discharge	1992 (since 1 May)	1993	1994 (first six months)
Completion of service obligation	13,530	13,823	6,341
Personnel organization measures	23,182	15,005	5,263
Not meeting the established requirements for service members	10,358	10,974	2,680
Actions besmirching the honour of the service	2,603	4,040	1,282
Other reasons	9,490	25,191	10,925
Total number of cadre officers discharged	59,163	69,033	26,491

Source: Krasnaya Zvezda, 2 August 1994.

taking part in sports and 209 educational establishments provided instruction for would-be sports teachers and coaches. Each major economic and social concern had its own sporting facilities and employed instructors. In 1972 'sports clubs' existed at 282 factories, 326 specialized secondary schools, and 22 collective and state farms. 'Sports clubs' formed the elite of the network of sporting associations, and often supplied athletes to national and international competitions (some 218,000 'physical culture groups' also existed, but rarely provided athletes at national level). In 1976, 56,326 professional athletes were employed by state structures.[16] Sporting instructors were the first to be laid off by firms. 'Sportsmen were the Regime's gems, well fed, cuddled, allowed to travel abroad, all acquainted with each other,' declared Lev Brekhman, a sports doctor. 'When the regime collapsed, they found themselves without the money to buy decent food and no skills to find an honest job.'[17]

Russia is a world leader in the production of arms, which can be bought without difficulty, both legally and illegally. Lack of morale and pressing economic problems pushed many members of the security services and the army to sell a considerable number of weapons on the black market. According to Gennadii Deinega, of the St Petersburg police investigation department, the local firearms black market offers, for the most part, weapons stolen from the army, KGB, and police units. Another significant source is the so-called 'conversion business'. Warrant officers at military warehouses often sell stolen weapons on the black market that are later listed as 'written off and destroyed'.[18] In 1993, the Defence Ministry reported 6,430 instances of weapons theft from military depots, a 75 per cent increase over the previous year.[19]

The Russian military remains 'the major and stable source' of arms used by criminals and those fighting in regions plagued by ethnic conflict, according to the Russian Ministry of Internal Affairs.[20] Aleksandr Dement'ev, the deputy head of the Ministry's Department for Combating Organized Crime, told *Interfax* that the bulk of illegally held arms came from warehouses of the Defence Ministry. He added that arms were also stolen directly from manufacturing enterprises. In 1994, the Ministry investigated a group who tried to deliver 4,350 hand guns from an Izhevsk arms plant to Grozny in Chechnya. Dement'ev said 1,247 thefts of arms and ammunition were reported in 1994, while nearly 17,000 crimes were committed involving firearms.[21] In the Ural city of Nizhnii Tagil, gangsters broke into an army tank training ground, overpowered security guards and seized a T-90 army tank. Subsequently, they used it in a battle with Muslim market traders, one of whom was killed and two seriously wounded, according to a Reuter report (3 April 1993). Similarly, Konstantin Tsyganov, a Ekaterinburg crime boss, and his men 'hijacked a tank from a military testing ground and parked it in the central square' in order to scare off a band of Chechens.[22]

Economically pressed army soldiers and officers are not the only suppliers of arms. A steady flow of weapons also comes from 'amateur manufactories': 'Any turner who has the basic skills can make hand guns,' says Deinega. Prices are not high: at the St Petersburg Sennoi market in 1991, hand guns were priced between 3,000 and 10,000 roubles, while a submachine gun cost 100,000 roubles.[23]

Poorly paid militia members, discharged army officers and soldiers, and sportsmen who found themselves suddenly unemployed were ready to take up the new opportunities offered by the private market for protection.

The *Krysha*

In Russian slang, the word for protection is *krysha* (lit. 'roof'). It was used during the Soviet period to refer to front activities for Committee of State Security (KGB), Military Intelligence (GRU), and Ministry of Internal Affairs (MVD) agents both in the country and abroad. Cultural institutions, publishing houses, embassies, and ministries all supplied a cover to people engaged in intelligence gathering. Since the Soviet Union collapsed, *krysha* refers to protection against ordinary criminals and 'unprofessional' racketeers, unruly business partners, and competitors. A *krysha* may ensure tax evasion and help in finding investment and credit opportunities. A Russian businessman, in his testimony to a US Senate committee, maintains that to operate a successful business in Moscow one must 'pay the right government officials' and 'purchase a *krysha*,... which has come to mean protection. The more important you are, the higher the roof must be.'[24] Reputable newspapers advise Russians to obtain a sound protection before starting any business. The search for a safe 'roof' is considered by *Komsomol'skaya Pravda* as the 'the most important element in the modern business world'.[25] Very practical suggestions on the pros and cons of various 'roofs' were given to entrepreneurs by *Argumenty i Fakty*.[26] Sportsmen and security personnel started to offer private protection in a variety of ways. Below, we review them.

Privately sold state protection

In an effort to raise money and reduce the outflow of quality personnel to private security agencies, the state itself started to sell private protection. In 1989, the Interior Ministry (MVD) issued an order allowing local Soviet policemen to enter into contracts with the co-operatives to provide security services for commercial establishments.[27] In 1989, contracts for such services totalling 600,000 roubles were signed by the Moscow militia (in 1989 a rouble was approximately one dollar). The Union of Veterans of Afghanistan and Moscow police formed a joint venture in 1991.[28] The head of the MVD suggested that policemen might form private cooperatives, which would be supervised by their own department.[29] A law passed in August 1992 allowed units within the MVD to offer 'extra-departmental protection'. Mark Galeotti, an expert on policing and security in the former Soviet Union, writes,

> Most police commands include a department known as the Extra-Departmental Guard (*Vnevedomstvennaya okhrana*) which is precisely there to offer [private protection] services. In some cases this is provided by regular police attached to the unit (and thus not available for 'proper' police work), in others by officers in effect moonlighting on their own time, but on behalf of their employer. Other agencies often provide such services, from army garrisons to Border Troops.[30]

The police ensure that potential customers are informed of the available services. In 1994, foreign companies in Moscow received by fax an advertisement from the city police offering a variety of protection services. Seven thousand roubles (then a little more than US$3) was quoted as the price to employ a policeman for one hour to protect one's business.[31] Where cash is short, the police accept payment in kind. In faraway Siberia, a Tadzhik fruit and vegetable import company pays for police protection in radio equipment and cars imported from the Far East.[32] A Russian–German joint venture called Malkom was obtaining extra protection from a very heavily armed police unit specially formed for the purpose. Subsequently, the special protection was taken over by the Extra-Departmental Guard. In this way, Malkom obtains protection from what is in effect a private protection agency, which has a market advantage over other agencies because it can ignore the restrictions on weapons (since it is a police unit) even though it is full-time attached to Malkom. Malkom first was paying for these services by subsidizing a local school and allegedly providing generous gifts to police officers, including the region's police chief. Afterwards, it simply paid a fee.[33]

Extra police protection is also available to criminals. Vasilii Naumov, the head of a Moscow gang, the *Koptevskaya* criminal group, was assassinated in January 1997. It later emerged that his bodyguards were members of Saturn, an elite police commando unit. He had simply hired them through the *Vnevedomstvennaya okhrana* in order to protect his company, Miranda.[34] This instance may be interpreted in two different ways: either Naumov was paying off the local police by signing a lucrative contract with the Extra-Departmental Guard, or he was in real need of extra protection, being unable to protect himself and his business. The police are either taking bribes or protecting (rather badly) criminals.[35]

Since criminal protectors offer protection services beyond the limits set by the law, some policemen complete directly with criminals and double as racketeers or private protectors unconstrained by the law. For instance, in the city of Tol'yatti a *militseiskaya krysha* [militia-provided protection] appears to be operating according to the rules of criminality. Officers as high-ranking as a lieutenant colonel are involved in racketeering and rumoured to be behind the murder of colleagues that threatened to expose their activities.[36] *Kriminal'naya Khronika* reported in 1995 of a band called 'white cross', formed by militia officers and headed by a man called Makeev.[37]

It may be the case that the Ministry of Internal Affairs has not pondered a perverse by-product of providing protection only to some commercial outlets: assuming that selective police protection is effective, thieves will be deterred from stealing from premises that enjoy extra police protection. Once these protected outlets become known to thieves, unprotected agents will easily be identified and crime will tend to be more concentrated in those places. Since protection is selective, it will be easier to spot the unprotected enterprises and target them.[38] The choice for entrepreneurs is between paying for extra police protection or being exposed to greater danger. The effect of such a policy is to shift the burden of crime onto the segment of the public, which does not pay the extra fee to the police officers. This in turn gives unprotected entrepreneurs a strong incentive to hire extra protection.

The use of privately sold state protection is not an indication that the state is fulfilling its role, just as the use of the Court of Arbitration is not an indication that the law works in Russia. On the contrary, it indicates that state protection is available to those who pay.

Private security firms

Private security firms (PSFs), a feature of post-Soviet Russia, are another possible 'roof'. Reportedly 500 such firms sprang up in Russia around 1989 and at least fifteen licensed training camps existed outside Moscow. By the end of 1999, 6,775 private security firms and 4,612 armed security services (attached to a specific parent firm) were registered in Russia. Licensed security personnel stood at 196,266 people,[39] while estimates of the State Duma Security Committee (reported in *Moscow Times*, 31 October 1995) suggest a total figure of 800,000 employees. Unregistered firms are also operating. The KGB claimed to have checked 6,000 such firms during one operation directed against them.[40] Unlicensed firms, according to *Argumenty i Fakty* (22/1997), employ no less than 200,000 people.[41]

A law passed in April 1992 allowed security firms and detective agencies to buy arms, including rifles. A new law 'on Private Detectives and Security' was passed in 1995. This law, as Galeotti writes, grants firms 'considerable powers of surveillance, search and even arrest, giving them far more latitude than envisaged in the 1992 law'. A firm must still obtain a licence to operate from the local police (cost was the equivalent of US$500 in 1997) and cannot employ individuals with a criminal record, although this requirement can be bypassed by registering one as a 'probationer' attached to a registered investigator.[42]

PSFs are staffed mainly by former officers of the KGB, the MVD, the GRU, and veterans of the Afghan and Chechen wars.[43] According to a study of the Russian Ministry of Internal Affairs (MVD), 17,000 former employees of the MVD and 12,000 from the KGB worked for registered and non-registered security and detective firms in 1995.[44] Prominent Soviet-era security officers have formed their own companies.[45] Close links between the PSFs and state securities and the police remain. Valerii Velichko, formerly chief of staff of the KGB's Ninth Directorate (in charge of VIP protection) and now head of Commercial Structures' Protection Bureau, says that his firm maintains 'good relations with the anti-mafiya [*sic*] unit RUOP'. 'That is', he adds, 'when we are not in a position to protect someone with our forces, we go to our [RUOP] colleagues, who can quickly render assistance.'[46] Private security companies may even be housed within military compounds. One security firm has been established at the paratroop school at Ryazan', 200 miles south of Moscow, according to *InterSec*, a newsletter specializing in private security.[47] The company employs 300 of the school's best ex-pupils, recently released from the army. They are available for hire by private commercial concerns or individual businessmen. The commandant of the school has given permission to the company to use its weapons, in return for a percentage of the profit the firm makes. The firm also makes use of the school's military transport. As reported by *InterSec*, '40,000 video-cassette players have already been transported across Russia on behalf of a Canadian firm'.[48]

These firms offer private security and investigation services (such as legal advice, security audits, and vetting of employees and possible partners and investors) to individual and corporate clients.[49] Among the first to be established was Alex, founded in Moscow in 1989 by former members of the KGB and promising four main services: 'Guarding objects, engineering security, information-analytical security, counter-terrorist activity.'[50] On the Alex internet home page one can find a brief

history of the company, including a reference to its services to the Russian government: 'In August of 1991 at government of Russia request our departments defended
the building of Russian White House. And in the October of 1993 we protected the
building of Russian TV centre from the thugs.'[51] Sherif is the largest firm currently
operating in Russia, uniting four detective agencies, eight security firms, and a
variety of other consultancies, with a total staff of nearly 1,000 and a branch office
in Kiev.[52]

At least two constraints should be analysed in regard to legal PSFs: costs and the
range of services. The first constraint is imposed on their clients by the firms
themselves. Substantial sums of money are required in order to purchase the services
of PSFs. The average price for posting a guard at a firm's office was US$1,000 a
month in 1994.[53] Small businesses and even kiosk owners can afford them only if
they join forces. One such case was reported in *Izvestiya* (12 March 1997): 'Kiosk
owners pool resources and hire a security firm with the stipulation that if a criminal
gets away, the guys in uniform will pay compensation for all losses.'

The second constraint is imposed by the state on both supplier and client and
limits the range of services that can be offered and demanded. PSFs are supposed to
provide *legal* protection against violent attacks. They are not supposed to engage in
activities such as twisting the arms of unwelcome competitors or settling disputes
outside the scope of the law. Certain businesses only require security services: the
nature of their interactions with the Russian business environment is quite limited or
they are safely protected by other arrangements, such as foreign government sponsorship. Foreign consulting companies, who come to Russia on fairly detailed
contracts with the Russian state, may qualify as businesses who do not require
illegal protection services. We should therefore expect them to opt more readily
for PSF protection. This seems to be the case with a US consultancy working in
Russia on a contract with the Russian government. When it was visited by four men
in long, black leather jackets proposing a protection deal, the firm refused and
turned for help to a British security concern allied with a squad of retired Russian
special forces troops. The Russians tracked down the four gangsters and warned
them off.[54] A further incentive for US-based firms to employ legitimate security
firms is the existence of a law that forbids American businesses to engage in 'corrupt
practices' abroad.[55]

Still, this does not always prevent PSFs from offering a wider range of services,
both legal and illegal, depending on the alternatives available to the customer. The
chairperson of a PSF called Bastion, a woman, told *Moscow Times*: 'To the bandits
we say we are a *krysha*, to the tax inspector we say we are consultants, and to the
police we say we are private guards.'[56] Most likely she is telling (part of) the truth to
all of them. A company was reported to offer protection and escort services to its
clients.[57] In the city of Krasnokamsk, in the Perm Region, the body of a man who
had been stabbed to death emerged from the waters of the river Las'va. The man had
been put into a metal container and cement was poured over him, a clear reference
to an 'Italian-style' mafia murder. It later emerged that the man was killed for failing
to return a debt. The employees of a private security firm based in the Kirovskii
district of Perm confessed to the murder.[58]

In a similar although not equally brutal case, the Stavropol' Saving Bank hired the
services of the firm MBK, which specializes in 'protection'. MBK signed a formal

contract for the recovery of debts outside of ordinary legal procedures. The Bank, in turn, pledged to provide MBK with a percentage of the value of all assets they recovered.[59] The contract provided for the supply of an illegal service: the violent recovery of assets outside the provision of the law contravenes article 200 of the Criminal Code of the Russian Federation, which can lead to a maximum six-month term of imprisonment.[60] Either the company MBK is a private security firm, which has started to compete with criminal firms offering illegal services, or it was criminal from the start. These examples point to the difficulty of distinguishing the two.

Some PSFs are closely connected to established criminal groups.[61] Skorpion, a St Petersburg-based protection firm established in 1993 and with over a hundred staff, reportedly was a front for the city's dominant Tambov gang. The police accused its director, Aleksandr Efimov (nicknamed Fima) of being a criminal *avtoritet*. The raid proved that several Skorpion staff had criminal records and the police revoked the firm's licence in March 1997. Efimov was arrested a year later in the Ukraine.[62] Ruslan Kolyak, nicknamed Pucheglazyi, also a member of the Tambov criminal group and accused of extortion, is the president of the Kuguar and Krechet security agencies.[63] Igor 'Rimer, with a long criminal record, and Vladimir Podatev, nicknamed Pudel', the most respected and feared criminal 'authority' of Khabarovsk, are the founders of Svoboda (freedom), a private protection firm. The firm has been involved in instances of extortion and kidnapping and is considered as a front for the criminal activities of Pudel'.[64]

PSFs are ready to offer services that go beyond those legally provided by their Western counterparts, thereby indicating that the state is only partially able to constrain them.

Internalization of protection

Major economic conglomerates have internalized protection, hiring a host of body-guards, which constitute in effect little private armies. The gas monopoly Gazprom has a 20,000-strong security service under Vladimir Marushchenko, a KGB veteran who also served as senior officer within the state tax service. The financial group Most can resort to more than 2,500 armed officers in Moscow alone, while Lukoil has an army of a similar size in its Novorossiisk oil terminal. These economic giants also employ commercial intelligence officers and a system of secure communications.[65] Economic conglomerates have benefited from the initial distribution of resources because of their connections with the political elite. Internalization of protection in these cases goes hand-in-hand with a privileged relationship with the state. Russian newspapers have pointed out that 'sizeable economic concerns...are quite often forced to "go under the roof", although in this instance we are referring to organs of state power, which are often law-enforcing agencies'.[66] Table 8.2 summarizes the most well-known connections for the mid-1990s.

The individuals listed under the heading 'political affiliation' offer a variety of favours, such as company tax concessions, protectionist measures against competitors, and exemptions from duties. These politicians are also able to mobilize violent resources and sometimes face confrontations of a military nature. *Izvestiya* reported that 'competition among different "legal roof-builders" in relation to the affairs of their "clients" often leads to quite violent confrontations [*razborki*]'.[67] On 2

Table 8.2 Russian conglomerates and their political affiliations, 1994–2000

Group/Head	Industrial holdings	Political affiliation
Oneksimbank/Vladimir Potanin	Owns 38% of Noril'sk Nickel, 26% of jet-engine maker Perm Motors, 26% of auto maker Zil, Sidanko, plus oil, metallurgy and real estate interests.	(then) President of Russian Federation, Boris Yeltsin and Anatolii Chubais
Menatep[a]/Mikhail Khodorkovskii	Most diversified conglomerate, with 78% of oil giant Yukos, plus controlling interests in plastics, metallurgy, textiles, chemicals, and food-processing companies. 10th largest bank in Russia.	Former communist apparatus
Rossiiskaya Metallurgiya	Links 14 institutes and troubled plants producing steel, alloys and other metals.	(then) Deputy Prime Minister, Oleg Soskovets
Most Group/Vladimir Gussinskii	Active in Moscow, its interests are spread across banking, real estate, government, construction, independent TV network NTV, and the paper *Segodnya*.	Moscow Mayor, Yurii Luzhkov
Gazprom/Rem Vyakhirev Lukoil/ Vagit Alegperov	This group links Russia's gas monopoly, its largest oil company and their jointly owned bank. Gazprom supplies gas to Europe and Lukoil deals with Libya and the Persian Gulf.	(then) Prime Minister, Viktor Chernomyrdin
Boris Berezovsky	LogoVaz, Aeroflot, Sibneft', Russia's fifth-largest aluminium producer Novokuznetsk, the Krasnoyarsk and Bratsk aluminium plants, *Kommersant-daily* newspaper, ORT TV Station, and SBS-Agro bank.	(then) President of Russian Federation, Boris Yeltsin and his family

[a]Menatep ceased to exist in 1998, although Menatep St Petersburg and Yukos are said to be its inheritors.

Source: Various newspapers including *Business Week Magazine*, 1 April 1996, *The Economist*, 21 January 1995 and 8 April 1995.

December 1994 the offices of Mostbank – protected by the Moscow mayor who was at that point in competition with the Kremlin – were raided by a group of masked men armed with automatic weapons. The men, who initially refused to identify themselves, turned out to be a detachment of President Boris Yeltsin's security staff. In order to protect their client, the troops of the city guard, led by Mr Sevost' yanov, intervened. At least two people were hospitalized.[68] Another incident of a similar nature occurred in March 1995. The headquarters of LogoVaz, an automobile consortium owned by Boris Berezovsky, were visited by a detachment of Moscow anti-organized crime unit (RUOP) in connection with the murder of television journalist Vladislav List'ev. Such an intrusion was quickly and successfully 'repelled' by FSK agents (the successor to the KGB). Different branches of the state apparatus protect different clients. *Izvestiya* concludes that, 'as a rule, the side whose "roof" is higher in the state hierarchy, wins'.[69]

Those who oppose major conglomerates may suffer severe consequences. Vladimir Petukhov, mayor of Nefteyugansk in western Siberia, was involved in a bitter fight against Yukos, the company headed by Mikhail Khodorkovskii. Petukhov opposed the sale of the local gas producer, Yugaskneftegaz, to Yukos and supported various actions against the company, including a demonstration protesting against delayed wage payments to workers. Allegedly, Yukos had a direct link with the President's administration and the General Procurator's office and, as a consequence, a probe into the way the city administration handled financial affairs was started.[70]

Criminals refrain from entering into conflict with political protectors. A deputy of Egor, one of the leaders of the Moscow's Izmailovskaya gang, granted an interview to Italian investigative journalist Cesare Martinetti. When asked whether the gang dealt in gas, he replied: 'No. We do not deal in gas because the government, or rather PM Chernomyrdin, controls it. We cannot reach those echelons, although recently we started to deal in gasoline.'[71] Similarly, Yurii Esin, a prominent member of the Solntsevo crime group with a fifteen-year prison background, started to deal in oil and gas between Italy and Moscow. Esin had set up a sophisticated network of high-profile connections in Rome, which included the former Deputy President of ENI, the Italian oil and gas agency. Esin's operation in Italy attracted the interest of the Italian police. In a telephone conversation recorded by the police, Esin warns his interlocutor to keep away from deals that might conflict with the interest of Lukoil: 'I do not want to have anything to do with Lukoil. Sure, they kill. And what do you want from me? Whoever gets hold of their oil becomes an obstacle on their path and is finished. You have no idea what sort of bitches they are!'[72]

Only sizeable firms can afford the high costs of internalizing protection. These firms also nurture connections with prominent political leaders. Politicians should act as 'agents' of the Russian people, uphold the law, and fulfil their election promises. Instead, they favour a corrupter who pays them a bribe in return for the use of the state resources. Economic conglomerates are not alone in engaging in corruption.[73] Their links are simply more high profile and more widely reported. Politicians depend on their tenure of office for supplying favours: access to state means of violence ends whenever a different president or city mayor is elected. For this reason, these conglomerates are both internalizing protection and are actively involved in sponsoring their own candidates.

Banditskaya Krysha

A report by the United Nations placed the number of individuals involved in organized crime in Russia at 3 million, employed in about 5,700 gangs.[74] These people come from a variety of backgrounds, including the police and sports. Russian Interior Minister Viktor Erin revealed in 1993 that 20 per cent of the professionals who left the police in 1992 'went over to the enemy', for a total of 12,600 individuals.[75] Criminal figures were quick to realize the importance of sportsmen and organized associations and charities in order to attract them. The most well-known patron of sports among Russian criminals was Otari Kvantrishvili.[76] He headed the Sportsmen's Social Protection Fund named after the Russian goalkeeper Lev Yashin and became one of the founders and the director of a Sports Academy, devoted to encouraging sports in Russia. In 1993 he even founded a party supposedly devoted to the interests of sportsmen – Sportsmen of Russia. Valentina Yashina, the widow of Lev, acknowledged Otari's role in the promotion of sports and the protection of retired sportsmen in a speech at Otari's grave. Among other things, she said, '[Kvantrishvili] was a man of great spiritual purity... Wherever his money came from, even if it may have come by coercion, this money went to the poor.'[77]

Criminal protectors are involved in a variety of sectors and, contrary to widespread belief, offer genuine services, at least in some cases. The owner of an Italian restaurant in Moscow described how he was initially forced into a contract with a criminal group but then the relationship evolved into one of genuine protection.

> After I rented these premises, restoration works started. One day, young lad comes in, looks around and says: 'You will need protection.' I hesitate and shortly afterwards my car is burned. At that point, a refined gentleman comes forward and tells me: 'Those young lads who offered you protection are just naughty boys. Let us handle the matter.' I am afraid so I pay. The gentleman visits me again. 'I see that restoration works are going rather slowly. If you wish, I could send in my crew.' I agree. The fee (*tangente*) increases, but the restoration works actually improve. After a month, the gentleman comes again: 'Don't you need credit?' To tell you the truth, I did. He recommends a bank, and so we became partners, so to speak. Better to make some profit, rather than none at all.[78]

The Filippov Report – a special report on organized crime in Russia prepared for the President of the Russian Federation and published in January 1994 – confirms that credit is accessed through criminal links. It is usually in the area of 'specific-purpose credit'. As stated by this report, 'In the banking sphere, the economic foundation of organized crime is centralized credits allocated outside the regular credit auctions. Such credits are provided in exchange for a 10–20 per cent commission paid in cash.'[79]

The collection of debts or delayed payments is one of the genuine services they offer. 'Bad bank credit, refusals to pay for goods delivered, non-delivery or partial delivery of goods, swindling and roguery: in order to seek justice in these spheres', writes Ladyzhenskii, 'it is useless to go to the court of arbitration.' In these cases, it is the 'roof' that 'steps in and helps'.[80] A correspondent for *Komsomol'skaya Pravda* from the city of Samara writes: 'In principle, all financial-ownership quarrels in our country should be decided by such an institution called the Court of Arbitration. However, as already noted, all attempts to use this method are condemned to failure. At present, the only effective way of settling a situation of conflict between businessmen is known as *strelka*.'[81] *Strelka* (lit. arrow) is slang referring to disputes settled with the help of violence.

One criminal *brigada* in the city of Samara is involved in recovering bad debts for established banks. In principle, banks should apply to the *Arbitrazh* court; however, they are afraid that the debtor may declare himself bankrupt.

> That is why banks operate in an unofficial way. They assign the task of recovering debt to an especially reliable and competent *brigadir*, who adjusts his tactics depending on the situation. For example, in one case, he simply scares the person; in another, he physically 'strains' him. The debtor is taken out of town (to the cemetery, to the forest, or by the river), beaten, threatened, and beaten again. In another case, the debtor is forced to apply for credit to another bank, in order to return money to the bank who hired the *brigadir*. This debtor is doomed to receive soon the visit of the brigade of the other bank.[82]

The article adds that an experienced *brigadir* might indeed cheat the bank, obtain from the debtor a sum, which ranges from 10 to 50 per cent of the debt, and report to the bank that the person in question turned to the department for the fight against organized crime and now he is under their protection.

Criminal groups, with the reputation for using violence, are called in to supply effective muscle against actual or potential competitors. As General Gennadii Chebotarev, Deputy Chief of Police for combating organized crime, declared to *Literaturnaya Gazeta*:

> Quite often, we hear that a businessman fell victim of criminals and when the police start investigating who issued the 'contract' for 'the hit', it appears that it was another businessman. So it transpires that businessmen are 'feeding' the bandits, extortionists and racketeers.[83]

Similarly, the police discovered that fifteen assassinations were ordered by one prominent industrialist caught up in a fight over the control of some natural resources in the Siberian city of Krasnoyarsk. In the same city, a businessman preferred to have his partner killed instead of buying him out. The reporter was told that it turned out to be cheaper to order a hit rather than to pay what the partner was entitled to.[84] A Moscow businessman, Sergei N., had been cheated by his partner and forced to give up his share of a jointly owned business. By chance he met a new protector: a surgeon friend had just operated on a powerful criminal, who said he was willing to look after Sergei's new business. The weekly *Stolitsa* reports: 'The wounded mafioso had guaranteed a good *krysha*...: for 25 per cent of profits, his boys were not only sheltering him from other bandits, but they also solved the many problems he was facing with local authorities, militia, and customs.' Sergei had also asked his 'roof' to kill his former partner, who was found dead some time later.[85]

The Filippov Report mentions the city of Tver', where criminals offer a competitive advantage to certain entrepreneurs, at the expense of others.

In Tver', entrepreneurs who want to set up a booth or open a store have to get permission from the unit leaders of gangsters' groupings. Local authorities will issue licences only with the gangsters' consent. The activity of independent entrepreneurs has been completely squeezed out of some provinces, since organized crime provides financing on very easy terms (for example, very large interest-free loans) to young people who are prepared to co-operate and who, as a result, have a significant advantage over their competitors (needless to say, when they achieve a certain degree of success, they turn over a sizeable portion of their profits as payment for the loan).[86]

The report adds that the additional 'tax' paid to gangsters, as well as the restrictions put on business activity with the aim of obtaining monopoly profit, 'leads to price increases of 20 to 30 per cent'. The losers are both the consumers, who pay higher prices for goods and services, and unprotected competitors.

There is at least one instance where a gang intervened to stop a workers' strike. It occurred in Vorkuta, a city of about 90,000 people located 160 kilometres north of the Arctic Circle. The strike leader, Konstantin Pimonov, was threatened at gunpoint in order to end a month-long strike against the company that owns the Vorgashurskaya coalmine.[87] This episode reminds one of American, Japanese, and Sicilian mafias' intervention in labour disputes.[88]

Coal mining is riddled with criminality in Russia.[89] Although most of the press refers to the mines as 'having been taken over' by the mafia, the picture is more complex. Vladimir Kudeshkin, head of the Barzasskaya mine in the Kemerovo region (western Siberia) since August 1999, complained about the criminals' interference with the operation of his mine. However, he added, they not only used violence to persuade him: 'They also have ready cash to pay the high railroad tariffs and the means to ship the coal through the crime-ridden ports.'[90]

Criminal protectors operate in a crowded market, competing with state protectors and legal security firms (PSFs). In turn, the latter two compete with each other over price and services for clients. As far as prices are concerned, police protectors can charge the same price as PSFs, although they can also free ride on existing state structures for equipment. They do have to pass on to the administration a portion of their earnings, but can keep most of them 'in-house'. Police protectors have less expenses and greater income than PSFs. They also have access to police files, can bypass restrictions on armament and carry a greater weight when dealing with the public. Police protectors are also supposed to supervise their own competitors and grant them permission to operate. Given that PSFs are at a disadvantage with police protectors, they expand the range of services by offering customers semi-legal enforcement and protection. This might lead the Extra-Departmental Guard to evolve in the same direction, competing with both criminals and PSFs over services.

Only severe intra-police competition might lead to police protectors being exposed by colleagues for providing illegal protection services. Still, potential for conflicts among different arms of the state is high. When different fragments of the state apparatus protect different clients, the state administration is drawn into the clients' conflicts. Military confrontation between the Presidential guard and Moscow city guard (as in a case involving Mostbank), or the Interior Ministry anti-mafia unit and the new FSB (as in the case involving Logo Vaz) are a by-product of the privatization of state protection. Business disputes are adjudicated not by independent tribunals, but by the use of compromising material, confidential police information, secret services reports, and ultimately the use of state violence.

Legal protectors operate in the same market as criminals and might even be prepared to use similar methods, although we should not conclude that they inevitably fight criminals, even for the wrong reasons (such as reducing competition). Instead they can eschew conflict in favour of tacit co-operation and agreements to share clients or segments of the market.

NOTES

1 Elster 1982.
2 Gambetta 1993a: 78.
3 Ibid.: 40–1.
4 Ibid.: 79.
5 In one survey of Muscovites, 26 per cent thought they themselves would become unemployed after the transition to the market (Jones and Moskoff 1991: 127. See also Peterson 1990: 4).
6 *Rossiya*, no. 9, 24 Feb. 1992.
7 *Kommersant*, 3 Feb. 1992.
8 *Interfax*, 2 Feb. 1993.
9 *Vladivostok News*, 29 Nov. 1996.
10 In 1990 it was estimated that there was a total of 475,000 personnel in the police as a whole. *TASS*, 27 June 1989 and *Radio Moskva*, 13 Mar. 1990.
11 The MVD troups are largely made of conscripts; Tsypkin 1989: 16.
12 *Trud*, 24 Aug. 1990.
13 *Izvestiya*, 9 July 1991.
14 *Kommersant-Daily* 16 Feb. 1993.
15 Louis and Louis 1980: 6.
16 Data from Louis and Louis 1980: 7–24.
17 *Repubblica*, 11 Sept. 1992. In Vladivostok there is even a gang called the 'sportsmen gang' that controls the traffic of stolen Japanese cars. Reportedly, it is headed by M. G. Mamiashvili and A. V. Slushaev (*Repubblica*, 11 Sept. 1992).
18 *Megalopolis-Express*, 11 Mar. 1991.
19 *Washington Post National Weekly Edition*, 20–26 Mar. 1995.
20 *Interfax*, 5 Apr. 1995.
21 Ibid.
22 *Moscow Times*, 2 Mar. 1994.
23 Respectively 43, 143, and US$1, 400, at the July 1991 exchange rate. *Megalopolis-Express*, 11 Mar. 1991.
24 Committee on Governmental Affairs 1996: 50.
25 *Komsomol'skaya Pravda*, 27 Dec. 1994.
26 See 'How to protect your business. A "Roof" is needed', by Vladimir Kavichev, *Argumenty i Fakty* no. 16, 1994.
27 In the Soviet period, industrial enterprises, collective farms, and ministries were protected by agencies that were formally part of the MVD apparatus but – as reminded by Galeotti (1998a: 3) – 'in practice they reported to local managers and authorities'.
28 See Galeotti 1995b: 61.
29 *Jones and Moskoff* 1991: 92. See also Trehub 1989: 21.

30 Galeotti 1998a: 7. See also Volkov 1999a: 748. See also Volkov 1999b.

31 *Corriere della Sera*, 14 Apr. 1994.

32 *Irish Times*, 3 Mar. 1999.

33 *Rossiiskaya gazeta*, 22 June 1996.

34 *Kommersant-Daily*, 13 Mar. 1997. See also *Moscow Times*, 25 Jan. 1997, 14 Mar. 1997 and 9 Apr. 1997; *International Herald Tribune*, 14 May 1997; Maksimov 1997: 260–6; Galeotti 1998a: 8; Volkov 1999a: 750.

35 Police officers at various levels consider the provision of private protection services not just a necessity but a positive development. Interpol National Bureau Department head Evgenii Malyshenko (1997) argues that it allows the police to have greater control over the private market for protection, closing down illegal or dubious providers. Also it helps to gather information that might be relevant for investigation, and it gives greater autonomy of police units to run their own superiors in the ministry. Closing down private agencies may however be motivated by a desire to reduce competition, while 'great autonomy' may lead to a breakdown of the chain of command.

36 *Kriminal' naya Khronika*, no. 3, 1999.

37 *Kriminal'naya Khronika*, no. 7, 1995. The 'white cross' is not to be confused with the 'white arrow', reportedly a detachment of policemen who secretly murder criminals (*Sovershenno Sekretno*, no. 7, 1998). There are doubts on the real existence of this 'Dirty Harry' type of organization (see esp. the film *Magnum Force*, 1973). There are of course various parallels in other countries. See, for instance, the results of the Lexow Committee's investigation into police corruption in New York at the end of the nine-teenth century. What the Committee found is that 'in return for pay-offs, they [police-men] protected gambling, prostitution, and other illicit enterprises. Officers extorted peddlers, storekeepers, and other legitimate businessmen who were hard pressed to abide by municipal ordinances. Detectives allowed con men, pickpockets, and thieves to go about their business in return for a share of the proceeds' (Fogelson 1977: 3 quoted in Block 1983: 19).

38 See Gambetta 1993a: 15–34.

39 Volkov 2000: 11. See also *Kommersant-daily*, 12 Mar. 1997.

40 See *ITAR-TASS*, 20 May 1997 and *Kommersant-daily*, 12 Mar. 1997.

41 According to Galeotti, total police strength is around 400,000 of the MVD's total of 540,000 police-related personnel. This amounts to a 3:1 ratio of security officers to police officers, which does not differ greatly from the US ratio (see Galeotti 1998a: 1–2, Moran 1995 and *The Economist*, 19 Apr. 1997).

42 Galeotti 1998a: 5.

43 Krishtanovskaya 1995: 95–6. According to a study of the Moscow-based Institute of Sociology, 80 per cent of the former members of the State Security Apparatus found employment in the private market for protection (*Golos*, no. 42/3, Oct. 1992). See also *Izvestiya*, 26 Jan. 1995; and *Izvestiya*, June 1995.

44 *Kommersant-Daily*, 21 Mar. 1995.

45 They include former KGB deputy Chief Leonid Shebarshin, once head of Soviet foreign intelligence, Mikhail Golovatov, former head of the Al'fa commando unit and founder of Al'fa-A security firm, Colonel A. Markarov, former army intelligence Colonel and founder of Alex, and Aleksandr Gurov, former deputy head of the Ministry of Interior Affairs (MVD) Research Institute and author of scholarly studies on organized crime. See Krishtanovskaya 1995: 95–6, Galeotti 1998a and Volkov 1999a: 750.

46 *Moscow Times*, 31 Oct. 1995.

47 *InterSec*, 1992: 116.

48 Ibid.

49 Galeotti 1998a: 6.

50   See Alex home page on the internet: http://www.alexsecurity.ru/.
51   Ibid.
52   Galeotti 1998a: 6. Other well-known companies include Legion and Bastion, based in Moscow. Foreign companies have opened offices in Russia (mainly Moscow and St Petersburg), such as Control Risks based in London, Coral Gables and Ackerman based in the USA, and the Israel-based firm International Security Services (the latter has a training centre in Moscow). Another company, Ranger, specializes in providing female bodyguards protecting women and children. See *Business Week*, 30 Aug. 1993; *Moscow Times*, 9 Apr. 1995; *Komsomol' skaya Pravda*, 5 June 1995; *The European*, 21–27 July 1995, *Moscow Times*, 14 Jan. 1998.
53   *Washington Post National Weekly Edition*, 20–26 Mar. 1995.
54   Ibid.
55   This is the Foreign Corrupt Practices Act of 1977 (see Noonan 1984: 680). Sheffet questions the overall efficacy of the FCPA ('It is difficult to determine whether the FCPA has made American corporations more ethical or merely more cautions', Sheffet 1995: 67). See however the recent FBI investigation into the activities of American businessman James Giffen, who allegedly paid bribes to Kazakh officials or their families, including President Nazarbayev (*Newsweek*, 10 July 2000). In 1997, a wider OECD convention combating bribery of foreign officials was signed (Moran 1999).
56   *Moscow Times*, 14 Jan. 1998.
57   *Business Week*, 30 Aug. 1993.
58   *Dos'e 02*, 4 Apr. 97.
59   Analiticheskii Tsentr 'Izvestii', 1994b.
60   See *Ugolovnyi Kodeks Rossiiskoi Federatsii*, 1993: 151.
61   'A large-scale operation recently conducted by the RF Ministry of Internal Affairs showed that, quite often, private bodygurad enterprises and security services are used by criminals as front for the business of armed robbery. Of the more than 5,000 firms checked last year, one-tenth turned out to be criminal.' *Izvestiya*, 12 Mar. 1997.
62   *Kommersant-daily*, 15 Mar. 1997.
63   *Kommersant-daily*, 2 Dec. 1998.
64   *Izvestiya*, 6 Jan. 1995; Martinetti 1995: 96; Razinkin 1995: 25.
65   Galeotti 1998b: 420. 'Vitalii Sidorov, Executive director of the Department of Security of the Association of Russian Banks, formerly Vice-Minister of Internal Affairs; Mikhail Shestopalov, Chief of Security Service of Bank Menatep, formerly Chief of OBASS, Chief of the Dep. for the fight against economic crime in Moscow; Vladimir Zaitsev, Chief of Security Service of Bank Stolichnyi, formerly Chief of Special Detatchment Al'fa in the KGB; Mikhail Gorbunov, Chief of Security Service of InKomBank, formerly Executive of the Intelligence Service' (Krishtanovskaya 1995: 96).
66   *Kriminal'naya Khronika*, no. 7, 1994.
67   *Izvestiya*, 14 Mar. 1995.
68   See RFE/RL, 5 Dec. 1994, *Moscow Times*, 3 Dec. 1994 and 7 Dec. 1994 and *New Yorker*, 20 Feb. 1995.
69   *Izvestiya*, 14 Apr. 1995. Similarly, M. Leont'ev writes: 'He whose "roof" is higher is right' (in *Segodnya*, 17 Mar. 1995). See also *Moscow Times*, 7 Mar. 1995.
70   On 26 June 1998, Petukhov was assassinated. Yukos denies any involvement in the murder. *Komsomol'skaya Pravda*, 30 June 1998. In a letter dated 16 June 1998 sent to President Boris Yeltsin, then Prime Minister Sergei Kirienko and leaders of the State Duma, Russia's lower house of parliament, Petukhov announced he was undertaking a hunger strike to protest against the 'cynical actions and murderous politics carried out by oligarchs from Rosprom-Yukos and Bank Menatep in the Nefteyugansk region'. The

letter calls on the government to bring criminal charges against Rosprom-Yukos for 'concealing taxes in large quantities from 1996 to 1998' (*Moscow Times*, 25 Aug. 1998).

71 Martinetti 1995: 176.

72 SCO 1997: i. 75.

73 This in turn leads to an equilibrium where corruption is pervasive and actors themselves simply consider the normal and acceptable method to deal with the state.

74 *UN Crime Prevention and Criminal Justice Newsletter*, nos. 26–7, Nov. 1995. By 1999, the official estimate is 4,600 groups.

75 *Kommersant-Daily* 16 Feb. 1993.

76 Otari Kvantrishvili (1948–94) started his career as a Graeco-Roman wrestler of international class. In the mid-1960s he was a member of a gang headed by a man nicknamed Mongol and a small-time card sharp. He was arrested for gang rape in 1966 and given a 10-year sentence, but was subsequently released and diagnosed as a schizophrenic. In the early 1980s Kvantrishvili was a coach at the Dinamo Club. Some of the wrestlers, boxers and weight lifters that grouped round him in this period later joined criminal gangs such as Lyuberetskaya, Baumanskaya, Domodedovskaya and Balashikhinskaya. He was a close friend of prominent criminals (the so-called *vory-v-zakone*) such as Invan'kov (Yaponchik), Kachiloriya (Peso), Bagdasaryan (Rafik-Svo) and others. In 1985 he started his own business, the 21st Century Association, and the Sportsmen's Social Protection Fund. He headed the Sportsmen's Social Protection Fund named after the Russian goalkeeper Lev Yashin and became one of the founders and the director of a Sports Academy, devoted to encouraging sports in Russia. In 1993 he even founded a party supposedly devoted to the interests of sportsmen – Sportsmen of Russia. In August 1993 his brother was killed in a day shoot-out with members of a Chechen criminal group. On 5 April 1994 he was killed in broad daylight outside a Moscow bathhouse. 'Moscow entertainment and athletic elite' attended his funeral (*Washington Post*, 16 Apr. 1994). Among many possible sources on Kvantrishvili, see *Komsomol'skaya Pravda*, 9 Apr. 1994; Martinetti 1995: 7–41; Modestov 1996: 276–89.

77 *Moscow Times*, 16 Apr. 1994. Private protection may also be supplied by gangs of young people who, out of pure pleasure, enjoy patrolling a certain area and exercising their physical strength on innocent victims. A gang of these young people, who make a cult of physical fitness, emerged in Moscow in the 1980s. The *Lyubery*, named after a working-class suburb of Moscow, are a party of clean-cut, karate-trained lads who in the early 1990s raided in the capital in order to 'cleanse' it of hippies, heavy-metal rock fans, and other representatives of 'Western decadence', apparently with the tacit support of police (Tsypkin 1989: 16). According to *Kommersant* (26 Dec. 1990), the gang made use of its skills in the market for protection, co-ordinating a prostitution ring. It is also reported to protect street players of shell games and other confidence games.

78 *La Repubblica*, 30 July 1994.

79 Filippov 1994: 1.

80 *Kriminal'naya Khronika*, no. 7, 1994. Gambetta documents how the Sicilian mafia intervenes to collect debts or delay repayment. See Gambetta 1993a: 167–71.

81 *Komsomol'skaya Pravda*, 27 Dec. 1994.

82 Ibid.

83 *Literaturnaya Gazeta*, 12 Jan. 1993.

84 *Irish Times*, 3 Mar. 1999.

85 This story has been reported by Alla Andreeva on the Moscow's weekly *Stolitsa* and recounted in Martinetti 1995: 119–22.

86 Filippov 1994: 1. On the Filippov's Report, see Varese (1999).

87 *St Petersburg Times*, 10–17 Feb. 1997.

88   In the US, the mafia offered its services both to employers in order to control trade unions in the harbour industry and to trade unions in order to scare employers off (Block 1983; Reuter 1987: vii). In Sicily in 1920 alone the mafia murdered four trade union officials. In the period 1945–65 the same hands killed 41 leaders of the peasant movement (Hess 1973: 141–2; Lupo 1996: 199). To the extent that the labour movement provides protection and ensures property rights to the peasants, it is a direct competitor of the mafia. The mafia would have no ideological reasons to refuse supporting workers but objects to others doing it (Gambetta 1993a: 93–4).

89   Not surprisingly, Kuzbass coal costs an average price of $26 to $28 per ton, compared with $12 to $15 a ton for US coal (*Moscow Times*, 4 Feb. 1998).

90   *Moscow Times*, 11 Feb. 1999.

REFERENCES

Analiticheskii Tsentr 'Izvestii' (1994a) *Ugolovnaya Rossiya. 1. Bespredel vremen peredela sobstvennosti* (*Izvestiya*, 18 Oct. 1994).

——(1994b) *Ugolovnaya Rossiya. 2. vory v zakone zanimayut ofisy* (*Izvestiya*, 19 Oct. 1994).

Block, A. A. (1983) *East Side West Side: Organizing Crime in New York 1930–1950* (London: Transaction Publishers).

Committee on Governmental Affairs (1996) *Russian Organized Crime in the United States. Hearing before the Permanent sub-Commitee on Investigation* (Collingdale, PA: Diane Publishing).

Elster, J. (1982) 'Marxism, Functionalism and Game Theory', *Theory and Society*, 11/4: 453–82.

Filippov, P. (1994) *Organizovannaya prestupnost' i perspektivy prikhoda k vlasti v Rossii natsional-sotsialistov*, in *Izvestiya*, 26/1: 1–2.

Fogelson, R. M. (1977) *Big-City Police* (Cambridge, MA: Harvard University Press).

Galeotti, M. (1995a) *Mafiya: Organised Crime in Russia* (*Jane's Intelligence Review*, Special report no. 10).

——(1995b) *Afghanistan: The Soviet Union's Last War* (London: Frank Cass).

——(1998) 'Private Security and Public Insecurity: The Rise and Implications of the Russian Security Industry' (mimeo).

Gambetta, D. (1993a) *The Sicilian Mafia* (London: Harvard University Press).

——(1993b) 'Trust and Co-operation', *The Blackwell Dictionary of Twentieth-Century Social Thought* (Oxford: Blackwell), 678–80.

Hess, H. (1973) *Mafia and Mafiosi: The Structure of Power*, trans. E. Oser (Lexington, MA: Lexington Books).

Jones, A. and Moskoff, W. (1991) *Ko-ops: The Rebirth of Entrepreneurship in the Soviet Union* (Bloomington: Indiana University Press).

Krishtanovskaya, O. (1995) 'Nelegal'nye struktury v Rossii', *Sotsiologicheskie Issledovaniya*, 22/8: 84–106.

Louis, V. E. and Louis, J. M. (1980) *Sport in the Soviet Union* (New York: Pergamon Press).

Lupo, S. (1996) *Storia della mafia dalle origini ai giorni nostri. Nuova edizione* (Rome: Donzelli).

Martinetti, C. (1995) *Il padrino di Mosca* (Milan: Feltrinelli).

Modestov, N. (1996) *Moskva Banditskaya* (Moskva: Tsentrloligrag).

Moran, J. (1995), 'Privatizing Criminal Justice', *Crime and Justice: The Americas*, June–July: 10–15.

Peterson D. J. (1990) 'New Data Published on Employment and Unemployment in the USSR', *Report on the USSR*, 2/1 (Jan. 5): 3–4.

Razinkin, V. S. (1995) *'Vory v zakone' i prestupnye klany* (Moskva: Kriminologicheskaya Assotsiatsiya).

Reuter, P. (1987) *Racketeering in Legitimate Industries: A Study in the Economics of Intimidation* (Santa Monica, CA: RAND Corporation).

Trehub, A. (1989) 'Hard Time for Soviet Policemen', *Report on the USSR*, 1/23, June 9.

Tsypkin, M. (1989) 'Workers' Militia: Order instead of Law?', *Report on the USSR*, 1/46: Nov. 17: 14–17.

Ugolovnyi Kodeks Rossiiskoi Federatsii (1993) (Novosibirsk: YuKEA).

Varese, F. (1999) 'The Russian Mafia' and 'The Filippov Report', in *The Mafia. 150 Years of Facts, Figures and Faces*, CD-Rom (Cliomedia Publisher).

Volkov, V. (1999d) 'Violent Entrepreneurship in Post-Communist Russia', *Europe–Asia Studies*, 51/5: 741–54.

——(1999b) 'Politekonomiya Nasiliya, Ekonomicheskii Rost i Konsolidatsiya Gosudarstva', *Voprosy Ekonomiki*, 70/10: 44–59.

——(2000) Between Economy and the State: Private Security and Rule Enforcement in Russia (Forthcoming, *Politics and Society*).

Chapter 9

The Agony of Mammon

Lewis H. Lapham

> Poverty is an anomaly to rich people. It is very difficult to make out why people who want dinner do not ring the bell.
>
> Walter Bagehot

Although in many ways bountiful and in some ways benign, the colossal mechanism that generates the wealth of nations (a.k.a. "The Global Economy," "Moloch," and "The Invisible Hand") lacks the capacity for human speech or conscious thought, a failing that troubles those of its upper servants who wish to believe that it is they who control the machine and not the machine that controls them. Their *amour propre* forbids them from picturing themselves as mere stokers heaving computer printouts and Montblanc pens (or shopping malls and movie studios and Mexicans) into a blind, remorseless furnace. They seek a more gracious portraiture (as masters of markets, captains of commercial empire), and so, every year in late January, they make their optimistic way from the low-lying places of the earth to the World Economic Forum in Davos, Switzerland, where, high up on the same alp that provided Thomas Mann with the setting for *The Magic Mountain*, they brood upon the mysteries of capitalist creation.

Given the chance last winter to make the annual ascent – the forum's sponsors having waived the $18,984 in various admission and subscription fees in deference to my occupation as an editor and therefore a prospective supplier of supportive adjectives – I didn't see how I could refuse to exercise the option. Here were the people to whom the world's governments assign the task of managing the world's money, and where else could I expect to learn how to divide the price of the deutsche mark by the number of fires in the forests of Brazil, or multiply the number of ships in the Suez Canal by the cost of bombing Iraq?

The advance publicity kindled the glow of great expectation at an altitude of 5,000 feet – five days and six nights of rarefied discussion attended by at least 2,000 gratifyingly important people from 150 countries (heads of state, finance ministers, policy intellectuals, Nobel Prize-winning physicists, corporate executives as thick upon the ground as pine needles), a schedule of continuous briefings on almost any topic that anybody might care to name (the bankruptcy in Djakarta, the future of the Internet, the outlook for Romania), maps of the oil fields around Baku, private viewings of George Soros and Bill Gates.

The forum had chosen "Priorities for the Twenty-First Century" as its theme for 1998, and the printed materials glistened with four-color advertisements announcing the presence in Davos of an impressive number of the world's leading corporations (among them DuPont, Volkswagen, Swissair, Texaco and Anderson Consulting) dressed up in full philanthropic regalia and setting about the work of "broadening horizons" and "finding harmony in diversity." A program of events listed the place, time, and principal speakers for each of the 310 sessions scheduled over the term of the forum in the Congress Centre's twelve halls and conference rooms as well as in one or another of twenty-seven resort hotels, and I was surprised to see that the expected briefings on political and economic topics were interspersed with a good many discussions of a more metaphysical nature – the implications of the human genome project, the problem of death and dying, the meaning of clones. The names on the program suggested a division of the prominent people on the set into three classifications – as many as 1,000 business executives representing corporate assets of roughly $4 trillion (i.e., a sum exceeding the collective net worth of all the member governments of the United Nations); 500 politicians; and 500 intellectuals in various denominations, a few of them famous, most of them futurists.

Kohl arrived late and spoke in German. His presence attracted a standing-room-only crowd to the Congress Hall, the largest of the forum's auditoria, and among the well-dressed heads in the audience I recognized several American news-paper columnists as well as a number of corporation presidents whose photographs I had seen in the pages of *Fortune* and *Business Week*. Cameras placed at different angles in the hall projected the chancellor's image onto a large television screen behind the podium, the magnification exaggerating Kohl's resemblance to a gigantic bird of prey gazing mournfully down on a row of field mice. He had come to say that the Economic and Monetary Union was an accomplished fact about which he didn't wish to hear any further complaint. Yes, it was going to be difficult – everything was always difficult – but what was done was done. The votes had been counted by the authorities in Brussels, the presses in Frankfurt were busy printing the new euro currency that would begin circulating on January 1, 2002, and Kohl was sick of listening to all the pointless talk about possible social and political consequences. His irritation prompted him to regret that the pessimists in London and Copenhagen never had the chance to know his mother, a marvelous woman, as wise as she was strong-minded, who taught her children to eat the meals placed in front of them on the kitchen table without sniveling objection. "We learned to clean up our plates," he said. Germany had cleaned up its plate (i.e., accepted the financial discipline required by the Maastricht Treaty), and now it was time for the Italians, and for everybody else in Europe, to clean up their plates. The euro was good for people, and the sooner they learned to like it the better.

Kohl spoke at ponderous length, and I noticed that we were free to wander out into the lobby for a phone call or an exchange of business cards before returning to our seats to listen to the chancellor's extended remarks. During one of my own brief absences, I ran across Peter Foges, a producer of television documentaries for PBS whom I knew in New York as a close student of both the stock market and German romanticism. He informed me that because I was a participant (white badge, not orange), I belonged to what the forum's sponsors denominated as the "Club of Media Leaders." The honorific brought with it an invitation to dinner later that evening at the Hotel Rinaldi, a dinner that Foges encouraged me to attend. He had been coming to the annual meeting in Davos for five years, most recently in his capacity as the producer of *Adam Smith's Money World*, and he recognized me as a novice in need of additional program notes.

The restaurant at the Hotel Rinaldi looked like a tourist postcard – beamed ceilings, beer steins behind the bar, decorative wood carvings, the waitresses dressed as if for a village scene in *The Sound of Music* – and most of the other media leaders in the room were American journalists with whom I was acquainted under their less exalted titles as staff writers for the *New Yorker*, contributors to *Newsweek* and the *Wall Street Journal*, the editor of *Foreign Affairs*.

Both the tenor and substance of the talk suggested that the American media leaders wished to be perceived as statesmen come to Davos to talk about matters of serious concern – about the devaluation of Thailand's baht, the collapse of the Indonesian rupiah and the Korean won, about the likely effect of the Asian economic crisis in Tokyo and Moscow, about why the United States Congress (a sad collection of provincial politicians, many of them barely literate, nearly all of them badly dressed) refused to ratify the fast-track trade legislation, blocked the appropriations for the International Monetary Fund, and declined to pay the $1.5 billion owed by the United States to the UN. The global economy apparently had replaced the Cold War as the heavy subject about which one was expected to be deeply informed if one was to retain one's standing as a journalist of rank. The old "domino theory" had been supplanted by the theory of "contagion," which referred to the spreading of fiscal and monetary disease from one country to the next. Whereas once it had been understood that unless communism could be contained in the jungles of Vietnam the virus would show up on the beaches of Southern California, now it was understood that large-scale bankruptcy in almost any of the world's markets (regional, emerging, peripheral) was likely to infect the prices on the New York Stock Exchange. Care must be taken, "crony capitalists" brought to book, irresponsible currency specula-tors made to swallow the pills of "austerity." The after-dinner speaker, an economics professor from MIT named Rudi Dornbusch, set forth the preferred attitude toward the financial ruin in the Indonesian archipelago.

"It's important that some people lose a lot of money," Dornbusch said. "Important that they be punished for their stupidity and greed."

His phrase "some people" embraced not only the friends and family of President Suharto but also the Japanese and European banks that had placed fanciful loans all over the roulette table of southern Asia, to no purpose other than their own selfish and myopic gain. The American journalists in the room received the professor's remarks with a show of complacent nods, glad of the chance to recover some of the pride they had lost to their foreign counterparts during the discussion of Saddam's intransigence and Monica's beret. Because American investors had underwritten a smaller share of the Asian risk, which was beginning to look as if it might cost the European banks upwards of $20 billion, the ladies and gentlemen from New York and Washington had found solace, at least for the moment, in a thinly smiling air of superiority.

They also took pleasure in the humiliation of Japan. Five or six years ago the Japanese economy was being touted as the wonder of the world; Japanese banks were buying California, Japanese businessmen were touring the Washington lecture circuit with little sermons about the spendthrift Americans who had lost their knack for making cars. But now that the Tokyo real-estate market had fallen upon stony ground, the shoe was on the other foot, and it was possible to speak of the once sovereign shogunate of the Pacific Rim as a nation famous for the incidence of suicide among the officials in its finance ministry.

Together with the gossip current in the corridors of the Congress Centre, the journalists at dinner offered suggestions about which briefings to attend, how to get invited to the Coca-Cola reception, where to find the Bolivians, when to order the raclette. The evening ended with the company ordering a last bottle of white wine, with Dornbusch deploring what he called "Dial 1-800-BAILOUT for reckless businessmen, greedy bankers, and corrupt politicians," and with a melancholy reprise on the theme of big Bill Clinton's penis.

"If you think that you're missing the point," Foges said, "don't worry about it. Everybody misses the point. Something more important is always happening some-where else."

Although each and every one of the forum's 2,000 participants was important, some were more important than others. The conversations apt to lead to a specific result (the building of a dam in Chile, say, or the writing of the Multilateral Agreement on Investments) took place privately, the time and place and principal speakers omitted from the program. The morning and afternoon discussions in the Congress Centre served the same purpose as the golf and tennis games arranged for the guests attending a conference at the Aspen Institute – a chance to acquire contacts, enlarge spheres of access, possibly drum up an invitation to dinner with the president of Mexico.

The division of interest that remained as constant as the weather – bright blue sky, the temperature at thirty degrees, no wind, very little ice – was the distinction between the buyers and the sellers. The buyers (bankers and industrialists from the wealthy nations) worried about transparency; the sellers (politicians and gov-ernment ministers from the poorer countries) worried about paying their hotel bills. The buyers delighted in grand abstractions and the illusions of omnipotence. Like the characters in Mann's *Magic Mountain*, they were accustomed to the deference of wine stewards, and although they couldn't draw upon the novelist's acquaintance with the music of Richard Wagner and the writing of Friedrich Nietzsche they were heirs to the dream of the *übermensch*, and they had brought with them in their hand-sewn luggage what the correspondent for London's *Financial Times* estimated at "roughly 70 percent of the world's daily output of self-congratulation."

The sellers hustled investment opportunities, and all their numbers were as bright and shiny as the exhibits at a trade show – low inflation, high growth, willing workers, beautiful girls, democratic institutions springing up like mushrooms, re-sponsible fiscal policies, broad vistas, a compliant press, courageous police. Their will to please spoke to the terms and conditions of postmodern imperialism – the lesser nations of the earth become colonies not of governments but of corporations, the law of nations construed as the rule of money, and the world's parliaments intimidated by the force of capital in much the same way that in the eighteenth and nineteenth centuries they had been intimidated by the force of arms. Once upon a time, and even as recently as forty years ago, the community of business interests tended to look upon the politicians as representatives of a superior power; merchants took the trouble to learn the languages south and east of Suez, to send sympathetic agents and maybe presents, seeking an audience with the empress or the king. No longer. Not under the dispensation of a global marketplace conducted in English and held together by McDonald's golden arches and the news on CNN. Now the kings and empresses kiss the ring of commerce.

An exceptionally blunt demonstration of the revised imperialist thesis took place in one of the Congress Centre's smaller meeting rooms before a discriminating audience of American oil-company presidents and French suppliers of municipal infrastructure. A Belgian business executive in a well-cut suit sat on a small stage with three Russian bureaucrats, all of whom looked as if they recently had escaped from one of Chekhov's provincial town meetings, and after introducing each of them in turn, he smiled upon his fellow participants as if he had brought them gifts of rare and precious fur.

"Here we have three active, successful, real-life politicians," he said. "They wish to make important statements."

The Russians spoke in succession from stage left to stage right, like accordion players performing a set of variations on *Moscow Nights*. Some of the translation was hard to follow, but not the principal points of interest: yes, it was true, Russia was a difficult business environment ("still some chaos"), but Russian enterprises had begun to pay salaries ("we have real government, real president, two chambers of parliament"); Russian exports weren't being dumped on international markets ("we wouldn't do that to our good friends, the Europeans"); crime was receding ("here in Russia we have learned how to get the criminals into the investment process"); foreign investors didn't pay taxes until their deals returned a profit ("remember America in the nineteenth century, wonderful place, no antitrust laws"); and 18,000 feet of pipe had been drilled into the Caspian basin without yet hitting bottom in what appeared to be an ocean of oil.

At the end of their recitation the Russians fell abruptly silent, their faces as stolid as cement, their hands clasped patiently on their knees, their innocent blue eyes staring innocently off into the innocent blue distance of the Siberian steppe. The Belgian sponsor was immediately on his feet, talking rapidly into the nearest microphone: "What we have heard, gentlemen," he said, "is exciting news. Stability in Moscow, flexibility in the regions, higher confidence for 'ninety-eight. A bumpy road, *meine Herren*, but in the end, great riches."

The buyers weren't so sure. What they had heard about Russia inclined them to think that foreign money had as much chance of surviving a Russian winter as did the armies of Hitler and Napoleon. Seventy-nine bankers had been shot to death in Moscow or St. Petersburg over the course of the last four years, and some of the other Russians in Davos – not the bureaucrats but the ones who arrived by helicopter with flashy blonde women and suitcases of American currency – didn't seem to have acquired, at least not quite yet, a proper sense of capitalist decorum. They preferred vodka to mineral water, they didn't attend the sessions about the prudent management of long-term corporate growth, and their female companions didn't sign up for horse-drawn sleigh excursions to the picturesque village of Clavadel.

Small windows of doubt drifted across the foreheads of the executives gathering their notes and making ready to depart for the next round of briefings. An oil-company president said that in Russia the criminals were easier to deal with than the politicians ("At least they stay bought"). Somebody else said, "Can you imagine meeting those three guys on a road twenty miles West of Sverdlovsk? They'd make a joke of forcing you to choose between giving them your wife or your car." The editor of a financial newsletter explained that it was no easy trick getting the oil safely away from the Caspian basin. No long-distance pipelines had been put in place, and the possible routes (via the Caucasus to the Black Sea or the Mediterranean, from Kazakhstan to China, through Iran to Kharg Island, via Pakistan and Afghanistan to India and the Arabian Sea, through Russia to Ukraine) were all, in the editor's word, "problematic." "We're talking about bandits," he said. "About people draining oil out of a pipeline in the same way they would take milk from a goat."

Worries about security – security for private investment, security for regional capital markets and corporate communications systems, security for public institutions, for civil society, for Western civilization – bulked large in the conversation at Davos, and the same questions kept coming up in different contexts, different languages, different conference rooms. Not surprisingly, given the ample wealth and assured status of the participants, most of the worry was about the future. For the time being, the good old invisible hand could be relied upon to distribute very handsome stock options, quite a few of them in denominations of $10 million and $20 million, but how long would the good fortune last, and if it wasn't going to last, where on the horizon could one expect to see the heralds of doom? Speaking in which language and bringing what blood-soaked remnant of whose severed head?

Not that anybody doubted the sacred truths of *laissez-faire* capitalism or questioned the sublime wisdom of the bottom line. All present understood that the free market was another name for God, but then again, when one got to thinking about it, the market, like God, didn't always answer everybody's prayers, and some of the more anxious members of the troupe had begun to wonder whether they remained (as the public-relations officers assured them they did) the masters of their fate and the captains of their destiny.

The abruptness of last year's financial collapse in Asia had come as something of a nasty surprise, and maybe the world was a more uncertain place than one might guess sitting here on the terrace of the Berghotel Schatzalp, admiring the plum cake and enjoying the view of the Rinerhorn. Just read the newspapers or listen to one of those policy-institute intellectuals at the Congress Centre talk about Rwanda or the Balkans, or about the Russians raffling off their inventories of nuclear weapons, or that awful story in the *International Herald Tribune*, the one about the Italian businessman kidnapped eight months ago in Brescia. The family had been slow with the ransom money, and the kidnappers were sending little pieces of the businessman's ears (last month the left ear, yesterday the right), as reminders of the outstanding debt.

No sir, it wasn't always easy to justify the market's ways to man. Not that anybody knew how else to proceed, but the market was damned hard to figure, and sometimes it could be downright mean. Which was the reason for all the walking around with the badges and the briefing books – to see if it might be possible to come up with a means of teaching the market how to behave in a civilized manner, maybe tempering its cruelty (which wasn't the market's fault, but merely a fact of its nature) with at least the facsimile of a conscience. A large project and a complex task, and not one to be addressed lightly, but if the men at Davos didn't undertake it, who else would? Who else could sow the wilderness of the free market with the seeds of moral scruple?

At session number fifty-three, "International Corruption: How Can Companies Play by the Rules and Still Win?" the participants assembled in the Salève Room reviewed the lessons of bitter experience. Seated in round, cream-colored leather chairs, they began by exchanging cautionary tales – about the legendary rapacity of Nigerian oil and finance ministers, about the different methods of laundering money in warm and cold climates, about the competitive advantage enjoyed by German manufacturers, who could write off their annual payments of $2 billion in bribes as a tax-deductible expense. The several narratives prompted a number of general observations. Corruption was more prevalent in those countries that insisted on stringent forms of government regulation because no poorly paid public servant in one of the dustier places of the earth could refuse a gratuity of $50,000 from a handsome CEO wearing Italian shoes and a British suit. The poor man would find it hard to look the CEO straight in the eyes, probably would think that he was looking into the face of Quetzalcóatl.

Even so, systematic bribery was preferable, at least in the short term, to random bribery, because "then it becomes a rational cost." But in the long term, bribery under any of its aliases was the enemy of global freedom and bad for economic growth. Bridges and dams collapsed because the money allocated for steel beams financed the prime minister's harem or the general's zoo, and people died in large numbers, which didn't improve local attitudes toward international business corporations. The habit of paying bribes also corrupted the people on the high side of the money. Let the fine gentlemen from London or Dusseldorf become overly adept at dealing dishonestly with others, and sooner or later they learned to become dishonest with themselves, and their own annual reports began to read as if they had been composed under a ceiling fan in Abuja.

Nor was it easy to know how to go about being both a good Christian and a successful capitalist, how to join the act of pitiless self-seeking with the gesture of turning the other cheek, how to balance the observation that what is moral usually doesn't pay against the belief that what pays is, by definition, moral. The delegate from Kenya expressed the dilemma in a remark about borrowing money from the World Bank, which required its loan applicants to first sign a protocol promising not to engage in corrupt practices. It was a handsome and uplifting thought, but standard African business practice being somewhat less than perfect, how then did one buy the tractors, the medicine, or the wheat? The international lending agencies also obliged their clients to protect the borrowed money with high interest rates, which preserved the integrity of the balance sheet but wrecked the hope of economic growth. On the other hand, if the borrowing country offered its citizens the privilege of cheap credit, the foreign banks took away the loans.

If the several concerns about security formed the highest-priority discussion in Davos, the next most urgent subject of general conversation was the euro – guesses as to how and why it would transform European society, speculation about its likely effect on the American dollar, theories about its political origin and historical meaning. The argument in favor of the new currency presented it as a *deus ex machina* guaranteed to make the collective European economy more competitive in the world's markets, and its promoters projected an immense upwelling of surplus energy: more jobs, greater profits, braver hopes, a vigorous rising from what were said to be the velvet sofas of the welfare state. The terms of the Maastricht Treaty obliged the signatories to reduce government expenditures for the comforts of everyday life (free education and health care, generous unemployment benefits, no end of music festivals, etc.), which was a decision none too soon in coming because the European corporate sector could no longer afford to pay the carrying costs. Not if the manufacturers of private wealth wished to keep pace with the Asians and the Americans.

The changes, of course, wouldn't take hold at once, and during the brief period of delay, while the benevolence of the public sector was being transferred to the no doubt equally benevolent offices of the private sector, a certain number of people might experience "disruptions" and "dislocations," possibly even a few moments of temporary "discomfort" and short bouts of "austerity." The inconvenience couldn't be helped, and it certainly wasn't anything to worry about – more like the few minutes of turbulence encountered on a weekend flight from London to Biarritz than like a bread riot in Weimar Germany.

The apostles of the new economic order were ripe with cautionary tales, and it wasn't much trouble to find a banker at one of the conference's café tables eager to talk about confiscatory tax rates and government bureaucracy suffocating the genius of invention – Germany cosseting its workers with six weeks of vacation and another twenty-seven days of sick leave, 3,000 young Frenchmen leaving Paris every month because no employer could afford to hire them (not at what amounted to § 140 an hour when one added the cost of the mandatory emoluments), unemployed workers in Lyon swollen with the gall to demand paid vacations from their paid idleness, the once industrious citizens of Hamburg become as lazy as Italians, as indolent as Greeks, refusing to condescend to menial labor because they enjoyed a higher standard of luxury when living on the dole. Some respondents spoke of leeches; others mentioned parasites or the rock of Sisyphus, but all agreed that the burdens were insupportable, the feckless charity synonymous with ruin. Look what happened to Russia, and know that socialism by any other name is still stupidity or disease; look at China and know that the keys of capitalist free enterprise can unlock even the most abominable of Marxist dungeons. The promoters of the euro never tired of citing the Chinese example, and they were especially fond of Li Lanquing, the vice premier of the People's Republic, who appeared one morning on the great stage of the Congress Hall to deliver what was regarded as an inspiring speech.

Sympathetic to the concerns of his capitalist friends confronted with the prospects of a little deprivation, Mr. Li began by observing that China was no stranger to the "challenges" of "economic restructuring and enterprise reform." In China, 87,000 state enterprises were on their way to being privatized, which in turn meant that 112 million workers probably would be scrapped. Not an easy or pleasant task, said Mr. Li, but one that must be squarely faced. For how else do countries find their way into the garden of prosperity if not by crossing the river of austerity?

"On the one bank of the river," he said, "we have the traditional planned economy; on the other, the socialist market economy. Now, most Chinese enterprises have crossed the river and are doing well after adapting themselves to the environment and law of the market economy... But some other enterprises are still struggling to cross the river by various means: some by swimming, others by boat, and still others by building bridges. I believe that in three years' time, most of them will get on shore successfully. However, since this is a river crossing, some may be drowned."

The audience in the Congress Hall welcomed Mr. Li's parable with grateful applause. A village tale, so simply and inspiringly told. Drowning in the Weser or the Marne was perhaps not as instructive as being washed away in the floodwaters of the Yangtze, but the lesson was the same and well worth bearing in mind when the bus drivers in Mainz or Lille began to complain about the loss of their paid vacation days.

Early the next morning at a breakfast table on the hotel terrace, high up in the light of a new day beginning its descent into the doll-like town of Davos, I made a list of the questions that I meant to ask Dr. Klaus Schwab, the World Economic Forum's founder, chief apologist, guidance counselor and spiritual director. We had arranged an interview for 10 o'clock, and although I didn't anticipate much of a resemblance to the Hofrat Behrens (no white coat, no stethoscope, a Swiss academic in place of the German clinician), I had been told, by Foges and a correspondent for one of the London papers, that Professor Schwab tended to classify the several forms of economic malady under the rubrics of physical illness, speaking of capital markets that were "feverish" or "consumptive," of a "palsied" GDP or a "suppurating" trade balance. It was also said of the professor that he appreciated careful preparation, and so, well-supplied with coffee and sweet rolls, I set about the chore of reading through what had become an extensive collection of scattered notes – informal asides entered in the margins of formal briefing documents (about "cross-cultural moral judgments" and "the outlook for Kazakhstan"), lists of possibly significant statistics (Japan's economy eight times larger than China's; 85 percent of the world's capital held by private investors; Korean Air Lines offered for sale at a price less than that of a single Boeing 747); fragments of conversations overheard in the corridors of the Congress Centre ("I'm a pacifist, but if we're going to have a war, we might as well win it"), descriptive phrases, remarks unavailable to attribution or direct quotation. Many of the notes were no longer valid, an impression acquired on Thursday having been corrected by a fact turned up on Friday, but a surprising number of them recalled a still memorable scene or tone of voice – Elie Wiesel, very much in the character of moralist-in-residence, parsing the text of the Davos meeting for a young woman from Mexican television ("Nowhere else will you find a conference at which so many captains of industry are speaking about the soul"); Archbishop Desmond Tutu, surrounded by a cadre of zealous admirers in the Photo Café, loudly demanding to know what the European central banks meant to do about rescuing the price of South African gold; Shoichiro Toyoda, the chairman of Toyota, defending the honor of Japanese business with an arrangement of clichés as flawlessly constructed as an origami heron, achieving at the end of his recitation the concision of a haiku: "personal trust must transcend history and culture," and, slightly more wistful, "a gentleman's agreement is fantastic if everybody is a gentleman"; Ingo Walter, director of the Salomon Center at New York University, an owlish man in a rumpled suit, very proud of his coining of a new acronym, BOBs, to signify the slings and arrows of outrageous fortune (a.k.a. "bolts out of the blue") that sometimes forced themselves upon the attention of the global economy.

Foges had described the forum's supporting cast of wandering scholars as "the cabaret," a troupe of singing historians and dancing economists, bearded futurists performing magic tricks with statistical levitations instead of with rabbits and silk handkerchiefs, philosopher clowns blowing the trumpets of doom. After only two days in Davos I could appreciate Foges' point, but I was more attracted to the metaphor of a medieval passion play. The corporate participants remained faithful to their program of exits and entrances, diligent in the study of their briefing books, no less earnest than the intellectual entertainment in their mumbling of ritual abstraction, and I could easily picture the company dressed in ermine cloaks and velvet hats, staging in the streets of Bayreuth or Oberammergau an annual perform-ance of the wonderful old Easter pageant, *The Agony of Mammon*.

But neither could I fail to admire the sincerity of their devotions or the wealth of their good intentions, and as I rummaged through the notes spread across a break-fast table at an altitude of 5,000 feet, I thought of the businessmen who hadn't bothered to come to Davos, who didn't think it worth their time and trouble to make the ascent from the low-lying places of the earth, Thomas Mann's "flatlands," where men flailed at one another with stupidity and knives. In New York on the night before I left for Zurich I'd been to dinner at Le Bernadin with three principals in a successful hedge fund who characterized the Davos meeting as a futile transfer of worthless platitudes. The action in New York City during the week in question might turn up something a helluva lot more interesting than snow, and who could afford the lost opportunity cost? Why bother to dress up the everyday cruelties of standard capitalist business practice with the rags of a Sunday conscience? To what purpose, and for whose benefit? Who was anybody kidding?

One of the gentlemen at the table ordered a $2,000 bottle of Latour, in celebration of their fund's triumphant short-selling of the Japanese yen, and when they had finished with the fish, they fell to talking about the prospect of a raid on the South African krugerrand. The sizeable sums of the speculations, their own and those of like-minded investors in London or Hong Kong or Buenos Aires, undoubtedly placed heavy strains on the troubled economies of the two countries, possibly even to the point of forcing the devaluation of both currencies and bringing into play the corollary effects customarily expressed as severe unemployment, high rates of inter-est or inflation, large-scale distributions of misery and fear. So what? Why should they concern themselves with the crying in a foreign wilderness? Self-interest was the name of the game, and if you didn't play to win, probably you were fool enough to go to Davos.

"Fool enough," Klaus Schwab said, "or maybe wise enough to know that there are many kinds of fool, quite a few of them running governments or guns."

He had arrived promptly at 10 o'clock, a balding, blue-eyed man in his early sixties wearing a gray overcoat and a wool scarf, taller than I had expected but otherwise confirming the rumor of a hopeful professor and a chronic idealist. Before bringing up the subject of the cynicism seated at the corner table in one of New York's more expensive restaurants, I'd asked enough questions about the World Economic Forum – its origins and purpose, the qualifications for membership, the nature of its influence – to know that Schwab probably could have guessed which of the investment bankers held season tickets to the Knicks games and which one had ordered the $2,000 bottle of Latour. The professor didn't require attendance on the part of the Wall Street betting crowd, and the forum directed its efforts to those happy few among the world's enlightened capitalists, not more than one in five, who were prepared to extend their sphere of interest beyond the frontiers of a wine list.

Schwab arranged the first Davos meeting in 1971 for the benefit of about 400 European businessmen interested in the societal definitions of the new American word "entrepreneurship." Then a professor of economics at the International Management Institute business school in Geneva, Schwab rounded up a program of speakers knowledgeable in the ways and means of freeing commercial enterprise from the bondage of government regulation. The meeting proved so successful that Schwab reconvened it in 1972. By 1973 it had become the World Economic Forum and an annual event, gradually broadening the range of its concerns and beginning to attract important politicians and prominent businessmen from Asia and the Americas as well as from Europe.

"Suddenly Davos was a place where they could talk to each other," Schwab said, "all at the same time, all in the same place, without having to travel to so many different countries, without having to work through a lot of embassies or appointment secretaries. If you can get them to sit down together, maybe something good will happen."

Organized as a club rather than as a think-tank or policy institute, the forum limits its membership to corporations supported by cash flows of at least $1 billion a year and graced by a chairman or chief executive officer known to take more than a passing interest in world affairs. The annual dues come up to $20,000, and the member corporations (their number fixed at 1,100 by the inventory of first-class hotel rooms in Davos) may send no more than one individual to the January conversations on the magic mountain. Every now and then the forum revises the guest list, retiring those of its members who, although still rich, no longer retain their place at the forefront of new technologies, new ideas. Not always an easy thing to do, shooting the old elephants, Schwab said, but how else did one stay current with the trend and temper of the times? Fifteen years ago the member corporations were mostly European, mostly banks and large-scale manufacturers; now the membership was more evenly balanced with Asian and American corporations, many of them embodying the forward-looking industries – communications, media, tourism, genetic engineering, the retail trades.

As supplements to the Davos meeting, the forum sponsors regional meetings, in Singapore or Cape Town or Washington, and Schwab had noticed that no matter what the latitude and time zone, the conversation over the last decade had been veering away from the sharply defined questions of means – How? At what price? – to a vaguely expressed questioning of ends – Why? For what purpose? He attributed the shift in emphasis to an awareness among the more thoughtful of the world's landlords that the global economy was a good deal more complicated than anybody had thought, and that in the absence of a coherent argument from the socialist left, even the most well-meaning corporate citizens found themselves marooned in a vacuum, a comfortable and well-furnished vacuum, of course, but still, unhappily, a vacuum.

We talked for no more than fifty minutes, Schwab fitting his remarks to the length of a college lecture, and as we descended together in the cabin of the hotel funicular with the late morning crowd of participants (freshly shaven and bright with the scent of expensive cologne, comparing notes about which of that day's sessions they planned to attend), I wondered if the World Economic Forum had discovered a means of assigning its pupils a passing or a failing grade.

Judging by my own observations of the class matriculating at Davos in the winter of 1998, it didn't seem likely that Schwab would find a surplus of honor students. Not because the lords and ladies of capitalist creation (mostly lords, not many ladies) weren't intelligent – a high percentage of them were a good deal more intelligent and considerably better informed than their analogues in the academic and literary guilds – but because they lacked the temperament for politics. They had achieved their success by virtue of their talent for organization, and they defined the dilemma of postmodern capitalism as a problem in management rather than as a search for metaphors. Their opinions largely shaped by the media that they also happened to own, they believed that the world's parliaments served at the pleasure of the world's markets, that politics was a subsidiary function of economics, and that democracy an agreeable by-product of capitalism. Legislatures came and went like football teams and fruit flies, and politicians belonged to one of only two familiar types, both untrustworthy – light-minded demagogues stirring up crowds, or "pesky legislators" constantly bothering people with demands for bribes. Markets might have their flaws, but government was worse. Ideology wrecked the free play of natural distribution, and government never knew how to manage anything – not roads, not dairy farms or gambling casinos or capital flows. All would be well, and civilization much improved, if only a healthy brand of politics (salt-free, risk-averse, baby-soft) could be manufactured in the way that one manufactured aspirin, cameras, and shampoo.

The point seemed so obvious to most of the participants that when John J. Sweeney, the president of the AFL-CIO, stepped up to the podium in the congress Hall on Saturday morning, his audience was predisposed to listen to another ten minutes of government-inspected cliché, resolute in the recognition of the "challenges" implicit in the mechanics of "economic restructuring and enterprise reform." If a Chinese communist could find his way out of the Marxist dungeon, surely an American labor leader could do the same.

But Sweeney turned out to be one of the few people at the forum willing to give public voice to the constituencies of private alarm. Like everybody else in Davos he acknowledged the feats of modern technology and the miracles of corporate production, but he failed to see how the enormous sums of new wealth had been made to serve the needs of the many as well as the pleasures of the few.

"Look around the world," he said: "Japan mired in recession, Asia in crisis... Russia plagued by a kind of primitive, gangster capitalism, Europe stagnant, Africa largely written off... Latin America adrift."

The straws were already blowing in the wind, and unless the profits generated by the global economy were more evenly distributed and equally shared, the nations of the earth could look forward to a siege of violence that "may make the twentieth century seem tranquil by comparison." Nor did Sweeney take much comfort in the proofs of American prosperity proclaimed by the rising prices on the New York

Stock Exchange. Yes, the United States was an economic success story, and some people were doing very well indeed, but one child in four was born to poverty, the schools were in shambles and so were the hospitals and the roads, and no system succeeds, at least not for very long, if the workers cannot afford to buy what they produce. Even in America, that rich and happy land, the widening chasm between rich and poor was becoming more difficult to cross; so were the distances between the literate and the illiterate, between the freedom granted to unregulated capital and the servitude imposed on non-union labor.

"If labor has no role," Sweeney said, "democracy has no future."

The observation evoked murmurs of disagreement and an impatient rustling of programs and briefing books. A Dutch banker rose to suggest that perhaps Mr. Sweeney hadn't been paying close attention in the conference rooms, perhaps had missed the news about the restorative tonic of privatization sure to cure the illness of the Asian and European economies by making them more fiercely competitive.

"What you are talking about," he said, "is protectionism, some sort of gift to American labor."

"No," Sweeney said. "Not protectionism. A fair division of the spoils. At the moment the workers get the austerity and little else. The speculators get the prosperity."

Sweeney's rejoinder dropped like a pebble into a well of indifference, and his remarks would have been dismissed without further notice if he hadn't been followed to the podium by George Soros, the financier as famous for his political philanthropy as he was venerated for his vast fortune. Who could fail to heed the utterances of George Soros, the voice of wealth incarnate and therefore omniscient? At Davos he was the man whom everybody wanted to see, the saviour of Eastern Europe and the patron saint of Prague, who had earned $1 billion in one week in 1992 by speculating against the British pound, a quasi-mythical figure believed to have discovered Rumpelstiltskin's secret of weaving straw into gold. Sweeney's words were of as little consequence as a scattering of sand, but Soros's words were as heavy as the stones on Easter Island, and Soros was as bleak as Sweeney.

Only imbeciles believed in the conscience of markets, Soros said, imbeciles and tenured professors of economics. Markets were as dumb as posts and as blind as bats, inherently unstable because dependent upon what people wish for, not what they have in hand, and therefore impossible to maintain in a state of equilibrium.

"Imagine a pendulum," Soros said, "a pendulum that has become a wrecking ball, swinging out of control and with increasing speed, knocking over one economy after another. First Mexico, then Indonesia and South Korea, and who knows what happens next? Maybe Brazil. Maybe Japan."

The murmuring in the Congress Hall turned suddenly apprehensive, and the pretty girls with the hand-held microphones found themselves besieged by participants wishing to offer an objection. The questions extended the remarks of the Dutch banker. What had happened to the blessings of privatization? To the infinite wisdom of the good old invisible hand?

"Market fundamentalism doesn't work," Soros said. "Without the intervention in Asia of the IMF and the World Bank, the whole system would have fallen apart."

The questions persisted until the time expired, Soros responding to them with an air of cheerful pessimism. Left to its own devices, he said, the global market undoubtedly would destroy itself. Not for any ideological reason, not because it resented rich people or failed to vote Republican, but because it obeyed the laws of motion rather than the rule of reason, and it didn't know how to do anything else except destroy itself. Certainly it would be nice if somebody could invent a set of international institutions capable of restraining the market, maybe something in the spirit of the old Bretton Woods agreement or along the lines of a Federal Reserve System. When economic catastrophes are "big enough to stop the music," Soros said, one needs a mechanism "to restart the lending." Several people rose to ask about the precise nature of the mechanism, wondering how the international institutions might be constructed, and from whom or whence they would derive the patents of authority. Soros smiled and didn't know the answers, and when the plenary session ended in what was still a clamor of anxious voices, he abandoned the company to its further investigations and bid them all a fond farewell.

The speeches and briefing sessions continued for another three days, but to the best of my knowledge nobody found a secret computer password, at least none that was posted on any electronic message board, solving the riddle of the global economy or justifying the market's ways to man. It wasn't that the participants didn't look. God knows, they looked – peering at documents, attentive to the simultaneous translations in Russian and Japanese, steadfast in their consumption of the plum brandy – but they never managed to discover the binding formulas of advanced technology that could invest Leviathan with a Christian conscience or a human face. The variables were too many and too hard to calculate, and even if they could be reduced to well-behaved rows of digital code, the printouts coming back from the Congress Centre's computers presumably would read like the ones issued by the fortune-telling machine in a penny arcade – sell gold, buy Islam, be home before midnight, and don't play Monopoly with Japanese banks.

The next day I left for Zurich, traveling by car instead of train because the journey was not as long and the wide turns in the road enlarged the view of the Grison Alps. Still in company with the canvas shoulder bag and its heavily increased weight of supplementary data, I looked for documents that I could leave conveniently behind, also for the stray observation that might suggest a summary paragraph or a last word. None was immediately forthcoming. At the end as at the beginning, I was still where Foges had found me in the bar at the Rinaldi Hotel, undoubtedly missing the point, certain that something more important had been happening somewhere else.

But neither had Foges been wrong about the number of participants wandering around as if lost or temporarily misplaced, or about the general sense of uneasiness, palpable but somehow weightless, drifting through the smoke-free atmospheres of the Congress Centre. Among the miscellaneous papers spread across the back seat of the car I came across a surprising number of marginal remarks attributed to business as well as media leaders that drew comparisons between the global economy and the *Titanic* – references to the band on the boat deck playing the theme from *The Lion King*, jokes about the emerging market in icebergs somewhere off the starboard bow. Other notes in other briefing books recalled the wistful, almost elegiac, tone that I'd heard in the voices of Shoichiro Toyoda and Professor Schwab, and in a few barely legible lines on an envelope I again encountered the gentleman from Kenya standing in the Congress Hall, very erect and very black, to remind the distinguished panel seated on the dais that in Africa the economic news was far from good, saying of his fellow Africans – not only in Kenya, but also in Rwanda, Nigeria, Zaire – "Don't forget us . . . we are here . . . we are a sleeping lion."

The members of the distinguished panel, American and European bankers who had been discussing the finer points of currency speculation, clearly didn't know much about lions, sleeping or awake, and after looking at one another for a few moments in hope of a helpful comment, they passed silently on to the next question, the expressions in their faces as empty as the deserts of the Sudan. I couldn't tell whether they were embarrassed or merely irritated, but their instinctive shying away from the prospect of catastrophe spoke, more eloquently than all the forum's briefing papers, to the nature of the dilemma placed before the splendid company assembled on a majestic alp in Davos. They were a parliament of managers, and Africa was beyond the pale of management; so were most of the other global propositions (terrorism, environmental degradation, ignorance, and war) brought to the podium in the Congress Hall with the pomp and fanfare of simultaneous translation and overhead projection.

How then were the participants to proceed? They wished to live in a world governed by clearly established rules: rules of contract, rules about the transfers of money and information, rules about the polluting of rivers and politicians. The exact wording of the rules mattered less than a willingness among the interested parties to obey the same rules. A polite thought and an admirable sentiment, but if the men of Davos didn't make the rules, who would? The men of Davos didn't know. They were managers, not the kind of people given to making rules – or laws, or revolutions, or moral codes, which tumbled into the world in a mess of blood and noise, torn untimely from the womb of the status quo.

But where was the comfort in the theory of a universe bound only by the rules of profit and loss? And if the wealth of nations came and went at the pleasure of the "free market," in many ways great and glorious but in other ways as mindless as a ballbearing, then what happened to the fond belief that it was the corporate magi on the magic mountain who controlled the engine of the global economy and not the other way around? How did they escape the thought that even they, the men of Davos, danced like red-hatted monkeys to an organ grinder's merry, witless tune?

The questions didn't invite attractive answers, didn't fluff up the pillows of self-congratulation, and so the men of Davos awaited a miracle born of a foundation grant and revealed as a wonder of high technology, in the meantime holding fast to their dream of virtual government in which careful adjustments made by the geneticists and Nobel physicists in their midst transformed the wayward and ferocious energy of the world's markets into a play of light on a computer screen.

Chapter 10

Governing by Numbers: Why Calculative Practices Matter

Peter Miller

Sociologists are busy rediscovering the economy (Callon 1998; Fligstein 1990; Granovetter 1985). The roles of networks that connect and form agents figure large in this revival of interest in the market as a social institution (Callon 1998: 8). Until recently, however, little attention has been devoted in the sociological literature to the calculative practices that make the economy visible and measurable *qua* economy (Callon 1998; Hopwood and Miller 1994; Miller 1998). In particular, the emergence and roles of the calculative practices of accounting have been overlooked or marginalized in the sociological literature. This chapter calls for greater attention to these practices, and argues that it is important to examine their emergence, and the ways in which new calculative practices alter the capacities of agents, organizations, and the connections among them. It also examines how they alter the power relations that they shape and are embedded within, and how particular calculative practices enable new ways of acting upon and influencing the actions of individuals. Calculative practices, in other words, should be analyzed as "technologies of government" (Rose and Miller 1992; 183) – as the mechanisms through which programs of government are articulated and made operable. Rather than focusing on the ways in which the economy is shaped by economics, attention is directed at the ways in which accounting shapes social and economic relations.

The concern here is not with the whole of accounting, but with that less visible aspect that is labeled managerial or cost accounting in Anglo-American contexts. This includes a variety of techniques for calculating costs, identifying deviations from standards, producing budgets and comparing these with the actual results attained, calculating rates of return for investments, setting transfer prices for intrafirm transactions, and much else besides. As a set of calculative practices, management accounting is a practice deployed not just in manufacturing and service industries, but also in areas as diverse as health, education, and social services. Management accounting today appears to offer a universal set of tools with which to manage an organization as an enterprise, and to act upon individuals and subunits as standardized entities for producing specified rates of return.

As a technology of government, one of the principal achievements of management accounting is to link together responsibility and calculation: to create the responsible and calculating individual. In its concern with individualizing performance, through its attempts to induce individuals to think of themselves as calculating selves, and through its endeavors to enroll individuals in the pursuit of prescribed and often standardized targets, accounting has become a body of expertise focused on exacting responsibility from individuals rendered calculable and comparable. Management accounting seeks to affect the conduct of individuals in such a way that they act freely, yet in accordance with specified economic norms. As a technology of power, management accounting is thus a mode of action that does not act directly and immediately on others. Instead, it acts upon the actions of others, and presupposes the freedom to act in one way or another. The agent who is acted upon thus remains an agent faced with a whole field of possible responses and reactions. Rather than tell individual managers which investments to choose, why not specify a percentage return to be earned on all investments and leave managers "free" to make the decisions as to which investments to choose? A similar attitude holds for budgets. Rather than confront individuals daily over the allocation of resources, why not provide funds to an individual who will have both the responsibility and the freedom to spend the money as they see fit? Why not, in other words, seek to produce an individual who comes to act as a self-regulating calculating person, albeit one located within asymmetrical networks of influence and control? And why not generalize this technology of government to as many spheres of social life as possible? Not only can the manager of a global corporation be governed in this manner, but so too can a doctor, a schoolteacher, or a social worker.

The image of accounting as a purely technical practice is thus displaced by an image of calculative practices as a key resource for a certain "liberal" form of government. Accounting helps to fabricate and extend practices of individualization and responsibility, and it also serves to establish a mutuality or reciprocity between forms of personal identity and the realm of economic calculation. The calculative practices of accounting thus help to create the calculating self as a resource and an end to be striven for. No longer an abstract entity entrapped within economic theory, the rationally calculating self is made operable by the mundane routines and practices of management accounting. To modify a phrase of Hirschman's (1977), management accounting provides a way of "harnessing the interests" of individuals, of utilizing their autonomy rather than seeking to suppress it. And, most important, this can now be achieved within the formally private domain of the large corporation as well as a range of not-for-profit organizations. The management of almost any organization can be transformed into a complex of incessant calculations. The political and the economic imperatives of liberalism are satisfied simultaneously.

The calculative practices of accountancy have one defining feature that sets them apart from other forms of quantification: their ability to translate diverse and complex processes into a *single financial figure*. Whether the processes are automobile manufacture, the assembly of electrical goods, or the administration of health care, management accounting can reduce them to a single figure, thus making comparable activities and processes whose physical characteristics and geographical location are widely dispersed. The labor efficiency variance, the return on investment of a division, and the net present value of an investment opportunity all share this elegance of the single figure. The objectivity and neutrality widely accorded to numbers achieves its most developed form (Porter 1995). The single figure provided by the calculative practices of accounting appears to be set apart from political interests and disputes, above the world of intrigue, and beyond debate. Of course, this is not to say that the single figure provided by diverse calculating machines answers the specifics of the problems it is called on to solve, or that it is always or even typically up to the task. But what is counted usually counts. The avalanche of numbers produced by management accounting links agents and activities into a functioning calculative network.

Sociology's neglect of the calculative practices of accounting is curious in view of its centrality to the sociological enterprise at its outset.[1] It is as if sociologists have been put off by a territory populated by apparently complex techniques; as if they have been too accepting of the view that these are neutral techniques and thus of little sociological significance; as if they have been more generally reluctant to enter the inner sanctum of the capitalist economy. Weber placed accounting at the heart of "rational" capitalistic economic activity. He argued that

> the modern rational organization of the capitalistic enterprise would not have been possible without two other important factors in its development: the separation of business from the household, which completely dominates modern economic life, and closely connected with it, rational book-keeping. (Weber 1992: 21–2)

To the extent that Weber's overriding concern was with the multidimensional rationalization of the conduct of life, or *Lebensfuhrung*, accounting in the sense of both budgetary management and capital accounting was central to the spread of the "specifically modern calculating attitude" (Weber 1978: 86). If one pairs Weber's concerns with the stronger formulations of Sombart (1979), according to whom double entry bookkeeping gave rise to capitalism, then one sees at least the rudiments of a sociology of calculative practices. Rather than relegating accounting to a subordinate and reflective role in economic processes, it becomes a constitutive and formative part of them, a legitimate object of investigation in its own right.

Marx also drew attention to the role of bookkeeping in the development of capitalism. In his ironic description of the activities of Robinson Crusoe on his desert island, he commented on Crusoe's need to divide his time between different activities:

> This our friend Robinson soon learns by experience, and having rescued a watch, ledger, and pen and ink from the wreck commences, like a true-born Briton, to keep a set of books. (Marx 1974: 81)

These pronouncements at the beginning of the sociological endeavor were followed by virtual silence on the part of sociologists for approximately half a century. It was not until the 1950s that a sociological interest in accounting resurfaced, at which point the focus was particularly on the group and its dynamics (Argyris 1952; Dalton 1959; Whyte 1955). And when "behavioral accounting" developed in the 1960s, and specialist journals examining accounting in its social context began in the mid-1970s, this took place largely outside the discipline and institutions of sociology.[2] A sociology of calculative practices was begun, or recommenced, by those academics who were closer to the practices, although they drew in a variety of different ways from the available sociological toolkit.[3]

To illustrate what is meant by a sociology of calculative practices, and how this might be conducted for those practices that go under the label of management accounting, two examples will suffice. The first will examine the emergence of standard costing in the early decades of the twentieth century. The second will address the introduction into accounting during the interwar and post-World War II years of net present value techniques for evaluating investment decisions.

A Standardizing Ambition

An early and decisive moment in the formation of that set of practices that now goes under the name of management accounting was the reformulation of cost accountancy in the first three decades of the twentieth century. Across these years, the vocabulary and techniques of cost accounting changed fundamentally. The notion of a "standard cost," which meant a cost determined in advance and against which "normal" or "actual" costs could be compared, was central to this transformation. Along with the related techniques of variance analysis and budgetary control, standard costing made it possible to apply an economic norm to every individual within the firm. Standard costing made it possible to specify in advance the normal or average cost of a particular operation, and to calculate how far actual costs had departed from this "standard cost." Variance analysis is the term that came to be applied to the various calculations that would enable one to say how and why there had been departures from the predetermined standards.

At the heart of standard costing was the ambition to shape the future. The actions of individuals, and the costs of those actions, were to be subject to a type and level of scrutiny previously unavailable. Cost accounting existed long before 1900, but before then it had only been possible to ascertain costs *after* they were incurred. With standard costing it became possible to predetermine costs by setting standards for the accomplishment of specified tasks. Standard costing supplemented the traditional concerns of accounting with the fidelity or honesty of the person (and with an eye toward making the individual governable by reference to prescribed norms of performance). It made it possible to calculate and analyze variances of actual from standard costs. As one of the principal exponents of standard costing expressed it, instead of leaving the "average man" to the mercy of his own inclinations, "we have set before him carefully determined standards of accomplishment rendered possible by standardization of conditions, and have given him scientific training supplemented by an efficiency reward" (Harrison 1930: 27–8). The calculative practice of standard costing made it possible to govern the future actions of the individual according to prescribed standards and deviation from an economic norm. Efficiency was now individualized.

The standardizing ambition in the costing literature, and its interest in governing the actions and outputs of individuals, was linked to other complementary initiatives. It owed much to the "scientific management" movement that originated in the United States. Taylor's (1913) writings contained many of the elements of what would later become standard costing. These, combined with the costing framework elaborated by Emerson (1919), an American efficiency engineer, helped shape subsequent formulations of a fully integrated standard costing and budgeting system. Together, these related initiatives sought to attack what were seen as the vast and largely invisible wastes that inhered in the daily actions of every individual. By making these wastes visible, and by giving them a financial form, engineers and accountants could collaborate in the common goal of detecting, measuring, analyzing, and removing inefficiencies. Standard costing made the engineering concept of scientific management visible and calculable in financial terms.

The calculation and predetermination of costs not only provides a mechanism through which the achievements of individuals may be compared with norms or standards. The calculation of costs is closely linked to the development and spread of a vocabulary of costs and costliness. This vocabulary helps to establish as legitimate and self-evident the importance of knowing and calculating the costs of activities and individuals. This in turn fuels the call for further calculations. The costly should be compared with the less costly, and product costs should be known more accurately (Hopwood 1987). The vocabulary of costs can operate as an organizing rationale around which debates can take place concerning individual product lines, organizational strategies, or the future of services such as education and health care.

In the United Kingdom an increasing preoccupation with the calculative practice of costing developed during World War I out of the government's attempts to control prices and profits (Loft 1986). Because of the difficulties in determining a "fair market price" for many of the items required for the war, in early 1916 a new clause concerning price was added to the Defense of the Realm Act. This clause stipulated that in determining the price to be paid, "regard need not be had to the market price, but shall be had to the *cost* of production of the output so requisitioned and to the rate of profit usually earned in respect to the output of such factory or workshop before the war" (quoted in Lloyd 1924: 58; emphasis added). A general clause bestowed the power to examine manufacturers' figures. Three basic methods could be used to verify and ascertain costs: technical costing (the estimation of costs by engineering experts); accountancy costing (which entailed ascertaining a contractor's actual cost of production by examining his books); and finally, use of the cost returns from national factories where similar articles were being produced. The last of these methods was widely used in an attempt to reduce the prices paid for munitions, drawing upon often sophisticated costing systems in place in the national factories.

The World War I experience thus expanded the calculable domain within the enterprise and endowed accountancy with a much broader legitimacy. As this expansion occurred, the calculative practices of accountancy moved up the organizational hierarchy and helped to transform the figure of the manager. Now it was not only possible to calculate the performance of workers; the activities of managers could also be subjected to the scrutiny of accountancy. And this was to take place in the name of acting upon the manager as a very particular type of person. Accounting was to take as its object the person of bounded rationality, a figure given clearest expression in the writings of Chester Barnard (1938). Seeking to install responsibility and to remedy deficiencies in rationality on the part of the manager, accounting would help transform the individual manager into a "decision maker" and in the process constitute management as a body of expertise defined essentially by this activity. With the subsequent development of such techniques as return on investment, the linking of managing and calculating was strengthened to the point where they have become almost indissociable.

As accounting has moved up the corporate hierarchy, the enterprise has increasingly come to be known through the calculative practices that have made it measurable and visible. Executive compensation plans, based on accountancy's ideal of summarizing the individual in a single financial figure, make possible comparisons with an economic norm. The manager can be represented as an object, evaluated and acted upon by others as a result of the visibility, calculability, and comparability that accounting provides. And the actions of managers can be linked with the calculations of others, whether these are financial analysts seeking to advise on optimal investment strategies for their clients, governments concerned with national economic performance, or boards of management keen to weed out loss-making divisions of an enterprise and those managers who do not deliver the economic returns sought.

Discounting the Future

If the actions of workers can be made calculable and governed according to an economic norm embedded in a standard cost, so too should it be possible to achieve something similar with respect to the actions of managers, and their investment decisions in particular. Where subjectivity and intuition once reigned, the calculative practices of accounting were to impose objectivity and neutrality. Such was the way in which the debate concerning the use of net present value calculations in investment evaluation came to be posed.[4]

In the 1930s in the United Kingdom a calculative practice hitherto not part of the repertoire of accountants was urged upon them. The notion of the time value of money (the idea that a given sum of money is worth more today than at some point in the future) was held to be a decisive and neglected aspect of investment decisions. Methods such as payback, which consisted simply in counting the number of years over which the original investment would be paid back, were held to be crude and inaccurate since they ignored the time at which future returns would occur. Discounting methods, it was argued, would bring science and objectivity into the investment process by demonstrating that a specified amount of revenue generated at the end of year one was worth more than an equivalent amount generated at the end of year two. As one of the key proponents of discounted cash flow argued in the late 1930s, "the influence of time must be eliminated and this is effected by discounting all receipts to their worth at a given date, say the date of the investment" (Edwards 1938: 14).

Applied to investment decisions, this principle suggested that the timing of future cash returns and the cost of capital were crucial. If one could routinely incorporate such factors within investment decisions made by individual managers, those decisions would no longer be guided, it was hoped, by impulse or subjective considerations, but would be based on a rigorous and calculable financial rationale.

Principles of compound interest existed long before they were used for investment decisions within the enterprise. They had been firmly established in actuarial practice as early as the sixteenth century, and by the late seventeenth century relatively standard annuity tables had been constructed. Moreover, the use of discounting and net present value had been articulated by developments in engineering and political economy in the late nineteenth and early twentieth centuries. But despite these previous developments, considerable hostility could be found in the United Kingdom as late as the 1930s to the suggestion that discounting might form part of accounting and aid the investment decision making of managers. And yet by 1965 views had changed substantially. Drawing on American experience and studies, a wide range of bodies, including government agencies, influential figures working for key firms, television programs, and the accounting profession were proclaiming the advantages to be gained from using discounting techniques for investment decisions. In an extremely influential article written in the *Harvard Business Review* in 1954, Joel Dean argued that discounting techniques offered a novel theoretical framework for managers to understand investment decisions (Dean 1954). Economic reasoning, especially with respect to the time value of money, should be reflected in all invest-ment decisions, he argued. The discounted cash flow method is "demonstrably superior to existing alternatives in accuracy, realism, relevance, and sensitivity" (p. 129).

The machinery of net present value calculations gave a particular visibility and calculability to investment opportunities, rendering them comparable and offering the promise that the subjective element of decision making could be curtailed if not eliminated. The individual manager would be transformed by the calculative prac-tice of discounting, which imposed an injunction to think in terms of the twin concepts of the time value of money and the notion of capital productivity. The headquarters of private firms, or the Treasury in the case of the nationalized indus-tries, would influence the decisions of individual managers by stipulating the precise discount rate to be applied to future cash flows.

In the United Kingdom the promotion of discounting techniques for investment decisions was linked to a wider debate concerning economic growth and the means to achieve it. Britain was seen to be falling behind in the growth "league" constructed out of the vast international statistical apparatuses of bodies such as the Organization for European Economic Cooperation and Political and Economic Planning in the United Kingdom, and discounting techniques were appealed to as an important mechanism that would help to deliver a higher rate of economic growth. Calculations at one level (within the firm) would be linked to calculations at another level (those for the economy as a whole). The calculative practice of discounting was to be a key device through which this economic revitalization would be operationalized. By encouraging or requiring managers to use discounting techniques rather than sup-posedly less sophisticated methods, the investment decisions of individual firms would be improved, and the entire economy would benefit. The United Kingdom could once again take its place alongside other successful industrialized nations.

The appeal of discounting techniques was not only that they held out the promise of replacing subjectivity with science, but that they also provided a simple way of governing the actions of managers. Net present value methods are based on a simple rule: only those projects with a positive net present value are acceptable. This is based on the reasoning that a project is preferable insofar as the returns to it exceed the cost of capital, or the return available by investing the capital elsewhere. The "productivity of capital" was to be the decisive test, a supposedly objective measure of the economic worth of individual investment proposals. Of course there are many ways in which managers can influence the inputs to the final figure that results from net present value calculations to achieve the result they seek, but this does not alter the role that this calculative practice plays in installing an economic norm within the firm. With the introduction of net present value, decisions and projects were given a visibility, calculability, and comparability that had been absent. The actions of managers could henceforth be tied to the calculations of others. In due course, this economic norm was to become a central ingredient in what Fligstein (1990) has termed the "finance conception of control"; that is, a conception of the corporation as a collection of assets to be evaluated by financial criteria alone that began to emerge in the mid-1950s. By the mid-1960s this finance conception of control had become the dominant model for the largest firms in the United States.

As with standard costing, net present value calculations sought to render the future knowable, calculable, and amenable to control. In different ways, they sought to bring the future into the present. Techniques of discounting applied to predicted future cash flows are the clearest expression of this capacity of accountancy to calculate and act upon the future. As a political technology, it not only links calculation and responsibility, but provides a tool by which the decisions of managers within firms can be made comparable to those taken outside the firm in the capital markets. A dense network of calculative practices can thus begin to form.

Conclusion

Even those most distant from the vast pedagogic and professional machine of accountancy are likely to be familiar with many of its concepts and calculative practices today. Terms such as budgets, costs, return on investment, and so forth are no longer the preserve of the specialist. The calculative practices and language of accountancy have seeped into everyday life to an extent that would have seemed improbable to an observer of economic and social life half a century ago. The preceding discussion has sought only to examine two of the principal events in the process by which the ascendancy of accountancy has occurred in a number of Western societies. Other moments in this process could have served equally well to illustrate this process, such as the invention of return on investment and its link to the emergence of the multidivisional firm. Significant also is the development of a range of cost concepts drawn from economics in the interwar years that provided managerial tools, such as cost-volume-profit calculations and break-even graphs. Concepts drawn from economics appealed to the importance of marginal cost and sought to link this concept firmly to that of decision, thereby helping instate a particular managerial vision of the role of accounting. More recently, developments such as activity-based costing have added to the repertoire of calculative practices available to accountants and would-be accountants.

Also of importance are the ways in which innovations in the calculative practices of accountancy are linked to transformations within firms, such as the design of new factory spaces, and how the development of new ways of calculating is linked to new forms of work organization and ideal images of new modes of economic citizenship (Miller and O'Leary 1994). The rearranging of persons and things on the factory floor – in accordance with the proponents of cellular manufacturing, just-in-time systems, and customer-driven manufacturing – calls forth new ways of calculating and new ways of governing individuals. The factory is a veritable laboratory, a site for invention and intervention in much the same way as the laboratory inhabited by physicists and chemists. New realities are created in the factory out of the dreams and schemes of diverse agents based in a multiplicity of locales. We need studies to unravel the complex networks that form within and between firms, and the wide range of related actors beyond their boundaries. We need studies that explore the roles particular calculative practices play in making operable the assemblage of ideas, practices, and people that forms from time to time.

As we enter the twenty-first century, the calculative practices of accountancy are intrinsic to and constitutive of social relations, rather than secondary and derivative. Accounting today exerts an influence on, and is influenced by, a multiplicity of agents, agencies, institutions, and processes. As a calculative practice, accounting represents one of the preeminent devices for acting upon individuals and intervening in their lives in an attempt to ensure that they behave in accordance with specified economic objectives. Accounting affects the type of social reality we inhabit, the way we understand the choices open to individuals and business undertakings, and even how we assess ways of maintaining the nation's health and education. It is fundamental to the manner in which we administer the lives of others and ourselves. Yet the calculative practices of accounting are largely invisible to the public eye, and have been neglected by sociologists.

Contrary to the popular phrase "cooking the books," accounting practices do much more than distort or modify results after the event. Studies of the misuse and abuse of accounting numbers are nontrivial, but they are secondary to the study of the constitutive role of calculative practices. Accounting practices create a particular way of understanding, representing, and acting upon events and processes. Accounting practices create the costs and the returns that can then become the basis for rewards and penalties, and define the profits and losses to which various parties react. They make up the financial flows that have come to achieve such a vital significance in contemporary society. And in so doing they provide a means for acting upon activities, individuals, and objects in such a way that they may be transformed. As one of the preeminent means of quantification in certain Western societies, accounting accords a specific type of visibility to events and processes, and in so doing helps transform them. By calculating and recording the costs of an activity, one alters the way in which it is thought about and made amenable to intervention. Accounting practices require and inspire particular organization forms. Entities such as profit centers, cost centers, investment centers, and strategic business units are unthinkable without the calculative practices of accounting. Equally, much performance measurement would be inoperable without accounting. Incentive structures based on specified rates of return, cost-reduction strategies devised by benchmarking costs against those of a key competitor, or simply a requirement to operate according to a budget are just some of the ways in which the calculative practices of accounting enable the government of individuals. Even when individuals seek to subvert or avoid the calculations made of them, their actions still take place in reference to an economic norm based on accounting numbers.

The calculative practices of accounting are always intrinsically linked to a particular strategic or programmatic ambition. Accounting practices are endowed with a significance that goes beyond the task for which they are deployed. Accounting practices are called upon not just to calculate costs or evaluate a particular invest-ment opportunity but to increase efficiency, to promote economic growth, to en-courage responsibility, to improve decision making, to enhance competitiveness. These rationales are assembled at various collective levels, including the firm, the nation-state, and a range of transnational as well as local entities and forums. They vary geographically, and over time. To understand the calculative practices of accounting as a technology of government, it is important to address these ration-ales, for it is through them that accounting is mobilized and appealed to. It is through them that conceptions of proper modes of governing persons and popula-tions are elaborated. And it is through them that accounting comes to appear essential to the government of social and economic life.

Insofar as accounting makes up the financial flows into which organizations come to be transformed, it actually constitutes the economic domain. It is through the calculative practices of accountancy that the disparate ways of producing and pro-viding goods are made visible in economic terms. Accountancy makes the abstract concepts of economic theory operable at the level of the firm, the organization, the department, the division, and the person. These entities can be construed as streams of discounted cash flows, costs of varying types, and collections of assets with varying rates of return. Rather than begin from the assumption that beyond social relations there exists a realm of irreducible economic events, the perspective is inverted. Economic events and processes are seen to be the outcome of the calculative practices of accountancy. Attention is thus drawn to the reciprocal relations between account-ancy and the social relations it forms and seeks to manage. The calculative practices of accounting are intrinsically and irredeemably social.

NOTES

1   For a more extended discussion of these issues, see Miller (2000).
2   The first journal dedicated to the sociological and organizational analysis of accounting was *Accounting, Organizations and Society*, founded in 1976.
3   For a review of the emergence of a sociology of accounting from approximately 1980 onward, see Miller (1994).
4   For a more extended discussion of these issues, see Miller (1991).

REFERENCES

Argyris, C. "The Impact of Budgets on People." School of Business and Public Administration, Cornell University, 1952.
Barnard, Chester. *The Functions of the Executive*. Cambridge, MA: Harvard University Press, 1938.
Callon, Michel, ed. *The Laws of the Markets*. Oxford: Blackwell, 1998.
Dalton, Melville. *Men Who Manage: Fusions of Feeling and Theory in Administration*. New York: John Wiley and Sons, 1959.
Dean, Joel. "Measuring the Productivity of Capital." *Harvard Business Review* (1954): 120–30.

Edwards, R. S. "The Nature and Measurement of Income." *The Accountant* (July 1938): 13–15.

Emerson, H. *Efficiency as a Basis for Operation and Wages.* New York: Engineering Magazine Co., 1919.

Fligstein, Neil. *The Transformation of Corporate Control.* Cambridge, MA: Harvard University Press, 1990.

Granovetter, Mark. "Economic Action and Social Structure: The Problem of Embeddedness." *American Journal of Sociology* 91 (November 1985): 481–510.

Harrison, G. C. *Standard Costing.* New York: Ronald Press, 1930.

Hirschman, Albert O. *The Passions and the Interests.* Princeton, NJ: Princeton University Press, 1977.

Hopwood, Anthony G. "The Archaeology of Accounting Systems." *Accounting, Organizations and Society* 12: 3 (1987): 207–34.

Hopwood, Anthony G., and Peter Miller. *Accounting as Social and Institutional Practice.* Cambridge: Cambridge University Press, 1994.

Lloyd, E. M. H. *Experiments in State Control at the War Office and the Ministry of Food.* Oxford: Clarendon Press, 1924.

Loft, Anne. "Towards a Critical Understanding of Accounting: The Case of Cost Accounting in the UK, 1914–1925." *Accounting, Organizations and Society* 11: 2 (1986): 137–69.

Marx, Karl. *Capital: A Critical Analysis of Capitalist Production.* Vol. 1. London: Lawrence and Wishart, 1974 [1887].

Miller, Peter. "Accounting Innovation beyond the Enterprise: Problematizing Investment Decisions and Programming Economic Growth in the UK in the 1960s." *Accounting, Organizations and Society* 16: 8 (1991): 733–62.

—— "Accounting as Social and Institutional Practice: An Introduction." *Accounting as Social and Institutional Practice.* Eds. Anthony G. Hopwood and Peter Miller. Cambridge: Cambridge University Press, 1994.

—— "The Margins of Accounting." *The Laws of the Markets.* Ed. Michel Callon. Oxford: Blackwell, 1998.

—— "How and Why Sociology Forgot Accounting." Paper presented at the *Accounting, Organizations and Society* twenty-fifth anniversary conference, University of Oxford, July 2000.

Miller, Peter, and Ted O'Leary. "The Factory as Laboratory." *Science in Context* 7: 3 (autumn 1994): 469–96.

Porter, Theodore M. *Trust in Numbers.* Princeton, NJ: Princeton University Press, 1995.

Rose, Nikolas, and Peter Miller. "Political Power beyond the State: Problematics of Government." *British Journal of Sociology* 43: 2 (June 1992): 173–205.

Sombart, W. *Sombart on Accounting History.* Trans. K. S. Most. Academy of Accounting Historians Working Paper no. 35 (1979). First published in *Der Moderne Capitalismus.* Vol. 2. Munich and Leipzig: Duncker and Humblot, 1919.

Taylor, F. W. *The Principles of Scientific Management.* New York: Harper and Bros., 1913.

Weber, Max. *Economy and Society: An Outline of Interpretive Sociology.* Berkeley: University of California Press, 1978 [1956].

—— *The Protestant Ethic and the Spirit of Capitalism.* London: Routledge, 1992 [1930].

Whyte, W. F. *Money and Motivation.* New York: Harper and Row, 1955.

Part IV Commodity Chains

Chapter 11

African/Asian/Uptown/Downtown

P. Stoller

In 1993 Moussa Diallo, a Malian, sold a variety of African crafts from his table on
125th Street in Harlem. In August of that year, he draped his aluminum card table
with a brightly colored African print cloth – a deep blue background with clusters of
variously sized red, yellow, and green circles that looked like sand dollars. On the
left side of the table he displayed dolls clothed from head to toe in African print
cloth. Behind them, he arranged Woodaabe Fulan jewelry from Niger – black leather
necklaces and bracelets into which were sewn cowry shells and round copper
ornaments. Varieties of silver Agadez crosses, which are fashioned by Tuareg smiths
in Niger and symbolize the Southern Cross constellation, glistened in the center of
the table. They were flanked on the right by reproductions of Ghanaian gold weights
and an assortment of tooled Akan earrings and necklaces also fashioned from
"gold." At the far end of the table, Moussa arranged a collection of kente cloth caps.

On a sun-splashed weekday afternoon in 1994, I went to 125th Street to find a
slow market day. After greeting the traders in the Nigerien section of the sidewalk on
the north side of 125th Street, I said hello to Moussa Diallo. Although he came from
Mali, he had lived many years in Niger and spoke fluent Songhay. I admired his
display of West African crafts and jewelry, and wondered about the kente caps.

"Do they make those caps in Ghana?" I asked Moussa, thinking that caps made
from traditional Ghanaian cloth would have been imported from Ghana.

"No," he answered. "I buy them downtown. You know, on Canal Street."

"Who do you buy them from?"

"I buy them from Asians, who give me a good price," he answered. "Most times
I go downtown to buy. Sometimes, they bring them uptown. The American blacks,"
he added, "like these caps. They sell very well in Harlem."

"Why do they come from Asians?" I asked, wanting to know about the circuitous
history of these objects.

"It's a long story," Moussa replied.[1]

Kente is the name of a colorful, intricate, handwoven silk cloth traditionally worn
by Asante nobles on ceremonial occasions. The antique cloths are colored with

vegetable dyes of deep blue, yellow, green, and red hues and are stitched in subtle and elegant patterns.[2] Large pieces of kente consist of many strips of cloth attached to one another. Kente has always been expensive – the province of members of the Asante nobility, who commissioned their wardrobes. As time has passed, however, old kente has become increasingly hard to find. Newer kente, moreover, pales in comparison to the antique cloth, for "the repertoire of patterns together with the technical skill needed has decreased."[3] In addition, the decline in the quality of yarn and the increase in price have limited the production of newer kente, which is often sold as individual strips. Silk and rayon kente strips – handwoven but admittedly inferior to the original cloths – gradually became popular in the United States. Many icons of African American cultural life began to wear these kente strips as scarves – colorful material badges of African identity.[4]

Sometime in the early 1990s, according to Moussa and his compatriot, Sidi Maiga, who in 1993 was a cloth merchant on 125th Street, enterprising Korean entrepreneurs saw an opportunity. Working from photographs of handwoven Ghanaian silk kente, they designed a cotton print cloth version – for a fraction of the original's cost. Soon their small textile factories in New Jersey began to spit out bolts of economical cotton print "kente," which were shipped to warehouses in and around Canal Street in lower Manhattan. The Asians contacted several West African buyers in Harlem who traveled downtown to inspect the new merchandise. The quality of the "kente" pleased them; the wholesale price per bolt made the cloth a fine business opportunity. Ever cautious with their investment dollars, they tried out samples on 125th Street. Patrons bought up the reasonably priced "kente" in short order, and soon West African cloth merchants in Harlem, boutique owners and street vendors alike, ordered many bolts of what Sidi Maiga called "New Jersey kente."

The reasonably priced New Jersey "kente," which in 1993 sold for 5 dollars per yard (4 dollars per yard for "special friends," large orders, or on slow days) sold well along 125th Street. When African Americans bought the cloth on the street, they'd take it to an African tailor, like Issa Trouré, who worked at Karta Textiles, located at 121 West 125th Street. For a reasonable fee, Issa, following the suggestions of his clients, would transform the New Jersey reproduction of traditional Ghanaian cloth into contemporary African American fashion – including "kente" cloth caps, sport jackets with "kente" cloth lapels, as well as dresses, skirts, and trousers. By 1994 a rather ironic symbolic reversal had presented itself on 125th Street: many African Americans – especially on Saturdays and Sundays during the summer months – would stroll along the sidewalk dressed in clothing fashioned from African print fabrics, including, of course, New Jersey "kente"; many West African vendors, by contrast, would sport the uniform of young urban African American males – baggy jeans or fatigue pants, T-shirts, baseball shoes, and leather hats worn backward or sideways.

Given the rapid transnational flow of people, information, and ideas in 1993, it is not surprising that the success of New Jersey "kente" shocked the African textile industry into action. Ghanaian textile factories, according to Sidi Maiga, had already reproduced the more popular West African cloth designs, undercutting the costs, but not exceeding the quality of their regional competitors. Now they reproduced, he suggested, one of their own traditional designs – kente cloth – and shipped it to New York City as well as to other West African markets. In his magisterial book, *Wrapped in Pride: Ghanaian Kente and African American Identity*, Doran Ross traces the machine reproduction of kente to the early 1960s. "Both Asante and Ewe weavers have serious problems with calling . . . these factory-made cloths 'kente' and view their industrial appropriation something of a copyright infringement. It is significant that these cloths are not produced by the textile mills in Ghana but are turned out in large quantities by mills in Benin, Togo, Côte d'Ivoire and Senegal among other countries (some of which are outside of Africa)."[5]

The "Ghanaian" reproduction of kente, whatever its origin, surpassed the New Jersey version in quality at a cheaper price. Small-time Asian factories, in the end, could not compete with state-sponsored industries. The New Jersey "kente" quickly lost its appeal, and following sound business instincts, West African cloth merchants in Harlem invested in bolts of what they called "Ghanaian kente." Sales of "kente" continued to be strong; profits increased. One Malian cloth merchant, Samba Soumana, claimed that his increased profits, part of which derived from the sale of "Ghanaian kente," enabled him to feed his entire village in Mali.[6]

Korean merchants in lower Manhattan, however, did not want to bow out of a lucrative market. And so they traveled uptown to invest in bolts of wholesale "Ghanaian kente," which they brought to their sweatshops in lower Manhattan, producing hundreds of "kente" caps at a price cheaper than one could get by buying cloth on 125th Street and commissioning an African tailor. Seeing samples of these new caps, West African street vendors traveled downtown to buy "African" merchandise, most likely sewed by indentured Asian immigrants using an African reproduction of an Asian reproduction of traditional African cloth. When these new caps appeared on 125th Street, they sold well and provided substantial profits.

"We told the people," Moussa Diallo said, "that they were kente caps. That's all. The African Americans were happy to buy them."

"Did your clients ever wonder if the cloth was 'true' kente or where they were produced?"

"Some think the caps come from Africa; others don't care where they come from. We don't talk about any of it. They just wanted to wear those caps, which make them feel more connected to the African tradition."[7]

On 125th Street in Harlem, African Americans bought "African kente" caps from West African street vendors who purchased the caps from Asian suppliers. The Asian suppliers manufactured the caps in downtown sweatshops in which mostly Asian immigrants, who were mostly undocumented, quickly produced large amounts cheap clothing. They produced "kente" caps, however, from "Ghanaian kente" cloth, a cheaper and higher-quality reproduction of New Jersey "kente" cloth, which Asian entrepreneurs had previously reproduced from the original handwoven kente. They manufactured this reproduction to sell to West African cloth merchants and African American boutiques.[8]

The convoluted story of the production and reproduction of "kente" caps is a gripping example of the central role of simulacra in contemporary economic social contexts; it is also a concrete case that demonstrates how economic and social networks work in transnational settings. I employ the Baudrillardian notion of simulacrum to unpack West African strategies of marketing Afrocentricity. Here, more briefly, we can compare what anthropologists have written about market behaviors and structures to the experience of contemporary West African street vendors in a global city like New York.

Economic anthropology has a long history in the discipline. Economic anthropologists have written a great deal about many subjects, including, of course, descriptions and analyses of individual market behaviors and the economic dynamics of urban and regional market systems. For example, Malinowski's classic work of the 1920s, *Argonauts of the Western Pacific*, describes and analyzes the mesh of economic and social relationships that made up the Melanesian kula ring, a striking instance of a regional economic network. Since Malinowski's time, economic anthropologists have focused on such varied topics as exchange, money, the economic behavior of hunters and gatherers, pastoralists, and subsistence horticulturists, markets, industrial agriculture, Marxism, and the informal economy.[9]

What conceptual insights can this literature provide a study of market relationships in a contemporary transnational setting? What can the literature tell us about the multidimensional relationships, among African American patrons on 125th Street, Harlem street vendors like Moussa Diallo, Sidi Maiga, Issifi Mayaki, and Asian suppliers in lower Manhattan?

This rich literature highlights some key concepts that underscore social relations in markets – transnational or otherwise. The transaction, for example, is the cement that binds economic relationships in markets. The transaction is "any change of status between a good or service between persons, such as a sale." There are two kinds of transactions: impersonal and personal. Impersonal transactions, like buying clothing from a salesperson in a shopping mall, present few or no social contours outside the context of exchange. Personal transactions, by contrast, are conducted among people, like peddlers and their suppliers, whose personal relationship extends beyond the transaction context; "they are embedded in networks of social relations."[10]

Most economic anthropologists agree that long-term personal economic relationships are superior in many situations. This assumption would most certainly apply to such informal economies as New York City street vending, in which transactions develop almost exclusively from the traders' various social networks. "The most important attribute of long-run exchanges is that they tend to be personalized, meaning that knowledge of the other's personality, family, history, church, and so on is relevant to the trust one has that the exchange will be satisfactorily completed. The riskier the economic environment, the more traders need additional information about a partner over and above the specific facts of the proposed deal."[11] The business connections among the buyers, sellers, and suppliers of New York "kente" cloth and "kente" products, for example, are based on a degree of trust that can only arise from ongoing personal relationships. West African cloth vendors, mostly Malians and Gambians, buy much of their inventory from Asian merchants in lower Manhattan, which means that the two parties have ongoing business relationships. These relationships, which transcend linguistic, religious, and cultural barriers, tend to be limited to economic contexts. Most West African traders know little of the personal or social lives of their Asian suppliers. Most Asian suppliers know little about the history and culture of West Africa. Asians offer the West Africans cheap merchandise – often counterfeits of designer clothing or bolts of New Jersey "kente" cloth. The West Africans usually pay cash for their merchandise, though some Asian suppliers extend them credit. As one West African street vendor put it. "The Asians like doing business with us Africans. We pay them cash, or if they extend us credit, we pay them back quickly. No funny business."[12]

Transactions, of course, involve goods and actors. Goods possess several attributes. Among the most important are the "search" and the "experience" quality of goods. The search aspect of goods includes such attributes as style, dimension, or color. The buyer's problem is to locate the right combinations in the marketplace. "Experience quality refers to those attributes revealed through use such as durability in clothing."[13] Here the buyer must have information about product quality before purchase. Buyers need more information from and more confidence in sellers who deal in riskier merchandise.

An example from the Malcolm Shabazz Harlem Market exemplifies these fundamental concepts. Several Senegalese traders used to sell pirated videocassettes at the market. They received their videocassettes from groups of Arab and Israeli traders who reproduced the cassettes illegally.[14] Cassettes from first-run films typically appeared at the market one to two days following the film's premiere. The cartels made their illegal copies from a stolen or bought original or by using a camcorder to video the film at the opening. Knowing that their Arab and Israeli suppliers had made thousands of copies of the videotaped films, the Senegalese traders knew that a cassette's quality could be somewhat off – a bit snowy.[15] They also knew that their clients would assume the worst about the quality of pirated videos. To bolster buyer confidence, the Senegalese allowed their clients to sample the quality of the videos on televisions that were hooked up in market stalls. As one Senegalese video merchant said: "With the TV my clients can see what they are buying. If they like what they see, they buy."[16]

We have already seen how Moussa Diallo and Sidi Maiga inserted themselves in African/Asian/uptown/downtown networks. Moussa Diallo bought "kente" caps from downtown Asian suppliers. Sidi Maiga bought New Jersey "kente" cloth from Asian suppliers, but eventually received cheaper and lower-priced cotton print "kente" directly from Africa. Issifi Mayaki, like all West African traders in Harlem, has also participated in several transnational economic networks in New York City. As we know, when he first came to New York City, Issifi sold African textiles that he had shipped from Côte d'Ivoire. He lived with fellow Hausa traders in a room at the Hotel Belleclaire and participated in an extended network comprised of his suppliers in the major textile-producing areas of West Africa (Mali, Ghana, and Nigeria), fellow Hausa traders in Abidjan, and fellow traders (Hausa, Songhay, Bamana, Malinke, and Wolof) in New York City.[17] After his financial difficulties when someone refused to pay him for a shipment of goods, Issifi lost all transaction confidence – a prime component in maintaining relationships in economic networks – and he temporarily severed most of the ties in his network of suppliers, transporters, fellow traders, and North American wholesalers.

Facing this loss of inventory, Issifi followed a time-honored practice and sought out members of his own ethnic group from his country of origin. These were people with whom he shared language and tradition – people he could trust. These men sold T-shirts, Africana (cheap crafts like dolls, jewelry, and "kente" strips), handbags, and hats at the informally organized 125th Street African market. Issifi, in fact, had met many of them when they shared space at the Treichville market in Abidjan, Côte d'Ivoire. Ever vigilant to the threat of theft, these traders maintained an informal fund from which compatriot traders who had suffered a loss, like that of Issifi's, might be extended credit to get started again. After hearing of Issifi's loss, his compatriots quickly provided him with a loan. One compatriot, Sala Fari, invited him to share an apartment on 126th Street. Loan in hand, Issifi decided to sell cassettes and CDs. Accordingly, another compatriot trader introduced him to downtown Asians who sold these items cheaply in their stores on and around Canal Street. Issifi paid cash for an inventory of cassettes and CDs – mostly rap, reggae, and rhythm and blues – and set up a table on 125th Street, where he sold his wares to local African Americans and Hispanics and to African American and European tourists.

When Issifi moved to the Malcolm Shabazz Harlem Market, he continued to sell cassettes and CDs, but the nature of his economic network shifted. He now established a formal relationship with the Masjid Malcolm Shabazz, administrators of the new market, which collected stall rents, policed the premises, and resolved disputes among traders. Dissatisfied with the profit margins obtained from selling cassettes and CDs, Issifi decided to return to trading West African textiles, but as a sedentary trader in Harlem. Besides, he didn't much care for rap music or rhythm and blues, preferring the music of Hausa musicians. Issifi also admitted that selling African cloth had brought him much pleasure. He had liked being surrounded by the bright colors and elaborate patterns and looked forward to hanging them again in his market stall. He especially appreciated the aesthetic contours of antique cloth, a few pieces of which he hoped to buy.

His Hausa compatriots and newfound Malian colleagues, the principal African cloth sellers in Harlem, introduced him to Malian, Nigerien, and Senegalese middlemen who wholesaled West African print fabrics in New York City. He also reestablished contacts with itinerant textile traders, whom he knew from his days in Abidjan, who specialized in antique cloth.

When he had firmly established IME African Cloth, I noticed that Issifi displayed a large piece of machine-made "kente" cloth. As an immediately recognizable symbol of Africa, the item attracted much interest in Harlem where the discourse of Afrocentricity has had significant commercial ramifications.

I asked Issifi where he had found the kente.

"I bought it in Midtown from Senegalese."

"Did they get it from Ghana?" I asked naively.

"No," he answered, "it comes from Tunisia. They're doing a lot of African cloth reproductions."

"Is it good for business?" I continued with interest.

"Very good," Issifi replied with considerable satisfaction.[18]

It is clear that the myriad economic relationships of Issifi Mayaki and his fellow traders are shaped through participation in a shifting array of socioeconomic networks. These networks respond with sophistication to the nuances of the global economy, which itself is affected by highly politicized regimes of supply, demand, assessment of profit, and state regulation.

The idea of the social network, pioneered by British social anthropologists, emerged from the analysis of social structure. Pioneers in social network analysis like James Clyde Mitchell and John Barnes had become increasingly frustrated with the inadequacy of British structural functionalism. They claimed that structural functionalism lacked the sophistication to probe the density of social relations in urban research sites.[19] From this perspective, a social network "refers to a set of points (individuals) defined in relation to an initial point of focus (ego) and linked by lines (relationships) either directly or indirectly to this initial point of focus."[20]

Anthropologists, according to Jeffrey Johnson, have considered social networks with one of two models: metaphorical and formal. Many anthropologists who are bent against formal models in sociocultural analysis see networks simply as a heuristic device.[21] They usually consider the network as a social "given." The great thrust of anthropological writing about networks, however, has been concerned with the formal analysis of social network data gathered primarily in complex societies.

There are many debates between culturally oriented cognitive anthropologists, who do network analysis of kinship, semantic fields, and self-report data, and the more sociologically oriented analysts who employ network analysis to generate more powerful explanations of social activities. Much of this formal literature has examined mathematical applications, schemes for sampling, tests for reliability of self-report data, and the nature of intracultural variation. Although this literature is inherently interesting, especially for anthropologists with formal training in mathematics, it is of only partial relevance to a study of the dynamics of New York's West African trading networks.

Of greater relevance are those studies that link ethnographic practice to social network analysis.

> There is no doubt that networks were an important element in the earlier work of social anthropologists in urban settings ... but it was more than the complexity of urban life that led these researchers to rely on these concepts so centrally in their work. Had they been survey researchers, it is doubtful that the notion of a social network would have had such a prominent place in their studies. Because they were ethnographers, engaged in the web of everyday life, an understanding of social networks was critical for obtaining the latest gossip, seeking information on hard-to-see events (e.g., rituals, drug use), and establishing friendships that would ultimately lead to the development of key informant relationships. It was the ethnographic context itself that, explicitly or implicitly, made understanding network relations so important.[22]

As Mary Noble stated more than a generation ago: "A network approach then appears to offer a deeper understanding of human behavior."[23]

This innovative analytic technique has resulted in several important studies of urban networks. Scholars have studied the personal networks of former mental patients and delimited urban structures by isolating overlapping cliques. Others have applied the same technique further afield. Thomas Weisner, for example, has focused on the dynamics of urban–rural networks in East Africa, discovering that network entanglements vary with clan, social rank, and location.[24]

There are two kinds of social networks that anthropologists have considered: personal and whole. The great thrust of anthropological writing has focused on personal, or ego-centered, social networks. Within these networks, according to Mitchell, social behavior is interpreted in terms of three orders of social relations:

structural, categorical, and personal. The structural order concerns the relation of the individual to some kind of institution (family, association, or trade union). The categorical order refers to how behavior is considered in terms of such broad social constructs as class, race, or ethnicity. The personal order, by contrast, is a framework for behavioral interpretation held in place by the mesh of the individual's personal relationships in a social network.[25]

When people in social networks interpret behavior from one of the three frameworks, they generate, in Mitchell's language, information, transactions, and expectations. Information that is exchanged between members of a social network is extremely important in economic contexts, for information about goods is central to ongoing transactions. After the theft of his cloth inventory, Issifi Mayaki integrated himself in the network of compatriot street vendors in New York City through which he acquired an informal loan. Issifi also received information from compatriot traders that enabled him to find reliable suppliers of cassettes and, later on, textiles, both original and reproduced.

Transactions define a key activity in the social networks of West African traders in New York City. People in these multiplex networks, which transcend ethnic and national categories, engage in continuous transactions. There are, of course, countless exchanges between West African merchants, with many permutations. Thus, it is possible to find

1 exchanges between compatriots of the same ethnicity (e.g., Nigeriens who are both Hausa);
2 exchanges between compatriots of differing ethnicity (e.g., a Songhay and a Hausa Nigerien);
3 exchanges between noncompatriots of the same ethnicity (e.g., a Malian and a Nigerien Songhay); and
4 exchanges between noncompatriots of differing ethnicity (a Malian Fulan and Senegalese Wolof).

The greater the degree of proximity between national identity, the greater the density of transaction. Compatriots of the same ethnicity exchange inventory and extend one another informal loans. Sometimes they combine resources to travel to what they call the American bush. In the summer of 1995, Soumana Harouna, Issifi Mayaki, Amadou Bita, Moussa Boureima, and Sala Fari, Nigerien Hausas all, frequently traveled in the American bush. These travels usually excluded non-Hausa and non-Nigeriens. Transactions in the informal economy of New York City, of course, are not limited to exclusive West African networks. As we have seen, West African street vendors are supplied by a variety of wholesale traders – Asians, Arabs, and Israelis. In Harlem, many traders enter informal agreements with African American, Korean, and Jewish store owners, who rent them storage space. In lower Manhattan, West African traders rent store and shelf space from Jewish and Arab store owners.

One must also consider to whom West African vendors sell their merchandise. Issifi Mayaki, for example, sells almost exclusively to patrons at the Malcolm Shabazz Harlem Market, which means that most of his clients are local African Americans. In addition, he sometimes sells items to tourists: Europeans, Japanese, and Americans, both African Americans and whites curious about Harlem, which, it should be added, has become a favorite tourist stop in Giuliani's New York. At the Malcolm Shabazz Harlem Market, entrepreneurs like Boubé Mounkaila, who has sold both leather goods from Niger and wristwatches from Korea and China, routinely ask tour group leaders to bring tourists to their booths – for a fee, of course.

Some of the traders at the market have engaged in both retail and wholesale activities. Issifi Mayaki has sold colorful African cloth to individual buyers at the market, but has also supplied cloth to various African American boutiques up and down the East Coast of North America.

Information and transactions result in varying amounts of economic satisfaction, which in turn generates multiple sets of expectations. In Mitchell's language, the normative content of social networks "refers to that aspect of the relationship between two individuals which can be referred to the expectations each may have of the other because of some social characteristic or social attribute the other may possess ... These perceptual categories exist as frameworks for evaluating the behavior of people in the appropriate situations."[26] Prior to the theft of his inventory, Issifi participated in the wide-ranging social networks associated with the African art and textile trade in the United States. The theft obliterated his trust in international textile traders, and as a result, his expectations of them, which had been based on Islamic precepts, shifted. Asian traders say they like to do business with West Africans because men like Boubé Mounkaila and Issifi Mayaki usually pay in cash. If they are extended credit, according to the Asians, they repay their informal loans quickly. Based on their transaction experience, Asians expect West Africans to be good trading partners. By the same token, they tend to be suspicious of African American informal traders, expecting them to be devious or dishonest. Such a belief may well be the result of their transaction experience or of what Mitchell calls the categorical order in which behavior – actual or expected – is judged in terms of a person's social category. In the latter case, the Asian assessment of African American traders seems to spring from a combination of actual experience and racist stereotyping, all of which affects how information and transactions course through the maze of socioeconomic networks.

With this focus on the personal, anthropologists have been less concerned with what Johnson calls "whole networks," more abstract structures that can be represented in matrix form. Studies of "whole networks" have considered "studies of relations, studies of structures, and statistical approaches to the study of networks."[27] More specifically, scholars working on whole networks are concerned with such issues as the dynamics of network formation, network density and clustering, formal treatments of how people communicate through networks and how network structures affect decision making.[28] Working specifically with economic networks, Borje Johansson constructs a variety of mathematical models that describe the dynamics of economic organizations that have "composite internal networks for resource flows and for communication and coordination of production and other activities. The links of such networks function as channels for information exchange and flow of resources. Attached to internal networks one can identify links which extend beyond the boundaries of each organization. Those links connect the organization with other economic units." After presenting a dizzying array of equations that construct models to predict market behavior, Johansson states that his work "suggests how and under which conditions the economic links remain, develop or disappear. The links form networks and these we claim to be an important ingredient in many types of markets."[29]

Although Johansson's equations are of questionable relevance to an ethnographic study of economic networks in transnational spaces, his framework is quite useful. The personal networks of individual West African traders do indeed consist of a series of what Johansson calls links across which information and goods flow. In New York City, moreover, the network of West African informal traders is linked to other networks that constitute other kinds of economic organizations: Asians in lower Manhattan; Arabs and Israelis in midtown Manhattan; Arabs, Jews, and Pakistanis along Canal Street; cloth and leather goods suppliers in Ghana, Cameroon, and Mali.

To render these networks a bit more precisely, let us reconsider the economic links of Issifi Mayaki in terms of network analysis. Consider figure 11.1, a schematic of Issifi's is part of a large network of West African traders in New York who are connected through ties of fictive kinship, ethnicity, and national identity. This network has varying degrees of density, determined by the frequency and nature of interaction between Issifi and his trading partners. The space closest to Issifi, noted as area 1, is reserved for people who like Issifi are Hausa and Nigerien. These men are Issifi's intimates, with whom he shares a wealth of information and resources that constitute a foundation of sociocultural, emotional, and economic support. Compatriots who do not share Issifi's ethnicity are linked in area 2. Issifi has frequent contact with these Nigerien Songhay and Fulan men, but he doesn't share an African language with them, and because of historical and sociocultural differences, the level of economic trust and social intimacy doesn't match that of his contacts in area 1.[30] Moving further from Issifi's center, we encounter traders from Mali, proximate to Niger, who share with Issifi neither ethnicity nor national identity. These men are Bamana, Fulan, and Soninke, ethnic groups with whom

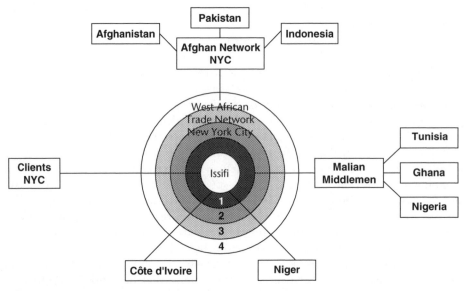

Figure 11.1 Issifi Mayaki's personal economic network.

Issifi has had extensive economic and social contact in Niger and Côte d'Ivoire. They are middlemen in Issifi's cloth dealings and occupy a more distant space in Issifi's network, area 3. Issifi has less extensive contact with Senegalese traders, mostly Wolof. Many of them are Mourids, who owe allegiance not so much to other West Africans in New York City as to their *cheik* in Touba City, Senegal.[31] In our depiction of Issifi's network, they are located in area 4. As we move farther out into the space of Issifi's West African trading network, the frequency of contact and degree of trust diminishes.

Issifi's economic network in New York, of course, is not limited to West Africans. He receives some reproduced cloth from Asians (Indians, Pakistanis, and Afghanis) who are, in turn, linked not only to Issifi but to their own Asian contacts in New York as well as to suppliers in India, Pakistan, and Indonesia. In Issifi's network, these non-African links are both literally and figuratively more distant than his West African connections. His interactions with the former are purely economic and short-lived. There is a lack of shared culture, although trust has built up over time through mutually satisfactory transactions.

Issifi's links to clients extend the space in his personal economic network. He has a few regular clients to whom he sells cloth. Most of his clients are either local African Americans or tourists – Americans of all backgrounds, Europeans, and Japanese. The social contours of specific transactions frame these socially distant, but economically productive, interactions.

Issifi's personal economic network among West Africans is not limited, of course, to New York City. He has economic and social ties to both Côte d'Ivoire, where his father and brothers reside, and to Niger, where his mother and her kin live. Like many West African long-distance traders, his kinship and economic networks are inextricably linked. This linkage, a process of using kinship idioms and ideology to shift social dislocation into culturally productive categories, transforms urban social instability and uncertainty into economically productive social continuity.[32] The linkage of kinship and long-distance trading has been common among African merchants. There are many traders in New York City, however, who are part of international networks that are not kin-based. Even so, as we have seen, the social continuity of these networks is ensured by the mutually binding system of rights and obligations characterized by West African systems of kinship.

The depiction of Issifi's transnational and transcultural interactions in figure 11.1, despite its complexity, is nonetheless incomplete, for it primarily plots Issifi's economic interactions. It says little about how political and legal regimes – and their representatives – affect his economic well-being. It reveals even less about how people in his personal network provide him social and emotional support.

Boubé Mounkaila refers to himself as a leather specialist. He has been selling African leather goods – purses, wallets, satchels, traveling bags, and attaché cases – since his arrival in the United States in 1990. Boubé says that he likes to sell African leather goods. He likes the ingenuity of their various designs as well as the opportunity they give him to meet a wide assortment of people – mostly women. Since 1996 he has complemented his African bag inventory with wristwatches. Between 1990 and 1992 Boubé sold from makeshift tables on 34th Street near Times Square. Although that spot in midtown Manhattan provided him substantial returns on his investment, he found it difficult to deal with continuous police pressure. "The police would come and ask if I had a permit. I didn't. But they liked me and didn't give me a fine and didn't ask me for my papers. They just told me to move on."[33]

After Boubé had some of his leather inventory confiscated, he decided, based on information gleaned from links in his personal economic network, to try to sell his wares on 125th Street in Harlem. His contacts told him that the police would not bother him uptown and that 125th Street, Harlem's main thoroughfare, attracted legions of shoppers. He set up his table with Sala Fari, on the north side of 125th Street between Lenox and 7th Avenues, where a cluster of Nigerien traders, Hausa and Songhay, had established themselves. The information he had received through his network proved to be correct. Even though he had no permit to sell his goods, Boubé operated his business openly without any interference from the police. At that time, New York's finest seemed more interested in ticketing illegally parked cars than enforcing city regulations, licensing agreements, or trademark statutes. As promised, legions of shoppers filled the streets during the week and especially on weekends.

Boubé's personal network, however, is far different from that of Issifi (see figure 11.2). Although both of them share links in a West African trading network, Boubé, who is a Songhay, gathers his economic information from a wider array of sources, many of whom are non-Songhay and non-Nigerien. Unlike the Hausa, who have a long history of relying on one another in long-distance trading situations, Songhay are more widely known for their warrior past than for their prowess as long-distance traders. Boubé, for example, has rarely traveled in the American bush with his compatriots. He routinely receives information on market and other economic

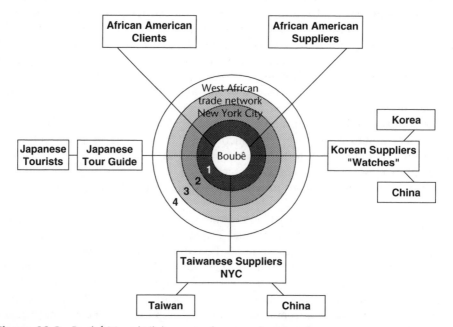

Figure 11.2 Boubé Mounkaila's personal economic network.

conditions from Senegalese traders and from African American clients and suppliers
– people who are more culturally and experientially distant from him.

He also has ongoing and productive economic relationships with Taiwanese and
Korean watch wholesalers. Since both the Taiwanese and Koreans supply Boubé
with knockoff goods (watches with "trademarked" logos), trust is a major component of their relationships. Boubé says he has always paid his Taiwanese and Korean
suppliers in cash, which, he says, instills confidence and ensures continuity. He also
says that his Asian suppliers have never complained to him about police harassment,
or citations, meaning, from Boubé's perspective, that they trust him with their
"unregulated" merchandise.[34]

In August of 1994 this trust was momentarily compromised – unwittingly so.
Boubé had invited me to meet his Taiwanese wristwatch supplier, who has a
showroom near Broadway and 28th Street, a section in Manhattan called the Gift
District. This neighborhood, which is mostly Asian, is well known for its wholesale
business in hats, caps, handbags, beads, and costume jewelry. Before entering the
shop, Boubé pointed out other Asian wholesalers – Broadway Bags and Ronette
Hats – major suppliers of West African traders. Accordingly, it was not surprising to
see many West African traders, mostly Senegalese, walking along streets with bags
filled with newly purchased inventory. We entered the showroom.

Two young Taiwanese greeted Boubé by name.

"This is my friend, Paul," Boubé said introducing me.

The Taiwanese men frowned and seemed visibly upset.

Sensing their discomfort, Boubé said: "He's been to my country and to my village
and he speaks my language. He's really an African," he said.

One of the young men said he didn't believe Boubé.

"Listen," Boubé said turning to me. In Songhay he said: "Speak Songhay to me.
These people think you're a cop who has come here to arrest them."

"Why do they think I'm a cop?" I responded in Songhay.

"They wonder why else would a white man wearing jeans accompany an African
trader on a visit to his supplier of knockoff watches?"

"I see," I said to him. I turned toward the two young Taiwanese and spoke to them
in English. "I lived in Boubé's country for seven years. Now I live near Philadelphia
where I work as a teacher. When I come to New York, I like to visit him and speak
his language. He invited me here to meet you."

With that explanation, some of the tension drained from their bodies and they
smiled a bit as they extended their hands to me.

"Boubé," one of the men said to me, "is a good customer. Always pays his bills."

The Taiwanese still seemed nervous. Boubé inspected the new inventory and
ordered 150 watches. One of the young men calculated the bill for the wholesale
goods; it came to $450.00.

"I'll come back tomorrow with cash and pick up the order," Boubé said.

"But, Boubé," one of the young men said, "you take the order now. We trust you."

"No thank you. You know that I'd rather pay and then pick up the order
tomorrow."

One of the Taiwanese smiled at me. "Boubé is a good customer."

After we left the showroom, Boubé said that the Taiwanese's nervousness hadn't
surprised him. "They think that a bearded white man wearing jeans," he said in

French, "is going to be the police or an undercover agent for the City [the Bureau of Consumer Affairs, which enforces trademark statutes]. These Chinese," he said, "are often suspicious of whites and African Americans, but usually get on well with African traders."[35]

I was pleased that my visit had not compromised Boubé's relationship with his wristwatch supplier, but it underscored the legal fragility of unregistered operations that are major links in the transnational networks that constitute much of New York City's informal economy. This fragility requires a bond of unflagging trust between economic partners, a trust that, given the conditions of informality in New York City trading, frequently transcends sociocultural and national boundaries.

Boubé's network has also been linked to African Americans in Harlem. Prior to 1997 he stored his inventory of leather goods in a battered black Econoline van. Although Boubé was at the time an undocumented alien who had no driving license in Niger or New York, he managed to buy the van from another West African – no questions asked. Enlisting the aid of compatriots, he procured liability insurance. In 1996, Boubé painted the address "1 Fifth Avenue," on one of the van's side panels, an address, he said jokingly, that gave his van an aura of economic authenticity. He proudly showed me his inspection stickers. Even with its 145,000 miles, the vehicle had easily passed.

The van became central to Boubé's operation. At the end of each business day, Boubé packed the van with his inventory and took it to a fenced-in "security" parking lot at 123rd Street and Park Avenue – just under the Metro North railroad tracks. He paid $150 a month to the African American attendants, which enabled him to park his vehicle there. After thieves broke into his "secured" van, Boubé found another parking/storage facility at Lexington Avenue and 125th Street. Because of his then undocumented status, he didn't report the theft to the police. Frustrated by the expense and time he had to devote to storage, Boubé eventually built and secured his own storage bins at the Malcolm Shabazz Harlem Market. "No more parking garages. No more dealings with the parking garage people."[36] By tapping into his network, Boubé had been able surmount a variety of economic challenges. By the winter of 1998, an improving economic climate combined with Boubé's commercial skills brought a flood of profits to his enterprise, enabling him to buy a Lexus.

We have sampled a slice of life at the Malcolm Shabazz Harlem Market and have seen the broader economic and social context within which West African traders in New York City operate. We have also considered how Islam and the history of long-distance trade in West Africa have influenced the trading practices of West Africans in New York City. Through those time-honored practices, West African traders have created complex and highly flexible transnational networks from which they derive valuable information, generate trust, and receive economic support.

I have tried to present an overview, then, of a community whose economic values are profoundly influenced by their faith and by their cultural and family histories. We also have a sense of how they have employed tradition to meet the economic challenges of a global city's informal economy. In short, we have seen how and why West Africans have established their informal enterprises in New York City.

NOTES

1 Interview with Moussa Diallo, August 17, 1994.
2 There are many fine studies of West African textiles. Among the best are Picton and Mack (1989) and Ross (1998).
3 Picton and Mack (1989: 124).
4 There are several African American enterprises that import handwoven kente strips from Ghana. Among the most important of these is Motherland Imports located in Los Angeles and Atlanta, which sells kente for pastors' robes, church choirs, sororities and fraternities, and for graduations.
5 Ross (1998: 27); also interviews with Moussa Diallo and Sidi Maiga, August 17, 1994.
6 Interview with Samba Soumana, July 24, 1994.
7 Interview with Moussa Diallo, August 17, 1994.
8 Interviews with Moussa Diallo and Sidi Maiga, August 17, 1994.
9 There is a vast literature in economic anthropology. Among the most significant studies, though this list excludes many fine works, are Malinowski (1961) Herskovits (1952); Bohannan (1955); Mintz (1974, 1985); Nash (1966); Sahlins (1972); Schneider (1974); Wolf (1966, 1982); Bloch (1975); and Godelier (1977).
10 Plattner (1989: 209, 210).
11 Ibid., 211.
12 Interview with Boubé Mounkaila, April 24, 1997.
13 Plattner (1989: 214).
14 Roberts (1996: 66–7).
15 Interviews with Boubé Mounkaila, March 15, 1993, and Garba Hima, August 1, 1994.
16 Interview with Jabar Tall, April 24, 1997.
17 The African art and textile traders had – and have – a warehouse in Chelsea, where shipments from Africa are stored and from which African art and textiles are shipped by van throughout the United States to boutiques, gallery owners, and private clients. In a future study, I hope to investigate West African traders who sell African art in North America.
18 Interview with Issifi Mayaki, April 24, 1997.
19 See Barnes (1954, 1969); Mitchell (1974, 1989); see also Johnson (1994: 118).
20 See Kapferer (1973: 84).
21 See Walsh and Simonelli (1986: 46); cited in Johnson (1994: 115).
22 Johnson (1994: 132).
23 Noble (1973: 10).
24 See Sokolovsky et al. (1978) and Foster and Seidman (1982) on urban networks; Weisner (1978) on urban–rural ties in Kenya; and for a recent study of a transnational trading network, MacGaffey and Bazenguissa-Ganga (2000).
25 See Mitchell (1973: 20).
26 Ibid.: 26.
27 See Johnson (1994: 116–17).
28 See Batton, Casti, and Thord (1995); see also Johnson (1994: 117).
29 Johansson (1995: 287, 305–6). Much of the literature on whole networks is highly technical; it is a key component of what some scholars have called mathematical anthropology. The sociological and economic literature on social networks is perhaps more mathematical than that of anthropology (see Batton, Casti, and Thord 1995). Many of the abstract models, sampling schemes, and computer programs used to locate network clusters seem rather far removed from the ground-level dynamics of network

interactions. Plattner criticizes some of this abstract modeling, suggesting that while some models "were...intellectually and graphically elegant" many of them "were not shown to be truly descriptive of real-world situations" (1989: 195). Bax (1978) criticizes much of the literature on social networks for its almost exclusive focus on modeling and statistical techniques.

30   There is a long history of ethnic enmity in Niger. As a consequence, there is much rivalry and bitterness between the Songhay, Hausa, Fulan, Kanuri, and Tuareg peoples. Considering the ethnic politics of the Republic of Niger, these deep-seated conflicts are far from disappearing. See Charlick (1991).

31   In the years since their founding in 1898, Mourid wealth and influence in Senegal have grown exponentially. The order's founder, Ahamadou Bamba, preached that hard work constituted the path to pious salvation. Adepts worked hard for the *cheik* and provided him a percentage of their earnings. This practice continues today among Mourid adepts, who make up a substantial percentage of the Senegalese population in New York City. See O'Brien (1971); Malcolmson (1997).

32   See Jacobson (1971: 641). Jacobson's essay is an attempt to understand the social processes involved in the construction of "kin"-based networks in urban settings, not unlike New York City, where social relationships are fleeting and filled with uncertainties. He writes: "Urban populations are typified by geographical mobility, which is often described as producing uncertainty and, potentially, social instability. Social stability, by contrast, requires an expectation of future interaction or continuity. One strategy, therefore, for coping with uncertainty in urban social life is to generate or confirm social continuity in social relations, a process which requires the actors' social perception of factors and circumstances affirming their future interaction" (ibid: 630).

33   Interview with Boubé Mounkaila, August 14, 1996.

34   Interview with Boubé Mounkaila, August 16, 1994.

35   Ibid.

36   Interview with Boubé Mounkaila, April 24, 1997.

REFERENCES

Barnes, John A. (1954) Class and Committees in the Norwegian Island Parish. *Human Relations* 7: 39–58.

——(1969) Graph Theory and Social Networks: A Technical Comment on Connectiveness and Connectivity. *Sociology* 3: 215–332.

Batten, David, John Casti, and Roland Thord, eds. (1995) *Networks in Action: Communication, Economics, and Human Knowledge*. Berlin: Springer-Verlag.

Bax, Mart. 1978. Figuration Analysis: A Better Perspective for Networks, with an Illustration from Ireland. *Anthropological Quarterly* 51: 221–30.

Bloch, Maurice, ed. (1975) *Principles of Marxist Anthropology*. New York: Academic Press.

Bohannon, Paul (1955) Some Principles of Exchange and Investment among the Tiv. *American Anthropologist* 57: 60–9.

Charlick, Robert (1991) *Niger: Personal Rule and Survival in the Sahel*. Boulder, Co: Westview Press.

Foster, B. L. and S. B. Seidman. (1982) Urban Structures Derived from Overlapping Subsets. *Urban Anthropology* 11: 177–92.

Godelier, Maurice. 1977. *Perspectives on Marxist Anthropology*. Trans. Robert Brain. Cambridge: Cambridge University Press.

Herskovits, Melville (1952) *Economic Anthropology*. New York: Knopf.

Jacobson, David (1971) Mobility, Continuity, and Urban Social Organization. *Man* 101: 630–44.

Johannson, Borge (1995) The Dynamics of Economic Networks. In *Networks in Action: Communication, Economics, and Human Knowledge*, ed. David Batten, John Casti, and Roland Thord, 287–309. Berlin: Springer-Verlag.

Johnson, Jeffrey C. (1994) Anthropological Contribution to the Study of Social Networks: A Review. In *Advances in Social Network Analysis*, ed. Stanley Wasserman and Joseph Galaskiewicz, 113–52. Thousand Oaks, CA: Sage.

Kapferer, Bruce (1973) Social Network and Conjugal Role in Urban Zambia: Toward a Reformulation of the Bott Hypothesis. In *Network Analysis: Studies in Human Interaction*, ed. Jeremy Boussevain and John Clyde Mitchell, 83–110. The Hague: Mouton.

MacGaffey, Janet, and Rémy Bazenguissa-Ganga (2000) *Congo–Paris: Transnational Traders on the Margins of the Law*. Bloomington: Indiana University Press.

Malcolmson, Scott (1997) West of Eden: The Mourid Ethic and the Spirit of Capitalism. *Transition* 79: 24–44.

Malinowski, Bronislaw [1922] (1961) *Argonauts of the Western Pacific*. London: Dutton.

Mintz, Sidney (1974) *The Worker in the Cane*. New York: Norton.

—— (1985) *Sweetness and Power*. New York: Random House.

Mitchell, James C. (1974) Social Networks. *Annual Review of Anthropology* 3: 279–99.

—— (1989) Algorithms and Network Analysis: A Test of Some Analytical Procedures on Kapferer's Tailor Shop Material. In *Research Methods in Social Network Analysis*, ed. L. C. Freeman, D. R. White, and A. K. Romney, 319–65. Fairfax, VA: George Mason University Press.

Nash, Manning (1966) *Primitive and Peasant Economic Systems*. San Francisco, CA: Chandler.

Noble, Mary (1973) Social Network: Its Use as a Conceptual Framework in Family Analysis. In *Network Analysis: Studies in Human Interaction*, ed. Jeremy Boissevain and John Clyde Mitchell, 3–15. The Hague: Mouton.

O'Brien, Conor Cruise (1971) *The Mourids*. Oxford: Oxford University Press.

Picton, John, and John Mack (1989) *African Textiles*. London: British Museum.

Plattner, Stuart (1989) Economic Behavior in Markets. In *Economic Anthropology*, ed. Stuart Plattner, 209–22. Palo Alto, CA: Stanford University Press.

Roberts, Johnnie L. (1996) Buyers Beware: Those Curbside Movie Videos May Be Cheap— But They're Pirated and Illegal. *Newsweek*, October 14, 66–7.

Ross, Doran (1998) *Wrapped in Pride: Ghanaian Kente and African American Identity*. Los Angeles, CA: UCLA Fowler Museum of Cultural History.

Sahlins, Marshall (1972) *Stoneage Economics*. Chicago, IL: Aldine.

Schneider, Harold (1974) *Economic Man*. New York: Free Press.

Sokolovsky, Jay, et al. (1978) Personal Networks of Ex-Mental Patients in a Manhattan SRO Hotel. *Human Organization* 37: 5–15.

Walsh, Anna C., and Jeanne Simonelli (1986) Migrant Women in the Oil Field: The Functions of Social Networks. *Human Organization* 45: 43–52.

Weisner, Thomas (1978) The Structure of Sociality: Urban Migration and Urban–Rural Ties in Kenya. *Urban Anthropology* 5: 199–223.

Wolf, Eric (1966) *Peasants*. Englewood Cliffs, NJ: Prentice-Hall.

—— (1982) *Europe and the People without History*. Berkeley: University of California Press.

Chapter 12

Retailers, Knowledges and Changing Commodity Networks: The Case of the Cut Flower Trade

A. Hughes

Introduction

The international cut flower trade provides a valuable case study through which to examine the power of retailers to shape commodity systems. First, it offers an alternative example of a commodity system from the much-researched agro-food chains. As cut flowers are a luxury product embedded in myriad practices of gift-giving and display in the sphere of consumption, it is important to consider how the design-based nature of cut flowers that ensues from these practices might affect the nature of production and trade. Second, research is required on the international cut flower trade in view of the considerable developments in the networks that link together consumers and producers. Such developments relate to the globalized nature of these links, where flowers being retailed and consumed in Europe and North America are increasingly being produced in developing countries in Africa, South America, the Caribbean and South Asia.

The objective of the chapter is to examine how UK retailers, as a significant set of actors mediating between the consumption and production of cut flowers, play a powerful role in shaping the relationships between some of these agents. To do this, I draw upon some preliminary fieldwork concerning trading links between UK retailers and cut flower producers in Kenya. First, though, my approach to this analysis is developed through a consideration of theoretical literatures on commodity chains, cultures, networks and knowledges.

Commodity Networks and Knowledge

There is a growing literature on commodity chains, cultures and networks, both within and outside the discipline of geography. As comprehensive reviews of this literature are constructed by other authors (see, for example, Cook et al. 1996b; Fine 1994; Jackson 1999; Leslie and Reimer 1999), the aim here is simply to consider the key ideas emerging from this body of work that might fruitfully be used to think about the contemporary dynamics of the cut flower trade.

Rethinking the morphology of producer–consumer relationships

One of the most pervasive metaphors for thinking about the links between the production, distribution and consumption of goods is that of *circuits of culture* (see, for example, Cook and Crang 1996a; Cook et al. 1996b; Jackson 1999; Jackson and Taylor 1996). Leslie and Reimer (1999) explain that taking a 'circuits of culture' approach treats the movement of commodities through phases of production, distribution and consumption as a non-linear circuit, rather than a linear chain. Such an approach both refuses to recognize beginning and end points in this movement and disrupts the prioritization of one moment of commodity circulation over another. Instead, the focus is upon the culturally inflected dynamics of the relationships between these moments. Embedded in a much broader literature on commodity cultures, the aim is to arrive at more contextual understandings of the meanings attached to goods in different times, places and phases of commodity circulation. As Cook et al. (1996b) reflect, such contextual understandings, which can be used to provide far richer geographies of commodity systems than those produced by commodity chain traditions, are underpinned by developments in economic anthropology, studies of material culture and critical ethnography (see, for example, Appadurai 1986; Bell and Valentine 1997; Carrier 1990; Howes 1996; Kopytoff 1986; Miller 1997, 1998; Weiss 1996). To counter approaches to the commodity chain that aim always to 'unveil' the economic realities existing at sites of production, both Crang (1996) and Jackson (1999) develop the literature on commodity cultures by suggesting that it is more fruitful instead to consider the complex ways in which goods are displaced from one site to another, and the ways in which various cultural knowledges inform, and are informed by, this process of displacement. Rather than prioritizing realities at the site of production, and simply searching for causal mechanisms responsible for these realities, then, work on commodity cultures aims to thicken descriptions of the meanings attached to goods through a cultural analysis of different phases of commodity circulation, including consumption. Studies of circuits of culture, more specifically, examine how meanings attached to goods get moved around the different phases of commodity circulation, for example between producers and consumers of advertising (Jackson and Taylor 1996).

Developments in the field of commodity culture therefore offer a rich understanding of the cut flower trade and the ways in which retailers are continually shaping it. However, Leslie and Reimer (1999) provide a cautionary note regarding this approach. They argue that the notion of an endless circuit of commodity culture

> may involve the loss of an important political stance: the foregrounding of exploitation. It is for this reason that we are hesitant to abandon the concept of the chain altogether…If the aim of commodity chain analysis is no longer to determine what forces are driving the chain, we are left with a question as to why chains should be reconstructed at all. (Leslie and Reimer 1999: 13–14)

It is important, then, while accepting the value of contextual understandings of commodity circulation, to retain some notions of where power lies in this process. This is not to suggest that ideas regarding circuits of culture should be abandoned, rather that these ideas are connected back in some way to the kinds of competitive pressures felt at the sites of production. This re-connection of production and consumption through notions of commodity culture and the use of ethnographic methods is actually performed by Cook (1994) and Cook et al. (1996b).

Another metaphor for rethinking the relationships between production and consumption, though, is the *network*. While this metaphor has been widely adopted in the social sciences, it has had a limited application to studies of commodities. However, it offers to resolve some of the contrasting difficulties associated with both the commodity chain and circuits of culture approaches to understanding the producer–consumer relation. Broadly defined, the metaphor of the network can be applied to the economy in order to describe how different kinds of nodes (people, firms, states, organizations, etc.) are connected to one another in complex and multi-stranded ways (Thrift and Olds 1996). While Thrift and Olds explain how the concept of the network has been used to represent the organization of social and cultural ties in economic linkages, they suggest that at the most general level of analysis it simply captures the pattern of webs of interdependence existing between different sets of actors in the economy (Powell and Smith-Doerr 1994). Inspired by concepts of the nervous system in biology and electrical networks in physics and engineering, Thrift and Olds (1996) argue that, 'The topological presupposition of the network is now in common usage in the social sciences as the emblem of an ambition to produce flatter, less hierarchical theories of the economy' (p. 322).

While still recognizing the existence of sets of actors (or nodes), whose work it is to shape the circulation of a particular commodity, the connections between these actors are seen as complex 'webs of interdependence' rather than fixed, vertical and uni-directional relationships. Such webs of interdependence not only connect firms through vertical commodity exchange relationships, but also bind together additional agents through the multi-directional flows of information and materials that variously support these exchange relationships. As such, the privileging of one sphere of commodity circulation over another is ideally avoided, as the network metaphor is extended to include, for example, sites of design, research and development, non-governmental organizations and consumer groups.

The analytical capacity of this metaphor can be extended through the development more formally of an actor–network approach, which has its origins in the new sociology of scientific knowledge. There is no space in this chapter to apply actor–network theory to the cut flower trade rigorously enough to do the approach justice. However, two of the central tenets of the theory are worth discussing here, in so far as they inform key developments in ideas about commodity networks. The first is that the agency in a network is driven by both humans and non-humans. In other words, material objects have a transformative capacity within the networks of which they are a part (Latour 1991, 1993; Murdoch 1997; Pile and Thrift 1995). An example of research specifically developing the concept of the commodity network, which takes up this idea, is Busch and Juska's (1994, 1997) study of rapeseed production networks. These authors argue that the extension of these production networks has, at least in part, resulted from the modification of relationships between people and plants through the development of rapeseed technoscience.

The second key tenet of actor–network theory worth mentioning here explicitly refers to the spatial morphology of networks. Put simply, the theory dictates that networks are always localized, working in real places and at specific times. As such, they can only be made known by accounts of their workings on the ground, and can only be considered as globalized in terms of their physical extension across space in practice (Murdoch 1995). From the perspective of actor–network theory, then, the globalization of a commodity network is considered primarily in terms of the extended spatial reach of associations between its key agents. This geographical slant on the morphology of commodity networks is also taken up by Busch and Juska (1997) in their study of the globalization of rapeseed production networks. They suggest that contemporary technologies permit new forms of action at a distance that pave the way for extending the physical distances over which these production networks can be practised. Whatmore and Thorne (1997) also develop this notion of 'network lengthening' in tracing the connections of fair trade coffee networks. Their application of the actor–network approach to agro-food networks is both rigorous and elaborate, and cannot be rehearsed here in full. The key point to pull out, though, is that the concept of network lengthening applied to their particular commodity network fruitfully problematizes the binary notions of core and periphery used in both the macro-scale political economies of food criticized by Cook et al. (1996b) and the GCC approach reviewed by Leslie and Reimer (1999). Instead, 'The power associated with global reach has to be understood as a social composite of the actions and competences of many actants' (Whatmore and Thorne 1997: 291).

A network analysis therefore recognizes that relations between producers in 'developing' countries and retailers and consumers in the 'developed' world are the product of complex flows between a whole host of interconnected actors that have become enrolled in the network. Leslie and Reimer's (1999) worries, regarding the failure of the circuits of culture approach to locate institutional power and stress the forces responsible for exploitation at sites of production, appear redressed to some extent by a network-based approach. Rather than explaining competitive pressures at sites of production in terms of the uni-directional, causal mechanisms though, explanations are traced through the multi-stranded connections forged between a variety of significant and interrelated actors. Applying the metaphor of the network, at least at its most general level, to the cut flower trade therefore offers a productive analytical framework within which both to adapt Gereffi's (1994a, 1994b) notion of buyer-driven commodity circulation and to identify the forces driving competitive pressures in the sphere of production. However, there is much to be gained from coupling this framework with ideas gleaned from the literature on commodity cultures. This literature, in particular, advances our understanding of how knowledge plays an active role in reshaping relationships between production and consumption.

Emphasizing the role of knowledge

That knowledge plays a vital part in reshaping the morphology of a commodity network and defining the flows within it is central to an understanding of how retailers shape the cut flower trade and influence the process of production in countries like Kenya. Indeed, asserting the significance of knowledge in the workings of commodity networks brings geographies of commodities in line with broader claims by theorists about the centrality of knowledge to the character of the economy and society in the late twentieth century. Such claims are reviewed by Knorr Cetina (1997) as speaking variously of a 'knowledge society' (Bell 1973), an 'information society' (Lyotard 1984) and a 'risk society' (Beck 1992).

Appadurai (1986), in the context of studies in economic anthropology, proposes that there are three sorts of knowledges at work in the social life of a commodity. First, there is knowledge that goes into its production. Second, there is knowledge required to consume it. And, mediating between these knowledges, is that which fuels commodity circulation and exchange. In contrast to traditional schools of thought, which tend to draw a rigid distinction between the sociability and localized knowledges of consumption with the profit-oriented, calculated and rational knowledge of commodity production and exchange. Appadurai argues that knowledges at work in each of the three moments can be at once technical, social and aesthetic. It is, of course, too large a task to consider how all of these different kinds of knowledges might be bound up in a commodity network. The more modest objective here is briefly to construct a framework for thinking about the knowledges that mediate between production and consumption, in order to inform my analysis of how retailers circulate knowledge to exert power in the cut flower commodity network. To do this, I consider how the aforementioned approaches to commodity circulation treat the role of knowledge.

While the role of knowledge is considered in network-based approaches, particularly in terms of its capacity to strengthen and order the configuration of a particular network (Whatmore and Thorne 1997), notions of knowledge developed in the literature on commodity cultures can also be usefully injected into a network analysis. Work on circuits of culture is particularly instructive here. While the metaphor of the network arguably offers the most useful way of envisioning the *morphology* of relationships between the production and consumption of commodities, for a consideration of knowledge it becomes necessary to think more about the constitution of the *flows* between nodes in the network. Here, the notion of circuits, of ideas and information moving around and between producers, retailers, distributors and consumers, is important. In contrast to the origins of the network metaphor, Thrift and Olds (1996) explain that the 'topological presupposition' of this kind of flow is inspired by biological notions of blood circulation and the physical circulation of energy.

Much of the work on knowledge and commodity cultures, particularly in the discipline of geography, concerns the sphere of consumption (see, for example, Cook and Crang 1996a; Gregson and Crewe 1997; Jackson and Holbrook 1995). Cook and Crang (1996a), for example, suggest that geographical knowledges in arenas of consumption, concerning a commodity's settings, biographies and origins, constitute the fetish that both obscures realities at sites of production *and* creates cultural and economic surpluses for consumers. More recently, though, Cook et al. (1998) apply a 'circuits of knowledge' approach to the phase of commodity circulation. They use this approach to provide a critique of corporate strategies based on 'category management'; strategies claimed by industry in the UK and USA to restructure relationships between retailers and their manufacturing suppliers based on the former's attempts to develop particular kinds of knowledge about consumers. In view of the position of retailers as mediators in commodity networks, it seems appropriate to consider their use of knowledge as circuitous. This is suggested at least by the *practices* of category management examined by Cook et al. (1998). The implication is that retailers' use of business knowledge, in order to lengthen and strengthen commodity networks to their advantage, continually draws upon, transforms and circulates commodity knowledges developed in spheres of production and consumption, as well as by additional actors in the network like designers and researchers.

The remainder of the chapter develops the idea of business knowledge circulated by retailers in the context of the cut flower commodity network. In line with Thrift and Olds (1996), two different kinds of 'topological presuppositions' are therefore suggested to coexist. First, the network is suggested as an appropriate metaphor to capture the morphology of the contemporary cut flower trade. And second, flows (or circuits) are the most useful metaphor for thinking about the movement of knowledge between nodes in this network. It is within this analytical framework that the power of UK retailers' buyer-driven business knowledges to reshape the cut flower trade is demonstrated.

The International Cut Flower Trade as a Knowledge-Intensive Commodity Network

The cut flower trade as commodity network

Many of the cut flowers that are bought for display and given as gifts in Europe and North America are produced in developing countries such as Chile, Colombia, Ecuador, the Gambia, India, Kenya, Uganda and Zimbabwe (see, for example, Detmers and Kortlandt 1996; Durham 1996; Maharaj and Dorren 1995; O'Hagan 1998; Shakespeare 1995; Shapley 1996; Stewart 1994; Wolf 1997). The conditions under which the flowers are produced in these national economies are frequently reported to involve great uncertainty and risk, as well as low wage levels for workers.[1] Mediating these conditions of production and 'Western' consumer cultures are power-laden operations of commercial capital, in which multinational corporations, influential development agencies and retailers play a significant role. The aim here is to describe some of the connections between these different agents in the cut flower trade and to demonstrate the applicability of the network metaphor to capture their morphology. Key trends in both the consumption and production of commercially grown flowers on an international scale are first outlined briefly to provide a backdrop against which to consider the composite networks that link them.

Goody (1993) presents an extensive anthropological account of 'the culture of flowers', containing rich cultural histories of the incorporation of flowers into everyday life. In the European context, he suggests that the use of flowers as gifts developed in the Netherlands during the Renaissance period. The use of flowers in various practices of display within Europe is also implied to have a long and complex history, significantly involving the importation of goods and ideas from the Far East in the sixteenth, seventeenth and eighteenth centuries. In many parts of Europe and North America today, the cut flower is considered a luxury commodity incorporated into everyday life in two main ways. First, cut flowers are often used in practices of display, from the adornment of bodies during ceremonies (for example, weddings) to the decoration of interiors (for example, the home or the workplace).[2] And second, flowers are bound up in practices of gift-giving, particularly during public festivals like Valentine's Day and Mother's Day, and on more private occasions such as birthdays and anniversaries. In addition, they are often presented at social events such as dinner parties, or given as 'thank you' or 'get well' gifts.

Historically, the production of flowers for such display and gift-giving, particularly in Europe, took place in the Netherlands. While the Netherlands retains a pivotal role in the cut flower trade today, the past thirty to forty years have seen the entrance of a number of other countries into the realm of production. Despite the markets for flowers being predominantly in Europe and North America, production has extended into Africa, South America, the Caribbean and South Asia, as mentioned above. The introduction of developing countries to the commercial production of flowers took place in the 1960s and 1970s, but their impact on international trade really took a hold in the 1980s (Maharaj and Dorren 1995). Table 12.1 illustrates the impact of Colombia, Thailand and Kenya, in particular, on world cut flower exports by 1992. In developing countries, the internal market for commercially grown flowers is small and typically confined to urban elites, owing to the high cost and luxury status of this commodity.

Cut flowers are therefore produced in these economies predominantly for export to Europe, North America and, increasingly, Japan. So, while flowers are still grown on a large scale in the Netherlands, Italy, Spain and France, and also on a smaller scale in the UK, the fight for market share is increasingly incorporating developing countries. Moreover, this competitive struggle is becoming progressively more intense amidst growing concerns in the trade that the market for flowers is becoming saturated; concerns that imply the shouldering of great risk and uncertainty on the part of individual producers. While workers on flower farms in developing countries are indeed connected to consumers in core regions of the world economy through a

Table 12.1   World cut flower exports, 1992

Country	Value of exports (000s of US$)
Netherlands	2,153,560
Colombia	395,644
Israel	146,120
Italy	111,120
Spain (including Canary Islands)	69,086
Thailand	67,579
Kenya	61,477
France	28,162
Ecuador	25,330

Source: COLEACP, document distributed at Floriculture Seminar, Trinidad and Tobago, 9–10 May, assembled on basis of European, American and Japanese sources, printed in Maharaj and Dorren (1995: 16).

set of vertical exchange relationships, including the central trading role played by the Dutch auction houses discussed below, there are a number of other chains of actors that lock into these exchange relationships and make them more complex. For example, a major change to the commercial production of flowers has been the significant application of technology to the growing process. Most notably, technology is used in the breeding of flowers, the cultivation process and in the development of pesticides to protect the crops (Maharaj and Dorren 1995). Flower breeding, or florigenetics, is used for cross-breeding flowers, introducing genes into plants to produce different colours, extending the vase life of flowers and creating new varieties. Most of the key laboratories involved in florigenetics are based in the Netherlands and Israel (Detmers and Kortlandt 1996). Once new breeds and colours of flowers have been developed satisfactorily in the laboratory, they are then ready to move to the trial beds of the farms where they are ultimately expected to go into full commercial production. There is an additional commodity chain concerned with the production and trade in florigenetic material, then, that exists to support and reshape the cut flower commodity chain.

Another additional chain of relationships that fuels the cut flower trade concerns fashion design. Recent innovations in bouquet design, incorporating new combinations of flower varieties and particular colour schemes, are tied in with contemporary trends in home furnishings. In addition, top florists such as Jane Packer and Paula Pryke are increasingly demanding high fees to produce designs and arrangements for high profile events, like celebrity weddings and sporting occasions, while also producing 'coffee table' books like Packer's (1997) *Living with Flowers* in which relatively simple ideas are communicated to a broad audience with an interest in more popular forms of floristry (Lane 1997). This trade in design-based ideas also significantly influences the nature of relationships between the producers and consumers of cut flowers. Added to a whole host of other significant actors, including development agencies, trade associations and consumer groups, the connection of these two chains of trade to the cut flower commodity chain appears to make the international cut flower trade a complex, multi-stranded commodity network. Rather than representing the trade as a linear commodity chain in which one set of buyers in a core region of the world economy dictate terms and conditions of supply to a producer in the periphery, the cut flower trade as commodity network brings together a range of influential agents in different parts of the world, including florigeneticists in Israel and the Netherlands, traders in the Netherlands and florists in the UK, who combine in intricate ways to shape the production process in a variety of developing economies.

A buyer-driven network

Historically, the key buying groups driving the trade have been connected with the Dutch auction houses. While one-fifth of all commercially grown cut flowers are produced in the Netherlands, three-fifths pass through this country during the circulation process. This is owing to the location in the Netherlands of nine major auction houses performing the role of distribution centres, where flowers are sold by exporters or import wholesalers and bought by buyers from wholesalers or retailers (Maharaj and Dorren 1995; Retail Business Market Survey 1996). In these vast auction houses, flowers pass on conveyor belts beneath a large electronic clock, which displays their starting price to buyers. The price on the clock then goes down until a buyer indicates their wish to purchase the product. In 1995, total sales of cut flowers and pot plants through these Dutch auctions were valued at £2.1 billion. Since their origins as far back as the sixteenth century, these auctions have held a pivotal position in structuring the dynamics of the international cut flower trade. In order for the majority of cut flowers to clinch a final sale to consumers today, they must first be accepted by the buyers operating in these auction houses. While their influence is waning slightly, as the retailers discussed below attempt to displace their function by forging more direct links with suppliers, these auctions still form a significant set of buyers directing the trade.

The way in which buyers based in both Dutch auction houses and retail chains actually drive the cut flower trade and shape the nature of the production process, though, has once again to be seen in the context of the commodity network. Rather than independently setting the standards against which flowers are judged, Dutch traders and retail buyers actually draw upon floricultural knowledges from other points in the commodity network in order to produce particular benchmarks in relation to pricing structures and aesthetics. Such knowledges are drawn, for example, from the sphere of consumption, designers, the media and market research-ers, as is discussed later in the chapter. This highlights the view that the dynamics of this buyer-driven network are actually energized through a complex 'web of interde-pendence', drawing on the metaphor developed by Powell and Smith-Doerr (1994) and discussed by Thrift and Olds (1996). Moreover, it makes the point that a central component of these buyer-driven dynamics is knowledge and its circulation.

A knowledge-intensive network

There is a vast range of knowledges circulating through the cut flower commodity network described above. Building on Appadurai's (1986) point, these knowledges are social, technical and aesthetic at all kinds of nodes in the network. In the realm of consumption, they incorporate purchasing knowledge, technical and specialist knowledge of flower care (Retail Business Market Survey 1996), aesthetic know-ledge of display (Lane 1997) and cultural meanings of flowers and gift-giving (Goody 1993). The production process is shaped by managerial knowledge of competition, traditional knowledge of horticulture and technoscientific knowledge of engineering in florigenetics. Rather than each of these knowledges formulating at isolated nodes in the network, though, they become pushed around between nodes. And as they get pushed around, they begin to reformulate the relationships between these nodes, as in the case of the relationship between florigenetics and commercial production, where the former has increasingly influenced the nature of the latter.

Rather than simply drawing on profit-oriented, calculated and self-interested knowledges of commodity exchange, as dictated by neo-classical economics and traditional political–economic thought, retailers circulate a whole range of know-ledges between different sets of actors and moments of commodity circulation (Cook et al. 1998). That is to say, retailers capitalize on the circulation of know-ledges between different points in the network, with the result of both reshaping the relationships between these points and strengthening their own position in relation to them. The knowledges can involve distribution, competition, marketing, design and more. It is therefore suggested, at least in part, that buyers (including retailers) drive the cut flower commodity network through the circulation of different kinds of knowledge. This suggestion is fleshed out through selected examples below, using the case study of trade between UK retailers and large cut flower producers in Kenya. First, though, the scene constituting this case study is set.

UK Retailers and Changing Cut Flower Trading Networks: The Case of Supply from Kenya

UK retailers are having a massive impact on the dynamics of the cut flower trade, both influencing patterns of consumption in their favour and reordering the supply channels that serve them. The key impacts are discussed here, in so far as they introduce the changing commodity networks that have been reshaped by buyer-driven business knowledge.

The total UK market for commercially produced cut flowers in 1995 was estimated to have a value of £871 million, compared with £420 million in 1986.[3] This UK market, though, is still considered to be underdeveloped in comparison with other economies, where fresh flowers are purchased for personal consumption to a far greater extent (see table 12.2).

With respect to the structure of the retail trade through which cut flowers are sold in the UK, traditional florists dominated up until the early to mid-1990s. And, often trading through these florists, were telesales organizations, such as Interflora which began business in 1924. However, the retail multiples, particularly Marks and Spencer, Tesco, Sainsbury, Safeway and Asda, have cut dramatically into the market share of these traditional florists and telesales companies (Marshall-Foster 1996). Between 1986 and 1995 the share of the UK cut flower market, by value, taken by the multiple retailers increased from 4 per cent to 30 per cent. Between the same years, the share held by traditional florists decreased from 47 per cent to 24 per cent.[4]

Up until the UK multiples became involved seriously in the sale of cut flowers, the distribution channels used by florists to source this product involved a variety of agents. Flowers would be passed in their country of origin to an exporter and then typically sent across to one of the Dutch auctions to be sold on to an importer in the UK. Then the flowers might have been sold to a wholesaler, before eventually reaching the florists for final sale. While most of these links are still maintained in the supply chain for flowers sold through telesales and traditional florists, UK retailers have recently begun to forge much more direct connections with the growers (Barrett et al. 1997, 1999; personal interviews). Barrett et al. refer to this as a retail-led, 'fully integrated' marketing chain, which allows the retail chains to maintain control over the supply channel.

Some of the largest and most significant suppliers of cut flowers to the UK retailers, which have become locked into this fully integrated supply channel, are based in Kenya. Barrett et al. (1997) note that 35,200 tonnes of cut flowers were exported from Kenya in 1996, to the value of US$80 million. Over 800 hectares of Kenyan land is devoted to the cultivation of cut flowers, with production being dominated by three large farms, two of which occupy around 250 ha of land each.

Table 12.2 International expenditure per head on cut flowers, 1995

Country	Expenditure (£ per year)
Switzerland	71
Norway	44
Finland	41
Austria	38
Belgium	33
Germany	32
Holland	31
Japan	29
Sweden	29
Italy	23
France	22
USA	17
UK	15
Slovenia	14
Greece	11
Ireland	9
Spain	9
Portugal	8
Croatia	5
Czech Republic	5
Poland	3

Source: Flowers and Plants Association, taken from Flower Council of Holland, December 1995.

There are then around thirty medium-sized farms of varying sizes above 5 ha and then several hundred much smaller farms taking up less than 5 ha each. The three largest growers are situated in Naivasha, drawing on the resources of Lake Naivasha, and attracting thousands of migrant workers from all over Kenya in search of employment. The two largest producers, Oserian and Sulmac, each employ over 5,000 workers, a small proportion of which constitute occasional rather than permanent labour (personal interviews). While Oserian is a family-owned business, its neighbouring competitor, Sulmac, is owned by Brooke Bond Kenya, which was taken over by the Anglo-Dutch multinational, Unilever, in 1984 (Maharaj and Dorren 1995) and subsequently by the Commonwealth Development Corporation in 1998. Today, it is the three large producers in Naivasha that lead cut flower production in Kenya, exporting mainly to Germany, the Netherlands and the UK, with direct business with UK retail chains forming an increasing proportion of their overall business (personal interviews). These large growers in Kenya, which are financially and organizationally able to meet the strict requirements of UK multiples in their quest for traceability and quality control, benefit from being plugged into a direct and integrated supply chain with guaranteed cargo space on flights from Nairobi and certain sales in the UK. In contrast, the smaller growers have to deal with more agents in the supply chain, weaker marketing links and the risk that their product may not even gain access to space on flights at all (Barrett et al. 1997).

In light of the aforementioned impacts that UK retailers are having on this particular supply channel in the cut flower trade, it serves as a useful case study through which to examine the more specific ways in which retail chains are reshaping the commodity network and strengthening their own position within it. The remainder of the chapter is an attempt to assert the centrality of knowledge to this process.

Retailers, Business Knowledge and the Transformation of Cut Flower Commodity Networks

Retailers, business knowledge and the strategic crafting of the producer–consumer relation

At the broadest level, one of the most significant ways in which UK retailers are proactively changing the morphology of cut flower commodity networks concerns their strategic moves to fabricate 'fully integrated' marketing and distribution channels, as mentioned above and discussed by Barrett et al. (1997). In making such strategic moves, these retailers effectively bypass the roles played by a number of previously significant agents in networks of cut flower circulation, including importers, warehousing services and the Dutch auctions. While these agents are far from displaced from cut flower trading networks altogether, the process whereby UK retailers forge more direct links with producers serves as a useful example of how a particular set of agents is proving capable of at least modifying the shape of a commodity network. Central to this process of modification, first, is the strategic deployment of knowledge about how the producer–consumer relation should be managed.

There are four main reasons why retailers have strategically developed fully integrated supply channels, identified by managers interviewed in both UK retail chains and the three large flower farms in Naivasha. First, the intention is to reduce the length of time the commodity journeys through the distribution system, not least because the cut flower is such a perishable item. Second, there is a desire to cut out the costs associated with using surplus commercial agents in the distribution system. Third, they wish to play a more proactive part in actually defining the nature of the commodity they eventually intend to buy, instead of purchasing the varieties that just happen to hit the market. And fourth, there is a need to comply with the 1990 Food Safety Act's requirement of traceability in the supply channel (Barrett et al. 1997, 1999); traceability that is far easier to attain if links with producers are direct.[5] These are important political–economic reasons for bypassing some of the traditionally pivotal agents in the cut flower commodity network. What strategically underpins the retailers' implementation of the direct links with producers is the notion of reducing the social and institutional 'distance' between producers and consumers, positioning themselves as key mediators in this process. As such, when corporate interviewees reflected on this strategy, the achievement of 'closeness' and 'proximity' to both producers and consumers was often cited as important to the attainment of greater control in the supply channel, as this consideration demonstrates:

Because we are now much, much closer to our customers, we understand what their needs and requirements are. Therefore, if the communication chain is shorter and we have a far greater influence over how the product is initially grown, then it means we have more opportunities to deliver the customers' expectations...It's two points. One, for communication. Secondly, for control...So, the closer we can get to growers, then the closer we can maintain control. And that's what it's about. (Interview with the Category Buying Manager, UK supermarket chain, March 1997)

While such closeness occasionally incorporates the face-to-face meeting of retailers with producers and consumers, it does not always refer to the physical proximity of agents in the commodity network. Notably, closeness refers to the supposed development of understandings between agents, or more accurately, the development by *retailers* of understandings of consumers and producers. And it is through this emphasis on understanding that knowledge plays such a central role in the mediation by retailers of the producer–consumer relation. This role of knowledge in the strategic assertion of closeness has much in common with the strategies of Category Management discussed by Cook et al. (1998), in that improved knowledges of consumers are supposedly used by retailers to direct their relationships with suppliers and the production process. This is exemplified by the following quote:

In terms of how we produce specifications for our product, we have very, very tight specifications...And then the supplier has to adhere to the spec. And if they don't, well, we *always* reject product if it's out of spec. The specifications in terms of variety mixes are being driven by customer research, which we've spent quite a lot of time doing. (Interview with the Horticulture Merchandiser, upmarket high street retailer in the UK, March 1997)

At the simplest level, knowledge of consumers is therefore constructed through customer research and translated into a set of specifications that are in turn used to manipulate the floricultural production process. But, while the one-way flow of knowledge about the consumers, from the point of consumption to the site of production, is propounded by managerial strategies, knowledge in practice tends to flow in circuits. My interviews with representatives from UK retail chains support this view. Customer research conducted by the retailers, in the form of panels, focus groups and mail-out questionnaires, for example, frequently questions consumers on existing bouquets and marketing and sales techniques. As such, it becomes difficult to separate consumer-driven knowledges from those that are driven by retailers. In addition, retail buyers do not always see fit simply to map the results of such customer research onto a set of specifications for cut flower producers to follow. In the case of the leading upmarket high street retailer interviewed, for example, innovations in bouquet design that are translated into directions for production are often generated through dialogue with other actors in the network, such as top-level designers, as well as consumers.

The following discussion of design-based knowledges aims to problematize the two key points that appear to be implicit in strategic formulations of managing the producer–consumer relation. First, it seeks to disrupt the notion that the producer–consumer relation for cut flowers is managed solely in the context of a vertical commodity chain. Rather, the metaphor of the network is applied in order to consider the critical roles played by a variety of actors. Second, the producer–consumer relation is shown to be energized through complex circuits of knowledge flowing between these actors, as opposed to a simple, unidirectional flow of consumer-based knowledge.

Circuits of design-based knowledges, the role of networks and the manipulation of the production process

Earlier in the chapter it was argued that the network is a more appropriate metaphor than the chain for the cut flower trade. Part of the reason for this was argued to be the presence of additional chains of actors that lock into and support the conventional exchange relationships existing between growers, retail buyers and consumers. In particular, it was highlighted that one such chain of actors is centred on the trade in design-based ideas that so strongly influences the cut flower commodity. In order most effectively to manage the producer–consumer relation in the cut flower trade, then, UK retailers not only utilize knowledge based on customer research panels, but they also harness the expert knowledges of top florists in the process of generating ideas for product development to be translated downstream to sites of production. In fact, as the following quote shows, customer knowledges are intricately tied to these expert knowledges of floristry, as the retailer uses the florist to gain an understanding of upmarket consumer trends, in order subsequently to shape more popular consumer fashions:

> We use Jane Packer's name [a leading florist, mentioned earlier]. She's obviously our consultant in the same way that [one of the leading supermarket chains] use Paula Pryke. And in magazines, you known you'll see the Paula Pryke name associated with [their] products and you'll see Jane Packer's name associated with ours. And we use part of her consultancy as a touch-base to check on the trends and, you know, what's happening in the florists' business in top shops and what influence that will have on the high street stores, perhaps in a couple of years. (Interview with the Horticulture Merchandiser, upmarket high street retailer in the UK, March 1997)

There is a clear circulation of knowledge here, then, where retailers enroll floristry experts into the cut flower commodity network, in order to play an active role in circulating knowledge on 'trends' between these experts, themselves and the consumers, until it becomes very difficult to establish any beginning and end points in the process of generating design-based knowledge. What is more, the resulting web of interdependence is made yet more complex by the way in which the leading florists are tightly connected to fashions in the home furnishings industry and their representation in so-called 'lifestyle' magazines, which in turn also influence popular consumer knowledges of flower designs:

> You will find that someone like Jane [Packer], who when we first knew her was totally country style and very much English cottage garden, has now moved to a brighter, bolder, clashing approach, because that's what's coming through in the lifestyle mags. Not even just the way-out ones, but the ordinary ones. (Interview with the Association Secretary, Flowers and Plants Association, March 1997)

There is a complex flow of ideas and knowledges centring on design, then, which get moved around the interconnected agents in the cut flower commodity network. The examples presented above illustrate briefly how this arrangement affects the retailer–consumer relation, involving top florists, the home furnishings sector and lifestyle magazines. As retailers attempt to forge the more direct relationships with growers discussed above, in the context of a buyer-driven commodity network, this circulation of design-based ideas has important implications for the production process on flower farms like those based in Naivasha, Kenya. The UK retailers are renowned by managers on these farms as being very demanding in terms of their requests for an increasingly sophisticated mix of product, as the following quotes from management of two of the largest Kenyan flower farms suggest:

> Some of our markets just demand a red carnation, or a white carnation. The supermarkets are a bit more fussy and some will demand a particular variety. (Interview with Managing Director, Kenyan flower grower, July 1997)
> You guarantee that once you've got last year's colours in, then they're out [laughs]. So we have a very broad colour range. We're not 100 per cent directed by one client... Having said that, the colour themes do change a lot. Pink and white, and yellow and white, have seemed to be big sales for the last ten years. But the supermarkets are getting much more adventurous... Now they're getting more and more European and really following Holland and Germany, and they are experimenting with all sorts of different fillers, different, very fancy, bouquets, which are far more complicated than they ever were... So we're having to very much tailor our growing to suit that, i.e. trialling new flowers all the time, different fillers just to keep ourselves ahead of competition. (Interview with Marketing Manager, Kenyan flower grower, July 1997)

These quotes support the view of buyer-driven commodity circulation. The second, in particular, illustrates effectively the way in which UK retailers' increasingly sophisticated bouquet designs are exerting competitive pressures upon these Kenyan suppliers. Rather than viewing these pressures as the direct effect of buying power on the part of the retailers, I suggest instead that they are best seen as resulting from the complex networks of relationships between retailers, designers and consumers, and the knowledges circulating between them. The power of retail capital in this process is still firmly acknowledged, then, but in the context of the interlocking relationships the retailers forge with a variety of agents.

In considering the pressures on the Kenyan producers to comply with the retailers' demands, the complexity of influential networks does not stop with the sway of design-based agents and knowledges. One of the problems posed by ever-changing demands for different colours and varieties of flowers concerns the need for growers continually to adapt their production process to meet them. The following reflection demonstrates this:

> If everything's Mediterranean again in the magazines for the summer coming, you'll know that you're fairly safe with sunflowers. And if it's very cottage garden, you might want to think more about peonies and stocks and delphiniums. So I think you have to react to what's fashionable. And I think the art is to have all the technical background done in advance, so that we're comfortable putting it on the counter, 'cos one of our major problems is getting things to survive through what we would call shelf life.

(Interview with the Horticulture Merchandiser, upmarket high street retailer in the UK, March 1997)

This implies that somehow new technical developments in florigenetics, which most appropriately create the physicality of the new flower designs to the high standards demanded by the retailers, need to be translated into full commercial production in advance. Interviews with Kenyan growers indicate that the risk of these developments not being in place in time to supply retailers with the commodity they demand is shouldered by producers. In other words, the growers are situated in the middle of a network constituted, at least in part, by two knowledge-intensive chains. On the one hand, there is the trade in ideas of flower design, in this case being shaped in the UK. And on the other, there is the trade in florigenetic knowledge and material mentioned earlier, originating primarily in the Netherlands and Israel. The growers invariably rely on the successful development and application of the latter to their production process, in order to meet the requirements of the former. Failure to achieve this risks the grower's position in the network being displaced by a competitor (personal interviews). This network of interdependence, which in part perpetuates the economic insecurity endured by Kenyan growers, problematizes the oversimplified notion of core–periphery relations proposed by commodity chain approaches. Once more, a network-based spatial imagination is therefore required to capture the uneven power relations between UK retailers and Kenyan cut flower producers.

There is a view developing in the trade, expressed below, that the retailers could tighten their control of changing cut flower networks still further by integrating the relationships between florigeneticists and the top florists:

I think that the better breeders are listening and looking and this is happening increasingly as well, in that they are keeping their eyes open for changes in colour and also perhaps talking more to people like the designers. And I suppose that's something that the supermarkets will assist with, that they do have control or influence on what is grown, certainly in developing countries, and that therefore the input for consumers and the designers may get back further to breeders that way. (Interview with the Association Secretary, Flowers and Plants Association, March 1997)

Such a view, while speculative, illustrates the power that this set of agents has in the modification of commodity networks. Moreover, it shows how the flow of different kinds of knowledge between different geographically positioned actors in the network is integral to the exercise of this power.

Discussion

While the examples of changing relationships between UK retailers and Kenyan cut flower producers discussed above are selective and fall short of capturing many of the varied cultural and economic dynamics of the cut flower business, they serve at least as a useful window on the power of retailers to drive change in a commodity network. Moreover, they show that it is impossible to appreciate the power wielded by these retailers without a consideration of the part played by knowledge.

Rather than constructing some kind of grand theory of uneven development caused, on the one hand, by the production of cut flowers amidst economic insecurity in developing countries, and on the other, by luxury-based consumption in Western economies, it is suggested that there is much to be gained by presenting more partial and positioned studies of specific links in the commodity network. Such positioned studies allow for more nuanced understandings of the way in which retail buyers, along with the networked relationships they forge, actually place demands upon producers and the growing process in a particular globalized trade.

The approach taken in the chapter has hinged on the use of a network metaphor to imagine the geography of complex links between the key actors in the international cut flower trade. While the linearity of global commodity chain approaches is appropriate to capture the strategic envisioning of the producer–consumer relation at its simplest level in the trade, these approaches fail to recognize the key roles played by the supporting cast of actors such as designers and flower breeders. A network approach that depicts more complex, multi-stranded relationships between a broad range of agents therefore appears to be far more appropriate for a study of cut flower trade dynamics. What is more, this approach also allows more complex geographies of commodity linkages to be realized, where agents in a variety of locations can be seen to combine to influence the production process, for example. Gereffi's (1994a, 1994b) notion of buyer-driven commodity circulation has therefore been adapted in my study, so that while the UK retailers are indeed acknowledged as a powerful set of buyers exerting control over the cut flower production process, it is the way in which they manipulate complex networks of consumers, designers and actors in supporting commodity channels that allows them effectively to practise this control.

Just as the network metaphor has been used to describe the morphology of relationships between the production and consumption of flowers, the concept of circuits has shed light on how knowledges move around between different sets of actors to alter the shape of these relationships. Supporting the conclusions of Cook et al. (1998), the flow of knowledge in the cut flower trade, as promoted in the rhetoric of supply channel management, is viewed as a simple, uni-directional movement of information generated by retailers about the sphere of consumption and translated upstream to the producers. However, this notion has briefly been shown to be destabilized in practice, by the complex way in which retailers push knowledges of design around between florists, representations in 'lifestyle' magazines and consumers, as well as being influenced by what designs of flowers are already being, or could be, produced. So, while the Kenyan producers are still viewed for the most part as being under pressure to respond to retailer-generated business knowledge, in line with the concept of a buyer-driven commodity network, this knowledge is seen to be complexly created by a variety of agents at different nodes in the network. Furthermore, the limits placed on the simple translation of this knowledge to the organization of commercial production, not least by the pace of change in florigentic knowledge and material, also challenges the simple 'cause and effect' model of uni-directional knowledge flow in buyer-driven commodity chains.

The combination of approaches based on networks and circuits of knowledge aids the development of a more dynamic understanding of how retailers powerfully generate change in the cut flower trade. The use of such approaches, in the context of my study, has aimed both to advance knowledge on retailer power and to contribute to debates on geographies of commodity systems. The capitalization on knowledge by retailers has been pivotal to both of these concerns. Indeed, the vital role played by design-based knowledges and networks, and their manipulation by retailers in the construction of 'value' (to use Marsden's 1997 term) in the cut flower industry, develops a key strand of debate that is intended to contribute to understandings of both the practice of retailer power and the dynamics of globalized commodity systems.

NOTES

1 Although the focus of the chapter is on connections between the retail of flowers in developed countries and their production in developing countries, it is important to note that conditions of work in the developed economies such as the Netherlands are also reported to involve insecurity and low wages.
2 As the focus of this chapter is upon cut flowers, this discussion is centred on practices of display in interiors, rather than looking at flowers grown to enhance the aesthetics of gardens and open spaces.
3 These figures are based on calculations made by Zwetsloots Ltd, a key British supplier of cut flowers to UK supermarkets. This supplier receives cut flowers imported from overseas and then sells them on to some of the major UK supermarkets, as well as independent florists.
4 These figures are based on calculations made by Zwetsloots Ltd.
5 Cut flowers appear to have been affected by the 1990 Food Safety Act because they are often treated as an integral part of the category of horticulture.

REFERENCES

Appadurai, A. (1986) Introduction: commodities and the politics of value. In Appadurai, A. (ed.), *The Social Life of Things: Commodities in Cultural Perspective*, ch. 1. Cambridge University Press, Cambridge, pp. 3–63.

Appelbaum, R., Gereffi, G. (1994) Power and profits on the apparel commodity chain. In Bonacich, E., Cheng, L., Chincilla, N., Hamilton, N., Ong, P. (eds), *Global Production: The Apparel Industry in the Pacific Rim*. Temple University Press, Philadelphia, pp. 42–62.

Barrett, H., Browne, A. W., Ilbery, B. W., Jackson, G. H., Binns, T. J. (1997) Prospects for Horticultural Exports Under Trade Liberalisation in Adjusting African Economies (R6139): Report Submitted to Department for International Development (DFID) (formerly ODA) (ESCOR).

Barrett, H., Browne, A. W., Ilbery, B. W., Jackson, G. H., Binns, T. J. (1999) Globalisation and the new consumer: the importation of fresh horticultural produce from Sub-Saharan Africa into the UK. *Transactions of the Institute of British Geographers* 4 (2) 159–94.

Beck, U. (1992) *Risk Society Towards a New Modernity*. Sage, London.

Bell, D. (1973) *The Coming of Post-Industrial Society: A Venture in Social Forecasting*. Basic Books, New York.

Bell, D., Valentine, G. (1997) *Consuming Geographies: We Are Where We Eat*. Routledge, London.

Bolger, A. (1997) Unions call for code to protect flower workers. *Financial Times.* 9 May 1997, p. 4.

Bowlby, S., Foord, J. (1995) Relational contracting between UK retailers and manufacturers. *International Review of Retail, Distribution and Consumer Research* 5, 333–61.

Busch, L., Juska, A. (1994) The production of knowledge and the production of commodities: the case of rapeseed technoscience. *Rural Sociology* 59 (4), 581–97.

Busch, L., Juska, A. (1997) Beyond political economy: actor networks and the globalization of agriculture. *Review of International Political Economy* 4 (4), 688–708.

Carrier, J. (1990) Reconciling commodities and personal relations in industrial society. *Theory and Society* 19, 579–98.

Cook, I. (1994) New fruits and vanity: symbolic production in the global food economy. In Bonanno, A., Busch, L., Friedland, W., Gouveia, L., Mingione, E. (eds), *From Columbus to ConAgra: The Globalization of Agriculture and Food.* University Press of Kansas, Kansas, pp. 232–48.

Cook, I., Crang, P. (1996a) The world on a plate: culinary culture, displacement and geographical knowledges. *Journal of Material Culture* 1 (2), 131–53.

Cook, I., Crang, P., Thorpe, M. (1996b) Amos Gitai's Ananas: commodity systems, documentary filmmaking and new geographies of food. Paper presented at the IBG/RGS Annual Conference, Glasgow University, January.

Cook, I., Crang, P., Thorpe, M. (1998) Category management and circuits of knowledge in the UK food business. Paper presented to the ESRC Commercial Cultures Seminar, University of Sheffield, September.

Crang, P. (1996) Displacement, consumption, and identity. *Environment and Planning A* 28, 47–67.

Crewe, L., Davenport, E. (1992) The puppet show: changing buyer–supplier relationships within clothing retailing. *Transactions of the Institute of British Geographers* 17 (2) 183–97.

Detmers, M., Kortlandt, J. (1996) Kenya's flower exports, a flourishing business. In Kortlandt, J., Sprang, U. (eds), *Make Way for Africa.* Association for North–South Campaigns, Amsterdam.

Doel, C. (1995) Market Development, Organisational Change and the Food Industry. Unpublished PhD thesis. University of Cambridge.

Doel, C. (1996) Market development and organisational change: the case of the food industry. In Wrigley, N., Lowe, M. S. (eds), *Retailing, Consumption and Capital: Towards the New Retail Geography,* ch. 1. Longman, Harlow, pp. 48–67.

Durham, M. (1996) Western tastes for prawns causes Third World misery. *Observer,* 12 May 1996, p. 15.

Fine, B. (1994) Towards a political economy of food. *Review of International Political Economy* 1 (3), 519–45.

Fine, B., Leopold, E. (1993) *The World of Consumption.* Routledge, London.

Flowers and Plants Association (1995) International Per Capita Spend.

Friedmann, H. (1993) The political economy of food: a global crisis. *New Left Review* 197, 29–57.

Friedmann, H., McMichael, P. (1989) Agriculture and the state system: the rise and decline of national agricultures, 1870 to the present, *Sociologia Ruralis* 29 (2), 93–117.

Gereffi, G. (1994a) Capitalism, development and global commodity chains. In Sklair, L. (ed.), *Capitalism and Development,* ch. 11. Routledge, London, pp. 211–31.

Gereffi, G. (1994b) The organization of buyer-driven global commodity chains: how US retailers shape overseas production networks. In Gereffi, G., Korzeniewicz, M. (eds.), *Commodity Chains and Global Capitalism,* ch. 5. Greenwood Press, Westport, CT, pp. 93–122.

Gereffi, G., Korzeniewicz, M., Korzeniewicz, R. (1994) Introduction: global commodity chains. In Gereffi, G., Korzeniewicz, M. (eds.), *Commodity Chains and Global Capitalism*. Greenwood Press, Westport, CT, pp. 1–14.

Goody, J. (1993) *The Culture of Flowers*. Cambridge University Press, Cambridge.

Gregson, N., Crew, L. (1997) The bargain, the knowledge, and the spectacle: making sense of consumption in the space of the car-boot sale. *Environment and Planning D: Society and Space* 15, 87–112.

Hartwick, E., 1998. Geographies of consumption: a commodity-chain approach. *Environment and Planning D: Society and Space* 16, 423–37.

Hopkins, T. K., Wallerstein, I. (1986). Commodity chains in the world-economy prior to 1800. *Review* 10, 157–70.

Howes, D. (1996) Introduction: commodities and cultural borders. In Howes, D. (ed.), *Cross-Cultural Consumption: Global Markets, Local Realities*, ch. 1. Routledge, London, pp. 1–16.

Jackson, P. (1999) Commodity cultures: the traffic in things. *Transactions of the Institute of British Geographers* 24, 95–108.

Jackson, P., Holbrook, B. (1995) Multiple meanings: shopping and the cultural politics of identity. *Environment and Planning A* 27, 1913–30.

Jackson, P., Taylor, J. (1996) Geography and the cultural politics of advertising. *Progress in Human Geography* 20 (3), 356–71.

Jackson, P., Thrift, N. (1995) Geographies of consumption. In Miller, D. (ed.), *Acknowledging Consumption: A Review of New Studies*. Routledge, London, pp. 204–37.

Knorr Cetina, K. (1997) Sociality with objects: social relations in positional knowledge societies. *Theory, Culture and Society* 14 (4), 1–30.

Kopytoff, I. (1986) The cultural biography of things: commoditization as process. In Appadurai, A. (ed.), *The Social Life of Things: Commodities in Cultural Perspective*, ch. 2. Cambridge University Press, Cambridge, pp. 64–91.

Lane, H. (1997) Of cabbages and catkins–jam jars, old pots, curious vegetation: welcome to the world of modern floristry. *Observer Life Magazine*, 20 April 1997, pp. 36–7.

Latour, B. (1991) Technology is society made durable. In Law, J. (ed.), *A Sociology of Monsters: Essays on Power, Technology and Domination*. Routledge, London.

Latour, B. (1993) *We Have Never Been Modern*. Harvard University Press, Cambridge.

Leslie, D., Reimer, S. (1999) Spatialising commodity chains. *Progress in Human Geography* 23 (3).

Lyotard, J. F. (1984) *The Postmodern Condition*. Manchester University Press, Manchester.

McMichael, P. (1998) Development and structural adjustment. In Carrier, J. G., Miller, D. (eds), *Virtualism: A New Political Economy*, ch. 4. Berg, Oxford, pp. 95–116.

Maharaj, N., Dorren, G. (1995) *The Game of the Rose*. International Books, Utrecht.

Marsden, T. (1997) Creating space for food: the distinctiveness of recent agrarian development. In Goodman, D., Watts, M. J. (eds), *Globalising Food: Agrarian Questions and Global Restructuring*. Routledge, London, pp. 169–91.

Marsden, T., Wrigley, N. (1995) Regulation, retailing and consumption. *Environment and Planning A* 27, 1899–1912.

Marshall-Foster, C. (1996) Petal pushing. *Fresh*. March 1996, pp. 25–7.

Mather, C. (1999) Agro-commodity chains market power and territory: re-regulating South African citrus exports in the 1990s. *Geoforum* 30, 61–70.

Meier, V. (1999) Cut-flower production in Columbia – a major development success story for women. *Environment and Planning A* 31 (2), 273–89.

Miller, D. (1997) *Capitalism: An Ethnographic Approach*. Berg, Oxford.

Miller, D. (1998) Coca-cola: a black sweet drink from Trinidad. In Miller, D. (ed.), *Material Cultures: Why Some Things Matter*, ch. 8. UCL Press, London, pp. 169–87.

Murdoch, J. (1995) Actor–networks and the evolution of economic forms: combining description and explanation in theories of regulation, flexible specialization, and networks. *Environment and Planning A* 27, 731–57.

Murdoch, J. (1997) Towards a geography of heterogeneous associations. *Progress in Human Geography* 21 (3), 321–37.

O'Hagan, A. (1998) A floral tribute. *Guardian Weekend*, 2 May 1998, pp. 10–19.

Packer, J. (1997) *Living with Flowers*. Conran Octopus, London.

Pile, S., Thrift, N. (1995) Mapping the subject. In Pile, S., Thrift, N. (eds), *Mapping the Subject: Geographies of Cultural Transformation*, ch. 2. Routledge, London, pp. 13–51.

Powell, W., Smith-Doerr, L. (1994) Networks and economic life. In Smelser, N., Swedberg, R. (eds), *The Handbook of Economic Sociology*. Princeton University Press and Russell Sage Foundation, Princeton, NJ and New York, pp. 368–402.

Rabach, E., Kim, E. M. (1994) Where is the chain in commodity chains? In Gereffi, G., Korzeniewicz, M. (eds), *Commodity Chains and Global Capitalism*, ch. 6. Greenwood Press, Westport, CT, pp. 123–41.

Raynolds, L. (1997) Restructuring national agriculture, agro-food trade, and agrarian livelihoods in the Caribbean. In Goodman, D., Watts, M. J. (eds), *Globalising Food: Agrarian Questions and Global Restructuring*, ch. 5. Routledge, London, pp. 119–32.

Retail Business (1996) Market survey, 3: cut flowers and pot plants. *Retail Business Market Reports* 459, May 1996, pp. 71–93.

Schrijvers, J. (1995) Preface. In Maharaj, N., Dorren, G. (eds), *The Game of the Rose*. International Books, Utrecht.

Shakespeare, J. (1995) Withering of the flower children. *Observer*, 9 July 1995, p. 16.

Shapley, D. (1996) Multiples see business blossoming. *Grocer*, 30 March 1996, pp. 45–6.

Stewart, S. (1994) *Colombian Flowers: The Gift of Love and Poison*. Christian Aid, London.

Thrift, N., Olds, K. (1996) Refiguring the economic in economic geography. *Progress in Human Geography* 20 (30), 311–37.

Watts, M. J. (1992) Living under contract: work, production politics, and the manufacture of discontent in a peasant society. In Pred, A., Watts, M. J. (eds), *Reworking Modernity: Capitalisms and Symbolic Discontent*, ch. 3. Rutgers University Press, New Brunswick, NJ pp. 65–105.

Watts, M. J., Goodman, D. (1997) Agrarian questions: global appetite, local metabolism: nature, culture, and industry in *fin-de-siècle* agro-food systems. In Goodman, D., Watts, M. J. (eds), *Globalising Food: Agrarian Questions and Global Restructuring*, ch. 1. Routledge, London, pp. 1–32.

Weiss, B. (1996) Coffee breaks and coffee connections: the lived experience of a commodity in Tanzanian and European worlds. In Howes, D. (ed.), *Cross-Cultural Consumption: Global Markets, Local Realities*. Routledge, London, pp. 93–105.

Whatmore, S., Thorne, L. (1997) Nourishing networks: alternative geographies of food. In Goodman, D., Watts, M. J. (eds), *Globalising Food: Agrarian Questions and Global Restruturing*, ch. 11. Routledge, London, pp. 287–304.

Wolf, J. (1997) Report on flower industry unearths dangers to workers, *Guardian*, 10 May 1997, p. 16.

Wrigley, N. (1993) Abuses of market power: Further reflections on UK food retailing and the regulatory state. *Environment and Planning A* 25, 1545–52.

Wrigley, N., Lowe, M. (eds) (1996) *Retail, Consumption and Capital: Towards the New Retail Geography*, Longman, London.

Chapter 13

Culinary Networks and Cultural Connections: A Conventions Perspective

Jonathan Murdoch and Mara Miele

Introduction

In *Sociology Beyond Society* Urry (2000) outlines a new global configuration of commodity chains and production networks. He describes innovative interminglings of social, technological, and natural phenomena within chains and networks and explains how 'human powers increasingly derive from the complex interconnections of humans with material objects, including signs, machines, technologies, texts, physical environments, animals, plants, and waste products' (Urry 2000: 14). Globalization refers to the increasing reach of economic networks as they align heterogeneous arrays of interrelated entities in ways that ensure their products and services are distributed widely.

Urry (2000) draws attention to the heterogeneous composition of global networks in order to indicate how traditional forms of stability associated with discrete societies have given way to a world of flows in which goods, images, peoples, technologies and other artefacts traverse long-established boundaries and borders. He takes this development as a starting point from which to argue that sociology – which has long taken social structures within nation-states as primary objects of analysis – should engage more whole-heartedly with *mobility*. Given the heterogeneous nature of global flows, Urry (2000) claims that sociology must study more than the 'social': it must focus on 'mixtures' and on zones where differing entities and artefacts 'exchange properties' (Latour 1999) as longer and more complex networks are constructed. Urry (2000) believes a new form of sociological analysis is required which can think 'beyond society' and recast its subject matter into the form of networks, commodity chains, fluid social spaces and global institutional forms.

This prognosis for sociology clearly has implications for geographical work on commodity chains, not least the need to examine the full range of interconnections between networks and spaces in a context of growing mobility (see also Castells 1996). The recognition that network 'heterogeneity' provides a useful starting point for investigating how commodity chains interact with spatially distributed resources is becoming increasingly evident within economic geography (Amin and Thrift 1995; Dickens et al. 2001; Murdoch 1995). In this chapter we develop this general approach further by considering different ways in which network relations might 'coalesce' with given spatial formations. In so doing, we introduce a note of caution into Urry's argument: we propose that while networks might appear to be increasingly mobile and increasingly disconnected from given spaces, they also act to 'condense' space and time. In other words, socio-economic networks and commodity chains emerge from spatially locatable values, symbols, products, practices and entities; and they serve to reflect and refine these phenomena within network forms (see also Bridge 1997; Kirsch 1995; Murdoch 2000). We believe this process of 'condensation' – which ensures a continuing interrelationship between networks and territorially distributed resources and entities – requires further analytical attention.

In looking more closely at how networks 'condense' space we concentrate on the role played by cultural frameworks in linking chains and territories. It has long been noted that the globalization of economic networks coexists with relatively stable cultural formations (Hannerz 1992), so that networks both of standardization and localized variability are invariably present in contemporary spatial configurations (Murdoch 1998). We therefore pay particular attention to the ways in which cultural frameworks interact with heterogeneous materials so that network and spatial formation reach some kind of (albeit temporary) accommodation with one another.

In connecting heterogeneous networks to cultural formations, we adopt a conventions perspective. This approach seeks to identify how social actors combine resources (including both things and people) in line with particular 'orders of worth' (Boltanski and Thevenot 1991; Lamont and Thevenot 2000). By focusing on the forms of calculation that lie behind 'orders of worth', the theory aims to understand how cultural norms and heterogeneous networks mutually consolidate one another. In other words, culture is encoded within complex arrangements of diverse materials, while diverse arrangements of materials are constructed according to cultural norms.

We apply conventions theory to an economic arena in which connections between heterogeneously composed networks and cultural formations remain relatively strong: the food sector. Although this sector has undoubtedly been 'globalized' in the sense that economic, social, technological and ecological aspects are promiscuously intertwined across vast spaces (Bonnano et al. 1994; Goodman and Watts 1997; Goodman 1999), regularities and stabilities in food production practices remain. Mobile networks of globalization continue to coexist with discretely spatialized production forms (cf. Whatmore 1994; Ilbery and Kneafsey 1998). It is thus likely that differential relationships between commodity chains and cultural formations will be evident within the food sector.

We also use the conventions approach to investigate how the composition of food commodity chains is linked to new patterns of food consumption (see Dixon 1999; Lupton 1996; Warde and Martens 2000). As global agro-food networks generate an abundance of food commodities (especially in advanced capitalist countries), consumers are provided with a wider range of food choices (Montanari 1994). It seems likely that increasingly sophisticated consumers will utilize a range of cultural repertoires in order to choose between a wider array of food products (Cook,

Crang and Thorpe 2000; Miele 2001). We can therefore speculate that cultural forms of evaluation will play an expanding role in shaping food commodity chains (Cook and Crang 1996; Lowe and Wrigley 1996; Miller et al. 1998).

We suggest that an analysis of heterogeneous networks from the standpoint of conventions theory may make it possible to consider how consumer conventions (linked to quality and value) come to be assessed against producer conventions (linked to efficiency and cost). However, in pursuing this approach it also is necessary to follow the commodity chain methodology by considering how 'intermediate' actors such as manufacturers, retailers, restaurant chains, caterers and food movements also promote given mixtures of conventions. By combining commodity chain and conventions perspectives we view food commodity networks as complex processes in which different conventions are 'traded' against each other (Wilkinson 1997).

In order to evaluate how conventions in food commodity chains come to be negotiated and aligned by a range of 'intermediate' actors we have chosen to focus in this chapter upon the 'culinary network', a concept that refers not to a single commodity (as in commodity chain analysis), but to the array of materials, actors and institutions that comprise *cuisines*. Cuisines are stable arrangements of foods, ingredients, practices and tastes, and comprise cultural and productive 'worlds of food'. The close connection between food and culture within cuisines makes the 'culinary network' an especially appropriate arena in which to link production and consumption using the conventions approach.

To facilitate an investigation of differing mixtures of actors and conventions in culinary networks we have selected case studies that highlight very different 'worlds of food'. The first is perhaps the archetypal example of 'globalization' in the food sector: McDonald's. Although this network is largely based upon standardized network relations, it also incorporates heterogeneous resources harnessed in line with specific cultural conventions. In particular, this assemblage reflects a set of cultural norms linked to the time and place of the restaurant chain's establishment: the postwar suburban United States. We examine how McDonald's acts to refine and disseminate cultural norms and we consider how a mix of conventions has become encoded in the heterogeneous materials that facilitate the flow of a 'McDonaldized' cuisine.

Having outlined the interaction between standardized network and cultural convention in the case of a global chain, we turn to examine a second case study which displays a markedly contrasting set of connections between network and culture. The Slow Food movement has arisen explicitly to challenge the 'McDonaldization' of cuisine and aims to reassert the values of foods in diverse spatial contexts. It emphasizes that cuisines should reflect localized cultural norms and practices. For Slow Food, cuisine variation goes hand in hand with cultural variation. The movement thus disseminates a range of conventions associated with local food cultures perhaps most evident in its country of origin: Italy.

In contrasting the two cases, we show that each network reflects the general repertoires of evaluation found within two main cultures of food, one 'fast' and the other 'slow'. While the networks might be seen to reflect these cultures in terms of the conventions employed, a recursive relationship between network and culture is evident; that is, the way a network condenses conventions has an impact on the culture of food. We therefore propose that networks and their (cultural) contexts mutually constitute one another. Before presenting this analysis we outline recent theories of food commodity chains in order to show how material complexity and multiple conventions have become of increasing concern to those studying the geography of food commodity networks.

Chains, Networks and Conventions in the Food Sector

The investigation of commodity chains or networks in the food sector has strong theoretical roots. The first examples of agro-food commodity chain analysis appeared during an early round of Marxist theorizing. The political economy of food chains identified an increasingly rapid destruction of traditional agricultural production forms (e.g. family farms) as the imposition of capitalist relations fuels a process of industrialization (de Janvry 1981). This industrialization process appears to be 'disembedding' food production from its pre-existing ('pre-industrial') economic, social and spatial connections. Work conducted in the United States by Friedland, Barton and Thomas (1981), for example, discerns differential rates of capitalist penetration in the agro-food sector but concludes that the process is well advanced across the food sector as a whole. Within each commodity chain, differing mixtures of technical, natural and economic resources are integrated so that distinctive industrial structures (of which agriculture is a diminishing part) are evident. The notion of 'commodity chain' is adopted because it shows how different commodity sectors are organized and highlights the complex sets of relationships invoked within each organizational segment.

The political economy of commodity chains was tailored to the sets of relations that are typically constructed around different agro-food commodities. Friedland (1984) summarizes the research focuses of the early studies as the labour process; grower and labour organizations; the organization and application of science and technology; and distribution and marketing. As this list indicates, commodity system studies dealt largely with the economic and social dimensions of industrialization (see Buttel, Larson and Gillespie 1990). Friedland (2001: 84) recently has admitted that analysts frequently took as their main concern 'agricultural mechanization and its social consequences'. They therefore tended to link network and spatial context primarily through an analysis of the industrial reconfiguration of space and how the industrial rationalization of the chains reconfigures production relations at the local level.

More recently food sector analysts have drawn attention to another aspect of commodity chain activity: the environmental or natural components that often are central to food chain construction both in terms of production (e.g. seasonality, perishability, pollution) and consumption (e.g. quality, health, safety). In early work, Friedland, Barton and Thomas (1981) noted that the specific nature of particular agro-food commodity chains often is determined at least in part by the natural properties of the commodity itself (e.g. the perishability of lettuce and tomatoes). This insight is developed by Goodman, Sorj and Wilkinson (1987) who suggest that the consolidation of capitalist enterprises in the food sector involves the replacement and substitution of natural processes as part of an effort to remove biological constraints from the production process. Goodman, Sorj and Wilkinson (1987) also argue that an expansion and lengthening of food networks tends to result from the progressive industrialization of food so that food products come to be transported over longer and longer distances. This lengthening of food chains increases their socio-technical complexity and leads to the emergence of global commodity chains.

Despite the wealth of valuable insights generated in these studies, commodity chain analysts tend to regard the development of specific chains as conforming to a simplified set of industrial rationalities. According to Busch and Juska (1997) it is usually assumed that the chains express multinationals' 'will to power' (cf. Bonnano and Constance 2001). This problem arises because commodity chain research tends to focus upon the impact of industrialization on agro-food labour processes. It thus neglects the role of retailers, restaurants, nutritionists, market researchers, advertisers and other actors located closer to the consumption end of the chain (Dixon 1999). As a consequence, there is little theoretical space to discern much deviation from the precepts of 'capitalist ordering' (either on the part of producers or consumers).

Building on this criticism, Whatmore and Thorne (1997: 288) suggest that the portrayal of commodity chains as 'systemic' and 'logical' tends to downplay miscellaneous forms of agency bound into material fabrics. In a discussion of 'fair trade' coffee, the authors propose that food networks must be conceptualized as composites of the various actors that go into their making. In doing so they argue that natural and technological entities as well as social actors be granted autonomy and causal powers. That is, multiple forms of agency should be considered when accounting for the establishment of (heterogeneous) relationships in food commodity chains.

Whatmore and Thorne (1997) claim that a greater understanding of agro-food networks can be gained if food chain analysts engage with actor–network theory (ANT) – an approach that sees both human and non-human actors as holding the ability to consolidate and disrupt network relationships. They believe this theory has the potential to achieve a more through understanding of how networks and their socio-natural constituents hang together through time and space. Unlike political economy which tends to see organizational forms (such as chains or networks) as emblematic of already stabilized power relationships, ANT 'problematizes global reach, conceiving of it as a laboured, uncertain, and above all, contested process of "acting at a distance"' (Whatmore and Thorne 1997: 290). ANT thus requires each network or chain to be studied in its own particularity and complexity (cf. Latour 1996).

In this view, networks are complex because they arise from interactions between differing entity types (Latour 1987). Entities coalesce, exchange properties, and (if the network is successfully consolidated) stabilize joint actions in line with overall network requirements (Latour 1999). It is in this context that Callon (1991: 133) defines a network as 'a coordinated set of heterogeneous actors which interact more or less successfully to develop, produce, distribute and diffuse methods for generating goods and services'. An emphasis on heterogeneity means that 'impurity is the rule' (ibid.: 139). For Whatmore and Thorne (1997: 291–2),

> people in particular guises and contexts act as important go-betweens, mobile agents weaving connections between distant points in the network...But, insists [actor–network theory], there are a wealth of other agents, technological and 'natural', mobilized in the performance of social networks whose significance increases the longer

and more intricate the network becomes...such as money, telephones, computers, or gene banks; objects which encode and stabilize particular socio-technological capacities and sustain patterns of connection that allow us to pass with continuity not only from the local to the global, but also from the human to the non-human.

That is, networks and commodity chains inevitably mobilize a multiplicity of social, natural and technological actors. The longer the networks and chains, the greater mobilization is likely to be.

Instead of the simplified world of capitalist ordering, we here encounter complex arrangements that comprise multiple rationalities, ordered in a variety of ways according to mixtures of entities assembled within the networks. However, an emphasis on the heterogeneous quality of network relationships does not necessarily imply that each chain or network is unique (a uniqueness that is determined only by the combination of heterogeneous elements). Networks are rarely performed in radically new or innovative ways; rather, incremental changes lead to 'new variations' on 'old themes'. Because network 'orders' tend to reflect widely dispersed 'modes of ordering' (Law 1994), we see patterns and regularities in network relationships. Modes of ordering – which can be conceptualized as discursive frameworks holding together knowledge about past performances of network relations – are 'instantiated' and stabilized in given networks arrangements. Networks perform multiple 'modes of ordering', which influence the way actors are enrolled and how they come to be linked with others (Whatmore and Thorne 1997: 294)

Because the notion of 'mode of ordering' is used in ANT to link discourses to networks it perhaps provides one means of establishing a connection between commodity chain and culture. However, ANT is less concerned with discourse than with non-human 'bits and pieces' that hold discursive formations together. It therefore tends to render ordering processes and network cultures in rather simplified terms. Having uncovered considerable socio-natural complexity in food commodity chains, for example, Whatmore and Thorne (1997) identify only two ordering modes: one that arranges materials according to a rationality of 'enterprise' and another that emphasizes the spatial 'connectivity' of entities and resources. Given that food networks come in many shapes and sizes, this two-fold typology seems unduly restrictive.[1]

A broader array of ordering modes can be found in conventions theory. Like ANT, this approach also proposes that network configurations stem from processes of negotiation between differing entities and discursive formations. However, conventions theory pays more attention to the different modes of ordering that operate across contrasting cultural formations. It reconceptualizes modes of ordering as 'repertoires of justification' and proposes that repertoires have arisen historically to evaluate actions taken in the name of a 'common' or 'collective' good (Boltanski and Thevenot 1991). Because it situates repertoires in varied cultural contexts, conventions theory is able to identify a broader range of modes of ordering than usually is evident in actor–network studies (cf. Lamont and Thevenot 2000).

Conventions theory proposes that the heterogeneous arrangement of any particular network can be linked via repertoires of justification to the surrounding cultural or discursive context. In general terms, Thevenot, Moody and Lafaye (2000) identify the following conventions as salient in providing this linkage:

'market performance', which evaluates worth based on the profitability, price or
   economic value of goods and services in a competitive market;
'industrial efficiency', which leads to evaluations based on long-term planning, growth,
   investment and infrastructure provision;
'civic equality', in which the collective welfare of all citizens is the evaluatory standard;
'domestic worth', in which value is justified by local embeddedness;
'inspiration', which refers to evaluations based on passion, emotion or creativity;
'renown' or 'public knowledge', which refers to recognition, opinion and general
   social standing; and, lastly,
'green' or 'environmental' justifications, which consider the general good of the
   collective to be dependent upon the general good of the environment.[2]

Thevenot, Moody and Lafaye (2000) argue that these justificatory repertoires exist
in various combinations in all cultural contexts and serve to 'enable' and 'constrain'
networking possibilities. In other words, they provide 'environments of action' in
which network 'bits and pieces' are put together (Storper and Salais 1997)

Whether or not the convention types listed above are exhaustive, they potentially
extend the range of ordering processes thought to operate within food networks.
Moreover, they allow us to specify the contrasting sets of linkages that might be
established between particular conventions and particular arrangements of materials.
As Lamont and Thevenot (2000: 7) argue, various evaluatory criteria will be employed
to link network entities in particular ways: 'the treatment of persons (as customers)
and things (as merchandise) that is required for market valuation is quite different
from their treatment as experts and techniques that is required for an evaluation in
terms of efficiency'. The final shape of any network can therefore be seen to both
reflect and enshrine convention-brokering processes. As differing conventions are
negotiated, entities and relations will be integrated in line with the convention 'mix'.

In applying this perspective to the food sector we must consider how mixtures of
conventions interact with combinations of natural, social and technological resources. Networks where modes of ordering reflect civic and domestic conventions
will align a different set of materials and actors to those based on industrial criteria.
Moreover, the brokering of conventions will extend from producers to consumers so
that the shape and composition of food commodities will be decisively shaped by
agreements enshrined within the material composition of commodity chains.[3]

Conventions theory thus finds a more complex interaction between cultural
repertoires and the consolidation of heterogeneous materials within networks than
either political economy or ANT. 'Modes of ordering' come in a variety of forms and
reflect both the composition of the network and the cultural repertoires woven into
its composition. In the remainder of the chapter we consider the interaction between
heterogeneous networks and conventions in the food sector by investigating two
culinary networks in which different evaluatory criteria link the enrolled elements in
distinct ways. We conclude with some thoughts on the globalization of cultural
conventions within food networks.

Fast Food Culture

The story of McDonald's is well known and we will not repeat it at length here (see
Love 1986; Schlosser 2001 for full, yet contrasting accounts). The company was

born in the United States in the years following the Second World War, at a time of rising wages, an expanding birth rate, suburbanization, mass ownership of the motor car and increased leisure time. Eating out became a standard pastime as hamburgers and other fast foods met the new suburban requirement for 'convenience, efficiency and predictability in ... food preparation and consumption' (Rifkin 1992: 260). Jakle and Sculle (1999: 143) similarly argue that fast food sprang from a cultural milieu of 'competition, the quest for volume, the sense of urgency about service, and the symbolic role of the pampered consumer'. The hamburger in particular came to reflect prevailing cultural aspirations, as its 'capacity for speedy preparation with uniformly satisfactory results ... mesh[ed] well with ... demands of consumer and entrepreneur alike' (Jakle and Sculle 1999: 144; Schlosser 2001).

It was in this context that Maurice and Richard McDonald opened their first restaurant in Pasadena, California. The first McDonald's 'drive-in' sold mainly hot dogs to car-bound customers. After the success of this venture the brothers moved to San Bernadino where they opened a larger and even more successful drive-in. However, the business was beset with problems, including high labour turnover: in a tight labour market the brothers experienced continuing difficulties in recruiting new workers. In the late 1940s they closed the drive-in and opened a new type of restaurant based on a refined system of food delivery. Under the 'Speedee Service System' the McDonald brothers dispensed with

> everything that had to be eaten with a knife, spoon, or fork ... [They] got rid of their dishes and glassware, replacing them with paper cups, paper bags, and paper plates. They divided the food preparation into separate tasks performed by different workers. To fill a typical order, one person grilled the hamburger; another 'dressed' and wrapped it; another prepared the milk shake; another made the fries; another worked the counter. For the first time, the guiding principles of a factory assembly line were applied to a commercial kitchen. (Schlosser 2001: 20)

By employing an 'assembly-line' process the McDonald brothers were able to diminish labour requirements but could still deliver large quantities of burgers at low cost: 'a 1.6 ounce hamburger, 3.9 inches in diameter, on a 3.5 inch bun with .25 ounces of onion sold for 15 cents – a standardized product of high quality but also low price' (Jakle and Sculle 1999: 141). In other words, the assemblage of heterogeneous elements within the McDonald's restaurant both reflected and refined a cultural convention of industrial efficiency.

The initial success of the Speedee Service System attracted the attention of a travelling milkshake mixer salesperson named Ray Kroc. Kroc apparently was impressed by the efficiency of the operation. Viewing the enterprise 'through the eyes of a salesman' (quoted in Schlosser 2001: 67), Kroc anticipated substantial market growth. The McDonald's brothers, however, had no plans to extend the system beyond the one restaurant. Thus Kroc acquired the franchise and embarked upon an expansion of McDonald's restaurants across the US. Initially restaurants were placed in suburban locations, but as competition increased McDonald's moved into the cities. Following the company's flotation on the stock market in the 1970s much expansion has taken place overseas. By the mid-1990s McDonald's comprised 25,000 restaurants in 120 countries and global earnings stood at around $11 billion.

According to Ritzer (1996), Kroc achieved a 'revolution' in the fast-food sector by assembling a network dominated by economic efficiency. Importantly, the convention of efficiency is stabilized in a range of non-human technologies: 'the food in a McDonald's outlet is prepared by the use of timing mechanisms, beeping signals, pre-measured quantities, and computers submerged in the cooking oil that fry foods to uniform specifications' (Fantasia 1995: 208). The same point is visible in Schlosser's (2001: 66) account:

> robotic drink machines selected the proper cups, filled them with ice, and then filled them with soda. Dispensers powered by compressed carbon dioxide shot out uniform spurts of ketchup and mustard. An elaborate unit emptied frozen french fries from a white plastic bin into wire mesh baskets for frying, lowered the baskets into hot oil, lifted them a few minutes later and gave them a brief shake, put them back into the oil until the fries were perfectly cooked, and then dumped the fries underneath heat lamps, crisp and ready to be served. Television monitors in the kitchen instantly displayed the customer's order. And advanced computer software essentially ran the kitchen, assigning tasks to various workers for maximum efficiency, predicting future orders on the basis of ongoing customer flow.

Heterogeneity is orchestrated within an industrial convention so that the whole process of food delivery is engineered in line with a logic of efficiency. This logic also is evident in processes of food preparation. Because the food arrives at the restaurant

> pre-formed, pre-cut, pre-sliced and 'prepared' [there is] usually no need [for the workers] to form the burgers, cut the potatoes, slice the rolls, or prepare the apple pie. All they need to do is, where necessary, cook, or often merely heat the food and pass it on to the customer. (Ritzer 1996: 103)

In the McDonald's system the industrial convention is materialized in the food preparation processes. This materialization extends to the restaurants themselves, which are designed to exact specifications, wherever they might be. McDonald's endeavours to make the consumption experience as repetitive as possible, with symbols, signs, colours, and layouts all repeating a basic formula: ' "kitchen" visible in the background, tables and uncomfortable seats, prominent trash bins, drive through windows and so on' (Ritzer 1996: 81).

While Ritzer's account usefully illustrates how an industrial convention is embedded in the heterogeneous materials that comprise the McDonald's food delivery system, his emphasis on an economic or industrial rationality neglects those network components that genuinely reflect the demands of consumers, and therefore the chain's 'market worth' (Kellner 1999; Smart 1994, 1999; Probyn 1998, 2000). As Gottidiener (1997: 132) suggests:

> fast food outlets are successful because they offer an easy solution to the method of purchasing food that depends little on spoken language, on the interpretation of the menu or personal relations with the waitress/waiter, as happens in other restaurants. These and

other themed environments, with their overendowed, instructive sign systems are fun places to be because they minimize the work we need to do for a successful interaction.

When entering McDonald's consumers need little prior knowledge of the consumption experience. Given McDonald's levels of marketing expenditure, consumers already will be familiar with the brand. Highlighting the importance of the 'reknown' convention in the network, Schlosser (2001: 5) notes that 'customers are drawn to familiar brands by an instinct to avoid the unknown. A brand offers a feeling of reassurance when its products are always and everywhere the same'. By repeating a basic formula, McDonald's transforms 'dining out' into a democratic process – anyone can (afford to) do it – and thereby expands its market.

It is arguable that we see here a civic convention in operation in which all consumers are equal before the food delivery system. Paradoxically it is the rigorous process of efficiency described by Ritzer (1996) that allows this civic convention to work: not only is the food relatively cheap, but also standardization allows consumers to adapt consumption spaces to their own requirements. Thus Kellner (1999) notes that in Taiwan restaurants have become study spaces for students, while in China and Russia they act as up-market eating establishments that provide welcome antidotes to the rather drab restaurants that surround them. McDonald's is therefore able to uphold a civic convention in varied spatial contexts. However, it is clear that the civic convention is closely tied to market worth and this appears to place limits on McDonald's ability to mobilize a civic conception of the 'common good'. It is more likely to assert a 'common good' via market criteria.

In short, McDonald's skilfully aligns heterogeneous elements to deliver a standardized cuisine that meets a range of consumer aspirations. The arrangement encodes conventions of industrial efficiency and civic equality within the heterogeneous fabric of the food delivery system. The system can be exported into differing socio-economic and cultural circumstances so that consumers bring individual civic repertoires to the consumption experience. However, the efficient nature of the system means that while these repertoires can be accommodated, they have little impact on the overall functioning of the food delivery process. That is, the civic convention is constrained by industrial and market criteria. As Fantasia (1995: 235) concludes in his study of fast food in France: 'with standardization the hallmark of the fast food business, there is little room for the restaurant itself to change and develop over time in relation to the people who inhabit it'.

Slow Food Culture

According to Urry (2000: 43), 'global flows engender multiple forms of opposition to their various effects'. Emergent opposition to McDonald's takes a variety of forms, including direct attacks on restaurants during the now frequent anti-globalization demonstrations. Our second case study represents a more long-standing form of opposition to this global network. It concerns Slow Food, a consumer movement established in Italy during the mid-1980s in direct response to the opening of one of the first McDonald's restaurants in Italy, in the famous Piazza di Spagna in Rome. The opening of this restaurant raised the possibility that traditional Italian eating habits might be under renewed threat from Americanized fast food. As part of the ensuing protest the food writer Carlo Petrini gathered chefs, authors, journalists and other intellectuals to discuss the most effective means of countering the spread of fast food in Italy. This first meeting in 1986 gave birth to a new consumer movement – Slow Food – which was to be devoted to the promotion of an 'anti-fast food' culture.

The initial aspiration of Slow Food was a celebration of cultural connections surrounding local cuisines and traditional products. The movement would target discerning consumers in order to heighten their awareness of 'forgotten' cuisines and the threats that these 'worlds of food' currently face. In this way it was hoped that new markets for traditional foods could be created. The main means of reaching potential consumers was to be a publishing house (Slow Food Editore) which would disseminate informed, interesting and accessible material on previously unknown or neglected foods. It was also intended that a network of local groups would be established in order to identify foods that are central to cuisines, to locate ingredients suppliers for these foods and to establish links to restaurants that would facilitate their consumption. Local groups would undertake activities explicitly aimed at tying actors more closely together in order to strengthen local cuisines. In other words, the network would give substance to the convention of domestic worth that is strongly present in Italian society.

The first edition of the movement's magazine, *Slow*, explicitly sought to oppose the spread of McDonald's and the other fast food chains. It claimed that the organization stood in opposition to the 'folly of fast life'. It proclaimed the need to nurture 'gentleness, pleasure, knowledge, care, tolerance, hedonism, balsamic calm, lasting enjoyment...culinary traditions...' The symbol of the snail was adopted as the movement's logo. As Petrini (1986) explained:

> it seemed...that a creature so unaffected by the temptations of the modern world had something new to reveal, like a sort of amulet against exasperation, against the malpractice of those who are too impatient to feel and taste, too greedy to remember what they had just devoured.

As the adoption of this symbol suggests, the emphasis in Slow Food is upon the need to decelerate the food consumption experience so that alternative forms of taste can be (re)acquired. However, Slow Food also has spatial significance: the movement is concerned about a rupture between spaces of production and spaces of consumption and seeks to bring consumers closer to spatially embedded foods. It also wishes to reassert the natural bases of food production (seasonality, ecological content) and the role of cultural context (tacit knowledge, culinary skills). In short, it wishes to embed food in territory.

Slow Food's main concern is thus for 'typical' or 'traditional' foods. According to Torquati and Frascarelli (2000: 343), 'typicality' in the Italian context is determined by 'historical memory (the product is associated with the history and with the traditions of the place of production), geographic localization (influence of the pedoclimatic environment), [and the] quality of raw materials and techniques of preparation'. However, while it attempts to bolster these components of local cuisines, Slow Food also recognizes that local and regional food products are disappearing because they are *too* embedded in local food cultures and ecologies:

they are not easily extracted and sold into modern food markets (for either cultural or ecological reasons, they often cannot travel the long distances covered by McDonald's burgers). So the movement attempts to attract consumers to traditional products by emphasizing aesthetic qualities. The magazine *Slow* promotes a highly aestheticized approach to consumption in lavishly illustrated articles. Slow Food Editore also publishes glossy consumer food guides that provide information on 'slow food' outlets. The best known, *Osterie d'Italia*, identifies typical restaurants in all the Italian regions, thereby giving new consumers (e.g. tourists) the opportunity to engage with previously hidden, but long-standing, local foods. This process of aestheticization indicates the importance of the reknown convention in the Slow Food culinary network.

While its roots are firmly within Italian food cultures, Slow Food seeks to promote 'typicality' much further afield. In 1989 it formally launched itself as an international movement and has subsequently spread to around forty countries (at the time of writing there are 70,000 members worldwide and offices in New York, Paris and Hong Kong). Local Slow Food groups are organized at the regional level into 'convivia'. Although the majority (over 300) are located in Italy, convivia now are operating in such differing national contexts as Australia, Brazil, India and the US. Essentially, a convivium is a consumer club made up of people who wish to 'cultivate common cultural and gastronomic interests' (Slow Food 1998). The definition of the local convivium area is given by cultural and culinary distinctiveness, so that each group is charged with promoting a particular local cuisine. Convivia usually undertake the following activities: identifying restaurants that enshrine the principles of 'slowness' (mostly those offering a good selection of regional dishes and wines); organizing tastings of typical foods and talks by speciality producers and others on gastronomic issues; and promoting an appreciation of local foods in schools and other public institutions. In the process convivia highlight the creativity and tacit knowledge that reside in local cuisines. In this respect they promote a convention of inspiration.

In general, Slow Food seeks to build up cultural diversity by establishing close associations between local cuisines and local systems of production. In so doing it conjures up collectives in which interactions between both people and nature are intense and close. In seeking to build these close associations the movement has come to recognize that many (ecologically sensitive) local producers and processors are precariously connected to consumers. It has thus decided to initiate more direct action in the production sector through a scheme called the Ark of Taste (Slow Food 2000). Along with the usual activities oriented to the dissemination of knowledge about endangered products, the Ark project aims to set up another local group structure ('praesidia') which will be encouraged to identify producers in need of support, develop appropriate support measures (e.g. new marketing channels), and raise funds in order to put these measures in place. In this endeavour, Slow Food is beginning to work like an extension agency whose activities are tailored to producers and processors of typical products. In providing support to producers, Slow Food hopes to promote ecological diversity in local areas in line with the ecological convention.

The Slow Food network thus provides a useful comparator to McDonald's. Where McDonald's imposes a standardized format upon each locality, Slow Food encourages and supports multiplicity; where McDonald's is based upon the dissemination of a simple formula (e.g. the Speedee Service System), Slow Food is built on an appreciation of diverse food cultures. However, there is a recognition in Slow Food that local diversity cannot simply be asserted as an alternative. Local cuisines and their constituent products first must be rendered transparent and made available to a wide number of potential consumers (this is done through the Slow Food publishing house). Second, cuisines must be protected by creating links between producers and consumers (this activity takes place through the convivia). Finally, producers must be economically enabled to remain in existence (such efforts are made under the Ark of Taste).

In undertaking these activities Slow Food condenses a set of conventions found more widely in surrounding cultures of food (notably in Europe but also elsewhere): an appreciation of domestic worth (e.g. close spatial linkages between place of production and place of consumption); an attachment to food as a source of creativity and inspiration (e.g. in production, processing and preparation); civic equality (e.g. everyone should have access to a distinctive and local food culture and should be provided with the opportunity to develop new tastes); and environmental connectedness (e.g. the diversity of foods is a necessary accompaniment to biodiversity). While Slow Food refines and condenses these conventions from its cultural context, it adds in a distinctive characteristic: renown. It does this by promoting a highly aestheticized culture of food in which the local, the traditional and the typical come to be seen as possessing considerable cultural value, even to consumers who understand little about the surrounding cuisine culture. In displaying food in this way, Slow Food not only seeks to provoke consumers into a reassessment of the traditional and the typical, but also to generate a set of conventions which might obstruct the further 'McDonaldization' of food.

Conclusion

The networks described in the previous sections assemble heterogeneous elements in line with the contrasting mixtures of conventions that can be found within differing social formations. McDonald's condenses aspects of an 'Americanized' food culture to distribute a standardized and ubiquitous product via an industrialized system. While it may tailor products to local circumstances to a limited degree (e.g. selling pizzas in Italy, few meat products in Muslim countries or providing luxurious restaurant fittings in Monte Carlo), its strength is based on an economically efficient mode of food delivery, which dispenses both cheap food to consumers and continuing profits to its shareholders. Slow Food, by contrast, is a consumer movement that promotes diversity in food production and consumption processes in order to safeguard the cuisine diversity that is found in Italy and other European societies. It therefore seeks to highlight connections between cuisines and regional natures and cultures and to strengthen markets for locally embedded products.

The two cases illustrate the different ways that global networks operate through space and time. McDonald's applies a uniform set of principles and seeks to turn all its network spaces into expressions of a single entity: 'McDonald's'. It also tends to efface the past in favour of a continuing present, a 'fast' present that can, again, simply be characterised as . . . 'McDonald's'. Alternatively, Slow Food ties together a host of cuisines within sets of relations that give aesthetic expression to spatial diversity. It also shows concern for multiple times: it seeks to reinvigorate long-established regional and local cuisines and wishes to maintain these so that gastronomic connections are extended from the past to the future. Where McDonald's 'economizes', Slow Food 'culturalizes': McDonald's combines civic, market and industrial conventions in ways that ensure the dominance of economic criteria, while Slow Food combines civic, ecological and market conventions in ways that favour cultural and environmental criteria. The outcome in the first is a set of products which enshrine the principle of economic efficiency; the second gives rise to more culturally and environmentally embedded forms of production and consumption.

Such space-time effects indicate the obvious need to critically evaluate the networks one against the other. Clearly any evaluation could begin to consider their differential impacts on surrounding societies, cultures and ecologies. It might point out that McDonald's seems to 'externalize' many of the most significant interactions between food and environment. Because it links heterogeneous entities within instrumental modes of evaluation, 'the low price of the fast food hamburger does not reflect its real cost' (Schlosser 2001: 261). Aspects of the production/consumption relationship (notably the health effects of the fast diet – see Vidal 1997) are therefore displaced so that 'the profits of the fast food chains have been made possible by the losses imposed on the rest of society' (Schlosser 2001: 261).

Slow Food, alternatively, appears to encourage some 'internalization' of costs within economic processes. In this network, market and industrial conventions are harnessed to those that highlight the cultural and environmental benefits of food. But this 'internalization' of cost means that many of the 'slowest' foods are relatively expensive. Thus, the Slow Food approach requires an 'aestheticization' of typical foods (that is, an increase in their 'reknown') in order to attract those consumers who are willing (and able) to look beyond price to a much broader set of criteria. The apparent success of Slow Food in establishing an extensive global network based on an aestheticized food culture seems to indicate that a growing number of (predominantly) middle-class consumers are disposed to assessing food in this fashion. However, upmarket constructions of slow foods may restrict their market reach, thereby weakening the movement's ability to challenge the global expansion of fast food.

Whatever critical stance is taken, the success of each network in mobilizing complex relays of heterogeneous entities such that their length is constantly extended indicates that they are able to coexist in the food sector. This state of coexistence points to a possible fragmentation of production/consumption relations and indicates that 'flows of food' may be proceeding in different directions simultaneously. It also serves to substantiate Urry's (2000: 43) claim that the activities of global networks (both multinational and oppositional) currently serve to 'detotalize' national social forms, thereby increasing the 'fluidity' of socio-economic life even further. In different ways McDonald's and Slow Food generate global flows that reach across national borders and cultures. Both cases highlight the existence of new (heterogeneous) interactions between networks and territories and suggest that spatial complexity will increase as global networks interact with discrete social formations to shape the practices of producers and consumers in diverse cultural contexts.

NOTES

1   A similar criticism might be made of Law's (1994) study, which provides the basis for Whatmore and Thorne's (1997) two types.
2   In certain circumstances – such as deep ecology or animal rights – any distinction between collective and environment breaks down as the former incorporates the latter.
3   For further insights on the relationship between negotiation and commodity network composition, see Cook, Crang and Thorpe (2000); Murdoch and Miele (1999); Murdoch, Marsden and Banks (2000); Wilkinson (1997).

REFERENCES

Amin, A. and Thrift, N. (1995) 'Institutional Issues for the European Regions.' *Economy and Society* 24: 121–143.

Boltanski, L. and Thevenot, L. (1991) *De la Justification: Les economies de le grandeur.* Paris: Gallimard.

Bonanno, A., Busch, L., Friedland, W., Gouveia, L. and Mingione, E. (eds) (1994) *From Columbus to ConAgra: The Globalization of Agriculture and Food.* Lawrence: University of Kansas Press.

Bonnano, A. and Constance, D. (2001) 'Corporate Strategies in the Global Era: Mega-Hog Farms in the Texas Panhandle Region.' *International Journal of Sociology of Agriculture and Food* 9: 5–28.

Bridge, G. (1997) 'Mapping the Terrain of Time-Space Compression: Power Networks in Everyday Life.' *Environment and Planning D: Society and Space* 15: 611–26.

Busch, L. and Juska, A. (1997) 'Beyond Political Economy: Actor–Networks and the Globalization of Agriculture.' *Review of International Political Economy* 4: 688–708.

Buttel, F., Larson, O. and Gillespie, Jr., G. (1990) *The Sociology of Agriculture.* London: Greenwood Press.

Callon, M. (1991) 'Techno-Economic Networks and Irreversibility.' In *A Sociology of Monsters: Essays on Power, Technology and Domination*, ed. J. Law. London: Routledge.

Castells, M. (1996) *The Rise of the Network Society.* Oxford: Blackwell.

Cook, I. and Crang, P. (1996) 'The World on a Plate: Culinary Culture, Displacement and Geographical Knowledge.' *Journal of Material Culture* 1: 131–54.

Cook, I., Crang, P. and Thorpe, M. (2000) 'Regions to be Cheerful: Culinary Authenticity and its Geographies.' In *Cultural Turns: Geographical Turns: Perspectives on Cultural Geography*, ed. I. Cook. London: Prentice-Hall.

de Janvry, A. (1981) *The Agrarian Question and Reformism in Latin America.* Baltimore, MD: Johns Hopkins University Press.

Dicken, P., Kelly, P., Olds, K. and Yeung, H. (2001) 'Chains and Networks, Territories and Scales: Towards a Relational Framework for Analysing the Global Economy.' *Global Networks* 1: 89–112.

Dixon, J. (1999) 'A Cultural Economy Model for Studying Food Systems.' *Agriculture and Human Values* 16: 151–60.

Fantasia, R. (1995) 'Fast Food in France.' *Theory and Society* 24: 201–43.

Finklestein, J. (1999) 'Rich Food: McDonald's and Modern Life.' In *Resisting McDonaldisation*, ed. B. Smart. London: Sage.

Friedland, W. (1984) 'Commodity Systems Analysis: An Approach to the Sociology of Agriculture.' In *Research in Rural Sociology and Development*, ed. H Schwarzweller. Greenwich, CT: Jai Press.

Friedland, W. (2001) 'Reprise on Commodity System Methodology.' *International Journal of Sociology of Agriculture and Food* 9: 82–103.

Friedland, W., Barton, A. and Thomas, R. (1981) *Manufacturing Green Gold*. New York: Cambridge University Press.

Garson, B. (1988) *The Electronic Sweatshop*. London: Simon and Schuster.

Goodman, D. (1999) 'Agro-food Studies in the "Age of Ecology": Nature, Corporeality, Bio-politics.' *Sociologia Ruralis* 39: 17–38.

Goodman, D., Sorj, B. and Wilkinson, J. (1987) *From Farming to Biotechnology*. London: Routledge.

Goodman, D. and Watts, M. (eds) (1997) *Globalising Food: Agrarian Questions and Global Restructuring*. London: Routledge.

Gottidiener, M. (1997) *The Theming of America*. Boulder, CO: Westview Press.

Hannerz, U. (1992) *Cultural Complexity*. New York: Columbia University Press.

Ilbery, B. and Kneafsey, M. (1998) 'Product and Place: Promoting Quality Products and Services in the Lagging Regions of the European Union.' *European Urban and Regional Development Studies* 5: 329–41.

Jakle, J. and Sculle, K. (1999) *Fast Food: Roadside Restaurants in the Automobile Age*. London: Johns Hopkins University Press.

Kellner, D. (1999) 'Theorizing/Resisting McDonaldization: A Multiperspectivist Approach.' In *Resisting McDonaldization*, ed. B. Smart. London: Sage.

Kirsch, S. (1995) 'The Incredible Shrinking World: Technology and the Production of Space.' *Environment and Planning D: Society and Space* 13: 529–55.

Lamont, M. and Thevenot, L. (2000) 'Introduction: Toward a Renewed Comparative Cultural Sociology.' In *Rethinking Comparative Cultural Sociology: Repertoires of Evaluation in France and the United States*, ed. M. Lamont and L. Thevenot. London: Cambridge University Press.

Latour, B. (1987) *Science in Action*. Milton Keynes: Open University Press.

Latour, B. (1996) *Aramis, or the Love of Technology*. Cambridge, MA: Harvard University Press.

Latour, B. (1999) *Pandora's Hope*. Cambridge, MA: Harvard University Press.

Law, J. (1994) *Organizing Modernity*. Oxford: Blackwell.

Leidner, R. (1993) *Fast Food, Fast Talk: Service Work and the Routinization of Everyday Life*. Berkeley: University of California Press.

Love, J. (1986) *McDonald's: Behind the Arches*. New York: Bantam.

Lowe, M. and Wrigley, N. (1996) 'Towards the New Retail Geography.' In *Retailing, Consumption and Capital: Towards the New Retail Geography*, ed. N. Wrigley and M. Lowe. London: Longman.

Lupton, D. (1996) *Food, the Body and the Self*. London: Sage.

Miele, M. (2001) 'Changing Passions for Food in Europe.' In *Agricultural Transformation, Food and Environment*, ed. H. Buller and K. Hoggart. Aldershot: Ashgate.

Miller, D., Jackson, P., Thrift, N., Holbrook, B. and Rowlands, M. (1998) *Shopping, Place and Identity*. London: Routledge.

Montanari, M. (1994) *The Culture of Food*. Oxford: Blackwell.

Murdoch, J. (1995) 'Actor–Networks and the Evolution of Economic Forms: Combining Description and Explanation in Theories of Regulation, Flexible Specialisation and Networks.' *Environment and Planning A* 27: 731–58.

Murdoch, J. (1998) 'The Spaces of Actor–Network Theory.' *Geoforum* 29: 357–74.

Murdoch, J. (2000) 'Networks – A New Paradigm of Rural Development?' *Journal of Rural Studies* 16: 407–19.

Murdoch, J., Marsden, T. and Banks, J. (2000) 'Quality, Nature and Embeddedness: Some Theoretical Considerations in the Context of the Food Sector.' *Economic Geography* 76: 107–25.

Murdoch, J. and Miele, M. (1999) '"Back to Nature": Changing Worlds of Production in the Food Sector.' *Sociologia Ruralis* 39: 465–83.

Petrini, C. (1986) 'The Slow Food Manifesto.' *Slow* 1: 23–4.

Probyn, E. (1998) 'Mc-Identities: Food and the Familial Citizen.' *Theory, Culture and Society* 15: 155–73.

Probyn, E. (2000) *Carnal Appetites: Food/Sex/Identities*. London: Routledge.

Reiter, E. (1991) *Making Fast Food: From the Frying Pan into the Fryer*. Montreal: McGill-Queens University Press.

Rifkin, J. (1992) *Beyond Beef: The Rise and Fall of the Cattle Culture*. New York: Dutton.

Ritzer, G. (1996) *The McDonaldisation of Society*. London: Sage.

Schlosser, E. (2001) *Fast Food Nation: The Dark Side of the All-American Meal*. New York: Houghton Mifflin.

Slow Food (1998) 'The Convivia.' *Slow* 15: 10–11.

Slow Food (2000) *The Ark of Taste and the Praesidia*. Bra: Slow Food Editore.

Smart, B. (1994) 'Digesting the Modern Diet: Gastro-Porn, Fast Food and Panic Eating.' In *The Flaneur*, ed. K. Tester. London: Routledge.

Smart, B. (ed.) (1999) *Resisting McDonaldisation*. London: Sage.

Storper, M. and Salais, R. (1997) *Worlds of Production*. Cambridge, MA: Harvard University Press.

Thevenot, L., Moody, M. and Lafaye, C. (2000) 'Forms of Valuing Nature: Arguments and Modes of Justification in French and American Environmental Disputes.' In *Rethinking Comparative Cultural Sociology: Repertoires of Evaluation in France and the United States*, ed. M. Lamont and L. Thevenot. Cambridge: Cambridge University Press.

Torquati, B. and Frascarelli, A. (2000) 'Relationship Between Territory, Enterprises, Employment and Professional Skill in the Typical Products Sector.' In *The Socio-Economics of Origin-Labelled Products in Agri-food Supply Chains*, ed. B. Sylvander, D. Barjolle and F. Arfini. Le Mans: INRA.

Urry, J. (2000) *Sociology Beyond Society: Mobilities For The Twenty-first Century*. London: Routledge.

Vidal, J. (1997) *McLibel: Burger Culture on Trial*. London: Macmillan.

Warde, A. and Martens, L. (2000) *Eating Out: Social Differentiation, Consumption and Pleasure*. Cambridge: Cambridge University Press.

Whatmore, S. (1994) 'Global Agro-food Complexes and the Refashioning of Rural Europe.' In *Globalization, Institutions and Regional Development*, ed. A. Amin and N. Thrift. Oxford: Oxford University Press.

Whatmore, S. and Thorne, L. (1997) 'Nourishing Networks: Alternative Geographies of Food.' In *Globalising Food: Agrarian Questions and Global Restructuring*, ed. D. Goodman and M. Watts. London: Routledge.

Wilkinson, J. (1997) 'A New Paradigm for Economic Analysis?' *Economy and Society* 26: 305–39.

Part V   Consumption

Chapter 14

Making Love in Supermarkets

Daniel Miller

For many purposes the main division in the street where I conducted fieldwork lies between the council estates on one side and the private housing on the other. But the significance of this division cannot always be assumed. Although she lives in an owner-occupied maisonette, Mrs Wynn comes across immediately as quintessentially working class. Her husband is an electrician but has been unemployed for several months owing to an injury. She is a childminder, taking into her home other people's children while they are out working. Between his injury and the fact that someone recently ran into their car while it was parked outside their house, they were not having an easy time of it. Nevertheless, as often proved to be the case, her concerns in shopping bear little upon the contingencies of the moment, and relate more to longer-term issues surrounding the personal development of each member of the family. She was pretty fed up with the consequences of these unexpected events, but shopping as a topic drew her back to things that at one level were more mundane. But these were relationships which she cared about a great deal and was constantly thinking about and forming strategies to deal with. In conversation she notes:

> A^1 My husband is quite fussy vegetable wise and he's a big meat eater, but yes I've been doing a lot of stir fries because I found I could get him to eat a lot more vegetables if I do stir fries, and he likes Chinese. He likes spicy stuff. He's got a lot better than when I first met him because his mum's Irish and over-cooked everything and was pretty basic and he's got so much better in the years.
> Q Do the kids eat the same as him?
> A No. Jack my son's got very fussy, definitely in the last year. I would say he's a good vegetable and fruit eater but he's the basic chips and burger and I'm afraid so.
> Q Do you cook separately for them?
> A Pasta he loves pasta. Yes, and separate times as well.

Later on in the same conversation she notes:

> A I try not to buy a lot of convenience [foods]. I do buy meat that is marinated and stuff like that and then think what can I do with it, but now and again I will sit down and get

my books out and have a look. I did it last week just because I was getting a bit tired of
things. But also what I will do is buy the sauces and the stir-fry things, stuff like that,
and then just add it to everything so it makes a bit of difference, but I seem to get stuck
doing the same things over and over again. So, every now and then, I've got to get my
books out to remind myself or think of some new things.
Q Is it you that's bored?
A No. He will say as well, we've had this a bit too much. I'm a great chicken eater and
he says chicken again!

Later still she starts discussing the purchase of clothing for the family, making it
clear that she buys her husband's clothes. She notes that out of preference he would
just wear some old T-shirts, and often would then go on to use these as cloths during
his work. It's not just his clothing she buys. In practice she prefers not to let him do
any of the shopping. She feels that if she lets him shop, then he misses things on the
list she has made, or buys himself things like biscuits on a whim.

A So it's more hard work. I'd rather him stay here and look after the children and I'll do
it. Then it's a break for me and you know.

These views were reiterated when we were out shopping in a local supermarket. She
again noted the problems with getting her children to eat what she wants them to eat
rather than what they would choose for themselves. She claimed to be quite strict
with the children that she was paid to look after, but with respect to her own
children, she tended to be much more lenient – 'anything for a bit of peace and
quiet'. Again and again her actual purchases are related back to household preferences. When she buys mint-flavoured lamb at the butcher's she notes in passing that
this had gone down really well the week before and that she had been asked to get it
again. Equally, some jam tarts purchased previously because they were under offer
(going cheap) had been well received. The only exceptions to this orientation to the
household in her shopping come with the purchase of some bread rolls and frank-
furters for a friend who will be coming round for tea. Also at another point in our
expedition she buys a fancy ice cream called Vienetta which she declares is 'a treat
for herself'.

By no means all the shoppers I accompanied were like Mrs Wynn, but she is
representative of a core of households. She should anyway be quite a familiar figure
from many previous feminist studies of the housewife. The feminist perspective on
such housewives will be discussed below, but many researchers have acknowledged
that which would be clearly evident here. However oppressive the outside observer
might find this subsumption of the individual to her husband and children, the
housewife herself insists that she merely expresses thereby a series of responsibilities
and concerns with which she strongly identifies and of which she is generally proud.

Mrs Wynn acknowledges that she is constantly monitoring, even researching, the
desires and preferences of her household. These include both foundational goods
which are expected to be constantly present and available in the house, but also
transient desires which arise from a preference for at least a subsidiary element of
change and innovation. But she would by no means regard herself as merely the
passive representative of these desires. Indeed if she merely bought what the other

members of her household asked for, shopping would be relatively easy. The problem is that she wishes to influence and change her husband and children in quite a number of ways. She is constantly concerned that they should eat healthier foods than those they would choose for themselves. By the same token she wants them to wear either better quality or at least more respectable clothes than those they prefer. She sees her role as selecting goods which are intended to be educative, uplifting and in a rather vague sense morally superior. It is precisely their unwillingness to be uplifted by her shopping choices that creates the anxieties and battles of shopping. In vindicating their decisions, such housewives often lay claim to a wider perspective than that of other family members. They see themselves as having the foresight to prevent the embarrassment and disdain that others might feel if they let their families dress as they choose, or determine their own food choices.

Of course, all these efforts could be reduced to her interests. It could be argued that she is buying better clothes because she feels she will be made to suffer the opprobrium of criticism by others if she doesn't. She buys healthier foods because she would have to look after the person who otherwise becomes ill. But for us to try to figure out whether the constant hassle of arguing with her family, in order to persuade them to adopt her preferences, actually pays some kind of long-term dividend is the kind of daft calculation we may safely leave to economists, socio-biologists and their ilk. There is no reason to suppose that Mrs Wynn engages in any such weighing up of cost or benefit. As far as she is concerned, the reasons that she researches their preferences and equally that she then tries to improve upon them are the same. Both are assumed by her to represent the outcome of a responsibility so basic that it does not need to be made explicit or reflected upon. In short, her shopping is primarily an act of love, that in its daily conscientiousness becomes one of the primary means by which relationships of love and care are constituted by practice. That is to say, shopping does not merely reflect love, but is a major form in which this love is manifested and reproduced. This is what I mean to imply when I say that shopping in supermarkets is commonly an act of making love.

One could use other terms than love. Care, concern, obligation, responsibility and habit play their roles in these relationships. So also may resentment, frustration and even hatred. Can these latter be the ingredients of something we may properly term love? As long as it is clear that we understand by this term 'love' a normative ideology manifested largely as a practice within long-term relationships and not just some romantic vision of an idealized moment of courtship, then the term is entirely appropriate. Love as a practice is quite compatible with feelings of obligation and responsibility. As Parker (1996) has noted, love for infants is inevitably accompanied by hatred and resentment, and this is perhaps rather more evident for partnerships. The term is certainly justified by ethnography in as much as these shoppers would be horrified by the suggestion that they did not love the members of their family or that there was not a bedrock of love as the foundation of their care and concern, though they might well acknowledge some of these other attributes as well.

I never knew Mrs Wynn well enough to be able to gain a sense of the more intimate moments within her household. I don't know how free she felt about expressing her love in explicit forms. In general, a reticence with regard to more overt expressions of emotion is regarded as a typically British characteristic, and was commented upon by those born elsewhere. But this reticence about love need not imply its absence, so much as its being essentialized as so natural that it becomes embarrassing to feel the need to express it. One consequence of this reticence is that love has come to be primarily objectified through everyday practices of concern, care and a particular sensitivity to others, within which shopping plays a central role.

During the course of this essay the term 'love', which first appears here as the common term by which relationships are legitimated, will become used to represent a value that leads us towards the problems of cosmology and transcendence. These terms are not intended to obfuscate or make complex some simple phenomenon. They merely remind us that within a largely secular society almost all of us still see ourselves as living lives directed to goals and values which remain in some sense higher than the mere dictates of instrumentality. Daily decisions are constantly weighed in terms of moral questions about good and bad action indicated in traits such as sensitivity as against style, or generosity as against jealousy. Though these may not be made explicit, the accounts we use to understand each other's actions depend on the continued existence of cosmology as a realm of transcendent value.

The terms 'cosmology' and 'transcendent' suggest values that are long lasting and opposed to the contingency of everyday life. They are intended to imply that although we focus upon the particular persons, children, partners and friends who occupy our concerns at a given moment of time, the way we relate to them is much influenced by more general beliefs about what social relations should look like and how they should be carried out. At one level then, love is a model of one particular type of identification and attachment. It is one we are socialized into and constantly informed about. This ideal is then triggered by an individual, such as a family member who makes it manifest. A relationship then builds its own specificity and nuance which (sometimes) goes well beyond the transcendent model with which we started. When the term 'love' is used, as here, in a more general sense, actual relationships are found to develop on the basis of much wider norms and expectations which pre-exist and remain after the relationship itself.

The term 'love' then indicates more than a claim to affection made during courtship. It stands for a much wider field of that to which life is seen as properly devoted. In later parts of this essay it will be more closely related back to devotional practices in which the term 'cosmology' is more obviously appropriate since the context is more clearly that of religion. The ethnography suggested that just as devotion is the taken-for-granted backdrop to the carrying out of religious rites in other times and places, so in North London love remains as a powerful taken-for-granted foundation for acts of shopping which will be argued to constitute devotional rites whose purpose is to create desiring subjects.

I would call Mrs Wynn a housewife, even though for the present she is the sole wage-earner of the family, because, for her, housewifery is her principal *raison d'être*. As feminist research has made clear, a person such as Mrs Wynn is more likely to view her earnings as simply part of her housewifery than as a job equivalent to that which her husband would be engaged in were he fit. As someone who identifies with being a housewife, the requests made by her family for particular foods are not viewed with resentment but are in fact desired by her. This is made quite explicit in another conversation with a working-class Cypriot woman.

Q Do you enjoy cooking?
A Yes I do, I'm afraid I do.
Q Does your family appreciate it?
A Oh yes, they do they love the food, my daughter when she comes home she says 'Oh mum food', she opens the fridge as soon as she comes in.
Q Is your husband particular?
A Oh he doesn't like very hot, very spicy food, but no he just eats what he's given really.
Q Does he make any requests?
A Oh I wish he would! No he doesn't.

Here, as is so often the case, there is no evident resentment at being identified unambiguously with housewifery. On the other hand, there is a considerable desire that this should be appreciated by the family members, and not taken for granted. A specific request for an item when shopping is taken as a kind of bringing into consciousness of the role played by the shopper and is most often viewed positively, even if it becomes a cause of contention. The subsequent argument is itself an opportunity for the housewife to demonstrate that she is only contradicting the request because of how much she cares for the person and therefore the consequences of what she buys. In general, the problem many housewives expressed was the lack of valorization, most particularly of the moral, educative and provisioning roles that housewives see as of immense importance. They would not normally use the term 'love' for such concerns, but it is clear from what they do say, that it is love alone that can satisfactorily legitimate their devotion to this work. It is also clear that to be satisfactory the subjects of love should desire and acknowledge that which the housewife sees as her ordinary devotional duty.

In the last two decades we have become far better informed about the work involved in keeping a home going and activities such as shopping. This is almost entirely thanks to a series of important empirical studies of housework inspired by the feminist critique of housewifery as unvalorized labour. Within a short time a normative pattern was uncovered and well documented which suggested that women tended to be largely responsible for the basic provisioning of the household, while men tended to be responsible mainly for extra items that were of particular interest to themselves, but were relatively unimportant in, for example, provisioning for children. Male work outside the home was found to be fully acknowledged through wages and through an endorsement of its centrality to the maintenance of the home, as in the phrase 'bringing home the bacon'. By contrast, women's work in the home was not only unpaid but even the homeworker tended to downplay the sheer weight of labour involved in keeping house. This degree of exploitation and the asymmetry of power was reinforced rather than redressed in consumption, where housewives were found to give the best of their labour in meals and comforts to others while often denying themselves the pleasure they strove to create for others.[2]

In general, our fieldwork revealed similar patterns to those uncovered in this previous work, and merely demonstrates that these generalizations still largely hold for the 1990s in this area of North London. Our research thereby also confirms the main conclusion of these other studies as to the basic asymmetry of housework and the exploitation of female labour. By the same token these previous studies provide the bulk of evidence for the centrality of love and care as the ideology behind mundane domestic activities such as shopping, to which this case study becomes merely an additional exemplification. The primary examples are these highly conventional expressions of care and concern within households. But there is a wide range of other ways in which love is expressed, which will be illustrated below. Examples include love within egalitarian couples, by the elderly, between friends, siblings and a gamut of other relationships. Even if love is extended to this degree, however, I am obviously not claiming it is ubiquitous. Not every shopping practice is about love; there are others that relate more to selfishness, hedonism, tradition and a range of other factors. What I will claim, however, is that love is not only normative but easily dominant as the context and motivation for the bulk of actual shopping practice.

Some Varieties of Love-making

Sheila, like Mrs Wynn, provides for a nuclear family within a clearly working-class milieu, in this case living in council housing. Her husband Bob works night shifts for the army and she works as a shop assistant. Unlike Mrs Wynn, however, their relationship is based on far more extensive sharing of activities such as shopping. This is in large measure due to the fact that his night shift is more compatible with shopping than her day shift. Beyond this is a more complex relation of gender. He works in the highly macho environment of the army, but is himself a clerk. He constantly expresses preferences for rather macho taste, but it is understood that this covers a rather less forceful disposition and a rather fearful personality. This comes over, for example, in his clear terror of the pigeons that fly around the high street and to which most people give little or no regard. The gender divisions are then traditional but not given, in that they have to be constantly re-expressed to hide what is otherwise a more confident and strong woman. For her part she does indeed want him to shop but because of her sense of love and family devotion she desires at the same time to protect his rather more fragile self-confidence from this aberration from their mutually conservative notions of gender differences.

The result of these contradictions was evident in the constant comic banter between the spouses when I accompanied them both shopping. In turn this was related to a clearly held view as to the importance of easy-going compromise as the foundation to their ideal of how their relationship ought to be. Shopping choices and negotiations then come to play their part in the constant reiteration of what they regard as the positive elements of their relationship. This ideal is made clear in earlier conversations.

> A But Sheila is normally easy because she always says to me 'Well we're pretty easy-going'. Like you know as long as we don't hate something, like we'll say Oh alright that's fair enough.
> Q What about other opinions?
> A No we don't, we're not for things like that. We get what we like. Well to be truthful the kids, they don't. They're like us, really easy-going, 'Oh that's alright yeah, that's it'. Charlotte, when we first did the wallpaper she said 'Oh it's disgusting', but a week later she said 'No it's nice, I like that wallpaper Dad'. Normally the kids are easy-going.

Within this idea of 'easy-going' is negotiated an arrangement whereby the indi-viduality of each family member is made explicit, but the demands that this individu-ality may put on the group limited. So the father is allowed to have tastes that are seen as natural to a 'proper man' as in:

> A They don't eat what I call proper. The whole household to me. I'm the only one who eats proper meat, what I call meat, I don't call them things beefburgers and all that, I'm talking about lamb chops, pork strips, legs of chicken.
> Q Butcher's?
> A Yeah a butcher's – exactly. I like my meat. I love my meat.

Similarly, the daughter is expected to have the propensities recognized as normal for a sixteen-year-old girl, but only in as far as they can be put together in a feasible shopping package. Demand for further autonomy is referred back to that individual, unless this seems to her mother to be a 'reasonable' request for special consideration.

> A Occasionally she'll ask for something, cotton balls or, and food wise she'll ask 'Oh I like them so and so I haven't had them for a while'. You know whatever. She likes them chicken bites doesn't she, she'll say 'dinosaurs [a shape of processed chicken] when are you getting some more dinosaurs', so I say 'If you want it just say what you want' 'cos Charlotte's not a real meat eater I mean she gets on me nerves sometimes.
> Q Do you still buy most things for her?
> A Oh yes, I'll say to her sometimes the day before 'Do you want a chilli tonight or something or would you prefer just something with chips or', but she'll let me know like in advance though.
> Q Things she gets for herself?
> A That's her hair things.
> Q Clothes, music?
> A Well we help with the clothes sometimes, but if she just wants to get a T-shirt, something like that, she'll get herself that out of her pocket money. She gets her hair sprays and hair colour whatever. The cleansing lotion we normally get because she can't use soap and water, so she has to have cleansing, so you know we get that for her.

During the shopping expedition the banter between them consists mainly of criticisms spun off as jokes. Sheila, as many North London housewives today, heads first for the National Lottery, while he takes the list for shopping. On her return he says to me in a loud – to be overheard – voice 'you didn't see how much she spent when she went off to buy cigarettes did you! She gave you the slip that time!' Later she interrogates him about a red-wine casserole sauce for chicken that he seemed to have slipped into the shopping basket without her seeing, and then again about some better-quality coat-hangers. She laughingly notes how 'You are going to see a fight now', and that he had better take them back. Yet this is said in a way that is clearly an acknowledgement that she accepts the purchase as a *fait accompli*. He tries but then fails to choose a jam, since he knows the kids don't like ones with pieces of fruit in, but doesn't know enough to be sure what they do like since 'the kids is her department'. Later at the shampoo counter she pretends she finds one for 'no hair' (since he is receding). 'She always gets one over me', he remarks. A key element within this comic banter is her constant criticism of his lack of shopping skills; for example, his forgetting to pack the bread in such a way as to prevent it becoming crushed. Taken in context, however, these criticisms are a mechanism she uses to affirm that as a man, although he may shop, he is not a natural shopper. He is thereby able to receive such 'criticisms' as praise for his natural manliness, something which he recognizes. I can see him light up with pride at each barb levelled against him. All such criticism is gratefully received.

Their individual shopping choices are part and parcel of the same shoring-up of conventionality. Compared to most shoppers, they tend to a much higher proportion of branded as against supermarket own-label goods. Also their food choices are amongst the most overtly 'British' of any of the grocery shopping observed. Apart from the elderly, most shoppers tend to take advantage these days of the highly cosmopolitan possibilities of the supermarket. But this family's shopping basket has mainly items such as mint sauce, chops, shortbread, corned beef, sage and onion stuffing, vinegar, pork belly and chipping potatoes, which together form a portrait of 'Britishness' in the rather 'bulldoggy' sense that he brings from his workplace. It is this that gives meaning to the cheap 'wine-based' casserole sauce being slipped into the basket as his guilty secret – his French bit on the side.

The couple also have to contend with a problem with their son, which time and again becomes a key point of contention for working-class shoppers on low incomes. Almost invariably sons desire the special football stripes (clothing) for their team and these are extremely expensive. In this case, the new Spurs (a football team) stripe would cost £66, which they really can't afford. In fact, they have resorted to borrowing the money from a building society account which contains funds given to their son from his grandparents. Although at one level they know they are stealing from their own son, they reason that it is more important to be able to provide something which has become a key element in a boy's constitution as a member of his peer group. Indeed, this is precisely the kind of 'love that cannot be denied' which can lead to theft by impoverished families, who, as in this case, would see themselves as scrupulously law-abiding by choice. I could never imagine this couple stealing on their own behalf, but they are simply too driven by love for this not to be imaginable as action on behalf of others. This example also makes clear that love should not be isolated as something opposed to wider social concerns. Here love takes the more exquisite form of parental anxiety over how the son will be treated if he does not live up to the expectation of his peers. Similarly, love may incorporate class consciousness, emulation and other factors discussed in research on consumption (see Slater 1997: 33–99 and Warde 1997: 7–42 for recent examples), in as much as these are turned into intra-household needs and anxieties.

Of course, this couple does not possess the eloquence of writers about household relations, such as the playwright Ibsen. Yet there is no reason why Ibsen could not be properly invoked. The family tensions and contradictions evident in their relationships are not just between individuals fulfilling roles, but revolve around the basic attributions of gender and its burdens of expectations in the form of male strength and female sentiment. These are precisely the issues found in Ibsen's fictional accounts of the classic bourgeois family. Shopping here allows for considerable play with performance and facade and the complex empathy and humanity that allows love to be the instrument rather than the victim of such contradictions. My contention is that this couple (as those writers) often reveal ways in which a larger sense of humanity struggles to express itself within a structure whose fundamentally oppressive nature would otherwise overwhelm them. It is hard to imagine a more unlikely figure of philosophy than Sheila, yet it was clear on the several occasions that I also observed her in the shop where she worked, listening and sometimes chatting extensively to fellow workers and customers, how she strives to bring to this, her second marriage, skills and sentiments gathered from her constant exposure to the trials and tribulations of other people's everyday domestic relations.

My next example requires us to cross, not only the road, but also that considerable boundary between the two major class contexts of British society, in order to review an extract from a much longer discussion about furniture shopping. Here are found a comparatively egalitarian couple, where the husband is said to do as much cooking as the wife, but their core shared interest is in art and design. The husband actually teaches design and the wife has a strong interest in the arts. For them, the emphasis on the commonality of taste becomes a particularly significant expression of their existence as a compatible couple in love.

> *A* Well we needed a sofa. We decided we didn't have enough seating in our house. We had a little sofa, then we had a couple of chairs so it was hopeless. So we were looking for a sofa and they're all so expensive and we were going around everywhere thinking 'Oh no', you know and they were all horrible. So we thought let's go to IKEA, they're fairly cheap there and the things seem fairly sturdy enough. We've got book cases and stuff from there before, and we went along, and we saw a sort of sofa bed we thought we'd get so we could have people come over and sleep, stay over, sort of dual purpose and we nearly went to buy one, and we were on our way out, when we went into the bargain basement corner, and there was this sofa, and we didn't immediately say 'yes that's it', we sort of went 'um yeah'. Actually we hadn't thought of leather, but yeah yellow's OK. Then I suddenly thought that would be just right, that'll just do us just fine so I sat on it while Allen went up to the cashier and said 'yes we want that sofa, I want to pay for it now before someone else gets it' 'cos there was only one like £750 and it was like £400 so and we squeezed it into the back of our Golf [car]. It could barely fit, took the legs off. We strapped it on, came home and my brother was like 'Hey you've got a new sofa' so it worked out quite well really. Allen's always worried that the cat's going to be scratching it up and stuff.
>
> *Q* Does the cat scratch?
>
> *A* Yeah yeah she just sort of walks around and hangs on. There are a few little bits but it's worn quite well. We're quite pleased with it really. I think it looks pretty good. It doesn't obviously look IKEA or anything so. Some of my friends really hate IKEA so you have to choose carefully what you get from there.

As in the case of the football stripes, this conversation demonstrates the interweaving of intra-household love, here expressed as the taken-for-granted sharing of taste, and the firm eye kept on the effect this has on the image of the couple exposed to external criticism.

These three examples express relationships that are already well established. Shopping can also shed light on relationships that are coming into being. There is a less common but equally germane case of shopping as a specific act of courtship – that is, part of a series of activities that enable a couple to decide whether they could or should be regarded as what is so eloquently termed 'an item'. We remain within the middle-class milieu of a young divorced woman, who is both a journalist and student at a design college, shopping with her boyfriend. Although he had not yet moved in with her, they had at least broached the topic of buying a house together. At this stage the crucial factor in shopping was my presence. This was an occasion to learn about each other's taste and forge a relationship in terms of shopping compatibility. But there was also the question as to how they appeared as a couple to an outsider. The sheer effort that I felt they were putting into showing me how happy they were together should not be seen as thereby false. It reflected their own question as to whether, when revealed in the reflected gaze of the anthropologist, they would find themselves to be in love.

They have both just bathed and dressed, they are in jeans, but are equally well trained at looking good in blue denim. Almost every shopping choice is exploited as an opportunity to construct an agreement as to whether to go his way, her way or in a way that could be defined in the future as 'their' way. This started from the decision as to whose car to use. During the journey they are exchanging knowledge about the best place to buy items (mainly car-related items). Although both have said that they do not normally enjoy grocery shopping, they are clearly out to have a good time. They have little gestures of fun; for example, she rushes to pick the bag of tea just before he gets there. She then holds it above the trolley and lets go in a kind of 'plop' gesture, as opposed to merely putting it in. They put their arms around each other, they perform little acts of showing off, such as when she pushes and then 'rides' on the trolley for a couple of feet. At one point she picks up a mini fudge to give him as an immediate gift. They also engage in conspicuous compromise: for example, at one point she picks up butter, he a low-fat spread, and they then decide to have a small tub of each. The shopping is not only about finding common tastes. Compared to most shoppers she spends quite some time simply picking up items she would not normally have considered. She does not buy any of them, but it is clear that the opportunity for changes represented by her new relationship is also a catalyst for her trying to imagine new possibilities for herself and whether she could be the kind of person who buys this or that product.

As so often with shopping, however, there are nuances and contradictions below the level of the more overt building of relationships. For one thing, the fact that she has stressed that this will be a small shop, and he that it will be a large one, is not unconnected to the fact that it is her turn to pay the bill. Furthermore, as so often with love, the relationship that is being forged while shopping is not based on equality. Even within what appears to be a feminist middle-class relationship with a more experienced divorcee, they establish a clear asymmetry. In general, she is trying to develop a more intimate knowledge of him and his desires, while he is establishing that he has the final word in most decision making. He vetoes choices such as a soyabean mix by saying he doesn't like soya, but I saw no cases of her vetoing him. They are both vegetarian but she sometimes eats fish. He wants them to end up with an agreement based on his preference, and manages to drop enough hints to make her say at one point: 'Why do you keep going on about it?' As decisions accumulate it becomes clear that although she will permit an unequal relationship, this should not be so overt as to prevent her from finding ways to hide this fact from herself. In addition they both have other relationships of care to mark. He normally takes his mother shopping and here buys extra goods for her. She has her daughter to think about, and as so often buys goods which are slightly less 'junky' versions of those requested by her daughter. These are accompanied with the typical explanation that 'I would like to wean her onto something healthier'. Within a few weeks of this shopping expedition the couple informed me they were engaged.

Few opportunities arose to observe such 'shopping as courtship' expeditions. Apart from individuals, the single most common shopping genre was also the most fraught, which is when mothers shop with infants. Here the relationship between power and love becomes far more explicit, as do the contradictions of love. Mothers with babies are constantly torn between a sense of pride and desire to show off their infant to appreciative fellow shoppers and the anxiety that mounts as babies lose 'patience' and start to cry, struggle and embarrass their parents. Such ambivalence continues as toddlers express often unmitigated greed, negating the sense of innocence and nature that the parent would wish them to express.[3] This is also the most unambiguous relationship of love in that no amount of anxiety, frustration or embarrassment can undermine the fundamental belief that the relationship being expressed and developed in endless battles and compromises should be called love.

Around those varieties of love that remain clearly within a normative centre lie other examples that are both more problematic and in some cases better regarded as exceptions. Clary illustrates the problems that arise when relentless poverty becomes in and of itself a constraint to the expression of such sentiments. Clary is a single mother living in a council flat, who simply cannot manage on the meagre government support she receives. Her present hardship is exacerbated by having been caught without a television licence, so that she is also paying off a fine. The father of her two children is much better off, and she feels particularly vulnerable because she simply cannot compete with his generosity when the children go and stay with him, and she is worried about the indulgences they become used to while there. In effect, her love is manifested largely as anxiety about shopping, rather than in shopping itself. The social science literature on consumption often seems to echo most journalism in making the daft assumption that it is mainly the rich who are materialistic. Clary, however, like most people I worked with who live in considerable poverty, is much more materialistic than the rich, because of the miserable consequences of her lack of goods. For Clary, this is reflected not merely in her persistent worrying about goods she cannot afford but also the deeper sense that she is a failure as a mother as a result of this. These anxieties constantly surface in conversations, as in a discussion about birthday parties for children at the school.

> A Yeah Ruth has been to quite a few, and one of Mark's friends had to go to McDonald's and it's really expensive, especially when there's about twelve or fourteen children, and I can't even afford to get Mark a birthday card let alone a party or anything. I mean it's his birthday on Tuesday and he's gone down to their [the father's] house for the week, so I mean I've only just sent a card down. It's all I can afford. It's very difficult when you're on your own and you haven't got any money, and I feel quite embarrassed when they have to keep going to parties, and I haven't really got a present but I sort of manage to get something.

The same anxiety permeates the experience of shopping with Clary. On one occasion – an extremely hot day – when we had walked to the shopping centre to save on fares, the children start to ask for drinks as soon as we arrive. I decide to buy ice lollies for all four of us (I was pretty thirsty too!). But Clary is immediately nervous. Eating slows them down. The lollies melt before they can be eaten properly and she has to hold her daughter's lolly for her, and eat some of the looser ice cream to stop it falling off. She then becomes upset about their sticky hands and faces, and makes clear by various gestures that I should not have bought them lollies – that she sort of knew that this is what would happen. She then buys a pack of tissues she cannot afford in order to clean the children up. Pride, love, guilt – one could attach so many labels to Clary's feelings and actions (and add insensitivity to mine). For most parents love is often subsumed within anxiety, but for Clary anxiety is often about all she has.

The concept of making love in shopping is even more problematic when the issue is not one of lack of money, but lack of a relationship to which love can be directed. In this particular area there are two main varieties of single-person household. The first and most numerous is that of the elderly. In general, these tend also to be amongst the most impoverished households, occupying the most run-down part of the council flats. There exist amongst the elderly some of the most self-obsessed individuals in the street; for example, one elderly male who had never married and clearly regarded other people (in particular inquisitive anthropologists) with considerable malevolence. Despite my perseverance in enquiry I could uncover very little beneath his armour of autonomy. It should be said, however, that this individualism did not always result in selfishness, and that he, along with a number of other elderly persons, took part in the routine shopping for those elderly in the flats who were invalids and unable to shop for themselves.

Many amongst the elderly show considerable ingenuity in turning shopping into acts of love for both their descendants and their ancestors. I will provide an example of the latter. This involved an older (she would not like to have been called elderly) woman who clearly shopped incessantly as a means of keeping occupied. The problem then arose as to how to keep such shopping going when in reality she had little in the way of goods she needed and little by way of money to buy them. In practice she develops 'projects' which fortunately are very hard to come to fruition. Several of these relate to gifts she will have to buy for Christmas, a wedding or a christening that she can start thinking about months, even years ahead. A more elaborate project revolved around an ancestral shrine. This consisted of the decoration of the flat with photographs of her parents and other deceased relatives. So, for example, she needed a particular photo frame to match exactly one she already had, but which she could never find, combined with other elements such as the right artificial flowers that would festoon the portraits. Through such devices she manages to engage herself in daily acts of shopping where most of the time is spent considering others and maintaining the same subsumption of the self that was crafted through decades of housewifery, but now returns as affection for her ancestors.

The other major form of single-person household in this area is that of single professional women who have developed strong career aspirations aided by feminism, but have had difficulty in finding men they regard as equal to themselves. Quite often, however, as in the couple described shopping/courting together, even where they are not in established households they have relationships of various degrees ongoing or on the horizon. Many of them seemed to have reached an age where their shopping is directed towards the imagined establishment of a household, though in practice this may well end up as a single-parent household. They are therefore closer to housewives than they are to the more clearly individualistic teenagers. Just as it should not be assumed that materialism is best associated with those who possess goods, so also it should not be assumed that it is the single person who is most individualistic. On the contrary, if anything it is the lonely who are more obsessed with relationships than those who can afford to take them for granted.

Perhaps most revealing of the problem of a lack of objects of love is Christine. She is a secretary and has few of the class and career aspirations of the dominant group of single women, and few aspirations with regard to partners either. Rather, she has entered a cycle of mild depression that saps the confidence that would help her in either one of these aims. For those who see shopping as a vicarious activity, where interest in commodities replaces the search for social relations, she might well have been a candidate for intensive shopping. But as I argued with respect to an earlier study of kitchen decoration in North London (Miller 1988), the evidence is quite the contrary. Concern for particular goods tends to come from the development rather than from the absence of meaningful relationships. An inability to relate to people usually means an inability to relate to goods also. As such, Christine finds little pleasure in shopping. Her conversation is replete with statements such as 'I haven't shopped for clothes for ages' or

Q Do you like shopping?
A No not really! I used to. I've gone off it now. I'm trying to decorate so I've been looking for furniture and that's just been awful.

Or

A I don't like shopping for food because it's too heavy to carry back. No I don't really enjoy the shopping, not at the moment, but that's probably my frame of mind at the moment, I'm not really interested in that sort of thing.

The only exception is when she can shop with a female friend, a shopping companion of ten years' standing – and then there is her cat. On several occasions the conversation also meanders wistfully back to a time when she did enjoy shopping, when there was some point to it.

There are, however, those for whom the generalizations I intend to develop on the basis of such material would not hold. Teenagers are certainly 'other' directed, but the other is often mainly a mirror (both literally and figuratively) in which they wish to gain a better sense of who they are. While they may talk of love rather more easily than their elders, they are less likely to conform to that version of love being described here. They may well be the group which comes closest to the conventional vision of shopping as devoted to the development of individual identity. There were cases of married women who could by no stretch of the imagination be seen as largely subsuming their own desires within service to their partners. There were relationships that were breaking up or where shopping was used to manifest rivalry and jealousy. But even taken together these amount to a minority perspective held against a norm of shopping as an expression of care and concern.

To conclude: the ethnographic evidence has been used to redirect attention from shopping as an expression of individual subjectivity and identity to an expression of kinship and other relationships. It could be argued that it is misleading to talk of making love when one has here such a variety of relationships, but this would be to ignore the crucial role of ideology in legitimating these relationships. As one listens to and takes part in the practice of these relationships it becomes clear that it is almost forbidden to understand or justify any dyadic formation except in the context of love. Parents are well aware of their responsibilities to their children and even of their legal requirements, but they would be highly offended by the suggestion that these alone are the cause of their devotion. Couples may have individual interests at stake and conflicts in practice, but they present the situation to themselves as founded on love, without which their relationship not only could but should be ended. Siblings and friends are understood to be cared for with more reason than obligation or reciprocity. Love is essential because it asserts the ideal of agency within any given relationship. What is rejected is any language of obligation that suggests we maintain relationships solely out of enforced behaviour. To define a relationship in any terms other than love seems to be taken as a debasement of that relationship.[4]

NOTES

1 Throughout this essay 'A' is the informant's answer to a question and 'Q' is the question asked. The speech is reported verbatim and I have not tried to convert it into formal grammar or 'accepted' words.
2 Examples for Britain start with Oakley (1976), and a good selection of the genre may be found collected together in Jackson and Moores (1995). Feminist research is complemented by other genres of sociological research of which Finch (1989) is a particularly important representative and whose results have largely confirmed the centrality of woman as carer and worker within the family.
3 For further details of this ambivalence as expressed in the tension between mothers and infants during shopping, see Miller (forthcoming).
4 This is notwithstanding that, according to Campbell (1986: 27), it was only in the eighteenth century that love was considered sufficient grounds for marriage in Britain. Now it is the only grounds that seems to be able to claim general legitimacy.

REFERENCES

Campbell, C. (1986) *The Romantic Ethic and the Spirit of Modern Consumerism*. Oxford: Blackwell.
Finch, J. (1989) *Family Obligations and Social Change*. Cambridge: Polity Press.
Jackson, S. and Moores, S. (eds) (1995) *The Politics of Domestic Consumption: Critical Readings*. London: Prentice-Hall.
Miller, D. (1988) '*Appropriating the state on the council estate.*' Man 23: 353–72.
Miller, D., Jackson, P., Holbrook, B., Thrift, N. and Rowlands, M. (1998) *Shopping, Place and Identity*. London: Routledge.

Oakley, A. (1976) *Housewife*. Harmondsworth: Penguin Books.
Parker, R. (1996) *Torn in Two: The Experience of Maternal Ambivalence*. London: Virago.
Slater, D. (1997) *Consumer Culture and Modernity*. Cambridge: Polity Press.
Warde, A. (1997) *Consumption, Food and Taste*. London: Sage.

Chapter 15

Window Shopping at Home: Classifieds, Catalogues and New Consumer Skills

Alison J. Clarke

Nothing, perhaps, more directly depends on early learning, especially the learning which takes place without any express intention to teach, than the dispositions and knowledge that are invested in clothing, furnishing and cooking or more precisely, in the way clothes, furniture and food are bought.

Bourdieu (1984: 78)

Material culture, its acquisition and appropriation, is integral to the construction and negotiation of social worlds and identities. The myriad decisions and complexities of household provisioning embody consumption as an arena of power in which social relations and knowledge are constantly rehearsed, rearranged and challenged.

In accordance with seminal works on the relationship between people, objects and consumption in modern societies (Douglas and Isherwood 1979; Bourdieu 1984; Miller 1986), this study posits the acquisition of commodities and goods as the very basis of households in industrial (or capitalist) societies. As Carrier, in his discussion of gifts and commodities in contemporary industrial societies, observes, 'a household exists in part because its members appropriate the commodities that are circulated and consumed within it' (Carrier 1995: 16).

This ethnographic study highlights the household as a crucial site of power and information. Focusing on two modes of informal acquisition, *Loot*, a localized classified paper, and *Argos*, a catalogue linked to a nationwide bulk distribution outlet, the study explores the development of consumptive skills. In conjunction with a range of other modes of acquisition, *Loot* and *Argos* highlight the dynamic of class, style and knowledge in consumptive activity.

Although *Loot* deals with non-standardized, second-hand goods or objects with 'histories' (Appadurai 1986) and *Argos* deals with alienable, mass-produced commodities, formal analysis of these two text-based mediums suggests a shared aesthetic appeal to social groups precluded from expensive high street shopping. Both *Argos* and *Loot* originated as non-formal modes of acquisition, offering cut-price goods and maximum choice through non-retail direct distribution. Neither source allows first-hand physical assessment of the goods offered for sale, or the intermediate sales advice of a third party.

While these methods of acquisition are motivated in part by utility and economics, this chapter frames such notions and consequent choices as culturally bound actions. The concomitance of commerce and sociality is played out through the everyday concepts of authenticity, newness, thrift and excess. Household issues ranging from romantic love and gendered divisions of labour to parental anxiety become manifest in chosen patterns of consumption.

While practices of consumption effectively illuminate social categories such as gender, class, ethnicity and age, exploration of the specifics of appropriation and material culture reveals the means by which these externally defined roles are understood and contested. Why is an impoverished family compelled to pay the maximum, high street price for a child's bed, available 'brand new' for half the price in a local classified paper (Caplovitz 1967)? Why would a household with soiled furniture and no bathroom be the home to fifty designer suits and a copy of *Debrett's Ettiquette and Modern Manners*?

Ultimately this ethnography reveals that provisioning is not only a question of obtaining goods, but also the application of particular schemes of knowledge and style to particular genres of information about goods. Poverty and wealth, as both Douglas and Isherwood (1979) and Bourdieu (1984) have pointed out, are based on a complex articulation between forms of knowledge and forms of possession. In this ethnographic encounter we see the experiential detail through which this articulation becomes manifest.

Shopping in 'the Street'

A street in north London forms the basis of this ethnographic enquiry into consumption. As a joint project, shared with Daniel Miller, the enquiry involves ethnographic study of the informal and formal aspects of acquisition. While Miller deals with the formal shopping habits of informants (accompanied supermarket visits, etc.) this portion of the research deals with ostensibly home-based and informal modes of acquisition.

The street, comprising private owner-occupied, rented and state-subsidized housing, forms the basis of this ethnography of consumption and social identity. A number of predominantly middle-class streets extending from the main street of our study have been included in the findings. The first phase of the research has included 76 households. The street proper is positioned between two major shopping areas, Wood Green Shopping City and Brent Cross Shopping Centre, which provide residents with the possibility of identifying with two distinct, formal shopping areas. The shopping facilities of central London, including the prestigious West End, are also easily accessible using public or private transport.

From the array of informal provisioning used by the street's householders (including stolen goods, Tupperware parties, Colour-Me-Beautiful sessions, jumble and rummage sales, clothing catalogues, cigarette coupons, door-to-door sales, etc.) *Loot* and *Argos*, in particular, defied simplistic definitions in terms of class, ethnic and gender patterns of usage.

Exchange and Mart, a well-known and established classified paper, acts as the significant precursor to *Loot*. *Exchange and Mart* offers new and used goods at bargain prices through the eradication of formal retail distribution expenses.

Its users describe it as a hard-edged, no-nonsense form of acquisition particularly useful for buying and selling used vehicles. It appeared to offer similar, but more convenient and assessable facets of a house clearance or car auction. Like the *Argos* catalogue, overheads of space, distribution and sales staff are visibly absent from *Exchange and Mart*'s classified pages. From their inception, both *Argos* and *Exchange and Mart* offered simple and accessible means of saving money on substantial household purchases and were aimed at a lower income population.

In recent years *Argos* has altered its customer profile. Its showrooms have expanded from cheaper inner-city sites to high street locations and *Argos* catalogues are now delivered, as a matter of course, to extensively middle-class areas. Similarly *Loot*, which unlike its competitors offers free advertising, has altered rapidly from a weekly to a daily publication considerably overshadowing the established role of *Exchange and Mart*.

Forms of acquisition, like commodities, carry with them ideological discourse. As Rutz and Orlove (1989: 6) state, 'consumption has an ideological character, in that it appeals to shared understanding and thus it allows for disagreement'.

Mainstream mail order catalogues, for example, bear the stigma of restricted, credit bound consumption. As a mode of purchase historically aligned, in British culture, to hire purchase and working-class credit functions, the mail order catalogue is bound to culturally and socially poignant meanings. Its overtly mass, non-personalized and visually based appeal have associated it with the alienation of modern commodity purchase (Carrier 1995). Unsurprisingly then, for informants it was this specific mode of purchase that provoked a familiar, socially and morally grounded debate regarding saving, spending, quality and value.

Mention of mail order catalogues warranted strong reactions from many, predominantly middle-class, informants, who disassociated themselves from the foolhardy practice of buying 'long-distance'. They frequently aligned this hazardous form of purchase with the quality and aesthetic of the goods themselves, to quote one such example: 'cheapy nasty girlie catalogues...with tacky underwear and leotards and things, oh no I'd never use them'.

Others removed themselves from the economic imperative suggested by catalogue use. Credit schemes and over-inflated prices seemed to have direct bearing on the goods themselves: 'those Littlewoods things...I'd never have those...I think it's a social thing...a class thing because, I mean you can buy in instalments and I used to have a cleaner who used to get all her Christmas presents through a catalogue'.

Many informants, although keen catalogue users themselves, depicted tawdry images of overdependent catalogue users; to quote one such opinion: 'I've met women who have furnished their entire homes top to bottom straight from just one catalogue!'

While for some shoppers Christmas presents, intimate apparel and home furnishings demanded less distanced and more proactive forms of acquisition, many informants relied entirely on catalogue purchases as a necessary budgeting measure. Far from taking advantage of the effortless leisure of mail order purchase, these consumers, economically precluded from formal shopping, used catalogues as a buffer against the risk and uncertainty of the marketplace and prided themselves on their discerning purchasing abilities.

Evidently, all modes of acquisition and their material culture carry with them culturally constituted meanings. In this sense *Loot* and *Argos*, in contrast to more established forms of acquisition, are being actively appropriated and redefined through new consumer knowledges and skills. The prominence of these genres across class, gender, age and ethnic households allows insight into the incorporation of recently formulated and historically specific modes of acquisition.

Loot

Loot is a London-based free-advertising paper sold daily at the price of £1.30. It describes itself as 'London's Notice Board' and according to many informants successfully operates in this fashion; many browse regularly with little or no intention of buying but merely to 'get a feel about what's out there'. In this sense it acts as a virtual marketplace where the excitement (and frustration) of rummaging and browsing are translated into the reading of obscure four-line prose:

> For Sale: Video Editor vanguard, 3 in 1 unit, AV,
> dubbing edit with picture enhancer,
> as new, £50. Gary 0181 [phone number] eves or
> 0171 [phone number] days Hammersmith

While *Loot* purports to offer 'Everything for everyone, everyday' (as its sales pitch reads) many readers spoke of 'frequenting' particular areas of the paper, deliberately imposing self-limitations in a sea of purchasing opportunities. Some informants referred to *Loot* in purely instrumental terms, confining their use to specific circumstance such as accommodation seeking or occasional car sales. Most, however, used *Loot* regularly and less strategically.

Many male informants used the paper as a staple read, browsing the section on cars even when they were not actively concerned with buying or selling a vehicle. For others, *Loot* functioned as a vital source of information for swapping in 'car conversations', and informants talked of enjoying vehicle descriptions and the sense of keeping 'in touch' through *Loot*.

While a small number of male informants read comparable classified papers such as *Exchange and Mart*, *Loot* was perceived as a more localized, community orientated publication – even though both papers shared the functional task of selling cars. Notably *Loot*, as a free-to-advertise publication, surpassed its commercial position and enhanced its value as a means of sale and purchase.

Acting as a form of non-corporate commercial exchange, *Loot* seemingly offers a type of democracy to otherwise marginalized shoppers, giving access to thousands of daily bargains. It is considered by many as an essential urban shopping guide, blurring the productive and consumptive aspects of household provisioning. A typical statement (from Barry, a long-term unemployed civil servant) proffers *Loot* as the most obvious and logical mode of enquiry into any proposed purchase: 'he [a friend] was looking for a computer and I said, "surely you've checked out *Loot*", you don't know what you're doing till you've looked in there'.

Recent developments, including a *Loot* property sales service, Internet link, and sister papers in the northwest and Midlands, reveal the growing significance of

Loot's appeal to informal economic activity. Originally a weekly publication, it now circulates each weekday using corresponding colours (blue, pink, gold, red, green) to emphasize its daily currency. Some *Loot* readers, newsagents pointed out, were becoming confused by the expansion and daily colour coding of the paper and lamented its new, unwieldy size.

'Whether you are collecting antiques, selling your property or looking for romance . . .' (as the promotional plea reads) *Loot* offers a diverse, informal consumption space. The paper is organized into ten separate sections, related to the goods and services of everyday life, beginning with introductory instructions on how to use the publication. Once initiated, the reader can peruse sections that include household goods, homes and family, cars, jobs, personal, computers, hi-fis, holidays and health and fitness. Private advertisers can advertise anything freely and are promised publication in the next day's issue provided they meet the appropriate deadline. The free advertisement appears once and charges are made if the advertiser requires a repeat advertisement for consecutive days. An individual can place up to three free advertisements for different items in each issue of *Loot*.

Columns and columns of private advertisements are interspersed with occasional trade advertisements. It is, however, ostensibly a forum for non-commercial, individualized exchange. While there remains a constant risk that divisions between commercial and private sales might blur, informants stressed the personalization of the sale as a major criterion for choosing *Loot*; 'when you go to have a look at the thing, it's then that you can usually tell that it's trade dressed up as private sale, and I mean I think that's just dishonest – if I want to use a shop I'll use a shop, but this is *Loot*'.

Loot's identity is based on its appeal as an unregulated free-to-advertise non-trade marketplace. Consequently its prices and goods are non-standardized and for some therefore overly daunting; to quote one informant, 'a lot of the time the prices are so contradictory to each other . . . and the British public if they are offered something that's a bargain they automatically think there's something wrong with it'. Finding a bargain among an array of unseen goods, whose product specifications are described by the partial vendor rather than through the distancing of formalized advertising and marketing terms, requires considerable skill, risk and time.

For some informants it was the appeal of preselection that made *Loot* a viable and attractive mode of consumption. The goods for sale had already been processed and evaluated by previous owners, their knowledge and selection adding a further 'depth' to their profile. Each advertisement brought together a product curriculum vitae to decipher. Some informants consequently felt that the recently expanded newspaper had become unwieldy, its simple-to-use and localized appeal lost in its hundred-odd pages and ever increasing variety and choice. Similarly advertisers felt that this decreased their ability to make a quick sale (due to the competition and lengthening of consumers' selection process). Consequently they were encouraged to increase (and pay) for longer advertising space; 'two years ago I advertised a sofa bed, there were maybe two other adverts and I sold it the same day. The other week I was looking for a sofa bed there were over twenty in there, so I gave up.'

Locality and description serve as the initial enticement but information proffered is often so minimal (for example, 'Sofas, 2 and 3 seaters, blue floral design') that the bulk of the selection or consumption process takes place via telephone. This transforms the advertisement into a potentially hazardous encounter where exchange and social relations merge, requiring totally different skills to those learned for formal shopping situations.

Georgie, a young single woman furnishing a newly rented home, commented that she had travelled over 50 miles tracking down sofa beds advertised in *Loot*. The first had been misrepresented as a 'good condition' item and turned out to be a stained and tattered specimen. The second, more suitable item, was eventually located the other side of London. She did not regret the purchase but commented that a 'real' *Loot* user would be able to distinguish truth from exaggeration during the initial telephone call. Georgie realized now that she had not 'asked the right questions' and also stressed that once the seller had spent time describing the item, she felt obliged to personally view it. The experience, she felt, had undermined her social capabilities.

John, a 35-year-old systems analyst, explained how he enjoyed shopping through *Loot* as a 'restricted' experience. Unlike shopping around the high street it was easier to 'rank and weight your decisions' and narrow down purchase possibilities effectively. The basic telephone questions John used when purchasing a second-hand amplifier from *Loot* were brand, age, condition and size. One reason John favoured this form of purchase (other than price) was his assumption that, unlike shop assistants selling commodities, *Loot* vendors would have intimate knowledge of their possessions. However, he expressed profound surprise at the ignorance of many *Loot* advertisers who, it seemed, had spent hundreds of pounds on items they had little knowledge of. Some vendors, he pointed out, were completely unaware of the brand, quality or specifications of the items they were putting up for sale. While this led to potential misunderstandings and inefficient purchase, the mismatch in skill and knowledge of purchaser and vendor created the ambiguity of an unregulated marketplace, and the potential for bargains as well as disappointments.

The dangerous ambiguity of *Loot* led many informants to refer to the power of 'the personal touch'. Barry, for example, ascertained that his mountain bike was a real bargain through chatting to the vendor about his forthcoming trip to the Himalayas and the need to sell off much-loved possessions (including the bicycle) to raise funds. This situation was validated by Barry's own personal situation; unemployed and fearful of bailiffs' intervention, he had been compelled recently to sell a professional synthesizer through *Loot* for half its original value. Barry, an avid and dedicated reader of *Loot*, firmly trusted it as a forum for real bargains: 'relatives are always dying and people need a quick place to sell things off'. He felt that British cynicism and suspicion made offering or appreciating a real bargain a major cultural dilemma.

The 'personal touch' praised by Barry made other informants deeply nervous. Chloe felt relieved that a neighbour happened to visit when two large 'Persian dealer types' arrived at her large, well-furnished house to view items of furniture she had advertised for sale in *Loot*. 'It could be dangerous', she reflected, 'people knowing your phone number' or 'may be giving out your address'.

Similarly, Sally, a council tenant with three children, bought a piece of carpet advertised in *Loot* and felt that she had been duped by personal friendliness when making her purchase. She travelled by public transport to the home of the vendor, a young mother of a similar age, several miles away and during a friendly chat was assured that the rolled-up carpet was in 'good condition'. On fitting the carpet Sally found that it had a visible burn mark in the centre and felt very let down by the seller. She would not consider asking for a refund as it was too far away to travel again. More significantly she felt personally offended (and humiliated for not being more vigilant and competent).

The more confident and competent users of *Loot* did not feel embarrassed to ask personal or extensive questions about articles over the telephone to ascertain their real worth. Chloe, a middle-class informant (married, mother of two, living in a semi-detached, four-bedroom house with an au pair) frequently uses *Loot* as a kind of 'home business' and hobby. When she is bored with a piece of furniture she 'tries' it in *Loot* to monitor the response. Only if she receives a good enough offer will she consider a sale. Similarly she purchases items cheaply through *Loot* and resells them at a profit ('with no overheads') back through *Loot*.

In this sense, many informants acknowledged *Loot* as a potentially 'subversive' arena where 'things might not be what they seem'. While a few informants distrusted certain types of advertisements as potentially criminal, others were unperturbed by the possibility of accidentally receiving or handling stolen goods. Chloe, for example, identified this subversive, black market potential as the linchpin of *Loot*: 'After all', she asserted, 'everyone appreciates a bargain, as long as it's not as traceable as a Cézanne painting'.

Loot operates simultaneously as a safe, logical derivative of the community-based classified pages of local newspapers and an anarchic, potentially subversive and ambiguous means of laundering goods and services. The free-advertising policy opens up a 'no loss', 'free-for-all' clause encouraging impulsive sales. The fast, 24-hour publication promise and lack of payment creates an instant non-formalized, fast-turnover marketplace where gratuitous browsing is encouraged. Previously treasured objects could, in effect, be turned into hard cash within a day. Accidental bargains from unassuming vendors coexist alongside deliberately misleading cajolery. While the 'personal contact' between buyer and seller might sanction and secure transactions, such self-regulating and non-formalized market relations for some offered too threatening a proposition.

Yet so socially pervasive is this 'ungoverned', communal marketplace called *Loot* that one critic (an educated, middle-aged male informant) viewed it as nothing less than a front for a censorious governmental organization: 'Of course . . . the police operate though *Loot* . . . what people advertise, it's constantly under surveillance . . . that's why it's free'.

The following case studies reveal *Loot* as a crucial mode of alternative acquisition for specific social groups. They highlight its use in 'expelling' and 'laundering' material culture within the negotiation of social relations and household moral economy. Within households *Loot* is used, in particular, as a mode of acquisition and dispossession during periods of upheaval and renegotiation. Usage of *Loot* fits into a romantic aesthetic of informal provisioning where authentic objects have 'histories' and negotiation of this literary, non-visual marketplace requires a particular urban, cultural currency and consumptive skill (for a comparative study see Soiffer and Herrmann 1987).

Case study 1: Romancing the artefact: objects with histories

Just as *Loot* is used to 'set up' new homes, with the acquisition of cheaper goods, it is also used as an effective means of 'expelling' or 'laundering' items made newly inappropriate to the household due to changing circumstances.

Michael and Jennifer are a couple in their late twenties. Jennifer has a 6-year-old son, Harry, from a previous marriage. Michael (her recent boyfriend) is in the process of leaving his flat and gradually moving in with Jennifer and her son. The flat is brightly painted, airy and light with informal uncluttered furniture arranged to allow optimum space. Interesting 'old things' and modern ethnic arte-facts decorate the apartment. The bathroom décor (featuring an original salvaged sturdy Edwardian basin) is inspired by a feature from the pages of *Elle Decoration*. Plain coloured and simple, it is decorated with real shells and starfish.

Jennifer has re-entered higher education to train as an arts administrator and Michael has a compatible career as a freelance arts journalist. Jennifer's newly formed relationship with Michael (he is several years her junior) has reintroduced her to the world of subculture and London nightclubs. There have been several emotional scenes during this process. Jennifer resents the fact that Michael retains dual status as bachelor and partner, and can always escape from the responsibilities of parenthood (which she bears the brunt of) by retreating to his own flat. Harry's natural father contributes little to the household, lives abroad, and sends only the occasional postcard and trinket to his son. As Harry places a miniature toy (given by his father) in his play house, Jennifer laments, 'I may not be a very good mummy but I'm the only one he's got'.

Jennifer is frustrated by the dilemma of whether or not to have a second child with Michael and attributes Harry's petulant behaviour and boredom to his status as a single child. The previous evening Jennifer, accompanied by Michael and Harry, had been babysitting for a 9 month old. Harry had enjoyed helping feed the baby its bottle. The dilemma of a second child seemed all the more poignant to Jennifer as Michael, having spent the night babysitting with Jennifer and her son, had returned to his flat the following morning to 'chill out and listen to some tapes'. This pro-voked envy, anger and resentment, ultimately directed towards Harry. Jennifer dreaded having her life 'taken away' again by a second child when she seemed only just to be living it again with Michael. Her burgeoning romance with Michael conflicted with the responsibility she felt towards her son.

Recently she had regained her sexual confidence, enjoying dancing and taking drugs in nightclubs she had not visited since her teenage. She knew, however, this offered only a glimpse of an unattainable identity. Barricading the kitchen door, leaving her pleading son outside, Jennifer expressed with shame the anger she sometimes felt towards her son and a pressing desire to have 'her own space'. She felt totally compromised. She was neither a single, self-determining girl, a 'proper' mother, nor a successful career woman.

Juxtaposed with this turmoil and emotional loneliness was the construction of a 'dream home'. Appreciating the idealist interiors featured in the style magazine *Elle Decoration* and browsing in antique shops in Ibis Pond, a local middle-class shop-ping district, fuelled her desire to move from her two-bedroom flat to begin a new life in a three-bedroom house with Michael. Car boot sales provided the ideal place for Jennifer to ponder the acquisition of interesting items for their new home. With her impatient, attention-seeking son in tow this seemed to be yet another luxury denied her. At times it seemed her son was the hindrance to the satisfactory pursuit of her dream as a whole.

Jennifer's homemaking was, she commented, 'on hold'. Since the departure of her ex-husband she had refrained from redecorating their home, a two-bedroom Victorian flat conversion. Many of its ornaments and utensils were attained as wedding presents. Although her homemaking was self-avowedly suspended, she and Michael shared an expedition to Carlton antique market to find an interesting old and battered enamel bread bin.

Both Michael and Jennifer shared an attraction to 'design classics', articles with known provenance and 'special' aesthetic status. This was embodied in Jennifer's car, a 1969 white Mini convertible which she adores, but regrets buying from a friend. Initially she had used *Loot* to choose her vehicle. But realizing a friend desperately needed to sell her car, thought it more beneficial all round to purchase from a close friend in need of the money. The friendship ended in disaster when the engine exploded a week after the purchase. With hindsight she favours the comparative safety of *Loot* as she had subsequently lost contact with her friend. While on a rational level she believed her friend had not set out to deceive her, the car and its ensuing expenditure acted as a constant reminder of the misconceived bargain.

The attraction to special things 'with history' combined with high style is manifest in Michael's Christmas gifts to Jennifer, which recently included an antique perfume bottle, black and white films (*It's a Wonderful Life*, *Casablanca*) and Muji, Japanese modernist make-up accessories. Jennifer's family gifts were confined to utilitarian and electrical appliances such as a JVC stereo system. This particular Christmas was a turning point in Jennifer and Michael's relationship as it was the first spent as a family with Harry; it included tree, trimmings and a traditional Christmas Day dinner. Jennifer stressed that only shopping for Michael had been a pleasure, the acquisition of other gifts had 'been a chore'. Her favourite gifts were those given by Michael, as, she said, he remembered her smallest likes and dislikes. Michael and Jennifer bought gifts for Harry individually and with little conference (choosing traditional games familiar to them as children such as Lego, Twister, Operation, Action Man, etc.). Unlike many married or established partners of their social group there was little debate around suitability and educational value of the toys (Miller 1995). Similarly the only joint gift they received, acknowledging their 'coupledom', was given by Jennifer's sister. They did not shop together as they gave no joint presents, instead buying separately for respective families. Publicly and privately, then, Jennifer and Michael's relationship is in a state of major negotiation. Material culture, as home, furnishings, gifts and toys, forms an integral part of this negotiation. As this case study demonstrates, *Loot* as a mode of acquisition constitutes a vital element in the creation of this 'romance'.

As a single mother living on limited means, just prior to her relationship with Michael, Jennifer used *Loot* to buy a computer. Lacking expertise in this area she travelled unaccompanied to south London to view a computer; feeling obliged, she purchased this and discovered it to be wholly unsuitable and overpriced. She realized how easily the newspaper could be used to 'flog off generally suspect gear'. The experience seemed to reiterate her vulnerable status as a single mother, isolated for several years from practising in what she described as the 'real world'. Michael, on the other hand, classed himself as a 'savvy' and practised *Loot* user. Indeed *Loot* had recently become the focus in the demise of his bachelor status. The previous week his guitar and leather jacket sold through *Loot* to a 'nice young man' from Richmond. Nowadays Jennifer and Michael frequently read *Loot* together, at the kitchen table with a cup of tea, comparing prices, considering potential bargains and 'play' arguing over fantasy purchases. Jennifer, for example, while having no intention of acquiring a pet, regularly browses the 'Animal' section to fantasize about 'a nice little Siamese cat'.

Jennifer described her attraction to *Loot* as an appeal to her 'jumble sale mentality' and its lack of association with formal marketing. She viewed regular readers of *Loot*, who understood the coded terminology of 'excellent condition', 'reluctant sale' and 'lovely runner' like the members of football collectors' cards or train spotters' clubs understood theirs, as a subcultural group. Although it was the ideal place to get rid of 'stolen and shoddy goods', Jennifer saw *Loot* as embodying a more positive ethic than commercial shopping, for it encouraged a sense of 'recycling' as opposed to wanton consumption.

Loot, with its variable contents and 'hands on' sales method, offers the chance to practise a particular urban aesthetic and set of skills. While offering a normative medium (it is a staple means of acquiring accommodation and selling cars in London) its format allows for overt display of informal sales skills. Jennifer and Michael use *Loot* as a shared celebratory consumption activity. Whereas Jennifer's experience of *Loot*, prior to meeting Michael, was wholly negative, the skills that Michael brings to the newly developing relationship reinvent *Loot* and its material culture as an arena of mutual fantasy making. Together they can peruse their romance for 'things with history' in an area of consumption deemed ethical in terms of its recycling, non-corporate dimensions. They have embraced the spontaneity of *Loot* to decisively expel the remnants of Michael's problematic 'unattached' status. Michael is seen to negotiate the danger of *Loot* with the same ease and daring he uses in his association with London's club life, a world he has made newly available to Jennifer. The use of *Loot* in the contestation of these shifting social identities is premised on cultural and aesthetic, rather than economic, imperatives.

Jennifer and Michael incorporate new, gendered, social skills into the household through the acquisition and dispossession of material culture. The changes and contestations of a household in flux are played out through a romancing, and expelling, of artefacts with histories.

Case study 2: Household hostilities and the aesthetics of consumption

Melissa and Jake have been married for four years and have a 6-month-old baby. Both are artists and Jake works as an art school lecturer. Their house (Victorian terrace, three bedrooms) was formally Jake's bachelor home which Melissa (inspired by features in *Elle Decoration* and her art school education) has transformed into a high style modern home. She is very house proud and has made painstaking attempts to capture a contemporary, almost 1950s Californian appeal. As well as contemporary furniture, Melissa has collected 'interesting' ornaments and curios; the fireplace features a sculptural architectural form salvaged from the demolished local church in which the couple were married. Melissa also managed to retrieve numerous rose bushes from the church garden which now flourish and bloom around the front door.

Auctions offer an arena where Melissa can make best use of her visual skills. Before the birth of their baby the couple attended Honiton auction rooms regularly to view every month. Their most celebrated acquisition was a Charles Eames chrome chair, a 'design classic' bought at a bargain price. It was now situated in the bathroom, having previously occupied the living room. Artists' easels, fire surrounds and art deco furniture proved the biggest attraction at such events. Melissa also used the same auction to get rid of Jake's unsuitable bachelor furnishings: 'In fact one of my husband's horrible old Turkish carpets he sold at the auction room because I hated it, I said I like those two but that one can go'. The main motive for auction going was the intrigue of 'old stuff, other people's stuff, things that people don't want'.

Melissa identifies her purchases as 'visually led' and so while she often browses *Loot* for attractive second-hand bargains she rarely (if ever) actually initiates a purchase, 'however good it might sound'. When her younger brother shared the marital home, he bought *Loot* 'religiously' to browse the vehicle section and discuss the merits of certain models with Jake. For them, *Loot* became a common feature of household life. While Melissa had never purchased through *Loot* she was thoroughly familiar with its format, readership and sales method. This familiarity had led her to use *Loot* as the site of major contestation in the relationship. She used *Loot* in an orchestrated protest designed specifically to challenge the household status quo.

Melissa's most valued and significant possession was a Henry Dartworth painting purchased from a gallery in Ibis Pond. The item exemplified the struggles and desires of her premarital identity. She had saved for six months while at college, working nights in a 'smelly pub' to purchase the picture, which now hangs prominently in the living room of the marital home. Recently she became disturbed by the picture; she felt that she was 'not appreciating it enough', that it was being 'wasted' in its present situation.

In a fit of rage, after a lengthy argument with Jake, she committed what she considered a desperate act of terrorism. She telephoned *Loot*'s 24-hour free-advertising hotline and within hours had offered her greatest fine art possession up for sale among gilt framed oil paintings of grazing sheep in 'the rococo style'. She joked that with hindsight *Loot* was the least appropriate place to sell contemporary fine art and that she did not receive one telephone enquiry over the sale. The gesture had not been intended as a serious sale attempt but to express the depth of Melissa's feelings. Publicly she had set out to sacrifice her most precious (premarital) possession through the 'lowly' pages of *Loot* (with its suspect goods and used cars). The act simultaneously undermined the values and knowledge associated with Melissa and Jake's shared world; they had, after all, met at the Ibis Pond Art Club; 'I was just trying to get back at Jake for something or other to make him feel bad, you know, about something horrible'.

Melissa's choice of medium for the painting's sale held particular poignancy. It was a gendered consumption space shared by Jake and her brother for perusing cars.

The meaning of the protest resided in the fact there would be little real risk of selling the article through such an inappropriate medium. Throwing her most prized and aesthetically superior possession, symbolically, to the wolves meant that Melissa had maligned its worth and signalled a major discontent.

Melissa and Jake share numerous other forms of informal provisioning, including fishing, pick-your-own produce, handicrafts and painting. Their relationship revolves around public and private interest in art and culture and its associated values. While other forms of informal acquisition are shared, the presence of *Loot* in the household was reminiscent of Jake's carefree car-hunting days. Melissa's own premarital identity, built on a series of unacknowledged sacrifices, had seemed subsumed by the pending birth of their baby. Like her highly valued picture, her premarital worth was going to waste, taken for granted and unappreciated. *Loot*, defined by its non-visual format, provided the ideal means of 'laundering' this dispute. Reducing her ultimate, inalienable possession to the stark world of commodification and low-brow, used goods, Melissa temporarily threatened the cultural values through which she shared her relationship with Jake.

Case study 3: 'Cultural capital' and the authenticity of subversion

In the course of the ethnographic research in north London a further case, which took place outside the street, illustrated the significance of 'authentication' and alternative acquisition. Phil and Spencer, both in their early thirties, share a two-bedroom flat, claim income support and have been unemployed for approximately a year. Prior to this period Phil had been employed as a temporary clerk in the professional sector and Spencer had worked in hotel restaurant kitchens. Their flat has no formal bathing facilities and is sparsely furnished with items salvaged from local skips. They pay a minimal rent and so accept this as a bearable sacrifice. The living room contains an oval marble-topped table with wrought iron legs, surrounded either side by a broken green velveteen sofa and a foam sofa bed with torn upholstery. There are no decorations or pictures on the wall. A table and four chairs stands in the window, and a bureau in the corner features the communal book and compact disc (CD) collection. Music is supplied by a Walkman CD with one speaker placed at an angle towards the ceiling. The kitchen sink has a permanent leak and a bucket has to be periodically emptied from beneath it. Spencer had just travelled to Germany and so had brought back duty-free goods including a bottle of Bombay Sapphire gin and several bulk boxes of Camel cigarettes kept on the marble coffee table for general consumption.

Despite living on limited incomes and in notably squalid surroundings, Phil and Spencer had developed an avid interest in luxury clothes and second-hand designer menswear. Their favourite shop is a gentleman's dress agency nicknamed. 'Fluffy Fleming's' after its camp ex-1950s couture milliner proprietor. 'Fluffy Fleming' hunts out appropriate styles from his stock and often puts things aside for the boys (whom he assumes are a gay couple) until they can afford the items. An Yves Saint Laurent suit worth £700 can be picked up at 'Fluffy's' for around £75 in excellent condition. Phil and Spencer usually begin their shopping trips with a strawberry milk shake in a local café and even when they have no money, they proceed to window shop at the places where their purchases normally take place.

Spencer insisted that his interest in clothes had evolved through age and the ability to 'carry a good suit off'. Under the tutelage of Phil, who keeps a copy of *Debrett's Etiquette and Modern Manners* and *Small Talk at Parties* on his bookshelf, he was continuing to learn the ropes. Phil joked that even in his native home of Urmston, Manchester, he had turned the tiny bedroom of a two-up-two-down terrace into a study equipped with pipe rack, leather chair and 'other affectations'. Spencer, who borrows Phil's clothes while he builds up his own collection, had, he commented, recently discovered 'the merits of a distinctive cologne'. Both were avid readers of P. G. Wodehouse novels.

Cheaper charity shops were used for what they described as 'practice shopping' where they learned, for example, to distinguish a French cuff or a quality cotton. Mistakes proved less disastrous when made in a cheap charity shop. Both considered the 'obvious' display of labels to be *gauche* and explained their attraction to designer wear as a concern for 'cut' and 'quality'. Spencer was proud that he could now confidently visit the menswear section of any upper-end department store and 'decipher' its contents without embarrassment. Phil and Spencer despised the attitudes of shop assistants in such places and defiantly shop-lifted expensive articles, using a pair of pliers to remove security tags. They once stole a small item from 'Fluffy's' shop but, as they now considered him a good friend, would never conceive of doing this again and regretted the initial act. However, they occasionally stole from charity shops which they condemned as overpriced. They justified their actions by explaining the fraud and colonialism associated with many charity organizations.

While they rarely purchase from *Loot* they frequently peruse the car section and had recently planned to buy a navy blue Jaguar XJ6 with a 'windfall'. Ironically this 'windfall' resulted from artful subversion of *Loot*'s potentially negative aspects. Phil and Spencer used *Loot* as an instrumental part of a recent, and successful, fraudulent household insurance claim. They placed a bogus advertisement in the music equipment section to sell two electric guitars. They stored Phil's massive collection of designer shirts, suits and accessories and their joint collection of CDs in a neighbour's house. They then contacted the police late that night to report a burglary.

On arrival at the scene of the 'crime', the major point of contention for the police was the lack of forced entry. Spencer explained this away by testifying that two young men, seeing the advertisement in *Loot*, had visited the flat to view the guitars offered for sale. They must have gained access to the house keys when Spencer briefly left the room to make coffee for his visitors. And, the police concluded, returned later that day to steal the guitars and other property.

After Spencer had spent four hours at the police station, trying (unsuccessfully) to identify the possible culprits, the police concluded that it was an opportunist burglary that illustrated the inherent danger of unregulated publications such as *Loot*. When visited by the insurance assessor and queried on the incongruous lifestyle the couple lived (with the strange juxtaposition of designer suits, odorous furniture and generally squalid living conditions) Phil explained that his compulsive clothes buying was the result of his intolerable living conditions. The insurance claim included photographs, swatches and some receipts for the majority of the missing suits. His remaining collection of accessories and shoes substantiated the claim. A week later a joint cheque for £15,000 arrived, two-thirds of their original claim.

Phil and Spencer had already begun to spend their booty. The previous evening they spent £200 dining at a four-star hotel restaurant; Spencer boasted 'we had asperitifs, Mersault, Sauternes and port' and looked 'dapper in our designer suits'. He was currently having a dinner jacket made-to-measure (and worked out the possible cost of each wearing in his lifetime as £150) and had that morning spent £160 on silk cravats. Still, he lamented his lack of visionary shopping skill and envied his flatmate's strategic shopping which he compared to the 'skill of Karpov'; he was always at least five moves ahead in envisaging the potential of purchases. Neither has yet fully decided which Jaguar to choose from *Loot*.

Due to long-term unemployment Phil and Spencer are precluded from formulating their identities in a formal workplace. Their limited economic means logically restricts their access to forms of non-essential consumption. They are at once excluded from a world of skilled labour and by extension, a world of playful and risk-filled luxury consumption. Instead, they invert their informal economic skills of theft, fraud and alternative acquisition to its disassociated lifestyle of conservative foppery and affluence. Moneys gained are reinvested in the improvement of skills of acquisition. Unlike the 'ordinary' income of the sporadic unskilled jobs otherwise available to them, their 'booty' finances the material culture and aesthetics of their shared relationship with consumption.

Like Michael and Jennifer and Melissa and Jake, Phil and Spencer shared a propensity for things with history and a sense of authenticity. Although Phil and Spencer are economically impoverished, they share a romance of 'authentic' masculine identity whose associated material culture has become the focal point of their lives. They are so advanced in the art of informal provisioning and alternative acquisition that they confidently invert the 'dangerous' and anarchic aspects of *Loot*. They parody the potential risks of *Loot* in a display of defiant and cynical disregard, and attain the ultimate 'bargain'.

Argos

While *Loot* demands interaction, one-to-one negotiation of social relations and skill to mediate and comprehend a chaotic array of goods, the *Argos* catalogue seems the ultimate handbook for the inactive armchair shopper. The *Argos* catalogue is a prominent form of alternative acquisition across all social groups in the street. Unlike *Loot*, the *Argos* catalogue provides a standardized, rigid repertoire of brand-new, visually represented alienable commodities. The catalogue, of approximately 500 pages, features over 5,000 products including jewellery, three-piece suites, domestic technology, sports equipment, toys, gifts, etc. Named after the 'argosy' ('a fleet of abundantly laden merchant ships') it is distinguished from other mail order catalogues in that it deals predominantly with hardware (no clothes or consumables) and acts as a portable shop window. Goods are chosen through the catalogue then ordered and purchased direct, in person, at a local showroom (larger orders, such as garden sheds, can be ordered by telephone and delivered). While the catalogue does not rely on offering a credit system, with users paying for their items in full, a £1,000 instant credit is made available through a personal account card. Some items offer six months' interest-free credit. The catalogue is published each season in full colour, spring/summer and autumn/winter. Each edition is eagerly anticipated by *Argos* users who can visit the showrooms to obtain the latest copy. The company also delivers catalogues to homes in the vicinity of the outlet.

The catalogue is designed to feature maximum products in the minimum space and locates products in a strict typology. For example, the jewellery section, beginning with diamond rings (4 pages, 132 items) progresses through 'His and Her' pendants, crucifix/St Christophers (1 page, 27 items), Sovereign rings, Mizpah pendants, to gold loop earrings (4 pages, 123 items). In total there are over 1,200 jewellery items offered for sale. Inset pictures feature models of different ethnicities sporting several of the items displayed in the catalogue. The household appliance section offers everything from hostess trolleys and deep fat fryers to electric toothbrushes. It features 46 vacuum cleaners ranging from £17.95 (for a hand-held model) to £199.99 (for a Dyson super model) and offers a choice of 19 different ironing boards, all fully illustrated. More recently selected goods are also displayed in the *Argos* shop window, as the outlets have moved to more prominent, high street locations.

Argos seems to offer a rationalized, simple, value-for-money way to shop where the consumer is in total control. Products selected from the catalogue are entered onto an order form using a coded number. The form is taken to the service point and during the payment transaction goods are delivered to the collection counter for the customer. A 16-day money-back guarantee offers the security of a conventional shopping outlet (if not more). Although the basic product types provide the core of the *Argos* catalogue, peripheral items such as 'Take That' bedspreads, 'Power Ranger' collectables, 'Barbie' watches, 'Baywatch' wall clocks and marble-effect telephones create a transient and fashionable dimension to the catalogue. These items circumscribe *Argos* as a contemporary, interactive catalogue as opposed to a strictly functional or blandly convenient consumptive encounter. While it provides an extensive variety of apparently mundane items, the substantial toy section de-notes its significant use for child-related consumption. Luxury and gift objects, and the suggestion of gift items (certain sections show symbols and text reading 'all items are gift boxed'), are prevalent throughout the catalogue.

What distinguishes *Argos* is its dual presence in homes where mail order cata-logues are otherwise considered an inappropriate, even divisive, means of acquisi-tion and those where traditional mail order catalogues are considered a staple and respectable form of consumption.

While *Argos* draws on the established working/lower-middle-class market of traditional catalogue consumers, the exclusion of clothing and 16-day money-back guarantee allows other (predominately middle-class) users to imbue its presentation and mode of purchase with the safe, respectable and educated functionalism of renowned department stores such as John Lewis (see Miller et al. 1997). The quantitative aesthetic of *Argos*, with its multiple brands and illustrations, made some informants critical of its mass 'plasticy and cheap' image. Others felt that bulk of choice coupled with the omission of a biased or manipulative shop assistant made *Argos* a minimum-risk, optimum-value consumption method. While inform-ants gave numerous examples of *Argos* products actually costing more than high street equivalents, they consciously opted for the security and self-determination offered by the pre-catalogue selection sales method. They enjoyed the *impression* of mass-produced, lowest-common-denominator goods offered at basic, understand-able, stratified prices.

Argos catalogue was considered a staple of contemporary living across all social groups in the ethnography (most could locate it instantly in a convenient magazine rack or, revealingly, in their child's bedroom). However, there were vital differences in the role it played in their household provisioning. A *Financial Times* (24 August 1995) article reported a massive growth in *Argos* shares and the exceptional success of its new 'Wedding List' service. While many consumers see *Argos* as an ideal source for gifts, some informants considered it as the least likely place to purchase gifts. One middle-aged woman typifying the latter view had recently used *Argos* to purchase a kettle and mattress cover, because, she pointed out emphatically, it was the only appliance store open on a Sunday: 'I use it very much as convenience shopping, I would never use it to buy presents or anything because I like to see what I'm buying before ... seeing it in a picture isn't enough for me, I need to touch and feel it'.

In stark opposition to this view, *Argos* was used by other informants as an essential guide for budgeting and identifying birthday, Christmas and anniversary gifts. Chris, a 19-year-old Greek/English youth working in a minimally paid government training scheme, who described himself as having a 'dangerously big family', used *Argos* to ascertain appropriate Christmas gifts on a limited budget. On Christmas Eve, when buying his brother a *Pin-Pad* executive game, he remembered the 'desperate scene' as people clambered to order and collect gifts.

Others viewed *Argos* as a source of consumption external (as opposed to integral) to their own provisioning, even if they made regular use of it. Some expressed an uncontainable sense of voyeurism flicking the pages of *Argos*, as if glimpsing a shopping 'underworld'; 'I normally find *Argos* catalogue quite entertaining because you always think "gosh, this is cheap", so it's quite good for cheap, less important birthday presents ... I find it quite entertaining', commented one middle-class informant.

Argos, then, shares with *Loot* an appeal to self-determining acquisition. The salesperson is replaced by series of descriptive product details, the formal shopping space is reduced to a format of numbered pages. Unlike *Loot*, however, *Argos* operates as a static, secure and trustworthy form of consumption used to anchor decisions and substantiate choices. As the following case studies reveal, this medium does not automatically exclude the play and fantasy making associated with *Loot*. But they accentuate *Argos* as a vital consumptive information system which, through its normative status, opens up the sociality of consumption.

Case study 1: Restricted choices and familial ties

Wayne and Gillian live in a small rented council flat with their four children. They are long-term unemployed and rely on income support and welfare benefit to support their family. Wayne has just completed a six-month government retraining programme. More recently expenditure (for example, on gifts) has been confined to the immediate family due to severe financial constraints. Wayne and Gillian always shop together as a couple, and use the nearest shopping centre regularly (about three times per week). They can see no advantage in travelling to the more upmarket and supposedly better equipped mall some miles away, especially as most of their shopping involves food provisioning. They recently cancelled a milk delivery as, using four pints per day, they found it more economical to purchase in bulk from the supermarket. Similarly the local shops are out of bounds except for the occasional ice-cream for the children and the Post Office for benefit. Mr McGrudie's local hardware store, however, was praised for the wealth of information the patron offered with goods he sold. This information and service counterbalanced the slightly higher prices he was forced to charge in comparison with bulk distributorship outlets. Despite their lack of funds and inability to socialize in formal settings they are a particularly sociable couple, receiving over seventy cards at Christmas. They get on well with neighbours but friendship is generally confined to greetings and conversations. Much of their leisure activity is provided by self-provisioning: the kitchen operates as a cottage brewery and distillery for various alcoholic drinks. A substantial proportion of their weekly budget is given over exclusively to this pastime, the National Lottery and smoking.

Wayne is proud of his dual role in provisioning the family and insists that he is not embarrassed to buy anything – even sanitary towels. With a large family, shopping frequently proved stressful and on a recent shopping trip Wayne had been reprimanded by an 'old dear' for hitting one of the kids in a supermarket. He felt morally justified as the child had been deliberately 'winding him up all day'. The children were expected to do their fair share of carrying shopping home and to learn to appreciate the cost of food. Gillian stressed, though, the nightmare of shopping with children during the summer holidays and her frustration with ill-organized shops. Places like Toys 'R' Us for example, enticed and over-excited children. In this context, *Argos* catalogue then was used as a controllable toy shop. Indeed the family relied almost exclusively on *Argos* for selection and purchase of the children's Christmas and birthday presents. As well as offering cheaper products than Toys 'R' Us, it allowed the children to indicate their choices and for their parents to respond accordingly. For them looking in *Argos* replaced the trauma of 'shopping around' with a restricted income. The variety and price range offered in the catalogue was tantamount to this selection process. It was used as a price barometer and a dependable source: 'If it's in *Argos* we normally get it from *Argos*'. Lamenting the lack of Christmas presents requested by their eldest son, Wayne and Gillian used *Argos* to identify the most sought-after and popular toys (in this case 'Power Ranger' plaster casts). Some of the children's presents are bought from bulk cut-price warehouses like Poundstretcher, but Wayne and Gillian pointed out that like Kwiksave, it was a horrible but necessary shopping experience. *Argos* on the other hand encompasses the positive experiences of 'shopping around' without the stress of outside intervention, but with an implicit sociality intact. The only downside to *Argos* shopping was the disappointment of out-of-stock items.

Varied and leisurely shopping is not a viable option for Wayne and Gillian. Illustrative of this position was their exclusion from 'sale' shopping and their inability to risk waiting for the 'right bargain'. Just before Christmas, for example, the family went to buy bunk beds from *Argos*; they dare not wait until the New Year sales as they feared the money would be subsumed by Christmas expenditures. They had already saved for a year and a half and desperately needed the bunk beds as the smallest child had outgrown her cot. In a two-bedroom flat, Gillian stressed 'bunk beds is the only way to get four of them in one room'. They had pre-chosen the beds through the *Argos* catalogue and collected the item flat packed for self-assembly.

Wayne and Gillian have a severely limited budget and are not able to engage in varied, leisurely or experimental shopping. For them, *Argos* provides a form of self-provisioning not just of goods but of shopping knowledge. *Argos* keeps them in touch with high street tastes and prices; through the normative sociality of *Argos* catalogue they prevent deeper isolation. Provisioning for a large family requires strategic action and with *Argos* they sustain a controllable, familial sociality through consumption. The children are socialized through shared food-buying trips and perusal of the *Argos* catalogue. Budgeting, Gillian pointed out, involved the use of 'nightmare shops' like Poundstretcher and Kwiksave which precluded imaginative or fantasy shopping of any kind. Such shops, based around utility, could not provide the necessary social resource that *Argos* provided.

Case study 2: 'Swings and Roundabouts': sustaining sociality

Philipa and her African–Caribbean husband Roger have three children aged 7 to 14. They are both in their late thirties and live in a three-bedroom council flat that is cosily decorated with knick-knacks new and old. Old sepia photographs of the husband's family ornament the walls and the living room has a comfortable, velour three-piece suite and large television. They shop mostly at bulk outlets such as Kwiksave, Iceland frozen foods and Tesco the supermarket, but Philipa enjoys variety and happily uses markets for clothes. Recently she treated herself to £30 of Amway products, purchased direct sale from her next-door neighbour, which she justified on the pretext of 'taking more care of herself at her age'. 'Besides which', she said, it was a question of 'swings and roundabouts' – what she saved on the arduous task of food shopping she could spend on a reward for herself. And her neighbour selling Amway benefited too.

Most of the household's non-food provisioning was supplied through catalogues. Philipa subscribed to both *Kays* and *Littlewoods* mail order catalogues as she perceived them as offering slightly different, interchangeable styles. Both mainstream catalogues, the former offered more conservative and old-fashioned clothes, and the latter, younger and more up-to-date versions. When a catalogue first arrives Philipa looks forward to browsing its pages as an enjoyable and exciting event. *Kays* catalogue provided T-shirts for the whole family in the summer and a pair of trainers for the 'old man'. Philipa controlled the purchase of items through catalogues but shared the browsing and decision making predominantly with the children. The Christmas provisions for the previous year, she stressed, had been almost exclusively reliant on catalogues. All the presents were purchased through catalogues which she believed forced her to keep to a fairly strict and manageable weekly credit limit. *Choice*, *Kays* and *Littlewoods* offered her a good combination of choice, and though *Littlewoods* do not offer commission, *Kays* gave a 10 per cent cash-back scheme. Accumulated 'cash back' was a major purchase incentive and could either be redeemed in the form of a cheque or, for a greater amount, be redeemed against future purchases. In the past Philipa enjoyed browsing the catalogues with friends and had once collated communal orders to accrue commission. In the process she discovered that some women furnished their entire houses through the catalogue. One neighbour, for example, bought three beds, a three-piece suite, display cabinets, bedroom suite, wardrobes, 'everything in one go' from *Freeman's* catalogue. The commission work, however, developed into a negative experience as many of her friends defaulted on their payments. Eventually she found the experience of badgering close neighbours and friends for their overdue payments too embarrassing.

Philipa's most recent large catalogue purchase was a professional sewing machine. She did not shop around for the item as she was already reliant on the catalogue's credit system. She had gained a new-found confidence, trying activities she had previously felt precluded from. She had used her sewing machine to make a costume for a jazz and tap dancing show she performed with a friend at a local dance school. There had been numerous time-consuming rehearsals and the whole family came to see the final performance. But ultimately she envisaged the sewing machine as a means to making clothes for her daughter, despite acknowledging that shop-bought clothes were cheaper in the long run. She could not yet justify the expense of the credit payments but saw the item as a major emotional and functional investment.

Her sewing machine projects had been on hold while she organized and arranged the silk flowers at her cousin's wedding. The arrangements for the wedding reception revolved around a bargain wedding dress purchased from the John Lewis department store at Brent Cross. Reduced from £500 to £250 due to being shop soiled, the dress was described as 'exquisite' and 'totally gorgeous', white with tiny pink sequins, glittering diamantés and a long train. This bargain, of which the bride and her relatives were extremely proud, had transformed the original decorative scheme from ivory to pink and white. This theme encompassed the bridesmaids' dresses, the bride's gown, the table settings, flowers and decorations. Philipa's mother-in-law made the dresses for the younger bridesmaids and a friend made the others. Philipa commented that her cousin's wedding had taken up a lot of energy and had been the main focus of the female relatives for the last five months. As well as creating the floral displays, Philipa had made the three tiers of the cake for her sister-in-law, a more proficient cake decorator, to ice.

Argos formed the focal point of gifting for the cousin's wedding list. With the main list placed with *Argos*, guests were asked either to choose from the catalogue or to donate *Argos* gift vouchers. Philipa had been able to afford only £20 but felt that at least her cousin could put this towards a bigger purchase. As the cousin already had an established home with two children she had preferred the notion of vouchers; but accepted that many guests would be uncomfortable giving money (despite the fact that *Argos* catalogue unequivocally indicates product prices and allows for direct comparison).

Philipa herself relied on the catalogue for the selection of gifts at birthdays and Christmas. In particular, the children used *Argos* for writing Christmas lists to Santa Claus. Their lists would include specific product selection, catalogue code number and exact price. Far from encouraging unbridled desire, Philipa used the catalogue to illustrate to the children that Christmas presents operated within a finite budget: 'I told them Father Christmas couldn't afford any products over £9.99 this year'. The children happily chose within the designated monetary limits.

Such comments were supported by the interviews conducted with local junior school children regarding Christmas gifting. They spoke of *Argos* catalogue as the dominant source of inspiration and identification of potential gifts. As another mother from the street noted, 'they see it on TV and look it up in *Argos* book to see how much it is ... the little one she can't write properly yet so she copies it all down including the price!' For many children, who fantasized about adulthood as the freedom to go 'in any shop you wanted', the catalogue acted as their own safe, fantasy shopping space. Notably at least two-thirds of all children identified themselves as *Argos* literate. Conversations among groups of children revealed a thorough and shared knowledge of the relevant *Argos* pages. As one parent in the ethnography commented, 'the children always use *Argos*...they all know what's on what pages and they all get their ideas what they'd like for Christmas out of it'.

Philipa and the family practise varied informal and formal shopping. While they budget with limited income, Philipa's social networks, particularly female kin, open up numerous links through which other advantageous forms of informal provisioning are pursued. A 'perk' of her work as the principal provisioner of the family is the occasional 'treat'. While an expensive purchase of cosmetics from the next-door neighbour seems irresponsible, such relations sustain other forms of advantageous informal provisioning. Philipa is frequently the beneficiary of stolen goods and neighbours often call on her husband Roger for paid repairs and home improvement chores which supplements an unstable family income. Like Wayne and Gillian, *Argos* is an invaluable means of controlling and mediating household consumption. It allows the children a productive and educative role in provisioning. *Argos* also forms the crux of normative consumption values within their given social group.

For Philipa, her broard range of provisioning supports an entire infrastructure of social and economic relations. The seemingly erratic consumption of treats and luxuries slots into a socialized web of female kin, neighbours and friends. The dual use of catalogues for acquisition and monetary provisioning, turning friendly neighbour into tiresome debtcollector proved too risky a venture as its commerciality overtly jeopardized this balanced array of vital relationships.

Within this social group *Argos* is a respectable and normative medium for self-provisioning and gifting.

Case study 3: A household in rehearsal: things without meaning

Joanna is a young, middle-class married mother ostensibly responsible for the household's provisioning. At the moment her partner is retraining as a medical student and so they are living on a limited income in a maisonette. The décor mainly consists of pastel colours, stripped pine and a number of items from IKEA. There are no items in the household that Joanna would describe as having 'sentimental' value or particular significance, except the ornaments and gifts given by her Canadian in-laws. The house contains predominantly new furniture and objects. Although Joanna had owned one antique, her grandmother's old chair, she had subsequently returned it to her mother as it was scruffy and too unwieldy for the small living room.

Although Joanna purchased a high ratio of brand new household products she considered *Argos* as 'last resort' shopping. While the house contained numerous objects purchased through the catalogue she disassociated herself from *Argos* as a recommendable form of shopping and described its products critically. *Argos* was considered as a basic, even degrading, form of shopping used merely to supplement practical items omitted from the couple's original wedding list. The living room magazine rack held a copy of the *Argos* catalogue which Joanna emphasized would be consulted only 'out of necessity, not for pleasure'. While the actual reasoning behind her using *Argos* was to control the purchasing experience and avoid pressure from assistants, Joanna described the visits to the shop as too hassle-ridden and stressful. She compared the uniformity, ritual and 'sheep-like behaviour' of the *Argos* users with pre-revolutionary Soviet Union bureaucracy. She did not deem *Argos* cheaper, just more instantly accessible: 'You can look at home and get yourself organized at home'. Her most recent purchase, a hair razor with alterable settings, was designed to save money on hair cuts for her husband and son. Three weeks after the purchase, she was still unable to operate the complicated appliance successfully.

To Joanna, *Argos* provided basic houseware at acceptably reasonable prices. In 'an emergency' she once purchased a pair of gold-plated earrings, chosen from the catalogue, to match a wedding outfit. Normally dismissing *Argos* and catalogues in general, for the acquisition of personal goods, she stressed the purchase as an act of desperation. She quickly realized 'the earrings were dreadful... horrible gold plate that tarnished quickly and were just not nice'.

Her mother similarly uses *Argos* 'in an emergency' where replacement, utility items are sought at a reasonable price. Neither would 'dream of getting real gifts from there' but saw it as a convenience hardware store. As well as precluding *Argos* as a store for meaningful or significant gifts Joanna would not consider using *Argos* for toys for her 5 year old, Sammy. Many of his items though were purchased through more acceptable alternative modes of informal acquisition, including the Ibis Pond Mother's Group jumble sales and the classifieds section of their monthly newsletter, the *Early Learning* catalogue and Usbourne and Red House educational book parties.

Joanna, living on a limited budget, consciously restricts the range of goods and methods of provisioning in the household. For Joanna, the present household is merely a household in rehearsal. Its objects have no overt sentimental ties and acquisition of household goods is actively neutral. It is as if the present contents are props, mock-ups to be replaced in a more stable, affluent future. *Argos* suffices as a bridging tool while quality valued provisioning (directly associated with the desired social and cultural group) is confined to the provisioning of the child.

Although Joanna's household is limited to a tight budget it is made understood, through the acquisition of material culture, that this is a temporary state.

Argos is viewed as an involuntary option, stress-filled and aesthetically deficient. Unlike Philipa's household, here *Argos* exemplifies the tawdry aspects of modern alienated consumption – receiving no service or individual attention Joanna feels like one of many passive, mass consumers choosing from a prescribed range of goods. She uses the stock of alienable commodities to prevent attachment to a transitional life-stage.

Conclusion

Loot and *Argos* are vehicles for the restriction and elaboration of consumptive choices. As alternative, non-formal modes of acquisition, they are incorporated and manipulated into broader systems of provisioning. Both act as crucial vehicles of sociality and knowledge formation.

Loot with its demand on time, skill and risk-taking appears to call on optimum 'cultural capital'. Driven by the aesthetic of authenticity rather than basic thrift, *Loot* seems best 'played' by those with the least at stake. Its literary, non-visual medium requires extensive interpretative skills and, to handle the exchange, competent social interaction. *Argos*, with its standardized, price-led, easy-to-use method of acquisition, appears in contrast to be a simplified option favoured by the unskilled shopper. Here the image replaces the word as a more obvious and instantaneous response-led means of representation. Shopping through pictures, with limited social interaction, seems to challenge consumption as a culturally informed practice. Like catalogues in general, critics berate *Argos* as a 'degrading' form of consumption, its users merely responding 'sheep-like' to a production line of goods. Closer examination reveals, however, that users of *Argos* were as skilled and practised in their acquisition as the wily *Loot* users. Skilled *Argos* consumers effectively inverted the outlet's commodified system, using the catalogue as an effective means of self-provisioning. Far from lacking skill and competence, consumers used *Argos* to control and manage the moral economy of the household, just as users of *Loot* used the medium to practise and test theirs. These choices are value-led rather than rationally and economically driven.

Just as goods, according to Douglas and Isherwood (1979: 75), 'are endowed with value by the agreement of fellow consumers', so too are modes of consumption. While *Loot* offers an element of thrift and bargain hunting that seems ideally suited to economically restricted or working-class consumption, in effect its risk-laden and time-consuming method leaves it firmly embedded in a middle-class style of knowledge use. Although *Argos* offers a more expensive range of goods it provides a basic resource for social groups precluded from mainstream leisure-imbued formal shopping.

Loot demands high mobility and the knowledge and resources to navigate the intricacies of London's suburbs, while *Argos* is based on a fundamental notion of immobility. For poorer households and those mostly confined to the home, such as elderly people and children, it allows home-based, self-regulated and containable provisioning. These practical implications relate to conceptual ideas of space: *Loot* expands the notion of local while *Argos*, as a chain store, brings the global to the local. As this ethnographic observation illustrates, modes of acquisition and material culture are not confined to rigid social groups. Skills culled from a range of knowledges (educational, class, subcultural) are brought to bear constructively on the opportunities opened up by these new forms of acquisition.

REFERENCES

Appadurai, A. (1986) *The Social Life of Things*. Cambridge: Cambridge University Press.

Bloch, M. and J. Parry (1989) *Money and the Morality of Exchange*. Cambridge: Cambridge University Press.

Bourdieu, P. (1984) *Distinction: A Social Critique of the Judgement of Taste*. London: Routledge and Kegan Paul.

Caplovitz, D. (1967) *The Poor Pay More: Consumer Practices of Low Income Families*. New York: Free Press.

Carrier, J. G. (1995) *Gifts and Commodities: Exchange and Western Capitalism since 1700.* London: Routledge.

Cheal, D. J. (1988) *The Gift Economy.* London: Routledge.

Douglas, M. and B. Isherwood (1979) *The World of Goods.* London: Basic Books.

Miller, D. (1986) *Material Culture and Mass Consumption.* Oxford: Blackwell.

Miller, D. (1995) *Acknowledging Consumption.* London: Routledge.

Miller, D. (in press) How infants grow mothers in North London. *Theory, Culture and Society.*

Miller, D., P. Jackson, B. Holbrook, N. Thrift, and M. Rowlands (1997) *Consumption and identity: A Study of Two North London Shopping Centres.* London: Routledge.

Rutz, H. and B. S. Orlove (eds) (1989) *The Social Economy of Consumption.* Lanham, MD: University Press of America.

Silverstone, R., E. Hirsch and D. Morley 1992. *Consuming Technologies: Media in Domestic Spaces.* London: Routledge.

Soiffer, S. S. and G. M. Herrmann (1987) Visions of power: ideology and practice in the American garage sale. *Sociological Review* 35 (1): 48–83.

Weiner, A. B. (1992) *Inalienable Possessions: The Paradox of Giving While Keeping.* Los Angeles: University of California Press.

Chapter 16

What's in a Price? An Ethnography of Tribal Art at Auction

Haidy Geismar

Introduction

This is an investigation of the ways in which price is constructed at the auction of tribal art objects.[1] The process of auction has traditionally been described as a simple formalization of price within a particular public space over a clearly delimited and public period of time: a fundamental index of the market (see Baudrillard 1981). This interpretation ignores the peculiar circumstances of the auction – as the culmination of a set of discursive, visual and socio-economic practices that may, at the final moment of sale, fail or be fundamentally subverted. This potential for subversion, and the subsequent unpredictability of price, exemplifies what Keane calls the 'ever-present potential for alienation, slippage or loss' (1997: 230) of economic consensus within the public interaction of persons and things. Thus, object identities, criteria of authenticity, and transaction histories are necessarily manipulated by buyers and sellers in order to tentatively ascribe price. Economics at auction can be filled with doubt, insecurity and surprise. Consequently, price is continually recreated, reflecting emotional as well as economic processes that cross-cut the unique event of each particular sale.

It is necessary to understand the peculiar commodity status of tribal art: each object's price is defined in relation to an identity selected from its various cultural histories. This selective presentation of the relation of object to context exploits a classificatory device commonly called 'authenticity', which, for the purposes of the tribal arts market, is used in a highly strategic and not necessarily consistent or coherent manner. In the art auction, all such objects, whether 'African', 'Native American' or 'Oceanic' have undergone processes of both *relocation* (they have moved from one place to another, their identities defined in the market by place of origin) and *delocation* (alienated entirely from place of origin, identities defined by processes of collection and dealing). The traditional 'ethnographic' context becomes an exploitable background over which the Western art market may be propagated. The concept of provenance, vital in the conferral not only of basic monetary prices but also of object identities, exemplifies this process. For the purposes of auction, the history of each item begins upon its entry into the market. An object's 'biography' (see Kopytoff 1986; Hoskins 1998) becomes one of Euro-American ownership and exchange, primarily between dealers, museums and private collectors. This is a market response to national and international cultural property legislation, whereby objects can only be sold if they are authentic enough for the market, but not so authentic as to be removed from the world of commerce and replaced in indigenous museums. This dilemma of the market relies on a self-conscious and highly ironic construction of authenticity that plays a vital role in the establishment of object identities within commercial transaction.

Such severance of objects from their sites of production has come to have profound political resonance, particularly as the Euro-American appropriation and representation of 'tribal' material culture has been increasingly contested (see Karp and Lavine 1991). The market is salient in the creation of origin myths and the presentation of object identities in a wide variety of contexts, from museum to auction salesroom. This study is a response to the recent proliferation of anthropological assessments of the art market,[2] most of which have attempted to locate the local production and consumption of art in terms of the global development of socio-political relations of exchange, often neglecting the tricky ways in which objects themselves enter into these relations.

In many studies, the 'market' becomes generic, cross-cutting cultural boundaries, often in tension with micro-level analyses. This needs to be picked apart as a fieldwork site. Steiner (1994) provides a multilocal ethnographic foil to transcend this divide, as he explores the market for African art, tracing historical trade links between Islamic African traders, village craftsmen, town bazaars, and New York galleries. His emphasis on the circulation of objects in local, national and transnational economies challenges the ethnocentricity of previous accounts of the market for art commodities (which often read 'Western' for 'global'). He demonstrates the need for historical analysis in understanding long-term culturally specific trade relations, and the importance of local knowledge for participants in the market. Studies such as this emphasize the social 'entanglement' and 'promiscuity' of object identities as they move within these particular economic relations (Thomas 1991). The interplay of culturally defined objects and persons in the market is subject to a complex geography, which must be kept in mind in any micro-analysis. Through study of one particular site of the art market (the tribal arts auction), I balance other ethnographic emphases on cross-cultural transactions with a case study that highlights how vital it is to ground economic analyses of the marketplace across time and space, both socially and materially.

Typically, anthropological work on the art market defines market value by reference to a particular geographic place, situating a global 'ideal' of the market in the context of various localities, and examining the inherent tension between substantive market 'place' and formal market 'principle' (see Dilley 1992). Steiner (1994: 63) writes (reflecting Appadurai's notion of 'tournaments of value'): 'The perceived value of an item is thus wholly dependent on where one is situated in the chain of economic transactions, and each transaction is characterized by the logic of its own system of value and mode of bargaining.' As a methodology for studying markets, this view suffers in the tension between the local and the global, from the 'situation' to the 'chain'. I analyse the art auction market as a complicated artefact in itself, following on from anthropological approaches to material culture (see Miller 1987, 1998), and rather literally from Strathern's exhortation to analyse 'artefacts as the enactment of events' in a context where 'performances are the artefacts of persons' (1990: 40, 32). Such 'material culture' approaches are invaluable to rethinking 'tournaments of value', or these previously divisive market spaces. By incorporating the social agency of both objects and persons into the construction of price we may view the auction as a performative tournament (with a catalogue-script, a stage, an audience, and so on) within a series of events taking place over a variety of places, times and media.

In undertaking research, I attended tribal arts auctions in London, Paris and New York, talking to dealers, auctioneers, curators and collectors. Research concentrated primarily on one of the biannual auctions of African and Oceanic art at Sotheby's New York (25 May 1999). The study is an empirically grounded illustration of the construction of price, and an examination of the ways in which objects both define and are defined by the particular economics of the auction house. For the sake of brevity, my examples focus on tribal art from the Pacific.

What Happens in Auctions?

There is a dearth of sociological writing about auctions. Smith's *Auctions: The Social Construction of Value* (1989) provides a useful introduction to the ambiguity of the socio-economic interactions between persons and things within a variety of auction contexts. Here, as elsewhere, 'value' and 'price' are used interchangeably. Within my own analysis, I focus upon the construction of *price* (as the monetary amount assigned to objects by the market), and use a working notion of *value* to suggest a set of judgements surrounding the assignation of price that are established in a multiplicity of ways – social, political and so on.

For Smith, 'auctions serve as rites of passage for objects shrouded in ambiguity and uncertainty' (1989: x), they are places where communities of value are continually recreated. Smith writes that value 'represents the collective judgement of the auction *community*' (p. 77, my emphasis). Value-as-price is thus inherently consensual. It is instilled within objects by the 'collective effervescence' of an economic community during the auction. Price is unpredictable, created anew within each exchange at auction:

> Objects are reborn in auctions. They acquire new values, new owners, and often new definitions. Sometimes they even acquire a new history. For these new identities to be accepted as legitimate, they must be seen as having a communal sanction. It is this search for legitimacy that underlies the communal character of the auction. (Ibid.: 79)

Smith's work sets the scene for an interpretative approach to auction economics that focuses on performance and theatricality in the fixing of price. However, his emphasis on 'community' and 'consensus' needs to be reassessed in three main ways. First, it is apparent from ethnographic research that whilst price *may* be consensually determined at auction, consensus within an auction 'community' is not fundamentally required. The *potential* for anyone to place any bid is the founding retail principle at auction. It is the potential for subversion, along with an ironic classification of authentic objects that paradoxically maintains the conservatism of the market. Ideals of 'community' are maintained despite actual social dissolution. Second, it does not fully account for durable object identities outside of auction, or for the idea that objects may have social agency in constructing their own prices (see Gell 1998). Third, it presents a market context that is entirely apolitical and ahistorical. Smith denies the existence of hierarchies of knowledge, of disagreements in attribution of meanings, or struggles for economic power; the auction itself becomes a singular social entity, independent in time and space. My research reveals that these struggles are the precise method by which price is set. As there is no need for consensus to set price at auction, nor is there a coherent *use* of the term 'value'. Instead, ideas about value are socially manipulated around objects, over several events (not just the sale) to fix price. This process is inherent in bidding, which sets the auction context apart from other retail transactions (also allowing price to be set without consensus). In bidding, exchange is rooted to a particular time and space *but* also simultaneously refers back to a history of prior exchanges: the estimated and reserve prices reflecting consultation between vendor and auction house, and previous sales. Price is thus the tangible result of these complex social negotiations of value, *across* space and time.

Smith's emphasis on consensus and on the day of the auction itself echoes Appadurai's work on commodity exchange. For Appadurai (1986) all exchange of objects is fundamentally rooted within a 'tournament of value'[3] – a precise, singular place of economic activity. Approaches such as these are useful in that they begin to think about the ways in which economic value is socially and politically constructed, and of the importance of market knowledge for those participating in the setting of price (see Geertz 1979), yet they lack focus on the ways in which knowledge is constructed, remembered and used in the market.

A representative of Sotheby's African and Oceanic Art Department described the auction as 'the only place where true price can be seen. Price at auction to me is the exact indicator of the state of the market, of demand and worth being decided at one particular time on one particular day.' Price at auction is viewed as the ultimate harbinger of value within an idealized marketplace. This synchronic focus fits in well with Appadurai's concept of a 'tournament of value', but denies a formulation of price and value for objects that transcends the auction event. As my ethnography of the auction demonstrates, each dealer or collector attends the auction with an idea of appropriate price, expressed in the estimate, reserve and final sale price. These ideas come from the experience of the catalogue and view (from the objects themselves), and from the degree of market knowledge (primarily the exchange histories each participant holds in mind). This type of imaginary value is built over time, ultimately consolidated onto the sites of objects. This 'formal' historical value needs to be understood as intrinsic to the fixing of price at auction sale.

A Brief History of the Western Auction

Herodotus' depiction of the auctioning of women in Babylon, in 500 BC is perhaps the earliest written account of the auction process we have. The term 'auction' originates from the Latin *auctio* meaning increase. The earliest Roman auctions were of booty, looted during war and sold *sub hasta*, where the auctioneer was a middleman taking a commission of 1 per cent.

The modern art auction developed during the destabilization of the rigid social hierarchies of the 'Great Chain of Being' in seventeenth-century northern Europe; intimately connected to changes in laws governing private property, particularly as they concerned ownership rights between state and private landowner (land being the definitive form of property). In 1556 the French government created the system of *huissers-priseurs* (bailiff-auctioneers) answering directly to the king as disinterested experts in property disputes. In 1715 their title changed to *commissaires-priseurs* and their numbers and practices were centrally regulated, as they are to the present. This marked the start of a tradition of state interest and intervention in commercial transaction that has resulted in the centralized system at the Hôtel des Ventes, Rue Drouôt, an auction house inhabited by independent experts: the dealers. The French system is distinguished by the *Droit de Presomption*, which allows any artefact approved by the governmental *Conseil Artistique* to be claimed on behalf of the state, overruling the outcome of any auction. For the French, the auction is not the last word on the ownership of an object. The free market is mediated by the state.[4]

In contrast to French state regulation, auction houses in Britain have been encouraged to become part of the 'free' world art market. This has led to problems in the development of a common European economic policy. Sotheby's and Christie's both have luxurious properties in Paris awaiting approval from Brussels to begin auctioning, to the chagrin of the French government. In Britain, Spink and Sons was the first auction house to open (1666), and the large houses began to proliferate in the 1680s after Cromwell's law banning the importation of paintings from Europe was revoked. Sotheby's was founded by Samuel Baker in 1744, his first auction of books held in 1745. Baker was joined by his nephew Sotheby in 1778, and the firm established itself as a bookseller and auctioneer of fine books. Meanwhile, Christie's was founded by James Christie in 1766; Philips, 'The Auction People', was established in 1796, by Harry Philips, previously chief clerk to James Christie; and Bonhams was founded in 1793, by William Charles Bonham and George Jones.

The British Settled Land Acts of 1882 allowed for the disposal of the contents of landed estates by inheritors tax free, if the proceeds from the sale went into trust. This resulted in widespread disposal of inherited property, mainly from large estates, in order to avoid death duties and other taxes, and as a method of liquidating assets. The auction houses became the focus for the dispersal of aristocratic property into the middle-class realm of mercantile commerce. It was in 1917 with the move to Bond Street, and the disposal of the Earl of Pembroke's collection of armour, pictures, drawings and prints that Sotheby's had come to rival Christie's in the disposal of property.

In 1927 the Auctions (Bidding Agreements) Act was passed in Great Britain making any prior agreement to the outcome of sales illegal.[5] Refinements in legislation over the past twenty years have resulted in the auction houses of Great Britain and USA being legally bound to state out loud at a sale if a lot has been 'passed over' (unsold). In 1975 Sotheby's and Christie's created a stir in the art world by announcing that they were to add a buyer's premium of 10 per cent into the commission structure, adding to the vendor's commission of 10 per cent and bringing up the auction houses' profits to 20 per cent, inflating the final cost of objects sold at auction. This resulted in a mass boycotting of the two houses by art dealers.

Philips to this day advertise their auctions as having 'no premium' above the auctioneers stand.

In 1954 the international auction market opened up to the United States after the deregulation of wartime currency regulations, resulting in a growth in the American market for European art and in the expansion of the major European auction houses across the Atlantic (Sotheby's taking over the American auction house Parke Bernet in 1964). The history of the twentieth-century auction houses has been dominated by the competition between Sotheby's and Christie's as they have floated successfully on the stock market (Christie's in November 1973, Sotheby's in May 1977). Ever since the Settled Lands Act the auction houses have frequently been the subject of state legislation to enforce and oversee the disposal of property. The auction house is an ideal local window through which to view the complex negotiation of price related to objects as cultural property, now within an international market.

A Background to the Tribal Arts Auction Market[6]

The George Ortiz sale held at Sotheby Parke Bernet, New York in 1978, under the direction of Richard Bleekley, marked the first occasion in which Sotheby's began to deal in tribal art apart from Antiquities, Islamic, Asian, and Oriental arts. At Christie's, London the same move was made in 1976 by Hermione Waterfield, with the sale of the James Hooper Collection. Due to the increasing rarity of pieces, both tiny departments are now gaining readily in importance. The market is intimately linked to institutionalized academic knowledge in museums and universities. These bonds between institutions must be examined if we are to trace the trajectory of economies of information defining value in the marketplace, and if we are to expand the concept of a 'tournament of value' to include such networks.

Within the Pacific art market, Polynesian art has historically been more successful at auction than Melanesian. The distinction hinges largely on the notion of 'contact', whereby pieces perceived to have been produced before the colonial period have greater authenticity, resulting in higher prices. The 'best' pieces are always the oldest. This hierarchy of value is a response to a tradition of collection whereby Melanesian contact history has been more recent and sporadic than the history of exploration and great collection within Polynesia. Almost all of the older Polynesian pieces are in museums, the museum collection being the ultimate reference point by which objects are judged, defining criteria of rarity, authenticity and desirability. Once more we can see the dilemma of the market: pre-contact (or untainted) pieces must be legitimated by Western institutions such as museums.

Webster and Oldman, both collecting from Britain at the turn of the nineteenth to the twentieth century, were the first commercial dealers of tribal arts; Oldman perhaps the biggest Oceanic collector of his time. In 1946 he offered his collection to the British Museum for £50,000; this was rejected and eventually sold for much less to the government of New Zealand. The tribal arts market has always been problematically internationalist, from the mass exportation of ethnographica during the colonial period, to the recent passionate debates concerning sales, the theft of cultural property, and repatriation.[7] Sotheby's and Christie's both moved their tribal arts departments out of London (to the free-market deregulation in New York and lax customs laws in Amsterdam respectively) after Peter Watson, an investigative journalist, exposed corruption and illicit trade in antiquities within the large auction houses (Watson 1997).

The sale of the George Brown collection highlights some of the problems of internationalism for the tribal art auction market, accentuating the importance of auction houses in the forming of cultural property legislation across national borders. The collection of objects from the Pacific was offered for sale in 1918 by the Brown family to the Australian Museum in Sydney, on condition that it remained together in both display and storage. The family eventually declined the Museum's offer and shipped the collection to Newcastle, England. In 1985 the Australian Museum registered an interest in acquiring the collection to both Sotheby's and the University of Newcastle, concerned that the collection would be lost for ever to its Pacific producers once sold at auction. Both the Australian Museum and the National Museum at Port Moresby failed as purchasers of the collection. The collection 'is now in four institutions, in two countries on opposite sides of the world' (Specht 1987). Despite this fragmentation, the case highlights the importance of the economically viable 'collection' of objects in constructing ideas of 'tribal' identities in a global market, demonstrating the importance of the international marketplace as forum for the dissemination of cultural identity politics across national borders.

The auctioning of the George Brown collection raises several key issues that highlight some problems facing the tribal arts market, and, indeed, the international art auction: the conversion of 'cultural heritage' into monetary values, of which there is no worldwide uniformity or guideline (and the subsequent unequal global distribution of cultural property within museums); the dual significance of ethnographic collections as markers not only of indigenous art histories, but also of the history of colonial collectors; and the vested interest that museums now have as consumers within the tribal arts market (and their concern to keep prices low so that they can still afford to collect at auction).

The tribal arts market has developed explicit and problematic relations with both museums and academia. A debate in *Anthropology Today* highlights some of the ways in which the linkage of market knowledge to other institutions has been critically assessed. The proposal of the journal to advertise forthcoming auctions by Philips, Christie's and Sotheby's was criticized by Peter Gathercole as 'wrong and unacceptable' on the grounds that auction houses exist primarily to make a profit, and that:

> Neither *AT* [*Anthropology Today*] nor the RAI should help to promote the sale of any culture's heritage in what is predominantly a private collector's market... Private collectors do not have to be publicly accountable... To advertise sales is to justify them *de facto*. Auction houses and private collectors continually seek academic endorsement, and would regard your proposal as just this... Advance publicity and academic justification usually put up prices... Are we all to be Thatcherites now? (Gathercole 1987: 22][8]

Sotheby's 'Important African and Oceanic Art'[9]

This brief ethnography of the auction aims to analyse the methods by which buyers and sellers in the market interact strategically with tribal art objects to construct price and value. Spatio-temporal complexity, and market knowledge, are marked by the formal qualities of each auctioned artefact, creating 'value histories' that are constructed by around objects. I have divided up the auction process into a series of events in order to demonstrate that the classic formulation of the auction as a singular economic event taking place in one fixed space and time is problematic when we come to assess the market in terms of objects as well as of social relations between persons.

The catalogue

In 1828 Joseph Halewood drew up for his friend Samuel Sotheby a set of 'Hints for a young auctioneer of books' in which his first criterion was 'Consider your catalogue as the foundation of your eminence and make its perfection of character an important study' (Cooper 1977: 96). The catalogue is the buyer's umbilical cord to the auction room. Sotheby's maintains its exclusive clientele primarily through the worldwide distribution of catalogues, also available over the Internet. In the run-up to the sale the catalogue is vital to initial projections of price (via the estimate) and has direct bearing on the outcome of the sale. For all but a privileged few, the catalogue is the first time that the objects to be sold are actually seen.

The auction catalogue as a temporal representation lies somewhere between the classic commercial (mail order) catalogue, as Clarke describes them: 'a standardized, rigid repertoire of . . . visually represented alienable commodities' (1998: 89), and the fine art exhibition catalogue, which is seen as an inferior substitute for the objects them selves, appearing *after* the fact as shadows or memories of the experience of viewing. As the first stage of the auction process, the catalogues become 'vehicles for the restriction and elaboration of consumptive choices . . . crucial vehicles of sociality and knowledge formation' (ibid.: 97). By the time a knowledgeable buyer comes to the auction salesroom for viewing, he or she is likely to have a clear idea of which pieces are potential purchases, which are 'sleepers' (lots underestimated by the auction house), and even which are fakes. In one way, the auction sale is simply an extension of the catalogue. The catalogue is the first instance whereby the retail/commercial aspect of the auction combines with fine arts aesthetic in order to set price.

The catalogue is an intrinsic part of the exhibition of objects at auction; indeed it may be seen as the script of the sale. It is the first conjecture of official value, by way of the estimate. It is the place where provenance is consolidated, ethnographica exploited and photography manipulated. It is the starting point of a complex series of information swapping and inference that continues all the way through the sale. The reserve price (the minimum an object can be sold for, agreed between the seller and the auction house) may be determined as a percentage of the estimate (a price or price range normally 10 per cent higher – although some pieces may be sold with no reserve). One can ascertain from this if the piece is being sold by a dealer or private collector (most lots are entered anonymously although some are from named collections or collectors).

The catalogue is the first place where object-values at auction acquire a singular language of description, a language of the market, that combines with photographic techniques to create visual value and price, firmly entrenched in a culture of commerce:

So, a seascape looking exactly like a coloured picture postcard, becomes a superb clipper under full sail by Montague Dawson. There is an *exciting* Art Nouveau lamp in sandblasted gun metal and frosted glass mosaic, a *ravishing* set of tablemats, painted with titmice by Beatrix Potter, a *magical* Jackson Pollock and a *noble* Munnings. (Reitlinger 1982, 3: 10)

Such language prepares one for the aggressive sales jargon that epitomizes the auction sale. The precedent was set by James Christie, well known for his flowery prose at auction which came to be termed as 'sale by epithet'. A contemporary caricature satirizes his declamation from the stand:

Let me entreat – ladies – gentlemen – permit me to put this inestimable piece of elegance under your protection – only observe – the inexhaustible munificence of your super-latively candid generosity must harmonize with the refulgent brilliance of this little jewel. (Cooper 1977: 23)

The catalogue uses this language to begin the ultimate seduction of the buyer via the interaction of image and text. In the Sotheby's auction of November 1998 the showcase of the catalogue and sale was lot 162: '*A Magnificent Maori Figure, poutokomanawa*, carved as a male figure, with rectangular pegs beneath the broad feet with distinct toes (some missing)...' and so on for three pages of provenance with an article by Terence Barrow PhD, three full-page colour photographs (two from different angles and one close-up). The figure was the cover piece for the entire catalogue, and during the viewing and sale came to be affectionately termed as the 'Maori Man'. Each photograph in the spread is taken portrait style, highlighting the human characteristics of the figure in a manner reminiscent of fashion magazines. This photographic personification was vital to the creation of a strong and memorable identity for the piece, transcending reputable anthropological knowledge and resulting in an unprecedented high price. The piece was catalogued 'estimate upon request' generating a secretive atmosphere; the estimate provided was $1,000,000, and it sold for this exactly ($1,102,500 including the buyer's premium). Despite this being the highest price ever achieved by a Pacific art object at auction, the lot went to an uncontested, absentee bidder.

The anthropological jargon used in the description of provenance describes a romanticized Maori culture, focusing on carving as 'fine art' transcending the trauma of colonialism and subsequent stylistic 'hybridity'. Stylistically, the figurative elements of the piece are emphasized in terms of a 'monumentality akin to that of the dynamic images of ancient Egypt and archaic Greece'. An entire paragraph is dedicated to a biography of Terence Barrow, of impeccable pedigree, justifying his knowledge claims: 'Of a pioneer New Zealand family, he has known as friends many Maori wood-carvers and the Maori people in general'. The tenuous construction of authenticity is illustrated perfectly here: the context of missionary colonialism mentioned just enough to give the piece historical credibility, and to establish it as an important representation of Maori 'culture', but not enough to be proved factually incorrect. Equally, the setting of the piece visually within a context more usually associated with 'fine art' allows it to be a timeless representation of a generic, static art tradition, fitting seamlessly into the fine arts auction market.

In these catalogues we are given a striking insight into the ways in which academic knowledge, photographic techniques, visual 'aesthetic' criteria, historicity, and provenance are all used in the construction of market values (estimated prices). Each piece is shown in isolation, standing upright, lit from above; the pose of standing alone visually expressing rarity, justifying price. We can see at once the necessity of visual aesthetics for the construction of value: techniques of carving, stylization, and the slick dark patina of aged wood. We see the same pieces again and again from year to year, the prices varying greatly. Provenance and historical pedigree are used as a technique of differentiation. Pieces are held together visually and separated verbally. Each is personified, not only by the way in which they are photographed individually, with particular stylistic emphasis on figuration, but also by their textual incorporation into real family trees, which not only include 'eminent' colonialists (and their families back home), but also institutions – the great museums and universities.

Leafing through back catalogues we can see that the more valuable pieces are shown to us individually, from several views (mainly front and side 'mug shots') emphasizing a correlation between visual display and price. This style of presentation mirrors the fine arts museum or gallery, in which we respect the material on view because of its particular context, often to the detriment of interaction with the intrinsic nature of the object itself (see O'Doherty 1986). Pieces in the catalogue are boldly lit to highlight the contrast of plane and tone following a traditional Modernist appreciation of primitive art. This style of presentation is continued on from the catalogue into the display of objects both in the auction view and sale.

What is most striking, as we compare the pieces through the catalogues across the years, is the similarity of representational convention. There can be no doubt that each piece is presented in a manner that best ties it to others, from catalogue to catalogue. There is a paradox here, borne out in the tension between the estimated price in the catalogue and the fact that the auction may unpredictably refuse to uphold that price. Each piece is at once presented as starkly separate original and individual, yet at the same time as a type or part of a wider group. This is the same ironic construction of the authentic object that we have earlier observed in the rhetoric of the auctioneers, dealers and collectors: pieces are unique, but not 'too unique'. Hence, the visual display of objects at auction is vital to the construction of value, and of price on the day of the auction.

The catalogues become indispensable reference points for the construction of 'value-histories' by which objects are compared across time, by criteria of ownership, provenance, material quality and previous price at auction. It would be impossible to begin the exercise of pricing (starting with the attribution of the estimated price) without a catalogue as fundamental reference point. The catalogue is the place in which value seems to congeal on the sites of objects. It allows us to observe the shifts in market prices, the movement of objects through the market (as private sales and ownership are outlined), and is a visual marker of the historical accrual of value for particular objects with reference to their object-types. It is a form of 'distributed object' (Gell 1998) in itself; each object maintains its position in any sale by its catalogue lot number and by its relationship to other similar objects in previous catalogues.

The notion of the catalogue as 'distributed object' itself becomes most apparent if we look at several auction catalogues together. The conventions of representation that carry on between each one take place on a limited number of objects: we quickly begin to anticipate what we might see at each auction. In the Oceanic art section, pieces quickly become generic: Tongan paddles and headrests; Maori feather boxes, greenstone pendants and ceremonial staffs; figurative sculpture from New Guinea; Asmat shields, Hawaiian calabashes. The objects valued must be ceremonial; if not pre-contact then at least harking back to the halcyon days before the colonial invasion. However, the Sotheby's auction included pieces collected as late as the 1950s and 1960s. In the realization that there are fewer and fewer old pieces, newer ones have to be incorporated to keep the market alive. The market begins to work through a highly specialized process of recognition by a select community of knowledgeable persons. The catalogue is the place where such information is displayed, leading directly to its exploitation at auction.

There are two catalogues from the Sotheby's sale (25 May 1999), the smaller, lots 220–35 entitled 'African and Oceanic from a Private Collection', kept separate in order to stimulate greater interest, generating the highest prices at the auction. The larger catalogue is divided into two sale sessions, lots 1–219, and lots 220–82. The smaller catalogue sale takes place in-between. The biggest, most important pieces are highlighted by colour photographs with extensive 'ethnographic' notes, usually broad generic descriptions. Less valuable pieces are photographed in black and white. Unlike Philips or Bonhams who only photograph the most important pieces at the auction, the Sotheby's catalogue illustrates every piece, making itself an invaluable reference tool for art historians and museum professionals. Catalogues are thus not disposable artefacts, but become pieces themselves, collected, archived, and cross-referenced.

The view

If the catalogue is where object-identities in the form of price are first established textually, visually and economically, the view and sale are places where this collection of objects engages directly with a community of persons; both groups acting *together* as market agents. Once the catalogue has been suitably perused from the comfort of home, the next step in the auction process is to visit the objects. The viewing is vital to the consolidation of one's opinions via the controlled sensuousness of the retail strategy of touching and feeling. Walking into Philips or Bonhams is like visiting a church bazaar or jumble sale. Elderly men in corduroy with leather elbow patches crouch on the floor, glasses on the tips of their noses, rifling through cardboard boxes of African masks crammed on top of Roman flints and Inuit spears. One is as likely to find an old Pitt Riverse museum label attached to the piece, or some old colonialist's spidery handwriting in ink on the underside of a shield, as one is to find worn masks bought in Nairobi airport only two or three years ago. Talk of the authenticity of objects lies fundamentally in the fact that there is always a tension between what the objects *are* and what they *may* be, as a London dealer commented: 'it is like the opposite of the antiques road-show mentality, where everything you thought was junk may be worth something. Here are things we think are worth something and a lot of it is junk.'

There is an air of fierce but humorous competition between dealers, who stroke and fondle each piece in turn, marking vigorously in their catalogues. The visitor is protective of the marks he or she has made in the catalogue. Showing too much interest in a piece will attract other buyers and potentially push up prices, yet it is vital to watch the other dealers out of the corner of your eye in order to verify the truth of your own hunches.

The champagne opening of the Sotheby's sale is an entirely different affair. Structured more along the lines of a fine art exhibition, from opening introductory panel to room headings, each piece is mounted on a plinth or laid carefully on the floor, lit to gallery standards. Yet unlike a gallery, the glass cases are open – although you may have to ask a steward to take out a piece for you to handle. Sipping wine delicately, collectors walk round with the Sotheby's experts from piece to piece, discussing ethnographic details, their recent purchases, and vigorously greeting others of their ilk.

Who are these people? From Philips and Bonhams, to Sotheby's New York, the group of buyers is a closed self-conscious community. Strangers are discounted as tourists or wild cards, objects sold to them are 'lost'. Most other objects are passed around from private collection to museum, to dealer, to private collection in and out of auction in the process. A curator comments that 'The main work of the dealer is to try to find out where the objects are'. Thus, despite the public nature of the auction space, it is not in the interest of the participants in the market to cultivate its penetration by unknown persons. Whilst it is theoretically possible for anybody to buy at auction, the kinds of knowledge necessary to make a successful purchase, and subsequent ambiguities involved, require membership of a complex social group that negotiates and enforces such value systems as price.

The preview is where the collectors come out in all their feathers. Objects are displayed in the context of the display of persons to one another. Arrive early in the morning on the day of the sale, and you will come across any serious buyer scrutinizing pieces intensely, checking back to the catalogue, squatting on the floor, crouching in front of cases. Buying decisions will generally have been made in advance of the opening of the sale; the view provides material consolidation (or repudiation) of these choices, and allows one to see what other people are thinking about buying. People predict outcomes of the sale knowingly. The eavesdropping researcher picking up on conversations held in front of the objects will never know of conversations held in Sotheby's offices, or of the telephone calls between dealers and potential buyers, which begin to organize the outcome of the bidding process itself. One curator described to me in detail the process of '*La revision*: when dealers get together and decide which things will be bought by whom and for how much. Thus the prices are agreed in the sale so that they are not in competition with each other, they eradicate the competitive side of the market between themselves.'

The sale

The view and sale are the places where the dynamics of the market become apparent, but to analyse the auction in Smith's terms as a piece of theatre where value is performed on the stage of the auction stand with a cast of dealers, private buyers, museum curators and savvy auctioneers, is to overestimate the importance of the day-event itself, and to underestimate the complex history that dictates behaviour at the sale. By including the cataloguing and viewing as intrinsic to the sale process,

I have tried to emphasize that the free-market notion of the auction as a spatially and temporally bounded production of value is an illusion. While it is difficult for the researcher to fully understand the complex social interaction that results in the fixing of price at auction, general conversation with auctioneers, dealers and curators highlights the necessity to view the auction in terms of an intricate economy of information centring upon objects. The fact that a buyer's physical presence is not required (that you may bid by telephone, by absentee bid or by proxy) should also be realized: knowledge is the prerequisite to the buying, not physical presence at the sale.

Legislation in Britain and America has stipulated that auctioneers must declare if a piece has not been sold, yet there is a premium on anonymity and secrecy: it is illegal for the auction houses to disclose the identity of purchasers to the public. The experience of attending an auction leaves one confused and perplexed. There is no place in an auction room, apart from the auctioneer's stand, where one may watch every bidder. Additionally, pieces are bought anonymously, over the telephone, by agents, by dealers for clients, by dealers for other dealers, and occasionally by strangers. The gathering of information at the auction itself is more often than not a Sisyphean endeavour.

Unlike Philips or the Drouôt, Sotheby's New York has an efficient system of revolving display which dispenses with the need for apronclad porters to hold up each piece. Lots revolve out from behind a curtain with a dramatic flourish. The sale continues the theme of fine art display. Each piece is showcased and spotlit, creating a visual link to both view and catalogue. Bidders have numbered paddles which they can raise to bid with, although eye contact with the auctioneer is the most important way in which the price is raised, making it hard for newcomers. At Philips, punters are given paper numbers like marathon runners, the auctioneer calls out the price to the person. At one auction I attended the auctioneer repeatedly took bids from 'the lady in red', much to the outrage of a slightly effeminate man in a red shirt sitting in the front row. It is much harder to gauge who exactly is buying at the Drouôt, as they do not describe or focus their attention on individual bidders. At Sotheby's there is also a second auctioneer who scans the right-hand side of the room to make sure that the principal auctioneer does not miss any bids. An electronic currency converter on the wall to the right of the lots keeps a clicking tab of the bidding process, only milliseconds behind the bids themselves.

The atmosphere at the outset of the auction is tense and breathless. Bidders are anxious to arrive as late as possible so that they can nab prime positions at the back of the room. The most serious bidding is done by those standing at the back, arms folded, scanning the room, minutely nodding as inconspicuously as possible. At the auction itself the objects fade into the background, as they sit smugly upon the revolving plinth. The real focus is on the development of price, and people have to concentrate hard upon each other to keep up with the proceedings. The object has been examined carefully before, now all it has to do is live up to its estimate.

The Sotheby show starts slowly, most lots selling for well within their estimates, often to absentee bidders. A large number of objects are passed over.[10] Of the Pacific pieces, a set of Maori greenstone pendants (lots 111–15) are all bought by telephone bids, probably by the same person, although it is impossible to verify this. A multi-millionaire, currently collecting Polynesian art very seriously, buys lot 121, a Solomon Islands outliers figure, for $10,350. Most of the bigger pieces fail to reach their estimates or are passed over. A major London dealer buys a series of small wooden Sepik River figures, all pictured together (provenance: 'collected by Inge-bourg de Beausacq in New Guinea in the 1950s') and New Guinea masks, all at higher prices than their estimates. People murmur among themselves about this. He also buys lot 153, one of the showcase pieces, 'a rare northern New Ireland mask'. This mask is lavishly illustrated in the catalogue, the value is conjectured primarily by its affinity to all aspects of primitivism that appeal to the moderns: the ground of the mask is deathly white, the cowrie eyes glare at you underneath a rust 'mohican' head-dress. Despite emphasis upon the rarity of the piece and that it comes from the area of specialization of a curator at the Metropolitan Museum of Art, the piece did not live up to its predicted value at auction. The estimate was for $40–60,000 and noticing the slowness of the bidding, the dealer buys it for the lowest estimate price. My neighbour whispers that the dealer used to own it himself. One could surmise that this is a safety purchase, an investment for the future, or that he had a particular client in mind. The cases of the New Ireland mask and of the Maori man demon-strate the fundamental unpredictability in the process of setting price. In a sense they are both failures of value, selling for the lowest possible price despite all efforts made by the auction house. This unpredictability accounts for the conservatism and premium on controlled information within the market.

The bidding really picks up at the start of the smaller catalogue. Prior to the sale it was assumed that this would be where the big money lay, indeed this sale made $2,900,350, including buyers' premium, for only 15 objects, as compared to the $2,372,191 of the larger sale of 220 lots. The first piece in the smaller catalogue (lot 220), 'A superb New Caledonian bird head club', sells above its $10–15,000 estimate for $21,850 to an anonymous bidder. Many of the other pieces sell for high prices over the telephone. The star of the show is lot 227, 'An important and rare Fang female reliquary guardian torso'. Estimated at $500–700,000, it sells for $1,542,500 to a man shaded by a hat at the back of the room. Later that week I meet one dealer in the Metropolitan Museum who tells me he bought the piece and that it 'just went up the road' in New York. The piece was given an added proven-ance of ownership by a Parisian dealer present at the sale. When this was announced the room collapsed into spontaneous hissing and booing. This occurred at another instance, when again, he added provenance to a piece. This mass expression of scepticism of dealer's provenance emphasizes the fact that those participants at auction are savvy members of a tightly knit clique, and is a direct expression of the ironies of authenticity that I have highlighted above.

The brief glimpse of the object that we get at the auction itself is the material consolidation of a complex process of historical value formation meditated by agents in the market. The unpredictability of bidding as process enforces a construction of value that must base itself within a complex economy of information stemming from the social relations of a relatively closed community of players. The auction exploits the notion of a public, free market, often to the advantage of private transaction. Each transaction references previous sales and will affect subsequent sales, both private and public, and is itself a complex negotiation between public and private. This elusive interaction between objects and persons forces us to look at the auction itself in a wider artefactual context, from museum, to auction catalogue and view, and then finally to the sale itself. The Sotheby's auction ends with a whimper, people trickling away for the last hour. It is raining outside as we leave, so the crowd of buyers quickly disperses into taxis and cars.

Conclusions

The auction sale is a theatrical production of price, created by market agents, that includes material artefacts as well as persons. It is a performance, complete with stage, lighting, object-props, catalogue-scripts and noisy interactive audience – a well-practised pantomine of price. However, the intensity of this performance may belie the complex and secretive preceding history of the market that dictates to the event of sale.

Viewing the auction as a series of processes rather than a singular event elucidates a working localized concept of value that is both grounded pragmatically and imaginatively constructed within a social hierarchy of information; both historical *and* momentary, material *and* abstract. Analysing auctions in terms of events enhances the interpretation of them as performative 'tournaments' of value. It is only by utilizing this form of 'historical' analysis that we can understand the ways in which objects are priced, primarily in terms of authenticity. The objects themselves play a vital role in marking and upholding these classifications, a role filled with what Gell (1998) terms social 'agency'.

The exploitation of criteria of authenticity is pervasive throughout each event. The value of the authentic, individual object is in a tense relationship with the generalized commercial value of commodities. Jamieson's notion of 'charismatic value' is useful here, by which value is ascribed 'in the first instance by the attitude adopted towards it' (1999: 9), highlighting a potential for instability, epitomized by the shifts of price performed at auction. This concept, linked to an awareness of transaction histories, allows us to transcend the spatio-temporal fixity previously accorded to auctions. However, we must also examine how the object itself is a link that also transcends this. As Keane comments: 'The materiality of words and things exposes actors and actions to the social world: as concrete media, words and things are accessible to a public, bearing formal properties that are open to the evaluative gaze of others' (1997: 231). This combined focus allows for the development of a more insightful methodology of the study of price construction in markets.

We can now begin to reassess the place of the tribal art object (and the materiality of commodities) within a reconsidered space of the market. Benjamin (1992) emphasizes an inherent 'modern' tension between the art object and its potential as reproduction or mass-produced commodity. For Benjamin, the 'reproduction' (or commodity), unlike any 'original', transcends particular time and space (or market). It has been my argument in this chapter that in the auctioning of tribal arts, the original, 'authentic' object also has the power to do this.

In tracing the place of the object in the auction system of value, we have observed its identification by ironic criteria of authenticity, as the focus of a dynamic group of market participants; its display both as commodity *and* reified art form in text, image (manipulated using technologies of mass reproduction, producing many original catalogue-objects, both in print and on the web), and in actuality. In Benjamin's often cited essay, technical reproduction engenders a shift from 'cult' to 'exhibition' value. Here, at auctions, the so-called cult (or authentic) value of the piece exists because of value fixed over a series of events, that is in turn exploited in the exhibition–performance that is price.

The object is the strand that holds the disparate components of the market together. This object, of paradoxical and ironic authenticity, its identity vacillating between that of frequently produced commodity and unique traditional artefact, is both exhibited in the market and sits at the head of a cult, its material form worshipped by the group of charismatic actors who sit in front of it and slyly bid.

NOTES

1 Synonymous with 'Primitive' art in market rhetoric, 'tribal arts' may include Antiquities, Pre-Columbian, African, Indonesian and Oceanic (or Pacific) arts, that are seen as inherently 'traditional' rather than 'contemporary'. Native American and Aboriginal Australian art are generally sold separately and are the only tribal arts that are marketed as 'contemporary' fine art.

2 The literature is extensive. See collected volumes edited by Appadurai (1986), Marcus and Myers (1995) and Steiner and Phillips (1999), also Thomas (1991, 1992) and Morphy (1995). A recent article in *Anthropology Today* by Raymond Corbey (1999) briefly describes the African art market in Brussels. Jeremy MacClancy (1988) does the same for the British market for Tribal Arts. Plattner (1996) has written one of the first 'ethnographies' of the Western art market, following on from debates in classic economic anthropology. Along with Steiner (1994) this has been one of the main stimulants of this study.

3 'Tournaments of value are complex periodic events that are removed in some culturally well-defined way from the routines of economic life. Participation in them is likely to be both a privilege of those in power and an instrument of status contests between them . . . Finally, what is at issue in such *tournaments* is not just status, rank, fame or reputation of actors, but the disposition of the central tokens of value in the society in question.' (Appadurai 1986: 21)

4 In a similar mechanism of state control, once objects have been purchased by the French state, they become inalienable. It is state policy to prohibit the practice of museums selling parts of their collections. This is a common practice in American museums where objects are frequently deaccessioned. See Parke Bernet catalogue (1967) for the auction of deaccessioned objects from the Rockefeller collection at the Metropolitan Museum of Art, New York. Douglas Newton (pers. comm.) comments that objects were deaccessioned if they were 'duplicates', highlighting the role of the auction houses in creating 'authentic' museum collections.

5 Although the recent scandal exposed by Christie's of the rigging of sale prices, and auctioneers' agreements, by both Sotheby's and Christie's demonstrates the ineffectual nature of such legislation, and the reliance of the market on secrecy and controlled information.

6 See Reitlinger (1982). 'Primitive Art' is discussed in volume 3, pp. 638–42.

7 Paul Bator's summary *The International Trade in Art* (1981) provides a useful introduction to some legislative problems concerning the international art market. With reference to Pacific art, Craig (1992) details the development of National Cultural Property legislation in Papua New Guinea, emphasizing the local dealings that supply the Western market. He uncovers a variety of illegal dealings, many involving dealer Wayne Heathcote who was a major buyer at the May Sotheby's auction: 'The activities of dealers such as Wayne Heathcote, Bruce Lawes and Barry Hoare rapidly inflated prices for significant old pieces.

Mackay's 1969 Report ... mentions a Karawari "cult hook" figure purchased in a village by Heathcote for $200 and sold to a Professor Carpenter for $7,000. When it suited the dealers and they could get away with it, they offered relatively small amounts to the owners of old objects. In due course, however, many of the villagers became aware of the overseas market value of their old heirlooms and asked for much higher prices; thus the market was even further inflated. Because of the profits to be made, the dealers were able, to some extent, to absorb these increases or to pass them on to their overseas clients. They were even able to use the situation to price the National Museum out of the local market. As late as 1982, Heathcote was offering double or more what the National Museum could offer and driving up the prices' (Craig 1992: 99–100).

8 The editorial response of *Anthropology Today* was 'We have decided not to publish in *AT* either advance information about auction sales, or advertisements by auction houses, since this might contribute to increases in price levels ... We intend to include retrospective news of the ethnographic art market from time to time' (Gathercole 1987: 22).

9 All prices in this study are as quoted in the published results of the auction houses. This includes (for Sotheby's) a buyer's premium of 15 per cent of the successful bid up to and including $50,000 and of 10 per cent on amounts in excess of $50,000. This price does not include sales tax which in New York City at the time of writing is 8.25 per cent (including buyer's premium).

10 At the Sotheby's sale, out of 382 lots in total, 147 remained unsold.

REFERENCES

Appadurai, Arjun, ed. (1986) *The Social Life of Things*. Chicago, IL: University of Chicago Press.

Bator, Paul (1981) *The International Trade in Art*. Chicago, IL: Midway Reprint, University Press.

Baudrillard, Jean (1981) *For a Critique of the Political Economy of the Sign*. St Louis: Telos Press.

Benjamin, Walter (1992 [1936]) 'The Work of Art in the Age of Mechanical Reproduction', in Hannah Arendt (ed.) *Illuminations*. London: Fontana Press.

Clarke, Alison (1998) 'Window Shopping at Home: Classifieds, Catalogues and New Consumer Skills', in D. Miller (ed.) *Material Cultures: Why Some Things Matter*. London: University College London Press.

Cooper, Jeremy (1977) *Under the Hammer*. London: Constable.

Corbey, Raymond (1999) 'African Art in Brussels', *Anthropology Today* 15 (6): 11–16.

Craig, Barry (1992) 'National Cultural Property in Papua New Guinea: Implications for Policy and Action', *Journal of the Anthropological Society of South Australia* 3 (2): 72–139.

Dilley, Roy (1992) *Contesting Markets: Analyses of Ideology, Discourse and Practice*. Edinburgh: Edinburgh University Press.

Gathercole, Peter (1987) 'Thatcherite Anthropology', *Anthropology Today* 3 (2): 22.

Geertz, Clifford (1979) 'Suq: The Bazaar Economy in Sefrou', in *Meaning and Order in Moroccan Society: Essays in Cultural Analysis*. Cambridge: Cambridge University Press.

Gell, Alfred (1998) *Art and Agency*. Oxford: Oxford University Press.

Hoskins, Janet (1998) *Biographical Objects*. New York: Routledge.

Jamieson, Mark (1999) 'The Place of Counterfeits in Regimes of Value: An Anthropological Approach', *Journal of the Royal Anthropological Institute* (ns) 5 (1): 1–11.

Karp, Ivan and Lavine, Steven, eds (1991) *Exhibiting Cultures: The Poetics and Politics of Museum Display*. Washington: Smithsonian Institution Press.

Keane, Webb (1997) *Signs of Recognition* Berkeley: University of California Press.

Kopytoff, Igor (1986) 'The Cultural Biography of Things', in A. Appadurai (ed.) *The Social Life of Things*. Chicago, IL: University of Chicago Press.

MacClancy, Jeremy (1988) 'A Natural Curiosity: The British Market in Primitive Art', *RES* 15: 163–76.

Marcus, George, and Myers, Fred, eds (1995) *The Traffic in Culture*. Berkeley: University of California Press.

Miller, Daniel (1987) *Material Culture and Mass Consumption*. Oxford: Blackwell.

Miller, Daniel (1998) *Material Cultures: Why Some Things Matter*. London: University College London Press.

Morphy, Howard (1995) 'Aboriginal Art in a Global Context' In D. Miller (ed.) *Worlds Apart: Modernity through the Prism of the Local*. London: Routledge.

O'Doherty, Brian (1986) *Inside the White Cube: The Ideology of Gallery Space*. Santa Monica/San Francisco, CA: Lapis Press.

Parke Bernet catalogue (1967) *Duplicates from the Collection of Governor Nelson A. Rockefeller and the Museum for Primitive Art*, May 4, 1967.

Plattner, Stuart (1996) *High Art Down Home: An Economic Ethnography of a Local Art Market*. Chicago, IL: University of Chicago Press.

Reitlinger, George (1982) *The Economics of Taste*. New York: Hack Art Books.

Smith, Charles W. (1989) *Auctions: The Social Construction of Value*. London: Harvester Wheatsheaf.

Specht, Jim (1987) 'The George Brown Affair Again', *Anthropology Today* 3 (4): 1–4.

Steiner, Christopher (1994) *African Art in Transit*. Cambridge: Cambridge University Press.

Steiner, Christopher and Phillips, Ruth, eds (1999) *Unpacking Culture: Art and Commodity in Colonial and Postcolonial Worlds*. Berkeley: University of California Press.

Strathern, Marilyn (1990) 'Artefacts of History', in Siikala, Jukka (ed.) *Culture and History in the Pacific*. Helsinki: Finnish Anthropological Society.

Thomas, Nicholas (1991) *Entangled Objects: Exchange, Material Culture and Colonialism*. Cambridge, MA: Harvard University Press.

Thomas, Nicholas (1992) 'The Cultural Dynamics of Peripheral Exchange', in Caroline Humphrey and Stephen Hugh Jones (eds) *Barter, Exchange and Value*, Cambridge: Cambridge University Press.

Watson, Peter (1997) *Sotheby's: Inside Story*. London: Bloomsbury.

Chapter 17

It's Showtime: On the Workplace Geographies of Display in a Restaurant in Southeast England

Philip Crang

For two and a half years I worked as a waiter in a barbecue-style theme restaurant, Smoky Joe's,[1] located in the southeast of England. Over the period 1987–90 I spent an average of two or three shifts a week in Smoky's, putting down my academic's books and putting on my waiter's silk waistcoat and bowler hat. In this chapter I report on some of the dialogues between my two jobs.

The Order of Service

Smoky's is a 'Southern American style' barbecue restaurant, that 'style' involving the playing of piped jazz and blues music throughout the restaurant, and the display of pictures of jazz and blues musicians on the walls. Smoky's was one of a chain of about ten restaurants in Britain when I worked there, although the multinational catering and leisure company that owns them planned to increase this to over fifty in the following five years. It includes a bar and a restaurant which seats up to 170 customers. It has a kitchen in the cellar beneath the restaurant seating area, but this is used for pre-preparation, and the final cooking is done upstairs in a windowed kitchen in the middle of the restaurant itself.[2] The number of staff fluctuates considerably because of high staff turnover, but on average there are about thirty employees of whom about half are full-time or part-time waiting staff. Of those waiting staff the vast majority are women, whereas most kitchen and bar staff are men. The menu is based around barbecued ribs, steaks and burgers and the 'average spend per head' or cost of meal was, when I left in 1990, approximately £12. Smoky's is therefore neither a fast-food restaurant – because of cost and because an average customer stays for just over an hour – nor traditional haute cuisine – much of the food is bought in pre-prepared and formal service etiquette is deliberately not adhered to. Instead it occupies what Mars and Nicod have classified as the 'ambiguous middle' between mass and individualistic consumption dispositions and service styles (1984: 36). Smoky's set its stall in that market by stressing its friendly, informal and fun service product, in turn linking that product to its geographical 'location', the Southern United States. In Finkelstein's terminology, Smoky's is a 'parodic restaurant', chosen by diners who wish 'to be amused and entertained' through its 'blatant . . . fully engineered atmosphere' (1989: 28–9).

The managerial surveillance and control of such a service style is, however, far from simply engineered. Of course, a standard routinization of service delivery is one potential, if partial, solution (Leidner, 1991, 1993), especially if standardization across a chain of outlets is desired (Christopherson 1989). To this effect, Smoky Joe's has an 'order of service'; that is, the company specifies a series of operations – twenty-three in total, involving sixteen visits to the table – which waiting staff must perform for every customer, and which set out the standard 'path' of the service they receive. As a waiter, I therefore began my encounter with a table and its customers by going over to them and beginning with a standard greeting – it went something like, 'Hi, my name's Phil and I'm your waiter tonight. Here's some popcorn for you while you look at the menu, and could I get you anything to drink now as well?' – and ended my contact with them with a standardized and specified farewell, calling 'see you again, good night!' as customers left. In between these two moments I was meant to follow the full order of service, which ran as follows:[3]

1   Go to table, introduce self, offer popcorn, and take drinks order (within two minutes).
2   Fetch drinks and deliver to table (within five minutes).
3   Take food order; offer choice of potatoes with all, choice of cooking on steaks and burgers. Suggest wine and side orders. Check drinks anyway.
4   Fetch drinks if necessary.
5   Deliver starters.
6   Clear starter plates, check drinks, and 'call table away'[4] to kitchen.
7   Take out correct main course cutlery and bibs if necessary (with ribs).
8   Take out main course food, do 'towel, napkin and tooth-pick speech' if eating ribs.[5] Offer ketchup, mustards (if steak) and relishes. Say 'Enjoy your meal'.
9   Check back on food (within two minutes), and ask about drinks.
10 Take out hot towels at end of main course if ribs.
11 Clear main course plates and empty glasses.
12 Take out dessert menus.
13 Take dessert order; suggest coffee and liqueurs.
14 Deliver desserts.
15 Deliver coffee, with mints, bill and comment card. Say 'pay me whenever you are ready', and draw attention to the comment card.
16 Take payment, close the table on the till, take back change.
17 Say 'see you again' as customers leave.

Such an order is not only a guide to staff; it specifies information for managerial surveillance, and enables intervention in the work of waiting staff. Both by panoptical gazing from vantage points in the restaurant – viewing whether dirty glasses are still on tables, how long diners remain unattended, whether food is getting cold on the kitchen counter – and through 'management by walking around' (Peters 1988; Peters and Waterman 1982) – overhearing conversations, chatting to customers to see if they are content – the restaurant managers could, aided by the division of the restaurant floor into sections of tables for which only one member of staff was responsible, monitor individual waitresses' and waiters' performance and try to enforce adherence to the order of service. In addition, corporate management from outside the branch sent in regular 'mystery diners' to produce service quality reports, which although not explicitly identifying an individual server formed the basis of general staff briefings on those parts of the order being neglected.

But such surveillance processes of information collection, work supervision and behaviour modification (Dandeker 1990) do not, in themselves, guarantee the production of a high-quality service product (Christopher 1984; Collier 1987; Klaus 1985; Lehtinen and Lehtinen 1991; Levitt 1980; Nightingale 1985; Saleh and Ryan 1991). For a start, such surveillance must not be too intense or it itself can harm product quality; managers looming over waiting staff and diners as they talk would both be intrusive and make rather too explicit the corporate functionality of the interaction. A workplace geography constituted through the co-presence of (some) producers and consumers has implications for the management of the former (Whyte 1948, 1949); in this case a disincentive to employ the kinds of minute scrutiny Braverman identifies in Taylor's scientific management (Braverman 1974; Taylor 1947) and to use looser forms of control, such as customer tips, to supplement the order of service. Thus in Smoky's, tips, and the social relations with customers that produced or did not produce them, were quantitatively and qualitatively central to the experience of waiting work. With no service charge they went directly to waiting staff, were kept by those they were given to (minus a small 'tip-out' for the kitchen staff), and accounted for the majority of our payment (in my case my wages from the company averaged about 30 per cent of my total earnings). If someone asked me 'did you have a good night?' I knew they meant 'did you get good tips?'

But there are also important pressures coming from the conception of the service product that tips are meant to reward. If cast as completely standardized then a tightly scripted and rigidly enforced and/or practised service delivery script can be used (fast-food outlets provide much cited examples; see Gabriel 1988; Leidner 1993). But many definitions of service – from producers and consumers, as well as from academics – place limits to such rigidity. For example, Mars and Nicod (1984), in their study of British hotels and their waiting staff, defined service as follows:

> '. . . service . . . refers to an action or material thing that is more than one might normally expect. In a transport cafe it can mean no more than passing the sauce bottle with a smile. In the Savoy it might mean making a prodigious effort to supply a rare delicacy. . . [it is] *that something extra . . .*' (p. 28, my emphasis).

Now an order of service can in itself try to provide some 'extras' – free popcorn in the case of Smoky's – but obviously this comes to be expected by regular customers, and in that sense stops being one. Moreover, there is a second element to the above definition: service as spontaneous, sincere, personally meant for you and you alone. An extra is thus not an extra not only if everyone gets it, but also if it does not 'mean' anything (that is, it is not meant). Orders of service, as standardized service routines, can therefore not only be non-contributory to, but actually directly problematic for, this ideal of service.

And it is such an ideal that is the advertised service style of Smoky's. As I have already said, it is situated in a growing, or at least reconstituted, middle market between haute cuisine and family restaurants on the one hand, and fast food on the other, thus cutting across simple dualisms of restaurant meals as 'convenience goods or luxuries' (Frisbee and Madeira 1986). Management frown on the stuffy formality and etiquette of 'traditional' restaurants but wish to distinguish Smoky's from cheaper fast-food competitors. In turn, such a distinction cannot really be achieved through either technical skill (both waiting staff and chefs are thoroughly deskilled in craft terms, allowing minimal training and the numerical flexibility of high turnover); or through a non-standardized menu (because of the extent of food pre-preparation); rather it has to be based in a slightly distinctive menu (with some Cajun dishes) and, above all, in the social relations of the restaurant, in particular those of waiter or waitress and customer (clearly more than the bare materiality of the food is being bought when dining out (for example, see Finkelstein 1989; MacClancy 1992; Mennell et al. 1989)). Smoky's is in its own corporate words 'the home of hospitality'. Thus, there may be an order of service, but the service and social relations that are ordered with the meal is deliberately indeterminate and individualized.

To recap, then, there was, in being a waiter or waitress at Smoky's, a necessary autonomy from direct managerial control, and in turn a managerial need to provide some surveillance of that autonomy, which arose for three reasons: first, because the geography of the workplace provided limits to the level of direct surveillance possible by management; second, because the order of service is not, and indeed in Smoky's is not meant to be, a definition of the service that the waitress or waiter must produce; and, third, because, given this, the provision of service by waiting staff remains what Crompton and Jones (1984) call an 'indeterminate skill', somewhat outside the scope of deskilling, not least because managers, and in the abstract, capital, need it to be incompletely rationalized and replicable. As such, experiences of doing the work were less dominated by a reduction of the self on display to a prewritten script, and revolved around rather more improvisational performances; performances that used and at times abused a script such as the order of service, but did not simply enact it; performances that involved social relations of display that were more than the projections of managerial surveillance strategies.

A Double Shift

I want to begin to illustrate the complexities of such performances by outlining a single double shift that I did on a sunny Friday in June 1989, written through – initially the day after, then in subsequent redrafts – in terms of four 'ideal type' periodizations of working time and space in Smoky's.

Quiet Days

I begin with a quiet weekday daytime (the restaurant was open from 11 a.m. to 11 p.m. daily):

> *The pace of work is relaxed with few customers, and waiting on tables is interspersed with my favourite tasks of preparation such as polishing pictures on the wall or stocking*

up desserts from the freezer in the cellar. There is only me 'on' so there are no sections and no one except the manager to answer to, and he is working in the office on paperwork. I have a real feeling of freedom and ownership. During the daytime, apart from lunch, the restaurant feels like a place out of its proper time. We are open to customers but the deliveries for the kitchen and bar have arrived and I am helping carry them in. It is a relaxed feeling of not quite having started work for real. Most waitresses have lots of cups of coffee during the day but not drinking the stuff I just find any excuse to sit at tables and gaze out the window (wiping and refilling salt and pepper pots is a good one; I did that for at least an hour today). Lunch is just about right; five tables, nicely staggered, all give OK tips, and are no real work. In the afternoon having tidied up there is only Sid in the kitchen and Piers in the bar, so we are chatting quite a lot. Piers makes a cocktail too big and gives Sid and me the leftovers.

Getting Going

After an hour break at 5 p.m. I return for the evening shift. More waiting staff begin to arrive; most begin at 6 or 7 p.m., and there should have been a total of eight of us by 8 p.m. (it is a Friday), but only six turn up:

It is 6.30 p.m. and the restaurant does not look like it will get really busy until about 8 p.m. as the weather is too nice. I have done all of the preparation during the day and time is dragging. The others are chatting in small groups around those places where they can find or pretend to find jobs to do, such as the popcorn machine, the dessert area or the dispense area [this is where the bar make drinks for the restaurant]. Now the managers have begun to patrol the restaurant floor and so we are all looking for jobs to do.[6] As my tables begin to arrive, relations with customers also have a slightly uneasy, restless quality. I have almost too little to do. Since I am bored I am 'pouncing' on my customers, when they arrive and in clearing away dishes etc. What is more, the jazz and blues music [that always plays] is turned up louder as the evening begins, and there is a general feeling of 'psyching up' or getting in the mood; I laugh with Jody that I feel like it's my party and I'm waiting for everyone to arrive. We laugh about that, and act out a little routine. She is pretty good [Jody was at drama school], which cracks me up. Kelvin [the manager] comes along and asks us what we are laughing about, and smiles to humour us. We move on to find something to do. I go down to dispense for a chat (Heather and Louise are there), and then I go down to the cold store to get some more cream, and sit down there doing nothing for a while. Even when tables arrive the general uneasiness, the waiting, is accentuated by what I can only call 'timing difficulties' with the customers. I normally try and exchange small talk with all my tables, to try and make sure that I have said something unique to each table, to be personal enough so it is hard for them not to tip, while at the same time not speaking for so long as to presume they are really interested in me as if I was a friend. When busy the breaking off of a conversation is fairly easy since there are other tasks to do. But now, when I am not busy, the break off is followed by standing doing nothing, looking a bit of a lemon. There's nothing more to prepare, so I just go back and stand by the till, and somehow the conventions and instrumentality of the talk I've just done seem really obvious and embarrassing. Generally I do not quite feel in the swing of it yet.

Waiting and Running Around

Once the evening shift had got busy the experience of the work changed totally. These are notes I scribbled at the end of that Friday night shift, the busiest for at least a month, aimed at recording how it had felt rather than what had happened:

> Bloody busy tonight. I'd forgotten what it was like. Had 8 tables in my section...and just about full from 8.30 on. The feelings were amazing. Panic – I screamed at Chris in the bar, and at John [the deputy manager] to stop giving me tables. I really wanted to cry. Now I'm great. It all clicked. I had a direction in my life, I was lost, like dancing. And good tips (£35). I feel so happy – its embarrassing but its true, I feel really great...

The next morning I added these notes:

> Very busy last night. I did 50 covers, the most I have done in ages (the night before I had done 30). Kelvin had decided to not turn anyone away even though we were short-staffed, which is what any manager would do, but everyone was really slagging him off for being a bastard. I had clutched my head and looked pretty desperate when he gave me an eighth table and I still had two I had not seen and one to clear. He told me to just get on with it. Wisely with Kelvin I then kept my head down...Everyone was losing their rag a bit. The chefs were shouting at the order machine every time an order came through. The atmosphere was pretty frantic, though June was calm like normal; John was telling me to calm down, but I hardly had time to listen. Lots of rows...I had to ask for some more barbecue sauce for 31, and the kitchen were already mad at me for asking where table 28's food was. They told me where to go. It wasn't my fault that they asked for it. I rushed down to the bar for 32's lager but it wasn't done. Everyone was moaning under their breath and staring at Chris the barman for being too slow with the drinks. I remember saying This is a joke'.

And I tried to summarize and reflect on the experience of the previous night thus:

> An initial panic and despair at not being able to cope with the pace of work, coupled with a demonstrative rushing around and impatience with any delay is eventually replaced by a fragile order, the reduction of customers to ticks on a list. All movement now has a direction, there is none of the earlier aimless congregating; I map out my priorities, I am heading somewhere all the time, and have the next four or five destinations planned out too. Yet this order is vulnerable. Firstly, any interruptions by customers are likely to throw it all into disarray. For that reason I try to control all contacts with tables, for example moving around all my tables to see if there are any queries when I have a spare minute rather than waiting to be called. Secondly, for me that sense of direction and the sheer amount of energy I'm expending mean I need a constant boost; and that is given by tips. If they don't come my motivation collapses. Luckily last night they were pretty good so that feeling of occasional despair as it all gets too much seems worth it.

Clearing Up, Winding Down, and Beyond

The final type of work time was the period of clearing up which usually lasted until at least 1.30 a.m., and on this occasion until 2.10 a.m., a period which saw the directionality to time and space collapsing:

I have a clear aim and that is to finish as quickly as possible, but I am shattered. Most of the others have gone to have a smoke, or a drink at the bar. I begin to skive too. I chat to Penelope as we sweep up, about what sort of night it has been. I take a long time to avoid being the one to clean the cappuccino machine. I manage it; Jody does it. She doesn't mind it, she says. I do the sweeping of the top, and wipe all the cutlery down with Heather. We chat about not very much; a little about me going full time for a while, about Kelvin letting the place be full, and a bit about my research. We also get some chips off Tony in the kitchen, before he chucks them. Heather says she's going out with Jenny et al. on Sunday, but I'm on a day shift. When we finally finish, I go and cash out, and by the time I've finished it's just about all done; just put out mints and napkins in the bottom. Kelvin inspects it all, especially the fridges, and says it's fine, so I get my stuff and buy some drinks with my hard earned cash while we wait for the taxis. Lean is reading some Julian Barnes book very conspicuously; she's such a pose. Dave is on the pinball machine. I sit by myself, until Jody comes over. She's still totally up, and starts pinching Dave's bum as he leans over. They chase around a bit. Her energy is limitless... By the time the taxis come, I can hardly be bothered to go home; I know when I do I will probably just flop and watch night-time TV (another French detective film with Alain Delon or The Hitman and Her). A load of people seem to be going to Heather's house, though interestingly none of the kitchen, where Donna has been having a party, and I'm tempted but after a double I'm just not up for it so I get the taxi to drop me off at home. Sit and watch TV till 4.30, then go to bed as it's getting light. Would feel good if I wasn't on again tonight.

Playing a Role

It's showtime!

In thinking through the sort of experiences inscribed above, and their complex relations of display, the motif of performance is a fairly obvious one to choose in Smoky's case. There is, after all, an explicit corporate aim to put on a show in the restaurant. The handbook given to all new staff bore the slogan 'It's showtime!' on its cover; a notice in the restaurant told customers to contact their 'show director' if they had any problems; the shift roster was headed 'cast performances'; and the uniform which 'packaged staff' (Solomon 1988) was, with its waistcoat and bowler hat, more like a costume. Exemplars of working practice and service content followed suit. The application form for the job asked explicitly for any dramatical experience, and many staff did come from stage backgrounds and used their skills as part of their work: for example, Jessica was a dance student and when her section was not busy often practised her routines around the tables to the piped jazz music; Vanessa was a budding singer, and spent one out of every five shifts singing live swing music in the restaurant. And, on a slightly different tack, during my first year at the restaurant perhaps the most praised waitress – she featured in a national corporate recruitment video – was 'Disco Dolly'. Disco Dolly was in fact the self-pronounced alter ego of Anne, the latter locating herself as a left-wing, middle-class lesbian, the former, located by Anne as a pastiche of the 'glossy' she was not. At her most buoyant Dolly would ironically dance around her purse in the middle of the restaurant, in mock imitation of the stereotype of women she scorned: the dolly birds of the disco dance floor. But even more generally, within Smoky's her alias was rarely dropped; Disco Dolly was what it said on her name badge; Dolly was what, except for those who knew her outside of the restaurant, we all called her.

Of course these extremes were not the norm. Later on in my time at Smoky's a staff competition was set up with a free weekend holiday for the best song and dance routine devised by staff to ask customers their orders. Dolly had left by then, and not even Jessica entered. In fact no one did. And corporate hype clearly does not equate with everyday realities. Shifts are called just that by staff; not shows or performances.[7] But the explicit use of dramatic metaphors by the corporate originators of Smoky Joe's highlights both the particular definition of the service product being sold and a more generally performative character to the waiting work being done; a character that many accounts of that work have drawn attention to. For example, in their study of waiters in hotels, Mars and Nicod (1984: 35–6) note:

> Whatever the level of hotel, waiters must always aim to meet the expectations of their customers. They do this by offering an idealized view of their situation, which involves concealing or underplaying activities, facts and motives which are incompatible with the impression they are attempting to put over. *They are actors putting on a performance...* (My emphasis)

And Hochschild (1983 and chapter 18, this volume), in examining the work of airline flight attendants, cogently demonstrates that such acting is not all on the surface; there is a deeper, Stanislavskian performing – an 'emotional management and labour' – in the work of caring about and smiling to customers.

Certainly the metaphor of performance was employed, and debated, by us waiting staff in Smoky's. And these performances felt emotional, albeit reflecting rather more amateur dramatics than the disciplined method acting Hochschild saw being trained for at Delta Airlines. Thus at the beginning of an evening shift people talked about 'getting in the mood', standing around doing their make work, chatting, and maybe half-dancing to the music; busy nights were emotional roller-coasters, full of swapped stories and swear words at the bar dispense area, the occasional shout of frustration at the chefs or barmen, the whispered obscenity when there was no tip, the satisfied grin and feeling of real pleasure when there was; somewhat symbolically, I found in my scratch notes the first words to me from Alice, a waitress on her first night (a busy Friday): 'Hi. God this place is weird. It's hysterical.'

Performative encounters

But the metaphor of waiting work at Smoky's as performative, as role playing, needs clarification and elaboration. How does such role playing work as a process? And what can it tell us about the character of waiting work as a social activity? I want to think about those questions by looking more explicitly at, to use a term from Goffman, what we might call the social 'encounters', the face-to-face interactions, between staff and customers, that make up much of the experience of waiting work (Goffman 1961, 1964, 1967, 1971, 1983; Kendon 1988). In part I do so in order to try to offer a slightly more subtle understanding of performance than that apparent in terms such as 'scripting' or 'engineering'; above all I want an understanding that allows for the interactional quality of mine and my colleagues' waiting work. But

I also use the idea of performative encounters because many commentators on so-called 'service employments' have understood their social significance by rhetorically stressing, if only scantily elaborating, the interpersonal character of some instances of such work; it is, they argue, about dealing with people not material things. For example, Bell (1973: 163) proclaims the coming of 'post-industrial' work by arguing that

> what is central to the new relationship is encounter or communication, and the response of ego to alter and back – from the irritation of a customer at an airline ticket office to the sympathetic or harassed response of teacher to student. But the fact that individuals now talk to other individuals, rather than interact with a machine, is the fundamental fact about work in the post-industrial society.

And more recently management literature on service provision returns to the theme of its interpersonal character, by stressing its constitution in innumerable 'moments of truth' (a phrase taken from the then chief executive of SAS airline, Jan Carlzon (1987)) or 'service encounters' (Czepeil et al. 1985). Now, what I want to do here is explicitly not to proclaim some epochal shift in employment experiences, but instead to use some of Goffman's concepts concerning social encounters to think in rather more detail about the character of service performances: and I will do that by briefly considering the ways in which that encounter in Smoky's is defined by participants, by looking at some aspects of the organization of the encounter itself, then turning to the forms of interaction it involves, before finally drawing out some observations on the resultant character of the encounter.

Defining the encounter

Perhaps the most fundamental import of Goffman's dramaturgical metaphor for social life, and of seeing that social life as made up by innumerable social situations of face-to-face interaction, is the stressing of the context dependency of social 'action'. That is, he suggests that the social role played by an individual is not a constant one, but dependent upon interactions in an encounter and the character of that particular encounter itself. He writes,

> The self...as performed character, is not an organic thing that has specific location...[the performer and] his body merely provide the peg on which something of a collaborative manufacture will be hung for a time. (Goffman 1956: 252–3)

Thus of crucial importance in the social relations of performative encounters are the defining processes of the situation or context of that 'collaborative manufacture'.

Such definitional processes are particularly significant at the outset of an encounter. Indeed, Goffman uses Whyte's earlier work on restaurants, and his concern with 'who gets the jump' between waitress and customer, as his exemplification of the point:

> The first point that stands out is that the waitress who bears up under pressure does not simply respond to her customers. She acts with some skill to control their behaviour. The first question to ask when we look at the customer relationship is, 'Does the waitress get the jump on the customer, or does the customer get the jump on the waitress?' (Whyte 1946: 132–3; cited in Goffman 1956: 5)

In this light, Smoky's order of service was in part a managerial attempt to define, crucially for customers as well as staff, the terms of the encounter envisaged, and it was used as such by waiting staff. Hence the name-giving speech we performed ('Hi, my name is Phil, I'm your waiter this evening . . . ') suggested both the character of the service (personalized), and the principle of monogamous possession (I am your waiter, you are my customers) that minimized disturbance for other waiting staff and anchored tips. And certainly, talk of 'awkward customers' (usually in less bland language) clearly identified them as those who refused the definitions that waiting staff or company wanted to offer: the table who wanted to be treated as if in a really posh restaurant, with individually chosen food rather than the standard menu choices; or those who would not talk to only 'their' waiter or waitress.

But there is more to this definitional process than a simple opposition. Indeed, the general tone of Goffman's body of work on social encounters carries with it a clear stress on the achieved character of situational definition, and on the necessity of that achievement (rather than solely oppositions over it) for social life to go on. He thus talks about the need for a 'working consensus' of the situation to be established and refined. So, far from simply imposing themselves and their definition of the situation on customers, we waiting staff, to some extent, tried to imagine – and if necessary reimagine – what the customer wanted. In part this involved employing terms to classify first impressions of customers, arranging them into types. Thus there were 'Garys and Sharons' (namings of middle-class English snobbery), 'Americans', 'students', 'lads', 'couples', 'regulars', 'snobs', 'foreign students', 'stag and hen nights', 'office parties', and people 'from the University' amongst others. Such classifications then acted as a starting point in gauging what role waiting staff themselves should play. They were a first step in the vital skill that our managers called 'knowing your customers'. Of course, they were only a first step. The definition of any encounter was being constantly monitored and negotiated as it progressed; as Turner puts it, 'Interaction is always a tentative process, a process of continuously testing the conception one has of the role of the other' (1962: 23).

Moreover, such testing and negotiation also involved working with and on other participants' conceptions of the encounter. Thus, for example, staff usually attempted to define the encounter as one where a tip was an expectation for reasonable service, but this had to be done in ways such that the information about it appeared to be 'given off' rather than simply 'given' (Goffman 1963). That is, this definition had to be made to appear as if unintentionally exchanged; even if it was not. To reveal its intentionality ran the risk of transforming the definition of the encounter, and thus its socially sanctioned behaviour, towards something rather different: say that of encountering a beggar or a mugger. Indeed I, for one, attempted to define the encounter and my role in it more generally through the giving off of information, not least through a tactic of 'notable' posing: for instance, when waiting for late food, I would, if I had time, be engaged in a deliberately furious looking at the kitchen, for although this did not make the food arrive any faster, as the chefs often fairly bluntly pointed out to me, that was not the point of the display in the first place. The aim was to define my role as the concerned waiter, the encounter as one where delays reflected on the restaurant not on me. Or, I and others used expressions of how busy we were, not explicitly directed at customers, but instead usually given to fellow members of staff in a waving of arms, or a holding of the head, and thus given off to customers as they gazed upon the restaurant space, to suggest how hard we were working for them.[8] Of course, in turn, customers could 'play' with the supposed latency of such definitions: at its most malicious this could be when a special 'favour' was met with the comment, 'Don't worry, we know you want a big tip'. There was no quick response to this, or at least I never developed one; just embarrassment (as given off information was taken as given), and powerlessness (because along with my preoccupation with tips, what was being made clear was the temporal inequality of the situation; the customers could, after all, still not tip).

Overall, then, the order of service simply provided a skeleton, and the showtime theme a managerial expectation, around which staff could build their roles through the initial reading of customers as sign-vehicles, and the refinement of those readings as the encounter continued in part with the cooperation of, and in part in a rather timid and petty guerrilla combat with, those being served.

Organizing the encounter

To supplement this account of some of the definitional processes of the service encounter in Smoky's, I want to make three brief points on their organization. First, Whyte's combative metaphor of 'getting the jump' stresses the crucial definitional impact of the initial stages of interaction, but in Smoky's the boundaries of that interaction did not simply comprise the opening and final gambits of the order of service. Rather, and to use Goffman's terminology, encounters between waiting staff and customers were made up of a number of 'focused' interactions – when customers and staff pursued a joint project, such as order taking, usually at the customers' table; 'unfocused' interactions, as both sets of participants gazed upon the displayed activities of the other but carried out separate projects – as when staff were dealing with other tables; and some breaks in face-to-face interaction – principally when restaurant staff were out of sight (in the kitchen, the dessert area, or more often, the bar), or when tables were engrossed in their own internal interactions. The coexistence of these various sorts of interaction impacted greatly on the overall encounter and, in particular, the odd combination of tact and competition that characterized them. In terms of tact, it was at such boundary points that the maintenance of the encounter often became most tenuous, and thus required the greatest work. It was at such points that norms of interest in and respect for fellow participants were most fragile. But, of course, where there is a requirement for tact and cooperation, there are also opportunities for powerful disruptions. Thus, whereas on the majority of occasions tables of customers and staff mutually dealt with the opening of a focused interaction – the table accepting staff had other duties, waiting for a chance to catch their eye politely, the waitress acknowledging their interest, paying attention to them from the other side of the room with a nod or a look, and signalling a desire to be with them as soon as possible – such openings were also opportunities for slights, and exhibitions of domination. Thus customers clicked their fingers – and staff muttered 'I'm not a dog'; and, on the other hand, staff ignored requests for attention – or rather, attempted to give off an appearance of not seeing them – until they could deal with them in their own time. Of course these two types of ruptures – by customers and staff – are not equivalent: customers who wished to exercise domination could do so explicitly, take pleasure in being seen to do it; staff's pleasures, at least if they still held hopes for the contractual fulfilment of a tip, were in implicit control, in keeping one's own choice of place and timing for interaction, whilst appearing to be serving another. But in both cases the spatio-temporal placing of various types of interaction is a vital component of the waiting service encounter.

Second, and given this, this encounter is about movements as well as stops. In the notes about a double shift earlier on, I tried to give a flavour of how staff moved in the course of their work: how when busy we rushed from table to bar, and back to table, to the kitchen counter, back to a table, and then to the till to put in an order and so on. Especially come the evening, the managers hated us being stationary, unless talking to a table: in part because it was idle, but also because movement made the restaurant buzz. In some ways a constant movement to our work enacted both a peculiar organizational structure, where customers' demands go straight to staff without any mediation by managers (see Whyte 1948), and cast waiters and waitresses as an embodiment of service and the power of the customer. And yet, this rushing around was not just the enactment of customers' demands; as tables kept being sat down it may have felt like working on a speeding up assembly line, but because it was us who moved and not the components (diners, food, drink, cutlery, etc.) (in contrast, for example, to the 'burgerline' of McDonald's (TIC 1987)) the politics of the performers' movements were not quite that neat. Although managers might insist we kept on moving from our various gathering and chatting 'stations' (dispense at the bar, the popcorn machine, the tills), and even stipulated forms of movement (for example, running was frowned on as both panicky and dangerous) we could use and manage that movement: so, for me, walking with a determinedly quick stride both expressed and maintained – by brushing off all but the most determined customer interruptions – that wonderful feeling of having my own direction, and at the same time tempered any frustration felt by customers with a notable performance of my dutiful work rate.

As for the stops, these too could be managed, negotiated and contested. In part this concerned when and where they happened; customers could be awkward not only by having a different definition of the encounter than us waiting staff but also by placing it or its moments differently (say, by asking for a drink as you stand by the till, rather than waiting until you come to their table). But precisely how a stop signalled a break from movement, and what sort of break it signalled, was also part of the performance: through deliberately keeping on moving, at least slowly, to signal the inappropriateness of a stop; to an efficient attentiveness when busy; or to a deliberately extended and more intimate stay where one might, expressing a desire to rest for a moment, sit down at a table for a stage of the order of service (a technique initiated by Disco Dolly, picked up by corporate managers as an advised service technique, but used only by some staff).

The third and final aspect of the organization of the encounters between waiting staff and customers that I want to look at leads on from this, and concerns the recognition – and blurring – of clear 'teams' in the interaction taking place (once more the term is Goffman's 1956: 47–65). In its basic structure the restaurant encounter is clearly about two different groups – producers and consumers, staff and customers – with slightly different interests, meeting in a face-to-face inter-action. The expressions of this were numerous, but included: the constant linguistic distinction of the two groups, including phrases that depersonalized the other group (waiting staff talked about 'tables' and 'covers' rather than customers); some distinction as to the areas of the restaurant into which staff and customers might venture; and sets of behaviour that tended to derogate, or at least lampoon, the other team in its absence, whilst building solidarity in one's own team.[9] But in Smoky's this dichotomy is only part of the story. Waiting staff partially cross sides. To acknowledge this goes beyond simply noting that the staging talk about 'them' and 'us' was different from the 'working consensus', the truce, established during the moments of encounter themselves. Instead, it emphasizes that we waiting staff worked at a corporate boundary (Adams 1976; Bowen and Schneider 1985), that a constituent part of the role we often played was to be our tables' ally: a 'mediator' dealing with the restaurant on their behalf (asking the kitchen for an extra portion of barbecue sauce, a few more chips, and so on); an 'informer', dealing the dirt on the restaurant, whilst staying as clean as possible themselves ('the kitchen staff are new tonight, so everything is a little slower than usual, but I'll get everything as fast as I can'); even a 'traitor' (bypassing the EPOS system and getting free desserts to 'keep' a tip).

Forms of interaction

The character of service encounters in Smoky's was not, however, completely determined through their processes of definition and organization. The form that interaction took also mattered. Thus, the experience of this waiting work in focused interaction was marked by the importance of talk, and, for valued service, of constructing a conversational form both pleasing to the customer (deferential, friendly, cheeky, whatever), and above all extending beyond the expected functional requirements of ordering and receiving a meal. And in unfocused interaction it was visual gazing that opened up the space for staff to perform their jobs. Of course such gazing varied in its character and direction: gazing was done by management – not only with regard to what staff did but also how they looked; by staff; and by customers. But much of it, unsurprisingly, used various gazes as instruments for masculine power: focused on women, defining subject and object apart, and the feminine as she whom is to be looked at rather than she who is to do the looking (Kappeler 1986; Mulvey 1975). Through such processes, and especially their coupling to the politics of encounter organization and definition outlined above, the geographies of display that characterized Smoky's could, and often did, make it a highly masculinist space. Let me give four illustrations, via research diary extracts: they in part concern, respectively, ogling and flirting in the restaurant as a whole; the kitchen staff reversing the gaze directed upon them by customers; and sexual harassment of waiting staff.

Research Diary (August, 1988) *42 covers on Saturday night, and I got off quite lightly as started late. Really brought home to me how different it is at weekends; less families apart from early on, the bar packed out, a lot of people my age or younger, everyone really dresses up. It's actually quite fun to be around it; just looking about, things going on, people looking good, its enjoyable to see it all, makes me feel like I've gone out...*

Research Diary (May, 1988) *Something really odd last night that I should probably begin with. The kitchen have got score cards made up, and every time a woman walks*

past their window, they hold them up in judgement. I thought Marcus [the manager]
would stop them, but he didn't say a thing. Heather and Lisa called them prats to me,
and I agreed... Contrast with notes a few weeks back about them being on display
behind that window, on show to customers; this was like them reversing that, behaving
as if they couldn't be seen, or at least like they were separate, and looking out, and
extending that really macho masculine ethos of the kitchen [all but two of the chefs in
my two and a half years at the restaurant were men]... Very different sort of gendering
to the restaurant, that more effeminate ogling I guess...

Research Diary (February, 1990) *Last night Kelvin finally agreed to ban stag parties.*
Julie had a table that were really obnoxious; she said they had kept on asking for Virgin
Coladas, Multiple Orgasms etc., asking her if she wanted one (ha ha) and really leering.
She was really pissed off with them, but said she wouldn't give them the satisfaction of
getting her to change tables, though Kelvin offered that I would take over (lovely!).
Eventually, she was saying at the till that she was acting really offy, not saying anything
at all to them, but they didn't let up; then, when she went to Table 29 [on the other side
of the restaurant] one of them shouted something like 'Julie's got great tits; I love your
tits, Julie'. His mates shut him up sort of, and Julie ignored them, but got Kelvin and he
asked them to pay their bill and leave (they were on their coffees anyway)...

Research Diary (January, 1989) *Also Julian got a bit of hassle last night from a table of*
blokes who kept calling him 'darling' and saying he wasn't their type and they wanted a
waitress. He was pretty upset I think. Oddly enough despite all the drunken men in here
the place is not normally terribly homophobic; it's not like a gay bar, but a lot of staff are
out, and that also seems to be part of the package sold here, a bit of homosexual frisson.

Such forms of interaction suggest that the situational selves performed in Smoky's
are, unsurprisingly, involved in everyday identity politics (see also Kay 1985). In part
this meant that 'looks mattered', in both senses of the phrase. Looking was a gendered
and sexualized activity, as was being looked at. And gendered conceptions of the body
and beauty infiltrated and sexualized the waiting work done in Smoky's (more
generally on the sexualizing of service work see Adkins 1992; Wolf 1990).[10] But
also it becomes clear here that gender and sexuality operate in the waiting performance not simply, to use Goffman's phrase, as 'ascribed characteristics' that inevitably
follow subjects into interaction to be used as definitional resources, but also as crucial
grounds of and stakes in that interaction. That is, gender and sexuality themselves
have to be performed, and performers are constantly held 'morally accountable', are
policed, for how they present their gender by those others with whom they are
interacting (Garfinkel 1967; Heritage 1984; McHoul 1986).

However, the above anecdotes on the masculine heterosexings of the restaurant's
visuality provide only a partial picture of Smoky's, which was not simply a straight
man's world (compare, for example, with Brady's bar as discussed in Spradley and
Mann 1975). For, although full of masculinist policing, gazing could be used in
different ways; by gay, bisexual and lesbian staff and customers gazing on each
other, such that Smoky's, although not a defined gay space, was multiply coded and
produced beyond or besides a dominant heterosexing (Bell et al. 1994). Or, especially in a 'parodic restaurant', gazing could be used in parody of dominant straight
masculinity: such that, for example, it was not only the sexuality police of homo-
phobia that made waiters' masculinity an issue; women customers could, occasionally, do likewise. Some recollections:

Research Diary (March, 1989) *Served a table of four students, all women. They were getting really pissed, but I was, I thought, really spot on [with the service]. They hardly left a tip though, and left a comment card on the table, where the only additional comment was 'Get hunkier waiters'...*

Research Diary (May, 1988) *Also last night I was stood at the till, writing on a bill, when this woman walked past and pinched me on the bum, then walking down to the loos killing herself with laughing.*

Research Diary (April, 1989) *Had a bit of a difficult lot of tables. Had a hen party on table 42, who were really rowdy initially, all whooping when I first came over to them; one shouted 'get your kit off' at me, but actually they were really nice and the others all tried to laugh it off. But somehow I couldn't play the game, I just felt awkward, and they all quietened down during the meal, and I knew I had sort of killed it off, dampened their night, by not joining in...*

Of course none of these, my personal tribulations, imply some equivalence of experience of performance between straight and gay waiters, or between waiters and waitresses. Events that reinforce, indeed magnify existing dominant power relations, and practices that overturn them, may stay locked in the same logic, but with quite different ends; symptomatically, my hen party reluctantly went quiet when I could not enjoy the game being played, whereas Julie's stag party became more and more abusive when she ignored them. I guess to that extent telling me I am not hunky is, if not to me, funny; commenting on a waitress's breasts is not. But the reminiscences above do suggest the role of Smoky's as a situation: a liminal place where dominant power relations are in many ways intensified, but at the same time a place where they can also be parodied, and where possibilities for still marginalized alternatives are made visible to all, if not dominant or equal.

Characterizing the encounter
Before amplifying these points on the kind of place that Smoky's is, and how that impacts on work experiences through defining the stage on which staff perform, I want briefly to summarize the character of the service encounter that I have been outlining. Perhaps most obviously, the work it involves is clearly based in routine geographies that involve the movement and stopping of the worker, the timings and placings of which are both matters of practical efficiency and 'political' contestation. But these routines are not sedimented; they involve creative spatial acts (see Thrift 1993). And in turn that creativity is regulated by negotiated norms of both content, and more importantly, process; norms that suggest ways of 'geting on' with this particular piece of production and consumption, as well as providing opportunities for powerful ruptures of that regulation by all participants. Central to these norms and their ruptures are the accommodations, the alliances, the battles, the power-plays, between consumers and producers, all of which involve questions of service delivery but which also enact other social relations of power.

Second, and following on from this, the politics of these service encounters are thus not reducible to those of disembodied producers and consumers. I briefly noted above the gendered and sexualized experiences of gazing and being gazed at. One might equally emphasize, though, the embodied character of the organization and defin-ition of encounters: thus, for example, the use of the encounter's norms to attempt a control of Julie by 'her' stag party, and the use of them by 'my' hen party to send me and masculinity up. Julie and I worked at the same job, but what we did in it – even as we both went to tables and took orders – could be radically different (see Crompton and Sanderson 1990). Or, to take another tack, one might examine how Smoky's is an arena not only of task-oriented, status-implicated definitions of server and served, but also one within which embodied 'cultural capital' (Bourdieu 1984) is both consumed and produced, and not only by customers: such that we employees had a preference for working in Smoky's rather than, say, Pizza Hut, not only for material reasons (better tips especially), but because of its perceived greater cultural capital to us (as a vaguely 'trendy, youth hang-out'); such that waiting staff were recruited as part of the cultural capital being sold, their selection involving matching a particular quality of cultural capital to the restaurant's product and market;[11] and in turn, such that both staff and customers could employ their adjudicated cultural capital in their relations, both as a passive defence, a 'status shield' (Hochschild 1983) ('I'm really an academic not a waiter'), and as an active attack (the puerile 'I've got more O-levels than all that table put together').

Third, the routines of these encounters involve a staging of display; a process that both marks out a political positioning that is often uncomfortable and oppressive for staff but which also involves an active inhabitation by them. This inhabitation is complex. It involves a variety of tactical manoeuvres, which, to classify some of the activities recounted above, combine processes that might be labelled as *hiding* (finding or constructing places shielded from the gaze of managerial or customer surveillance), *masquerading* (appearing to be doing what one is not), *distancing* (separating oneself from the restaurant *in toto*; either by emphasizing one's individuality or conversely by using a standardized script for a rest from that emphasis), and *posing* (using surveillance, especially by customers, to strike a pose, to send a particular message) (what Hebdige 1988 calls 'hiding in the light'). These tactics cannot be cast either as unequivocally effective resistance and subversion, or as superficial co-optations that leave the fundamental power relations of the workplace untouched. They are ways of getting by that combine resistance (contradicting managerial and/or customer control), avoidance (escaping that control oneself, but leaving it otherwise untouched), parody (a symbolic revolt, a laughing at control practices), and adaptation (the use of games that in fact defuse any attempt to fundamentally transform the workplace social relations) (Burawoy 1985).

Fourth, the kinds of tactics codified above are metaphors for, as well as practices of, the relationship of self to labour in this job. As such, the performative encounters that I have identified as central to customer – staff relations in Smoky's suggest the crucial place of the self in the practices of this employment: such that the surfaces of the self are bound up in interpersonal relations that do not simply surround the task in hand, but comprise it; and so that those performances reach into the 'deeper' self of emotions and feelings (see Hochschild 1983; Seabrook 1988). The implications are twofold: first, that the labour done becomes bound up with – and does not simply replace – realms held apart from labour in traditional images and conceptions of capitalist employment (chiefly various moral regulations of social activity); and, second, that the self is consequently not excluded from the labour done (contrast with Gouldner 1969), but increasingly implicated in it. To that degree Smoky's service, as provided by the waiting staff, is neither purely personal, nor simply mechanical and impersonal; it is *personalized*. It is in that mutual entanglement of self and capitalist production that this waiting work sits.

NOTES

1   Smoky Joe's is a pseudonym.

2   A map of the interior of Smoky's is not included in this chapter as its shape is distinctive.

3   The full order of service sets out the form of contact with a table of customers, but not all the necessary tasks to achieve that. At the simplest level, for example, it does not refer to the need to enter all orders made into the computerized electronic point of sale (EPOS) terminals. Once entered, these orders are then automatically sent to a printout terminal at the bar, the kitchen or the dessert area. Getting onto a terminal soon after an order is therefore vital. Nor does it allude to the pre-preparation of a table, and the restaurant more generally, upon which the order of service relies: for example, the presence of condiments, napkins and toothpicks on a table, or, at the restaurant level, enough clean cutlery or mustard or relish or hot towels to give to a table when they need them. In addition, at a more complex level, there are clearly a number of social relations between waiting and other staff, and between waiting staff and other customers, that are bound up with meeting the order of service, and its time limits, for a particular table.

4   This simply means saying 'Table x away' over the counter to the kitchen staff once the starters are finished; one of the chefs (usually the head chef) then moves that table's order printout along a metal strip to the section where main courses that need cooking are displayed.

5   This involves a preset form of words that includes three pieces of information; my slight adaptation was 'As you're having ribs, and they get pretty mucky [gentle laugh], I'll bring you a hot towel to wipe yourself down with at the end of the meal. But there are toothpicks and paper napkins on the table if you need them before then [point to both in the middle of the table].'

6   Goffman (1956: 68–9) calls this response to surveillance 'make work'.

7   I was somewhat worried about my already rather weak credentials as a participant-observer when I noticed the labelling on the roster only after a whole year's work at Smoky's; but at least when I then asked all the other waitresses working at that time about it, not one of them had ever noticed either.

8   This attempt to give off an expression of 'busy-ness', and often near panic, had the intention of demonstrating the hard work being put in by a waiter or waitress on behalf of his or her table. It ran the risk of simply demonstrating amateurism, but as I will elaborate later, in the situation that was Smoky's with its informal service style, this was rather less problematic than might be thought.

9   Again I necessarily speak from my own side of the divide, in noting that waiting staff did this in two main ways: first in various sorts of talk about 'tables', usually out of earshot from them in somewhere like the dispense, the dessert, or the kitchen counter areas (Goffman calls this generic commentary on another team 'staging talk'); and second, in acted out pastiches of customers, especially prevalent when covering the mutual embarrassment of table and waitress when the former comprised existing or past restaurant staff (see Goffman 1956: 107–31).

10 At Smoky's there was not a strict 'beauty qualification' in the application process for a waiting job, or at least it was not as strict as in some rivals (the nearby 'Frank's Place' was renowned among waiting staff as somewhere where only 'beautiful people' got jobs; and perhaps reflecting this, always had, even in a city with labour shortages at this time, a

waiting list of aspirants hoping to be selected), but staff still clearly reflected corporate and managerial tastes. Waitresses, on the whole, were not expected to conform to any weight limits, but were, according to dominant male norms, 'pretty', and usually young; only a very powerfully projected personality – often involving elements of comedy and self-parody – shifted such criteria. As for waiters, on the whole, we were fairly effeminate, slim not muscular. The bar and kitchen both contained a greater variety of looks.

11   Thus staff had to be capable of being informal, young (usually biologically but youthfulness was not totally reduced to age), friendly, with the 'right' skills of emotional control and deference; and have the 'right' sort of gendered body and style of presenting it. With regards to the last of these, I once asked Kelvin the manager why it was that kitchen staff were not allowed to walk from the kitchen across a small bit of the restaurant to get a cup of coffee. He jokingly replied, 'Well look at Dave [the head chef], he'd put you right off your food wouldn't he!' Dave was fat, he had his front teeth missing; he was not, we might say, tasty. And in Smoky's not only the food had to be.

REFERENCES

Adams, J. (1976) 'The structure and dynamics of behavior in organizational boundary roles', in *Handbook of Industrial and Organizational Psychology* ed. M Dunette (Rand McNally, Chicago, IL) pp. 145–81.

Adkins, L. (1992) 'Sexual work and the employment of women in the service industries', in *Gender and Bureaucracy* eds M. Savage, A. Witz (Blackwell, Oxford) pp 207–28.

Bell, D. Binnie, J. Cream, J. Valentine, G. (1994) 'All hyped up and no place to go.' *Gender, Place and Culture: A Journal of Feminist Geography* 1: 31–48.

Bourdieu, P. (1984) *Distinction: A Social Critique of the Judgement of Taste* (Routledge and Kegan Paul, London).

Bowen, D. Schneider, B. (1985) 'Boundary-spanning-role employees and the service encounter: some guidelines for management and research', in *The Service Encounter Managing Employee/Customer Interaction in Service Businesses* eds J. Czepiel, M. Soloman, C. Surprenant (Lexington Books, Lexington, MA) pp 127–47.

Braverman, H. (1974) *Labour and Monopoly Capital: The Degradation of Work in the Twentieth Century* (Monthly Review Press, New York).

Burawoy, M. (1985) *The Politics of Production* (Verso, London).

Christopher, M. (1984) 'The strategy of consumer service.' *Service Industries Journal* 4: 205–20.

Christopherson, S. (1989) 'Flexibility in the US service economy and the emerging spatial division of labour.' *Transactions of the Institute of British Geographers*, New Series 14: 131–43.

Collier, D. (1987) 'The customer service and quality challenge.' *Service Industries Journal* 7: 77–90.

Crompton, R. Jones, G. (1984) *White-collar Proletariat: Deskilling and Gender in Clerical Work* (Macmillan, London).

Crompton, R. Sanderson K. (1990) *Gendered Jobs and Social Change* (Unwin Hyman, London).

Czepeil, J. Soloman, M. Surprenant, C. (eds) (1985) *The Service Encounter: Managing Employee/Customer Interaction in Service Businesses* (Lexington Books, Lexington, MA).

Dandeker, C. (1990) *Surveillance, Power and Modernity: Bureaucracy and Discipline from 1700 to the Present Day* (Polity Press, Cambridge).

Finkelstein, J. (1989) *Dining Out: A Sociology of Modern Manners* (Polity Press, Cambridge).

Frisbee, W. Madeira, K. (1986) 'Restaurant meals: convenience goods or luxuries?' *Service Industries Journal* 6: 172–92.

Gabriel, Y. (1988) *Working Lives in Catering* (Routledge and Kegan Paul, London).

Garfinkel, H. (1967) *Studies in Ethnomethodology* (Polity Press, Cambridge).

Goffman, E. (1956) *The Presentation of Self in Everyday Life*. Edinburgh Research Monograph Number 2, Social Sciences Research Centre, University of Edinburgh, Edinburgh.

Goffman, E. (1961) *Encounters: Two Studies in the Sociology of Interaction* (Bobbs-Merrill, Indianapolis, IN).

Goffman, E. (1963) *Behaviour in Public Places: Notes on the Social Organization of Gatherings* (Free Press, New York).

Goffman, E. (1964) 'The neglected situation.' *American Anthropologist* 66 (6): 133–6.

Goffman, E. (1967) *Interaction Ritual: Essays on Face-to-face Behaviour* (Doubleday Anchor, New York).

Goffman, E. (1971) *Relations in Public: Microstudies of the Public Order* (Basic Books, New York).

Goffman, E. (1983) 'The interaction order.' *Americal Sociological Review* 48: 1–17.

Gouldner, A. (1969) 'The unemployed self', in *Work: Twenty Personal Accounts*. Volume 2 ed. R. Fraser (Penguin Books, Harmondsworth) pp. 346–65.

Hebdige, D. (1988) 'Hiding in the light: youth surveillance and display', in *Hiding in the Light: On Images and Things* (Comedia, London) pp. 17–36.

Heritage, J. (1984) *Garfinkel and Ethnomethodology* (Polity Press, Cambridge).

Hochschild, A. (1983) *The Managed Heart: Commercialization of Human Feeling* (University of California Press, Berkeley).

Kappeler, S. (1986) *The Pornography of Representation* (University of Minnesota Press, Minneapolis).

Kendon, A. (1988) 'Goffman's approach to face-to-face interaction', in *Erving Goffman: Exploring the Interaction Order* eds P. Drew, A. Wootton (Polity Press, Cambridge) pp. 14–40.

Klaus, P. (1985) 'Quality epiphenomenon: the conceptual understanding of quality in face-to-face service encounters', in *The Service Encounter. Managing Employee/Customer Interaction in Service Businesses* eds J. Czepeil, M. Soloman, C. Surprenant (Lexington Books, Lexington, MA) pp. 17–33.

Lehtinen, U. Lehtinen, J. (1991) 'Two approaches to service quality dimensions.' *Service Industries Journal* 11: 287–303.

Leidner, R. (1991) 'Serving hamburgers and selling insurance: gender, work, and identity in interactive service jobs.' *Gender and Society* 5: 154–77.

Leidner, R. (1993) *Fast Food, Fast Talk: Service Work and the Routinization of Everyday Life* (University of California Press, Berkeley).

Levitt, T. (1980) 'Marketing success through differentiation – of anything.' *Harvard Business Review* January/February, pp. 149–65.

MacClancy, J. (1992) *Consuming Culture* (Chapmans, London).

McHoul, A. (1986) 'The getting of sexuality: Foucault, Garfinkel and the analysis of sexual discourse.' *Theory, Culture and Society* 3 (2): 65–79.

Mars G, Nicod M, 1984 *The World of Waiters* (George Allen and Unwin, London)

Mennell, S. Murcott, A. Van Otterloo, A. (1992) *The Sociology of Food: Eating, Diet and Culture* (Sage, London).

Mulvey, L. (1975) 'Visual pleasure and narrative cinema.' *Screen* 16 (3): 6–18.

Nightingale, M. (1985) 'The hospitality industry: defining quality for a quality assurance programme – a study of perceptions.' *Service Industries Journal* 5: 9–22.

Peters, T. (1988) *Thriving on Chaos: Handbook for a Management Revolution* (Pan Books, London).

Peters, T. Waterman, R. (1982) *In Search of Excellence: Lessons from America's Best Businesses* (Harper and Row, New York).

Saleh, F. Ryan, C. (1991) 'Analysing service quality in the hospitality industry using the SERVQUAL model.' *Service Industries Journal* 11: 324–43.

Seabrook, J. (1988) *The Leisure Society* (Blackwell, Oxford).

Solomon, M. (1988) 'Packaging the service provider', in *Managing Services: Marketing, Operations and Human Resources* ed. C. Lovelock (Prentice-Hall, Hemel Hempstead) pp. 462–72.

Spradley, J. Mann B. (1975) *The Cocktail Waitress: Woman's Work in a Man's World* (John Wiley, New York).

Taylor, F. (1947) *Scientific Management: Comprising Shop Management, the Principles of Scientific Management, Testimony before the Special House Committee* (Greenwood Press, Westport, CT).

Thrift, N. (1993) 'The arts of the living, the beauty of the dead: anxieties of being in the work of Anthony Giddens.' *Progress in Human Geography* 17: 111–21.

TIC. (1987) *Working for Big Mac*. Transnationals Information Centre, 9 Poland Street, London WIV.

Turner, R. (1962) 'Role-taking: process versus conformity', in *Human Behaviour and Social Processes: An Interactionist Approach* ed. A. Rose (Routledge and Kegan Paul, London) pp. 20–40.

Whyte, W. F. (1946) *Industry and Society* (McGraw Hill, New York).

Whyte, W. F. (1948) *Human Relations in the Restaurant Industry* (McGraw Hill, New York).

Whyte, W. F. (1949) 'The social structure of the restaurant.' *American Journal of Sociology* 54: 303–10.

Wolf, N. (1990) *The Beauty Myth* (Chatto and Windus, London).

Part VI   Economy of Passions

Chapter 18

Feeling Management: From Private to Commercial Uses

Arlie Hochschild

If they could have turned every one of us into sweet quiet Southern belles with velvet voices like Rosalyn Carter, this is what they would want to stamp out on an assembly line.

Flight attendant, Delta Airlines

On PSA our smiles are not just painted on.
So smile your way
From LA
To San Francisco

PSA radio jingle

When you see them receiving passengers with that big smile, I don't think it means anything. They have to do that. It's part of their job. But now if you get into a conversation with a flight attendant...well...no...I guess they have to do that too.

Airline passenger

When rules about how to feel and how to express feeling are set by management, when workers have weaker rights to courtesy than customers do, when deep and surface acting are forms of labor to be sold, and when private capacities for empathy and warmth are put to corporate uses, what happens to the way a person relates to her feelings or to her face? When worked-up warmth becomes an instrument of service work, what can a person learn about herself from her feelings? And when a worker abandons her work smile, what kind of tie remains between her smile and her self?

Display is what is sold, but over the long run display comes to assume a certain relation to feeling. As enlightened management realizes, a separation of display and feeling is hard to keep up over long periods. A principle of *emotive dissonance*, analogous to the principle of cognitive dissonance, is at work. Maintaining a difference between feeling and feigning over the long run leads to strain. We try to reduce this strain by pulling the two closer together, either by changing what we feel or by changing what we feign. When display is required by the job, it is usually feeling that has to change; and when conditions estrange us from our face, they sometimes estrange us from feeling as well.

Take the case of the flight attendant. Corporate logic in the airline industry creates a series of links between competition, market expansion, advertising, heightened passenger expectations about rights to display, and company demands for acting. When conditions allow this logic to work, the result is a successful transmutation of the private emotional system we have described. The old elements of emotional exchange – feeling rules, surface acting, and deep acting – are now arranged in a different way. Stanislavski's *if* moves from stage to airline cabin ("act as if the cabin were your own living room") as does the actor's use of emotion memory. Private use gives way to corporate use.

In the airline industry of the 1950s and 1960s a remarkable transmutation was achieved. But certain trends, discussed later in this chapter, led this transmutation to fail in the early 1970s. An industry speed-up and a stronger union hand in limiting the company's claims weakened the transmutation. There was a service worker "slowdown." Worked-up warmth of feeling was replaced by put-on smiles. Those who sincerely wanted to make the deeper offering found they could not do so, and those who all along had resisted company intrusions on the self came to feel some rights to freedom from it. The job lost its grip. When the transmutation succeeded, the worker was asked to take pride in making an instrument of feeling. When it collapsed, workers came to see that instrument as overused, underappreciated, and susceptible to damage.

Behind the Demand for Acting

"A market for emotional labor" is not a phrase that company employees use. Upper management talks about getting the best market share of the flying public. Advertising personnel talk about reaching that market. In-flight service supervisors talk about getting "positive attitude" and "professional service" from flight attendants, who in turn walk about "handling irates." Nevertheless, the efforts of these four groups, taken together, set up the sale of emotional labor.

The purpose of Delta Airlines is to make a profit. To make a profit, Delta has to compete for passenger markets. Throughout the postwar years, for example, Delta competed with Eastern Airlines for markets along routes they both serviced. (It now shares 80 percent of its routes with Eastern.)[1] The Civil Aeronautics Board (CAB), established in 1938 in recognition of the national importance of air transport and the threat of monopoly, was granted authority to control market shares and prices. Until 1978 it established uniform prices for airline tickets and sharpened competition by offering parallel route awards. Companies competed by offering more frequent flights, more seats, faster flights (fewer stops), and – what is most important here – better service. After 1978 the airlines were deregulated and price wars were allowed.[2] Yet a brief price war in 1981 and another shake-out of weaker companies has been followed by a general rise in prices. As it was before deregulation, service may again become a main area of competition. When competition in price is out, competition in service is in.[3]

The more important service becomes as an arena for competition between airlines, the more workers are asked to do public relations work to promote sales. Employees are continually told to represent Delta proudly. All Delta workers once received, along with their paychecks, a letter from the president and chairman of the board asking them to put Delta bumper stickers on their cars. The Delta Jogging Club (which included two vice-presidents) once ran a well-publicized 414-mile marathon from Dallas, Texas, to Jackson, Mississippi, to commemorate Delta's first commercial flight. Virtually every employee is asked to be "in sales."

But of all workers in an airline, the flight attendant has the most contact with passengers, and she sells the company the most. When passengers think of service they are unlikely to think of the baggage check-in agent, the ramp attendant, the cabin clean-up crew, the lost and found personnel, or the man down in commissary pouring gravy on a long line of chicken entrées. They think of the flight attendant. As one Delta official explained: "For each hour's work by a flight attendant, there are 10.5 hours of support time from cabin service, the billing department, maintenance, and so on. Altogether we spend 100 hours per passenger per flight. But the passenger really has prolonged contact only with the flight attendant."

As competition grew from the 1930s through the early 1970s, the airlines expanded that visible role. Through the 1950s and 1960s the flight attendant became a main subject of airline advertising, the spearhead of market expansion.[4] The image they chose, among many possible ones, was that of a beautiful and smartly dressed Southern white woman, the supposed epitome of gracious manners and warm personal service.[5]

Because airline ads raise expectations, they subtly rewrite job descriptions and redefine roles. They promise on-time service, even though planes are late from 10 to 50 percent of the time, industrywide. Their pictures of half-empty planes promise space and leisurely service, which are seldom available (and certainly not desired by the company). They promise service from happy workers, even though the industry speed-up has reduced job satisfaction. By creating a discrepancy between promise and fact, they force workers in all capacities to cope with the disappointed expectations of customers.

The ads promise service that is "human" and personal. The omnipresent smile suggests, first of all, that the flight attendant is friendly, helpful, and open to requests. But when words are added, the smile can be sexualized, as in "We really move our tails for you to make your every wish come true" (Continental), or "Fly me, you'll like it" (National). Such innuendos lend strength to the conventional fantasy that in the air, anything can happen. As one flight attendant put it: "You have married men with three kids getting on the plane and suddenly they feel anything goes. It's like they leave that reality on the ground, and you fit into their fantasy as some geisha girl. It happens over and over again."

So the sexualized ad burdens the flight attendant with another task, beyond being unfailingly helpful and open to requests: she must respond to the sexual fantasies of passengers. She must try to feel and act as if flirting and propositioning are "a sign of my attractiveness and your sexiness," and she must work to suppress her feelings that such behavior is intrusive or demeaning. Some have come to see this extra psychological task as a company contrivance. A flight attendant once active in Flight Attendants for Women's Rights commented: "The company wants to sexualize the cabin atmosphere. They want men to be thinking that way because they think what men really want is to avoid *fear of flying*. So they figure mild sexual arousal will be helpful in getting people's minds off of flying. It's a question of dollars and cents...Most of our passengers are male, and all of the big corporate contract business is male."[6]

The advertising promises of one airline tend to redefine work on other airlines as well. So although Delta's advertising has assiduously avoided explicit sexualization of the role, Delta's flight attendants must cope with the inflated image of the flight attendant put out by other companies. There may well be an economic pattern to sexual innuendo in these ads: the economically marginal companies seem to aim a sexual pitch at the richest segment of the market, male businessmen. United Airlines, which was ranked first in revenues in 1979, has not attached suggestive words to the female smile; but Continental, ranked tenth, and National, ranked eleventh, certainly have. But in any case, when what Doris Lessing has called a fantasy of "easily available and guiltless sex" is encouraged by one airline, it is finally attached to air travel in general.

As the industry speed-up and union pressure have reduced the deep acting promised and delivered in American-based companies, there are signs that the same corporate logic that reached its nadir in the 1950s in the United States is now emerging abroad. *Fortune*, in an article about Singapore International Airlines entitled "An Airline Powered by Charm" (June 18, 1979), notes:

> [SIA's] advertising campaign glamorizes the cabin hostess as "the Singapore girl"...To convey the idea of in-flight pleasure with a lyrical quality, most SIA ads are essentially large, soft-focus color photographs of various hostesses. In a broadcast commercial a crooner sings: "Singapore girl, you look so good I want to stay up here with you forever." [The chairman of SIA has said] "We're fortunate in having young people who get a Western education, speak English, and still take an Asian attitude toward service."

This may be the service-sector version of a "runaway shop," including not only runaway-shop labor ("with an Asian attitude toward service") but "runaway" imagery to advertise it.

We might add that the first, and nonsexual, significance of the advertised smile – special friendliness and empathy – can also inflate the expectations of passengers, and therefore increase their right to feel disappointed. Ordinary niceness is no longer enough; after all, hasn't the passenger paid for extra civility? As every flight attendant knows well, she can expect to face surprisingly deep indignation when her expressive machine is idling or, worse yet, backfiring.

Behind the Supply of Acting: Selection

Even before an applicant for a flight attendant's job is interviewed, she is introduced to the rules of the game. Success will depend in part on whether she has a knack for perceiving the rules and taking them seriously. Applicants are urged to read a pre-interview pamphlet before coming in. In the 1979–80 *Airline Guide to Stewardess and Steward Careers*, there is a section called "The Interview." Under the subheading "Appearance," the manual suggests that facial expressions should be "sincere" and "unaffected." One should have a "modest but friendly smile" and be "generally alert, attentive, not overly aggressive, but not reticent either." Under "Mannerisms," subheading "Friendliness," it is suggested that a successful candidate must be "outgoing but not effusive," "enthusiastic with calm and poise," and "vivacious but not effervescent." As the manual continues: "Maintaining eye contact with the interviewer demonstrates sincerity and confidence, but don't overdo it. Avoid cold or continuous staring." Training, it seems, begins even before recruitment.

Like company manuals, recruiters sometimes offer advice on how to appear. Usually they presume that an applicant is planning to put on a front; the question is which one. In offering tips for success, recruiters often talked in a matter-of-fact way about acting, as though assuming that it is permissable if not quite honorable to feign. As one recruiter put, it: "I had to advise a lot of people who were looking for jobs, and not just at Pan Am...And I'd tell them the secret to getting a job is to imagine the kind of person the company wants to hire and then become that person during the interview. The hell with your theories of what you believe in, and what your integrity is, and all that other stuff. You can project all that when you've got the job."

In most companies, after the applicant passes the initial screening (for weight, figure, straight teeth, complexion, facial regularity, age) he or she is invited to a group interview where an "animation test" takes place.

At one interview session at Pan American, the recruiter (a woman) called in a group of six applicants, three men and three women. She smiled at all of them and then said: "While I'm looking over your files here, I'd like to ask you to turn to your neighbor and get to know him or her. We'll take about three or four minutes, and then I'll get back to you." Immediately there was bubbly conversation, nodding of heads, expansions of posture, and overlapping ripples of laughter. ("Is that right? My sister-in-law lives in Des Moines, too!" "Oh wow, how did you get into scuba diving?") Although the recruiter had simply asked each applicant to turn to a neighbor, in fact each woman turned to her nearest man "to bring him out." (Here, what would be an advantage at other times – being the object of conversational attention – became a disadvantage for the men because the task was to show skill in "bringing out" others.) After three minutes, the recruiter put down her files and called the group to order. There was immediate total silence. All six looked expectantly at the recruiter: how had they done on their animation test?

The recruits are screened for a certain type of outgoing middle-class sociability. Sometimes the recruitment literature explicitly addresses friendliness as an *act*. Allegheny Airlines, for example, says that applicants are expected to *"project a warm personality* during their interview in order to be eligible for employment." Continental Airlines, in its own words, is "seeking people who convey a spirit of enthusiasm." Delta Airlines calls simply for applicants who *"have* a friendly personality and high moral character."

Different companies favor different variations of the ideal type of sociability. Veteran employees talk about differences in company personality as matter-of-factly as they talk about differences in uniform or shoe style. United Airlines, the consensus has it, is "the girl-next-door," the neighborhood babysitter grown up. Pan Am is upper class, sophisticated, and slightly reserved in its graciousness. PSA is brassy, funloving, and sexy. Some flight attendants could see a connection between the personality they were supposed to project and the market segment the company wants to attract. One United worker explained: "United wants to appeal to Ma and

Pa Kettle. So it wants Caucasian girls – not so beautiful that Ma feels fat, and not so plain that Pa feels unsatisfied. It's the Ma and Pa Kettle market that's growing, so that's why they use the girl-next-door image to appeal to that market. You know, the Friendly Skies. They offer reduced rates for wives and kids. They weed out busty women because they don't fit the image, as they see it."

Recruiters understood that they were looking for "a certain Delta personality," or "a Pan Am type." The general prerequisites were a capacity to work with a team ("we don't look for chiefs, we want Indians"), interest in people, sensitivity, and emotional stamina. Trainers spoke somewhat remotely of studies that indicate that successful applicants often come from large families, had a father who enjoyed his work, and had done social volunteer work in school. Basically, however, recruiters look for someone who is smart but can also cope with being considered dumb, someone who is capable of giving emergency safety commands but can also handle people who can't take orders from a woman, and someone who is naturally empathetic but can also resist the numbing effect of having that empathy engineered and continuously used by a company for its own purposes. The trainees, on the other hand, thought they had been selected because they were adventurous and ambitious. ("We're not satisfied with just being secretaries," as one fairly typical trainee said. "All my girlfriends back in Memphis are married and having babies. They think I'm real liberated to be here.")

The trainees, it seemed to me, were also chosen for their ability to take stage directions about how to "project" an image. They were selected for being able to act well – that is, without showing the effort involved. They had to be able to appear at home on stage.

The training at Delta was arduous, to a degree that surprised the trainees and inspired their respect. Most days they sat at desks from 8:30 to 4:30 listening to lectures. They studied for daily exams in the evenings and went on practice flights on weekends. There were also morning speakers to be heard before classes began. One morning at 7:45 I was with 123 trainees in the Delta Stewardess Training Center to hear a talk from the Employee Representative, a flight attendant whose regular job was to communicate rank-and-file grievances to management and report back. Her role in the training process was different, however, and her talk concerned responsibilities to the company:

> Delta does not believe in meddling in the flight attendant's personal life. But it does want the flight attendant to uphold certain Delta standards of conduct. It asks of you first that you keep your finances in order. Don't let your checks bounce. Don't spend more than you have. Second, don't drink while in uniform or enter a bar. No drinking 24 hours before flight time. [If you break this rule] appropriate disciplinary action, up to and including dismissal, will be taken. While on line we don't want you to engage in personal pastimes such as knitting, reading, or sleeping. Do not accept gifts. Smoking is allowed if it is done while you are seated.

The speaker paused and an expectant hush fell across the room. Then, as if in reply to it, she concluded, looking around, "That's all." There was a general ripple of relieved laughter from the trainees: so that was *all* the company was going to say about their private lives.

Of course, it was by no means all the company was going to say. The training would soon stake out a series of company claims on private territories of self. First, however, the training prepared the trainees to accept these claims. It established their vulnerability to being fired and their dependence on the company. Recruits were reminded day after day that eager competitors could easily replace them. I heard trainers refer to their "someone-else-can-fill-your-seat" talk. As one trainee put it, "They stress that there are 5,000 girls out there wanting *your* job. If you don't measure up, you're out."

Adding to the sense of dispensability was a sense of fragile placement *vis-à-vis* the outside world. Recruits were housed at the airport, and during the four-week training period they were not allowed to go home or to sleep anywhere but in the dormitory. At the same time they were asked to adjust to the fact that for them, home was an idea without an immediate referent. Where would the recruit be living during the next months and years? Houston? Dallas? New Orleans? Chicago? New York? As one pilot advised: "Don't put down roots. You may be moved and then moved again until your seniority is established. Make sure you get along with your roommates in your apartment."

Somewhat humbled and displaced, the worker was now prepared to identify with Delta. Delta was described as a brilliant financial success (which it is), an airline known for fine treatment of its personnel (also true, for the most part), a company with a history of the "personal touch." Orientation talks described the company's beginnings as a family enterprise in the 1920s, when the founder, Collett Woolman, personally pinned an orchid on each new flight attendant. It was the flight attendant's job to represent the company proudly, and actually identifying with the company would make that easier to do.

Training seemed to foster the sense that it was safe to feel dependent on the company. Temporarily rootless, the worker was encouraged to believe that this company of 36,000 employees operated as a "family." The head of the training center, a gentle, wise, authoritative figure in her fifties, appeared each morning in the auditorium; she was "mommy," the real authority on day-to-day problems. Her company superior, a slightly younger man, seemed to be "daddy." Other supervisors were introduced as concerned extensions of these initial training parents. (The vast majority of trainees were between nineteen and twenty-two years old.) As one speaker told the recruits: "Your supervisor is your friend. You can go to her and talk about anything, and I mean *anything*." The trainees were divided up into small groups; one class of 123 students (which included three males and nine blacks) was divided into four subgroups, each yielding the more intimate ties of solidarity that were to be the prototype of later bonds at work.

The imagery of family, with mommies and daddies and sisters and brothers, did not obscure for most trainees the reminders that Delta was a business. It suggested, rather, that despite its size Delta aspired to maintain itself in the spirit of an old-fashioned family business, in which hierarchy was never oppressive and one could always air a gripe. And so the recruit, feeling dispensable and rootless, was taken in by this kindly new family. Gratitude lays the foundation for loyalty.

The purpose of training is to instill acceptance of the company's claims, and recruits naturally wonder what parts of their feeling and behavior will be subject to company control. The head of in-flight training answered their implicit question in this way:

> Well, we have some very firm rules. Excessive use of alcohol, use of drugs of any kind, and you're asked to leave. We have a dormitory rule, and that is that you'll spend the night in the dormitory. There's no curfew, but you will spend the night in the dormitory. If you're out all night, you're asked to leave. We have weight standards for our flight attendants. Break those weight standards, and the individual is asked to resign. We have a required test average of 90 percent; if you don't attain that average, you're asked to resign. And then we get into the intangibles. That's where the judgment comes in.

From the recruit's point of view, this answer simply established what the *company* conceived of as "company control." In fact, this degree of control presupposed many other unmentioned acts of obedience – such as the weigh-in. Near the scales in the training office one could hear laughter at "oh-my-god-what-I-ate-for-dinner" jokes. But the weigh-in itself was conducted as a matter of routine, just something one did. The need for it was not explained, and there was no mention of the history of heated court battles over the weight requirement (most of them so far lost by the unions). One flight attendant commented, "Passengers aren't weighed, pilots aren't weighed, in-flight service supervisors aren't weighed. We're the only ones they weigh. You can't tell me it's not because most of us are women." Obviously, discussions of this issue might weaken the company's claim to control over a worker's weight. The trainers offered only matter-of-fact explanations of what happens to the weight gainer. If a flight attendant is one pound over the maximum allowable weight, the fact is "written up" in her personnel file. Three months later, if the offender is still one pound over, there is a letter of reprimand; if another three months pass without change, there is suspension without pay. People may in fact be fired for being one pound overweight. Outside the classroom, of course, there was a rich underground lore about starving oneself before flights, angrily overeating after flights, deliberately staying a fraction over the weight limit to test the system, or claiming "big bones" or "big breasts" as an excuse for overweight. (One wit, legend has it, suggested that breasts be weighed separately.) Officially, however, the weigh-in was only a company routine.

The company's presumption was supported by several circumstances. It was difficult to find *any* good job in 1981, let alone a job as a flight attendant. There was also the fact that Delta's grooming regulations did not seem particularly rigid compared with those of other airlines, past and present. Flight attendants were not required to wear a girdle and submit to the "girdle check" that Pan American flight attendants recall. There was no mention of a rule, once established at United, that one had to wear white underwear. There was a rule about the length of hair, but no mention of "wig checks" (to determine whether a worker had regulation hair under her wig), which were used by several companies in the 1960s. There was no regulation, such as Pan Am had, that required wearing eyeshadow the same shade of blue as the uniform. There were no periodic thigh measurements, which PSA flight attendants still undergo, and no bust–waist–hips–thighs measurements that formed part of an earlier PSA routine. In an occupation known for its standardization of personal appearance, Delta's claims could seem reasonable. The company could say, in effect, "You're lucky our appearance code isn't a lot tighter." Under a more stringent code, those who could be judged a little too fat or a little too short, a little too tall or a little too plain, could feel pressured to make up for their physical deviations by working harder and being nicer than others. Some veteran workers ventured a thought (not generally shared) that companies deliberately tried to recruit women who were decidedly plainer than the official ideal so as to encourage workers to "make up for" not being prettier.

The claim to control over a worker's physical appearance was backed by continuous reference to the need to be "professional." In its original sense, a profession is an occupational grouping that has sole authority to recruit, train, and supervise its own members. Historically, only medicine, law, and the academic disciplines have fit this description. Certainly flight attendants do not yet fit it. Like workers in many other occupations, they call themselves "professional" because they have mastered a body of knowledge and want respect for that. Companies also use "professional" to refer to this knowledge, but they refer to something else as well. For them, a "professional" flight attendant is one who has completely accepted the rules of standardization. The flight attendant who most nearly meets the appearance code ideal is therefore "the most professional" in this regard. By linking standardization to honor and the suggestion of autonomy, the company can seem to say to the public, we control *this* much of the appearance and personality of *that* many people – which is a selling point that most companies strive for.

At the other extreme, workers were free of claims over their religious or political beliefs. As one Delta veteran put it: "They want me to look like Rosalyn Carter at age twenty, but they don't care if I think like she does. I'm not going to have power over anyone in the company, so they lay off my philosophy of life. I like that."[7]

Between physical looks and deeply held belief lies an intermediate zone – the zone of emotion management. It was particularly here, as the head of in-flight training put it, that "we get into the intangibles." The company claim to emotion work was mainly insinuated by example. As living illustrations of the right kind of spirit for the job, trainers maintained a steady level of enthusiasm despite the long hours and arduous schedule. On Halloween, some teachers drew laughs by parading through the classroom dressed as pregnant, greedy, and drunk passengers. All the trainers were well liked. Through their continuous cheer they kept up a high morale for those whose job it would soon be to do the same for passengers. It worked all the better for seeming to be genuine.

Trainees must learn literally hundreds of regulations, memorize the location of safety equipment on four different airplanes, and receive instruction on passenger handling.[8] In all their courses they were constantly reminded that their own job security and the company's profit rode on a smiling face. A seat in a plane, they were told, "is our most perishable product – we have to keep winning our passengers back." How you do it is as important as what you do. There were many direct appeals to smile: "Really work on your smiles." "Your smile is your biggest asset – use it." In demonstrating how to deal with insistent smokers, with persons boarding the wrong plane, and with passengers who are sick or flirtatious or otherwise troublesome, a trainer held up a card that said "Relax and smile." By standing aside and laughing at the "relax and smile" training, trainers parried student resistance to it. They said, in effect, "It's incredible how much we have to smile, but there it is. We know that, but we're still doing it, and you should too."

Beyond this, there were actual appeals to modify feeling states. The deepest appeal in the Delta training program was to the trainee's capacity to act as if the airplane cabin (where she works) were her home (where she doesn't work). Trainees were asked to think of a passenger *as if* he were a "personal guest in your living room." The workers' emotional memories of offering personal hospitality were called up and put to use, as Stanislavski would recommend. As one recent graduate put it:

> You think how the new person resembles someone you know. *You see your sister's eyes in someone sitting at that seat.* That makes you want to put out for them. I like to think of the cabin as the living room of my own home. When someone drops in [at home], you may not know them, but you get something for them. You put that on a grand scale – thirty-six passengers per flight attendant – but *it's the same feeling.*

On the face of it, the analogy between home and airplane cabin unites different kinds of experiences and obscures what is different about them. It can unite the empathy of friend for friend with the empathy of worker for customer, because it assumes that empathy is the *same sort of feeling* in either case. Trainees wrote in their notebooks, "Adopt the passenger's point of view," and the understanding was that this could be done in the same way one adopts a friend's point of view. The analogy between home and cabin also joins the worker to her company; just as she naturally protects members of her own family, she will naturally defend the company. Impersonal relations are to be seen *as if* they were personal. Relations based on getting and giving money are to be seen *as if* they were relations free of money. The company brilliantly extends and uses its workers' basic human empathy, all the while maintaining that it is not interfering in their "personal" lives.

As at home, the guest is protected from ridicule. A flight attendant must suppress laughter, for example, at seeing a passenger try to climb into the overhead storage rack, imagining it to be a bunk bed. Nor will she exhibit any idiosyncratic habits of her own, which might make the guest feel uncomfortable. Also, trainees were asked to express sincere endorsement of the company's advertising. In one classroom session, an instructor said: "We have Flying Colonel and Flying Orchid passengers, who over the years have always flown Delta. This is an association they're invited to join. It has no special privileges, but it does hold meetings from time to time." The students laughed, and one said, "That's absurd." The trainer answered, "Don't say that. You're supposed to make them think it's a real big thing." Thus, the sense of absurdity was expanded: the trainees were let in on the secret and asked to help the company create the illusion it wanted the passengers to accept.

By the same token, the injunction to act "as if it were my home" obscured crucial differences between home and airplane cabin. Home is safe. Home does not crash. It is the flight attendant's task to convey a sense of relaxed, homey coziness while at the same time, at take-off and landing, mentally rehearsing the emergency announcement, "Cigarettes out! Grab ankles! Heads down!" in the appropriate languages. Before takeoff, safety equipment is checked. At boarding, each attendant secretly picks out a passenger she can call on for help in an emergency evacuation. Yet in order to sustain the *if*, the flight attendant must shield guests from this unhomelike feature of the party. As one flight attendant mused:

Even though I'm a very honest person, I have learned not to allow my face to mirror my alarm or my fright. I feel very protective of my passengers. Above all, I don't want them to be frightened. If we were going down, if we were going to make a ditching in water, the chances of our surviving are slim, even though we [the flight attendants] know exactly what to do. *But I think I would probably* – and I think I can say this for most of my fellow flight attendants – *be able to keep them from being too worried about it.* I mean my voice might quiver a little during the announcements, but somehow I feel we could get them to believe . . . the best.

Her brave defense of the "safe homey atmosphere" of the plane might keep order, but at the price of concealing the facts from passengers who might feel it their right to know what was coming.

Many flight attendants spoke of enjoying "work with people" and adopted the living room analogy as an aid in being as friendly as they wanted to be. Many could point to gestures that kept the analogy tension-free:

I had been asked for seconds on liquor by three different people just as I was pushing the liquor cart forward for firsts. The fourth time that happened, I just laughed this spontaneous absurd laugh. [Author: Could you tell me more about that?] Part of being professional is to make people on board feel comfortable. They're in a strange place. It's my second home. They aren't as comfortable as I am. I'm the hostess. My job is really to make them enjoy the flight. The absurd laughter did it, that time.

Others spoke of being frustrated when the analogy broke down, sometimes as the result of passenger impassivity. One flight attendant described a category of unresponsive passengers who kill the analogy unwittingly. She called them "teenage execs."

Teenage execs are in their early to middle thirties. Up and coming people in large companies, computer people. They are very dehumanizing to flight attendants. You'll get to their row. You'll have a full cart of food. They will look up and then look down and keep on talking, so you have to interrupt them. They are demeaning . . . you could be R2–D2 [the robot in the film *Star Wars*]. They would like that better.

This attendant said she sometimes switched aisles with her partner in order to avoid passengers who would not receive what the company and she herself wanted to offer. Like many others, she wanted a human response so that she could be sincerely friendly herself. Sincerity is taken seriously, and there was widespread criticism of attendants who did not act "from the heart." For example: "I worked with one flight attendant who put on a fake voice. On the plane she raised her voice about four octaves and put a lot of sugar and spice into it [gives a falsetto imitation of 'More coffee for you, sir?']. I watched the passengers wince. What the passengers want is real people. They're tired of that empty pretty young face."

Despite the generous efforts of trainers and workers themselves to protect it, the living room analogy remains vulnerable on several sides. For one thing, trainees were urged to "*think* sales," not simply to act in such a way as to induce sales. Promoting sales was offered to the keepers of the living room analogy as a rationale for dozens of acts, down to apologizing for mistakes caused by passengers: "Even if it's their fault, it's very important that you don't blame the passengers. That can have a lot of impact. Imagine a businessman who rides Delta many times a year. Hundreds, maybe thousands of dollars ride on your courtesy. Don't get into a verbal war. It's not worth it. They are our lifeblood. As we say, the passenger isn't always right, but he's never wrong."

Outside of training, "thinking sales" was often the rationale for doing something. One male flight attendant, who was kind enough to show me all around the Pan American San Francisco base, took me into the Clipper Club and explained: "This club is for our important customers, our million-mile customers. Jan, the receptionist, usually introduces me to some passengers here at the Clipper Club. They go in the SIL [Special Information Log] because we know they mean a lot of money for the company. If I'm the first-class purser for one leg of the journey, I note what drink they order in the Clipper Club and then offer them that when they're seated in the plane. They like that." The uses of courtesy are apparently greater in the case of a million-mile customer – who is likely to be white, male, and middleaged – than in the case of women, children, and the elderly. In any case, lower-income passengers are served in segregated "living rooms."

"Think sales" had another aspect to it. One trainer, who affected the style of a good-humored drill sergeant, barked out: "What are we always doing?" When a student finally answered, "Selling Delta," she replied: "No! You're selling yourself. Aren't you selling yourself, too? You're on your own commission. We're in the business of selling ourselves, right? Isn't that what it's all about?"

In this way, Delta sells Southern womanhood, not "over their heads," but by encouraging trainees to think of themselves as *self*-sellers. This required them to imagine themselves as self-employed. But Delta flight attendants are not making an independent profit from their emotional labor, they are working for a fixed wage. They are not selling themselves, they are selling the company. The *idea* of selling themselves helps them only in selling the company they work for.

The cabin-to-home analogy is vulnerable from another side too. The flight attendant is asked to see the passenger as a potential friend, or as like one, and to be as understanding as one would be with a good friend. The *if* personalizes an impersonal relation. On the other hand, the student is warned, the reciprocity of real friendship is not part of the *if* friendship. The passenger has no obligation to return empathy or even courtesy. As one trainer commented: "If a passenger snaps at you and you didn't do anything wrong, just remember it's not you he is snapping at. It's your uniform, it's your role as a Delta flight attendant. Don't take it personally." The passenger, unlike a real friend or guest in a home, assumes a right to unsuppressed anger at irritations, having purchased that tacit right with the ticket.

Flight attendants are reminded of this one-way personalization whenever passengers confuse one flight attendant with another ("You look so much alike") or ask questions that reveal that they never thought of the attendants as real people. "Passengers are surprised when they discover that we eat, too. They think we can go for twenty hours without being allowed to eat. Or they will get off the plane in Hong Kong after a 15-hour flight – which is a 16- or 17-hour duty day for us – and say, 'Are you going on to Bangkok?' 'Are you going on to Delhi?' Yes, right, sure – we go round the world and get sent back with the airplane for repairs." Just as the flight attendant's empathy is stretched thin into a commercial offering, the passenger's try at empathy is usually pinched into the narrow grooves of public manners.

It is when the going gets rough – when flights are crowded and planes are late, when babies bawl and smokers bicker noisily with nonsmokers, when the meals run out and the air conditioning fails – that maintaining the analogy to home, amid the Muzak and the drinks, becomes truly a monument to our human capacity to suppress feeling.

Under such conditions some passengers exercise the privilege of not suppressing their irritation; they become "irates." When that happens, back-up analogies are brought into service. In training, the recruit was told: "Basically, the passengers are just like children. They need attention. Sometimes first-time riders are real nervous. And some of the troublemakers really just want your attention." The passenger-as-child analogy was extended to cover sibling rivalry: "You can't play cards with just one passenger because the other passengers will get jealous." To think of unruly passengers as "just like children" is to widen tolerance of them. If their needs are like those of a child, those needs are supposed to come first. The worker's right to anger is correspondingly reduced; as an adult he must work to inhibit and suppress anger at children.

Should the analogy to children fail to induce the necessary deep acting, surface-acting strategies for handling the "irate" can be brought into play. Attendants were urged to "work" the passenger's name, as in "Yes, Mr. Jones, it's true the flight is delayed." This reminds the passenger that he is not anonymous, that there is at least some pretension to a personal relation and that some emotion management is owed. Again, workers were told to use terms of empathy. As one flight attendant, a veteran of fifteen years with United, recalled from her training: "Whatever happens, you're supposed to say, I know just how you feel. Lost your luggage? I know just how you feel. Late for a connection? I know just how you feel. Didn't get that steak you were counting on? I know just how you feel." Flight attendants report that such expressions of empathy are useful in convincing passengers that they have misplaced the blame and misaimed their anger.

Perspectives elicit feeling. In deep acting, perspectives are evoked and suppressed in part through a way of speaking. One way of keeping the living room analogy alive is to speak in company language. In a near-Orwellian Newspeak, the company seems to have officially eliminated the very idea of getting angry at the passenger, the source of revenue. Supervisors never speak officially of an *obnoxious* or *outrageous* passenger, only of an *uncontrolled* passenger. The term suggests that a fact has somehow attached itself to this passenger – not that the passenger has lost control or even had any control to lose. Again, the common phrase "mishandled passenger" suggests a bungle somewhere up the line, by someone destined to remain lost in the web of workers that stretches from curbside to airplane cabin. By linguistically avoiding any attribution of blame, the idea of a right to be angry at the passenger is smuggled out of discourse. Linguistically speaking, the passenger never *does* anything wrong, so he can't be blamed or made the object of anger.

In passenger-handling classes one trainer described how she passed a dinner tray to a man in a window seat. To do this, she had to pass it across a woman sitting on the aisle seat. As the tray went by, the woman snitched the man's desert. The flight attendant politely responded, "I notice this man's dessert is on your tray." The dirty deed was done, but, the implication was, by no one in particular. Such implicit reframing dulls a sense of cause and effect. It separates object from verb and verb from subject. The passenger does not feel accused, and the flight attendant does not feel as if she is accusing. Emotion work has been accomplished, but it has hidden its tracks with words.

Company language is aimed not only at diffusing anger but at minimizing fear. As one Pan Am veteran recalled:

> We almost turned upside down leaving Hong Kong. They call it an "incident." Not an accident, just an incident. We went nose up and almost flipped over. The pilot caught the plane just before it went over on its back and made a big loop and dropped about 3,000 feet straight down and then corrected what happened. They pulled out at 1,500 feet over the harbor. We knew we were going to die because we were going nose down and you could see that water coming. I was never really afraid of flying before, but turbulence does shake me up now. I'm not as bad as some people, though.

The very term *incident* calms the nerves. How could we be terrified at an "incident"? Thus the words that workers use and don't use help them avoid emotions inappropriate to a living room full of guests.

Finally, the living room analogy is upheld by admitting that it sometimes falls down. In the Recurrent Training classes held each year for experienced flight attendants, most of the talk was about times when it feels like the party is over, or never began. In Initial Training, the focus was on the passenger's feeling; in Recurrent Training, it was on the flight attendant's feeling. In Initial Training, the focus was on the smile and the living room analogy; in Recurrent Training, it was on avoiding anger. As a Recurrent Training instructor explained: "Dealing with difficult passengers is part of the job. It makes us angry sometimes. And anger is part of stress. So that's why I'd like to talk to you about being angry. I'm not saying you should do this [work on your anger] for Delta Airlines. I'm not saying you should do it for the passengers. I'm saying do it for *yourselves*."

From the beginning of training, managing feeling was taken as the problem. The causes of anger were not acknowledged as part of the problem. Nor were the overall conditions of work – the crew size, the virtual exclusion of blacks and men, the required accommodation to sexism, the lack of investigation into the considerable medical problems of flight attendants, and the company's rigid antiunion position. These were treated as unalterable facts of life. The only question to be seriously discussed was "How do you rid yourself of anger?"

The first recommended strategy is to focus on what the *other* person might be thinking and feeling: imagine a reason that excuses his or her behavior. If this fails, fall back on the thought "I can escape." One instructor suggested, "You can say to yourself, it's half an hour to go, now it's twenty-nine minutes, now it's twenty-eight." And when anger could not be completely dispelled by any means, workers and instructors traded tips on the least offensive ways of expressing it: "I chew on ice, just crunch my anger away." "I flush the toilet repeatedly." "I think about doing something mean, like pouring Ex-Lax into his coffee."[9] In this way a semiprivate "we-girls" right to anger and frustration was shared, in the understanding that the official axe would fall on anyone who expressed her anger in a more consequential way.

Yet for those who must live under a taboo on anger, covert ways of expressing it will be found. One flight attendant recalled with a grin:

> There was one time when I finally decided that somebody had it coming. It was a woman who complained about absolutely everything. I told her in my prettiest voice, "We're doing our best for you. I'm sorry you aren't happy with the flight time. I'm sorry you aren't happy with our service." She went on and on about how terrible the food was, how bad the flight attendants were, how bad her seat was. Then she began yelling at me and my coworker friend, who happened to be black. "You nigger bitch!" she said. Well, that did it. I told my friend not to waste her pain. This lady asked for one more Bloody Mary. I fixed the drink, put it on a tray, and when I got to her seat, my toe somehow found a piece of carpet and I tripped – and that Bloody Mary hit that white pants suit!

Despite the company's valiant efforts to help its public-service workers offer an atmosphere perfumed with cheer, there is the occasional escapee who launders her anger, disguises it in mock courtesy, and serves it up with flair. There remains the possibility of sweet revenge.

Collective Emotional Labor

To thwart cynicism about the living room analogy, to catch it as it collapses in the face of other realizations, the company eye shifts to another field of emotion work – the field in which flight attendants interact with each other. This is a strategic point of entry for the company because if the company can influence how flight attendants deal with each other's feelings on the job, it can ensure proper support for private emotion management.

As trainers well know, flight attendants typically work in teams of two and must work on fairly intimate terms with all others on the crew. In fact, workers commonly say the work simply cannot be done well unless they work well together. The reason for this is that the job is partly an "emotional tone" road show, and the proper tone is kept up in large part by friendly conversation, banter, and joking, as ice cubes, trays, and plastic cups are passed from aisle to aisle to the galley, down to the kitchen, and up again. Indeed, starting with the bus ride to the plane, by bantering back and forth the flight attendant does important relational work: she checks on people's moods, relaxes tension, and warms up ties so that each pair of individuals becomes a team. She also banters to keep herself in the right frame of mind. As one worker put it, "Oh, we banter a lot. It keeps you going. You last longer."

It is not that collective talk determines the mood of the workers. Rather, the reverse is true: the needed mood determines the nature of the worker's talk. To keep the collective mood stripped of any painful feelings, serious talk of death, divorce, politics, and religion is usually avoided. On the other hand, when there is time for it, mutual morale raising is common. As one said: "When one flight attendant is depressed, thinking, 'I'm ugly, what am I doing as a flight attendant?' other flight attendants, even without quite knowing what they are doing, try to cheer her up. They straighten her collar for her, to get her up and smiling again. I've done it too, and needed it done."

Once established, team solidarity can have two effects. It can improve morale and thus improve service. But it can also become the basis for sharing grudges against the passengers or the company. Perhaps it is the second possibility that trainers meant to avoid when in Recurrent Training they offered examples of "bad" social emotion management. One teacher cautioned her students: "When you're angry with a passenger, don't head for the galley to blow off steam with another flight attendant." In the galley, the second flight attendant, instead of calming the angry worker down, may further rile her up; she may become an accomplice to the aggrieved worker. Then, as the instructor put it, "There'll be *two* of you hot to trot."

The message was, when you're angry, go to a teammate who will calm you down. Support for anger or a sense of grievance – regardless of what inspires it – is bad for service and bad for the company. Thus, the informal ways in which workers check on the legitimacy of a grievance or look for support in blowing off steam become points of entry for company. "suggestions."

Behind the Supply: Supervision

The lines of company control determine who fears whom. For flight attendants, the fear hierarchy works indirectly through passengers and back again through their own immediate supervisors.[10] As someone put it, "Whoever invented the system of passenger letter writing must be a vice-president by now." Any letter from a passenger – whether an "onion" letter complaining about the temperature of the coffee, the size of a potato, the look of an attendant, or an "orchid" letter praising an attendant for good service – is put into the personnel files. These letters are translated by base supervisors into rewards and punishments. Delta flight attendants talked about them as much as they talked about the reports of those in the official line of authority – the senior attendant on the crew, the base supervisor, and the plainclothes company supervisors who occasionally ghost-ride a flight.

In addition to the informal channels by which passenger opinion passes to management and then worker, there are more formal ones; company-elicited passenger opinion polls. The passenger is asked to fill out a questionnaire, and the results of that are presented by letter to the workers. As one male flight attendant, seven years with United, describes it:

> We get told how we're doing. Twice a year we get sent passenger evaluations. They show how United, American, Continental, and TWA are competing. Oh, passengers are asked to rank flight attendants: "genuinely concerned, made me feel welcome. Spoke to me more than required. Wide awake, energetic, eager to help. Seemed sincere when talking to passengers. Helped establish a relaxed cabin atmosphere. Enjoying their jobs. Treated passengers as individuals." We see how United is doing in the competition. We're supposed to really get into it.

Supervision is thus more indirect than direct. It relies on the flight attendant's sense of what passengers will communicate to management who will, in turn, communicate to workers. (For the indirect "bureaucratic" control more common to the modern workplace, see Edwards 1979: ch. 6.)

Supervisors do more than oversee workers. At this juncture in Delta's history, the fear hierarchy bends, and supervisors must also pose as big sisters in the Delta family – bigger but not by much. These largely female, immobile, and nonunionized workers are not greatly feared by underlings, nor much envied, as the comment of one flight attendant suggests:

> It's not a job people want very much. Some girls go into it and then bounce right back on the line. The pay is an inch better and the hours are a whole lot worse. And you have to talk oat-meal. My supervisor called me into her office the other day. I've used seven out of my twenty-one days of available sick leave. She says, "I don't want to have to tell you this. It's what I have to tell you. You've used up too much of your sick leave." She has to take it from her boss and then take it from me – from both ends. What kind of a job is that?

Supervisors monitor the supply of emotional labor. They patch leaks and report breakdowns to the company. They must also cope with the frustrations that workers suppress while on the job. As one Delta base manager explained: "I tell my supervisors to let the girls ventilate. It's very important that they get that out. Otherwise they'll take it out on the passengers." So the supervisor who grades the flight attendant on maintaining a "positive" and "professional" attitude is also exposed to its underside. For example, one flight attendant recalled coming off a long and taxing flight only to discover that her paycheck had been "mishandled." She said she told her supervisor, "I can't take this all day and then come back here and take it from *you*! You know I get paid to take it from passengers, but I don't get paid to take it from you. I want my money. I just got my teeth cleaned three months ago. Where's my check? *You* find it!" What is offstage for the flight attendant is on stage for the supervisor. Managing someone else's formerly managed frustration and anger is itself a job that takes emotional labor.

Achieving the Transmutation

To the extent that emotion management actually works – so that Bloody Marys do not spill "by accident" on white pants suits, and blowups occur in backstage offices instead of in airplane aisles – something like alchemy occurs. Civility and a general sense of well-being have been enhanced and emotional "pollution" controlled. Even when people are paid to be nice, it is hard for them to be nice at all times, and when their efforts succeed, it is a remarkable accomplishment.

What makes this accomplishment possible is a transmutation of three basic elements of emotional life: emotion work, feeling rules, and social exchange.

First, emotion work is no longer a private act but a public act, bought on the one hand and sold on the other. Those who direct emotion work are no longer the individuals themselves but are instead paid stage managers who select, train, and supervise others.

Second, feeling rules are no longer simply matters of personal discretion, negotiated with another person in private, but are spelled out publicly – in the *Airline Guide to Stewardess and Steward Careers*, in the *World Airways Flight Manual*, in training programs, and in the discourse of supervisors at all levels.

Third, social exchange is forced into narrow channels; there may be hiding places along shore, but there is much less room for individual navigation of the emotional waters.

The whole system of emotional exchange in private life has as its ostensible purpose the welfare and pleasure of the people involved. When this emotional system is thrust into a commercial setting, it is transmuted. A profit motive is slipped in under acts of emotion management, under the rules that govern them, under the gift exchange. Who benefits now, and who pays?

The transmutation is a delicate achievement and potentially an important and beneficial one. But even when it works – when "service ratings" are high and customers are writing "orchid" letters – there is a cost to be paid: the worker must give up control over *how* the work is to be done. In *Labor and Monopoly Capital* (1974) Harry Braverman argues that this has been a general trend in the twentieth century. The "mind" of the work process moves up the company hierarchy, leaving jobs deskilled and workers devalued.[11] Braverman applies this thesis to physical and mental labor, but it applies to emotional labor as well. At Delta Airlines, for example, twenty-four men work as "method analysts" in the Standard Practices Division of the company. Their job is to update the forty-three manuals that codify work procedure for a series of public-contact jobs. There were no such men in the 1920s when the flight engineer handed out coffee to passengers; or in the 1930s when Delta hired nurses to do the same; or in the 1940s when the first flight attendants swatted flies in the cabin, hauled luggage, and even helped with wing repairs. The flight attendant's job grew along with marketing, becoming increasingly specialized and standardized.

The lessons in deep acting – acting "as if the cabin is your home" and "as if this unruly passenger has a traumatic past" – are themselves a new development in deskilling. The "mind" of the emotion worker, the source of the ideas about what mental moves are needed to settle down an "irate," has moved upstairs in the hierarchy so that the worker is restricted to implementing standard procedures. In the course of offering skills, trainers unwittingly contribute to a system of deskilling. The skills they offer do not subtract from the worker's autonomous control over *when* and *how* to apply them; as the point is made in training, "It will be up to you to decide how to handle any given problem on line." But the overall definition of the task is more rigid than it once was, and the worker's field of choice about what to do is greatly narrowed. Within the boundaries of the job, more and more actual subtasks are specified. Did the flight attendant hand out magazines? How many times? By the same token, the task to be accomplished is more clearly spelled out by superiors. How were the magazines handed out? With a smile? With a *sincere* smile? The fact that trainers work hard at making a tough job easier and at making travel generally more pleasant only makes this element of deskilling harder to see. The fact that their training manuals are prepared for them and that they are not themselves entirely free to "tell it like it is" only illustrates again how deskilling is the outcome of specialization and standardization.

Sensing this, most of the flight attendants I observed were concerned to establish that theirs was an honorable profession requiring a mastery of "real" skills. I was told repeatedly that there was a law school graduate in the incoming class at the Training Center and that a dentist, a librarian, and a botanist were serving on line. At the same time, they generally expressed frustration at the fact that their skills in rescue and safety procedures were given soft play (how many tickets can you sell by reminding passengers of death and danger?) whereas their function as meal servers was highlighted. As one flight attendant put it eloquently:

> I have a little bit of pride in what I do. Of course I'm going to haul ass and try to do everything I conceivably can to get that breakfast for 135 people completed in forty minutes. That means that 135 people get meal trays, 135 people are supposed to have at least two beverages, 135 trays are collected and restowed. You can imagine how many seconds we have left to give to each passenger. But what kind of condition does that put me in when I finally reach the jump seat at the end of the flight, the time when a crash is relatively more likely? And do I even notice that man slumped over in his seat? *That's* really my job.

Thus because passengers see them – and are encouraged by company advertising to see them – as no more than glamorous waitresses, flight attendants usually resented the *appearance* of working at a low level of skills, and had to cope with this resentment. But the ways in which these two functions – managing rescue operations and serving food – are combined, and the relative priority given to each, cannot be influenced by the workers or even the trainers. Such things are determined by management.

The Transmutation That Failed

When an industry speed-up drastically shortens the time available for contact between flight attendants and passengers, it can become virtually impossible to deliver emotional labor. In that event, the transmutation of emotion work, feeling rules, and social exchange will fail. Company claims about offering a smile "from the inside out" (Delta) will become untenable. The living room analogy will collapse into a flat slogan. The mosaic of "as if" techniques will fall to pieces, and deep acting will be replaced by surface displays that lack conviction.

This is approximately what has happened in the US airline industry. Flight attendants who had worked during the 1960s spoke, sometimes nostalgically, sometimes bitterly, of a "before" and an "after" period. In the "before" period they were able to do what they were asked to do, what they often came to *want* to do. As one twenty-two-year veteran of Pan American reminisced:

> On those old piston-engine Stratocruisers we had ten hours to Honolulu. We had three flight attendants for seventy-five passengers. We had a social director who introduced each of the flight attendants personally and asked the passengers to introduce them-selves to each other... We didn't even use the PA system, and we had a vocal lifeboat demonstration. There was more of the personal touch. The plane had only one aisle, and we had berths for the passengers to sleep in. We used to tuck people into bed.

There was time to talk to passengers. Layovers between flights were longer. Flights were less crowded, the passengers more experienced and generally richer, the work more pleasant. Descriptions of flying today are much different:

> Now we have these huge planes that can go forever. I mean, we have twelve-hour duty days, with 375 people to tend [on the Boeing 747]. The SP [Special Performance plane]

is smaller, but it can go fifteen or sixteen hours without refueling. We used to fly with the same people, and there were fewer of us. We would just informally rotate positions. Now you come to work all set to argue for *not* working tourist class.

When we go down the rows, we avoid eye contact and focus on the aisle, on the plates. People usually wait for eye contact before they make a request, and if you have two and a quarter hours to do a cocktail and meal service, and it takes five minutes to answer an extra request, those requests add up and you can't do the service in time.

The golden age ended sometime after the recession of the early 1970s when the airlines, losing passengers and profits, began their campaigns to achieve "cost-efficient" flying.[12] They began using planes that could hold more people and fly longer hours without fuel stops. This created longer workdays, and more workdays bunched together.[13] There was less time to adjust to time-zone changes on layovers, and less time to relax and enjoy a central advantage of the work – personal travel. Like the airplane, the flight attendant was now kept in use as long as possible. Pan American shortened its port time (the time before and after flights) from one and a half to one and a quarter hours. One American Airlines union official described the result of the speed-up:

They rush us through the emergency briefing...They're even briefing us on the buses getting out there. When you get on the plane, you just start counting all the food and everything and start loading passengers. They'll shut the door and pull away and we'll find we're twenty meals short.

Now if we worked in an auto assembly line and the cars started to come down the line faster and faster we'd call it a speed-up. But on the airplane they give more passengers to the same crew. They ask us to do a liquor service and a dinner service in an hour, when it used to be an hour and a half...and we do it. Now why is it we don't call that a speed-up?

With deregulation of the airlines, the price of tickets dropped, and the "discount people" boarded in even larger numbers.[14] Aboard came more mothers with small children who leave behind nests of toys, gum wrappers, and food scraps, more elderly "white-knuckle flyers," more people who don't know where the restrooms, the pillow, and the call button are, more people who wander around wanting to go "downstairs." Experienced business commuters complain to flight attendants about the reduced standard of living in the air; or worse, they complain about less experienced "discount" passengers, who in turn appeal to the flight attendant. The cruise ship has become a Greyhound bus.

The companies could increase the number of flight attendants, as the unions have asked, to maintain the old ratio of workers to passengers. One union official for Pan American calculated that "if we had the same ratio now that we had ten years ago we would need twenty flight attendants on board, but we get by with twelve or fourteen now." One reason the companies have not done this is that flight attendants cost more than they used to. With regulations that assured their removal at age thirty-one or at marriage, flight attendants used to be a reliable source of cheap labor. But since the unions have successfully challenged these regulations and also secured higher wages, the companies have chosen to work a smaller number of flight attendants much harder. While some flight attendants find it hard to refute the corporate logic, others continue to question why this female labor was so cheap to begin with.

In the early 1980s there has been a super speed-up. The vice-president for In-Flight Service at United Airlines explained the economic background of this: "United has to compete for the travel market with low-cost, nonunion planes, with companies with lower overhead, who only lease planes – companies like PSA, Pacific Express, Air California." In response to this greater competition, United instituted its Friendship Express flights. After only a year and a half, such flights accounted for 23 percent of all United flights.

On Friendship Express the fares are lower, the service is minimal, and the seating is "high density." It is not unusual for a flight attendant to handle a thousand passengers a day. The ground time is limited to a maximum of twenty minutes. (One United flight attendant said, "We don't send Friendship Express flights to St. Petersburg, Florida, because with the number of wheelchair passengers there, we couldn't make our twenty minutes deboarding time.") With such limited groundtime, four segments of travel can be squeezed into the time of three. There is no time to clean the cabin or replace supplies between trips: "If you're ten lunches short on the Friendship Express, well you're just out ten lunches. You have to live with the complaints." But the old ways of handling complaints are no longer available. Faced with disappointed passengers, the flight attendant can no longer give out free decks of cards or drinks. The main compensation for mishaps must be personal service – for which there is virtually no time.

The recession has required United, like many airlines, to lay off baggage checkers, gate personnel, ticket personnel, and managers. Lines are longer. Mishaps multiply. There are more ruffled feathers to soothe, more emotion work to be done, but fewer workers to do it. The super speed-up has made it virtually impossible to deliver personal service. Even those who have long since abandoned that ideal – passengers as well as airline workers – find the system stressful.

Management, however, sees no escape from the contradictory policy of trying to meet the demand for emotional labor while promoting conditions that cut off the supply. The companies worry that competitors may produce more personal service than they do, and so they continue to press for "genuinely friendly" service. But they feel compelled to keep the conveyor belt moving ever faster. For workers, the job of "enjoying the job" becomes harder and harder. Rewards seem less intrinsic to the work, more a compensation for the arduousness of it. As one veteran of thirteen years with Pan Am put it:

> The company did, after all, pay relatively good salaries and give us free or reduced rates for air travel. There was a seniority system, so the longer you flew, the better most things got – vacations and layovers got longer and more pleasant. The fact that none of us was really happy on the job didn't matter – that wasn't why we were flying. We were flying for money, men, adventure, travel. But the job, the work on the plane, was the most strenuous, unrewarding, alienating concentration of house work and waitress-type drudgery to be found anywhere.

Before the speed-up, most workers sustained the cheerful good will that good service requires. They did so for the most part proudly; they supported the transmutation.

After the speed-up, when asked to make personal human contact at an inhuman speed, they cut back on their emotion work and grew detached.

NOTES

1 For a detailed picture of the Delta–Eastern competition in the postwar period, see Gill and Bates (1949: 235).

2 The Airline Deregulation Act, passed by Congress in October 1978, provided for abolition of the CAB by 1985, after the transfer of some of its functions to other agencies had been accomplished. In 1981 the CAB lost all authority to regulate the entry of air carriers into new domestic markets.

3 Despite fierce competition in some arenas, airlines cooperate with each other. According to the airlines, flying is safe but, in fact, airplanes occasionally crash. When they do, the efforts of their public relations offices call for surface acting and sometimes border on illusion making. For example, the head of Delta's public relations office received a call during my office visit. "A crash in Mexico City? Seventy-three died? It was a DC – 10, too?" He turned to me after hanging up. "After that last Eastern crash, I was getting 150 calls a day. We don't have any DC – 10s, thank God. But I try to keep the press off of Eastern's back. I say, 'Don't mention those planes.' Eastern does the same for us when we're in trouble."

4 When an airline commands a market monopoly, as it is likely to do when it is owned by a government, it does not need to compete for passengers by advertising friendly flight attendants. Many flight attendants told me that their counterparts on Lufthansa (the German national airlines) and even more on El Al and Aeroflot (the Israeli and Russian national airlines) were notably lacking in assertive friendliness.

5 A black female flight attendant, who had been hired in the early 1970s when Delta faced an affirmative action suit, wondered aloud why blacks were not pictured in local Georgia advertising. She concluded: "They want that market, and that market doesn't include blacks. They go along with that." Although Delta's central offices are in Atlanta, which is predominantly black, few blacks worked for Delta in any capacity.

6 Many workers divided male passengers into two types: the serious businessman who wants quite, efficient, and unobtrusive service; and the "sport" who wants a Playboy Club atmosphere.

7 Delta does officially emphasize "good moral character," and several workers spoke in lowered voices about facts they would not want known. They agreed that any report of living with a man outside marriage would be dangerous, and some said they would never risk paying for an abortion through the company's medical insurance.

8 Most of the training in passenger handling concerned what to do in a variety of situations. What do you do if an obese passenger doesn't fit into his seat? Make him pay for half the fare of another seat. What do you do if the seat belt doesn't fit around him? Get him a seat-belt extension. What do you do if you accidentally spill coffee on his trousers? Give him a pink slip that he can take to the ticket agent, but don't commit the company to responsibility through word or action. What do you do if you're one meal short? Issue a meal voucher that can be redeemed at the next airport.

9 Most anger fantasies seemed to have a strong oral component, such as befouling the troublemaker's food and watching him eat it. These fantasies inverted the service motif but did not step outside it. No one, for instance, reported a fantasy about hitting a passenger.

10 At Delta in 1980 there were twenty-nine supervisors in charge of the 2,000 flight attendants based in Atlanta.

11 Braverman (1974) argues that corporate management applied the principles of Frederick Winslow Taylor and systematically divided single complex tasks into many simple tasks so that a few parts of the former complex task are done by a few highly paid mental workers while the remaining simple parts of the task are done by cheap and interchangeable unskilled workers. To management, the advantage is that it is cheaper and there is more control over the work process from the top, less from the bottom. Braverman applies this thesis to factory work, clerical work, and service work, but he fails to distinguish between the kinds of service work that involve public contact and the kinds that do not (p. 360).

12 Between 1950 and 1970 the annual growth rate of airline companies was between 15 and 19 percent. In 1970 growth slowed, and air traffic grew about 4 percent annually. Periods of financial hardship have led to the failure of weak companies and increased concentration. Of the thirty-five airlines regulated by the Civil Aeronautics Board (CAB) the largest four – United, TWA, American, and Pan American – earned 43 percent of the 1974 revenues (Corporate Data Exchange 1977: 77).

13 Companies are trying to eliminate "soft-time trips" and increase "hard-time trips." A hard-time trip is one on which the flight attendant puts in more than her projected daily quota of flying hours. On a soft-time trip she works below that quota. In cases where a flight attendants' union – as at American Airlines – has won the right to per diem pay for nonflying time, the company is correspondingly eager to eliminate occasions on which the workers can use it.

14 In 1979 discount fares accounted for 37 percent of Delta's total domestic revenue from passenger service.

REFERENCES

Braverman, Harry (1974) *Labor and Monopoly Capital*. New York: Monthly Review Press.

Corporate Data Exchange, Inc. (1977) *Stock Ownership Directory. No. 1. The Transportation Industry*. New York: Corporate Data Exchange.

Edwards, Richard (1979) *Contested Terrain: The Transformation of the Workplace in the Twentieth Century*. New York: Basic Books.

Gill, Frederick W. and Gilbert Bates (1949) *Airline Competition*. Boston: Division of Research, Graduate School of Business Administration, Harvard University Printing Office.

Stanislavski, Constantin (1965) *An Actor Prepares*. Trans. Elizabeth Reynolds Hapgood. New York: Theatre Arts Books. First published 1948.

Chapter 19

Negotiating the Bar: Sex, Money and the Uneasy Politics of Third Space

Lisa Law

Stereotypical representations of sex tourism in Southeast Asia have abounded for the past three decades. Images of middle-aged Western men debauching adolescent Asian girls in the red light districts of Patpong in Bangkok or Ermita in Manila, or of servicemen 'letting loose' in the R&R districts surrounding American military bases have inspired extensive critiques of American colonialism, cultural imperialism and the commodification of Asian sexuality. It is difficult to imagine these commoditized sexual relations without at least contemplating the structural inequalities and patterns of globalization which have enabled the development of sex industries catering to foreign men. Indeed, it has been through the important interpretive frames provided by feminist, nationalist and anticolonial accounts of sex tourism that the stereotypical encounters between 'voyeuristic' Western men and 'submissive' Asian women have gained a politically strategic coherence.

The popular representation of go-go bars as sites of foreign oppression underpins, and plays a major role in sustaining and authenticating, political mobilization against sex tourism in Southeast Asia, as well as internationally. Within the language of advocacy, prostitute identity is metaphorically fixed within a rich-Western-male/poor-Asian-female dichotomy, ultimately conveying a powerful subject/disempowered other. While this representation plays an important role in highlighting the economic, political and social bases of inequality, it simultaneously reinforces the hegemonically constructed identities of the 'oppressor' and the 'victim' through naturalizing them as fixed identities and subject positions. In so doing, it offers little room to manoeuvre, to negotiate identity or to resist the complex power relations constructed at points where class, race and gender intersect.

The aim of this chapter is to destabilize the naturalness of the encounter between Western men and Southeast Asian women through an analysis of space, and more specifically, to deconstruct and reconstitute the places of sex tourism as negotiated spaces of identity. This is not to deny the relations of power in the sale of sex; it is a rather different conception of power which enables us to conceive more nuanced geographies of resistance. In this way, it can be suggested that the white, male gaze is not merely an autonomous voyeurism – it has its own difficulties and uneasiness due to the gaze from the supposedly powerless bar women, who have their own sights/ sites of power, meaning and identity. It can also be conveyed that bar women are capable of positioning themselves in multiple and intersecting relations of power – which include but are not exclusive to their encounters with men – and that it is in these spaces that subjectivities, capable of resistance, are forged. By analysing the space of the bar in this manner, the presumed identity of women *as prostitutes* and men *as customers* is called into question, as well as the moralizing discourses upon which these social/political portraits of oppression depend.

To examine the places of sex tourism as negotiated spaces of identity, I situate this conception within a particular space: a bar in Cebu City.[1] The bar is owned by an Australian, managed by a Filipina, employs approximately 20 Filipina women, and is primarily frequented by white, Western men. Despite its vernacular status as a 'foreigner bar'. however, its space is far from being clearly indigenous or foreign: it is neither and both depending on how it is framed and experienced. Nor, as many pro-would argue, is the space of the bar clearly liberating or oppressive; it simultaneously offers the possibility of both liberation and oppression, together with a range of other experiences. While there is no 'true' reading of this landscape, the space itself is not entirely innocent. For the space of the bar is also situated within other spaces of political, religious and moral significance, and these conflicting and interpellative discourses play a role in how this real-and-imagined space is experienced and understood. Indeed, the bar is the place where the real and the imagined merge to mediate the performance of identity.

Because Cebu's bars, and the encounters occurring within them, are beyond dualistic economies of meaning and power. I begin by specifying an understanding of 'third space', as well as its implications for strategies of resistance. This is followed by a narrative of the everyday social relations in a bar in Cebu City, mapping a space for a Filipina subject. The bar is a space where dominant images and stereotypes are contested, where people speak from spaces beyond conventional representations of sex tourism, and where resistance, in potentially subversive forms, is possible. At the same time, however, it is the uneasy politics of third space encounters which invite the performance/visibility of fixed identities – identities which are thoroughly intelligible through representations which simultaneously circumscribe the stereotypes of the 'oppressor' and the 'victim'. I conclude by asking questions about the constitution of subjectivity in space and the spatial constitution of subjectivity, and how an understanding of third space can aid in our conception of geographies of resistance.

The ontology of this approach is not apolitical: instead, elaborating the negotiation of power and identity – revealing ambiguity, displacement and disjunction – refuses to totalize experience and therefore offers the potential to locate where more subtle sites of resistance are enunciated. There have been many ways of articulating the 'problem' of sex tourism within various political discourses in the Philippines, but these discourses remain largely dominated by the interpretations of middle-class activists. This is at least partially due to the reality that comprehending the political, economic and colonial dimensions of sex tourism does not necessarily provide a basis for understanding the more personalized modes of identification which form around issues of race, gender and sexuality. In short, emphasizing the determined character of prostitution ironically tends to alienate its subject. Elaborating a negotiated space in order to find contemporary sites of collaboration and contestation and new perspectives on identity, power and resistance provides a means to imagine more ambivalent deployments of power, and how space is constitutive of this process. For what if meaning and power are not necessarily mobilized through stereotypes and their associated dichotomies? Culture generally, and strategies of power in particular, are not found in predetermined categories of identity and experience, and power has the potential to be mobilized through ambivalence.[2]

'Third Space', Identity and Resistance

> Meaning is constructed across the *bar* of difference and separation between the signifier and the signified.[3] (Bhabha 1990: 210, emphasis added)

Drawing on recent writing in feminist and postcolonial studies. Pile (1994: 255) has argued that dualisms are 'intended to mark and help police supposedly fixed, natural divisions between the powerful and the disempowered', and that 'if we accept these dualisms then we collude in the reproduction of the power-ridden values they help to sustain'. As dualisms are more fluid than their architecture would suggest. Pile outlines an alternative to dualistic epistemologies which incorporates the notion of a new geometry of knowledge, or a 'third space'. This space is a location for knowledge which (a) elaborates the 'grounds of dissimilarity' on which dualisms are based: (b) acknowledges that there are spaces beyond dualisms; and (c) accepts that this third space itself is 'continually fragmented, fractured, incomplete, uncertain, and the site of struggles for meaning and representation' (ibid.: 273). An epistemology which uses the concept of third space therefore encourages a politics of location which recognizes the 'social construction of dualisms as part of the problem', as well as 'places beyond the grounds of dissimilarity – collectively named the third space' (ibid.: 264).[4]

This conception of third space is useful for examining the articulation, transgression and subversion of dualistic categories: indeed, in a metaphorical and material sense, this third space is the bar. The bar is the location of difference, particularly of the cultural, racial and sexual differences between white, Western men and Filipino women. It is, therefore, the location where various bar experiences are articulated and assigned meaning by bar employees, the men who frequent these establishments, and researchers such as myself. Yet this third space does not contain preconstituted identities which determine experience, nor does it possess an authentic character or identity. Instead, identities are continuously negotiated through this space of difference – apropos Bhabha's (1990) opening quote to this section – and therefore constituted through encounters with otherness. To elaborate this concept of negotiation. Pile draws on Bhabha's notions of hybridity and identification. For Bhabha,

> the importance of hybridity is not to be able to trace two original moments from which the third emerges, rather hybridity... is the 'third space' which enables other positions to emerge. This third space displaces the histories that constitute it, and sets up new structures of authority, new political initiatives, which are inadequately understood through received wisdom. (Bhabha 1990: 211)

Moreover, in enabling such other positions, this third space is therefore

> not so much [about] identity as identification (in the psychoanalytic sense)...identification is a process of identifying with and through another object, an object of otherness, at which point the agency of the identification – the subject – is itself always ambivalent, because of the intervention of that otherness. But the importance of hybridity is that it bears the traces of those feelings and practices which inform it, just like a translation, so that hybridity puts together the traces of certain other meanings or discourses. It does not give them the authority of being prior in the sense of being original: they are prior only in the sense of being anterior. The process of cultural hybridity gives rise to something different, something new and unrecognizable, a new area of negotiation of meaning and representation. (Ibid.)

I quote Bhabha at length due to the complexity of his statements, drawn – as Pile (1994) observes – from the psychoanalytic and poststructuralist traditions. What is stressed here is the ambivalence, and not fixity, of the construction of identity. 'Prostitutes' and 'customers' are actively produced through inherently unstable social encounters, and it is through these intersections of power and difference that they locate their oppositional identities. Both bar women and customers, for example, are conscious of the moralizing discourses of sex tourism, yet their constructions of prostitution draw from various and different cultural, historical and gendered positions. While some Western men might be inclined to construct the issue around the moral and secular perspectives of Western feminism (e.g. the subordination of women), Filipinas might be more inclined to situate their employment within the struggles of everyday life and Catholic beliefs (e.g. suffering, shame and martyrdom). Yet the result of negotiating these differences may be the articulation or subversion of prevailing notions of powerful/powerless in terms of how they experience their encounters: a 'submissive' Filipina may simultaneously be striving for self-actualization, a 'voyeuristic' Western customer may be humbled by an awareness that his masculinity is yoked to his pocket book. The third space is therefore capable of disrupting the 'received wisdom' which portrays sex tourism as an uncomplicated relation of domination.

Homi Bhabha's 'interstitial perspective' has most recently been criticized by feminist geographers as a disembodied – and gendered – perspective (Rose 1995). While a feminist critique of Bhabha is beyond the scope of this chapter, it is important to acknowledge at least some of these criticisms. First, Bhabha's attempts to disrupt the dominant gaze in colonial encounters spoke to my understanding of the relationships between men and women in Cebu's bars (which were simultaneously about race, class and sexuality). Bhabha's perspective appeared to be a useful way beyond the stereotypical representations of the voyeur/victim, opening a space for alternative subjectivities capable of differentially engaging the relations of the bar. Second, and if our theories are to be embodied, then hybridity and third space reflect my position as a researcher, as a white, Western woman who simultaneously identified with both *Western* men and Filipina *women*. It was not possible to locate myself at either the margins or the centre in this space – such a move would be dubious privilege. Third, while Bhabha's conception of third space stands accused of lacking critical possibilities or a radical potential, what I attempt here is to develop Bhabha's project in ways which take these concerns into account.

If the bar is a third space, an ambivalent space of negotiation, and a site of struggle for meaning and representation, then this approach to understanding power and identity poses interesting questions for geographies of resistance. In the context of Cebu's bars, these questions circulate around issues of how Filipino women find ways to engage Western men in ways which are not outside power, but are in interstitial spaces between power and identity. By dancing on the bar, and negotiating interstitial spaces through their own perspectives, women resist the power of the voyeuristic gaze through disruption rather than covert opposition. Yet this approach to resistance necessitates a different conception of power – one that is transient, flexible and ambivalent. Writing on resistance has traditionally relied on an assumption of power which was thought to oppress coherent human subjects. Resistance was therefore anchored to an essential measure of agency (usually class) as a point from which to undertake political projects.[5] The theoretical displacement of the human(ist) subject has most recently inspired critiques of these studies, which are said to neglect the complex layerings of meaning and subjection which inform social encounters, as well as how the deployment of power is frequently laced with contradiction, irony and compromise (Abu-Lughod 1990; Kondo 1990). Indeed, Kondo (1990: 219) has asked if 'articulating the problematic of power in terms of resistance may in fact be asking the wrong question'.

If everyday sites of struggle occur in places of overlapping and intersecting forms of subjection, and if domination is never achieved without ambivalence, then how are we to envision power and resistance? What is evident is that Foucault's (1978: 95) formulation 'where there is power, there is resistance' is no longer sufficient. One way forward is Abu-Lughod's (1990) reformulation 'where there is resistance, there is power', and resistance is understood as a 'diagnostic' of changing relations of power. Although Abu-Lughod's focus is on gender relations, by analysing resistance on its own terms, she displaces abstract theories of power with subjectivities capable of contingent and flexible modes of resistance. Through focusing on these resistances, we can begin to ask questions about precisely what relations of power are at play in different contexts. This approach therefore addresses the problem of attributing people with consciousness which is not a part of their experience, as well as opening the possibility for examining the more localized contexts of resistance. Within the internal politics of the bar, for example, bar women are not merely resisting white, Western men: they are resisting stereotypical encounters with men, their co-workers and researchers such as myself, where the categories of race, class, gender and sexuality place them in uneasy positions of coherence.

Now I introduce a new border – a shift to a narrative voice – to explore this conceptualization further. Drawing on the critical style of Malcomson (1995), I strategically destabilize the boundaries between self and other by replacing a first person narrative ('I') with a second person narrative ('you'). Malcomson's essay on the multiple identities performed by customers in a bar in Bulgaria formed the inspiration for this narrative, particularly his emphasis on the fluidity of bar patron identity. The second person narrative is not meant to reject or dismiss my own gaze, but rather to decentre and destabilize it – allowing 'you' to imagine and experience presumably discrete identities in different contexts.[6] It is also a device of memory, where the academic 'I' remembers the fieldworker (in this case 'you'), and a modality which reflects my own resistance to the confines of an academic discourse which occludes the smoke, beer, laughs, intimate chatter and secrets which permeate the space of the bar.

The Dialogics of the Dance: An Evening at the Brunswick

It's 5:30 p.m. and you're in the Brunswick waiting for Cora. She agreed to meet for a beer before work so you could talk about her life in Cebu. Last month she told you she was completing high school in Leyte a few months ago when her poverty-stricken parents forced her to migrate to Cebu to seek paid employment. Because of her lack of education, she resorted to working in a bar: 'I had no choice,' she'd said, 'what else could I do?' You know this is a common story in and around the growing metropolis, but Edna – another employee of the Brunswick and your friend for almost a year now – said they worked together in a bar around the American military bases before the Mount Pinatubo eruption. 'That's why she got those breast enlarge-ments', Edna elaborated, 'and where did you think she learned to speak Pampangan? Of course she's been working in a bar before.' You're interested in hearing Cora's side of the story.

It's 6:30 p.m. and you sit at the bar watching women trickle into the Brunswick from the crowded streets of Fuente Osmeña. Anna, Edna, Maryann and some new women have arrived, but there's no sign of Cora. While you wait, you spend some time talking to Fely, the manager, who has proven to be an endless source of anecdotes about life in the Philippines. Most of the bar women believe Fely used to work as a prostitute in Manila, where she met her husband, the Australian owner of the bar. Fely disregards such *tsismis* (gossip) as pure jealousy over her elevated social status, however, and tells you grand stories about working in various jobs around the Philippines.

Fely spends time talking to you because she too is taking note of recent arrivals; indeed, she is waiting for them. Each night she sits at the bar writing each woman's name onto a list as they arrive. The list is very much like a roll call – Fely is very strict on attendance and punctuality – but will also serve as the dancing order and an inventory of the ladies' drinks each woman earns for the evening. Fely's air of formality and strictness contrasts with the chatting and laughter emanating from the back rooms where her employees are spending their time preparing for the night: dressing up, putting on make-up, eating dinner, chatting about last night's business or their boy-friends and wondering if the night's business will be good.

Cora shows up at almost 7:00 p.m., and you know she doesn't have time to talk. She just strolls past by you, barely catching your eye and not saying a word. Later Edna will inform you that Cora cannot separate your identity from that of a religious or social worker, and after dealing with your frustration – you've emphasized your support and don't want people to hold that opinion of you – you accept that as a good strategy for women who have been previously condemned for their employment. 'Anyway,' Edna will say, 'she'll never understand and you have lots of friends who want to talk to you in the bar already.'

This passage is simultaneously a story about identity, power and resistance. Cora's refusal to separate my identity (as a student/researcher) from a religious or social worker[7] can be read in many ways. First, it can be seen as resistance to confronting the power of moralizing discourse; Cora resisted such power through refusing to talk. Second, Cora's identification of herself as a particular subject – an immoral Filipina – relates to prevailing attitudes about prostitution. Most bar women are aware that in many Western countries, as in the Philippines, prostitution is conceived of as an immoral form of employment, although Western men and women are more inclined to understand the context of poverty in the Philippines. While this identification may have been ambiguous for Cora, it nonetheless impeded our ability to communicate. Edna, on the other hand, was pleased to inform me that I had many friends in the bar already, and that my research did not require a formalized interview with Cora. This identification – where to Edna my interest developed from research to empathy and friendship – led to a new area of negotiation between friends like Edna and myself, where I learned that constructing her as a subject was only possible through my academic pursuits. To Edna I was merely a student at the local university who was interested in the lives of bar women and, while she patiently answered my many questions. I assumed part of that identity too.

Cora's breast enlargements are one example of how the bodies of Filipina bar women – or more appropriately, 'dancers', as they refer to themselves – become marked through the selective incorporation of features of an imagined Western sexuality. Other examples would be the use of cosmetics, and various drugs to control their weight. These practices are often interpreted by middle-class Filipinos as a purely Western influence – large breasts and skinny bodies are not highly valued in the Philippines, but are dominant in imported pornography and television programmes – but they could also be read as the psychological dynamics of resistance which allow women to retain control of their bodies. Dancers re-learn their bodies in new and often revolutionary ways during their employment in the sex industry, and this is often equated with 'becoming modern'. Yet while dancers' bodies express modernity they also bear the marks of being Filipino. Their dancing styles and entertaining costumes, for example, follow distinctively Filipino fashion trends. It is precisely this hybridity – exotic otherness and a sexualized modernity – that male customers are often attracted to (cf. Manderson 1995).

Finally, it is important to note Cora's assertion of having 'no choice' but to work in a bar, which bears resemblance to Foucault's (1978) notion of a 'reverse discourse'. In the Philippines, political mobilization against sex tourism has primarily been based on analyses which situate prostitution within the political economy of colonialism, militarism and sex tourism.[8] By emphasizing the structural determinants of why women enter the sex industry, however, Filipina dancers are cast as 'victims' who have no choice. While it could be argued that this representation victimizes women, denies agency and distorts the complexity of experience, here it is important to note that the naturalness of the choice issue can be appropriated by women themselves, where having 'no choice' simultaneously becomes a source of agency, a resistance to moral judgements and justification for their employment.

> It's Maryann's night to do manicures so you go out to the back room to get one yourself. Maryann is very petite and shy, and is fussy about the customers she goes out with, so Fely has agreed she can earn extra money from this side-business one night a week. This used to be Maryann's regular employment in her *barangay* (suburb) until her husband was sent to jail last year and she needed more money to support her two children. Everyone agrees Maryann's manicures are very good, and she needs the money, so you splurge and get your toes done with red polish too.
>
> While you get your manicure, you realize that your own *placement* in the bar is related to your relationships with the women – it took a long time until you were invited to this back room, for example, or until you were comfortable sitting out front by the

dance floor. You also wonder about the recent government AIDS information campaign about sterilizing manicuring equipment between customers, but know this is not the time nor place to mention it. Whenever you've tried to get to this aspect of your research – to discuss AIDS as an issue for sex workers – this space becomes awkward and silent. You've wondered if AIDS has been delimited as an impossible subject, and if there are too many borders for you, as an outsider, to cross. Of course they use condoms whenever they can, but by virtue of the fact that you are not a dancer, it is difficult for you to participate in discussion of the times when they don't. Dancers are obliging in terms of discussing their sexual lives with you, but condom use, if discussed in a rational or clinical way, is difficult. You end up feeling like a City Health Official and the answers you get are rehearsed.

The recent government AIDS education campaign did not go unnoticed by bar women in Cebu. This was partially due to the increased information drive at their weekly check-ups at the City Health Department, but also because there had been several interested non-government organizations through the bar over the past year asking them to fill out KAPB (knowledge, attitude, practice and belief) questionnaires. The most profound effect, however, came from the release of a Filipino film, *The Dolzura Movie*, which was a more emotionally charged perspective on a woman who had contracted the virus. While bar women were happy to answer KAPB questionnaires and discuss the movie in terms of their fear, they located these discussions in two distinct discursive realms: KAPB questionnaires were part of an official education campaign they were required to participate in, while the film dealt with personal circumstance, emotions and love.

There are several academic and activist 'theories' regarding why women in the sex industry do not use condoms for every sexual encounter. In the Philippines it is emphasized that women in the sex industry do not use condoms with their regular partners, and while at work, have less negotiating power due to the oppressive nature of the business. While it is true that bar women tend not to use condoms with their regular boyfriends in order to separate work from pleasure, to equate the non-use of condoms with general disempowerment distorts the issue. The non-use of condoms, in what would appear to be unreasonable circumstances according to middle-class sensibilities, has more to do with Filipino conceptions of *bahala na* – translated by Enriquez (1990: 302) as 'risk-taking in the face of the proverbial cloud of uncertainty and the possibility of failure' – than with disempowerment or a lack of negotiating skills. Many women employed in these establishments are looking for a future husband, and the use of condoms in these instances – that is, with a prospective husband – is seen to impede the achievement of intimacy, and ultimately, an opportunity to exit the industry.

Awkwardness, particularly in the form of silences and bodily discomfort, is a common phenomenon in the bar. Such awkwardness occurs in the space between attempting to comprehend a situation, and articulating a (suitable) response to it. In a sense this uneasiness may embody the third space concept, and is what makes the bar a 'special' space. If third spaces are merely spaces where dualisms are worked out, then all spaces in a sense are third spaces. But in the Brunswick, as in most bars, uneasy silences and bodily discomfort are better conceived as the result of uncertain identities in tension. In the back room of the Brunswick, for example, discussions of HIV/AIDS had previously provoked the performance of official, public health identities, but these identities were inappropriate/d for a space which was usually used for chatting and socializing. Rather than interrupting this space with what could be considered an interrogation, I opted instead to listen to stories about Maryann's children, her previous employment and the high quality of her beautician skills.

Although discussions on HIV/AIDS in the back room fell outside appropriate codes of conduct, the public area of the bar is a space where dominant codes can be transgressed. Dominant codes of morality, for example, prohibit commerical sex between Western men and Filipino women. It is the possibility of precisely this kind of sex, however, that creates a third space of bodily discomfort and a quest for an individual subject position. If the third space is a 'space' of negotiated identity, and more specifically, if it is a space beyond dualisms, then both the bar and the body can be conceived of as sites of ambivalence and negotiation. In this space dancers are awkward on their first nights in the business, and new customers tend to be rather gauche. Researchers are 'out of place' in this environment, so negotiating an appropriate subject position – whether it be in the back room discussing HIV/AIDS or sitting out front watching a dancer perform – is hardly surprising.[9]

A few customers arrive. You look at them and suspect they're probably tourists, and probably here for the first time. They look nervous and unsure of what to do or where to sit tonight, but by tomorrow you know they'll be acting like regulars. You've stopped being so self-conscious and aware of the white, male tourist gaze for some time now, and briefly wonder why they're staring at you. One of them looks as if he is about to engage you in conversation, but Edna comes over to remind you about the birthday party in her *barangay* the next day. You're grateful you don't have to talk to this man after being berated by a drunken Australian the week prior. He had demanded to know why you were in the Brunswick, and when you told him, he accused you of wasting Australian tax money by carrying out research in bars, and particularly because you're Canadian.

Edna's neighbour Lorna, who works at a nearby bar, comes in to see what's going on in the Brunswick. She's on a steady barfine this week: she's enteraining a young Australian 'boyfriend' who's she's been travelling around Cebu with. Last night he took her to a beach resort where they went jet-skiing and skinny-dipping, and today she's lost her voice so cannot work. She and the Australian are playing pool in a nearby pub, the Richmond, and she asks you if you'd like to join them. The Richmond is a staple hangout for foreigners, particularly for local expats and tourists who have come to Cebu to scuba dive. Lorna knows all of the bartenders and waitresses – many of her customers bring her here to socialize – so you stop to chat and compare notes on Lorna's boyfriend. Fely has unofficially banned all Brunswick employees from entering the Richmond unescorted, however, because she says it makes them look cheap because they have no reason to be there apart from 'hunting'. Lorna points out the 'hunting girls' that are working the bar tonight. 'Hunting girls', she tells you, 'aren't dancers, and don't work in a bar. They're just working when they want to, and looking for a man who will give her all their money – no barfine – and may be she'll tell them she's not working, it's just for fun.'

You play a few games of pool and think the Australian is OK. You want to check him out because Lorna is pretty serious about him. This is his second trip to see her, and he sent her twelve red roses for her birthday last month. She confides that she's planning to have his baby, while you're happy she's happy, you wonder what she needs another baby for; she already has two Amerasian children from when she was working in Olongapo. But you say nothing of the sort because you're happy for her, you know how much Filipinas love children, and how dancers often see children as an opportunity to solidify a relationship.

The community where Lorna and Edna, and several other Fuente Osmeña bar women live has an extensive history of women migrating to work in the bars around the American military bases at Angeles and Olongapo. The first bar woman is rumoured to have migrated in the late 1960s, after which time a series of personal recruitments produced a steady flow of women to both cities. Many families rely on remittances from daughters elsewhere in the Philippines, or from daughters who have married American men and are now living in the United States. The Mount Pinatubo volcanic eruption in 1991 saw the unequivocal departure of American servicemen, however, and this event also displaced thousands of dancers in both cities, many of whom came from communities such as Lorna's. Both Lorna and Edna migrated back to Cebu in 1992, and obtained employment in the bars of Fuente Osmeña. In contrast to the perspectives of those who strive to abolish sex tourism, it is important to note that they do not see themselves as victims to American imperialism.

The phenomenon of 'hunting' should not pass unremarked, although my contact with these women was fleeting and occasional. The women I spoke to who were 'hunters' either currently, or had previously, worked in a bar in Cebu. They were frustrated with the bar owners' commissions on their 'barfines', which were perceived to be an unfair reduction to their salaries (primarily thought to be obtained from dancing and entertaining customers in the bar).[10] In this case hunting provides the opportunity to transgress the boundaries of a dancer identity which, as evidenced in Fely's strictness in attendance and punctuality, as well as her ban on employees in the Richmond, is also one of 'employee'. Hunting emphasizes women's looking and agency, revealing their ambivalence in negotiating their identities with Western men in different spaces.

> It's 10:00 p.m. and you walk back to the Brunswick. Some of the regulars are around and the space feels more comfortable: there are more people around, there is less overt staring and the women are happy because they're earning drinks. One of the regulars is May's German customer Hans, but that doesn't stop a group of women from coaxing him to buy them a drink: Alice is telling him about her sick mother, and Anna is telling him she needs a break from working but her family cannot afford it. Ladies' drinks cost the customer from P50 to P100, and the women receive a P25 to P50 commission for each drink. The women know Hans is sometimes generous and, anyway, May has a Filipino boyfriend at home. You look at May, she's acting so confident – she knows she'll be out making money on short time tonight – and you remember that she's almost 35 years old although she looks much younger. She's been working in the business off and on since she was 18, and has lived with two former husbands in Europe and the Middle East respectively. She always gets the German customers because she speaks their language.
>
> You go and join the group and say hello to everyone. The women are chattering in Cebuano and you hear them discussing how cheap Hans is because he won't buy anyone but May a drink. Behind their backs such customers are 'cheap charlies' or 'kuripot' (in Tagalog, the national language, this is the word for 'cheap'), but Hans has

been in the Philippines long enough to speak Tagalog, so they're calling him '*tahik*', which is the Cebuano translation. You ask him if he's buying rounds, but he tells you – for what is probably the fifth time – that he just runs a scuba-diving shop and earns Filipino wages. You laugh but understand his point and so does Edna, who tells everyone to go look somewhere else for a drink. Hans buys the three of you a beer.

You ask May about the women soliciting drinks and she reminisces about a time when things were different. 'These girls we have right now, they're only interested in money', she tells you, 'like if they can get a customer that night. You see how they react if a customer walks in, and I hate that. Our old group was not like that before. I mean, we wait, give him a chance. Not like now, one customer and five girls at the table, its supposed to be the customer wants her or likes her, you know, and then they cannot say anything because they are too embarrassed to say.' You agree but wonder if a round of drinks isn't really that expensive after all.

While Edna and Hans talk about scuba-diving, you and May notice one of the new dancers on the stage. She looks extremely uncomfortable because tonight is her first night, and May informs you she's a virgin. She was recruited by a friend who also took a job in the Brunswick as a virgin but married her first customer, a Norwegian man, after only three days on the job. 'I talked to her tonight', May tells you, 'and I said if you are dancing, dance with the music. Don't dance and look around because you don't know how you're reacting on the stage. You know, it's boring. The customer, instead of saying "hey she's nice", says "hey she's boring". So I told her that if you dance, don't think about the girls around you. Listen to the music and dance with it, then you will feel good. That's what I did before.'

Calling Hans cheap to his face, but in another language, can be understood as a source of resistance; but it is a resistance directed not only at Hans, it is also directed at May. Hans is an expatriate with a Filipina wife, and only engages in 'short time' with May. Both May and Hans have Filipino partners they return to each night, and neither are interested in an emotional relationship. Because Hans is not a prospective husband for women in the bar, but also because they know his wife – she used to work at the Brunswick a few years ago – many dancers question both his and May's morality. It is frequently insinuated that Western men differ from Filipino men in that Filipino infidelity is more concealed, and therefore more respectable. Therefore, while Hans' ineligibility and infidelity should deter women from soliciting drinks so staunchly, their inclination to solicit May's customer in particular is derived from wanting Hans to pay for his pleasure, on the one hand, while questioning May's morality on the other. Many women justify their employment in the sex industry through their desire for a better life, symbolized by their desire for relationships with customers. It is precisely this absence of desire in May that vexes them.

Although my purpose here is not to analyse 'romance', the centrality of love and emotional pursuits should not be denied. Indeed, May's attraction and 'short time' with Hans are criticized by many women because they are not interested in 'love'. It would be unfair to cast dancers as merely seeking the allure of wealth or an escape from poverty, because their relations with foreign men – even if they desert or disappoint them – are most often seen fairly favourably. Furthermore, Catholic ideas about victimhood and martyrdom play a constitutive role in terms of their emotional desire. It is difficult to place their desire outside the pursuit of happiness via foreign men, marriage and more children, and this desire also connects to the non-use of condoms to achieve intimacy with customers. *Contra* Hochschild's

(1983) position on the professionalization of emotions in the hospitality industry, however, there are 'real' relationships that form in the bar, happy marriages are consummated, and these relationships often provide both the dancers and the customers with opportunities for marriage. These contradictions, which are marginalized within current debates on sex tourism, are important in the constitution of dancer subjectivity.

Because of her age and long-term employment in the bar, May usually takes it upon herself to initiate new women through advice on interacting with customers, other bar women, as well as miscellaneous tips on personal hygiene (usually on condoms, personal and customer genital health and how to avoid being diagnosed positive for STDs at the City Health Department). May's advice on dancing in this passage is interesting because she identifies an important gaze as coming from the women themselves (i.e. not the customers). Most women identify their first few weeks of employment in the sex industry as tremendously difficult, and this is at least partially due to the look May specifies. Because the bar is a space that breaches dominant codes of morality, new dancers must negotiate the way this space is understood. As the opinion on May's involvement with Hans indicates, it is also a judgemental look that continues throughout the course of bar work.

> It's almost midnight and a man you might call a holiday regular comes in. His name is Derek, he's a successful businessman in Australia, and he spends all of his holidays in Cebu. You've had the opportunity to talk to him before because his good friend is your current housemate's boyfriend; you've all been for dinner, dancing and hanging around to enjoy the relative luxuries of the Graduate Hotel. The bar is crowded and one of the few seats left is beside you. He comes over to join you. May, Hans, Edna, and what would appear to be Edna's impending barfine. Derek asks you how your research is going and you tell him you're doing fine. He always wants to talk about your research because he's certain that he's an expert whose opinion you should solicit. You do want to talk to him, since his presence plays an important role in dancers' lives, and you recognize that customers all have their own constructions of bar work. Tonight Derek wants to talk about how the bars in Cebu are no different from the pick-up bars in Australia, except that the women in Cebu get paid for their sexual liaisons. He dissociates prostitution in Cebu from prostitution in Australia because in Cebu the women are interested in more than sex, and are willing to spend more of their time with him. 'It's really a much better deal for your money', he says, 'I've been coming here almost every month for two years.'

Derek's perceived parallel between Cebu's bars and pick-up bars in Australia is partly a denial that he is paying for sex, and therefore, by implication, that he is morally degenerate and sexually inadequate. At the same time, however, it must also be acknowledged that dancers in Cebu consider themselves more than prostitutes, they are also city guides, interpreters of local culture, prospective wives, and so on. Both dancers and customers maintain these impossible spaces for themselves – as pick-up artists, as prospective wives – spaces that subvert dominant codes of behaviour and morality in interesting ways. Resistance in these spaces is about negotiating uneasy and contradictory feelings and desires.

Furthermore, it is important to note Derek's dissociation of these bars, and his desire for relationships which are about, but are also more than, sex. As mentioned above, customers are often attracted to the hybridity of dancer sexuality, but in some emotional relationships the contradictions of these desires may not be resolvable. While some men desire the sexy selflessness of Asian women, for example, it is also true that employment in the sex industry is constitutive of dancer's self-actualization. In this sense the women's intentions contradict the assumptions of the 'submissive' stereotype, emphasizing that this identity is not accepted without struggle. Yet the desire for a sincere relationship does exist on the part of some customers, a large proportion of whom are divorced and in their forties and fifties. While such desire meshes well with dancers' desires for marriage, it is also true that many of the women do not find many of the men physically attractive. These men are therefore in a position where their allure is their wealth. While this position is a form of power, it also underlines the contradictory relationships between sex, money and the uneasy politics of third space.

Dancing on the Bar: Mapping Geographies of Resistance

> [Nietzsche] insisted on a new type of philosophy or knowledge, one which, instead of remaining sedentary, ponderous, stolid, was allied with the arts of movement: theatre, dance, and music. Philosophy itself was to be written walking – or preferably, *dancing*. (Grosz 1994: 127, emphasis added)

Dancing on the bar, as a play on words, is one way to imagine the subjectivity of Filipino dancers. First, it bears in mind the importance of dancing to employment in Cebu's sex industry. Working in a bar is about, but also exceeds, the exchange of money for commercial sex. Second, dancing *on* the bar is an attempt to displace the dominant representations of sex tourism which, through emphasizing the oppressive relationship between Western men and Filipino women, fails to recognize the production of identities through the negotiation of the sex tourism encounter. Finally, it is a way to stress the importance of the kind of *dancing* to which Grosz refers: that is, a way to recognize that women in Cebu's sex tourism industry are capable of manoeuvring to position themselves within multiple and intersecting relations of power.

The relationship between resistance and subjectivity, however, is more problematic. It might be helpful first to differentiate between identity and subjectivity, demonstrating how the performance of particular identities can itself be understood as resistance, while at the same time recognizing that the performance itself tells only part of the story. In their analysis of Rio Carnival, for example, Lewis and Pile (1996) have suggested that the performance and masquerade of identity (in this case, femininity) can be a form of resistance that renders that particular identity indeterminate and unknowable. Following Butler (1990, 1993), they maintain that the most productive effect of power is to secure these identities as visible/intelligible. Within this framework it could be argued that dancers in Cebu are aware of, and perform, their status as objects (of Western desire) and subjects (immoral Filipinas). Many incorporate features of an imagined Western identity (e.g. the use of cosmetics, tobacco, and the attainment of an ideal breast size or weight), for example, particularly as they 'become modern'. Furthermore, and within more traditional understandings of performance, women often perceive their sexual relations in emotional terms. Although these fantasies and incorporations only become visible through stereotypes which deny the lived experience of sex work, reading them in this way also has the potential to undermine resistance as either reproducing stereotypes or as participating in their own oppression. It is therefore important to acknowledge that as these women 'become modern' and experience emotional attachments, new images and desires are simultaneously being produced.

These new images and desires exist in a third space of possibilities which are not capable of being understood within current theorizing on sex tourism in the Philippines. At the same time, however, it is precisely these possibilities which are constantly engaging meaning and power: the bar is one site: the body, however, is another. Yet by restricting an analysis of resistance to the performance of identity, demonstrating how dancers ritually escape dualistic economies of meaning and power, dancers are reduced to a series of 'subject effects' which have little internal coherence (Ortner 1995). Instead of focusing on these 'effects', it is useful to focus on what becomes defined as contested terrain, and how resistance can, and does, surface.

Cora's refusal to speak to me, reactions to Alma's engagement in 'short time' with Hans, and Derek's dissociation of prostitution in Cebu are good examples of how power can be produced through stereotypes (and not through a clear relation of domination), and how dancers can refuse to occupy particular subject positions which place them in uneasy positions of coherence. In a sense these resistances are, indeed, effects. An alternative approach would be to replace these effects with a subject capable of resistance, but this runs the risk of essentializing the subject and 'romanticizing' the concept of resistance (Abu-Lughod 1990). To focus instead on how individual resistances reveal power in particular contexts and how these resistances, taken together, play a role in defining the contested terrain of politics in/at the bar may be another way to conceptualize resistance while simultaneously displacing dichotomized relations of power. Within these domains there are mobile and multiple points of resistance which surface in dancers' relationships with customers, researchers, management and between themselves, and at issue are more personalized questions of self-actualization, personal ethics, friendship, morality and so on.

One evening in the Brunswick, and this approach to resistance raises interesting questions about what assumptions of power, agency and encounters between people have been assumed in traditional analyses of resistance. In reconceptualizing the space of the bar as a negotiated space, a third space where identities are negotiated and ambivalent, performed and not fixed, it becomes possible to question the positioning of dancers as 'victims'. While the 'reality' of sex tourism in the Philippines is a historically specific reality, the practice of sex tourism, and the various identities of the bar are certainly more ambiguous. Understanding the manner in which points of resistance surface in the contested terrain of the bar offers a way to conceptualize the politics of meaning within the sites of sex tourism, as well as our comprehension of geographies of resistance.

NOTES

1 Cebu City is the second largest city in the Philippines with a metropolitan population of approximately 1 million people. The events described here are not fictional: they occurred

in many of the different bars in which my research was carried out (between November 1992 and March 1994). The names of all people and places have been replaced with pseudonyms.

2 Cf. Bhabha (1994: 38, 66–7).

3 Bhabha's (1990) 'bar' is derived from the space between signifier/signified and he is primarily concerned with 'culture' and issues of meaning in translation. I have borrowed this quote and highlighted the *bar* to spatialize this concept within the entertainment establishments of Cebu City.

4 Many authors, particularly within feminist and cultural studies, have sought to theorize this space. See, for example, Irigaray (1985); hooks (1991); Grosz (1994); Bhabha (1990, 1994); Keith and Pile (1993).

5 The work I refer to here is the well-known literature on the English working class (Willis 1977) and peasants in Southeast Asia (Scott 1985). Ong's (1987, 1991) important work on factory women in Malaysia also focuses on classbased resistance, but the brings issues such as indigenous religious systems and Japanese management techniques to bear on the concept of resistance.

6 See also Murray (1995).

7 'Social worker' was the term Edna used to describe a range of government and non-government professionals, whether involved in health, employment or community development issues.

8 For a review of some of these perspectives, see Enloe (1989). Miralao et al. (1990) and Sturdevant and Stoltzfus (1992).

9 Geographers have also discussed the phenomenon of personal comfort in terms of the production of private and public space (e.g. Valentine 1989), and gay and straight space (e.g. Bell et al. 1994).

10 A barfine is the amount a customer pays to take a woman outside the bar, although dancers often refer to their paying customers as barfines as well. Barfines in Cebu were approximately P300 during 1992–4, and were usually split 50/50 between the woman and the bar. A night's salary for dancing and entertaining customers ranged from P100 to P150. During this time the exchange rate was approximately US$1 = P25.

REFERENCES

Abu-Lughod, L. (1990) 'The romance of resistance: tracing transformations of power through Bedouin women', *American Ethnologist* 17 (1): 41–55.

Bell, D., Binnie, J., Cream, J. and Valentine, G. (1994) 'All hyped up and no place to go', *Gender, Place and Culture* 1 (1): 31–47.

Bhabha, H. (1990) 'The third space: interview with Homi Bhabha', in J. Rutherford (ed.) *Identity: Community, Culture, Difference*, London: Lawrence and Wishart.

—— (1994) *The Location of Culture*, London and New York: Routledge.

Butler, J. (1990) *Gender Trouble: Feminism and the Subversion of Identity*, New York: Routledge.

—— (1993) *Bodies that Matter: On the Discursive Limits of Sex*, New York: Routledge.

Enloe, C. (1989) *Bananas, Beaches and Bases: Making Feminist Sense of International Politics*. London: Pandora Press.

Enriquez, V. (1990) 'Indigenous personality theory', in V. Enriquez (ed.) *Indigenous Psychology*, Quezon City: Akademya ng Sikolohiyang Pilipino.

Foucault, M. (1978) *The History of Sexuality: An Introduction*, Volume 1. London: Penguin Books.

Grosz, E. (1994) *Volatile Bodies: Toward a Corporeal Feminism*, St Leonards, NSW: Allen and Unwin.

Hochschild, A. R. (1983) *The Managed Heart: Commercialisation of Human Feeling*, Berkeley, CA: University of California Press.

hooks, b. (1991) *Yearning: Race, Gender, and Cultural Politics*, London Turnaround.

Irigaray, L. (1985) *This Sex Which is Not One*, trans. C. Porter with C. Burke, Ithaca, NY: Cornell University Press.

Keith, M. and Pile, S. (eds) (1993) *Place and the Politics of Identity*, New York: and London: Routledge.

Kondo, D. (1990) *Crafting Selves: Power, Gender and Discourses of Identity in a Japanese Workplace*, Chicago, IL: University of Chicago Press.

Lewis, C. and Pile, S. (1996) 'Woman, body, space: Rio Carnival and the politics of performance', *Gender, Place and Culture* 3 (1): 33–41.

Malcomson, S. (1995) 'Disco dancing in Bulgaria', in M. Henderson (ed.) *Borders, Boundaries, and Frames: Essays in Cultural Criticism and Cultural Studies.* New York: Routledge.

Manderson, L. (1995) 'The pursuit of pleasure and the sale of sex', in P. Abramson (ed.) *Sexual Nature/Sexual Culture: Theorising Sexuality from the Perspective of Pleasure*, Chicago, IL: University of Chicago Press.

Miralao, V. A., Carlos, C. O. and Santos, A. F. (1990) *Women Entertainers in Angeles and Olongapo: A Survey Report*, Manila: Women's Education, Development, Productivity and Research Organization (WEDPRO) and Katipunan ng Kababaihan Para Sa Kalayaan (KALAYAAN).

Murray, A. (1995) 'Femme on the streets, butch in the sheets', in D. Bell and G. Valentine (eds) *Mapping Desire*, New York: Routledge.

Ong, A. (1987) *Spirits of Resistance and Capitalist Discipline: Factory Women in Malaysia*, Albany: State University of New York Press.

—— (1991) 'The gender and labour politics of postmodernity', *Annual Review of Anthropology* 20: 279–309.

Ortner, S. (1995) 'Resistance and the problem of ethnographic refusal'. *Comparative Studies in Society and History* 37 (1): 173–93.

Pile, S. (1994) 'Masculinism, the use of dualistic epistemologies and third spaces', *Antipode* 26 (3): 255–77.

Rose, G. (1995) 'The interstitial perspective: a review essay on Homi Bhabha's *The location of culture*', *Environment and Planning D: Society and Space* 13: 365–73.

Scott, J. (1985) *Weapons of the Weak: Everyday Forms of Peasant Resistance*, New Haven, CT: Yale University Press.

Sturdevant, S. Pollock and Stoltzfus, B. (1992) *Let the Good Times Roll: Prostitution and the US Military in Asia*, New York: New Press.

Valentine, G. (1989) 'The geography of women's fear', *Area* 21 (4): 385–90.

Willis, P. (1977) *Learning to Labour: How Working Class Kids get Working Class Jobs*, Farnborough: Saxon House.

Chapter 20

A Joint's a Joint

S. Denton and R. Morris

It is the last night of the twentieth century. In extravagant worldwide programming to befit the occasion, television networks from the United States and several other countries beam their live satellite coverage back and forth among the major cities of the world. Most of the focus is on the great centers of Western civilization and commerce: Paris, London, New York – and Las Vegas.

As the day and evening wear on, it is striking: in a half-dozen languages broadcast to an audience of hundreds of millions, no metropolis, no locale on the planet, receives more attention, has more of its entertainment, color, and imagery portrayed to the world, than the city in the southern Nevada desert that scarcely existed when the century began. The extraordinary television coverage reflects a consensus of producers, and a careful demographic survey of what the universal viewers want and expect. The cameras register a reality of power. On the eve of the millennium, Las Vegas is a global capital.

The backdrop of the city's mammoth, towering resorts tends to dwarf the special New Year's Eve correspondents standing in front of them to deliver their reports. Television's latest digital cameras swivel, zoom, and then retreat in vain efforts to encompass the famous Strip. Las Vegas has changed so much so rapidly over the last decade, says commentator after commentator, that the city would be unrecognizable to those who had not been there recently. Yet so many millions of people have visited the city over the last half century that reporters seem to take for granted the audience's fascination with the place, their easy familiarity with the most famous street on earth.

Straining to picture the panorama, one network positions a crew atop the 1,149-foot-tall Stratosphere Tower casino, only 200 feet short of New York's World Trade Center and the tallest building west of the Mississippi. Another camera hovers nearby in the cabin of a blimp 1,500 feet above the Las Vegas Valley floor. No lens, no single vantage point seems able to take it all in. But then the sweep of the city has never been easy to discern, whatever its scope.

What the cameras are trying to convey is the result of a transformation so complete that the familiar phrase 'building boom' seems a trivializing description.

The Las Vegas of the later 1980s, though an impressive national showcase and already the country's major tourist attraction, seems shabby in comparison to what stands here now.

In 1989 Steve Wynn builds on a South Seas theme the Strip's first wholly new resort in sixteen years, the luxurious $610 million Mirage, with more than 3,000 guestrooms in three thirty-story towers, atop grand ballrooms larger than any tsar's. In 1990 Circus Circus Enterprises, under its president, Bill Bennett, opens the $300 million 'medieval' Excalibur, the first theme park concept resort casting Las Vegas as a family playground, though beneath its castle turrets is a casino the size of four football fields.

In 1993 Bennett expands on an Egyptian theme to open the $375 million Luxor, with more than 2,500 rooms and the world's largest atrium in a thirty-story bronze and glass pyramid, entered through a sphinx of matching magnitude. That same year Wynn and his associates open the $430 million Treasure Island, a 2,900-room resort on a Caribbean theme with three thirty-six-story towers and a 100,000-foot casino designed on the model of a pirate city. By now, too, Kirk Kerkorian has built his new $1 billion MGM Grand Hotel, Casino, and Theme Park, the world's second-largest hotel, with more than 5,000 rooms, and the biggest casino on the planet, featuring 3,500 slot machines and 170 tables around the motif of *The Wizard of Oz* and Hollywood.

In 1996 Bob Stupak builds Las Vegas's own space needle, the towering $550 million Stratosphere with its 100,000-square-foot casino, and amusement thrill rides as high above the street as the top floors of the Empire State Building. That year, too, Wynn and other partners build the $344 million Monte Carlo as an expression of what they call the 'popular elegance' of Monaco; its 3,000 rooms make it the seventh largest hotel in the world.

In 1997 a consortium of Kerkorian and other associates who own Nevada casinos outside Las Vegas build New York New York, a $2 billion replica of what they call the 'Best of the Big Apple,' complete with copies of famous skyscrapers, street mimes, a Statue of Liberty, a Brooklyn Bridge, a Coney Island roller coaster, and a casino cashier's cage designed after the Manhattan financial district. In 1998 Wynn opens the $1.8 billion luxury Bellagio, with its thirty-five stories and 3,000 rooms. The same year Circus Circus Enterprises inaugurates the $1 billion, 4,000-room Mandalay Bay, set in a 'rainforest,' and featuring at the entrance to its Red Square restaurant and vodka bar a larger-than-life statue of Lenin imported as a trophy from the former Soviet Union.

In the last year of the century, computer trade show promoter Sheldon Adelson brings on his $2 billion Venetian Hotel Resort and Casino, with two ornate thirty-five-floor towers and 6,000 accommodations – all suites. Also in 1999 Arthur Goldberg, formerly of Bally's and now the head of Park Place Entertainment (merging Bally's and Hilton), opens the $750 million, fifty-story Paris with 3,000 rooms and a two-acre swimming pool.

To make way for it all, monuments of the past are erased, a grand publicity stunt made of the destruction. Two hundred thousand people gather on an October night in 1993 as Wynn throws the switch to implode floor by floor the old Dunes, with the Sands, Hacienda, and Landmark soon to follow, more hotel rooms demolished in a few years than most cities have come to possess over the century. Off the Strip, hundreds of millions of dollars in public as well as private funds have gone to rebuild and modernize, and the result is the 'Fremont Street Experience,' a five-block-long pedestrian mall (enclosed by 2 million lights), the city's old Glitter Gulch, including the Horseshoe, California, El Cortez, Four Queens, Fremont, Golden Nugget, and Las Vegas Club. And beyond the Strip and downtown are a string of showy new satellite casinos set about the valley – among them the Rio, the Boulder, the Sunset, and the Palace Stations.

Opulent beyond anything Las Vegas has ever known, the new Strip mega-resorts, with their $400-a-night accommodations, house world-famous gourmet cafés, and fashionable international boutiques with such tenants as Armani, Chanel, Lagerfeld, Hermès, and Gucci. The new casino complexes, self-contained bazaars of luxury, mark Las Vegas's appeal to the richest and increasingly prosperous top 5 percent of America's population. Though the city still draws and depends upon the general populace – striving 'to sell its elitism to the masses,' as one local journalist puts it – it has always been a place where ordinary people come to feel extraordinary. But now that the preponderance of visitors cannot afford the sumptuous new rooms and restaurants, they troop through the new resorts and their enclosed malls with Paris street names or Italian marble walkways, peering at the window displays and ornate lobbies as if they were passersby in the exclusive blocks of some Gilded Age city.

Yet beyond the glamor and massiveness of the once again reinvented city, its essence never changes. The new corridors of affluence and pretension still lead to the gigantic casinos that are the heart of the matter, the reason for all the rest. However discreetly lit or adorned, electronically encased or programmed, the racket works now as it always has, with the single ultimate purpose of taking the public's money in a manner no other industry in the world can match. Those who see that reality most clearly, the few who knew the old Las Vegas, are unfazed by the new facade. 'A joint's a joint,' says a casino manager who came to the city with Meyer Lansky.

As the millennial midnight approaches, ABC's Connie Chung appears outside the Bellagio to interview longtime Las Vegas entertainer Wayne Newton, now a jowly, heavily made-up intimation of the plump teen star of Glitter Gulch, under contract to play the Stardust for the entire first decade of the new century. They chat for a while, Chung visibly searching for something amusing and interesting to say. What will Las Vegas be like in the new millennium, she finally asks the singer, adding in jest one of the city's forbidden questions: will the mob come back to run it? she asks him with a smile. But instead of dismissing the question as the banter it was meant to be, Newton flares in nervous alarm, revealing how close beneath the surface the elaborately masked reality still is. For those who understand the city, Chung's question is no lighthearted joke. 'Oh, I wouldn't know anything about that,' Newton says too quickly in utter seriousness, looking at the camera as if at an audience he can see in the flesh. 'I just want everyone to know that I don't have anything to do with that kind of thing.'

But the unease of the performer is soon forgotten in the extravaganza of the evening's climax. As the clock strikes midnight Pacific time, the grand finale of the continent's millennium celebration shows the dancing waters of Steve Wynn's 1,000 carefully lighted fountains in front of the Bellagio, sending choreographed streams as high as 240 feet in the air to the accompaniment of Handel's *Messiah*. It is a moment of the sensational and the sacred, fittingly broadcast from the American Mecca.

Ten days after the millennium-eve spectacle, headlines blared the largest corporate merger in history, a $350 billion deal between US communications giants Time Warner and America Online. The looming media–Internet conglomerate, determining so much of what the public might see, hear, and read in a seductive new computer technology, seemed to many a stunning sign of the trend toward corporate monopolies of unprecedented reach and force. 'In our lust for profits,' wrote columnist Jill Nelson, 'we have forgotten democratic principles.' Yet viewed from the Strip, the new behemoth seemed only another version of the kind of concentrated power Las Vegas had seen over the past decade and before. Once again, the city had been an augury for the nation.

By any measure economic or political, the oligarchy that ruled Las Vegas at the millennium was – as it had been in essence for fifty years – an exclusive regime. As always in the city, the juice belonged to a handful of prominent men, representing larger, less conspicuous interests behind them, and with their own power inseparable from their emblematic pasts. The umbrella companies of end-of-century Las Vegas were with few exceptions traded on Wall Street. 'America, Inc. Buys out Murder, Inc.,' was how David Johnston summed up the apparent advent of corporate chain ownership of casinos and what Las Vegas would officially celebrate as yet another cleansing crossing of casinos into 'mainstream American business.' Yet, as in the city's earlier passages with Del Webb, Hughes, Parvin-Dohrmann, Continental Connectors, Recrion, Argent, and dozens more publicly chartered entities, the corporate veil remained in many ways as thin and deceptive as it had always been. The operational decisions still remained in the hands of a few. Seventeen of the twenty largest, most consequential casinos on the Strip, and thus most of its jobs and the bulk of its profits, were effectively controlled during the 1990s by five men – MGM's Kerkorian, Bennett leading Circus Circus Enterprises, Wynn atop his Mirage, Inc., Adelson with his Las Vegas Sands, Inc., and Arthur Goldberg presiding over the Park Place Entertainment combine. The rest of the city's casinos of any note were divided among less than a dozen other owners, including hotel chains like Hilton and a few inheritors of venerable local names and companies – Jack Binion, Michael Gaughan, and Bill Boyd, the sons of families who had been in Las Vegas since the 1940s. But it was the five mega-resort giants who clearly dominated.

In the fashion and ritual of the times, like Milken's lavish meetings with his bond buyers that they called the Predators' Ball, the Strip CEOs at the statutory intervals would parade their profits and plans before shareholders. In that venue, they might be subject to the predictable power-plays – not unlike their Syndicate forerunners, after all – as when a falling out with big investors eventually drove Bennett from the chairmanship of Circus Circus in the mid-1990s. But behind the brand-name logos, portfolios, and casting of ballots, the men at the top were resonant of the order they ostensibly replaced.

Genealogies and corporate customs aside, what was most revealing about the latest Las Vegas monopolists – what placed them in a lineage with their predecessors – was how they ran gambling's ever-growing tyranny over the city and state. By the 1990s the industry's economic weight alone was crushing. The eleven largest companies in Nevada were all casinos, eight of them bigger than state government. Of the twenty-five largest employers statewide, seventeen were Las Vegas resorts. The Strip's security guards were a legion four times the size of the Clark County police force. It left gambling more than ever 'the sacred cow that all Nevada politicians treat with deference,' a historian of company power in communities wrote in 1999. 'Company towns only grow beyond their roots when the politicians stop giving the company everything it wants.'

In Nevada, that had long since been political suicide, and by century's end the casinos were not simply resting on their massive, preemptive presence but commanding the political process as never before. As a 1999 study recorded, in almost every political campaign of any import in Las Vegas or statewide for decades, half and often more of the campaign funds of winning candidates had come from the casinos and their masters. The permanent axiom of Nevada politics was that no one could win without them. The rare exceptions were, as always, effectively isolated and neutralized. In cities and towns the *de facto* dictatorship ensured any public easement or added infrastructure helpful to the casinos. In Carson City it maintained the sanctity of the meager gambling tax, barely raised in 1991, again by a fraction, to only 6.25 percent on gambling profits, a rate lower than any other state's. While its comparatively meager declared revenues paid for more than one-third of Nevada's public expenses, what the industry continued to abscond from the state held the society hostage. The new business culture and managerial regimes of the resorts imposed a pervasive conformity with even more impact than the crude violence of the past. 'The heavy hand of the industry controlled virtually every area of life in the Las Vegas valley,' a team of out-of-state reporters concluded at the end of the century. 'The concept of pluralism that is crucial to the stabilization of democratic systems is foreign to Las Vegas,' wrote Chuck Gardner, a lawyer and editor, of the respected *Nevada Index* in 1998. 'A culture of influence and corruption has permeated all walks of political life.' The resulting bleakness of the human landscape was more stark than anything recorded by writers since the 1950s.

Over the last decades of the century Clark Country had grown by more than twenty times – 'a record no other large US country even comes close to matching,' as one account described the incessant boom. All along the way there were warning signs of unmet crises, and of an underlying social dysfunction as constant as the city's phenomenal growth – overcrowded schools, a depleted and polluted water supply, an alarmingly high rate of violent crime, unrelieved traffic congestion despite new roads, and runaway construction described by one writer as 'an unreadable chaos of non-planning.'

The gambling industry in Las Vegas and Nevada had become one of the most profitable in human history. Nevada's senators over the years were among the most powerful in the nation. Metropolitan Las Vegas was five times again larger. In the late 1990s a team of journalists from the University of California at Berkeley led by former *Wall Street Journal* correspondent David Littlejohn took much the same measure of the city as the earlier academic survey of the Fund. Their findings coincided with the research of a handful of local scholars and writers around the same period. If Las Vegas still led the nation in growth, it was also the highest in total crime, automobile accidents, alcohol consumption, teen pregnancies, and births to unwed mothers; the city also had one of the higher percentages of citizens lacking health insurance. Suicide rates were still double the national number. Las Vegas had one of the highest air pollution indexes in North America, fed by a profit-driven grid of sprawl, thrown across the valley with scant public transportation. There were less cultural and recreational facilities relative to its population than in any other comparable metropolitan area in the nation. Outside the casinos' increasingly expensive entertainment, it had no accredited civic symphony, opera, or major art museum. Its school district was the ninth largest in the United States, and one of the most overcrowded and outmoded. It welcomed its tens of millions of visitors to America's twelfth-busiest airport, which many pilots and air traffic controllers thought dangerously strained by laggard funding.

As always, the lights of the Strip – and now its well-paid corporate publicists – seemed to dazzle the rest of the country, many visiting journalists oblivious to the reality behind the neon. In 1994, in a cover story typical of much of the coverage of the moment, *Time* declared Las Vegas 'an All-American city,' what it called 'the new American hometown.'

The toll hardly stopped at the edge of the valley. The Nevada that Las Vegas casinos now dominated and cheated still had one of the highest per capita and median incomes in the nation, statistics that reflected the vast wealth of Las Vegas but said nothing about the actual distribution of income, much less power. Thus it also had one of the highest proportions of bankruptcy in the United States, as well as one of the worst high school dropout rates. Despite graduate schools, buildings, and other monuments named after some of the city's most infamous predators, its system of higher education remained relatively starved and neglected, as always by the ruling mega-resorts, which drew the preponderance of employees from the ranks of those with a high school education or less, and most of their top executives from out of state.

Even beyond gambling's stranglehold there might have been other sources of revenue to address the state's needs. By the 1990s, in an ironic reprise of the Comstock boom, Nevada led all states in gold and silver production, though with the same piracy and colonial exploitation in public policy. A 'sort of informal agreement since 1989' had existed 'between the casino and mining industries to respect each other's interests regarding tax policy,' as Nevada historian Eugene Moehring recorded in 1999. 'Nevada has once again served as a bank where mining companies have used their under-taxed profits . . . to fund mining operations in other states and nations.'

Not surprisingly, the governor presiding over the mining–gambling collusion and much else was Bob Miller, the son of the Riviera mobster. With the rise of the former Clark County district attorney to the Governor's Mansion in 1988, the last figment of any ostensible separation between politicians and gamblers was erased. The man who had been in a blind-trust casino partnership with Allen Dorfman and others, who had been less than zealous to prosecute the depredations at Binion's Horseshoe, was the Strip's own – enjoying 'political support from nearly every major casino owner in the state,' as Moehring noted, and on any issue of importance doing their bidding.

In the last presidential election of the twentieth century the national political power of the city – long wielded for the most part discreetly, if not covertly – came dramatically into the open. Unlike the millions of gamblers who went to Las Vegas seeking a windfall, the 1996 candidates, Clinton and Bob Dole, seemed to beat the proverbial Las Vegas odds. Both parties, in equal measure, raked in gambling money as never before, gratefully taking official record contributions of more than $5 million and millions more generated from its collateral businesses and influence. But much of the real game remained hidden, and the house would be the only winner in the end.

If the Strip had once quietly given Jack Kenney a valise with a million dollars at one of the Rat Pack parties at the Sands, if Marcello had made his secret payoffs to Lyndon Johnson and Hughes to Richard Nixon through poker-faced middlemen, if Reagan had taken their campaign backing by way of Sunbelt and Teamster proxies, if Laxalt only a few years before had given up a run for the White House because of the city's taint, now the passing of the cash was one more public show.

In June 1995, with some fanfare, Senator Dole went to Shadow Creek – Wynn's 320-acre, $48 million private golf course, a guarded preserve where the staff was sworn to secrecy and the few guest players, required to have a minimum credit line of $100,000 at one of the Wynn casinos, were served caviar on the fairway. But Dole had no trouble getting in. At a $5,000-a-plate luncheon, where the guests included Frank Fertitta and Blake Sartini of the Station Casinos, Binion's son Jack, and other wealthy Las Vegans, Dole raised a half-million dollars. In 1994 Wynn had hosted a breakfast that gave the GOP another $540,000 at one sitting, though the cash from both events was only a fraction of the more than $7 million Las Vegas interests put into local races throughout the country, as well as 'soft money' coffers of both parties over the early 1990s. After the Shadow Creek golf outing, Wynn personally would go on to raise more than another $1 million for Dole, including some $90,000 from his family and Mirage, Inc., employees, and Wynn's close friend and associate John A. Moran became Dole's finance chairman. There was not simply an extension of gambling's political investment – there was an explosion. By the first weeks of 1996 the Strip had contributed eight times more cash to the presidential race than in 1992.

Republicans had been ahead at first in what one candidly called 'Vegas winnings,' but the Democrats soon hit their jackpot. In June 1996 President Clinton had lunch at the home of *Sun* publisher Brian Greenspun, a long-time friend and sometime Shadow Creek golfer whose wife, Myra, had recently given $35,000 to the Democratic National Committee. Dark-windowed limousines jammed the streets of an exclusive subdivision of Green Valley – the now lush suburb built on desert Hank Greenspun had bought decades earlier – as the city's wealthy ate salmon catered by Spago at $25,000 a couple, and executives of the Sands, Bally's, and Circus Circus, as well as the peripatetic Wynn, gave some $650,000 to the Democrats. It was only the beginning of Las Vegas cash for Clinton's reelection, with still more money generated by his good friend Ghanem.

Tracking Clinton and Dole, the national media now began to discover in earnest, if not in some shock, that behind all the highly publicized and bipartisan good fortune there were enormous stakes. The Las Vegas interests now inserting unprecedented amounts of money into the political process had expanded throughout the nation. More and more localities fiscally ravaged in the 1980s had turned for revenue to the apparent rescue of casino gambling, from riverboats to Indian reservations to huge new carpet joints coast to coast. The industry now commanded the attendant political influence not only in Nevada, but in governors' offices, legislatures, county commissions, and city councils in forty-seven other states, where it spent more than $100 million in lobbying and contributions in the 1990s. Corporate casinos boasted heavily staffed 'government relations' departments, conducting sophisticated polls on issues and candidates on all sides. While Laxalt himself served as a senior consultant to Dole, his old crony, the elaborately coiffed Fahrenkopf who had succeeded him as GOP chairman, was now the $750,000-a-year head of the industry's American Gaming Association in its ceaseless Washington lobbying.

Moreover, Americans were gambling their money as never before – and losing more than $40 billion a year. Uncertain of the present and future, suffering 'a collapse of confidence in the utility of work,' as A. Alvarez wrote in the *New York Review of Books*, the nation was now spending six times more on gambling than all other forms of entertainment combined, more on slot machines, cards, and numbers rackets than on movies, theme parks, cruise ships, and recorded music altogether.

'We're not US Steel,' a colleague of Wynn's was quoted as saying about the industry's still shady image. Only a few noticed the unintended mockery. In the popular 1974 movie *The Godfather*, the Meyer Lansky character had turned to his younger Italian partner at one point to characterize their international gambling empire. 'Michael,' he breathed in words borrowed from an actual FBI wiretap of Lansky, 'we're bigger than US Steel.' It had been true enough during the time depicted in the movie – the late 1950s – but now even more salient as gambling surpassed not only the money generated by the nation's decaying manufacturing base but also the profits of the thriving new sectors of high technology and service. With 30–50 percent profits, double the average of most businesses, the trillion-dollar gambling industry had become a force like few others in the nation's history. From Las Vegas as its global headquarters, the gambling industry unabashedly and conspicuously dictated the politics of much of the nation as it had long dictated to Nevada. 'In the old days, casino owners just gave money to politicians and stayed in the background,' *Review-Journal* columnist Smith would say in a passage quoted by the *New York Times*. 'Now it's an open orgy of power. If politicians don't give back what they want, they run them out.'

Once again in the 2000 election, the casinos, planning heavy contributions to both presidential nominees, would have their bets covered. That cash and the power it bought made Las Vegas a kind of shadow capital, in political as well as socio-economic terms, and the masters of the Strip and Glitter Gulch knew a good thing when they saw it. No matter what happened in the first elections of the twenty-first century, the Vegas connections would win. As the founders of the city always understood, parties and personalities were minor compared to the stakes now shared among an ever-expanding group of profiteers. Corporate veils and Wall Street brokering had made thousands of stock-owning individuals and institutions, from the Harvard University endowment to the California State Employees Pension Fund, the successors to Costello, Luciano, Siegel, Giancana, and the others as the capital funders of the gambling empire. More than Lansky could ever have known, it was a form of the grand alliance of upperworld and underworld that he had founded and developed over half a century – not simply a city but a nation in which gambling was openly and unashamedly an integral part of a political economy that had always been in the shadows, where the only real winners were the few who owned the house and controlled the game, and the losers were all the rest. It was an ultimate corrupt capitalism in which the Polish immigrant boy's place of angels, 'somewhat like heaven,' had become so largely his 'paradise of suckers.'

President Clinton – raised in Hot Springs, his family deeply involved in the back-room gambling there in the 1950s when it rivaled Las Vegas, his own political career launched by the backing of his uncle Raymond, who ran slot machines in the town for the Marcello family – seemed to understand the city's bipartisan politics as clearly as any politician of the century. He spoke a kind of jovial epitaph on the system when he attended a $10,000-a-person luncheon in October 1999, held in the gourmet restaurant of the new Paris Casino's Eiffel Tower, with its dramatic view of the Strip. 'One of the things that I like about Arthur Goldberg and a lot of the others of you who have been my longtime friends here, is that you have a sense of enlightened self-interest,' he told a select group of backers, including Elias Ghanem. 'You're intelligent enough to support Democrats so that you can continue to live like Republicans.'

It was still business as usual in Las Vegas. In 1995 publisher Lyle Stuart's Barricade Books had included among its new titles *Running Scared: The Life and Treacherous Times of Las Vegas Casino King Steve Wynn*. Written by John L. Smith, a fourth-generation Nevadan and a popular award-winning *Review-Journal* columnist, the biography was the first critical book-length look at the city by a local journalist since *The Green Felt Jungle* by Ed Reid and Ovid Demaris more than three decades before. Though Smith never called Wynn a creature of the Syndicate, he made clear his skepticism about the casino owner's adamant denials of any questionable associations, and that he believed the old Las Vegas differentiation between 'gang-sters' and 'friends of gangsters' was a distinction without meaning. The young journalist was also among the first to report some of the controversial Scotland Yard material from Wynn's aborted application for a London gambling license more than a decade earlier.

Well before Smith's *Running Scared* was published, Wynn filed a multi-million-dollar libel suit against Stuart in Nevada for the publisher's catalogue copy, and subsequently brought a separate lawsuit against the book in Kentucky. As Smith's book appeared, legal battles raged over reliance on Scotland Yard information that Wynn angrily denounced and attacked as untrue and unsubstantiated, but which now gained unprecedented notoriety and dissemination – including a quoted passage from British investigators: 'The strong inference which can be drawn from the new intelligence is that Stephen Wynn, the president of GNI [Golden Nugget, Inc.] has been operating under the aegis of the Genovese family since he first went to Las Vegas in the 1960s to become a stockholder in the New Frontier Casino.' It was this assertion in the British intelligence files that Stuart paraphrased in his catalogue copy, though substituting the term *front man* to describe Wynn because the pub-lisher assumed that bookstore owners in Nevada and elsewhere would not under-stand the meaning of the word 'aegis,' and it was that catalogue summary of the book that Wynn contended was libelous.

The message of the Wynn litigation was plain along the Strip. 'He wants to bust you out,' Stuart, himself a frequent high roller, told Smith in an all-too-accurate gambling metaphor. In addition to a battery of lawyers who filed suits in Nevada and Kentucky, Wynn would have his own figurative bust-out crew at the Las Vegas trial. Nevada governor Ross Miller and former car salesman become Las Vegas mayor Jan Jones appeared as fulsome character witnesses for the plaintiff, depicting him as a 'gee-whiz guy.' Hearing the Las Vegas case was one of Miller's appointees, Judge Sally Loehrer, who narrowed the defendant's discovery from a requested 10,000 items to eventual receipt of only 6 pieces of paper. Loehrer would go on to be elected to the bench and lead a judicial effort to defeat a term-initiative for judges in a campaign financed heavily by Mirage Resorts. When the trial was over, more than two years after the book appeared, Smith himself had been dropped from the Nevada suit, and Wynn would withdraw his Kentucky action as well. But eight Las Vegas jurors ordered the publisher, Stuart, to pay the casino mogul $500,000 for emotional distress suffered from the catalogue copy, as well as more than $1.5 million for damage to reputation and professional standing, and another $1 million in punitive damages. 'We live in a town with no standard of obscenity, but criticizing a casino boss is a sin,' Smith would tell reporters at one point. The victor was not in the courtroom when the verdict came in. Wynn was back at the Mirage with President Clinton, hosting a meeting of the nation's governors.

As a result of the jury award, Stuart's Barricade Books filed for bankruptcy, and as the publisher's appeal of the verdict wound through higher courts in Nevada, Wynn's lawyers would threaten to drag Smith back into the lawsuit. In the summer of 2000 the case was heard before the Nevada Supreme Court.

For his part, Smith continued to write his 'On the Boulevard' column – chronicling the Strip's colorful characters with the toughest, most insightful reporting since Ned Day. Yet Wynn's retribution left a palpable chill. 'In the old days the casinos sent their hit men. Now the corporations sent their lawyers after you,' said a retired newsman. 'The point is never how they do it, but that they just do it over and over one way or another. The town gets the message. Everybody accepts the silencing and censoring just like always.' Though the object of intimidation in the form of thuggish slurs in public places as well as the posturing of attorneys, Smith emerged from his libel ordeal still loving his city without illusion. 'This is a frontier town peopled by a lot of good souls,' he told an interviewer in December 1999. 'But never forget that the evil is ten feet deep.'

Meanwhile, however, in the customarily polite Las Vegas press, there seemed not a cloud on Wynn's horizon. Nevada officials had just given him a tax break on his $400 million art collection – a concession crafted for Wynn by legislators in Carson City he had backed with bipartisan contributions, and where he was reputed to be the most powerful man in the state. He was also thought to have neutralized the Nevada journalist most knowledgeable about him, John L. Smith. In the late winter of 2000, just as Wynn was teetering on the edge of his corporate summit, he was still riding high in his hometown papers. The *Independent* of London summed up his writ in a March story with a directness and candor all but unknown in the Las Vegas press. 'Politicians jumped at his command, candidates prostrated themselves to seek his endorsement and his campaign contributions. City planners re-routed roads and sewers at his behest, water authorities allowed him to siphon off millions of precious gallons to feed his private golf course.'

Outwardly, Ken Mizuno had been one of the more notorious Asian high rollers along the Strip in the 1980s. When the former baseball star moved to open a gourmet Japanese restaurant and health spa in the Tropicana and applied for a liquor license, even the usual desultory investigation uncovered his long-standing associations with the Yakuza, Japanese organized crime. Initially, the Clark County commission had denied Mizuno the license; but in a subsequent session a few weeks later – a distant echo of Bugsy's experience with the same body – the commissioners promptly reversed themselves. For nearly a decade Mizuno would be one of the city's leading international citizens, attended by his own personal hostess at the Mirage, where he gambled hundreds of millions.

Then, in the 1990s, wealthy Tokyo investors pressured Japanese police to implicate Mizuno in a $853 million golf club pyramid scheme. His fall was mourned by casinos where he had been known as a 'whale' for his $100,000-a-hand bets at baccarat, and Mizuno eventually ended up in a Japanese jail. His fall was long in coming.

In 1991 the small US Customs office in Las Vegas received warnings about Mizuno from the Customs attaché at the US Embassy in Tokyo. Las Vegas agents began to trace not the gambler's links to the Yakuza, or the massive expatriation of funds to foreign organized crime – one of the city's thriving industries, and to law enforcement a more familiar pattern – but rather the pouring into Las Vegas of hundreds of millions through foreign criminal combines. At one point following a path from the Federal Reserve Bank in San Francisco to the Las Vegas Strip with bills bound in casino wrappers, the Customs agents traced an enormous traffic. While Mizuno had a locker at Shadow Creek next to Wynn's, and was a popular high-tipping man-about-town, he was bringing in as much as $220 million through bank channels, wire transfers, and other means that escaped currency reports. There were additional indicators that he transferred to southern Nevada as well much of the remainder of his $800 million take from the Tokyo fraud – altogether hundreds of millions more than even he wagered at Las Vegas tables.

As the investigation continued, many of the trails led to the luxury Mirage. Mizuno's girlfriend turned out to be working in the 'international department' of the casino. The high roller himself was 'said to have ... dropped upwards of $75 million in two years' at the Mirage tables. Often met by a Mirage limousine at a private landing strip when he returned from trips abroad, and then whisked to the casino behind darkened windows, arrangements that defeated Customs surveillance, Mizuno went on to buy from his close friend Wynn a personal DC-9 jet later seized by Customs authorities and implicated in the massive financial crimes they suspected. Agents as well as at least one prosecutor familiar with the accumulating evidence came to believe that looming behind Mizuno was the shape of a vast new criminal investment in, and thus control of, the new mega-resorts going up on the Strip, casinos like Treasure Island and others supposedly funded entirely by Wall Street investment in their new corporate proprietors. Even the sums visible in Mizuno's 'gambling' – a minimum of $150 million by one account at a time when

Kerkorian had purchased both the Desert Inn and Sands for $167 million – made the Customs calculus only too plausible.

Early in the investigation the small five-man Customs office in Las Vegas had been overwhelmed by the magnitude of the traffic, the intricacy and sophistication of the means, the network of legitimate institutions around and behind the crimes, and not least by the obdurate secrecy and refusal of casinos to share more than the minimally required information. As agents told their stories later, they could not even enter a casino to observe Mizuno, much less interview employees, without encountering the house's heavily armed force of security retainers. 'It is a world unto itself,' said one investigator, echoing Yablonsky and others. 'I've been in enemy territory as a soldier in battle and felt more at home.' But when the beleaguered Las Vegas agents asked their superiors for the obvious support a major investigation required – more personnel, undercover money, and authority to go to the top of what they termed under the federal racketeering statute 'the continuing criminal enterprise' they saw in and behind Mizuno – their requests were effectively denied, buried or put off in organizational delays, never openly rejected with any individual liability or record but quietly stifled by bureaucratic device. Eventually Customs would seize more than $60 million in Mizuno's assets, including golf courses in the Las Vegas Valley and Palm Springs, real estate and other assets in Clark County. By most measures it might have seemed a success – the largest single non-narcotics money-laundering case in American history. But agents on the inside knew, as one described it, that it was only 'the tip of an iceberg here in the middle of the desert.' The agents never knew why they had been called off before following the case to its conclusion.

On the heels of the truncated Mizuno case there would emerge the silhouette of the even larger, more dramatic, more sweeping national system that at once was central to Las Vegas and by now far transcended it. Beginning in 1996, and for the next two and a half years, Customs agents based in Los Angeles had conceived and carried out a unique investigation of the money-laundering at the core of the drug trade: Operation Casablanca, a sting of Mexican bankers, organized crime figures, and others. By the late 1990s Mexico accounted for 70 percent of the cocaine sold in the United States, far more than the notorious Colombian cartels or any other channel. The traffic yielded much of what the United Nations had carefully docu-mented as the $25-million-an-hour, $600-million-a-day laundering of drug profits at the end of the century, the surge of a criminal fortune far larger than the wealth of many countries. Organized crime, long in control of the presidency and government of Mexico, effectively headquartered in the National Palace in Mexico City, had also captured Mexico's financial system. By converting drug cash into bank drafts, highly liquid currency difficult to trace, Mexican banks legitimized billions in illegal income and official graft, taking out their own huge fees.

To penetrate the system, US Customs operatives had set up their own illicit enterprise, a sham import-export firm named the Emerald Empire Corporation with an office and warehouse in Santa Fe Springs, fifteen minutes outside Los Angeles and a short drive from the frontier. The innocuous storefront offered crucial services in the laundering; its undercover agents picked up drug proceeds from couriers or warehouses in New York, Chicago, Houston, Miami, and a dozen other American cities, and then returned the cash to Los Angeles, where it was either taken across the border or deposited in designated accounts to be wire-transferred directly to Mexican banks. From there, in turn, 'clean,' untraceable bank drafts payable in American dollars were drawn on financial institutions in both the United States and Mexico, for final distribution to the traffickers and their facilitators. Throughout the process, just as in Mizuno's operation, transactions in the millions of dollars evaded tax or Customs reports ostensibly required for deposits of $10,000 or more. Channeling smoothly into the fraud, Emerald Empire quickly established its credibility. 'We are not criminals,' an undercover man in Santa Fe Springs assured a wary Mexican banker, pointing to a plaque on the wall. 'We are accepted by the Chamber of Commerce.' The clients were grateful. 'May God bless you,' one drug dealer said to an agent after a lucrative transaction. The operation lured them on with more laundered profits – and with visits to Las Vegas, where they often met to discuss business and celebrate their successes during the two-and-a-half-year collusion.

From a series of midnight arrests by Customs officers in May 1998 on a highway outside Las Vegas and elsewhere across three continents, unprecedented indictments of drug traffickers and their attorneys, and especially thirty-one Mexican bankers from the largest financial houses in that country, charges against three Mexican banks, and the seizure of $35 million along with two tons of cocaine, followed. Evidence filed in court, congressional testimony, internal Customs reports, and other intelligence documents began to chart the magnitude of what Operation Casablanca had glimpsed from its storefront. Laundering only a small fraction of the traffic, undercover agents had handled more than $180 million. 'We were so conservative,' one reflected. 'We could have done not millions of dollars, but hundreds of millions.' At a safe house for dealers in Illinois, agents found a ledger of $200 million in profits over a few weeks by a minor part of the network.

Operation Casablanca incriminated some of the highest officials of the Mexican regime. Undercover Customs agents in the 1990s joined the drug trade, like Meyer Lansky and Bugsy Siegel fifty years before, by making payoffs to Mexican federal police and intelligence officials. On four different occasions, Casablanca records would show, they delivered money in bulging suitcases in the lobby or suites of a luxury hotel along the fashionable Reforma in Mexico City. 'Bags of cash for Mexican intel,' a US agent would describe it matter-of-factly. Outsized luggage crammed with bills was commonplace in the operation. At one videotaped rendez-vous an undercover agent would be seen straining and staggering as he tried to heave a suitcase of bribe money onto a hotel bed, almost falling backward under its weight.

The cash emptied into a well of corruption. Testimony would implicate the offices of Mexico's president and attorney general in the drug trade. Casablanca operatives dealt repeatedly with emissaries of the Mexican minister of defense, General Enrique Cervantes, seeking to launder $1.15 billion in graft. Fifteen audio- and videotapes of exchanges with two drug traffickers and at least four bankers left the role of Cervantes and others 'indisputable,' as a US agent would testify to Congress. In April 1998 one of the men representing the minister warned undercover US contacts about caring for the billion plus. 'He said it could be very dangerous if it got screwed up,' a Customs agent recalled, 'because the money belonged to "all of them, includ-ing the President."' Moreover, Washington's codebreakers, the National Security Agency, had intercepted communications incriminating Cervantes, texts seen by the chairman of a congressional committee, Customs agents, and other high-ranking government officials.

But then, as Casablanca records would also show, Cervantes and his Mexican cohorts were hardly alone. Of the $180 million handled by US undercover agents, every transfer had been arranged with the cooperation if not criminal complicity of an American bank. 'Not a dollar was laundered by a Mexican bank,' an undercover agent would recall, 'that wasn't in a US account under American scrutiny at one time or another.' Operation Casablanca would document over a hundred money-laundering accounts in the case tracing to more than seventy US banks, including many of the nation's most powerful and respected – among them, Chase Manhattan, Bankers Trust, Bank of New York, Chemical Bank, Citibank, Great Western, Nationsbank, Norwest, American Express Bank, and scores of others. In Florida alone some twenty banks were implicated, along with several South Florida trading companies, part of what agents discovered to be a parallel laundering conduit in fraudulent trade transactions costing the public an added $50 billion a year in tax revenue.

In the first days and weeks after the midnight arrests near Las Vegas in the spring of 1998, it seemed Casablanca would erupt into one of the great international scandals of the century. But only a year later – after the guilty pleas of two Mexico City banks, along with the conviction of a handful of Mexican bank employees and the acquittal of others – the episode was all but forgotten. What had happened, much as in the Mizuno investigation, was a case called off short of its connections in Las Vegas, Washington, the nation, and the world.

The forces and impulses killing the investigation were much the same confluence of interests that had come together to serve the power of Las Vegas. Confronted with the unwanted findings, politicians, bureaucrats, and bankers had all behaved predictably. When the Mexican government and the anxious American creditors of its financial system angrily protested the one-sided blame of Mexico as well as the fingering of General Cervantes and others, the State Department and White House had quickly and characteristically moved to contain the diplomatic and political damage, including the staving off of any Mexican counterexposé of American complicity. At the time of the arrests in 1998, Treasury Secretary Robert Rubin had called the money-laundering revealed by Casablanca 'the lifeblood of organized crime,' yet most other Washington leaders, including the president, the secretary of state, the attorney general, and not least a Congress beholden to the Strip, would not even acknowledge the existence of 'American organized crime,' so long after the death of the 'Mafia' in Las Vegas and elsewhere, let alone its 'life' or 'blood.'

Meanwhile, in the bureaucracy, ranking officials jealous of or compromised by an operation run, like the Mizuno investigation, against the odds of civil service lethargy, found their own reason to discredit and inter the investigation. Finally, an American business and banking community, itself so widely compromised like its Mexican counterparts, gave no voice or impetus to pursue what Casablanca had only begun. 'We were at the edge of unraveling Las Vegas,' a Customs agent in Nevada would say of the Mizuno case. 'We were about to get at the whole damned system,' a Casablanca agent would say in grimly identical terms. But in both cases, yet again, the house had won.

In June 1999 Las Vegas elected its last mayor of the twentieth century and its first of the new millennium. Richly symbolic of what the city was and had become, the landslide winner would be the lawyer Oscar Goodman. Apologist for the worst of the Strip's past and present, the 59-year-old Philadelphian had been 'juiced in' since his arrival in 1964. Since then, as lawyer, spokesman, and social friend of a retinue of some of the vilest clients in organized crime, he had won local fame and fortune not simply as a constitutional defense lawyer but as the Syndicate's on-call publicist and legal manipulator.

Soon after Goodman's election, and even during the campaign, at startling moments in interviews with British television, the *New York*, *60 Minutes*, and others, Goodman could descend suddenly into a gritty cold venom that lay just beneath his exterior of bravado and banter – lapses he lamely dismissed afterward as jokes no one understood. In one documentary broadcast not long before his political debut, he had been caught in an unexpected confrontation with an old adversary from the FBI. 'The former agent gets the better of him in their shouting match, saying that Goodman turned the world upside down to suit his ends, making evil good and good evil,' the *New Yorker*'s Connie Bruck would write in describing the scene. 'Goodman starts to leave, and then, turning – with a look and a tone that bespeak the company he has kept for nearly thirty-five years – says "Drive Safely."' But the too obvious public snarling was no barrier to his election in Las Vegas. Goodman's mania and reputation would make it possible once again for many not to take the city seriously.

The summer Goodman took office, crowds along the Strip were bigger than ever, building toward the turn of the millennium when, despite the threat of terrorism and national uncertainties about computer failures, hundreds of thousands would throng the surreal corridor where sirocco winds across the empty desert once whipped Bugsy Siegel's gabardine topcoat. Las Vegas expected more than 50 million visitors in the year 2000.

Las Vegas would continue to offer them, as it had for decades, a kind of controlled nostalgia. There would be souvenirs, posters, and other memorabilia of the already legendary performers in this long unrivaled capital of entertainment: carefully posed portraits of the first Copa Girls; candid shots of Sinatra and his Rat Pack cavorting at the Sands; a bloated, perspiring Elvis stuffed into one of the sequined leisure suits that became his last costumes; a pompadoured Liberace smiling across his own Las Vegas–scale white grand piano, and a long troop of sentimental lounge favorites. There are pictures and memorials, too, in tribute to the vanished casinos, some of their famous neon signs and symbols restored like precious artifacts and displayed in the canopied 'Fremont Experience' downtown. In curio shops and bookstores off the Strip, in a place where both tourists and residents seem revenous for the city's raucous and bloody history, there are the inevitable grainy depictions of Bugsy. The long-dead gangster stares out harmlessly from a past officially as bygone and ancient as the prehistoric bones still turned up at Tule Springs, the crumbling adobe of the old Mormon Fort in North Las Vegas, the first crude safety helmets, hard-boiled in tar, worn by the muckers, highscalers, and powder monkeys at Boulder Dam. In the cumulative effect of this commercialized, often kitsch, history there are memories for generations of Americans, the tens of millions of losing gamblers – one statistic the number-spewing city never evokes – and the equally impressive hordes who come for all the Las Vegas reasons, and despite the odds will remember it fondly, will come back again.

Still, for all the commemoratives, the new millennium's crowds along the Strip will be accompanied by other ghosts as well, whose heritage is too complex, and often too ominous, for tourist consumption. Casino to casino, from the old Horseshoe and Golden Nugget downtown to the new Mandalay Bay at the far end of the Strip, through the fresh luxury and aged seediness, across the lots traded in dizzying land deals and the new corporate facades built over the rubble of the old joints, Las Vegas's indomitable customers will walk wide-eyed, if unseeing, with them all: politicians naive and corrupt; moneymen visionary and venal; hoodlums banal and vicious; hustlers charming and maniacal; journalists courageous and compromised; unions plundered and persevering; police heroic and hireling. Not least, the visitors will see the spectral reflection of the rest of America whose underworld Las Vegas only copied in the open, and whose upperworld came to adopt the city as its own. The apparitions will all be there, many as faceless to the public and the people of the town as the real owners of the city over the years, as the banks and groups of investors behind the Strip at the millennium, as invisible to history as to gaming control authorities.

Chapter 21

Marking Time with Nike: The Illusion of the Durable

Celia Lury

Marks, Things, and Property

Defining the brand as a process of objectification requires attention to the means by which objective properties of things are constituted and thus demands a concern with brands-in-use, with objects as occasions and results of active experience, and with bodies in time and space – with doing.[1] But one problem that immediately arises in the attempt to observe Nike is that more than one mark makes up its logo(s). These include, among others, the graphic mark Swoosh, the graphic mark Jumpman, the words Swoosh and Nike, and a set of associated words and acronyms including Just Do It, Total Body Conditioning, Zoom-Air Cushioning, P.L.A.Y., and NIKEF.I.T. Each mark operates in multiple registers, moving in diverse media and directing the movements of the bodies of both producers and consumers. Indeed, as what Malcolm Quinn (1994) calls a migratory image, the brand is continuously being placed and displaced; while having ambitions to define its own context as universal, it only becomes visible, recognizable, and mobile through processes of selection and exclusion.

Moreover, each mark is synesthetic and operates within a topological space that opens onto an ever expanding perceptual field, the space of contemporary techno-aesthetics. This internally fissured field is made habitable, in part, by means of images of place, not only the visual representations of photographs, films, and videos but also images in the broader sense of 'emotional residues of perception' (Shields 1996a: 1). Simultaneously then, these marks resonate with both the depth of perception that is a person's bodily, affective memory and the cultural history of the perceptual mechanics of motion – the techno-artistic conceptions of speed and movement. It is in this complex, internally contradictory, heterogeneous field that the Nike brand operates.

To follow the movements of the Nike logos I draw on interpretations of the field that understand it as a set of interactions producing both objects and space (Hayles 1990). The project that results – moving between tenses and times and across places and spaces – might be called a *visual sociology*. In it, photographs and video stills function not as illustrations but as nonverbal and nondiscursive interpretations of brands. This use of the visual is especially important because so much of people's use of things is nonverbal, bodily, habitual, unreflective. In these visual records of practice, the properties or qualities of things are revealed: images in visual sociology compose moving hypotheses of lines, shapes, and volumes – hypotheses of things-in-motion; they call attention to time, to the time of seeing and to the editing of seeing. With this in mind, let me move into the field or, rather, to the beach.

In/of the Field

We sit and watch people cycling, roller-skating, roller-blading by; the insignia on their clothes are usually too small to see until they have passed us.[2] As Rob Shields (1996b: 4) observes of Rodeo Street, Seoul: 'So much happens so quickly that 180 degree vision would be necessary to begin to "observe" such a scene.' Here, by Manhattan Beach in Los Angeles, you have to be on the move to see whether it is Adidas or Nike. If we, too, were on blades, we could move up behind people, overtake them, hang back, or turn around to get a second look. Imagining this movement, the placing of insignia on the back of clothing suddenly makes sense: you still have a face, even when your back is turned. The insignia are communication in movement, moving communication, not turn-taking but turn and turnabout, as fronts and backs of people move past and around each other.

Sitting on the beach we watch two boys playing in the waves, each wearing Nike shorts with the letters *NI* and *KE* printed on separate legs. One boy is bigger, the other smaller. The shorts unite them: the boys are larger and smaller versions of each other. The shorts flicker a message as the boys dart in and out of the waves: a visual message, but with an aural accompaniment, a bit like a football chant, or at least a crowd chant: NI-KE! NI-KE! Here, the brand's register is not face-to-face communication but the topography of the body: sounds and profiles, silhouettes and shapes, and, most of all, *passing by* – the body in movement. But in what time and space does this moving communication occur?

Some indication of the multiply mediated framing that characterizes this time and space is provided by filmmaker Spike Lee, an ambiguous figure in the creation of the Nike brand. In a recollection of the making of his early film *She's Gotta Have It*, Lee (1997: 18) describes a complex juxtaposition of frames, apparently disconnected in topological time and space, that create a space in which the Nike brand can emerge:

> I was living on Adelphi Street in Brooklyn. There we would get a shot where Mars [a character Lee plays in the film] is on the phone with Nola; the poster is in the background – [Michael] Jordan lifting off, life-size. Simple art direction, cheap stuff...I didn't even know if we'd get through *She's Gotta Have It*, let alone that Island Pictures would put it on release in August 1986; or that it would be accepted into the Cannes Film Festival; or that Jim Riswold and Bill Davenport at Wieden and Kennedy, an advertising agency in Portland Oregon that had the Nike account, would later see *She's Gotta Have It*; or that they would then get the extraordinarily bright idea of pairing Mars Blackmon with Michael Jordan in a long series of commercials for Nike Air Jordans – what got Jim off was seeing the tight shot of Mars's feet in untied Air Jordans shuddering orgasmically. I had no way of foreseeing it at all.

As Lee observes, the space in which Nike moves, is, in part at least, that of the poster and the screen, the basketball court and the television: a space in which sport, technology, and art combine. This is a space from which, Lee says, he can't foresee what the future will bring; but he sees something – 'simple art direction, cheap stuff' – and this seeing has effects.

In the shopping malls we visit the next day. I observe how the careful positioning of Nike logos situates their wearers' bodies in three-dimensional Cartesian space: the marks or logos are often at right angles to each other. I notice this most clearly as I observe someone sitting down, one leg at a right angle to the other, the ankle of one leg resting atop the knee of the other. There is a Swoosh in a contrasting colour on the sole of the shoe, looking out at me. This perpendicularity of space is also apparent as I watch people walking by in Nike socks, the Swoosh riding high on their ankles. Although their legs move in sequential time, although they are clearly in three-dimensional space, the wearers are repositioned by the logos or marks. It is as if the mark of the brand collapses foreground into background, sliding now into then, and moving these Sunday morning window-shoppers into and out of multiple planes in space and dimensions of time. The mark – as a conceptual outline or trace of movement – presses against an enveloping surround of space and time which can simultaneously seem far away *and* near, right here *and* already gone, over there. In short, the mark of the brand functions as a recalibration machine in time and space.

Jacques Aumont (1997) writes that physical space is typically described in terms of the Cartesian geometry of three axes of coordinates. These three dimensions. Aumont postulates, can be understood with reference to the human body. The vertical dimension is the direction of gravity and the upright body; the horizontal dimension is the line of the shoulders, parallel to the visual horizon; the third dimension is depth, corresponding to the body moving forward in space. Recognizing that in everyday life the perception of space is almost never entirely visual. Aumont observes that the idea of space is fundamentally linked to the body and its movement. But is this always so, or is it always so in these ways?

Trying to understand the space of the brand in relation to the bodies and movements just described, I recall a man seated opposite me on the bus on my way home from work in London. The man wore a jacket with Nike written horizontally (first dimension) across the front of his chest and a Nike ribbon hanging vertically (second dimension) from the jacket's zip. He also wore a baseball cap, peak forwards, with a Swoosh, also facing forwards, visible on the top of the cap. There was something written across the cap's peak, but initially I could not read it. I stared, looking away whenever he seemed to notice me. I shuffled round in my seat, half stood up, then sat down again. I saw the word *Michigan*. I was going home; he was moving forward to Michigan.

The peak of the cap intrigued me. When the cap is worn backwards, the peak covers the neck. Functionally, it can be seen as a sunscreen for the delicate region of the back of the neck. But I know that is not the point. I think of a well-known image of the boxer Mike Tyson, taken from behind, cropped so that just his head and neck are visible. His neck is thicker than his head. This makes me reconsider the cap worn frontwards: it is, as Aumont indicates, a marker of moving forwards, of depth – the third dimension of space. It is also, because of the difficulty of seeing what is written there from an ordinary bodily position, a marker of another space, a space from within which other, four- or five-dimensional movements can be seen, and in being seen can be embodied. I come to see the cap's peak as somehow refiguring the wearer's body, opening up Aumont's third dimension to what Virilio (1994) calls the time of exposure, the time of the editing of seeing.

In these observations the brand redefines the limits of the human body by placing it in a newly extended field: the space of the screen, or techno-aesthetic space, a space which, while not immaterial, is both material and imagined, objective and subjective, mechanical and embodied. The space in which Nike moves, in other words, is both ordinary, physical. Cartesian space and also the space of the rhythm. NI-KE! NI-KE! It is a space in which the gap between individual and the mass might be closed; it is the space of the frame in which foreground and background can be brought into and out of focus mechanically, a space that we are in and at a distance from: the space of 'life on the screen' (Turkle 1995).

This space is complex: scale is to be interpreted not only in terms of distance or perspective but also as enlargement and miniaturization. In the brand's production of space, distance is a function of the body (of perspective, standpoint, and gravity) as well as an effect of the lens, the machine, and technology; hence, size is at once a property of the body *and* of an image that can be manipulated at will. (Other examples of the capacity of the brand to up- and down-size include giant Calvin Klein advertisements on the sides of dilapidated buildings in New York and huge hoardings that people ancient squares in Italy with Benetton faces.) The time of the brand is also multiple. It is not only referenced chronologically but simultaneously indexed as the time of a still in which the rhythms of movement linger like the traces of car headlights caught in time-lapse photography. The time of the brand is neither simply cut up by the clock nor caught up in a narrative; it is barely a sequence. Time takes place in a repetition of sound, in a loop of video, in a space that is right here and over there. As I consider the beams of light caught in time-lapse cityscapes. I draw a connection. The stripes on the legs of tracksuits, the markings on socks, shorts, shirts, and caps are like the stripes and dots that marked human limbs in the movement-study photography of nineteenth-century physiologist Etienne-Jules Marey. The photographs produced in these studies were simultaneously records of spatialized, abstracted time *and* images in which time is arrested, in which temporal relationships are dense, knotted, and multiple, in which time disrupts and extends three-dimensional space.

The Line and the Brand

In *A Passion for the Trace* (1992), François Dagognet shows the significance of Marey's studies of animal and human motion for modern expressions of movement and contemporary understandings of speed. At the end of the nineteenth century Marey captured and dismantled the diverse phases of motion, thereby making it possible to reassemble them in, for example. Taylorist workplace practices and mechanical devices of abstract speed, such as the airplane. Dagognet (p. 12) argues that in this process, however, Marey presented a distinctly dynamic image of life: 'He gave life to images, which henceforth flew like birds,' thus saving the image from torpor. As Dagognet writes, Marey 'hastened the reign of speed' in technological modernism and contributed to the conception of movement elaborated by artistic modernism.

Underlying this double impact, Dagognet argues, was a novel understanding of the relationship between science and art, between the real and figuration. This relationship, I will suggest, is being reworked at the end of the twentieth century in the animation of communication instantiated by the set of marks that compose the brand. Marey developed a set of mechanisms with which he caught movement's signature, its rhythms and variations, in the form of graphic lines. By adjusting scale and modulating time, Marey's mechanisms could reduce the enormous or enlarge the tiny, slow down the second or speed up the hour; in short, he made machines able to impose rates and proportions. Rejecting both experiment and observation, he drew on and expanded technologies of notation 'to force a "direct writing" from [movement]' (p. 40). His project consists finally in showing 'what one could learn from a curve,' from interpreting 'the message from the lines themselves' (p. 62).

The dots and stripes I recalled while watching the movements of the Nike logo in the mall are components of what Dagognet describes as the middle phase of Marey's studies. During this phase Marey developed a technique, which he called 'partial' or 'geometric' photography, to image human motion. In this process the (male) human subject, dressed completely in black (his outline invisible against a black background), wore strips of silver along the axes of his limbs, the movement of which Marey recorded with a specially modified camera. The result was both a flight of lines and a line of flight; as Anson Rabinbach (1992: 108) puts it, 'the body became a trace on a glass surface, a trajectory of decomposed movement.'

Marey's graphic writing shook up not only the biological sciences but also representational art 'by simultaneously valorizing it [the graphic mark] and assaulting it, demanding its modification [to include energy]' (Dagognet 1992: 149). In both cases the challenge came from Marey's conception of movement – of the 'moving image of and for man' (Marey quoted in Dagognet 1992: 176). It was a distinctively modern conception of dynamism. As Marta Braun (1992) puts it in her study *Picturing Time*, Marey's photographs shattered the spatial and temporal unity that, since the advent of the linear perspective in the Renaissance, the frame had been understood to enclose. Perhaps this shattering is why I find it so hard to see what is going on by the beach and in the mall with my naked eyes, and why Spike Lee could not foresee what others would see in what he saw through a camera lens.

As a number of commentators have noted, the emphasis on dynamism was part of a whole series of shifts in artistic and scientific thought emerging from the eighteenth century onwards, in which the location of truth moved from spatial order to organic structure and thence to motion and thermodynamics. Summarizing the later stages of these developments, Marey (quoted in Rabinbach 1992: 91) writes, 'The shift from organic structure to dynamics and the "interplay of organs" was a shift to mobility and to "motor function."' Indeed, as Dagognet (1992: 60) points out, Marey was one of the chief proponents of the theory of the 'animal-machine'; for him, 'energy was bound up with machinery and arose wholly from it.' Central to Marey's investigation of the motion of the animal-machine was his attempt to map the internal physiological time, or duration, present in any physiological process. In the words of one of Marey's most important scientific predecessors, Hermann von Helmholtz (1971), this was '*temps perdu*,' time lost. This lost time was seen to consist in the interval between the reception of a nervous shock or impulse by the muscle and the muscle's contraction. The development and application of Marey's studies of the 'language of duration,' the *'langue inconnue'* of physiological time, was in large part informed by the desire to recover this lost time (Rabinbach 1992: 94, 95).

For Rabinbach, Marey's work is important insofar as it contributes to a general understanding of energy and fatigue; specifically, an understanding of a perceptual system entrenched in quantification and abstraction. Rabinbach concludes his study with the claim that the conception of the human as machine no longer holds sway in contemporary culture. However, while that notion, which underpinned Marey's understanding of motion, may indeed be in decline, the quest for the spatialization of time remains underway, as does the project to recover *temps perdu*. As more recent studies of movement emphasize – especially those concerned with speed – the process of recovery remains linked to the operation of technologies of inscription and visualization, and the body remains a site of this inscription. Indeed, the image of the body – especially the image of the black male body, the body merchandised as a depthless surface Other of the white self – is continually illuminated.

Marey's tracing mechanisms dismantled human motion to a degree beyond that possible in unaided human perception: his cameras caught all but a few fragments of lost time. As Mary Ann Doane (1996) points out, however, Marey was continually confronted by a spatial difficulty. In his photographs of horses in motion, for example, his images were blurred, limited, as he says, by 'interference from super-position and consequent confusion' (quoted in Doane 1996: 328). What Doane calls the legibility of time was restricted by the available spatial field. With the develop-ment of contemporary imaging technologies, such as the digital camera and com-puter-aided animation techniques, however, a new field of spatialization is emerging: one in which previously lost time is made visible. And the newly visible is quickly put to work, not only in the ubiquitous presence of the brand but also in the 'real time' of the computer and the WWW; in the cross-national, racialized, and gendered spatialization of a 'just-in-time' division of labor; in the open-wall prison discipline of electronic tagging and video surveillance; and in the 'on-demand' accessibility of database transactions. This extended field is one realization of what Doane (1996: 341) describes as Marey's desire for 'sheer, undivided extension, of a "real time" without significant moments.' It is the expanded field of techno-aesthetics, a space in which most of us still feel a little lost, since, as Doane points out, we suffer from a confusion about where or why to look. In this milieu the Nike emblem and other global logos, I argue, compose a series of wayfinding devices, directional signals in this new space of the time of exposure that harness what Doane (ibid.) calls the 'capacity to represent the unforeseen.' As such, they are a means of organizing and controlling social space – traces of, if not automated, then informed movement in the age of animation.

Marking Time

While the Nike corporation does not actually manufacture shoes or clothes itself (CEO Phil Knight describes Nike as a marketing company), it is the operation of its brand that directs the movements of capital and labor in the processes of just-in-time production across the globe.[3] The brand marks this time as its own. The *Just* in Just Do It is a sign of this animated, informated spatialization of time; it is the linguistic transposition of the Jumpman logo, a figure suspended in the space of now/here (Friedland and Boden 1994), absolutely relaxed and at the peak of exertion in time so brief that it escaped Marey.[4] Obeying the dictum Just Do It, one enters a present without a past or a future, inhabiting the moment in a jump of simultaneously going up and coming down, rising and falling, flying and dying, caught in an instant which is no more than a shiver of time, a chronic ecstasy.[5]

The bodies in motion in this extended field (the global) are both those of the people who make the products that are the brand's effects, trapped in movement that keeps them just alive, and those of the people who buy and wear the products, whose liveliness is animated by the brand, who just do it. These movements – of livelihood and of liveliness – are coordinated but unconnected.[6]

Paul Gilroy (1994) has identified what might be considered another consequence of this feature of the brand, of coordinated disconnection: the replacement of the densely coded, verbally mediated dialogue that previously vivified the black public sphere by 'morbid phenomena like the Americo-centric image of the black public sphere as the inner-city basketball court' (p. 56). Certainly, the global brand must be seen in terms of selection and exclusion. While accomplishing a violent erasure of historical links between people, places, and practices, the brand contributes to a shift from organic and historical understandings of the nation-state to expansionist and market-led notions of territory whose limits are those of speed, not space (Quinn 1994). That brands contribute to this shift is a consequence of their owners' ability to pose a question that requires no reply other than an acceptance of their (exclusive) right to ask: 'Where do you want to go today?'[7] The ease with which this acceptance has been secured is a consequence of the brand's ability to mark time, to offer some direction in the extended field of techno-aesthetic space.

Paul Virilio, who argues that we are seeing the ongoing automation of perception, has charted the contemporary expansion of this field in some detail. Virilio (1994: 61) points out that any visual 'take,' mental or mechanical, is simultaneously a 'time take' in which 'sight travels from a long way off.' The take necessarily involves 'some degree of memorization (conscious or not) according to the speed of exposure.' The time of this memorization, the time of a perceptual activity 'that starts in the past in order to illuminate the present, to *focus on* the object of our perception' is an apt formulation of Marey's lost time (p. 62; my emphasis). For Virilio, the continuing attempts to recuperate that loss are today most significantly undertaken by the military–industrial development of visual technologies of stealth and surveillance – another form of speeding-up in which lost time is captured, dismantled, and reassembled.

But this process of speeding up is also occurring in relation to the brand. The capture, dismantling, and reassembling of time is evident in the phenomenology of the last second shot, as described by Michael Jordan: 'The first time you hit a jump shot with no time on the clock, you can always go back to that moment. You have the confidence because you've done it before...I was in that situation and I came through. Now when I get in that situation, I don't weight the negatives and the positives and hope the positives win. I just go back to my past successes, step forward and respond' (Vancil 1995: 36). To inhabit this time (the time of 'no time on the clock') was Roland Barthes's desire; indeed. Barthes argues that what Marey had done as an operator, that is, to decompose, to enlarge, to retard the image, is what he wants to do as a spectator. For Barthes, insofar as these processes are experienced as bodily, they provide the spectator with time to know, to feel, to see (Barthes 1981). With the development of the digital camera, however, as Virilio points out, there is no need of a support, a material substrate; no longer is a body necessary to the production of knowledge, affect, or action. The problem, as Virilio poses it, is that because of the limitations of the depth of time of our (human) physiological take (the way in which we lose | ourselves in | time), our seeing will be replaced in this military-technological, global world by the artificial vision of synthetic-perception machines. Our seeing will be foreseen for us by the phatic image, the 'image that grabs our attention and forces us to look ... to inscribe itself in some unfolding of time in which the optic and the kinematic are indistinguishable' (Virilio 1994: 62–3).

The suggestion here is that the perceptual activity that starts in the past in order to illuminate the present, our focus on the object, is completed beforehand in the brand. This process of focusing on an image – whether an advertisement, a program, a frame, or a product – is anticipated by market research 'focus groups,' resulting in items produced in conformity to standardized reactions, expectations, and regula- tions – that is, branded objects. Thus the logo is an indefatigable phatic image, a perception that anticipates the object that it brings into focus. Such images prolifer- ate, writes Virilio (1994: 14), 'like beak-nosed carp in the polluted ponds they depopulate.'

These perceptions are not new, but they describe increasingly pervasive practices. While the realization of this perceptual field – the depth of time – is enabled by new technologies of vision, it relies on a conception of surface that was already present in artistic modernism. Indeed, this understanding arose in the late nineteenth and early twentieth century when the use of relief in sculpture underwent a fundamental shift, visible in Auguste Rodin's *Gates of Hell* (1880–1917). By depicting figures as emerging from background into foreground, relief was traditionally used to articu- late the temporal values of narrative or history. But in *Gates of Hell*, as Rosalind Krauss (1996: 23) writes, 'the relief ground acts to segment the figures it carries, to present them as literally truncated, to disallow them the fiction of a virtual space in which they can appear to expand.' This disallowing, rather than simply reducing meaning leads, in the artistic history Krauss outlines, to the development of a belief in the manifest intelligibility of surfaces.

Krauss (1996: 27) describes the gestures of the figures in one panel of *Gates of Hell* as 'unsupported by appeals to their own anatomical backgrounds' and unable to 'address themselves logically to a recognizable, prior experience within ourselves.' The consequence, Krauss argues, is not only a decline in the plausibility of certain notions of cause as they relate to meaning but also an increase in the possibility of meaning independent of the proof of verification of cause. Effects themselves become self-explanatory, reliant on a groundless ground.[8]

What the groundless ground implies might be learned through a consideration of semiotic phenomena in the framework proposed by Charles Peirce, who argues that a sign refers to a ground through its object. For Peirce, the ground is an attribute of the object insofar as the object either has been selected in a certain way or some of its attributes have been made pertinent in a sign. In this sense, grounds are only ever meaning components of objects and signs. As Umberto Eco shows, for Peirce this interdependence of signs and grounds, rather than leading to an infinite semantic regression (in which grounds for one sign are themselves always signs in relation to other grounds), is meaningful insofar as a sign is understood in relation to purpose, to immediate responses, or to habit, a regularity of behaviour in the interpreter or user of that sign.

What the notion of a groundless ground suggests in the case of the global brand is not simply that reorientation of purpose or shift in habits that in Peirce's pragmatic terms is an inevitable and ongoing outcome of semiosis but, rather, a fundamental reconfiguring of the casuistry of interpretation. It involves a novel rearticulation of the elements of purpose, which Peirce 1991 provisionally describes as 'immediate, dynamical and final' (and which have been redescribed in more recognizable terms as emotional, energetic, and logical by Eco 1987). The effect of the groundless ground of the brand is a reorientation of the relationship between semiosis and action and, in particular, a reevaluation of what Peirce calls the final or logical aspects of purpose – 'why' some action should be taken. How this is accomplished by the Nike brand is the subject of the next three sections.

The Illusion of the Durable

In his discussion of Marey, Rabinbach considers the comparison drawn by Henri Bergson, who was a colleague of Marey's at the Collège de France, of Marey's chronophotographs of a galloping horse and the rendition of the gallop in the Parthenon frieze by Phidias. For Bergson, the comparison had value because it revealed the difference between art and chronophotography and illuminated the critical feature of modern time consciousness:

> It is the same cinematographical mechanism in both cases [Phidias and Marey] but reaches a precision in the second that it cannot achieve in the first. Of the gallop of a horse our eye perceives chiefly, a characteristic, essential or rather schematic attitude, a form that appears to radiate over a whole period and so fill up a time of gallop. It is this attitude that sculpture has fixed on the frieze of the Parthenon. But instantaneous photography isolates any moment; it puts them all in the same rank, and thus the gallop of the horse spreads out, into as many successive attitudes as it wishes, instead of massing into a single attitude, which is supposed to flash out in a privileged moment, and illuminate a whole period. (Rabinbach 1992: 112)

For Bergson, both images are cinematographical in that they produce stable images of bodies from multiple objects in time. The images differ in that while Phidias's gallop freezes the true image of time, a single moment of illumination in which the passage of time in duration is captured. Marey's image is an example of the modern, concrete illusion of objective time consciousness. In the modern image of objective time, moments of experience are organized spatially, and in this process quality is reduced to quantity. As Rabinbach (1992: 114) puts it, for Bergson, 'the ancients "composed" the visual and temporal field; the modern sciences "decomposed" it.' In Virilio's (1994) terms, what we are seeing with the emergence of the global brand is the field's recomposition: while art removes objects from the automatism of perception, brands replace them in the perception of automatons, or at least in informated perception. What we see in the brand, rather than simply an image of objective time, is the image of the commercial object itself – what might be called the illusion of the durable.

The importance of time, memory, and duration to conceptions of the object is often overlooked. Yet, as the commercial qualifier 'durable' indicates, one of the key qualities of objectivity is endurance, that is, persistence in time. The durability of an object, the ability of an object to persist, is a much valued attribute; it is operative, for example, in the luster of age known as patina and explicitly manipulated in the creation of fashion items (McCracken 1988). What the argument I am presenting here suggests, however, is that the durability of the brand is, in many respects, independent of the durability of the products which are its effects. Moreover, this should not, as in the case of fashion, simply be seen as a consequence of the commercial imperative of novelty. Through the operation of the brand, Nike does not attempt to come first in a race of product fashions but to displace the temporality of fashion altogether.[9] In an attempt to lever profits higher, to avoid the cycles of popularity and outdatedness, the brand operates in lost time. Its independent durability is related to the extent to which the brand can substitute itself for past memory, intervening in and occupying the time of exposure, reconstituting habit through surface effects. In this process, the product is merely a means to an end.[10] Absolutely vital to the brand's success in persisting, in substituting itself for past memory, is repetition.

As Arjun Appadurai (1996: 67) has noted, 'repetition characterizes the commodity culture of consumer capitalism' at a very general level: this is because consumption is typically centered on techniques of the body that are 'repetitious, or at least periodic.' More contentiously, Appadurai argues that it is more appropriate to see mediated acts of exchange as *indices*, rather than as *icons*, of the rites with which they are associated. Temporalities of consumption, as they relate to strategies of exchange, often constitute the primary significance of events, rather than simply building on already existing meanings: 'Consumption creates time and does not simply respond to it' (p. 70). The brand, as a particular form of mediated exchange, can thus be seen as an index rather than or as well as an icon of contemporary strategies of accumulation and divestiture.

But the indexical functions of the marks of the Nike brand are also subsumed within their symbolic elements, which relate to the indefinite future. Roman Jakobson (Jakobson and Pomorska 1983: 92) argues: 'The value of a symbol . . . lies in the fact that it 'gives us the possibility of predicting the future' . . . It is a potentiality whose mode is the *esse in futuro*.' Drawing on Peirce, Jakobson asserts that the symbol is not itself an object but a 'frame law' that gives rise to different contextual 'occurrences.' It is in the context of each occurrence that the invariant of the sign – its general meaning – acquires new particular meaning. Since the context is frequently variable, the particular meaning of the sign is continually renewed: 'Through this creative force, the sign opens a path toward the indefinite future, that is, it anticipates, it predicts things to come' (p. 92). Nike manipulates this creative force, inserting the brand, transparently, into the occasions or frames in which its objects are given practical and imaginative uses, transforming the relation between action and semiosis, and, through its reconstitution of purpose, providing new possibilities of embodment and new kinds of politics.

The Jumpman

Take the Jumpman, the silhouetted figure of Michael Jordan that adorns a line of Nike apparel. What does this silhouette represent? Michael Jordan. But of what is Michael Jordan a symbol? Spike Lee (1997: 20), a not uninterested contributor to the value of the Nike brand, has this to say about Jordan:

> Michael Jordan changed ball. Jordan was multi-dimensional, up in space, in the air, explosive, and saw all the horizontal creative passing angles, with added shot-blocking and psychological warfare edge...Jordan is now the top of the line. I doubt we'll see anything like him again.
>
> I can't say I saw Babe Ruth, Jack Johnson, Ty Cobb, Joe Louis, Jim Thorpe, Josh Gibson, Sugar Ray Robinson, Ben Hogan, Cool Papa Bell, the Herculean guys, but now we are in the presence of one of the greatest athletes ever and we're able to see this gentleman perform.
>
> I consider Jordan an artist. Not all athletes are. Not all make it to that level. Jordan is like John Coltrane. Louis Armstrong, Ella Fitzgerald, James Baldwin, Toni Morrison, Paul Robeson, Jean-Michel Basquiat. When we speak of Afro-American artists. I think we now have to include Michael Jordan. Muhammed Ali would be up there too.

Clearly Michael Jordan is a lot of things to Spike Lee.[11] He is up in space, in the air, the top of the line, a gentleman, an artist. He is all of these things because he 'changed ball.' He changed how people throw a ball around in space, and in doing so he changed space. In seeing Jordan in this way, in looking back and locating him in a lineage of African American artists. Lee looks forward, anticipating a continuing trajectory of black creativity. But this seeing has unforeseen effects.[12]

The Jumpman silhouette catches Michael Jordan, stops the artist, arrests the gentleman moving in space, and in transferring that trace of movement onto shoes and clothes opens up an entry point to a new space – the depth of time – for the Nike corporation. As a symbol, the Jumpman signals not a specific movement but imaginary movement, movement in abstraction, movement in the continuous, unending artificial light of 'a world that does not stop coming, that we can't stop waiting for' (Virilio 1991: 59). As Krauss might put it, there is no relief, only surface application. But how is the indexical, temporal function of particular marks subsumed within this, the symbolic aspect of the brand?

As Peirce and Jakobson both argue, the medium through which individuals rummage to assign meaning to a sign is the context of their personal experience or action. If there is no past action – or if that personal action is consistently repeated or superimposed within other contexts – then it is the context of the repetitions or superimpositions that comes to provide the meaning. In the case of the Jumpman logo, the relationship between background and foreground does not project the temporal values of lineage and history. The repetitive application of the silhouette to a product line of clothing and shoes is not a technique by which a potential future is imagined. Jordan's leap is 'unsupported.' The basis for an address 'to a recognizable, prior experience within ourselves' is undermined by the superimposition of the logo within the multiply mediated frames articulated by the brand. Its repetition is thus another of the ways in which focusing is already completed for us: It is how the brand intervenes in the time of exposure. Spike Lee situates Jordan/Jumpman in a tradition of black creativity, a tradition that he believes has left a cultural imprint. But on other occasions and for other people, the Jumpman. I suggest, is able to substitute itself for past memory. This substitution, rather than any kind of precision of representation, is what gives the emblem teleological and topographical (rather than or as well as topological) depth. It is an example of what Alexander Kluge calls the attack of the present on the rest of time (in Huyssen 1995: 26).

As Richard Dyer (1997) notes, conventionally the black man tends to be posed in profile or near silhouette so as to emphasize his 'emblematic' qualities while denying him the workings of individuality. A further reason for the silhouette in the case of the Jumpman might be that it signals a kind of pre- and postchemical photography. While emulating the trace that is most obviously nature's expression – the shadow, a trace that lengthens and shortens with the passing of the day – the Jumpman silhouette fixes itself to a day that never ends, the 24-hour working day of the global economy. In this contemporary revival of the brand, in which memories of the slaveowner's mark persist, the black body continues not only to be marked but also to be the mark, the medium of a reconfiguring of what it is to be human. The Nike brand is a powerful example of this. What Paul Gilroy (1994) calls a store-house of alterity is here misrecognized, objectified, and reified, deployed to make possible new spaces and new times for objectifying processes, the circulation of goods, the creation of intellectual property, and the expansion of capital in a speeded-up economy. In contradistinction to the overembodied, mostly black, fig-ures of Nike spokespeople (of whom Jordan is only the foremost) are the under-embodied, mostly white, figures of Nike management (of whom Knight is foremost).[13] Knight and the faithful among his employees (ekins, as they are some-times called) have tattooed their bodies with the Nike Swoosh. It is as if the repetition of the mark of the brand, its permanent inscription in the flesh, will support the corporation's claims of authenticity, legitimacy, and ownership, as it is continually challenged by the bodily actions of others, by bodies whose time is not their own.

In its use of these marks the Nike brand continues the functions of heraldry: of presenting the colors of kinship and the graphics of group membership. Its logos herald an absent or delayed meaning, the loss of power to reenact the body, individual and collective, in an organic or historical sense; they are simultaneously its defensive shield and the sign of a body that escapes the pull of the earth, that proffers immortality (Quinn 1994). The anti-organic, anonymous tendency of such figurations both has a utopian dimension and encapsulates the rationality of com-modity exchange. The figures represent capital's abstraction of labor and bodies, the black male working body in particular, while signaling capital's apparently infinite mobility. As the border and the limit of the techno-aesthetic field in which the brand is perceived, the figure of the black male is thus simultaneously erased and endlessly applied. He marks time in the global economy; he is going up and coming down, rising and falling, flying and dying.

Transparency

To suggest that the power of the phatic image is such that the brand operates independently of the durability of its products is not to suggest that there is no relationship between the brand and the ways in which 'things become different kinds of property.' The nature of this relationship can perhaps be understood by considering further the notion of surface-effects. A 'turn to the surface,' a tendency towards externality, has been noted not only by Krauss but also by many commentators of mass culture. Recently, in Sherry Turkle's (1995) study of the use of computers, surface features as transparency. Turkle writes specifically about the iconic interface of the Macintosh computer, but her argument also signals a cultural shift. Rather than encouraging its users to 'look beyond the magic to the mechanism,' as was true of the early IBM PCs, Macintosh, Turkle writes, tells its users 'to stay on the surface.' The iconic style of the Macintosh does 'nothing to suggest how [its] underlying structure could be known'; it is instead 'visible only though its effects' (p. 23). In place of the assumption that 'an object is transparent if it lets the way it works be seen through its physical structure,' this transparency is 'somewhat paradoxically... enabled by complexity and opacity' (pp. 79, 42).

More generally, this is a shift from 'why' to 'how' reasoning or interpretation, and it has profound implications for object relations in contemporary society. The consequence of cause-and-effect or 'why' thinking has been that objects are understood in terms of a set of internal properties or qualities: as this understanding is displaced by 'how' reasoning, the object is understood in terms of its interface. As Turkle notes, however, the implications of this shift are ambivalent. On the one hand, the shift might encourage the acceptance of opacity and lead to a willingness to abdicate authority: on the other hand, it can 'confront us with the dependency on opaque simulations we accept in the real world.' This confrontation, she points out, can feed into either 'simulation resignation' or 'simulation denial': then again, it can also pose a challenge 'to develop a more sophisticated social criticism' (p. 71).

It is in the creation of this confrontation with transparencies and in the management of the surface effects that follow that Nike has been most adept. This project has included not only advertising but also the sponsorship of athletes ('contracted symbols') and athletic teams, and the design and use of retail space. In the Portland Niketown, for example, I observed many instances of this confrontation. In one section of this store there are nine television screens set three by three into the floor. I tapped my foot gently on one before seeing what it feels like to walk on transparency, on glass that lets you see through not to the other side but into the brand, for what are showing, of course, are Nike promotions. I then watched four children play on and around the screens. Initially, one of the girls, like me, was apprehensive of walking on them at all and sat on the bench beside them and watched. Then, somewhat timidly, she walked across the screens, looking down as she did. Finally, she joined another girl in jumping and skipping from one screen to another, as if in a game of hopscotch. Meanwhile, a boy stamped his foot on the screen, as if it were ice and might crack.

The effectiveness of the notion of transparency identified by Turkle is supported by the development of what Norman Klein (1993) calls consumer cubism. As Klein (1993: 210) has written. 'The door of a refrigerator (or any appliance) became the ultimate grid for consumer gratification, opening like a little diorama into the new highway or the new airport. By cartoon logic, the consumer object arrived (or was packaged) to the happy consumer at right angles.' Klein provides a wonderful example: in a cartoon titled *Design for Leaving*, Daffy Duck as salesman chases

Elmer Fudd up and down his house, trying to sell him robotic gadgets designed to bring the world to him, such as a hydraulic device for bringing the second floor downstairs, thereby eliminating the need of taking the steps. This design logic is a bit like that which informs the construction of Niketowns. Indeed, Klein argues that cartoon memory has entered into real space, in, for example, the grid of new suburbs and shopping centers in 1950s United States, and, more recently, in themed environments. This spatial organization produces. Klein argues, 'pleasure designed off a short, grid-like menu.' This is a system 'based on co-ordinated pauses' in consumer space, what Klein (1993: 211) calls the architectonic spaces of cartoon nostalgia.

The Nike brand is transparent in both of the senses Turkle identities. It is transparent in the sense that it enables one to see 'why' Nike shoes and apparel are fit for particular sports activities. Promotional and advertising materials explain the technology and scientific rationale for the shape, size, materials, and styling of specific products: they explain *why* you should use Nike products. The F. I. T. acronym (Functional Innovative Technology), for example, designates a range of Nike materials that direct air, water, and heat in ways supposedly advantageous to athletic activity. DRI F.I.T is a Nike 'base layer' material, a 'High performance microfiber polyester that manages moisture and dries quickly. Acts as a wicking layer next to the skin in cold or warm weather to keep you cool and provide warmth when needed. This soft, cotton-like jersey fabric is ideal as a technical replacement for 100% cotton polos' (from Nike promotional leaflet).

Other components of the Nike logo, however, are transparent in the sense that they show you not why but *how* the Nike logo works. Indeed, it is this second sense that seems to predominate. Nike publicity sustains the view that Nike shoes and clothing are designed with the athlete or sportsperson in mind (the advertising copy is insistent: 'To all athletes and the dreams they chase, we dedicate Niketown'; 'Nike is a shoe company. Excuse me, an *athletic shoe company*'; 'This is not a shoe for shopping. This is not a shoe for gardening. This is an athletic shoe with maximum-volume Nike-Air cushioning'). Yet, 60–80 percent of purchases are acknowledged to be for leisure or everyday use. The use of special (inert-gas-based) cushions in the soles of Nike shoes did not contribute to their commercial success until it was made visible as 'air' through a window or bubble in the sole of the shoe.[14] Despite the emphasis on *why* the 'special' properties of Nike shoes make them superior, it was the presentation of these properties as part of the interface between shoe and wearer that made them commercially successful.

In Turkle's terms, the Nike brand is opaque but enables complex actions. For example, the Swoosh is iconic, comparable to the icons of the interface communication of the Macintosh screen; it is not discursive but presentational. In many of its promotional and everyday uses, the Swoosh presents observers with manifold ensembles of signs; the observer can attend to the whole of the frame and then to its parts or vice versa. In movements like those described above (by the beach, in the mall, on the bus), these ensembles are in sequences, but these sequences operate and are perceived not just in three-dimensional space and linear or sequential time but in the articulated frames of the extended field of techno-aesthetic space. Indeed, what the observations and images above indicate is that the presentation of Nike emblems coordinates the articulation of these frames. Their effect is to organize how the observer sees the movement of these frames. Their effect is to organize how the observer sees the movement of the whole (or some) of the parts of the frame into another frame, then the next, and so on. Adapting terms from linguistics and anthropology, and following Virilio, the brand is a form of both phatic communication and communion.

In linguistics, the phatic is the name given to the signals which maintain discourse or dialogue and have little or no intrinsic meaning, for example, 'How are you?' In graphic media such as comics, phatic communication refers to panels, framing devices such as lines, balloons, rules, and escapements, and motifs such as speed lines or arrows (Eisner 1985). The branded product is intended to act in exactly this way. Consider how a designer describes the design of one particular Nike shoe:

> When I was designing the first cross-training shoe for Bo [Jackson], I watched him play sports, I read about him, I absorbed everything I could about him. Bo reminded me of a cartoon character. Not a goofy one, but a powerful one. His muscles are big, his face is big – he's larger than life. To me, he was like Mighty Mouse. So we designed a shoe called the Air Trainer that embodied characteristics of Bo Jackson and Mighty Mouse. Whenever you see Mighty Mouse, he's moving forward. He's got a slant to him. So the shoe needed to look like it was in motion, it had to be kind of inflated looking and brightly colored, and its features had to be exaggerated. That's how we came up with the larger-than-life, brightly colored Stability Outrigger and the similarly colored, inflated-looking rubber tongue top. (Willigan 1992: 93)

Phatic devices capture and direct the attention of observers: they indicate possible relations between separate frames: they maintain movement, change location, shift focus, and direct the action.

Such devices, both linguistic and graphic, proliferate in the American retail environment. To give one example, the greeting 'How are you today?' disturbed me as I wandered around sports stores. What worried me was *today*: as if the speaker know how I was yesterday and was interested to know whether I was any better now. If I was disturbed (I tried not to be, to take it in my stride), it was because I was taking seriously the nowness of the statement, its attempt to bring me – including some recognition of my past, some supposition that I was not just someone who had walked into the store and was just about to walk out – into its frame. But this nowness functions only to move me along to the follow-up frame: 'Can I help you?' or 'What can I get you?' As the Swoosh moves me, its transparency constitutes both the objective and subjective capacities of the brand: it coordinates the making of objects, and defines their properties, positioning me relative to their use. It shows *why* I should use Nike products, and *how* to move, how to see movement in techno-aesthetic space. Moreover, through these self-explanatory demonstrations of effect, through phatic communication and communion, the brand creates community. It is in this sense that the brand constitutes the objective properties of things in new ways.

The Redoubling of Effort

Rob Shields (1996a) argues that different forms of interaction are registered not only in corresponding architectural forms but also in the diverse uses and actualization of urban space. The latter though, he points out, leave fewer enduring traces. Yet these traces, which were once relatively fleeting, are now caught in the processual flow of video images.[15] If, as I have argued, these traces now not only are caught in the flow of video images but also endure in the indefatigable marks of global brands directing phatic communication, in the inscription of marks on over- and underembodied figures, what types of activity, what kinds of movement, which bodies, are coming to be seen as fit for this space? Which movements fall into the gutter, the name given to the nonspace between panels in a comic strip cartoon (Eisner 1985)? What relationships are possible between the actualization of place in traces and the prescriptions of space in brands?

Something about this dynamic between space and place is caught by Spike Lee when he identifies the secondary effects of a series of advertisements for Nike that he both directed and featured in, paired as his character Mars Blackmon with Michael Jordan. Lee (1997: 18) writes, 'Some say Mars helped Jordan pierce the culture at large. I think Mars and Michael helped each other in that way. I truly believe that those commercials, going to Knicks games, having the best seats in the house, have given me more visibility than I got from being a film maker. It wasn't my astuteness. It was an accident. I had no idea what would happen to Michael. He was thrilling to watch, and was the only one with his own shoe.' The ambiguity of the phrase 'given me more visibility than I got from being a filmmaker' is central here. In one reading, this is simply a statement about the symbiotic nature of the commercial relationship in which Lee (as Mars) and Jordan (as AirJordan and Jumpman) helped to make each other – and Nike – into internationally recognized figures, into symbols, into hyper real-estate (Lukes 1995). But it is also a statement about how those commercials and their making in the context of Lee's biography, his lifelong interest in basketball, his fandom – and the fact that Michael was 'the only one with his own shoe' – helped Lee to see and be seen. In this interpretation, Lee's visibility emerges from a complex embodied *and* automated, indexical *and* symbolic, topo- logical *and* topographical field, in which his decision to attend game seven of the NBA Finals rather than watch his father give a jazz concert at Cami Hall is as important to Lee's artistic success as the day he bought a Super 8 camera.

Undoubtedly Lee is a special case; he sees better or from a more privileged viewpoint than most of us: not only is he a filmmaker as well as a fan – he has the best seats in the house.[16] Virilio's beak-nosed carp – the phatic imagery of global brands – have depopulated what even Lee agrees are polluted waters. But consider the intriguing way in which cartoonist Chuck Jones (quoted in Klein 1995: 219) has described the fanatic: 'The fanatic is someone who redoubles his effort, when he has forgotten his aim.' The fan then is someone who perhaps no longer plays the sport, has forgotten how to aim, but nonetheless doubles his or her effort. Such doublings may, perhaps, have at least the potential to disturb the logo's repetitions, to disrupt the legibility of the superimpositions of the brand.

Coda

I have suggested here that the global brand reverses not only the relationship between the perceiver and the perceived but also the relationship between the product or object and the image. The brand operates by controlling the translation from the two dimensions of the image to the three dimensions of the product. If the brand is successful, the individual supports it by buying the product. Put another way, the object or product is now an effect of the brand. As Virilio (1994: 52) writes, 'the image is no longer solitary (subjective, elitist, artisanal): it is solidary (objective, democratic, industrial).' The rationale behind this reversal of the relationship between object and image in the brand is that the serious profits are to be made in the long-term (Castells 1996), and in particular through the management of sustained relationships with consumers. The brand assists in this process through its role in the management of phatic communication and the creation of phatic communion. In this sense the brand is a powerful example of the ways in which 'things become different kinds of property' and is of a piece with more general trends in the global economy.

I have further suggested that as a phatic image the brand intervenes in the processes of memorization which bring any object into focus. Its repetitions occur in what Manuel Castells (1996: 446) describes as 'timeless time.' the time of the flows of a global economy characterized by the 'breaking down of rhythmicity, either biological or social, associated with the notion of a life cycle.' However, this intervention is necessarily complex. In a reorientation of the inter relationship between semiosis and action, the brand grows in strength through its appropriation of surface effects. The changing uses and meanings of a product – including the effects produced in the shift from why to how reasoning – are retroactively refigured as attributes of the brand, thus enabling the global economy 'to escape the contexts of its existence, and to appropriate selectively any value each context could offer to the ever-present' (p. 433). Nevertheless, there is simultaneously the possibility that if the subject redoubles his or her efforts, the repetitions of the brand in the time of exposure will be confused, its movements rendered illegible.

While Appadurai (1996: 82) notes that *ersatz* nostalgia or 'nostalgia without memory' is increasingly central to mass merchandising, there is still the possibility that we might lose ourselves in time when doing things with objects. This may be considered to be nothing more than child's play, what Virilio calls picnoleptic auto-induction, as in a child's enjoyment of spinning around, rapid turnings and somersaulting, the game of Freeze. But play can be serious. Indeed, Virilio argues for the preservation of what he calls picnoleptic savoir-faire, suggesting that its usual confinement to child-society is a loss to adults, since it enables the use of sensations of vertigo and disorder as sources of imagination and pleasure. More than this, 'the picnoleptic onset would be something that could make us think of human liberty, in the sense that it would be a latitude given to each man to invent his own relations to time and therefore a kind of will and power for minds' (Virilio 1991: 22).

NOTES

1   This essay draws upon Roman Jakobson's (Jakobson and Pomorska 1983) notion of marked time to describe a constituent of subjective time.
2   Most of the observation discussed in this piece was conducted with Deirdre Boden; and some was recorded by one or other of us with either a still or a video camera. She and I are members of a research team investigating. 'The global biographies of cultural products,' a project funded by the Economic and Social Research Council in the UK. The other members of the team are Scott Lash. Vince Miller, Dan Shapiro and Jeremy Valentine.

I would like to thank them all and the editor and referees for *Public Culture* for their comments on earlier versions of this chapter.

3   Tom Vanderbilt (1998: 84) notes that 'the Air Max Penny is a truly global product... the shoe is designed in Oregon and Tennessee ... with input from technicians in South Korea and Taiwan. It is manufactured in South Korea and Indonesia with some fifty-two components from five countries (the United States. Taiwan, South Korea, Indonesia, and Japan). During the assembly process, a single shoe is touched by some 120 pairs of hands.'

4   Michael Jordan is renowned for his apparent ability to defy gravity: this 'special effect' is known as hangtime.

5   This term was suggested by Scott Lash.

6   While numerous strategies have been deployed to highlight the conditions of those who manufacture the products that Nike identities as its own. Nike remains unrepentant. PUSH, a Chicago-based civil rights organization, launched a boycott of Nike products in 1989 on the grounds that Nike has a 'zero' policy. This means, the organization claimed, that zero African Americans hold executive positions: zero African American-owned newspapers, magazines, radio and television stations carry Nike advertisements; and zero African American professional service providers have contracts or do business with Nike. In addition, numerous strikes and campaigns, both by the largely female workforce in Asia and by various groups in Europe and the United States, have sought to highlight the conditions of workers who make the products that Nike brands.

Nike's response is legible in the following advertising statement:

Yep, we're capitalists.
We want you to wear our shoes.
Because we want to be there when your body corrupts every notion of doubt your mind ever had.
Because we cherish photo finishes and muscle memory and the gasps of a crowd when an athlete spits on anonymity and does something very, very big.
Because we believe obsession is a very fine belief.
Because we make athletic shoes. Great ones.
And if we make a buck in the process, we ain't going to apologize.

7   'Where do you want to go today?' is an advertising slogan of Microsoft.

8   This term is introduced and developed, in a different sense to that indicated here, in Lash 1999.

9   However, recent reports suggest that Nike has not been entirely successful in this attempt and that the fluctuations of fashion have undermined the persistence of the brand. So, for example, Sawyer (1998: 15) argues that, despite its explicit attempts to position itself above fashion. Nike has became fashionable and therefore subject 'to fashion's strange fads and vagaries.'

10   CEO Phil Knight describes 'the product' as Nike's 'most important marketing tool' (Willingan 1992: 97).

11   Cheryl L. Cole (1996) argues that as an 'All-American' figure. Jordan is both an effect and an instrument of modern power.

12   For a discussion of Lee's own responsibilities as artist, gentleman, and capitalist, see Christenson (1991) and Mitchell (1991).

13   See Berlant (1993) for a discussion of the body, individuality, and the workings of what she describes as racial hieroglyphies in a bourgeois capitalist economy.

14   Phil Knight (Willigan 1992: 92) recognizes the importance of this second notion of transparency in his description of Nike as 'a marketing oriented company': 'For years,

we thought of ourselves as a production-oriented company, meaning we put all our emphasis on designing and manufacturing the product. But now we understand that the most important thing we do is market the product.'

15   Virilio (1991: 64) writes. 'The question today therefore is no longer to know if cinema can do without a place but if places can do without cinema.' He answers this question with the claim that 'from now on *architecture is only a movie*' (p. 65).

16   Lee has recently taken up a position as creative director with the advertising agency DDB Needham. A newspaper account (Armstrong 1996: 13) of the deal noted. 'Finally, a mainstream ad agency has officially stood up and said "black America is the single most important force in determining global youth culture and we're desperate to get a piece of it."'

REFERENCES

Appadurai, Arjun (1996) *Modernity at Large: Cultural Dimensions of Globalization*. Minneapolis: University of Minnesota Press.

Armstrong, S. (1996) Buy the right thing. *Media Guardian*, December, 9, 13.

Aumont, Jacques (1997) *The Image*, trans. Claire Pajackowska. London: British Film Institute.

Barthes, Roland (1981) *Camera Lucida: Reflections on Photography*. trans. Richard Howard. New York: Hill and Wang.

Berlant, Lauren (1993) National brands/national body: *Imitation of life*. In *The Phantom Public Sphere*, ed. Bruce Robbins. Minneapolis: Minnesota Press.

Braun, Marta (1992) *Picturing Time: The Work of Etienne-Jules Marey (1830–1904)*. Chicago, IL: University of Chicago Press.

Castells, Manuel (1996) *The Rise of the Network society, vol. 1. The Information Age: Economy, Society, and Culture*. Oxford: Blackwell.

Christensen, J. (1991) Critical response: Spike Lee and corporate populism. *Critical Inquiry* 17: 582–95.

Cole, Cheryl L. (1996) American Jordan: P.L.A.Y., consensus, and punishment. *Sociology of Sport Journal* 13: 366–97.

Dagognet, François (1992) *Etienne-Jules Marey: A Passion for the Trace*, trans. Robert Galeta with Jeanine Herman. New York: Zone Books.

Doane, Mary Ann (1996) Freud, Marey, and the cinema. *Critical Inquiry* 22: 313–43.

Dyer, Richard (1997) *White*. London: Routledge.

Eco. Umberto (1987) *The Role of the Reader: Explorations in the Semiotics of Texts*. London: Hutchinson.

Eisner, Will (1985) *Comics and Sequential art*. Tamarac, FL: Poorhouse Press.

Friedland, Roger, and Deirdre Boden eds. (1994) *NowHere: Space, Time, and Modernity*. Berkeley: University of California Press.

Gilroy, Paul (1994) 'After the love has gone': Bio-politics and etho-poetics in the black public sphere. *Public Culture* 15: 49–76.

Hayles, N. Katherine (1990) *Chaos Bound: Orderly Disorder in Contemporary Literature and Science*. New York: Cornell University Press.

Helmholtz, Hermann von (1971) *Selected Writings*. ed. Russell Kahl, Middletown. CT: Wesleyan University Press.

Huyssen, Andreas (1995) *Twilight Memories*. New York: Routledge.

Jakobson, Roman, and Krystyna Pomorska (1983) *Dialogues*, trans. Christian Hubert. Cambridge, MA: MIT Press.

Klein, Norman M. (1993) *Seven Minutes: The Life and Death of the American Animated Cartoon*. London: Verso.

Krauss, Rosalind (1996) *Passages in Modern Sculpture*. Cambridge, MA: MIT Press.

Lash, Scott (1999) *Another Modernity. A Different Rationality*. Oxford: Blackwell.

Lee, Spike (1997) He's gotta have it. *Guardian Weekend*, September 13, 14–20.

Lukes, T. (1995) New world order and neo-word orders: Power, politics, and identity in informationalizing globalities. In *Global Modernities*. ed. Mike Featherstone, Scott Lash, and Roland Robertson. London: Sage. 91–107.

McCracken, Grant (1988) *Culture and Consumption: New Approaches to the Symbolic Character of Consumer Goods and Activities*. Bloomington: Indiana University Press.

Mitchell, W. J. T. (1991) Critical response: Seeing Do the right thing, *Critical Inquiry* 17: 596–608.

Peirce, Charles Sanders (1991) *Peirce on Signs*. ed. James Hoopes. Chapel Hill: University of North Carolina Press.

Quinn, Malcolm (1994) *The Swastika: Constructing the Symbol*. London: Routledge.

Rabinbach, Anson (1992) *The Human Motor: Energy, Fatigue, and the Origins of Modernity*. Berkeley: University of California Press.

Sawyer, M. (1998) It's not working out. *Observer Life*, May 3, 12–17.

Shields, Rob (1996a) Urban images, identity, and flexible sociality. Unpublished paper.

——(1996b) Research programme on the flexible sociality thesis. A comparative study of Toronto and Seoul. Unpublished paper.

Turkle, Sherry (1995) *Life on the Screen: Identity in the Age of the Internet*. New York: Simon and Schuster.

Vancil, Mark (ed.) (1995) *I'm Back! More Rare Air*. San Francisco, CA: HarperCollins.

Vanderbilt, Tom (1998) *The Sneaker Book: Anatomy of an Industry and an Icon*. New York: New Press.

Virilio, Paul (1991) *The Aesthetics of Disappearance*. New York: Semiotext(e).

——(1994) *The Vision Machine*. London: British Film Institute.

Weiner, Annette (1995) Culture and our discontents. *American Anthropologist* 97: 14–40.

Willigan, Geraldine E. (1992) High performance marketing: An interview with Nike's Phil Knight. *Harvard Business Review* July–August: 90–101.

Index